W9-BIH-734

Launching New Ventures
An Entrepreneurial Approach

Third Edition

Kathleen R. Allen

University of Southern California

Houghton Mifflin Company

Boston • New York

To the students and alumni of the Lloyd Greif Center for Entrepreneurial Studies at the University of Southern California, where the entrepreneurial spirit continues to grow.

Editor-in-Chief: George T. Hoffman
Associate Sponsoring Editor: Susan M. Kahn
Senior Project Editor: Tracy Patruno
Senior Manufacturing Coordinator: Jane Spelman
Marketing Manager: Steven W. Mikels

Cover image: © FPG International

Printed in the U.S.A.

Library of Congress Control Number: 2001135732

ISBN: 0-618-21481-X

123456789-CW-06 05 04 03 02

Contents in Brief

Contents

All chapters include an Overview, New Venture Checklist, Issues to Consider, Experiencing Entrepreneurship, Additional Sources of Information, Internet Resources, and Relevant Case Studies.

Preface

Entrepreneurship has permeated every industry and arguably every career choice. Today, more than ever before, you must take charge of your career, manage it, and turn yourself into a business of one, proving your value at every turn. The days of spending an entire lifetime in one job or even in one career seem to be a thing of the past. It is critical to develop skills that can move from one job to another, from one career to another. Being opportunistic, building social networks, and becoming a resource gatherer and a critical thinker are vital. These are some of the skills of an entrepreneur. Whether you start a new venture, join an entrepreneurial venture, acquire a business, or create a new venture inside a large organization, you will need entrepreneurial skills to navigate an increasingly complex world. One of the major goals of *Launching New Ventures* is to help you acquire those skills.

Launching New Ventures, Third Edition, represents the most current thoughts, ideas, and practices in the field of entrepreneurship. In fact, since the first edition, *Launching New Venture* has been ahead of its time:

> *Launching New Ventures* has always been at the forefront of entrepreneurial thought and practice, usually ahead of its competition in its vision.

> Whereas many texts are just beginning to convey how the customer contributes to the entrepreneurial venture, the customer-centric vision has always been pervasive in *Launching New Ventures.*

> Technology has always played an important role in the book in defining an entrepreneur's competitive advantage.

The third edition reflects the enormous changes that have occurred in the marketplace in the past three years due largely to technology and the availability of capital. While the world continues to change at a rapid pace, the fundamental entrepreneurial values, attitudes, and skills discussed in *Launching New Ventures,* Second Edition, continue to be relevant. With the rise and fall of the dot coms, many businesses that started three years ago no longer exist. In their place are new businesses and entrepreneurs who learned from the failures of the dot coms that no matter what kind of business you have, you must create value and you must give customers what they want and need. This text recognizes that whether you are starting a lifestyle business to support your family or the next biotech giant, there are certain fundamental truths about entrepreneurship and new ventures that make them very different from established companies.

Entrepreneurship is about the creation of new ventures. But it is much more than just a set of skills for starting a business; it is a mindset—an approach to the world. To successfully compete in a rapidly changing environment, you have to understand and develop this entrepreneurial mindset—the values and attitudes—and constantly scan the environment prepared to adapt to change. This book was designed to immerse the reader in the entrepreneurial mindset and provide the critical thinking skills required to successfully recognize and evaluate an opportunity.

Today aspects of entrepreneurship are incorporated into many different kinds of academic courses and into a variety of business situations. Even large corporations are spinning off entrepreneurial ventures and encouraging the entrepreneurial mindset in their environments. For example, executive education programs are using *Launching New Ventures* to introduce and teach the entrepreneurial mindset to middle level managers and CEOs of large companies.

One of the most important aspects of entrepreneurship is passion. The passion of the entrepreneur is like energy. It can change, but it can never be destroyed—it simply takes on another form. When an entrepreneur's business venture fails, the passion doesn't die with it; rather, it sustains the entrepreneur in an effort to start again. Passion is not something that can be taught. It is something that happens when a person discovers what he or she was *meant* to do. No one has a monopoly on passion. Some of the most successful entrepreneurs have been teachers, engineers, psychologists, musicians, and filmmakers. Many have had no college education at all, but in every case they were lifelong learners and they believed in themselves. As Will Rogers once said: "Know what you are doing. Love what you are doing. Believe in what you are doing." That is the spirit of the entrepreneur. And that is the spirit of *Launching New Ventures*.

Content, Organization, and Unique Coverage

Launching New Ventures is organized around the process of creating a new venture, from the recognition of an opportunity to the launch of the business. It is designed to help the reader organize and plan for venture creation by going through all the various activities that entrepreneurs typically undertake. Because the book focuses on the pre-start-up phase of venture creation, it explores these pre-launch activities in more depth than the average entrepreneurship book.

Part I introduces the foundations of entrepreneurship that are important to understanding the decisions that entrepreneurs make, the environment in which they make those decisions, and the tasks they must undertake before launching a new company. In Chapter 1, students will learn the entrepreneurial mindset and understand the nature of entrepreneurial ventures and how they are distinct from other types of businesses. Chapter 2 explores the increasingly important topics of vision, ethics, and social responsibility. The value system of a new business creates the culture and reputation it will have to live by into the future. Students will be challenged to define a vision for a new venture based on the values they believe to be important. They will also gain a greater understanding of the need for ethics and social responsibility in any business. Chapter 3 introduces the subject of opportunity and how entrepreneurs recognize and create opportunities for themselves. This part closes with Chapter 4, "Learning an Industry," which is a critical activity students need to undertake if they are to find good opportunities appropriate to their goals. The chapter discusses how to evaluate an industry and learn how it works.

Part II addresses the essence of entrepreneurial activity, the testing of a new business concept through feasibility analysis. Chapter 5 begins this part with an overview of feasibility analysis and how it is used to help the entrepreneur make decisions about the conditions under which he is willing to go forward with a business concept. The development of a business concept that can be tested is the focal point of the chapter. Chapter 6 addresses the issue of analyzing the risks and benefits of the primary customer for the new business. It guides students through the gathering of primary research with the customer to determine needs and level of demand. Chapter 7 explores the product/service being offered and considers such things as product development, prototyping, and intellectual property issues. Chapter 8 analyzes the founding team and discusses how to determine what gaps in experience and expertise may exist in the team and how to compensate for them with such solutions as strategic alliances and independent contractors. In Chapter 9, the financial risks and benefits of the business concept are examined. A method is given for calculating how much capital and other resources will be required to start the venture and carry it until it achieves a positive cash flow on its own. Part II closes with Chapter 10, which discusses how to analyze the value chain to create a competitive advantage. At this point, the feasibility portion of the start-up process is complete and a decision can be made about going forward with the concept and constructing a business plan.

Part III deals with developing a business plan to execute the feasiblility concept. Chapter 11 sets the stage by providing an overview of the business planning process and comparing it to the feasibility analysis. In Chapter 12, the legal forms of organization are discussed with the goal of helping the reader determine the most effective legal form for the type of business and its stage of development. Chapter 13 looks at the management and operations strategy of a new venture and considers such things as decision criteria for selecting a location and organizing company personnel. Chapter 14 focuses on the production of products and services and deals with issues of manufacturing, quality control, and customer service. Chapter 15 helps the reader construct a marketing plan for the new venture, while Chapter 16 assists the reader in preparing a complete set of financials and financial ratios for a new venture.

Part IV focuses on planning for growth and change in the new organization. Chapter 17 opens this part with a discussion of growth strategies for start-up ventures. This chapter prepares the reader for Chapter 18, which considers financial strategies for start-up and growth including private and public offerings. Chapter 19 closes this part with a discussion of planning for change. It deals with the kinds of changes most ventures face such as the loss of a key employee, a decline in sales, or a product liability issue. It also discusses harvest, or exit, strategies and provides an overview of bankruptcy law relevant to entrepreneurs.

Special Features in the Third Edition

The third edition contains a variety of features of value to professors and students.

- ▶ *Overviews* highlight the key topics for each of the chapters.

- ▶ Entrepreneur *Profiles* that begin each chapter provide real-life examples to illustrate the application of chapter concepts and to inspire students. In addition, smaller profiles are scattered throughout the chapters to maintain the real-life tone of the book.

- ▶ *Boxed inserts* highlight additional examples, strategies, and entrepreneurial tips.

- ▶ The *New Venture Checklist* serves as a reminder of the tasks that need to be completed at a particular stage of the entrepreneurial process.

- ▶ *Issues to Consider* are questions at the end of each chapter that provoke interesting discussions in class.

- ▶ *Experiencing Entrepreneurship* is a series of activities at the end of each chapter that gives students a chance to learn about entrepreneurship by getting involved in entrepreneurial activities and interacting with entrepreneurs and others in an industry in which the student is interested.

- ▶ *Additional Sources of Information* lists books that will give the student more in-depth information about a topic.

- ▶ *Internet Resources* are provided as a current source of additional information.

- ▶ Several new *Case Studies* have been added to the third edition to reflect a wider variety of businesses and entrepreneurial types. The cases include discussion questions.

Supplemental Materials

An *Instructor's Resource Manual with Test Items* features suggestions for planning the course; instructional tips; learning objectives; lecture outlines; answers to end-of-chapter questions; a test bank with true/false, multiple choice, and essay questions; and instructor's notes for the case studies.

The *Web Site* contains resources for both students and instructors. For students it provides links to other useful sites on the web, ACE self-test questions, and examples of feasibility studies and business plans. For instructors it includes sample syllabi, PowerPoint slides for classroom presentation, and downloadable files from the *Instructor's Resource Manual* so instructors can edit the material for their particular course needs.

Acknowledgments

Many people helped make this third edition happen—entrepreneurs, university students, professors, and, of course, the publishing staff at Houghton Mifflin. In particular, I would like to thank Associate Sponsoring Editor Susan Kahn whose patience and humor got me through a tough production schedule. In addition, appreciation is due to Elisa Adams, Tracy Patruno, and Books By Design.

I want to thank the instructors who used the second edition and gave me feedback and my students at the Lloyd Greif Center for Entrepreneurial Studies at the University of Southern California who willingly shared their ideas and comments with me. I also thank those instructors who provided formal manuscript reviews at various stages of the revision process for this and previous editions:

Donna Albano, *Atlantic Cape Community College*

Joeseph S. Anderson, *Northern Arizona University*

Richard Benedetto, *Merrimack College*

Edward Bewayo, *Montclair State University*

Janice Feldbauer, *Austin Community College*

Todd Finkle, *University of Akron*

Susan Fox-Wolfgramm, *San Francisco State University*

Frederick D. Greene, *Manhattan College*

Jeffry Haber, *Iona College*

Steven C. Harper, *University of North Carolina at Wilmington*

Timothy Hill, *Central Oregon Community College*

Sandra Honig-Haftel, *Wichita State University*

Tom Lumpkin, *University of Illinois at Chicago*

Clare Lyons, *Hagerstown Community College*

Steven Maranville, *University of Houston—Downtown*

Ivan J. Miestchovich, Jr., *University of New Orleans*

Stephen Mueller, *Texas Christian University*

Eugene Muscat, *University of San Francisco*

Terry Noel, *Wichita State University*

Robert Novota, *Lincoln University*

Fred B. Pugh, *Kirksville College of Osteopathic Medicine*

Juan A. Seda, *Florida Metropolitan University*

Randy Swangard, *University of Oregon*

Charles N. Toftoy, *The George Washington University*

Lynn Trzynka, *Western Washington University*

Barry L. Van Hook, *Arizona State University*

John Volker, *Austin Peay State University*

Gene Yelle, *SUNY Institute of Technology*

Mark Weaver, *University of Alabama*

Dennis Williams, *Pennsylvania College of Technology*

And finally, I would like to thank my husband, John; and my children, Rob, Jaime (a writer herself), and Greg for supporting my writing efforts and forgiving my relentless schedule.

K.R.A.

About the Author

Kathleen R. Allen, Ph.D., is the author of several texts, including *Growing and Managing an Entrepreneurial Business, Bringing New Technology to Market, Entrepreneurship and Small Business Management,* Second Edition, and a variety of trade books in the field of entrepreneurship. Her academic research focuses on high-tech entrepreneurs and their ventures.

A professor in the Greif Entrepreneurship Center of the Marshall School of Business at the University of Southern California, Allen has helped hundreds of entrepreneurs realize their dreams of starting new ventures. She received the Marshall School of Business Innovation in Teaching Award in 2000 for the development of an entrepreneur course in feasibility analysis that brings scientists, engineers, and business students together to form e-teams to bring new technologies to market. At USC, she is also Director of the Technology Commercialization Alliance, a collaboration of the schools of business, engineering, and medicine to work with researchers to commercialize USC technologies. She also leads a National Science Foundation project, N2TEC, with several university and public/private partners to build a national commercialization network with the goal of raising the level of innovation, facilitating the sharing of knowledge and resources, and increasing the transfer of university technology to the marketplace.

As an entrepreneur, Allen has been involved in commercial real estate development for the past ten years, having co-founded a development firm specializing in office, industrial, and apartments; and a brokerage, which she sold. She is the co-founder of two technology companies and regularly consults to high-technology companies, with a particular interest in biotech and biomedical device companies.

PART ONE

The Foundations of Entrepreneurship

1

Understanding Entrepreneurship

Develop a vision, and never lose sight of that vision.
Sandy Gooch,
Sandy Gooch Enterprises

Overview

Two Friends, Two Choices

The decisions people make and the reasons for those decisions are always an interesting study. But when two friends with similar backgrounds and interests attend the same university, join the same fraternity, take the same degree program—entrepreneurship—and then make completely different decisions about what to do when they graduate, the reasons become more interesting. Jon Weisner and Bryan Rosencrantz met at the University of Southern California in 1992. Rosencrantz came to the university from Portland, Oregon, knowing from the beginning that he wanted to major in business. He had grown up in an entrepreneurial family: his uncle founded a major chain of discount stores; his grandfather founded the largest steel company in the western United States; his father was a successful real estate developer. The family generally expected that Rosencrantz would graduate from college and enter one of the family businesses. It seemed only natural, since he had been involved in them since childhood and wouldn't have to make a difficult transition. But the entrepreneurial spirit that infused his family also burned in Rosencrantz, and he became determined to start his own business and make it on his own.

Naturally impatient to make things happen, Bryan Rosencrantz didn't wait until graduation to start his business. By the end of the first semester of his senior year, in 1995, he had gotten Fit-Net off the ground. At that time, the World Wide Web was relatively young, and there were countless opportunities for someone with vision and the ability to pull together the right resources. Rosencrantz, who had a great interest in the fitness industry, decided to become the biggest online clearinghouse for information, equipment, and resources for fitness enthusiasts. He readily admits that, although he didn't have unlimited funds, he did have the advantage of significant resources from wise investments in the stock market. He knew that it would be a while before this Internet-based business would make money, and he was aware that he was risking his savings.

As the business grew, he established Fitscape, an umbrella company offering total Internet service provider services, including web page design for his clients' web sites. To distinguish his company from others in the market, Rosencrantz developed a software product called iWell, designed as a preventive nutritional program. He first tried seeking customers over the Internet; it was a long, slow process and did not yield the kind of results he was looking for. So he shifted his focus to corporations and insurance companies hoping to achieve a user level that would allow him to make a profit. Recently, he licensed the iWell program to Blue Cross, which uses the software to help its two million covered customers remain healthy, and another insurance company, United Healthcare, is using and marketing the product as well.

Rosencrantz takes a philosophical approach to his business. He knows that if the business fails, he can always fall back on the family businesses. That confidence gave him the cushion he needed to start his business in the first place. His Fitscape site is one of the oldest on the Internet; he has survived and that is something to be proud of. And what does the future hold? He may decide to sell the business at the right time and take a break—work with other health-related businesses and his family's companies. At 28, he has already been through a lifetime of experience. His conclusion: "I think I've accomplished something. If everything fell apart tomorrow, I'd know I did something."

To learn more about his friend Jon Weisner's choice, see Profile 1.2.

Entrepreneurship has assumed such an important presence in the U.S. economy that everyone from the dry cleaner to the biomedical engineer wants to refer to himself or herself as an entrepreneur. Entrepreneurs grace the covers of an increasing number of business magazines and books and stare back at us from myriad television shows dedicated to new businesses and the people who create and grow them.

There is nothing wrong with that level of enthusiasm, but it's important not to lose sight of what entrepreneurship really is because it plays a critical role in economic well-being. An entrepreneur is someone who creates a new opportunity in the marketplace and assembles the resources necessary to successfully exploit that opportunity. Entrepreneurs have the ability to see opportunity where others do not because they have a well-developed opportunistic mindset. The businesses they create are generally growth-oriented and innovative; they create value where there was none before; they disrupt the economic equilibrium; and they change the way we do things. Entrepreneurs lead exciting, challenging, and interesting lives. Is it any wonder that so many people want to be entrepreneurs?

If you decide to become an entrepreneur, the odds are in your favor. One out of three U.S. households is home to at least one adult with some level of experience as a founder or business owner.[1] And, since 1995, entrepreneurship was revitalized with the advent of the Internet. In 1993, there were no Internet businesses and no web sites. By June 1996, over 200,000 web sites had been launched; by early 2000, 15.7 million web sites were registered.[2] The Internet is definitely the new frontier for entrepreneurs.

This book takes the view that entrepreneurship is about innovation, creating value, and growth, all of which are accomplished through the medium of a new venture. Whether that venture is large or small or exists inside a larger company, the entrepreneurial mindset drives its creation. In this chapter, you'll get a good grounding in the field of entrepreneurship and come away with a sense of whether or not this is where you belong. Even if you have no intentions of becoming an entrepreneur now or in the future, learning the entrepreneurial mindset and developing entrepreneurial skills will give you invaluable assets to use in whatever you choose to do.

New Economy or Variations on a Theme?

Entrepreneurs today are faced with an environment that is changing so rapidly that it's difficult to keep up with, let alone get ahead of, all the changes. Since 1995, when Netscape Communications went public and saw its stock value more than double in twenty-four hours, we have seen the new venture landscape shift to technology in all its many iterations: the Internet, information systems, telecommunications, gene therapy, wireless technology, nanotechnology, and thousands of variations on these themes. We also saw a gold rush of sorts—entrepreneurs who hurried to start the latest dot com business, only to see their dreams of an initial public offering (IPO) and untold wealth dashed in the dot com bust of April 2000. For those who did not understand the need to create real value in their businesses to generate a profit, the dot com bust was a rude awakening. One of the biggest and perhaps most surprising failures was that of e-Companies, the dot com incubator started by Earthlink founder Sky Dayton and Disney executive Jake Winebaum. Most of the thirty-three companies it incubated or invested in have been closed, sold off, are cash-strapped, or in hibernation.[3] All e-companies expected of potential incubatees was a compelling story that could scale out quickly to a mass market. The idea of creating value was, unfortunately, never part of the picture. For Dayton, Winebaum, and the venture capitalists whose money was driving the rush to dot com, it was a humbling lesson in the fundamentals of business.

It is interesting to note that in the years leading up to April 2000, we were beginning to see businesses become more customer-centric, not just touting customer service, but working diligently to satisfy customer needs in the ways that customers wanted them satisfied. When the dot com gold rush hit, all that went out the window and a new type of entrepreneur emerged—the young Turk who defined success by the amount of money he or she was able to raise and the speed with which his or her Internet company could go public. Thousands of hopeful, would-be entrepreneurs rushed to find the next concept that could scale out quickly to a mass audience. Successful entrepreneurs like Sky Dayton, the founder of Earthlink, placed their bets in the dot com arena in a big way by creating incubators designed to push ideas from concept to business in 120 days. Writers everywhere proclaimed the end of business as usual and the birth of a new economy that would put non-Internet businesses out of business in a very short time.

That didn't happen, and everyone from seasoned entrepreneurs and venture capitalists to first-time Internet chief executive officers (CEOs) felt the pain and learned the lesson that fundamental economic principles are still alive and well in a digital world. Still, technology—and particularly the Internet—has had a lasting impact on business and society in general, and while it may not have changed economic principles, it certainly has given them a new look. In the following sections, we look at some of the changes that affect the way entrepreneurs structure their business models.

● *First-mover with a Scalable Concept*

The Internet provides huge potential for rapid growth and the ability to scale out or reach millions of potential customers with a simple mouse click and a mass e-mailing at little or no cost. So it is no wonder that one of the notions that arose out of the dot com rush was that to succeed in business it was necessary to be the first to market (first mover) and scale out quickly so that you could grab the bulk of market share before anyone had a chance to catch up.

There are two fallacies in this premise. First, the first-mover advantage has not often been successful, particularly in the technology arena. In fact, it is more often the second, third, or fourth mover that wins the day. PalmPilot, the highly successful personal digital assistant (PDA), was not the first of its kind. It actually arrived on the market years after Apple's failed Newton MessagePad. Microsoft's Internet Explorer web browser was very late to the game; yet it now dominates. The first-mover advantage lies in the "quiet time" during which your company holds a temporary monopoly and can establish its brand and foothold in the market. But often, being second allows you to learn from the mistakes of the first mover and do a better job of satisfying customers as PalmPilot did.

The second fallacy is that scaling out quickly wins the day. The problem with that notion is that to grow effectively requires an infrastructure and systems and controls that most new entrepreneurial ventures don't have and can't afford to acquire. Moreover, as a company grows quickly and aims to reach as many customers as possible, it doesn't take care of the customers it has, so the customer turnover rate is high and the cost of acquiring new customers keeps going up.

● *Scarcity*

Knowledge has become the intellectual property of choice in a digital economy. Economists often have trouble with the fact that knowledge defies the law of scarcity. For example, if you sell your house, you no longer own it, but if you sell an idea, it is still yours. In fact, you can sell it over and over again, as many times as you like, because it will never be used up. Moreover, with knowledge and information products, such as software, books, and movies, there are increasing returns rather than the classic diminishing returns described in economic theory. Information products are costly to produce but inexpensive to replicate and thus provide superior economies of scale that create strong barriers to entry for companies that benefit from them.

● *Monopoly*

The term *monopoly* often carries with it a negative connotation suggesting that it's wrong for an entrepreneur to enjoy a period of time with no rivals. Classical economist Joseph Schumpeter (1883–1950) asserted that monopolies actually

How Do You Really Feel about Business?

It is important that you seriously consider a number of key issues that may relate to the kind of business you want to own. If your feelings on these issues conflict with the type of business you start, you will in all likelihood be very unhappy and less successful in that business. So, how do you feel about:

- Taking responsibility for the success or failure of a business?
- Paying yourself last?
- Using debt or having a highly leveraged business?
- Dealing with unions and union workers?

- Hiring and managing employees?
- Dealing with government regulation and paperwork?
- Working with people from other areas of the United States or the world?
- Dealing with ambiguity and insecurity, such as not receiving a paycheck from the business for up to two years?
- Traveling?
- Sharing ownership of the business?
- Working long hours and on weekends, particularly in the beginning?
- Dealing with crises, like not making payroll?

stimulate innovation and growth because they allow a new firm this quiet period to get established. The U.S. Patent and Trademark Office (USPTO) was originally created to give inventors a temporary monopoly on their work. Without it, they would never be able to recoup their development costs before they had to compete on price. In short, for innovation to occur, there has to be a mechanism in place to allow for a temporary monopoly. That being said, it's important to observe that not only has the time from concept to market declined sharply, but the time for a temporary monopoly has as well. To learn more about intellectual property, see Chapter 7.

● Quality, Speed, Price

The entrepreneurial environment today is characterized by the demand for superior levels of quality, faster time to market, and lower prices, goals that often come into conflict. The challenge for entrepreneurs is to find ways to achieve all three through a customer-centric organization, efficient production methods, and the ability to provide real value that customers perceive so that price does not become the sole bargaining chip.

The Nature of Entrepreneurs

It is an interesting fact that many of the characteristics normally associated with entrepreneurs also exist in some managers and, in fact, in anyone who is highly successful in his or her career. What characteristics are typically found in entrepreneurs and in people who have the entrepreneurial mindset? Research points to the ability to take calculated risks, an achievement orientation or intense drive

PROFILE 1.2

Two Friends, Two Choices Continued

Recall from Profile 1.1 that Bryan Rosencrantz was impatient to start his own business from the day he started in the Entrepreneur Program at USC. His friend Jon Weisner, on the other hand, had a completely different perspective as he approached graduation. He had chosen to study entrepreneurship to learn how to create a business and how to write a business plan. He recalls his first day in class with 140 other students majoring in entrepreneurship as an overwhelming experience: "I was in this room with all these very serious people who were going to start businesses, and I was there to learn about business plans." At that point, he wondered what he was doing there. Weisner suspected that he wanted to own his own business someday, but—unlike his friend Bryan Rosencrantz—he knew he had much to learn about how to do it. He always saw himself as the type of person who "thinks a lot about something" before he does it.

Jon Weisner had also grown up in an entrepreneurial environment, but in the entertainment industry. His father, a highly respected personal manager in the recording industry, has represented some of the great artists of our time. So Weisner grew up surrounded by entertainers, and his family and friends, like Rosencrantz's, naturally expected him to go into business with his father. That certainly would have been the easy choice, and he knew he could handle the work well. But Weisner found himself surrounded by other interests that took him away from the music industry to encompass his hobbies: computers and electronics. Fortunately, in his senior year, 1994–95, the entertainment industry and technology were beginning to converge. A new industry was emerging, one that satisfied both his interests. In the realm of technology he recognized an opportunity he could pursue for his business plan.

One day as he was playing with his calculator in class, he began contemplating the liquid crystal display (LCD) and the way the light reflecting on it affected the visibility of the numbers. He wondered whether it was possible to control the visual display in more ways than just on and off. Curiosity moved him to investigate the technology behind LCDs, and he began talking with key people in the industry in an effort to find some clue to the answer. Throughout the first semester of his senior year and after hours of research, he developed a primitive prototype of a system he would eventually call Weisner Windows. This innovative system allowed the user to control the opacity of windows electronically in a manner similar to the way a dimmer controls the degree of light from a light bulb. Almost immediately he saw a market niche for the product: using it on car windows to control the level of tint. As he began to improve on his prototype and it began looking more and more like a feasible product, Weisner filed a notice of disclosure with the USPTO to protect his efforts.

As his senior year progressed, Weisner was fast reaching a crossroads. He had to make a decision about his future. Even though he found the Weisner Windows concept fascinating and people appeared interested in helping him do it, Weisner knew he wasn't ready to start his own business and be responsible to investors for its success. The decision to work for someone else was not difficult even though people thought he was crazy for not starting the business. The difficult decision was where to work. The easy route would have been a job in the entertainment industry, where he knew a great many people and could make money quickly. The more difficult choice was to find a type of work that might make a difference in his life—a job that would have meaning. Toward the end of his senior year, an opportunity presented itself to work with technology at the Survivors of the Shoah Visual History Foundation. Shoah (the Hebrew translation for the Holocaust) was founded by producer/director Steven Spielberg. This nonprofit foundation is archiving the testimonies of Holocaust survivors and storing these records in a digital library system so that future generations can learn from them. The pay for this position was certainly not what he could have earned in the for-profit world, but Weisner saw this as an opportunity to learn levels of technology that he could not have learned in school and to meet some very fascinating people. It was also a chance to develop some business savvy, so that when he did start his own business, he might not make the mistakes of a novice. The decision was made more difficult by his awareness that his friend Bryan Rosencrantz was deeply involved in his own business, and several other friends had taken high-paying positions in industry. For a student coming out of school ready to earn some real money for a change, the temptation was great. Yet the more Weisner learned about the Shoah Foundation, the more he became convinced that he needed to work there.

In taking the position, Weisner's strategy from the very beginning was to learn everything he could about the whole business, not just his particular position at the foundation. The strategy worked. Within two years, he became the system administrator for the foundation's global network and was working with state-of-the-art technology developed by the leading companies in the world. In 1998, after more than three years at the foundation and networking with the people associated with the foundation, Weisner discovered the opportunity to join a project that was developing new technology in the visual collaboration area. He jumped on the opportunity, realizing that it would give him the chance to learn a new indus-

try—telecommunications—and also come as close as possible to starting his own business without actually taking on the risk of start-up alone, something he was not yet ready to do. As the project took off, Weisner learned quickly how to create a technology prototype, test it, and bring it to the place where legal and accounting professionals could be enticed to help the project develop a business model for making money with this new visual collaboration technology. The team became skilled at how to identify customers and find out what they wanted in terms of functionality in the technology; that led to successfully testing their business concept at twenty different sites in the entertainment industry. All of a sudden, they had something that looked like a real business, and in late 2000, they made it official and took the major step of incorporating. The year 2001 was difficult for a lot of technology companies and Weisner's company was certainly affected by the downturn in the economy. He is presently restructuring the company so that it can move forward successfully in a rapidly changing market and has great hopes that he will continue to be an important player in the visual collaboration environment.

The choice to become an entrepreneur is a difficult one, and a person reaches it in his or her own way. For some, like Bryan Rosencrantz, there is no option but to "just do it"; they have no intention of working for someone else, at least not before trying it on their own. For others, like Jon Weisner, a more conservative approach is called for. No one approach is better than others. Just as there are many types of entrepreneurs, there are many routes to entrepreneurship. The important thing to remember is that becoming an entrepreneur is a personal decision that should be made after careful consideration of who you are and what you want in your life.

to succeed, a sense of independence, an internal locus of control, and a tolerance for ambiguity. Recall the profiles of Bryan Rosencrantz and Jon Weisner. Which of these characteristics did you see in them? (Remember that not all entrepreneurs have all these characteristics. They were derived from statistical averages.) Let's look at each of them in more depth.

● Entrepreneurial Characteristics

Risk-Taking

The consensus of the research on risk-taking in entrepreneurs is that they are not big risk-takers.[4] Instead, they are moderate, calculated risk-takers who define the risks inherent in any venture and attempt to minimize them or manage them while remaining focused on opportunity. Not being a big risk-taker is certainly not a deterrent to entrepreneurship. As discussed in the previous section, entrepreneurs tend to be highly optimistic about their potential for success. It seems likely that this optimism is closely related to their determination to reduce risk as much as possible. Entrepreneurs see challenges as opportunities and roadblocks as simply temporary pauses in their journey.

Need for Achievement

Entrepreneurs tend to have a high desire to be personally responsible for solving problems and setting and reaching goals—in other words, they have a need for achievement,[5,6] often referred to as "the burning gut," "fire in the belly," or simply "passion." Entrepreneurs are innately driven to make things happen. They are not generally daunted by failure but tend to keep trying until they succeed. The exploitation of opportunity provides a stimulating environment for achievement.

A Sense of Independence

Entrepreneurs also seem to purposely seek independence—to be their own boss in situations that allow them to assume a higher degree of personal responsibility for their decisions and achievements. This need for independence, however, often makes it difficult for entrepreneurs to delegate authority. This inability to delegate has often been referred to as the dark side of the entrepreneur.

Internal Locus of Control

Locus of control describes the source to which we attribute the things that happen to us. Those who believe they have control over aspects of their environment and destiny are said to have an *internal* locus of control, whereas those who feel controlled by their environment are said to have an *external* locus of

Should You Become an Entrepreneur?

Here are some questions to consider before you decide to become an entrepreneur. There are no right or wrong answers, but it is important to acknowledge that these issues affect every entrepreneur to some degree.

1. What are your reasons for wanting to own your own business? If money is the goal, you need to consider that there are easier, less risky ways to make money. Most entrepreneurs start businesses for reasons other than money, although they fully intend to create wealth through their companies.

2. Are you in physical and emotional shape to start a business? Launching a new business requires tremendous amounts of time and energy, as well as support from family and friends. It can also be very stressful, so you have to be in good health and physically fit to withstand the pressures.

3. What kind of lifestyle are you looking for? Will your business and its location provide the kind of life you want?

4. In what type of business environment do you like to work? If you prefer the outdoors, don't start a business that keeps you inside at a desk all day long.

control. Many studies have determined that entrepreneurs have a strong internal locus of control, which gives them a level of confidence in their ability to manage the entrepreneurial process.[7]

Tolerance for Ambiguity

The start-up process is by its very nature dynamic, uncertain, complex, and ambiguous. Entrepreneurs, however, seem to work well in this type of environment, possibly because it is challenging and exciting and offers more opportunity than a structured environment. Researchers have found that entrepreneurs have a greater tolerance for ambiguity,[8] and that those who have a tolerance for ambiguity are more likely to start new ventures.[9]

● *Entrepreneurial Behavior*

The origin of the word *entrepreneur* is found in the French economics literature, where an entrepreneur is described as someone who embarks on a significant project or activity—a behavior. So the entrepreneur is also distinguished by what he or she does. Much research suggests that it is the behaviors of entrepreneurs that set them apart from others who might have the same characteristics or traits.[10] The act of creating a business—perceiving an opportunity, assessing and risking resources to exploit the opportunity, managing the process of building a venture from an idea, and creating value—is the entrepreneurial act. Those who have the passion to build innovative businesses from the idea stage and who continue to act entrepreneurially, making strategic decisions that engage the business in risk-oriented activity, growth, and consequent high performance, are considered entrepreneurs.

In line with the behavioral approach, recent research has proposed that entrepreneurship is about the process of organizing,[11] which includes but is not limited to:

▶ Committing resources to an opportunity

▶ Establishing procedures for the use of resources

▶ Identifying, assembling, and configuring resources

▶ Interacting with people

▶ Coordinating and establishing routines

Why Entrepreneurs Start Businesses

Entrepreneurs start businesses for a variety of reasons. Sometimes their progress is blocked at the company for which they work or they see a better way to do something, or they just want to see whether an idea will work. In 1999, Scott Savitz and Craig Starble, two investment bankers, were watching all the start-ups on the Internet and decided that they wanted to try e-tailing, or retailing on the Internet.[12] They went in search of a product to sell just to see whether they could do it and finally settled on shoes. They reasoned that the mail-order market for shoes was $2.5 billion, so a lot of people were willing to purchase shoes without trying them on first, and it appeared that no one was really selling shoes on the Internet at the time. Savitz and Starble also discovered that they needed no sales force, no inventory, no warehouse, and a minimal number of employees to return a 30 percent net profit. Only time will tell whether their projections were correct but as of spring 2002 they were successfully in business at www. shoebuy.com.

Some entrepreneurs have started their businesses after taking a course in entrepreneurship at a community college or university. Todd Stennett studied entrepreneurship in the MBA program at the University of Southern California. There he completed a feasibility study and business plan on a concept for doing 3D mapping of terrain using technology he could license from the federal government. Learning the process of developing a business concept, testing it in the market, talking with more than 450 people about his concept, and then using the business plan process to build a plan for execution gave him the confidence to actually start the business.

Others start businesses for very personal reasons. This was the case for Sandy Gooch, who suffered from toxic reactions to artificial additives in food. Learning that many others also suffered in this way, Gooch decided to become an expert on natural foods, and in 1977 she founded Mrs. Gooch's Natural Foods Market in the Los Angeles area. By 1993 the company had seven stores, was doing about $80 million in annual revenues, and had over 800 employees. In 1996, Gooch sold her company to Whole Foods and went on to found several other companies. (See Case Studies at the end of the book.)

Still others simply want to own their own businesses. After World War II, Masaru Ibuka started a company in a rented room of a bombed-out department store in Tokyo with $1,600 of his own savings and seven employees, but no idea what the business should be. After weeks of brainstorming, he and his workers decided to produce a rice cooker. Unfortunately, it didn't work the way it was supposed to. However, Ibuka and his team persisted in spite of failure. Their company is known today as Sony Corporation.

Preparing to Be an Entrepreneur

Whatever the reason, most entrepreneurs have the intense desire—the passion—to start a business long before they know what that business will be. It is that internal need to be independent and create something, "the burning gut," that drives entrepreneurs. It is probably the one thing that cannot be taught; you either have it or you don't. The reason passion is so important is that starting a business is hard work that doesn't always go smoothly. The drive to succeed sustains the entrepreneur through the difficult times.

Several skills you can easily acquire will help you prepare to become an entrepreneur.

Creativity

Entrepreneurship is more art than science. No two start-ups experience exactly the same things. No two entrepreneurs approach a venture in exactly the same way. This is what makes entrepreneurship at once so exciting and so difficult. There are no hard and fast rules for how to go through the process; there are only examples from which to choose those things that seem most appropriate for a given situation. To successfully craft a start-up strategy requires creativity—the ability to juxtapose things that are normally not found together. For example, the drive-through bank was the result of combining banking and the fast food model. In Chapter 3, you'll learn more about developing your creativity and the role it plays in opportunity recognition.

Business Knowledge

One of the best ways to prepare for entrepreneurship is to learn as much about it as possible, through magazine articles, books, newspapers, and—most importantly—talking to entrepreneurs. Study the environment in which you plan to do business and look for trends and patterns of change. Increasing your entrepreneurial knowledge will reduce your risk and enhance your chances of success.

Critical Thinking

Because entrepreneurs operate in a world of uncertainty, the ability to analyze a situation, extract the important and ignore the superfluous, compare potential outcomes, and extrapolate from other experiences to the current one is vital. Entrepreneurs also regularly have to weigh options in complex situations. All these things are part of critical thinking. You improve critical thinking skills through practice and by observing how others, who have well-developed skills, work through a problem-solving situation.

Values Assessment

When all is said and done, business is about relationships—with partners, with customers, with suppliers. Successfully building relationships requires honesty and integrity. It requires giving value and delivering on your promises. Your core values become the foundation for your business. Spend time assessing the values that are important to you and that you want to convey in the business. You'll learn more about core values in Chapter 2.

● *Types of Entrepreneurs*

Entrepreneurs are as varied as the kinds of businesses they start. For every characteristic or behavior that defines one successful entrepreneur, you can find another completely different, yet successful, entrepreneur who displays different characteristics and behaviors. There are many paths to entrepreneurship and in the following sections we look at four broad categories: the home-based entrepreneur, the cyber entrepreneur, the serial entrepreneur, and the traditional entrepreneur.

The Home-Based Entrepreneur

Would it surprise you to learn that more than 24 million people operate home-based businesses?[13] Many of these are hobby businesses, consulting, and freelance type businesses, but many others are entrepreneurial ventures that compete in the same arena as brand-name businesses with large facilities. Technology has made it possible to do business from virtually anywhere, so you don't have to work in a traditional office space to start or run a business. Moreover, home-based business owners can tap into more resources than ever from their desktops to locate help for any problem they may be facing, from finding business forms to seeking legal advice to learning how to start and run a business. In addition, U.S. tax laws have become friendlier to home-based business owners who can take a deduction for their home office space and appropriate business expenses.

PROFILE 1.3

The Case of the Serial Entrepreneur

I t is not uncommon for entrepreneurial types to start more than one venture in their careers. In fact, many entrepreneurs enjoy the start-up process so much that they start several ventures sequentially or simultaneously, take them to the point where they can hand off the management to someone else, and move on to the next start-up. That process certainly describes Scott Purcell well. Purcell is a good example of the new breed of entrepreneur who grew up with technology and at age 40 has had three Internet-related ventures.

Purcell grew up in an entrepreneurial family. His father's first business was as an independent electronics representative for several manufacturers; his second with a partner was Encad, a company that produced and distributed a new line of computer printers called plotters. The younger Purcell began his entrepreneurial career at age 9, when one day he noticed the lunch trucks that served the construction crews building homes in his neighborhood. He and a cousin watched the timing of their arrival and decided to go into business. They purchased sandwich and drink items at the grocery store and set up shop every day a few minutes before the lunch trucks typically arrived. Their fledgling business was so successful that the lunch truck company called the sheriff and put them out of business. Purcell was undeterred by this first challenge and vowed to himself that he would one day own his own business.

Upon completing his business degree, Purcell tried his hand at starting several financial service businesses and ended up building a trust company to $1.4 billion in assets. He recognized early on that he was a strategic thinker who had a knack for seeing the big picture. To compensate for his lack of interest in details, he surrounded himself with good management people who would look after the day-to-day details of the business operations. In 1995, Purcell founded his first Internet-related venture—Epoch Networks Inc. in Irvine, California—an Internet service provider (ISP). To grow his company, he began to look for other companies to acquire. In 1996, he bid for a struggling ISP in Atlanta. To ensure that he would win the bid, he started turning around the company and kept it in business before he ever closed the deal. One of the assets of the new acquisition was the domain name www.com, which Purcell retained when he left Epoch to start yet another venture.

www.com is Purcell's biggest effort to date— the world's largest Internet broadcast network focused on entertainment, travel, news, e-mail, and sports. It has the largest online radio network. In 1999, www.com became part of Microsoft's Windows Media Broadband Jumpstart Initiative to increase the use of broadband applications. In 2000, Purcell signed an agreement with the Recording Industry Association of America (RIAA) that gave it a license to webcast millions of songs produced by RIAA's top artists. Purcell has displayed all the characteristics of a serial entrepreneur. Will this be his last venture? Only time will tell.

Sources: Dan Morse, "Planning: How Much Is Too Much?" *The Wall Street Journal Interactive Edition,* February 21, 2000; http://www.epoch.net: "WWW.COM Joins Microsoft Windows Media Broadband Jumpstart Initiative at Streaming Media West Conference." *PR Newswire,* December 7, 1999; "WWW.COM Signs Agreement with RIAA—Largest Webcaster to Have the Rights to Broadcast Music." *PR Newswire,* February 9, 2000.

Many entrepreneurs with growth intentions start from home to save on over-head and reduce the risk of start-up. Once the concept has proven itself, they often move out to acquire facilities that will support the growth of the company and the addition of employees. Some small business owners do what it takes to just support their lifestyle. One such person moved to Hawaii and began selling handmade necklaces and beads to tourists at the southernmost tip of the United States, where there is nothing but ocean all the way to Antarctica.

Some entrepreneurs choose never to have office space but rather to enjoy the ability to move around. Such is often the case for the next type of entrepreneur—the Internet entrepreneur.

The Cyber Entrepreneur

The birth of the commercial Internet gave rise to the cyber entrepreneur, who takes pride in the fact that he or she does not have a bricks-and-mortar operation. Cyber entrepreneurs transact all their business with customers, suppliers, strategic partners, and others on the Internet and deal in digital products and services that do not require bricks-and-mortar infrastructure like warehousing and physical distribution.

MrSwap.com (www.mrswap.com) is a San Francisco-based company that provides consumers a market to swap used CDs, DVDs, and video games. The firm makes money by charging swap recipients a shipping and handling fee for each transaction. Customers earn Swap-Points for the items they list that they can use to purchase anything from other swap items to shipping fees. This company needs no warehouse or distribution.

The Serial Entrepreneur

Many entrepreneurs enjoy the pre-launch and start-up phases so much that when those activities are over and running the business takes over, they become impatient to move on to the next start-up. It's the thrill of starting a business that keeps them going; they prefer to leave the management issues to someone else.

Consummate entrepreneur Wayne Huizenga is a classic serial entrepreneur. He started with a single garbage truck and grew his company truck by truck to become Waste Management Inc., the largest garbage hauler and waste management service in the world. Huizenga then went on to tackle the video rental business with Blockbuster Entertainment and the used-car industry with Auto Nation.

The Traditional Entrepreneur

If there really is such a thing as a "traditional entrepreneur," it would probably be that entrepreneur who starts a bricks-and-mortar business and builds it to a point where the wealth created can be harvested. When Jack Shin started his small business in 1987 in Portland, Oregon, his goal was to target the serious photographer and build strong supplier relations. His Camera World operation consisted of a retail outlet and a very popular mail-order catalog that accounted for 70 percent of his revenues.

In 1992, Shin computerized his fulfillment operations, which gave him better information about his customers. Then in 1995 sales began to flatten, digital cameras were on the horizon, and Shin knew something had to be done to infuse new life into the business; he also knew he was not going to be the person to do it. He decided to harvest the wealth his business had created by selling it to someone whose goal was to take this old-fashioned company and turn it into an Internet firm. From 1998 to 1999, Camera World's annual revenues grew from $80 million to over $115 million. Shin, the traditional entrepreneur, had stepped aside in favor of a serial entrepreneur with the funding to take the business in a new and timely direction.

Traditional entrepreneurs will not disappear as long as there is a need to build sustainable companies, especially in sectors like food services, manufacturing, and retail that are not highly technical.

The Nature of Start-ups

The entrepreneur is only one component in the process of new venture creation. (See Figure 1.1.) The behaviors and experience of the entrepreneur interact with all the other components of the new venture process to create a business. The second component, the environment, is the most comprehensive in the venture creation process. It includes all those factors, apart from the entrepreneur's personal background, that affect the entrepreneur's decision to start a business. These environmental variables, which can be broken down into four categories (see Figure 1.2), have a significant impact on a new venture's ability to start and grow and will vary depending on the specific nature of the industry in which the new business will operate. For example, entrepreneurs who start high technology companies, such as computer and electronics companies, face an environment at once highly dynamic and very complex. In contrast, entrepreneurs who start restaurants face a more technologically stable and less complex environment. The more favorable the environment when the entrepreneur starts the business, of course, the better the chance the new venture will grow and become successful.

The environment for starting new ventures is generally characterized by:

▶ Global competition

▶ Faster product development cycles

▶ Rapidly changing technology

▶ High expectations for quality and service

FIGURE 1.1

The New Venture Process

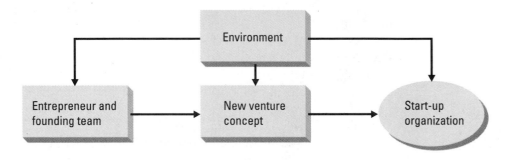

FIGURE 1.2

Environmental Variables

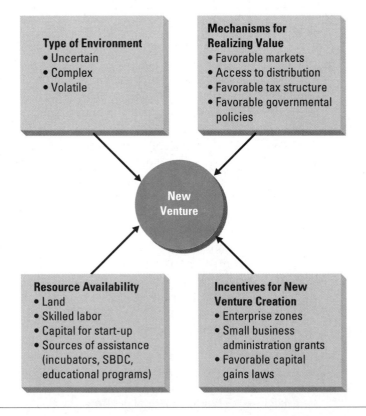

> ▶ The need for strategic alliances

> ▶ A decline in traditional financing sources

Within specific industries and in specific geographic regions, environmental variables and their impact will differ.

The Business Formation Process

Entrepreneurs go through a number of activities in the process of creating a new venture. Although the research literature can't agree on where the process starts and where it ends, it has been suggested that the process starts when one or more people decide to participate in the formation of a new business and devote their time and resources to founding it.[14,15] Empirical research has shown that the process is iterative, nonlinear, and nonsystematic.[16] While entrepreneurs may go in many directions during the process, they typically adhere to identifiable milestones to measure their progress.[17] These include deciding to start a business, researching the concept, preparing for launch, securing the first customer, obtaining the business license, and many other activities that signal that the business is in operation.[18]

Business Failure

The intent to start a business is not enough to make it happen. Many potential entrepreneurs drop out of the process as they move from intention to preparation. And a very high number give up before the new business makes the transition to an established firm.[19] The Small Business Administration Office of Advocacy reports that, in 1999, about 588,990 firms hiring new employees outnumbered the 528,600 firms experiencing business closures by 8.8 percent.[20] It is important to note that not all business closures are failures. In fact, 57.4 percent of employer firms were successful at closure, while 38.2 percent of firms without employees were successful at closure. The Office of Advocacy also reports that about 66 percent of all new businesses survive at least two years; 49.6 percent survive at least four years; and 39.5 percent survive at least six years.[21] As of 1999, small businesses continued to employ more workers than large companies.

One body of research views failure as a liability of newness; that is, the firms that are most likely to survive over the long term are those that display superior levels of reliability and accountability in performance, processes, and structure. Because these factors tend to increase with age, failure rates tend to decline with age.[22] Young firms have a higher chance of failure because they have to divert their scarce resources away from the critical operations of the company in order to train employees, develop systems and controls, and establish strategic partnerships. Another body of research sees failure as a liability of adolescence, claiming that start-ups survive in the early years by relying on their original resources, but that as those resources are depleted, the company's chances of failing increase.

Many researchers and others view failure as a negative outcome of the entrepreneurial process, but history shows that the failure of first-mover entrepreneurs has actually precipitated emerging industries.[23] For example, research laboratories such as MIT, Stanford, and Lucent Technologies are developing speech recognition technology. They are the first movers in their particular technologies. Early examples of companies commercializing this technology are Dragon Systems, Nuance Communications, and Applied Language Technologies. When speech recognition technology becomes more widely adopted, these companies that deliver products and services based on the technology will likely earn the bulk of the profits, while the original developers of the technology often benefit far less.[24]

The vital issue is not avoiding failure but minimizing the cost of a possible failure. That comes from starting with a robust business model and testing it in the marketplace prior to starting the business.

New Business Requirements

An idea is an important beginning for a new business, but it's only that—a beginning. For an opportunity to become a business requires four things: a benefit you're providing the customer, a business model, a team that can execute the model, and resources.

Customers purchase benefits. These come in the form of products or services that solve real needs, not just make life more pleasant. Products and services that provide real value by satisfying a need are easier to fund than those that do not, because customers will typically satisfy needs before wants.

The business model is simply the way you plan to make money, including what you sell, who pays you, how they pay you, and how often they pay you. Your model will dictate the way you structure your business. Most businesses make money in more than one way, even for the same product or service. For example, suppose your company produces and sells herbal supplements. You'll plan to make money from the products you sell; you could also provide consulting services for an hourly fee and hold workshops with a nominal attendance fee supplemented by profits from the sale of products after your presentation. Businesses with the best chance for survival and funding earn some form of recurring revenue from the sale of consumable products that customers purchase repeatedly. You will learn more about business models in Chapter 9.

Most businesses today are started with teams because the environment is too dynamic and complex for any one person to have all the knowledge and all the answers. The most effective teams include people with different skill sets but common values and work ethic. Teams will be the subject of Chapter 8.

Whether you acquire it from other people or use your own resources, every business needs money. The unfortunate fact is that new businesses typically spend a lot of money before they ever make any. You may need to purchase start-up inventory or raw materials for manufacture, and you may need to hire employees to help you. You will learn about start-up capital in Chapter 9.

Entrepreneurial Ventures versus Small Businesses

It is important to make a clear distinction between entrepreneurial ventures and small businesses because their visions and goals differ. Therefore, decisions, resources, and strategies will differ as well.

In general, entrepreneurial ventures have three primary characteristics; they are

1. Innovative

2. Value-creating

3. Growth-oriented

An entrepreneurial venture brings something new to the marketplace, whether it be a new product or service (the fax machine or an executive leasing service), a new marketing strategy (viral marketing on the Internet), or a new way to deliver products and services to consumers (*The Wall Street Journal Interactive Edition*). The entrepreneurial venture creates value through innovation, through bringing new jobs to the economy that don't merely draw from existing businesses, and through finding under-served niches in the market. The entrepreneur typically has a vision of where he or she wants the business to go, and generally that vision is on a regional, national, or, more often, global level.

By contrast, small businesses are generally started to generate an income and a lifestyle for the owner or the family. Often referred to as mom-and-pop or "lifestyle" businesses, they tend to remain relatively small and geographically bound. Here is an example to illustrate the differences.

If you were to start a company that builds parts for local manufacturers, you would be starting what is termed a small business, in this case a job shop, because the business concept in and of itself is not innovative and your employees would likely come from similar businesses. If, however, you were to specialize in remanufacturing certain types of machinery, using the latest technology or developing proprietary technology, marketing the company on an international level with a plan to go public in a few years, you would have started an entrepreneurial venture. It would be innovative and therefore would create value by offering something that doesn't currently exist and has a life of its own beyond its founder; it would create new jobs; and it would have a growth orientation. Logically, many small businesses have the potential to become entrepreneurial ventures. The reason they don't is often a conscious decision on the part of the founder to keep the firm a small, lifestyle business.

Choosing what kind of business you will start is very important, since it influences all your decisions and determines the kinds of goals you are able to achieve. For example, if your intent is to grow the business to a national level, you will make different decisions along the way than if your intent is to own and operate a thriving restaurant that competes only in your local community. Generally, a small business requires good management skills on the part of the owner, since the owner must perform all tasks associated with the business as it grows. By contrast, entrepreneurs typically do not have the skills to handle the management aspects of the business and would prefer to hire experts to carry out that function, leaving the entrepreneurial team free to innovate, raise capital, and get involved in public relations.

Many would-be entrepreneurs think their venture must attract venture capital immediately, so they look for a concept that is complex and scalable, requiring significant management skills. That approach may do nothing more than cause frustration because it's too much for a first-time entrepreneur to take on. A better approach may be to get your feet wet with a simpler venture, using personal resources, where you can test your entrepreneurial skills without risking too much. You will be able to refine your skills, experience some success, and build your confidence level for taking on the next venture. Alternatively, consider a business concept that will not require a fast start, so that you can grow the business when you're ready and feel you have the skills and resources to do it.

Corporate Venturing

Entrepreneurs can choose to start a new venture from scratch, buy an existing business and build it, or start a venture inside a large existing organization. The choice is a function of the type of business, the opportunity, and the support for such a venture inside the existing organization if any.[25] For example, when capital markets make it difficult to find funding, entrepreneurs are less likely to start new ventures from scratch. By contrast, they are more likely to start new ventures on their own when the incentives inside large organizations are weak or nonexistent, when the opportunity requires individual effort, and when the normal scale advantages and learning curves do not provide advantages to the large organization.[26] Entrepreneurs also choose the start-up process when industry entry barriers are low, when the environment is more uncertain, and when the opportunity they seek to exploit involves a breakthrough or disruptive technology that will make previous technology obsolete.

Large organizations are finding it increasingly necessary to provide for entrepreneurial activity to remain competitive. As they saw themselves lagging behind small, young companies in finding great opportunities, they began to look for ways to restructure their organizations to allow creative employees to search for new opportunities the company could exploit. Recognizing that it is nearly an impossible task to re-engineer and redesign an entire organization, many companies have chosen the "skunk works" route (named for Lockheed's unit that developed the Stealth fighter jet). Skunk works refers to an autonomous group that is given the mandate to find and develop new products for the company that may even be outside the company's core competencies. Other companies attempt to encourage **intrapreneurship,** or entrepreneurship inside the structures of their existing organization. This approach at best has been difficult to achieve because the bureaucratic structures of most large organizations—the restrictions of hierarchies of decision making, their inherent avoidance of risk, and strict budgets—all challenge even the most enthusiastic of corporate entrepreneurs.

For an entrepreneurial mindset to succeed inside a large corporation requires:

▶ *Senior management commitment.* Without the support of senior management, it will be difficult to move any entrepreneurial project forward fast enough and far enough to be successful.

▶ *Corporate interoperability.* You must provide an environment that encourages collaboration and gives the intrapreneur access to the knowledge and resources of all the company's functional areas.

▶ *Clearly defined stages and metrics.* Entrepreneurial ventures inside large organizations need a timeline with stages at which decisions can be made about whether to proceed and if additional or different resources are required. They also require a way to measure progress and success that is not based on the corporation's benchmarks but rather on benchmarks appropriate to start-up ventures with limited resources.

▶ *A superior team.* Only the best people should be put in corporate venture situations, because by definition they are riskier than projects based on the company's core skills and products. The new venture team also needs a champion among the top management who will find help for the team when the project reaches the inevitable roadblock.

▶ *Spirit of entrepreneurship.* Entrepreneurship is about opportunity—recognizing it, seizing it, and exploiting it—but it's also about failing sometimes. A company that encourages corporate venturing must not penalize its intrapreneurs for failure but support them as they take what they have learned to a new project.

This book is not intended to address the specific needs of corporate venturers, but the process of opportunity recognition, feasibility analysis, and business planning are certainly relevant in the corporate environment.

A Brief History of the Entrepreneurial Revolution

The term *entrepreneur* has existed in our vocabulary for more than 250 years. The United States was founded on the principle of free enterprise, which encouraged entrepreneurs to freely assume the risk of developing businesses that would make the economy strong. However, it was not until the 1980s that the word *entrepreneur* came into popular use in the United States, and an almost folkloric aura began to grow around men and women who started rapidly growing businesses. These formerly quiet, low-profile people suddenly became legends in their own time, with the appeal and publicity typically accorded movie stars or rock musicians. From the founding of this country, individuals with an entrepreneurial spirit have started the businesses that are the basis of the free enterprise system. With a careful eye on trends and consumer needs, they have supplied us with new technology and new products and services of every conceivable type while also creating jobs. Beyond all this, the most successful entrepreneurs affect our lives, the way we do things, and the choices we make.

Marc Andreesen, young entrepreneur and cofounder of Netscape Communications, was responsible for bringing the wealth of information on the Internet to the average person through a user-friendly graphic interface. Under the leadership of Howard Schultz, Starbucks rekindled our love of coffee and turned coffee drinking into an art form. Entrepreneurs like these shake up the economy. They look for unsatisfied needs and satisfy them. Today small businesses—those with fewer than 100 employees—account for about 90 percent of all new jobs created. How has this happened? Figure 1.3 summarizes the evolution that has taken place since the 1960s.

● The Precursors to Entrepreneurship as a Discipline

In the mid-1960s, gigantic companies were the norm. General Motors in the 1960s was so large that it earned as much as the ten biggest companies of Great Britain, France, and West Germany combined.[27] The reason U.S. companies enjoyed such unrestricted growth at that time was that they lacked competition from Europe and Japan. Therefore, job security for employees was high and companies tended to diversify by acquiring other kinds of businesses.

The 1970s saw the beginning of three significant trends that would forever change the face of business: macroeconomic turmoil, international competition, and the technological revolution. A volatile economic climate pervaded the 1970s, the likes of which had not been seen since World War II. The Vietnam War economy brought inflation, the dollar was devalued, food prices skyrocketed due to several agricultural disasters, and the formation of OPEC sent gas prices up 50 percent. Furthermore, by the late 1970s the Federal Reserve had let interest

FIGURE 1.3

The Entrepreneurial Evolution

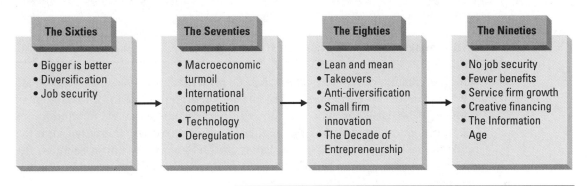

The Sixties	The Seventies	The Eighties	The Nineties
• Bigger is better • Diversification • Job security	• Macroeconomic turmoil • International competition • Technology • Deregulation	• Lean and mean • Takeovers • Anti-diversification • Small firm innovation • The Decade of Entrepreneurship	• No job security • Fewer benefits • Service firm growth • Creative financing • The Information Age

rates rise to a prime of 20 percent. The result was no borrowing, no spending, and a recession that spilled into the 1980s, bringing with it an unemployment rate of 10 percent.[28]

To compound the effects of the economy on business, by 1980 one-fifth of all U.S. companies faced foreign competitors that had far more favorable cost structures, which included much lower labor costs. Imports, particularly in the automobile and machine tools industries, were suddenly taking a significant share of the market from U.S. businesses.

The third event affecting business was the technological revolution brought about by the introduction of the microprocessor by Intel in 1971, the Mits Altair personal computer in 1975, and the Apple II computer in 1977. Microprocessors succeeded in rendering whole categories of products obsolete—such things as mechanical cash registers and adding machines, for example—and effectively antiquated the skills of the people who made them.

Increasing the pressure on business, the government ushered in a new era of business regulation with the Environmental Protection Agency, the Occupational Safety and Health Agency, and the Consumer Product Safety Commission, all of which increased costs to businesses. On the opposite front, deregulation forced planes, trucks, and railroads to compete, and in general big companies no longer had control of the marketplace.

By the early 1980s, business was in terrible shape. The Fortune 500 saw a record 27 percent drop in profits.[29] Large mills and factories were shutting down; manufacturing employment was declining; yet, ironically, productivity remained the same or increased. New, smaller manufacturers were still generating jobs—and not only manufacturing jobs, but service jobs as well. How was this possible?

To become competitive, the smaller, more flexible, entrepreneurial manufacturers had hired subcontractors who could perform tasks such as bookkeeping and payroll more efficiently. These service firms developed to support the needs of the product sector, but they inspired the creation of other service firms as well—people who work often need day-care or maid services, so even more jobs were being created.

• The Decade of Entrepreneurship

With the creation of all these jobs, it is no wonder that the 1980s has been called the "Decade of Entrepreneurship" by many, including the dean of management science, Peter Drucker, who was not alone in asserting that the United States was rapidly and by necessity becoming an entrepreneurial economy.[30] On the heels of the emergence of Silicon Valley and its legendary entrepreneurs, the mainstream press began to focus on business activities, creating many popular magazines such as *Inc.* and *Entrepreneur.*

Responding to this entrepreneurial drive, big business in the 1980s found it necessary to downsize and reverse the trend of diversification it had promulgated for so long. If big companies were going to compete with the dynamic, innovative smaller firms and fend off the takeover bids so prevalent in the 1980s, they would have to restructure and reorganize for a new way of doing business. This restructuring and reorganizing actually resulted in improved performance, increased profits, and higher stock prices. It also meant, however, that many jobs would no longer exist, employees would receive fewer benefits, and the only "secure" jobs left would be found in civil service.

All these events moved this country toward a period that required the vision, the resources, and the motivation of the entrepreneur to seek new opportunities and create new jobs in a vastly different global environment electronically linked via the Internet.

The interest in entrepreneurship has not waned since the earliest days of the 1980s. According to recent research, demand for and supply of entrepreneurship faculty have increased dramatically in the period from 1989 to 1998.[31] The number of faculty positions increased 253 percent, while the number of candidates available for these positions increased by 94 percent. This is a direct result of demand from students, which is particularly noteworthy because in most schools, entrepreneurship remains an elective subject dependent on student interest.[32] Still, today there are over 400 U.S. and international schools offering courses in entrepreneurship.

Researching the Entrepreneurial Phenomenon

While entrepreneurs and their ventures became the subject of media attention, they also spawned a new field of research to study the phenomenon. As the instrument by which concepts born in laboratories and in the minds of scientists and engineers are transferred to the private sector in the form of useful products and services, entrepreneurship is the intersection of two phenomena: lucrative opportunities and enterprising individuals.[33] It is worth repeating that neither one nor the other, but the two phenomena interacting, result in entrepreneurship.

In the field of entrepreneurship, researchers study

- sources of opportunities;

- processes of discovery, evaluation, and exploitation of opportunities;

- individuals and teams who recognize the opportunities, evaluate them, and exploit them.[34]

Thus, entrepreneurship is not about people and their attributes and behaviors independent of the situations in which they are found.[35] In fact, entrepreneurs represent such a diverse group in their traits and behaviors that it's unrealistic to believe that people are entrepreneurs, or are not entrepreneurs, all the time.

Furthermore, entrepreneurship does not require the creation of a new venture or organization; it can also occur inside an existing organization.[36] This phenomenon is known as corporate venturing and was discussed earlier in the chapter.

● *Opportunity Recognition*

For entrepreneurship to exist and thrive, there must be opportunities to develop new goods and services, gather the resources to produce those goods and services, and mechanisms to bring them to market at a price greater than their cost of production. What differentiates entrepreneurial opportunities from other profit-making opportunities is that to exploit entrepreneurial opportunities one must discover a new means to an end, with unknown outcomes and resources not yet under the control of the entrepreneur.[37] Exploiting opportunity means that the entrepreneur must assume a risk. Furthermore, there must be differing viewpoints on the value of resources so that the entrepreneur can discover a value that was not previously identified.[38] This scenario is what is commonly termed "finding a niche in the market." In a situation where more than one entrepreneur perceives the same value for a resource, in other words, finds the same niche, competition for profit occurs. The entrepreneur must then seek another source of value, another niche to differentiate himself or herself from the competition. It has long been known that innovation and entrepreneurship drive the economic change process. Schumpeter identified entrepreneurship as the engine of change when he proposed that the job of the entrepreneur is creative destruction. Entrepreneurs disrupt the economic equilibrium—and from that disequilibrium come new ideas, new businesses, and even new industries.[39] Disequilibrium provides an ongoing supply of new information about resources so that entrepreneurs can continually find new ways to use resources to create wealth.

For entrepreneurs to recognize an opportunity, they have to possess prior information from experience that is compatible with the new information they receive from scanning the environment.[40] The new information may be in the form of a customer need, a niche that is not being served, or the juxtaposition of two opposing ideas that triggers an entrepreneurial opportunity. However, an entrepreneurial opportunity will never reach the marketplace if the entrepreneur can't identify a way to make it happen.[41] That is the reason so many inventions do not become commercialized. Their inventors are unable to visualize their commercial applications and it often takes teaming with a business entrepreneur to complete the commercialization process.

Opportunity Exploitation

Recognizing an opportunity is only part of the equation; deciding to exploit that opportunity is the other part. Why do entrepreneurs choose to act on an opportunity when others do not? How do entrepreneurs choose the opportunities worthy of exploitation? Not every opportunity has a sufficiently high expected value to warrant action. The return on the investment of time and effort must be large enough to offset the opportunity cost of exploiting another opportunity or doing something else (like taking a job).[42] Moreover, entrepreneurs also consider their ability to acquire the necessary resources—capital, land and equipment, human resources, etc. Some research suggests that entrepreneurs who have ready access to capital and strong connections to resource providers are more likely to choose to exploit an opportunity that meets their other criteria.[43]

Another factor that seems to propel entrepreneurs to move forward with an opportunity is information from previous employment and industry experience that serves to reduce the cost of commercializing the opportunity and increase the probability that the opportunity will be exploited.[44]

More recent research tells us that entrepreneurs' decisions to exploit an opportunity are influenced by their level of optimism. In fact, entrepreneurs typically perceive their chances of success as much higher than they may actually be. Entrepreneurial optimism tends to minimize the amount of information the entrepreneur requires to make the decision to exploit an opportunity and is reflected in overly optimistic forecasts of sales and profits.[45] Entrepreneurs also display a tendency to act first and analyze at leisure.[46]

The Network Effect

Networking is the exchange of information and resources among individuals, groups, or organizations whose common goals are to mutually benefit and create value for the members. Research in the field of entrepreneurship has learned much about the positive effects of networking. For instance, entrepreneurship has been found to be a relational process. Entrepreneurs do not act autonomously but are "embedded in a social context, channeled and facilitated or constrained and inhibited by people's positions in social networks."[47] These social networks consist of strong and weak ties. **Strong ties** are the entrepreneur's close friends and family members whom he or she knows well, while **weak ties** are the entrepreneur's acquaintances and business contacts. In general, acquaintances are not socially involved, that is, entrepreneurs do not generally spend their nonbusiness hours with acquaintances.[48] Nevertheless, these weak ties play an important role in the entrepreneurial process because entrepreneurs typically move forward faster with the help and support of weak ties who are not biased by a prior history with the entrepreneur. Family and close friends, on the other hand, tend to restrict the entrepreneur's potential because they look at the impact on them of the entrepreneur's business activities. In short, if you have a new concept for a business and you want objective advice, your chances of getting the advice you seek are better if you approach one of your weak ties than either family or close friends.

Entrepreneurs who successfully use their networks to build their businesses generally are committed to the success of the people in their network, are active listeners, and approach every contact with an open mind.[49] In that way, they derive the maximum value from their network ties.

Looking Ahead: The Organization of the Book

Starting a new venture is a process that begins long before the business ever opens its doors. That process is rarely linear. More often it is an iterative—even chaotic—process, but one with a direction and goals. Consequently, this book takes a process approach to starting an entrepreneurial venture. This chapter serves as an introduction to the field of entrepreneurship and the environment in which entrepreneurs start new ventures today. Chapter 2, another foundational chapter, addresses the critical area of ethics and social responsibility and their relationship to entrepreneurs and start-up ventures. The topics discussed in Chapter 2 are fundamental to all the topics presented in the book.

At Chapter 3, the process of entrepreneurship begins with the recognition of an opportunity and the testing of the business concept arising out of the opportunity in the marketplace through a series of analytical tools that comprise feasibility analysis. Feasibility analysis is depicted in Figure 1.4 as a series of concentric circles. The entrepreneur begins with the largest circle—the industry—and makes his or her way through each circle and its respective analytical tools to the decision point. The tools in each of the circles are discussed in Chapters 3 through 10.

Once you have a feasible concept, you will create a business plan to execute the concept. Whereas the feasibility process worked from the largest area of study—the industry—inward, in the business planning process the entrepreneur works from the inner circle out, as depicted in Figure 1.5. The creation of any

FIGURE 1.4

Feasibility: Test the Concept

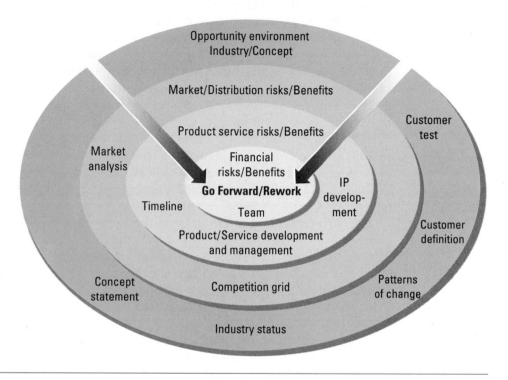

company should start with a consideration of the purpose, core values, mission, and goals that form the basis for all the decisions made about the company. The business plan documents the creation of a new company—the business model, operating plan, management plan, financial plan, and execution plan. Chapters 11 through 19 deal with the development of the business plan.

In the next decade, entrepreneurial skills will be the key not only to economic independence and success, but literally to survival. The marketplace places a premium on creativity, initiative, independence, and flexibility, and entrepreneurs who develop those behaviors and display those characteristics will be more likely to succeed.

FIGURE 1.5

Build the Company from the Inside Out

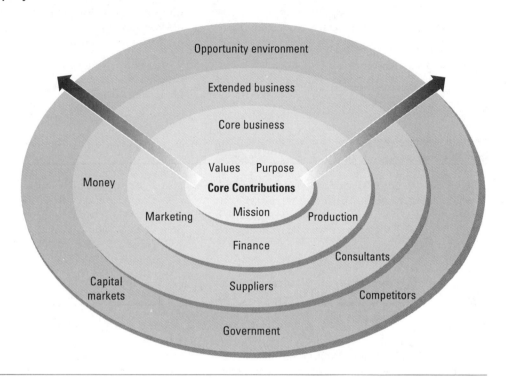

NEW VENTURE CHECKLIST

Have you:
- ☐ Concluded that you have what it takes to be an entrepreneur?
- ☐ Determined why you want to start a business?
- ☐ Decided whether you will start an entrepreneurial venture, an intrapreneurial venture, or a small business?
- ☐ Determined how the trends for the new millennium will affect your search for a business idea?

ISSUES TO CONSIDER

1. Why is it so difficult to assign "typical" characteristics to entrepreneurs in order to describe them?

2. What impact does the environment have on your ability to start a business?

3. What are the steps you should take to prepare yourself for entrepreneurship?

4. Choose a typical "small business" in your community and discuss how you could turn that business into an entrepreneurial venture.

5. Which of the trends for the next decade do you believe hold the most promise for business opportunity and why?

EXPERIENCING ENTREPRENEURSHIP

1. Interview an entrepreneur in an industry or business that interests you. Focus on how and why this entrepreneur started his or her business. Based on your reading of the chapter, what type of entrepreneur is this?

2. Visit an entrepreneurial venture and a small business. Compare and contrast them in terms of the distinctions discussed in the chapter. Which type of business is more suited to your personality and your goals?

ADDITIONAL SOURCES OF INFORMATION

Allen, K. (2001). *Entrepreneurship for Dummies.* Chicago: IDG Books.

Catlin, K., and J. Matthews (2001). *Leading at the Speed of Growth: Journey from Entrepreneur to CEO.* Chicago: Hungry Minds.

Drucker, P.F. (1986). *Innovation and Entrepreneurship.* New York: Harper & Row.

Gerber, M.E. (1995). *The E-Myth Revisited.* New York: HarperBusiness.

Koehn, N.F. (2001). *Brand New: How Entrepreneurs Earned Consumers' Trust from Wedgwood to Dell.* Boston: Harvard Business School Press.

INTERNET RESOURCES

E-Business Research Center
http://www.cio.com
Good source of case studies on e-commerce businesses.

EntreWorld
http://www.entreworld.org
Resources for entrepreneurs and links to magazines, journals, and trade associations.

ZDNet Small Business
http://www.zdnet.com/smallbusiness/
A clearinghouse for information on Web-based small businesses.

AllBusiness.com
http://www.allbusiness.com/
A site that provides tools, services, and information to help start, manage, and grow a business.

RELEVANT CASE STUDIES

2

Ethics, Social Responsibility, and the Start-up Venture

Some say knowledge is power, but that is not true. Character is power.
Shri Sathya Sai Baba

Overview

Vision and values

Ethics

Social responsibility

Core values and success

From the Ivory Tower to the Real World: A Lesson in Ethics

Eric Van Merkensteijn has always believed in the basic goodness of people—that beneath the outward appearance and behavior lies a basically honest and trustworthy human being. And he regularly conveyed that philosophy to his skeptical MBA students at the University of Pennsylvania's Wharton School. So confident was he that he was right about people's inherent goodness that he decided to prove his theory by retiring from his 25-year teaching career and starting his own business, Van M's Music Bar & Grille, in Philadelphia.

Van Merkensteijn had no way of knowing that with that decision his long-held belief about people's integrity was about to change. He hired the employees he needed to prepare for the restaurant's opening, and thought he had picked people who were trustworthy and loyal. He quickly discovered, however, that some of them were stealing from the company to the tune of tens of thousands of dollars. What he did not know about the industry was that there was a culture of restaurant people who moved from new restaurant to new restaurant because they knew the restaurants were not yet in good shape and they could take advantage. Bartenders would serve customers regular drinks, ring them up as premium drinks, and pocket the difference. Waiters would alter tip amounts on credit cards, and busboys and cooks would hide expensive meats in the bottom of trash cans, which they collected at the end of the evening. Van Merkensteijn felt that his basic belief about people had been destroyed. Would he have to assume that everyone was out to get him—that no one could be trusted?

No, Van Merkensteijn was undaunted and determined to make a difference with his restaurant. In an industry where the interests of the owners always come before the well being of employees, Van Merkensteijn decided to do things differently. He began giving everyone, from the dishwasher on up, stock in the company after three months of employment and educated them on the finer points of marketing strategy and return on investment. Van Merkensteijn believed that rewarding the least skilled workers instills pride of ownership and higher ethical standards, and, in a restaurant, the performance of the least skilled workers can mean the difference between success and failure.

Despite his forward-thinking approach, Van Merkensteijn will not have an easy time of it. In late 1999 when he opened his restaurant, Philadelphia was in the midst of a restaurant boom, the likes of which it hadn't seen since the 1970s. The total number of restaurants more than doubled in the space of five years. Still, Van Merkensteijn doesn't see that as a negative; in fact, the influx of new competitors has fed his enthusiasm. In his words, "the more the merrier. If a new restaurant opens up across the street from me, I celebrate that." He foresees a day when he *and his competitors join forces to create a network to share advertising, human resources, and knowledge—another opportunity to test one of the many human resource theories he taught as a professor at Wharton.**

SOURCES: Leigh Buchanan, "Into the Frying Pan," *Inc. Magazine,* January 2001; John McCalla, "New Wave of New Eateries," *Philadelphia Business Journal,* August 11, 2000; Scott Robinson, "Ex-Wharton Prof Tries on Proprietor's Hat," *Philadelphia Business Journal,* June 2, 2000. http://www.van-ms.com.

Never before has an entrepreneurial business needed an ethics policy more than it does today. The very nature of the so-called new economy or digital economy puts business owners in situations that test their value systems on a daily basis. Just to keep up, businesses must create new and better products and services at lower prices and faster speeds than ever before. Shareholder value is often more important than basic human values, and everyone is learning to deal with uncertainty. The pressure to achieve unachievable goals and survive in such a chaotic environment causes stress; and when people suffer stress, they don't always make wise decisions. Moreover, the global economy, made more accessible than ever through the Internet, has juxtaposed U.S. businesses with cultures that may define morality in terms of very different contexts, values, and codes of ethics. Yes, it's a challenging environment, but those entrepreneurs who understand their value systems and create a code of ethics for their businesses can successfully maneuver through the challenges without forsaking their principles.

This chapter looks at three key issues for entrepreneurial companies, issues that will become increasingly important as companies interact more frequently in the global marketplace: vision and values, ethics, and social responsibility. The profile of Van M's Music Bar & Grille clearly demonstrates that every industry is looking for ways to reinvent itself and deal with the many ethical challenges it faces. The chapter closes with a discussion of the components of success and how to make sure your success is congruent with your vision and values.

Vision and Values

Every great company begins with the entrepreneur's vision of what that company will become. Just as top professional athletes envision every play of an upcoming game in their minds before they ever set foot on the playing field, so do entrepreneurs envision the kind of company they want to build. That vision acts like a beacon, guiding the company in the right direction. It's the company's true north.

While it's possible to have a successful company without a vision, it is difficult, if not impossible, to become a great company without a vision. Researchers Jim Collins and Jerry Porras back up this belief. The authors of *Built to Last: Successful Habits of Visionary Companies,*[1] Collins and Porras found that the num-

*Today Van M's is successfully offering a full menu of great musical events and good food.

ber one company in every industry outperformed its number two competitor by a significant amount in terms of revenues, profits, and return on investment. The primary reason was that the number one companies each had a strong vision based on core values that it regarded as inviolable. Vision is made up of core values, purpose, and mission. The following sections are based on the work of Collins and Porras.

● *Core Values*

Core values are the fundamental beliefs that a company holds about what is important in business and in life in general. Your company's core values represent your philosophy of life because core values derive from the personal values and beliefs of the founder. They are not something that can be created or invented for the company out of thin air. Your company's core values tell the world who you are, what the company stands for. Because they are so fundamental to the existence of the company, they rarely change over time. For example, Nortel Networks' core values are as follows:

> We create superior value for our customers.
> We work to provide shareholder value.
> Our people are our strength.
> We share one vision. We are one team.
> We have only one standard—excellence.
> We embrace change and reward innovation.
> We fulfill our commitments and act with integrity.

Source: http://www.nortelnetworks.com/corporate/community/ethics/practices.html. Reprinted with permission of Nortel Networks.

For more on Nortel's core values, see Profile 2.2.

Core values endure beyond the tenure of the founder; in fact a company is known by its core values. Companies like Walt Disney Company, Sony Corporation, and Merck have become the leaders in their industries because of their core values, which have guided all their decision-making processes.

One way to test whether a value (for example, "the customer is always right") is a core value or not is to ask yourself whether you would ever relinquish it if you were going to be penalized in some way for holding it. If you are willing to let go of the value, then it's not a core value for your company.

● *Purpose*

Your purpose is the fundamental reason you're in business. It is the answer to the question, "why does the business exist?" It is not necessarily a unique characteristic of the business; in fact more than one business may share the same purpose. What is crucial is that the purpose be authentic; that is, you must mean

---

PROFILE 2.2

Nortel Networks Focuses on Values

"At Nortel Networks, we recognize the importance of credibility, integrity, and trustworthiness to our success as a business. We are committed to upholding high ethical standards in all our operations, everywhere in the world. We believe in the principles of honesty, fairness, and respect for individual and community freedoms."

These are the opening words on the web site home page of Nortel Networks, a global Internet and communications business. When visiting Nortel's web site (see below for URL), you get the unmistakable feeling that it takes these words seriously. Not only does it educate employees on

all aspects of ethical behavior, it provides guidelines for dealing with typical situations its employees might encounter.

For example, employees are told that they are not to use improper means to gather competitive intelligence: bribes, gifts, electronic eavesdropping, or any other illegal means. Then they are given suggestions as to how to obtain help when needed.

Nortel's core values, the basis for all the ethical standards it has, and those core values are infused into everything it does.

Source: Nortel Networks web site: http://www.nortelnetworks.com/corporate/community/ethics/index.html

---

what you say. A properly conceived purpose will be broad, enduring, and inspiring.[2] For example, Jordan Neuroscience is in the business of "saving brains" through remote monitoring of brain waves in emergency room patients.

● *Mission*

A company's **mission** is the way to bring everyone together to achieve a common objective and is closely related to the company's purpose. According to Collins and Porras, a mission is a "Big Hairy Audacious Goal" designed to stimulate progress. All companies have goals, but a mission or BHAG is a daunting challenge, an overriding objective that mobilizes everyone to achieve it. The natural metaphor is mountain climbing. The mission is *to scale Mt. Everest,* a major challenge to be sure. To get there, however, will require smaller goals like *reaching base camp in one week,* but the bold and compelling mission is what drives us forward.

A company's mission is communicated through a mission statement. A mission statement precisely identifies the environment in which the company operates and communicates the company's fundamental philosophy.[3] Here are three examples of mission statements—the first two are brief but compelling and the third is more comprehensive.

To preserve and improve human life — Merck
To give unlimited opportunity to women — Mary Kay Cosmetics

FIGURE 2.1

The Components of Vision

Core Values
What you believe to be true

VISION
Where you see your business going

Purpose
Why you're in business

Mission
Big, hairy audacious goal

Goals
Milestones on the way to the mission

Strategies
Plans for accomplishing goals

Tactics
Means for implementing strategies

America West will support and grow its market position as a low-cost, full service nationwide airline. It will be known for its focus on customer service and its high-performance culture. America West is committed to sustaining financial strength and profitability, thereby providing stability for its employees and shareholder value for its owners.

● *Strategies and Tactics*

Look at Figure 2.1 to get a broad view of the components of vision and their relationship to each other. To review, the vision for the company stems from the founder's core value system. It becomes the guideline for all the decisions made by the company as it grows and operates. The company needs a compelling mission that is congruent with its core values—a BHAG to propel it forward—and goals or operating objectives, which are milestones along the way to achieving the mission.

Once goals have been set, you need to develop strategies, which are the plans for achieving those goals and ultimately the mission. You will also need tactics, which are the means to execute the strategies. An example will make these points clearer. Suppose your company's mission is *to be number one in your industry.* Two goals or milestones you might set to help you accomplish the mission could include 1) to create an Internet presence and 2) to achieve brand recognition. Now you need some strategies for achieving these goals, such as building a web site to accomplish goal #1 and developing a marketing campaign to build your brand (goal #2). You will then have a variety of tactics or ways to implement the strategies. For example, to implement the strategy of building a web site, you might employ the following tactics.

▶ Determine the purpose and focus of the web site.

▶ Hire a web designer and developer.

▶ Purchase a server.

▶ Plan for content.

Merely setting a goal is not enough. You must also have a plan for achieving the goal and that is the role of strategy. But strategy is not enough to achieve your goals. You will also need some good tactics or action items.

Ethics

Ethics, or the moral code by which we live and conduct business—essentially our concept of right and wrong—come from the cultural, social, political, and ethnic norms with which we were raised as children. We don't often sit down to think about our value system; we merely act instinctively on the basis of it. It's only when we're faced with a dilemma that appears to us to be immoral or un- ethical that we may consciously ask ourselves what is the correct thing to do. Harvard Business School conducted a survey of its alumni to find out what it needed to teach future business leaders. The top responses included leadership, technology, entrepreneurship, and globalization. But the response cited most often overall was ethics, morals, and values.

Many people believe that if they follow the Golden Rule (do unto others as you would have them do unto you) they're safe from ethical dilemmas. Unfortu- nately, most ethical dilemmas in the business environment are complex and offer gray areas that are troubling when one attempts to apply an ethical principle. One Oregon construction company hired a subcontractor to do a $15,000 concrete job. That particular subcontractor did not have solid bookkeeping practices and never submitted an invoice to the construction company for the work it did. The construction company could have kept quiet, but instead sent the subcontractor a copy of the plans, specifications, and names of workers on the job, and told the subcontractor how much to bill it. The gray area here is the decision point—whether to notify the subcontractor of its failure to invoice. The construction company demonstrated its ethical values by contacting the subcontractor to ask for the invoice.

Another ethical decision had to be made by a marketing company that received two checks from a client for the same $50,000 project. There was no way the client would have discovered it, yet the marketing firm immediately sent the second check back. These kinds of ethical dilemmas occur every day in business. Although these two entrepreneurs did what they believed to be ethically correct, not everyone operates under the same standards of ethics. The employee who steals notepads, pens, and computer disks because "the employer won't miss them," the executive who abuses his or her expense account, and the business owner who evades taxes by not reporting employee income demonstrate the lack of a clear ethical standard that is accepted too widely and costs entrepreneurs both time and money. Entrepreneurs face special problems when it comes to ethical issues. Their small companies generally are more informal and lack systems and controls. They often don't have the time or resources to focus on ethics during their attempts to keep their businesses alive, and they often take for granted that everyone in their organization and everyone with whom they do business share their values. This is a mistake, because unethical behavior can contaminate a business for as long as it exists.

Another very practical reason why small firms should pay attention to the ethics of employees concerns their ability to defend themselves against criminal action in a court of law. The U.S. Sentencing Commission's guidelines assert that an effective ethics program can serve to protect a company from criminal penalties, or at least in lessening their impact, if an employee violates federal law.[4]

In general, ethics dilemmas in business are found in four areas: conflicts of interest, survival tactics, peer pressure, and pushing the legal limit.

● *Conflicts of Interest*

Conflict of interest is one of the most universal problems in business today. A conflict of interest occurs when a person's private or personal interests clash with professional obligations. Business owners have vested interests in many areas of their lives: careers, a business, family, community, and their investments, to name just a few. It is rare for all these interests to be in complete harmony with one another. A potential conflict of interest occurs when there is a discrepancy between an individual's private interests and his or her professional obligations such that an independent observer might reasonably question whether the individual's professional actions or decisions are influenced by personal gain, financial or otherwise. For example, you may want to continue an important manufacturing process that provides many jobs and profit for your company, even when your community claims that the process is not good for the environment.

Conflict of interest has also found its way into e-commerce. Today an online company can use its web site to gather information about customers, profile them, and send the right message to the customer at the right moment. Through cookie technology, a company can track customers' movements online. Over time it will have compiled an enormous amount of data that it can use to better target its marketing messages. A company that uses cookie technology will usually offer a notice of privacy to its customers, promising not to sell the information it gathers to other companies.

Unfortunately, many an Internet company has gone back on its promise to protect customers' privacy. When Internet ad company DoubleClick (DCLK) was exposed for matching online and offline databases (essentially matching cookie data to real names, addresses, and phone numbers), it was hit with a Federal Trade Commission inquiry, investigations by the states of New York and Michigan, six lawsuits, and a lot of bad press.[5] The Electronic Privacy Information Center (EPIC) wants to require companies to obtain customer consent before creating a profile. Proponents of profiling claim that advertising is the "lifeblood" of the Internet and if it's too highly regulated, content may no longer be free. This conflict of interest is one that will not go away for a long time because there is so much potential marketing benefit in consumer profiling.

The issue of privacy, however, is big enough to warrant a watchdog, and that watchdog is TRUSTe, a nonprofit organization dedicated to auditing and approving online privacy policies. Designed to reassure customers that the business they're dealing with online is sticking to its promises, the TRUSTe seal of approval is the most displayed banner on the Internet, but it has its critics. More than one famous Internet company, while sporting the TRUSTe seal, has been caught violating its privacy clause. As a result, TRUSTe has competitors like The Council of Better Business Bureaus and most of the Big Five accounting firms.

● ## *Survival Tactics*

Many are the stories of entrepreneurs who did whatever it took to survive, even violating their own standards. Survival is the area where most people's ethics really face a test. It's easy to be ethical when things are going your way, but what if you're facing bankruptcy or can't make payroll? What do your ethics look like then? Small firms, especially in the early years, are vulnerable to setbacks that would not negatively affect a large organization. The loss of a major customer or supplier could put a small business out of business. In these types of life or death situations, a small business owner's commitment to ethical practices can force the company to make some difficult decisions. Again, we reiterate the importance of sticking to your ethical code, because what you do today out of desperation, you will live with for the rest of your business career.

One entrepreneur whose company, Haven Corporation—a manufacturer of products for the mail-order industry—had a history of cash flow problems finally reached the point where it was time for him to close the doors. It was a tough decision because the entrepreneur felt a profound sense of duty to his fanatically loyal employees and customers who would be stranded by his decision. But, as he said in the e-mail he sent out to his customers and suppliers, the company could not pay its bills and he was personally $100,000 in debt. Little did the entrepreneur know but his e-mail tactic turned out to be a survival tactic. Over 400 customers began communicating with each other to seek technical help, to bemoan the loss of the company and to begin to generate some ideas for how to resurrect it. Out of the rush of communications came the person who would ultimately raise the money to breathe life back into the company.*

● *Peer Pressure*

There are many stakeholders in your business, and they all want what's owed them when it's owed them. Stakeholders include any person or organization that has an interest in seeing the company succeed—investors, shareholders, suppliers, customers, and employees, to name a few.[6] Every business, no matter how small, has stakeholders.

One area of research has focused on what the business ought to do in terms of the "ends it pursues and the means it utilizes."[7] For many entrepreneurs, there are times when managing the demands of stakeholders becomes a real juggling act. For example, to grow the company to the next level, you may decide to consider an IPO. Once you throw that hat into the ring, you'll find lots of stakeholders pressuring you to move forward, even when you're not sure it's the best thing to do. These stakeholders include investment bankers who get a fee for doing the deal; business partners who may be able to cash out of some of their holdings in the company; and lawyers who want the additional business. All these stakeholders want to be served, and the entrepreneur must hold to his or her code of ethics and base decisions on it and not the personal agendas of stakeholders who may not have the best interests of the company at heart.

● *Pushing the Legal Limit*

Some entrepreneurs look for ways to bend the law as much as possible without actually breaking it. Entrepreneurs who regularly play too close to the edge of legality eventually get caught, and the price is often their businesses and their reputations. Ethical entrepreneurs don't play those games, but they're always on the alert for companies that might use quasi-legal practices against them to gain an edge in the market. These types of tactics must be dealt with strongly. For example, a large water-meter repair company that operated within the law was

---

*You can read this interesting story in the February 27, 2001 issue of *Inc. Magazine*. The article is written by Donna Fenn and is entitled "Rescue at cc:."

attacked by a competitor in collusion with a newspaper reporter. The competitor entrepreneur accused the company of bribing public officials. It was a false accusation, clearly unethical but perhaps not illegal. Still it caused the innocent utility company a great many problems and a lot of money defending itself.

Learning from Real-Life Dilemmas

There is no better way to fully understand the role of ethics in any business than to encounter real-world dilemmas and determine how they might be solved. Here are some examples of real-life ethical dilemmas. Think about what you might do to deal with them.

▶ Your struggling Internet company is not producing revenues at the rate you originally projected; at the same time your burn rate (the rate at which you spend your cash) is increasing as you continually seek new customers. Your site claims to protect the privacy of visitors who purchase your products and services and that's something you take pride in. However, you're concerned that if you don't find a quick source of income, the company may not survive. You have heard that you can sell your customer information lists to companies that will pay a lot of money for them. You have also heard that if you start tracking which web sites your customers visit, you can sell that information to major advertising firms for use in targeted advertising, another source of revenue. These tactics will violate your customers' privacy, but if you don't do something quickly, you may have no business to offer them. What should you do?

▶ One of your best customers has asked for a specific product from you. After telling him the price, you learn from the customer that a competitor is selling the same item at your cost. You know that this competitor has unethical business practices. Should you tell your customer about the competitor or let the customer purchase where he can get the best price?

▶ One of your employees confides in you that another employee is planning to leave the company in two months to start her own company as a competitor. Armed with this knowledge, you are tempted to fire this employee immediately, but she is in the middle of a major project that is critical to the company and will be completed within two weeks. What should you do?

▶ You have hired an engineering design firm as an independent contractor to design and build an e-commerce site for your company. You paid a large portion of the fee, $25,000, up front to begin the work. The owner assures you that the work is on schedule to be completed on time, but as of a week before the due date, you have yet to see any designs. You schedule a meeting at the engineer's office to check on the status of the project. While wait-

An Ethical Dilemma

Superior Machine Works had developed a new type of generator that was environmentally friendly and could be controlled from a distance. Superior's research had determined that the market was quite large and had the potential to be very profitable.

Superior was marketing two models: a small, lightweight version for people who would use it to power small tools and a bigger, heavier version used generally as backup power for an office or home in addition to supplying power for a variety of electrical tools. The smaller version retailed for $895, while the larger version sold for $1,500. The larger version had a patented noise reduction feature on it that significantly reduced the decibels of sound the machine produced. Studies on similar equipment had shown that over a long period of time the noise level of the small machine could produce hearing loss.

Meanwhile, Superior's main competitor was also developing a generator very much like Supe-

rior's small version and that company was also aware of the noise problem and the potential for deafness over time. Still, it was going ahead with the product. Superior was faced with a real dilemma. If it didn't move quickly to get its smaller version to market, it would lose its first-mover advantage to its competitor. At the same time, did Superior want to market a product that was known to cause deafness over time? If it only marketed the larger machine, it would quickly lose market share to its competitor's smaller, lighter machine. If Superior could not introduce a successful product quickly, it would have to lay off many of its workers. Considering the downward trend in its current sales, the company might fail if it couldn't introduce its product quickly.

1. What options does Superior have and what are the consequences of each?
2. What should Superior do and why?

ing at the office, you overhear employees talking about the impending closure of the business. You also hear that the programmer assigned to your project has not been paid and there is no money to pay him. The owner mentions nothing of this during your meeting and assures you that the project will be completed as planned. You suspect that he is not being truthful. You know that if the business closes and you have not received the designs and software for the project, you will be out $25,000 and will have to file a lawsuit. Should you talk to the programmer and reveal what you've heard? Should you confront the owner? Should you approach his disgruntled employees to find a way to gather the data you need to win a lawsuit?

▶ You are about to begin doing business in another country where it is well known that paying bribes to officials makes business transactions move more quickly. You know that paying bribes is illegal in the United States, the home base for your business, but this contract will insure that you establish a foothold in the global market before your competitors. What should you do?

These are all difficult choices when often the very survival of your business is at stake. For one more example, see the sidebar. Aristotle, the Greek philosopher, said that courage is the first of the human virtues because without it, the others are not possible. How we make these difficult and courageous choices is the subject of the next section.

Developing a Code of Ethics

Most of the research on ethics has been in large organizations, so we have very little information about small businesses. However, work done by Longenecker and others found that small-business owners have more stringent ethical views on such things as favoritism in promotion, acquiescence to a dangerous design flaw, misleading financial reporting, and misleading advertising. But surprisingly, they view with much greater tolerance padded expense accounts, tax evasion, collusion in bidding, insider trading, discrimination against women, and the copying of computer software.[8]

Research has also found that the ethical behavior of employees is very much influenced by the code of ethics of the company.[9] When a code of ethics is written, people in the organization take it more seriously. So it would seem to be important for a business owner to develop a formal code of ethics for the business. After all, the best way to handle ethical dilemmas is to have in place a mechanism for avoiding them in the first place. Look at Profile 2.3 for an example of a company whose employees live and breathe the company's code of ethics.

The Code of Ethics Development Process

The process of developing a code of ethics begins with a company self-examination to identify values held by individuals and alert everyone to inconsistencies in how people deal with particular issues. For a new company, this means getting the founding team together to discuss how certain issues should be dealt with. For a larger company, forming a committee to oversee the process may be appropriate.

The Josephson Institute of Ethics developed a list of ethical values that should be considered.[10]

▶ Trustworthiness: loyalty, honesty, integrity

▶ Respect: privacy, dignity, courtesy

▶ Responsibility: accountability, pursuit of excellence

▶ Caring: compassion, kindness, giving, consideration

▶ Justice and fairness: impartiality, consistency, equity, due process, equality

▶ Civic virtue and citizenship: law abiding, community service, protection of environment

As you think about a code of ethics for your business, think about behaviors that would allow your business to display these characteristics.

PROFILE 2.3

Setting Standards in the Jewelry Industry

Trust is a significant issue in the jewelry business. Customers must rely on the integrity of the jeweler because they usually aren't able to judge quality with any degree of success. But the jewelry industry is highly competitive and that breeds unscrupulous retailers. The Jewelers of America (JA) tried to address that issue by establishing a set of standards for all its members. It also wanted to recognize members who upheld the standards with a special designation that they could place in the windows of their stores. In this way customers would feel more comfortable shopping there.

It began by developing a Code of Ethics and Rules of Professional Conduct and Business Practices. Basically, the Code spells out the need to 1) act in a professional manner in all their dealings; 2) continue to improve their expertise; 3) keep promises and commitments; and 4) deal honestly with customers. The Rules of Professional Conduct then explain how the jeweler can achieve these goals. The ERC (Ethics Resource Center, www.ethics.org) helped JA to develop the procedures for monitoring compliance and dealing with customer complaints.

To get members to buy into its effort, the JA chose to use a positive approach, presenting the Code to its regional affiliates as the new standard for the industry. It is now the largest trade association in the industry with more than 10,000 members who sign on to the Code of Ethics. You can visit the site at http://www.jewelers.org/.

As part of the code of ethics, business owners should ask three questions about any ethical decision to be made.[11]

1. Will the actions taken result in the "greatest good for all parties involved"?

2. Will the actions respect the rights of all parties?

3. Are the actions just? Would anyone be hurt by the actions?

A fourth question puts everything into perspective.

4. Would I be proud if my actions were announced in my local newspaper?

This question gets to the heart of how you determine what is ethical in a situation. It has the further advantage that most people can immediately and intuitively answer it.

Characteristics of an Effective Code

The most effective code of ethics will have these characteristics:

▶ The code and its attendant policies will be clear and easy to understand.

▶ Specifics regarding special situations that need further explanation will be included (e.g., political factors in certain countries).

▶ Where employee judgment may be required, descriptions and examples make it easier for the employee to make the decision.

Employers should make sure that all employees are aware of and understand the code as well as the values and culture of the company. The following are some guidelines for insuring that your code of ethics is implemented and maintained over time.

▶ Model the behavior expected of others in the company. In some companies the ethical behavior of management and employees in tough situations can become legendary and part of the company culture to remember over and over again.

▶ Educate employees about ethics through workshops that put employees in hypothetical situations. For example, "What would you do if you found out that your best customer was harassing your administrative assistant?"

▶ Demonstrate commitment to the ethics program by mentioning it on a regular basis and providing examples of appropriate behavior that employees display during the course of their work.

▶ Share your code of ethics with customers, so they understand your commitment and are assured of your company's integrity.

▶ Provide a channel for reporting and dealing with unethical behavior.

▶ Reward ethical behavior through recognition, bonuses, raises, and so forth.

You will find an example of a code of ethics in the sidebar on page 49.

Once you have developed a sound code of ethics and business practices, you need to take some steps to ensure that the standards you have established become part of the company culture.

▶ As the leader of your business, you need to be the role model for ethical behavior. Be sure you treat everyone from employees to customers with the highest level of integrity.

▶ Give your employees the opportunity to achieve both personal and professional growth.

▶ Give your employees the right and responsibility to treat customers ethically.

▶ Reward the ethical behavior you find in your employees.

▶ Share your code of ethics with your customers.

There is no way to avoid the ethical problems that business brings. But developing a strong ethical code and getting the cooperation of everyone in the business will go a long way toward making those problems easier to deal with.

The MVK Group Code of Ethics

MVK is an office products-related sales agency that serves manufacturers and customers in the Southeast. The following is its code of ethics.

1. Maintain the highest standard of personal and professional conduct in our dealings with both principals and customers.
2. Encourage and promote the highest level of ethical and professional conduct within our profession.
3. Maintain loyalty to the principal who hires us and pursue our principal's objectives in ways that are consistent with the public interest and that are fair to the principal's customers.
4. Strive to continually keep our principals informed of matters that may adversely affect our relationship with them and their ability to compete in the marketplace.
5. Maintain confidentiality of privileged information entrusted to us by our customers and principals.
6. Always communicate matters concerning our principals and their customers in a truthful and accurate manner.
7. Recognize and discharge our responsibility to uphold all laws and regulations governing the policies and activities of our profession.
8. Be courteous and professional in our dealings with other reps in our industry. Work with them for the advancement of all rep agencies in our industry.
9. Respect the rights and interests of my competitors.

Source: http://www.mvkgroup.com/ethics.html. Reprinted with permission of MVK Group. All rights reserved.

Social Responsibility

Today it's not enough to have a successful business and make a profit. Your business must hold itself to a higher standard of social responsibility by giving something back to the community or communities in which it does business, and through them to society as a whole. According to Business for Social Responsibility (http://www.bsr.org/), a nonprofit organization dedicated to helping companies become socially responsible, social responsibility is "operating a business in a manner that meets or exceeds the ethical, legal, commercial and public expectations that society has of business." This means obeying the law, respecting the environment, and being mindful of the impact the business has on its stakeholders, the industry, and the community in general.

The benefits to businesses that seek to become socially responsible are many.[12]

- Improved financial performance
- Reduced operating costs by cutting waste and inefficiencies
- Enhanced brand image and reputation
- Increased sales and customer loyalty
- Increased productivity and quality

◗ Increased ability to attract and retain employees

◗ Reduced regulatory oversight

Some business owners have chosen to define their businesses publicly as "socially responsible businesses." But when their goals are too ambitious, their businesses do not always succeed. In 1989, Ben & Jerry's cofounder Ben Cohen launched Community Products Inc. (CPI) whose purpose was to save the rainforest and contribute to a number of worthy causes by donating an astronomical 60 percent of its profits to these causes. But things didn't turn out the way Cohen intended. The idea was to import nuts for the company's ice cream products (namely Rainforest Crunch) from the local economies in the region of the rainforests. This vision was newsworthy so Ben & Jerry's received a lot of free publicity, helping to generate revenues of $3 million within the first year.

CPI then partnered with Cultural Survival Enterprises, a nonprofit organization dedicated to finding markets for products from developing countries, but soon found that its goals were not compatible with CPI's. Cultural Survival was charging high prices for its nuts and was not controlling quality. But more important, the products received from Cultural Survival contained a number of foreign substances, everything from glass to rocks to insects. Then there were CPI's operating problems, poor working conditions, and constraints on its ability to pay workers because of the requirement that 60 percent of its profits must go to charity.

By 1993, CPI was losing money and the glow on the "save the Rainforest" vision was merely a glimmer. By 1997, the company was in bankruptcy. While Ben Cohen's goal was certainly lofty, it was highly unlikely that one corporation could do what entire nations had been unable to accomplish. So for all practical purposes, CPI was setting itself up for failure. Furthermore, since a company like this puts its social goals into all its publicity and advertising, it is held to impossibly high standards by the public and the media, who are ready and willing to remind it of its failure to achieve its goals. Although CPI gave away a half million dollars to save the rainforest, it ultimately crashed, leaving its creditors hanging.

Stories like this should never discourage a company from being socially responsible. But they should warn entrepreneurs of the importance of choosing a mission that is achievable. Paul Brainerd founded a company, the Brainerd Foundation, in Seattle, Washington, for the purpose of helping entrepreneurs to give back strategically. He suggests that entrepreneurs follow two rules:

1. Don't wait until you're older to begin giving back. Start when you and the business are young.

2. Don't go for something huge. Start at the grassroots level, where help is needed the most.

● *Effective Ways to Become Socially Responsible*

Your company does not have to be a large, multimillion-dollar company to begin to give something back to society. Even a very small company can have an impact on its community if it does a few things first by way of preparation.

▶ Set some goals for your company. What do you want to achieve with your social responsibility efforts?

▶ Pick a cause that is yours. It's always better to focus your efforts on one cause than to use a shotgun approach.

▶ Consider partnering with a nonprofit organization. The nonprofit contributes its expertise in the social issue. Your company contributes its expertise and the time of its employees to the nonprofit.

▶ Get everyone in your organization involved. There is strength in numbers.

▶ Get your customers involved.

Once you have your goals in place and have chosen a cause that fits your company's core values, there are several things you can do with your new venture that will establish positive relationships in your community and benefit both the company and the community.

Donate Your Product or Service

One of the least expensive ways to do good is to donate the products or services your company produces. Saint Louis Bread Company gives bread, muffins, and so forth to the homeless to the annual tune of $700,000 retail. Stanford Coaching Inc. serves wealthy clients who need academic test tutoring, but it has found a way to give back by giving away its services through scholarships to needy students. Volunteers from Stanford's employees, who are never in short supply, provide those services.[13]

Get Other Companies Involved with You

In the spirit of networking, consider putting together a group of small businesses so that your combined efforts produce results with more impact. Just Desserts, a San Francisco bakery, put together a group of thirty-five businesses to adopt an elementary school. With its combined financial strength, the group planted trees on the school grounds, painted the school, and refurbished the classrooms, creating a positive environment for students.

Offer Your Expertise Free of Charge

Some organizations in the community need the expertise your company has developed. Abby Margalith, who owns Starving Students of San Diego, a moving company, has relocated more than 100 women and children from abusive homes. Her crews volunteer to do the work and she collaborates with the local YWCA.[14] Jay Backstrand used his technology expertise to develop a web site, Volunteer America, which merged with Impact Online in October 1996, to match nonprofit organizations with people looking for opportunities to volunteer (http://www. impactonline.org).[15]

Contribute to Your Community

Many entrepreneurs have found cost effective ways to give back to their communities without breaking the bank. In fact, they have made social responsibility a regular part of their businesses.

Each store of a bagel chain in New Hampshire adopts a local nonprofit organization for a year. Customers vote for their favorite charity, and the winning choice receives a cash donation, bagels, meeting space, and a place to advertise its services in the store. They also get volunteer help from the bagel employees who do their deeds on company time.

Another entrepreneur shares the benefits of his success with his community by providing ski trips for underprivileged children, food drives for the hungry, highway cleanups, and the Easter Seals poster-child campaign among many other things.

As you can see, there are many ways to demonstrate social responsibility through your business. It doesn't have to cost much time or money to make a significant difference as long as you focus your efforts where they will count the most.

Core Values and Success

Why are we talking about success in a chapter on ethics and social responsibility? Because your personal definition of success—what it means to be successful—is really a function of your core values and the vision you have for your life. A business's success is easily measured by total revenues, earnings, return on investment, and so forth, but entrepreneurs don't typically measure their personal success solely in these terms. In fact, research has shown that the personal rewards that motivate entrepreneurs to start businesses are independence and freedom.[16] Entrepreneurs are goal-oriented and tend to cite being one's own boss, being in control of one's destiny, and having the ultimate control of the success of the venture as reasons for going into business.[17] They measure their personal success by their achievement of those goals.

Wally Amos of Uncle Noname Cookies believes that success is "turning lemons into lemonade." For Sue Szymczak of Safeway Sling in Milwaukee, success is "being happy with what you're doing and feeling as though you're accomplishing something." One group of entrepreneurs decided that measuring the financial performance of the business did not totally reflect their definition of success, even at the company level. These are the entrepreneurs who started many of the so-called "socially responsible" businesses that we discussed earlier. They intend to take their personal definitions of success to the company level. This is possible if at the same time the business is conducted effectively so that it can achieve its financial goals and give the entrepreneur a vehicle for his or her social responsibility efforts.

No matter how you define success, there are some constants. One of these is *purpose*. To feel successful, entrepreneurs need to know that what they are doing is taking them in the direction of a goal they wish to achieve. True success is a journey, not a destination—even the achievement of a goal will be just a step on the way to the achievement of yet another goal.

The second constant is that life has its ups and downs. *Failure* is the other half of success, and most entrepreneurs have experienced several failures of one sort or another along the way. Still, they do not fear failure, because they know intuitively that those who obsessively avoid failure are doomed to mediocrity. To avoid failing, one has to virtually retreat from life, to never try anything that has any risk attached to it. Most entrepreneurs are calculated risk takers, so they make sure that every time they come up to bat they give it their best; then, win or lose, they strive to learn from the experience and go on. Entrepreneurs are generally optimists who believe that failure is a normal part of the entrepreneurial process.

The third constant is a *sense of satisfaction* with what you are doing. The most successful entrepreneurs are doing what they love, so their satisfaction level is usually very high. Does satisfaction with the work result in success, or does success bring satisfaction? Probably a little of both, which suggests that it's important to know yourself well enough to recognize what kinds of tasks and activities will give you satisfaction in business.

The fourth constant of success is that there is *no free lunch*. Success rarely comes without work. Entrepreneurs do not have the luxury of a nine-to-five workday; they usually are married to their businesses twenty-four hours a day. It is not just the number of hours of work that distinguishes entrepreneurs, of course, but the way they use their time. Entrepreneurs make productive use of odd moments in their day—while they're driving, on hold on the telephone, in the shower, walking to a meeting. Because they love what they're doing, it doesn't feel like work, and that's probably why, wherever entrepreneurs are, they're always working on their businesses in one way or another.

NEW VENTURE CHECKLIST

Have you:
- ☐ Developed a code of ethics for your business?
- ☐ Listed possible ways that your business can be socially responsible?
- ☐ Defined what success means to you?

ISSUES TO CONSIDER

1. Do you believe that your code of ethics should stand firm in any situation? Why or why not?

2. Suppose you are doing business in a country where paying fees (bribes) to get through the process more quickly is standard practice. In the United States, bribery is against the law. How will you deal with this conflict in ethical standards when you're doing business in that country?

3. In addition to the suggestions given in the chapter, name two ways that your company can demonstrate its social responsibility.

4. Would you require your employees to give back to the community as part of their work contract with your company? Why or why not? If yes, how could you implement this policy?

5. How do you define your personal success? How can your definition be applied to your business?

EXPERIENCING ENTREPRENEURSHIP

1. Choose an industry that interests you and interview a manufacturer, a distributor, and a retailer about the code of ethics in that industry. Does the industry have ethical problems? If so, what are they and how are people responding? If not, how are they avoided?

2. Choose two companies in different industries. Interview management in each company about its code of ethics and its stance on ethical standards. Compare their answers and account for any basic differences.

ADDITIONAL SOURCES OF INFORMATION

Cohen, B., and J. Greenfield (1997). *Ben & Jerry's Double-Dip: Lead with Your Values and Make Money Too.* New York: Simon & Schuster.

Houck, J.W., and O.F. Williams (Eds.) (1996). *Is the Good Corporation Dead?: Social Responsibility in a Global Economy.* Lanham, MD: Rowman & Littlefield.

Murphy, P.E. (1998). *Eighty Exemplary Ethics Statements.* Notre Dame, IN: Notre Dame Press.

Reder, A. (1995). *75 Best Business Practices for Socially Responsible Companies.* New York: J.P. Tarcher/Putnam.

Rushworth, M.K. (1995). *How Good People Make Tough Choices.* New York: William Morrow and Company.

Seglin, J. (2000). *Good, the Bad, and Your Business: Choosing Right When Ethical Dilemmas Pull You Apart.* New York: John Wiley.

Solomon, R.C. (1999). *A Better Way to Think about Business: How Personal Integrity Leads to Corporate Success.* London: Oxford University Press.

Trevino, L.K., and K.A. Nelson (1999). *Managing Business Ethics: Straight Talk About How to Do It Right.* 2d ed. New York: John Wiley.

INTERNET RESOURCES

Business Ethics Magazine
http://condor.depaul.edu/ethics/bizethics.html
Delivers timely news, commentary, and features on social responsibility and ethics.

Corporate Conduct Quarterly
http://www.singerpubs.com/ethikos
A bimonthly publication that examines ethical and compliance issues in business.

International Business Ethics Institute
http://www.business-ethics.org
Deals with issues of transnationalism in business ethics.

The Online Journal of Ethics
http://www.depaul.edu/ethics/ethg1.html
Contains cutting-edge research articles in the field of ethics.

RELEVANT CASE STUDIES

Case 1 Mrs. Gooch's

Case 2 Franchising a Dying Business

Case 6 Highland Dragon

Case 8 Alcoholes de Centroamerica, S.A. de C.V.

3

Recognizing and Creating Opportunity

Few ideas are in themselves practical. It is for want of imagination in applying them, rather than in acquiring them, that they fail. The creative process does not end with an idea—it only starts with an idea.

John Arnold,
Massachusetts Institute of Technology

Overview

The nature of creativity

Challenges to creativity

Removing the roadblocks

Sources of new product/service ideas

PROFILE 3.1

A Creative Way to Generate Ideas

Dr. Yoshiro Nakamatsu is truly the essence of a creative, innovative person. He holds more than 2,300 patents, more than double the number that prolific American inventor Thomas Edison held. For example, Nakamatsu is responsible for the floppy disk, which he licensed to IBM (and he does get a royalty on the millions of disks sold every year), the compact disk and disk player, the digital watch, and the water-powered engine.

As a child Nakamatsu was encouraged by his parents to be creative and not focus solely on learning. This was important, because Japanese children are typically made to memorize great quantities of information and aren't allowed to free-associate until they reach their twenties. Nakamatsu believes that this discipline and the freedom that follows is what results in genius. He also believes that trying too hard stifles creativity.

Nakamatsu has a very creative way of generating ideas. He starts the creativity process by sitting calmly in a room in his home, which he calls the "static room" because it has only natural things in it, much like the meditation gardens in Kyoto, Japan. It is in this room that he opens his mind to the creative flow of new ideas—he freeassociates, letting his mind go where it wants to go. He then moves to the "dynamic room," a dark room with the latest audio/video equipment. Here he listens to jazz, easy listening music, and Beethoven's Fifth Symphony—one of his favorites. In this room new ideas begin to form. Following a period of time in the dynamic room, he heads for the swimming pool, where he swims underwater for extraordinarily long periods of time. It is underwater that he finishes the process of "soft thinking" or playing with the idea and is ready to move on to the more practical phase of considering how to implement the idea. He even records his ideas on a special Plexiglas writing pad underwater.

Nakamatsu, by the way, also swears by the brain food he eats, which he dubbed "Yummy Nutri Brain Food": dried shrimp, seaweed, cheese, yogurt, eel, eggs, beef, and chicken livers!

SOURCES: Linda Naiman, "Dr. Yoshiro Nakamatsu," http://www.creativityatwork.com/Nakamats2.html; Chic Thompson, "Dr. Yoshiro Nakamatsu," http://www.creativityatwork.com/Nakamats1.html.

Have you ever wondered where people get those great ideas that turn into extraordinarily successful businesses? Is the ability to recognize opportunity something you're born with? Not necessarily. Can it be learned? Absolutely! It is important to distinguish between an idea and an opportunity. Everyone has ideas; in fact, you probably have hundreds of them every day. However, a *business* opportunity is an idea that can be turned into a business or commercialized in some manner. In fact, the very act of developing a business concept and successfully testing it in the marketplace with potential customers is what may turn an idea into an opportunity.

Certainly some people have an easier time generating ideas than others, but that's the case only because they may possess better-developed awareness and creativity skills. This is good news, because even if you have never thought of yourself as a creative person, you have the ability to become one.

What does creativity have to do with entrepreneurship? Very simply, creativity is that behavior that results in innovation, which is finding a new way to do something, a key ingredient in entrepreneurial success. In the new century, entrepreneurs face a rapidly changing environment brought about in large part by the speed of technological change. The combination of rapid change and the resulting uncertainty for what the future holds presents a fertile ground for new opportunities. It is a curious fact of life that a healthy economic climate results in more jobs and less incentive to start new businesses, while the worst business conditions (such as a recession) inspire creative men and women to find opportunities and ways of adapting to the environment, making it work for them. So the worst times often bring out the best entrepreneurs.

On the other hand, it is precisely in strong economic times that entrepreneurs' skills at running a business are most tested. Prosperous customers demand a steady stream of new and innovative products and services, and entrepreneurs find that they have to adjust their thinking to encompass many types of change, which sometimes take place simultaneously. But, surprisingly, the greatest ideas come out of chaotic environments where inventors and entrepreneurs are pushed to the edge.

Some entrepreneurs use their creativity to improve on what they currently do or do better what everyone else does. This is the process of opportunity recognition, innovating based on a product or service already in existence. Other entrepreneurs do things that no one else is doing. This is the process of opportunity creation or starting from scratch. The highest level of creativity and innovation is doing things that seemingly can't be done, which is called radical innovation.

No matter what the environment throws at entrepreneurs, if they put their creative talents to work, they can find ways to succeed. Opportunity recognition and creation begin with a creative mindset. In the next section, you'll learn how to bring out your natural creativity and develop some skills that will put you in a better position to recognize or create a business opportunity for yourself.

The Nature of Creativity

Creative people are curious and strongly aware of their surroundings. They ask questions and aren't afraid to do things differently. They are open to all ideas, believing that every one is worthy of at least initial consideration, and they seem to have a high tolerance for ambiguity. However, some people resist creativity and ambiguity; they are uncomfortable in uncertain environments and don't know how to use their creative skills to survive. This is not surprising when you consider that many schools do not challenge students to be creative, but instead expect them to follow a structured plan laid out by the professor, which includes coming up with only the expected correct answers.

Entrepreneurship is a creative, not a scientific, process. From the generation of the business idea to the development of the marketing plan to the management of the growing business, it is creativity in all aspects of the venture that sets the most successful new businesses apart from those that merely survive.

What Is Known about Creativity

Creativity has been defined from both a functional and an outcome perspective. The **functionalist perspective** dominates the literature and proposes that creativity is the production of novel and useful ideas.[1] The **outcome perspective** focuses on the generation of valuable, useful products and services, procedures, and processes.[2]

The earliest research on creativity focused on the individual, in much the same way that early research on entrepreneurship focused on the entrepreneur. Researchers looked at personality factors and cognitive skills such as language, thinking processes, and intelligence.[3] From the individual level of examination, they moved to looking at the context in which people are creative and found that a number of environmental settings are conducive to creativity, among them absence of constraints, rewards, and team effectiveness.[4]

The newer models of creativity incorporate organizational variables, which include such things as policies, structures, culture, and training. However, little is really known about the specific conditions that promote creativity in individuals inside organizations.[5] Furthermore, research finds that creativity takes place at both an individual and a group level and is a matter of choice on the part of the person involved.[6]

Creativity as a Process

As discussed in the previous section, most researchers have looked at creativity more as an outcome than a process, so the models they describe are static. However, one group of researchers has proposed that time is an important variable in the creative process, and that creativity is not a linear process but an iterative, chaotic one.[7] This view is compatible with research on the new-venture process.

The creation or invention process is not formulaic, but research suggests that some definable patterns and activities occur in any creative process. They are connection, discovery, invention, and application.[8] See Figure 3.1. The activities are labeled in order to provide clarity in explaining them, but the graphic should not

FIGURE 3.1

The Invention Process

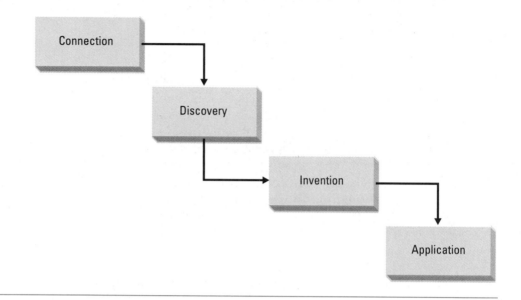

suggest that this is a linear, step-by-step process. Using the example of Leonardo da Vinci, one of the greatest inventors of all time, we can describe the creative process.[9]

Connection

A connection occurs when two ideas are brought together using various devices like metaphor, analogy, symbol, or hypothesis. Da Vinci saw a connection between the branches of trees and the canal system he was designing for the city of Florence, Italy. He verbalized this connection as a metaphor: canals are tree branches. It is interesting to note that nature has been the metaphor for many an invention, including Velcro® and nanotechnology—the use of micro machines whose functions are based on processes in nature.

Discovery

Once you have a connection established, you begin to explore it in depth. Da Vinci did this by drawing tree branches, examining them closely, and conducting experiments. Through his in-depth research he learned how trees manage the flow of nutrients and water through their systems. This gave him a better understanding of how water flows through canals. Discovery often occurs when we look at something that already exists but see it in a new way.

Invention

Inventions are the product of effort once a discovery has occurred. They usually arise out of needs in the market, but they can be serendipitous as well. Da Vinci's insight into the inner workings of tree branches aided the development of hydraulic devices to control water levels so a boat could cross a bridge. His other inventions led to a means to create a waterway from Florence to the sea.

Application

Going beyond the initial invention to other applications, da Vinci came up with ideas for mills powered by wind and water. It is interesting that many inventors never see beyond the initial invention to all the other possible applications in other industries and in other situations. The highest levels of creativity occur when you can find applications outside the areas with which you're familiar.

Challenges to Creativity

Entrepreneurs are often their own worst enemies when it comes to creativity. They unintentionally place roadblocks in their paths that keep them from thinking out of the box. Some of these roadblocks are discussed in the following sections.

● No Time for Creativity

Letting yourself get so busy that there is no time to think and contemplate can keep you from exercising your creative skills. Most people rely on routines to keep their lives organized and under control. But relying on routines too heavily can prevent you from taking the time to let your mind generate new ideas outside those routines and adapt to a changing environment.

● No Confidence

Taking the familiar path out of fear of being criticized will keep an entrepreneur from fully realizing her potential because she will be continually held back by the need for her ideas to be acceptable and rational to others. Rationality is not often associated with the best opportunities. Certainly Ken Hakuta, the Harvard-educated king of fad products, wasn't thinking about rationality when his mother sent him an octopus-shaped rubber toy from Japan. When you threw this toy against a wall, it would stick; then gravity would force it to crawl down the wall. Hakuta saw an opportunity to bring this toy to the United States, which he did, calling it the Wacky Wallwalker. During the 1980s, he sold more than 250 million of these little beasts, generating about $20 million. A lot of products that we now use every day—the fax machine and the personal computer to name two—would not have come about if the people who invented them hadn't had the courage to go against the general thinking at the time.

● *No Creative Skills*

All these roadblocks can stifle creativity, but believing that you aren't a creative person, that you have no creative skills, is perhaps the most damaging because it keeps you from even trying to be creative. Everyone can learn how to become more creative and develop some creative skills. In the next section, you will discover some ways to prepare yourself for creative success.

Removing the Roadblocks

As you begin your journey to more creative thought, it's important to keep a journal of your thoughts and ideas with you at all times. You may not be ready to work on a particular idea at the moment you conceive it, but you may want to return to it in the future. As much as we might believe that we'll never forget the idea, it does happen.

There are a number of things you can do immediately to remove the roadblocks in your path to more creative thinking. The process starts with preparing an environment that makes it easier for you to think imaginatively and then moves to some techniques for enhancing your creative skills. This chapter cannot present all the possible creativity tools and skills available, so check the end of the chapter for some additional resources.

● *Preparing for Innovation*

Great inventors and highly creative companies owe their success to the environments they created that simulated high levels of innovation. Thomas Edison's greatest invention was arguably not the light bulb but rather the concept of a research and development laboratory that provided an incubator for radical innovation. Likewise, Disneyland was not the greatest invention of the Walt Disney Company. Disney Imagineering, its Edison-like laboratory, is the source of its celebrated ideas.

The environment in which a person works can either stimulate or dampen the creative juices.[10] For example, suppose your business has a very rigid and hierarchical structure with many layers of management. For this type of environment to be effective, its operations must be standardized so that everyone does things in the same way. That kind of environment is not conducive to thinking out of the box. Here is another example. Suppose you have an advertising and public relations firm that has to meet many deadlines. A fast-paced environment like this leaves little time for contemplation, which is essential to higher levels of creative thought.

Even in environments like these, there are techniques for making the setting more conducive to creativity and innovation. Here are a few suggestions:

❿ Minimize distractions. Give yourself permission to close your door or shut off the phone when you want to do some creative thinking.

❱ Devote some time each day to quiet contemplation. Doing this on a regular basis will train your mind to shift quickly to creative mode. It will also help make creative thinking a habit.

❱ Pay attention to the places where you find yourself being the most creative and spend more time there.

❱ Develop a creative culture in your company so that your employees contribute to the company's ability to innovate. For example, Premiere Radio Networks, a Los Angeles-based producer and distributor of radio broadcasts, lets its creative writers design their own office space to reflect their personalities. Comedy writer Jaime Case has adopted an eclectic blend of random souvenirs and toys collected during her travels. She refers to her office theme as "F.A.O. Schwartz on steroids," but it provides just the right type of surroundings to suit her particular style of creativity.

❱ Mix people up. Another way that companies have achieved a more stimulating environment is to mix people up, that is, take them out of their familiar surroundings and put them in a new setting that forces them to think outside their normal mode. For example, put your technology person in the marketing group for a month and place one of your marketing people inside the technology group. The cultures of the two groups are typically very different, so the marketing person will bring a new perspective to technology issues and vice versa. One entrepreneur looks for unusual places to locate his businesses because he believes that you can't generate truly creative ideas in a typical office setting. So he located one of his businesses in a Victorian mansion and another in an old Army building in the Presidio in San Francisco.

● ### Starting with the Familiar

It is a myth that entrepreneurs only build businesses based on concepts that never existed before. Most business concepts derive from existing ideas that the entrepreneur intends to improve on. And most business ideas stem from a problem or opportunity that the entrepreneur sees in his or her immediate environment. Your own neighborhood or community is a rich source of opportunity, and as you learned in Chapter 1, finding opportunity in things with which you have experience is the most common and effective way to achieve entrepreneurial success. Research supports this notion. One study at the University of Illinois at Chicago identified the following sources of new venture ideas.[11]

❱ Prior experience (73%)

❱ Business associates (33%)

❱ A similar business (26%)

❱ Friends or relatives (19%)

- ◗ Hobby/personal interest (17%)

- ◗ Market research (11%)

- ◗ Serendipity (11%)

- ◗ Other sources (7.4%)*

These are just a few examples of the many familiar sources of creative inspiration. Of course, reading current newspapers, magazines, and trade journals is another excellent source of ideas and trends.

Notice that prior experience was cited more often than any other source. Entrepreneurs do frequently find new opportunity in the familiar. Howard Schultz, founder of Starbucks, did. He found a new use for coffee as a designer beverage that creates an experience. Johann Gutenberg took two unconnected ideas—the wine press and the coin punch—and came up with the printing press and movable type. The mechanism for roll-on deodorant was the motivation for the ball-point pen and the sticky burr was the inspiration for Velcro®. Look at Profile 3.2 for another example of two entrepreneurs who took something familiar and found a new niche in the market.

The federal government or your state government can also be great sources of new venture ideas. New laws and regulations often require the use of a product or service that didn't previously exist. For example, the establishment of the Occupational Safety and Health Administration (OSHA) provided an opportunity for people who could provide training to businesses on everything from meeting the stringent requirements in the workplace to filling out the incredible amount of paperwork associated with those requirements. City ordinances that require certain products, such as glass and plastic, to be recycled have produced many businesses that provide new uses for these materials.

● ## *Identifying a Problem and Solving It*

One of the most effective ways entrepreneurs have of finding opportunity is to see a problem and seek a solution. Most people do this out of habit every day; they just don't realize it. For example, how many times have you not been able to find a particular tool you needed (say, a hammer), so you substituted something else (the handle of a screwdriver). That's using creative thinking to solve a problem. Todd Smart saw that small independent towing companies were having a difficult time surviving and getting new customers in a world of big, brand name companies. So he brought many of these little companies together under one umbrella, Absolute Towing and Trucking, which handled customer acquisition and management activities for the owners so they could do what they do best—tow vehicles.

*Respondents to this survey were allowed to indicate more than one source.

Making Creativity Work

Two young New Yorkers pitch their latest product—Red Sox Monster Crunch cereal—and the audience, a large grocery chain, yawns. What else is new? Yes, Jason Bauer and Michael Simon, founders of Famous Fixins Inc., are relatively new to the supermarket industry, but their concept is not. Putting celebrities, especially sports stars on cereal boxes has been standard practice for mega companies like General Mills and Kellogg's. But Famous Fixins main competitor, PLB Sports Inc., a Pittsburgh, Pennsylvania-based food marketing company, has really built the niche with products like Flutie Flakes and Miami Dolphins mustard. Its creativity in branding products for particular markets has allowed it to find coveted shelf space in crowded supermarkets around the country. And this is no small accomplishment when you consider that slotting fees (the cost for shelf space) range from $1,000 to $10,000 per item, per supermarket.

Creativity and bootstrapping go hand in hand for Bauer and Simon. When they discovered that they would have to pay approximately $10,000 for the rights to use stock photos of the Parthenon and the Greek Islands on their bottles of Olympia's Greek Salad Dressing (named for Academy Award winning actress Olympia Dukakis), they spent $2,000 instead to travel to Greece and take their own photos.

Like PLB, Famous Fixins donates profits to charities, and athletes have a role in designing its packaging. But the key advantage Famous Fixins has over PLB is that it can offer shares in its company.

Sources: Michelle Prather, "Thinking Out of the Box," *Entrepreneur*, June, 2000; http://www.famousfixins.com; http://www.plbsports.com.

Problems and needs are everywhere; the trick is to become more observant of things around you. One way to practice doing that is to go to some place familiar to you, a place that you usually go to for a purpose and rarely if ever spend time contemplating, for example, the airport. Park yourself in a spot where there's a lot of activity, then observe. Watch what people do and how they do it, and look for sources of stress or ways to make what people are doing easier. You will be surprised how many needs you can find. Then put your mind to work to brainstorm some ways to satisfy those needs. You may very well identify a product or service that could become a business opportunity for you.

Using a Personal Network

The second most commonly cited source of new venture ideas is business associates. A personal network—your circle of friends, associates, and acquaintances—is not only a rich source of innovative ideas, it also helps open your mind to new ways of thinking and new possibilities. Contacts within your personal network can help you put ideas together that you might not have thought of on your own because you were relying solely on your personal experiences.

They can help you refine your ideas and direct you to resources that will assist you in testing the business concept that you develop from your ideas. Personal networks don't happen by accident but from the concerted effort of entrepreneurs to go out and meet new people on a daily basis. Once you've identified an industry in which you're interested, begin meeting and talking with key people in that industry: suppliers, customers, distributors, and so forth.

● *Making Time for Creativity and Innovation*

When potential entrepreneurs don't see themselves as creative people, it's often because they don't give themselves the time to exercise their latent creative skills. To enhance your chances of successfully becoming an entrepreneur and spotting that great opportunity, you must give yourself time each day. Here are some suggestions for doing that.

When does your mind relax and become more open to new thoughts? It could be while you're jogging, floating in your pool, or simply lying in a hammock in the back yard. Be sure to schedule at least twenty minutes a day in a place that lets your mind wander. Whenever you choose, make sure it's a time when there are no distractions—when you won't be interrupted.

Some people find that music helps them become more contemplative (remember Dr. Yoshiro Nakamatsu from Profile 3.1). Writers often find that the music of Mozart is good for clearing mental blocks. The important thing is to give yourself a chance to let your mind wander. The best new ideas do not come about because you forced them to happen, but rather because you placed yourself in an environment where they could occur naturally.

● *Returning to Your Childhood*

Many creativity and innovation gurus use toys to get their clients to respond more creatively. Legos and K'NEX are great for stimulating creativity because you start with a simple brick or connector piece, and from there the sky's the limit. Take that one step further and play with children. In that way, you will see unfettered imagination in action. Try suspending your adult intellect for a while and become a child again. Creativity guru Doug Hall, whose famed Eureka Mansion near Cincinnati has been the birthplace of thousands of new product ideas, uses games and toys to make people more comfortable doing things they've never done before and coming up with ideas that previously they would have dismissed as strange or unworthy.

● *Thinking in Opposites*

Great ideas often spring from imagining the opposite of what is normal. For example, when you think about what you can do with a telephone, you probably don't consider eating it. At one point, AT&T was brainstorming some new mar-

Generating Business Ideas

Here are some exercises you might try to spark some new ideas and new ways of looking at things.

List some geographic areas that are not being serviced by a particular product or service.

1. _____
2. _____
3. _____

List some market segments (populations) that are underserved.

1. _____
_____

2. _____
_____

3. _____
_____

List some big or troublesome problems for which the solution could turn into a potential business.

1. _____
_____

2. _____
_____

3. _____
_____

keting tactics when marketing people asked themselves what a telephone is NOT. It's not something you eat, so they came up with the idea of making chocolate telephones to send to their best customers.

Another example can be found in the paradox of recessions. Most people regard recessions or economic downturns as negative events, but looking for what is good about a recession is a useful creative exercise. A recession brings about many more needs and problems from which to find opportunity. For example, during a recession, many people lose their jobs and go back to school to retrain themselves for new careers. Educational entrepreneurs know this, so they start private schools offering courses and workshops to people wanting to take a new direction in their careers or needing to retrain after losing a job. Publishers know this as well, so they develop books geared toward retraining and refocusing careers.

Sources of New Product/Service Ideas

Organizations that monitor the growth of industries believe that the sectors of the economy that will attract sales and investment in the coming years are in the health industries, particularly home health care, and in computer-related industries, specifically companies working on networking and the Internet as well as intranets. Intranets are closed internets accessible only by the companies that own them. The list of the fastest-growing industries contains significant diversity.[12]

- Computer and data processing services

- Home health care services

- Miscellaneous health services

- Automotive services, except repair
- Residential care
- Security and commodity exchanges and services
- No-store retailers
- Management and public relations
- Local and suburban transportation
- Personnel supply services

The most successful firms in these industries, generally high-tech and high-growth firms, flourish in an environment of change. Let's consider some of the major technological trends that will affect opportunity and every new business concept to some degree into the coming decades. You might also look at Profile 3.3 to find out how one entrepreneur found an opportunity for a very interesting business.

Technological Trends

It is also important to note that three disruptive technologies (those that obsolete previous technology) will play a significant role in many of the business opportunities we see for the foreseeable future: gene therapy, nanotechnology, and wireless technology.

Gene Therapy

Perhaps the most important scientific finding of the last decade was the mapping of the human genome, first announced in June 2000. Mapping the structure of human genes opens the door to therapies targeted to a person's specific genetic makeup and ultimately the ability to cure devastating diseases like cancer. It also makes possible the use of cloning to create duplicate organs and potential duplicate human beings, an outcome that is facing huge ethical challenges.

The Human Genome project will result in hundreds of business opportunities. For example, companies like PE Biosystems Group make equipment that genomics companies use to sequence and assemble genes. Entrepreneurs with diagnostic laboratories like BioForce Laboratories, a young entrepreneurial firm, will find new opportunities in gene-based diagnostic tests. Entrepreneurs interested in gene therapy will be able to license new technologies for which they can create new applications in the marketplace.

Nanotechnology

Nanotechnology involves processes that occur at the molecular level. (A *nano* is one billionth of a metric unit, and 10 nanometers is 1,000 times smaller than the

PROFILE 3.3

If It Looks Like a Duck ...

Ideas for businesses can come out of virtually anywhere. In the case of Andrew Wilson, a Boston investment banker, opportunity hit like a bolt of lightning. In 1992, tired of working 100-hour weeks, he traveled across country to visit family and friends. Along the way he stopped in Memphis to visit the legendary Graceland, estate of Elvis Presley. It was there that he first came upon a World War II amphibious military vehicle known as the "duck," which had been converted to a kind of tour bus. It occurred to him that the amphibious nature of the vehicle was perfect for land and water tours of Boston.

The City of Boston wasn't as sure as Wilson. In fact, Wilson had to deal with more than 100 government agencies to get the 29 permits he needed to go into business. Part of the problem was that Wilson didn't even own a "duck" that he could show the city leaders. It took him 9 months to discover a funeral home director, Manuel Rogers, who happened to be a collector of military vehicles; he owned a duck. Not only did he lend it to Wilson to convince the city officials to let him

start his business by giving sample tours, he helped raise start-up capital as well to add to the $30,000 that Wilson had invested. Everyone thought his idea was crazy and off the wall, but Wilson persisted. He painted his ducks bright colors and configured each to carry 32 passengers. In the spring of 1994, Wilson launched his ducks in the Charles River. By fall, 33 investors had placed their faith in Wilson to the tune of $1.25 million. The company was officially in business in October 1994. By 1996, Boston Duck Tours, sporting 12 boats and 19 Coast Guard licensed "captains," was carrying 250,000 riders and boasted revenues of $3.4 million. By 1999, sales had reached over $7 million, and Boston Duck Tours is one of the biggest attractions the city offers. Wilson has plans to open tours in other cities that have plenty of history—and water as well.

Which niche in the market did Wilson's opportunity serve and how?

Sources: Michael Barrier, "The Mighty Ducks," *Nation's Business,* October 1997, pp. 78–79; Laura Tiffany, "Making Waves," *Entrepreneur,* June 1999.

diameter of a human hair.) Scientists and engineers are developing molecular machines, such as microscopic-level diagnostic chips, that a person can swallow so that a doctor can track what's happening in that person's body. The ability to create microscopic machines and robots opens the door to thousands of new products and services that never existed before.

Wireless Technology

The ability to communicate without physical connections will also open up many opportunities to provide new products and services. Today anyone with a web-enabled cell phone or PDA can check on inventory levels and shipping progress for customers, and send and receive e-mail. And that's only the beginning. Many entrepreneurs interested in this area believe that people will become walking Internet portals with wearable wireless technology. They will be able to extend their senses and become an interface for everything they need wherever they go.

● *The Next Great Idea*

If you are looking for the next great idea and are having trouble finding it, take heart. The most successful businesses—the leaders in any industry—did not start with a great idea but rather with a team that wanted to build a great company. Like Sony's first product—the rice cooker—many ideas fail, but a creative and opportunistic person or team will eventually produce something of value out of industry knowledge, familiar things, the need to solve a problem, or a combination of all three, like the entrepreneur in the following story.

In 1951, a young Bette Nesmith approached a new secretarial position with some trepidation because for the first time she would be working on an electric typewriter. Her job required that she rapidly create error-free documents, but the electric typewriter seemed destined to keep her from that goal. The slightest touch produced a stream of letters across the page and the ability to erase a mistake was made nearly impossible by the new carbon ribbons.

Recognizing that the key to her survival was to find a solution to the error problem, Nesmith tried putting some white water-based paint into a nail polish bottle and literally painting over her mistakes. For five years she refined and used the concoction she called "Mistake Out" as others in the office began asking her to supply them as well. A business was born.

Nesmith soon changed the name to Liquid Paper, believing it to be a better brand name, and by 1966 she was producing 9,000 bottles a week. In 1979, Gillette purchased her company for $48 million; it was generating $38 million in sales. Nesmith found her great idea in an industry she knew, with a problem she understood, and in a familiar environment. She was neither an entrepreneur, nor an inventor by trade, nor did she consider herself to be particularly creative, but she discovered her latent creativity and used it to become a successful entrepreneur. In Chapter 4, you'll begin to practice your own creative skills by learning about an industry.

✓ **NEW VENTURE CHECKLIST**

Have you:
- ☐ Identified the roadblocks that keep you from being creative?
- ☐ Developed a plan for removing the roadblocks?
- ☐ Started a file to keep track of business ideas?
- ☐ Started networking and reading in your industry?
- ☐ Identified an industry or trend that interests you?

ISSUES TO CONSIDER

1. Give an example to demonstrate that you understand the difference between an idea and an opportunity.

2. Why do you suppose many people shy away from talking about failure?

3. Pick a business in your community and find a creative way to change either the product/service or the way it is delivered to the customers. How does your innovation add value to the business?

4. Identify the challenges you face in becoming more creative. What three things will you do to address those challenges?

EXPERIENCING ENTREPRENEURSHIP

1. Spend an afternoon walking around your community or your university or college campus. Don't look for anything in particular. Observe the things that you don't normally see when you're in a hurry. Watch people—what they do and don't do. At the end of the afternoon, write down all the thoughts that come to you based on your afternoon of observation. Which of these ideas could possibly become a business opportunity and why?

2. Pick one of the trends discussed starting on page 68 of the chapter. Using the Internet or your library, develop a report on the current status of that trend using articles and sources no more than two years old.

ADDITIONAL SOURCES OF INFORMATION

Crouch, T.D. (1992). "Why Wilbur and Orville? Some Thoughts on the Wright Brothers and the Process of Invention." In *Inventive Minds: Creativity in Technology,* edited by R.J. Weber and D.N. Perkins. New York: Oxford University Press, 80–96.

Gelb, M.J. (2000). *How to Think Like Leonardo da Vinci: Seven Steps to Genius Every Day.* New York: Dell Books.

Gladwell, M. (1999). "Six Degrees of Lois Weisberg." *New Yorker* (January 11): 52–63.

Habino, S., and G. Nadler (1990). *Breakthrough Thinking.* Rocklin, CA: Prima Publishing.

Hall, D., and D. Wecker (1995). *Jumpstart Your Brain.* New York: Warner Books.

Pfenninger, K.H., V.R. Shubik, and B. Adolphe (2001). *The Origins of Creativity.* London: Oxford University Press.

Smith, R. (1997). *The 7 Levels of Change.* Summit Publishing Group.

van Oech, R. (1990). *A Whack on the Side of the Head.* New York: Warner Books.

Weick, K.E. (1993). "Small Wins in Organizational Life." *Dividend* 24 (1):2–6.

INTERNET RESOURCES

Business Opportunities Handbook: Online
http://www.ezines.com/
Features articles about running a small business. Also lists business opportunities.

Creativity Web
http://www.ozemail.com.au
Yes, it is located in Australia, where it appears they are very much interested in creativity. On this site, you will find many articles on various aspects of creativity. It is your one-stop shop for resources on creativity. Check out the article called "What Can I Do to Increase My Creativity?" to get started. It's at http://www.ozemail.com.au/~caveman/Creative/Techniques/intro.htm

Where Really Bad Ideas Come From
http://www.inc.com/articles/details/
1,,CID1114_REG6,00.html
This great article by Ron McLean takes about how entrepreneurs learned from their failures.

Where Great Ideas Come From
http://www.inc.com/articles/details/
1,,CID908_REG6,00.html
This is the corollary article written by Susan Greco.

Thinking Up a Storm
http://edge.lowe.org/
A brief article on brainstorming that will help you generate more ideas.

RELEVANT CASE STUDIES

Case 1 Mrs. Gooch's

Case 2 Franchising a Dying Business

Case 3 Overnite Express

Case 4 Beanos Ice Cream Shoppe

Case 5 Earthlink.net: The Journey to Recognizing an Opportunity

4

Learning an Industry

Now here, you see, it takes all the running you can do to keep in the same place. If you want to get somewhere else, you must run at least twice as fast as that.
Lewis Carroll

Overview

Really Cooking in a Tough Industry

If you look at a ranked listing of the industries in which venture capital is most likely to be spent, you'll typically find restaurants and food services at the bottom, right next to retail. That's because the restaurant industry is notorious for its high failure rate. So to succeed in the restaurant business, you have to understand the industry inside out, and you have to find a niche.

Joaquim Splichal came to the United States in 1981 from Spaichingen, a small village in Germany, in his early thirties, having worked in the hotel and culinary businesses from the age of 18. His years in Holland, Switzerland, and France, serving as an apprentice to some of the great chefs, had earned him many culinary awards when he took his first job in the United States as executive chef for the Regency Club in Los Angeles. Later he became part of the launch of the successful Seventh Street Bistro, also in Los Angeles. Then, in 1984, he had his first entrepreneurial opportunity when one of his customers gave him a minority stake in his own restaurant, Max au Triangle. Again, the food he created was outstanding, but, unfortunately, he knew nothing about managing a restaurant and very soon the restaurant closed. For the next five years, he took consulting jobs until he was ready to try his luck at entrepreneurship again.

In 1989, he opened Patina, an upscale French restaurant in Los Angeles, with an investment of $650,000 from people who believed in him. He also took advantage of the expertise of his wife, Christine, who has an MBA in international management and who runs the management and investment end of the business. Where Joaquim was the visionary, Christine was the one who executed the concept. This time, their restaurant was a huge success, paying back its investors to the tune of 110 percent in fifteen months.

With investors paid, the Splichals now owned 50 percent of the company. But with typical entrepreneurial vision, Joaquim Splichal determined early on that more restaurants were part of his dream. At Patina, he was the chef and was in the kitchen every night. He wanted to build a company that endured beyond him, that didn't require him to be in the kitchen. Splichal knew that he had no desire to build a brand based on his persona like his good friend, the renowned chef Wolfgang Puck, had done. He wanted to take a more low-profile approach. In 1992, an opportunity presented itself to purchase a failed French restaurant in the San Fernando Valley. He turned that site into Pinot Bistro and once again paid back the million dollars in investment capital in less than two years to retain a 60 percent interest in the restaurant.

Splichal's biggest concern with this new restaurant was that he had developed an image for Patina that was upscale and expensive. Pinot was intended to be a different experience, less expensive and not the super high quality of the original restaurant. Would customers accept the difference? After a short period of confusion, they did and the restaurant succeeded. To achieve his goal of not being the chef at the restaurant, he hired a very talented chef who became his executive chef and who trained all the chefs he would later need in his subsequent restaurants.

Splichal went on to develop four more restaurants, all rooted in classic French cuisine, but with a touch of California whimsy. But restaurants were not the only undertaking of this multi-talented entrepreneur. Catering became one of the most important divisions of his ever-growing company. In 1995, he hired a catering manager, who promptly won the Emmy Awards dinner that next year. The catering business began earning $1 million a year, and by 1999 had reached $6.2 million in revenues.

In 1998, the Splichals consolidated all their holdings under The Patina Group (http://www.patinagroup.com), which now made the company more attractive to lenders and investors. When they received a lowball offer from Restaurant Associates (RA), who wanted to expand to the West Coast, the Splichals figured it was time to retain the services of an investment bank. Their subsequent association with an investment banking firm almost doubled the value of their business, and in 1999, after much thoughtful consideration, the Splichals merged the business with RA in a deal said to be worth about $40 million. At that time, The Patina Group consisted of seven restaurants, four museum cafes, and the catering company, and employed 700 people while grossing $35 million in annual revenues.

The Splichals are as busy as ever. With the huge resources of RA behind them, they are expanding at a rapid pace. They are even looking into vineyards in Europe, perhaps to find his next entrepreneurial venture.

SOURCES: Restaurant Associates, "Joachim Splichal" and "News: The Patina Group Merges," *Nation's Restaurant News,* January, 1997, http://www.restaurantassociates.com; Arthur Lubow, "Recipe for a $40 Million Score," *Inc.,* October, 2000.

One of the factors that affects both the creation of new ventures and the strategies they adopt is the environment in which they will exist. This environment includes:

1. The industry in which a business operates

2. The market the business serves

3. The state of the national—and perhaps the international—economy

4. The people and businesses with which the business will interact

Looking at the business environment at the broadest level, we find the industry in which the business intends to operate, which is essentially a grouping of similar businesses that interact in a common environment. Recall from Chapter 3 that ideas for new ventures frequently come from understanding and having experience with an industry. Knowing an industry inside and out opens the door not only to discovering an opportunity but to finding strategic partners, customers, venture capital, and strategies for success when you build a business to turn your idea into reality. Taking a strategic position in a growing, dynamic, healthy industry can go a long way toward ensuring a successful venture. A young, growing industry with many new entrants will present at once a highly competitive environment for the new venture and a chance to gain significant market share This was the case in the telecommunications industry in the 1990s. By contrast, a weak position in a mature industry may sound a death knell for the business before it even opens its doors. A more mature industry, may have already passed through the period of "survival of the fittest" and will now consist of a few firms with large market shares, like the automobile, semiconductor, and airline industries, to name a few.[1]

In this chapter, you will discover the various types of information that can be used to describe an industry so that, as an entrepreneur, you can determine if the industry is receptive to your business concept. Those areas of information include the way the industry is structured, potential opportunities or threats, and competitors. With a good understanding of the industry, you will be able to develop a strong entry strategy that will give your new venture a chance to survive.

A Framework for Understanding Industries

It is often helpful to put a framework around the concept of an industry. The early work of Starbuck and others has identified three dimensions of the industry environment that help the entrepreneur grasp the nature of an industry and a new venture's potential for success in that industry: carrying capacity, uncertainty, and complexity.[2] We will now look at each of these in more detail and then discuss the industry life cycle.

● Carrying Capacity

Carrying capacity or **degree of saturation** is the extent to which the industry can support growth, from both the entry of new ventures and the growth of existing ones. Entrepreneurs typically seek out an industry that can support expansion, thus allowing the new venture to grow and to obtain the resources it needs. Difficulty entering a specific industry due to many competitors, major companies that control needed supply chains, or economies of scale suggests that the industry may be approaching saturation—that is, the production capability of the existing firms may equal or exceed customer demand for their products. The only way to enter such an industry is through the introduction of new technology or the discovery of a niche where a need has not been met. Vidal Herrera understood the medical services industry well. That's why he was able to spot a need that was not being served and that became the impetus for his business concept. (Read more about Herrera's venture in the case study Franchising a Dying Business.)

● ## Uncertainty

Uncertainty is the degree of stability or instability and ambiguity in an industry. A dynamic, uncertain environment is one that is difficult to predict because it is in constant flux. Industries that operate in volatile environments, like the biotech industry, contain higher degrees of uncertainty or risk. Consequently, the rewards are usually higher as well. Dynamic, even chaotic, environments also provide a fertile growing ground for new opportunities and have given birth to many successful companies.

● ## Complexity

Complexity is the number and diversity of inputs and outputs facing an organization. Firms that operate in complex industries usually have to deal with more suppliers, customers, and competitors than firms in other industries, and they regularly produce a greater number of dissimilar products for global markets. Industries with a high degree of complexity, such as the electronics industry, are by their very nature difficult for new businesses to enter. They are also extremely competitive; therefore, new ventures often find a great deal of hostility rather than collaboration in those industries. Telecommunications and biotechnology are both industries with a high degree of competition and government regulation and in which product life cycles are very short.

● ## Industry Evolution

Industries do not remain static or stable over time on any of the three aspects of the framework just discussed. In fact, they are in an almost constant state of evolution. Like people, industries move through a life cycle that includes birth, growth, maturity, and ultimately decline. The stages of the industry life cycle are identified by the different kinds of activities occurring at each stage. Figure 4.1 displays this life cycle.

1. *Birth:* A new industry emerges often with the introduction of a disruptive technology like the Internet.

2. *Growth and adaptation:* The new industry goes through a volatile stage, and companies and their respective technologies jockey for position and the right to determine the standards. Proprietary rights give companies a brief "quiet" period to gain acceptance by customers.

FIGURE 4.1

Industry Growth Cycle

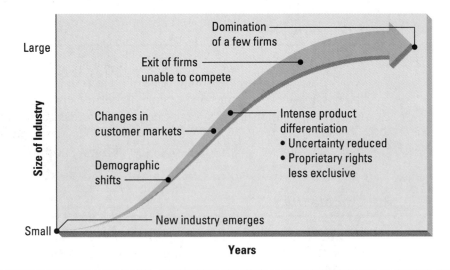

3. *Differentiation and competition:* As more firms enter the industry, intense product differentiation occurs as the industry established standards and proprietary rights no longer provide the exclusivity they once did.

4. *Shakeout:* When competition is the most intense, those companies that are unable to compete leave

5. *Maturity and decline:* The industry reaches a mature state with several major players that dominate. If research and development in the industry do not produce a resurgence of growth, the industry could face decline.

Of course, for every industry, these life cycle stages occur at different times and vary in duration. The video rental industry presents a classic example of an industry in transition. In the early stages it was comprised of small independent (mom-and-pop) owners. Wayne Huizenga sought to consolidate the industry by developing Blockbuster Video, a video megastore. In just a few years, independents were disappearing in favor of large-volume chain outlets. In the not-too-distant future, the megastores will likely give way to video on-demand, available over cable television and even the Internet.

When you study an industry in which you're interested, you will want to look for these five signs to discover which stage of the life cycle the industry is in. Reading the analyses of industry watchers in trade magazines and talking with people who regularly work in that industry are also good ways to learn where your industry is in the life cycle.

The Special Case of Emerging Industries

Emerging industries are those that are just coming into being. Some examples are interactive television and genetic therapy. In these types of industries, there are no rules initially. Instead, technical uncertainty exists until the major technology developers enter the industry and it becomes apparent which technology is the best. Consequently, in the beginning, there is no standardization of products or processes for some time, and as a result, costs to produce are high. Securing sufficient raw materials may also be difficult.

Buyers in an emerging industry are, for the most part, considered early adopters. They will pay a premium for the product at its introduction but will usually see that price decline significantly as competition increases and standardization of technology occurs.

For entrepreneurs, an emerging industry is at once exciting, challenging, and extremely risky. Certainly the strongest position is to own the technology being introduced and be able to enter the market with sufficient resources to establish a firm market share and brand identity—to create the killer application that causes a technology shift and sets a new standard. If, however, others are also entering the market at the same time with similar proprietary technology, resources will have to be directed toward promoting the benefits and superiority of the entrepreneur's technology. This was the case for Microsoft's Windows, which ultimately overcame the threat of IBM's OS/2 technology.

If major companies from other compatible industries are entering the new industry, the task is that much harder. That is the situation for new ventures hoping to garner a piece of the action in the telecommunications industry, where they are competing for market share against the likes of AT&T and Nortel Networks.

Studying an Industry

Now that you have the broad picture of the nature of industries, you need to understand how your specific industry works—its structure, opportunities, and potential threats. For years the work of Michael Porter has provided a way of looking at the structure of an industry. Porter's basic premise is that sustaining high performance levels in an industry requires a well-thought-out strategy and implementation plan based on knowledge of the way the industry works. Porter asserts that there are five forces in any industry that affect the ultimate profit potential of a venture in terms of long-run return on investment. His Five Forces framework is a way to classify the industry structure so that a strategy for entry and sustained growth can be developed.

While Porter's work still serves as a useful guide for strategic planning for most businesses, it may not, in its classical form, meet the needs of businesses in the new economy, particularly those in cyberspace. Researchers Larry Downes and Chunka Mui assert that any industry whose primary product or service includes information is in the process of major technological shifts and cannot wait for traditional planning processes.[3] They balk at the notion that the future in information-based industries can be predicated on current conditions, claiming that the frequent technology shifts since 1996 have made forecasting a difficult task. Furthermore, every industry is affected by information technology and is experiencing the revolutionary changes it has wrought. So, while not every industry is as volatile as the digital industries, every industry must understand the changes, adapt to them, and use them to their competitive advantage.

Table 4.1 compares and contrasts a traditional view of an industry with the more recent digital view.

Both these views of an industry have merit. For the rest of this section, we will use Porter's Five Forces framework and add a sixth force, technology, as suggested by Downes and Mui, to discuss the kinds of information about an industry you will need to collect. The six forces are as follows:

1. Barriers to new businesses in the industry

2. The power of suppliers to affect your strategy

3. The threat of substitute products

4. The power of buyers to affect your strategy

5. The degree of rivalry among competitors in the industry[4]

6. Technology

These are the forces that drive competition and affect the long-run profitability of the new venture as well as of other firms in the industry. Such things as economic forces, changes in demand, material shortages, technology shifts, and so forth, by contrast, affect short-run profitability. Let's look at each of these forces in more detail.

● *Barriers to Entry*

In some industries barriers to entry are high and will discourage a potential entrepreneur from attempting to enter. These barriers may include the following:

Economies of Scale

Many industries have achieved **economies of scale** in marketing, production, and distribution. This means that their costs to produce have declined relative to the price of their goods and services. A new venture cannot easily achieve these same economies, so it is forced into a "Catch-22" situation. If it enters the industry on a large scale, it risks retaliation from those established firms in the industry. If it enters on a small scale, it may not be able to compete because its costs are high relative to everyone else's. Another version of this dilemma is an

TABLE 4.1

The Traditional versus the Digital View of an Industry

	Traditional	Digital
Nature of Industry	Static	Dynamic
Environment	Physical	Virtual
Discipline for Responding to the Industry	Analytical	Intuitive
Time Frame for Planning	3–5 years	12–18 months
Key Pressure Point	Five Forces	New forces
Key Technique	Value chain leverage	Value chain destruction
Participants	Strategists, senior management	Everyone (including business partners)
Technology's Role	Enabler	Disrupter
Output	Plan	Killer apps

industry in which the major players are vertically integrated; that is, they own their suppliers and/or distribution channels, which effectively locks out the new venture. What most new ventures attempt to do when faced with economies of scale is to form alliances with other small firms to share resources and compete on a more level playing field. We see this collaboration happening more and more often as businesses realize that the marketplace is too complex for any one company to have all the resources and intellectual property to control a portion of a market. This strategy has been prevalent in the grocery industry where independent grocers join forces to achieve more buying power. In the fiber optics industry, smaller companies like Galileo Corporation have banded together with their competitors to make a bigger impact. The most difficult part of a competitor alliance? CEO ego. You will learn more about strategic alliances in Chapters 8 and 18.

Brand Loyalty

New entrants to an industry face existing products and services with loyal customers, so an extensive marketing campaign focused on making the customer aware of the benefits of the new venture's products will be required. The cost of undertaking this strategy can be a significant barrier to entry unless customers are dissatisfied with the competing brands. On the Internet, it has become clear that when they set up shop in cyberspace, companies like Barnes and Noble and The Gap retain the brand presence they have already established in their bricks-and-mortar stores—they can be profitable immediately. Alternatively, it takes a company like Amazon (with the strongest online brand recognition) years to become profitable, if ever.

Capital Requirements

The cost of entering many industries is prohibitive for a new venture. These costs may include up-front advertising, research and development (R&D), and expenditures for plant and equipment to compete on par with established firms in the industry. Entrepreneurs often overcome this barrier by outsourcing to or partnering with established companies to leverage their resources and industry intelligence.

Switching Costs for the Buyer

Buyers in most industries don't readily switch from one supplier to another unless there is a demonstrated reason to do so. Switching costs the buyer money and time. For example, users of the Microsoft Windows graphical interface will not readily switch to a different system because they have spent a lot of time learning the Windows environment and are used to it. A new entrant, like Linux, will need to spend considerable time and money convincing customers that the product is worth switching to.

Access to Distribution Channels

The new venture must persuade established distribution channel members to accept the new product or service and must prove that it will be beneficial to distributors to do so. This persuasion process can be costly for the new venture. One solution is distributing via the Internet, which is a direct method of reaching the customer.

Proprietary Factors

Barriers to entry also include proprietary technology, products, and processes. Where established firms hold patents on products and processes that the new venture requires, they have the ability to either keep the new venture out of the industry or make it very expensive to enter. Most favorable location is another form of proprietary barrier. Often entrepreneurs will discover that existing firms in the industry own the most advantageous business sites, forcing the new venture to locate elsewhere. The Internet diminishes such location advantages somewhat, but the ability of customers to find a Web address quickly through the major search engines also becomes a location advantage. These proprietary factors are all substantial barriers to entry for a new venture.

Government Regulations

The government can prevent a new venture from entering an industry through strict licensing requirements and by limiting access to raw materials through laws or high taxes and to certain locations via zoning restrictions. Food products and biochemicals must obtain FDA approval, which is a significant barrier to entry. Isis Pharmaceuticals, a drug-development company located in Carlsbad, California, recognizes that any delay in approvals can result in millions of dollars lost. It invested in a local area network for its company and an Intranet on the Web; now it can manage its FDA-mandated clinical trials on thousands of patients without losing time. By submitting its required forms electronically, it cuts several months off the FDA's normal fifteen-month review process.

Industry Hostility

Some industries are extremely retaliatory toward new businesses that attempt to compete in the industry. This typically occurs where there are many well-established firms that have sufficient resources to spend the time and money going after a new entrant. It is also common in mature industries where growth has slowed, so rivalry for market share intensifies as profits decline. Weaker firms ultimately are forced to exit the industry. But today it's also common in technology industries where companies are finding it difficult to maneuver the intellectual property minefields. For example, with the barrage of broadly defined business method and software patents hitting the U.S. Patent and Trademark Office (USPTO), it is clear that many companies are going to find it difficult to compete without infringing on someone's patent. The USPTO is not set up to find all the bad patent applications, so court battles like the one over Amazon's one-click patent will become more and more common.

● Threat from Substitute Products

A new venture must compete not only with products and services in its own industry but also with those that are logical substitutes in other industries as well. Generally, these substitute products and services accomplish the same basic function in a different way or at a different price. For example, movie theaters regularly compete with other forms of entertainment for the consumer's disposable dollars. The threat from substitute products is more likely to occur where firms in other industries are earning high profits at better prices than can be achieved in the new venture's industry.

● Threat from Buyers' Bargaining Power

In industries where buyers have bargaining power, it is more difficult for a new entrant to gain a foothold and grow. Examples of buyers that have this type of bargaining power are Price/Costco, Barnes and Noble, and Toys 'R' Us. Buyers like these can force down prices in the industry through volume purchases. This is particularly true where industry products comprise a significant portion of the buyers' requirements—books for Barnes and Noble, toys for Toys 'R' Us. Under this scenario, the buyer is more likely to achieve the lowest possible price.

The largest buyers also pose a threat of backward integration, where they actually purchase their suppliers, thus better controlling costs and affecting price throughout the industry. The more buyers understand the nature of the industry and the more the products are standardized, the greater the likelihood that these buyers will have significant bargaining power.

● *Threat from Suppliers' Bargaining Power*

In some industries suppliers exert enormous power through the threat of raising prices or changing the quality of the products that they supply to manufacturers and distributors. If the number of these suppliers is few relative to the size of the industry, or the industry is not the primary customer of the suppliers, that power is magnified. For example, suppose your company is in the construction industry. You purchase lumber at good prices because the construction industry is one of the primary purchasers of lumber. But when you need steel, you pay a premium because your company is not a volume purchaser in the steel industry.

A further threat from suppliers is that they will integrate forward—that is, they will purchase the outlets for their goods and services, thus controlling the prices at which their output is ultimately sold.

It is interesting to consider labor as a source of supply. In certain industries where highly technical skills are required or where unions are strong, labor as a supplier has enormous bargaining power and can significantly affect costs for the new venture. Key employees who have highly marketable skills and are mobile can demand higher salaries and perks than the new venture can afford. In the high-tech arena engineers command exorbitant salaries, signing bonuses, perks, and stock options.

● *Rivalry among Existing Firms*

In general, a highly competitive industry will drive down profits and ultimately the rate of return on investment. To position themselves in a competitive market, firms often resort to price wars and advertising skirmishes. Once one firm decides to make such a strategic move in the industry, others will follow. The clearest example is the airline industry; when one airline discounts its prices significantly, most of the others immediately follow.

The problem with this tactic is that it ultimately hurts everyone in the industry and may even force out some smaller firms, because competitive prices drop below costs. Most new ventures can't compete on price and can't afford costly advertising battles to build an image. To compete in an industry that is highly competitive, they must find a market niche that will allow them to enter quietly and gain a foothold. Many entrepreneurs seeking entry into industries like software and telecommunications deliberately position themselves to be acquired by the larger rivals rather than try to compete against them.

Technology

Technology is no longer just an enabler of business goals and change; it's a driver of change and of competitive advantage. Technology is the dynamic component of a business's operations. That is why traditional strategic planning, which tends to be static and is done in cycles by top-level executives, is ineffective in a highly volatile industry.

The role of technology in business today forces a new way of planning that occurs almost constantly and is undertaken by everyone in the organization. In fact, it is the very people who work with the customer, or work at an operations level, who are most likely to see change coming in time to do something about it. Strategy now is implemented quickly, often without a lot of thought, in an attempt to take advantage of a rapidly shrinking window of opportunity. This is the new environment that technology has wrought.

Once you have a clear understanding of the way your industry works and what some of the opportunities and threats are, you will also want to undertake a competitive analysis.

Competitive Analysis

Within any industry, it is important to hypothesize about the competitive strategy of the competition—in other words, to know the competition as well as you know your own business. Studying the history and management style of major competitors will give insight into what motivates them and how they may react to your strategy. You need to identify their current strategy to learn how they have positioned themselves in the industry. In the same way that you would analyze your strategy's strengths, weaknesses, opportunities, and threats, you should also study theirs.

Not all of your competitors will exhibit the same strategy, so it is useful to categorize them to get a handle on what the new venture is facing. A competitive grid (Figure 4.2 displays an example) will make it easier to see differences and recognize opportunities. Start by listing competitors in the first column. Subsequent columns will depend on your needs, but in general you will want to compare product or service, benefit, distribution, and marketing strategy. Be sure to include your company so it's easy to see what your strengths and weaknesses are relative to the competition.

FIGURE 4.2

Competitive Grid for Nutritional Concepts

	Product	Unique Features/Benefits
Enutrition.com	• Online supplements and beauty products	• Boast great customer service • Wide selection • Detailed descriptions of their products
Ediets.com	• Online health evaluation with meal plans and support staff	• Largest support group community including message boards • Large staff with good personalization
Mothernature.com	• Natural products and information distributor	• Product supplement planner • Widest selection of product categories from supplements to groceries to fashion • Message boards
Wholepeople.com	• Online shopping from natural foods to supplements along with nutritional advice	• Will offer wide selection of food and supplements with retail store backing them
Vitaminshoppe.com	• The largest selection of vitamins and supplements	• Wide variety • Easy search categories • Have 78 retail locations to go with web site • Resource center
NutritionalConcepts.com	• Personalized health evaluations complete with all implementation tools (supplements, groceries, books, and beauty products)	• The only web site offering a complete personalized health evaluation with home delivery of the products necessary to implement the plan • Live support staff • A personalized web page for members

Source: Created by Mike Minsky while a student in the Greif Entrepreneurship Center at the University of Southern California.

Price	Promotion	Weaknesses
• Depends on amount of products purchased	• Free shipping on orders $20 or more • Free newsletter • Ads in magazines, on radio, and Internet	• No personalized health evaluation available • No article and resource information available • Advertisements confusing in correlation with business mission
• Free brief evaluation • $10 start up fee for detailed evaluation and plan • $10 a month (minimum 3 months)	• Free brief evaluation • Ads on the Internet, radio, and magazines • Free newsletter	• Very small selection of supplements • No groceries or online database • Confusing to know if they sell anything besides their evaluations
• Depends on products purchased • $3.95 for shipping	• Free shipping for purchases over $50 • Ads on TV, magazines, and radio • Free newsletter	• Does not focus on personalization • Evaluation very weak • Core team not outwardly focused on
• Advice is free	• None	• Failure of first e-commerce site • Personalization and products not integrated
• Depends on products purchased • Shipping dependent on purchase (minimal)	• Free color catalog • Ads in newspapers, magazines, billboards, and radio	• No online community • Does not focus on personalization • Core team not focused on • No grocery or book purchases
• Personal health evaluation, $50 • Membership after evaluation, $15 per month • Product sales per customer and delivery costs dependent on amount purchased	• Free delivery for purchases over $75 • 1 month free membership for new members and existing clients • Ads in local Chicago newspapers, local cable, and billboards • Free newsletter	• Size and awareness on a national scale

● *Identifying the Competition*

There are three types of competitors for a product or service: direct, indirect or substitute, and emerging. Identifying specifically who these companies are—their strengths, weaknesses, and market share—will put the new venture in a better position to be a contender in the industry and particularly in the target market.

Direct Competitors

Those businesses supplying products or services that are the same as or similar to yours, or are a reasonably good substitute for yours, are **direct competitors** to the new venture. However, be careful: the term *competition* is not quite that simple. Suppose you are going to open an entertainment center that offers virtual reality computer games in a shopping mall. One possible direct competitor that comes to mind is a video arcade. But if you consider your venture to be in the entertainment business, you will see that other direct competitors for the consumer dollars you are seeking are movie theaters, miniature golf courses, bowling alleys, and video rental stores. That certainly complicates the picture, and you will need to have a strategy for competing against each different type of competitor you have now identified.

Indirect or Substitute Competitors

Indirect competitors may not even be in the same industry as the new venture but do compete alongside it for consumer dollars. For example, consumers may choose to spend their limited dollars at the movies rather than on an expensive restaurant. Or, a business looking for videoconferencing capability may choose an Internet-based system delivered through an application service provider (ASP) rather than purchase and maintain equipment. When you're considering who your competitors might be, you must look outside the immediate industry and market for alternatives to what you offer.

Emerging Competitors

Assess not only the existing competition but also the potential for future competition—**emerging competitors.** In many industries today, technology and information are changing at such a rapid pace that the window of opportunity for successfully starting a new venture closes early and fast. Consequently, the entrepreneur must be ever-vigilant to new trends and new technology, both in the industry in general and in the specific target market. For example, one engineer/entrepreneur spent several years developing a video-streaming technology. Now that he is ready to consider commercializing that technology, he has discovered to his dismay that not only are there competing (and in some cases better) technologies already in the market through major companies like Microsoft, but there are emerging technologies from major companies that will make his technology obsolete in a very short time. How do you avoid such a calamity? You need to stay in touch with your industry and look not only at technologies already in the market, but look at what types of research and development projects are going on at major research universities that might foretell a shift in technology. Journals like *MIT Technology Review* regularly look ahead to see where the world of technology is going. In other industries, trade journals, conferences, and trade shows are excellent sources of emerging competitors.

Gathering Competitive Intelligence

Collecting information on your competitors is one of the most difficult parts of researching the industry. While it's easy to gain superficial information from the competitor's advertising, web site, or facility, the less obvious types of information like revenues, operating strategies, and the like are another matter. If your competitors are public companies, you will find much of this information in annual reports and other filings required by the Securities and Exchange Commission (SEC). Unfortunately, most start-up companies are competing against other private companies that will not willingly divulge sensitive data.

Some of the data that is helpful to gather includes:

▶ Current market strategies

▶ Management style and culture

▶ Pricing strategy

▶ Customer mix

▶ Promotional mix

A well-conceived plan for collecting information on competitors will help you get what you need. Here are some suggestions.

▶ Visit your competitors' web sites or the outlets where their products are sold. Evaluate appearance, number of customers coming and going, what they buy, how much, and how often. Talk to customers and employees alike.

▶ Buy your competitors' products. This will not only help you understand the differences in features and benefits, but in doing the transaction you will learn much about how they treat their customers.

▶ Search the Internet. There are a variety of search engines on the Web where you can begin your investigation. Some of the more popular ones include Yahoo.com, MSN.com, AltaVista.com, and Infoseek.com.

▶ Find information on public companies to serve as benchmarks for the industry. You can investigate a public company through Hoover's Online (www.hoovers.com), the U.S. Securities and Exchange Commission (www.sec.gov) and One Source (www.onesource.com).

▶ Search the government web sites. You will find a list of some of these in the Additional Sources of Information section of this chapter.

▶ Seek out trade associations and other organizations dedicated to your industry.

Competitive Entry Strategies

Armed with industry information, you are in a good position to devise a strategy for entering the industry. Of course, that strategy will also be a function of the type of business you choose to start, but in general there are three broad strategies: cost superiority, product/process/service differentiation, and niche.

● Cost Superiority

Cost superiority entails entering the industry with an organizational structure that is lean and mean, with tight controls on costs. Accomplishing this usually requires designing the production process and distribution mechanisms to operate under strict controls and to meet stringent quantity targets. This strategy is very difficult for a new venture to implement in that it is more often the result of being further along on the experience curve and producing in high volumes. A new venture from the beginning typically does not have the infrastructure and resources in place and sufficient product/service demand to allow it to use cost superiority as an entry strategy. However, in an emerging industry where everyone suffers from the same disadvantage, a new firm can gain an advantage if it can keep overhead costs down, outsource expensive, noncore activities, and keep labor to a minimum. Tom Nadeau imports and wholesales wood furniture from Indonesia, India, Mexico, and China. He successfully competes on cost superiority because he has contracted with the best furniture crafters in each country and he offers his furniture distributors huge discounts for taking the shipment FOB (freight on board) in the country of origin. He keeps his overhead as low as possible and saves on collection expenses by maintaining excellent relationships with his suppliers.

● Differentiation

Differentiation is a strategy that distinguishes the new venture from others in the industry through product/process innovation, or a unique marketing or distribution strategy. Differentiation often creates brand loyalty among customers, thereby making the product or service less sensitive to price. Consequently, margins are usually increased, which better insulates the company against supplier and buyer bargaining power, and moves the focus away from the cost to produce. Additionally, substitute products are less likely to be a threat where differentiation is the strategy.

When Marianne Szymanski created Toy Tips, Inc., an independent toy research company, she refused to accept money from toy manufacturers and thereby differentiated herself from other companies that were evaluating toys and that regularly accepted payment for those evaluations. With this strategy, she made her firm the only independent toy research company in the United States.

If your business is competing in the mainstream market, as opposed to focusing on a niche (see the next section), it will be vitally important to differentiate yourself from others in the market. Otherwise, how will you answer the crucial question "Why will they buy from my company?"

● *Niche Strategy*

The third strategy is often referred to as a **niche strategy,** which means that the new venture focuses on a particular customer group or specific geographic region not currently served effectively by the industry. By selecting a segment of a market, niche entrepreneurs attempt to insulate themselves from market forces such as competitors and the barriers to entry in an industry. You can create a niche by focusing on any of the key elements of the business: customer, product design, price, service, packaging, geographic focus, and distribution.

Many a new venture has entered an established industry via a niche by finding a gap in the market that allows the company to compete without going head to head with the major companies in the industry. Where competition is weak and exposure to substitute products is a minor issue, the niche strategy offers a safer route to establishing a foothold in the industry. Jordan NeuroScience entered the established neuro-diagnostic field via a niche. It provides hospital emergency rooms, which had not previously monitored trauma patients for brain injury, with remote EEG monitoring of brain waves. Jordan NeuroScience created a niche that it intends to dominate and for which it has set the standard.

The important thing to remember about niche creation is that it allows a small company to define and own that segment of the market. Working in a niche gives the company time to develop, to become stronger and better able to compete against companies in the mainstream market. Be aware, however, that niche strategies can fail where the costs to serve the niche exceed the size of the market, so you need to choose a niche that makes sense for your product or service. Niches, by their very nature, are small and usually only serve to provide an entry strategy, not a sustainable strategy for long-term viability. Some high-tech entrepreneurs gather several niches in a Pac Man type of strategy that lets them build sustainable strength.

Conducting Industry Analysis

Any good analysis needs a plan. You've learned about the kinds of information needed to understand an industry. Now you need to consider how to go about finding that information.

To avoid wasting time, turning up old or inadequate information, or not knowing what to do with the data you collect, take the following steps:

▶ Identify the industry

▶ Examine secondary resources

▶ Conduct primary research, including talking with people in the industry

▶ Analyze the data and draw conclusions

● Identifying the Industry: North American Industry Classification System (NAICS)

Identifying your industry typically begins with the classification system developed by the United States, Canada, and Mexico to identify industries and allow for common standards and statistics across North America. **The North American Industry Classification System** (NAICS) is replacing the traditional U.S. Standard Industrial Classification system (SIC) and will soon change the way we view our economy. You can learn the new coding for industries you're interested in by going to the U.S. Department of Commerce National Technical Information Service (NTIS) web site at http://www.fedworld.gov/ntis/.

NAICS covers 350 new industries that have never been coded before. Some of these industries reflect high-tech developments such as fiber optic cable manufacturing, satellite communications, and the reproduction of computer software. However, far more of them identify less technological changes in the way business is done: bed and breakfast inns, environmental consulting, warehouse clubs, pet supply stores, credit card issuing, diet and weight reduction centers.

NAICS industries are identified by a six-digit code, in contrast to the four-digit SIC code. The longer code accommodates the larger number of sectors and allows more flexibility in designating subsectors. It also provides for additional detail not necessarily appropriate for all three NAICS countries.

NAICS is organized in a hierarchical structure much like the existing SIC.

▶ The first two digits designate a major Economic Sector [formerly Division] such as Agriculture or Manufacturing.

▶ The third digit designates an Economic Subsector [formerly Major Group] such as Crop Production or Apparel Manufacturing.

▶ The fourth digit designates an Industry Group, such as Grain and Oil Seed Farming or Fiber, Yarn, and Thread Mills.

▶ The fifth digit designates the NAICS Industry such as Wheat Farming or Broadwoven Fabric Mills.

The international NAICS agreement fixes only the first five digits of the code. The sixth digit is used for industrial classifications in other countries where necessary. With the NAICS code, you can find statistics about size of the industry, sales, number of employees, and so forth.

● Secondary Sources of Industry Information

Once you have identified your industry with the NAICS code, you can begin a search of secondary data sources—journals, trade magazines, reference books, government publications, and annual reports of public corporations—normally available in a university or community library and on the Internet. Historical data, such as annual reports over a ten- to fifteen-year period, can often help you spot trends, cycles, and seasonal variations in the industry. Trade magazines provide a good sense of key firms and of the directions the industry may be taking.

After the secondary data are collected, you need to organize and analyze them. In general, answer the following key questions about the industry:

1. *Is the industry growing?* Growth is measured by sales volume, number of employees, units produced, number of new companies entering the industry, and so forth.

2. *Where are the opportunities?* Does the industry provide opportunities for new businesses with strategies involving new products and/or processes, innovative distribution, or new marketing strategies?

3. *What is the status of any new technology?* How quickly does the industry adopt new technology, and does technology play a significant role in the competitive strategy of firms in the industry?

4. *How much does the industry spend on research and development?* Expenditures on R&D will tell you how important technology is, how much you will need to spend, and how rapid the product development cycle is.

5. *Who are the major competitors?* Which firms dominate the industry?

6. *Are there young, successful firms in the industry?* This will give you an indication of how formidable the entry barriers are and whether or not the industry is growing rapidly.

7. *What does the future look like?* What appears likely to happen over the next five years? What are the trends and patterns of change?

8. *Are there any threats to the industry?* Is there any chance that new technology will render obsolete either the industry or that segment of the industry in which you're doing business?

9. *What are the typical margins in the industry?* Looking at gross margins in the industry gives you an indication of how much room there is to make mistakes. You derive a gross margin by dividing gross profit by sales. It tells you how much money is left to pay overhead and make a profit. If the industry typically has 2 percent margins or less, like the grocery industry, you will have to sell in large volumes and keep overhead costs to a minimum. Where margins run at 70 percent or more, there is a lot more room to play, but generally these industries (like software) have relatively short product life cycles, so R&D costs are high.

● The Importance of Primary Data

Secondary research paints the broad picture of the industry; however, given the lead-time from data gathering to print, it is rarely the most current information available. Therefore, to access the timeliest information, it is extremely important to gather primary field data on the industry. (See Figure 4.3.) In other words, you need to talk with people in the industry—"pound the pavement," so to speak. Some of the sources to tap are as follows:

▶ *Industry observers,* who study particular industries and regularly report on them in newspapers or newsletters or through the media.

▶ *Suppliers and distributors,* who are in an excellent position to comment on the health of the industry in terms of demand for products and services, as well as on the financial strength and market practices of major firms.

▶ *Customers,* who can be a clue to satisfaction with the industry and the product or service supplied.

▶ *Employees of key firms in the industry,* who are a good source of information about potential competitors.

▶ *Professionals from service organizations,* such as lawyers and accountants, who regularly work with a particular industry.

▶ *Trade shows,* which give a good indication of who the biggest competitors are and who has the strongest market strategy.

Tactics for Talking with Key Industry People

Field research is usually accomplished via interviews or casual discussions with people in the industry. Getting them to open up and talk will be easier if you follow a few simple rules.

▶ Where possible, secure an introduction from someone who knows the interviewee. You will find that once you talk with the first person, that person

FIGURE 4.3

Sources of Field Data

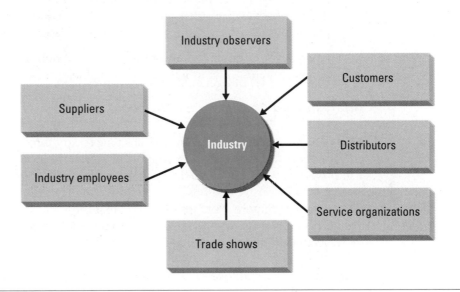

will recommend someone else, and you'll be on your way to gathering more information than you could ever use.

▌ Seek out individuals who regularly deal with the media, since they are easier to approach; however, be aware that they are also accustomed to being very careful about what they say.

▌ Allow sufficient lead-time for scheduling the meeting or phone call, since you probably are dealing with very busy people on tight schedules. If a source can't meet with you personally, suggest an e-mail interview.

▌ Offer something that might be of value to interviewees, such as a summary of the results of the industry analysis, a popular book in the field, or a subscription to a business magazine—or take interviewees to lunch.

▌ Be honest about your affiliation with a university or a business. Interviewees want to know that you understand the value of their time.

▌ To give yourself credibility, demonstrate your knowledge of an interviewee's business. (Research the business before the meeting.)

▌ If possible, take a colleague or business partner along to ensure that you obtain all the needed information and catch all visual cues. This is particularly true when talking with potential competitors.

▶ Carefully observe the surroundings when you're on site. Physical clues and nonverbal communication are often excellent indicators of the nature of the industry. For example, note whether the business environment seems quiet or bustling, whether the office space is a showplace or a barebones place to work, and whether the equipment is kept in good working order.

▶ Be sure your opening questions are easy and nonthreatening and show a genuine interest in your interviewee's business.

● *Analysis and Conclusions: The Ideal Industry*

Once you have gathered all your data, it's time to sort through it and decide how all the pieces come together to support or refute the notion that this industry will provide a good environment in which to start a business. While no industry is perfect, an industry comprised of the following features offers more opportunity for a new venture. You are cautioned that these are general benchmark figures across all industries. The analysis of your particular industry will provide more accurate figures.

▶ An industry with over $50 billion in sales will probably have niche markets of sufficient size to allow for the attainment of an adequate market share.

▶ An industry that is generally growing at a rate greater than the gross national product (GNP) offers more potential for growth of the new venture.

▶ An industry that allows for after-tax profits of greater than 5 percent of sales within three to five years will enhance the new venture's chances for success.

▶ An industry that is socially and environmentally responsible will be compatible with current societal and political trends and consequently may be eligible for special grants and other types of funding.

New ventures entering an emerging industry will not have the luxury of a track record that can indicate potential for growth and profits. They can, however, look to the experiences of other recently formed industries similar to their own to predict patterns and potential market demand. These characteristics are merely benchmarks. With so many variables involved, no one can guarantee that a new venture will survive or become a success, even if the industry possesses all the requisite characteristics. However, the more information the entrepreneur has, the better his or her chances are of avoiding costly mistakes.

NEW VENTURE CHECKLIST

Have you:

- ☐ Identified the NAICS code for the industry in which your new venture will operate?
- ☐ Collected secondary data on the industry?
- ☐ Conducted field research by interviewing suppliers, distributors, customers, and others?
- ☐ Developed an industry profile that will tell you and others if the industry is growing, who the major competitors are, and what the profit potential is?

ISSUES TO CONSIDER

1. Considering the framework presented in Figure 4.1, what do you believe are the two most important industry factors, and why?

2. Which primary and secondary information will tell you if the industry is growing and favorable to new entrants?

3. What kind of information can suppliers and distributors give you?

4. How will you decide on an entry strategy to an industry? What factors will you consider?

EXPERIENCING ENTREPRENEURSHIP

1. Choose an industry that interests you. Create a status report using the Internet, Lexis/Nexis, current periodicals, and interviews with people in the industry. In your estimation, is this an industry that has a great potential for new business opportunities? If so, where do those opportunities lie?

2. Interview a producer, a supplier, and a retailer or wholesaler in an industry that interests you. What is their role in the industry? Compare and contrast how they view the status of the industry.

ADDITIONAL SOURCES OF INFORMATION

Cornwall, J.R., and B. Perlman (1990). *Organizational Entrepreneurship.* Homewood, IL: Irwin.

Darnay, A.J. (Ed.) (1994). *Manufacturing USA: Industry Analyses, Statistics, and Leading Companies.* Detroit: Gale Research Inc.

Elster, R.J. (Ed.) (1998). *Small Business Sourcebook.* 12th ed. Detroit: Gale Research Inc.

Jasinowski, J., and R. Hamrin (1995). *Making It in America: Proven Paths to Success from 50 Top Companies.* New York: Simon & Schuster.

Miller, J.P. (2000). *Millenium Intelligence: Understanding and Conducting Competitive Intelligence in the Digital Age.* Medford, NJ: CyberAge Books.

Porter, M. (1980). *Competitive Strategy: Techniques for Analyzing Industries and Competitors.* New York: Free Press.

Porter, M. (1985). *Competitive Advantage.* New York: Free Press.

INTERNET RESOURCES

The Competitive Intelligence Guide
http://www.fuld.com
Advice on how to seek competitive intelligence and links to specific industries.

Department of Commerce
http://www.doc.gov
Links to many web sites of interest to business owners.

Federal Web Locator
http://www.infoctr.edu/fwl/
Links to economic news, export information, legislative trends, and more.

IndustryLink
http://www.industrylink.com/
Offers links to web sites of interest to people in a number of industries.

The Industry Standard
http://www.thestandard.com/research/metrics
Maintains an extensive database of information on the Internet.

Mediamark
http://www.mediamark.com
Provides general Internet statistics.

PR Newswire
http://www.prnewswire.com/
Good source of immediate news from corporations worldwide.

Securities and Exchange Commission
http://www.sec.gov/
Good source for researching specific industries.

SEC Edgar Database
http://www.sec.gov/edgarhp.htm
Contains documents that publicly traded companies must submit to the SEC.

Thomas Register
http://www.thomasregister.com:8000/
This is the online version of the Thomas Register of American Manufacturers. Contains information about products, services, and companies.

Wall Street Journal Interactive
http://www.wsj.com/
There is a charge for this web site, but it may be worth paying for the latest news from around the world. It also contains good information about the economy and specific companies and industries.

RELEVANT CASE STUDIES

Case 1 Mrs. Gooch's

Case 2 Franchising a Dying Business

Case 4 Beanos Ice Cream Shoppe

Case 6 Highland Dragon

Case 7 Roland International Freight Service

PART TWO

Feasibility: Testing a Business Concept

5

Developing and Testing the Business Concept

I'd rather have a Class A entrepreneur with a Class B idea than a Class B entrepreneur with a Class A idea.
Gifford Pinchot III*

Overview

Developing a business concept

The nature of feasibility analysis

Presenting the feasibility study

*The International Institute of Intrapreneurs, *Intrapreneuring* (Harper & Row, 1986).

Follow the Dough

Attorneys have long been associated with dough—the green kind, that is. But entre-preneur Doug Low had been an attorney for twenty-one years in the Central Val-ley of California when he decided he might prefer cookie dough to the green type. That was in 1993. Over the next four years, he worked on recipes to find the per-fect cookie. He was constantly testing his product with potential customers. His plan was to open a shop next to the law firm and put his wife, Marsha Eichholtz, a paralegal, in charge. She agreed on the condition that he come up with a recipe that was "really, really good." He did just that. The market told him he had a prod-uct that people wanted. In February 1997, Low and Eichholtz opened Doug-Out Cookies and claimed to be "the only law office in town that has four different kinds of coffee."

Opening Doug-Out, a baseball-themed shop, meant working twelve to fifteen hours a day, six days a week. Eichholtz started the day at 5:00 a.m., mixing dough for thirty-two different recipes for a variety of baked goods, including the now-famous baseball cookie. By 8:00 a.m., Low was in the law office or at the Workers' Compensation Appeals Board. By 5:00 p.m., they were both back at the law office, where the work day ended at 7:30. Seven months into the business, they were still testing the waters but breaking even, slowly building up a loyal customer base in-cluding several restaurants that purchased what Low calls "season tickets," or the right to regular deliveries of Doug-Out products.

But, beginning in December 2000, Low and Eichholtz discovered a variety of ways to grow the business. They expanded to two additional storefronts and se-cured agreements to supply a Southern California theme park, several drive-through coffee houses, an airline, and a retail outlet that uses cookies as gifts for their clients. They also learned that charitable and sporting events are excellent venues to promote their products. Today their latest idea is a partnership with Profit Spe-cialties, a fund-raising facilitator, to offer tins of cookie dough as a fund-raising item. Recognizing the popularity of themed food concepts, Low and Eichholtz now have plans to franchise the business nationally and take their concept to baseball stadiums around the country.

SOURCES: Greg Ahlstrand, "Doug-Out Lineup Is Big League," *The Fresno Bee,* September 19, 1997; Doug-Out Cookies (http://www.doug-out.com/), 2001.

In today's chaotic business environment, it's easy to have the impression that business concepts are developed on a napkin during dinner, and within two days the business is funded and operating. But, even for Internet businesses, that exciting scenario is a stretch. Just because you build a business does not mean that customers will come. In reality, a substantial amount of planning must take place and a great deal of effort must be put forth before a company's products or services ever successfully reach the market. Part of that planning and effort took place when you studied the industry in which you're interested. (See Chapter 4.) Chances are the business opportunity you find will come from your knowledge of an industry. Mark Alessi saw huge inefficiencies in the industry he knew well—comic-book publishing, an industry that saw its sales shrink from $850 million in 1993 to $275 million in 2000.[1] The industry is comprised of freelance artists who juggle many assignments simultaneously for several different publishers and generally have no incentive to remain loyal to a particular publisher. Alessi wanted to create an environment that would encourage people to do their best and allow publishers to better meet deadlines and demands for quality. He founded Cross-Generation and offered the artists he hired the highest salaries in the industry, benefits, and an equity stake in the company. As a result, his titles hit the news-stands on time, and in just one year CrossGeneration became the fifth-largest comic-book publisher in the United States.

Industry knowledge is a powerful source of opportunity that puts you in a stronger position to succeed. But, before you spend the time and effort to start a business, you need to develop a concept, test it, and prove it in the marketplace. You can do that through a process called *feasibility analysis*. Feasibility analysis is a set of tools and a process for examining a business concept in a way that gives you confidence about the conditions under which you are willing to move forward. The results of feasibility analysis tell you:

▶ Whether or not there is market acceptance for the concept—the level of demand.

▶ What conditions must be present for you to move into the business planning stage—the nature of the genesis team, start-up capital requirements, distribution channel, and so forth.

Estimation of demand is a vital step in deciding whether you have a viable business concept, for there is no business without enough satisfied customers. Once you have concluded there is adequate demand for the product or service, other issues such as the operational and organizational requirements can be undertaken and a business plan completed. There is no need to spend time and effort on these issues if the feasibility analysis indicates insufficient interest in your product or service.

Before going further, it's important to distinguish between a feasibility study and a business plan, which is the subject of Chapter 11. A feasibility study is a way to test your business concept in the market to see whether it makes sense to develop it and enter the market. By contrast, a business plan assumes a feasible concept. The purpose of the business plan is to describe the creation of a company to execute the concept. In short, feasibility is about an idea; the business plan is about a company.

Even though the feasibility study is a tool geared primarily toward providing information to the entrepreneur, it's often possible to attract outside interest in your concept at the feasibility stage if the results are positive. That interest may result in some funding to help you complete a comprehensive business plan, conclude product development, and start the business. The feasibility study may also assist in attracting quality people to the founding team. To test a business idea requires that you first formulate the business concept.

Developing a Business Concept

A business concept is a concise description of an opportunity that contains four elements: the product/service, customer definition, value proposition (benefit to the customer), and distribution channel. Assume that your business concept is about importing unique types of furniture from all parts of the world. By answering the following questions, you can arrive at an effective business concept that can be tested.

1. *What is the product or service being offered?* In this case it is a product—furniture—and a service that will provide U.S. retailers with access to furniture that they could not achieve on their own.

2. *Who is the customer?* The customer is the smaller U.S. retailer of furniture.

3. *What is the benefit?* The retailer can purchase from one supplier (you, the importer) to find unique pieces of furniture from many parts of the world. In short, the benefits are convenience and access.

4. *How do you get the product or service to the customer?* You plan to reach the customer through a combination of a catalog service, web site, and showroom. You will warehouse the furniture and deliver direct to the customer.

The complete concept statement might look like this.

> Worldwide Imports provides smaller U.S. furniture retailers with the ease and convenience of worldwide access to unique pieces of furniture. Worldwide will reach its customers through a catalog service, web site, and showroom, and will deliver direct to the customer from its warehouse.

It's important to state your business concept in a couple of clear and concise sentences, so that when someone asks about your new business, you can get the information out quickly rather than stammering and talking around the key points, which only causes confusion. Some entrepreneurs refer to this two-sentence statement as their "elevator pitch." Pretend that you find yourself in an elevator with a potential funder. You only have the duration of an elevator ride to interest him or her in your business concept. What would you say? If you can get the concept out in two to three sentences, you've given the listener the critical elements and caught his or her attention sufficiently so that the conversation might continue after you leave the elevator.

Here's an example of an effective concept statement done in elevator pitch style.

> I'm working on a concept for a health education company called Smart Choice Software that helps young college students learn about the dangers of substance abuse. I plan to develop and distribute interactive software on CD-ROM that delivers objective, nonthreatening, entertaining, and flexible programs to my customers, college and university health centers, to help them reduce the overall cost of dealing with drug and alcohol related issues.

Defining the Business You're In

The question of what business you're in is important to the development of a business concept because many entrepreneurs define their businesses so narrowly that they have nowhere to go as they grow. In the case of the foregoing example, Smart Choice Software is in the health education business. Notice that it doesn't define itself as being in the software or CD-ROM business because that would limit its potential as technology changes. Instead, Smart Choice places itself in the broader health education arena and doesn't restrict itself to a particular distribution channel. In this way, the company can take advantage of new technological media as they become available.

So, the concept statement also defines what business you're in. Two additional questions often arise out of the development of a concept statement.

1. What is the difference between a benefit and a feature?

2. Why is money *not* part of the business concept?

Let us consider each of these questions.

Features versus Benefits

It is common for entrepreneurs to think they're focusing on the benefits they're providing to the customer when actually they're describing features. For example, using the furniture importer example discussed earlier, the typical entrepreneur may say that he or she is providing retailers with unique pieces of furniture from many parts of the world. That certainly is true, but *uniqueness* is a feature or characteristic of the furniture, not the benefit to the customer. The benefit to the cus-

TABLE 5.1

Features versus Benefits for an Online Trading Floor for Importers and Exporters

Features	Benefits to Importers
Virtual trading floor with a database of goods available for import	Reduction of the time and expense it takes to find suppliers of goods to import from all over the world
Chat room	Acquisition of new contacts and sharing of information
Industry database	Ability to learn more about a region of the world to determine feasibility for importing

tomer is those factors that encourage the customer to purchase from you over your competitors. The benefit is what's in it for the customer and it's typically something intangible like convenience, better health, speed, or reliability. Look at Table 5.1 to see an example of features versus benefits for a different type of business.

The Role of Money

Money is always assumed to be the most necessary component of a successful venture. While it's true that money is important, it is only an enabler; its presence does not confirm that the business concept is feasible. In fact, the dot com bust of spring 2000 proved that a large investment in a business idea will not make it feasible if customer demand and an effective business model are not present. Until you know that customers are interested in what you are offering and will pay for what you are offering, all the money in the world will not make your venture feasible.

However, once you have successfully determined feasibility, you can begin to think about where you will get the funding needed to start the venture.

Quick-Testing the Concept

With your preliminary business concept in hand, it's helpful to do a quick test to see if a full-blown feasibility study is warranted. Many weak business concepts can be quickly eliminated from consideration by asking yourself a few simple questions. Answering these questions will not require any research; you can simply rely on your own knowledge and the thoughts of people you seek out when you want to get some objective opinions.

1. *Am I really interested in this business opportunity?* If you develop this concept, it is going to take all the time and energy you can give it, so it's important that you be passionate about it. Many potential entrepreneurs have gone forward with concepts that others suggested to them only to discover, after they have spent considerable time and effort—not to mention money—that their heart wasn't in the business. The most successful businesses come from the passion of the entrepreneur for the business concept.

2. *Is anyone else interested?* You can't have a business without customers, and you may need investors, so you had better be sure that others are interested in what you plan to offer.

3. *Will people actually pay for what I am offering?* Often when people hear about a new product or service they express interest, even excitement, over it. But what are they willing to pay for it? And how much? If they are not willing to pay what you believe it's worth, you may need to rethink the idea.

4. *Why me?* Why are you the right person to execute this concept? Knowing what assets you bring to the concept is an important part of deciding if it's doable.

5. *Why now?* Why is this a good time to launch this business? And why has no one done this before? Or have they?

If you can answer all these questions to your satisfaction, then it's time for a more formal level of investigation: the feasibility study.

The Nature of Feasibility Analysis

It is no understatement to say that feasibility analysis is one of the most important skills you can acquire if you want to become an entrepreneur or use your entrepreneurial mindset inside a large corporation. Feasibility analysis forces you to do some serious research, to think critically about the business concept, to answer the fundamental questions, and to reach a high level of confidence about your willingness to go forward and actually start the business.

In general, the research that you do to conduct the feasibility analysis answers the following three questions:

1. Is there a customer base and a market of sufficient size to make the concept viable? Research will provide real numbers that you can convert to sales forecasts. Those forecasts and additional numbers that describe the costs of doing business will help you decide if you can make money with this concept—that is, if it's worth your time and effort. Some market niches are not large enough to allow the entrepreneur to make a suitable profit once competitors enter the market. Knowing that about a market in advance allows you to make adjustments in the concept to perhaps broaden

FIGURE 5.1

Layers of a Feasibility Analysis

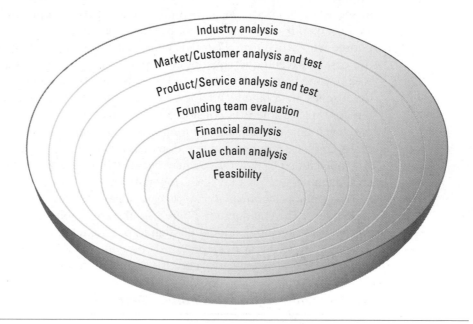

Industry analysis

Market/Customer analysis and test

Product/Service analysis and test

Founding team evaluation

Financial analysis

Value chain analysis

Feasibility

the market niche or decide not to go forward with the business before you've spent time and money starting the business.

2. Do the capital requirements to start, based on estimates of sales and expenses, make sense? Can you start this business with an amount of capital that you either have or will be able to raise?

3. Can an appropriate start-up or genesis team be put together to execute the concept? Recall that most successful start-ups involve teams rather than solo entrepreneurs. In an earlier question, you asked yourself why you should be the person to lead this venture. Now, based on your research, the question becomes what kind of team can you put together to comprise all the skills needed to effectively execute the concept. A team consists of the founders and any strategic partners, which can be people or other businesses with capabilities your business requires.

Conducting feasibility analysis is a little bit like zeroing in on a target or peeling away the layers of an onion to get at the core. In this case, the core is the feasible business concept, and the layers are simply the layers of analysis you must go through to get to the core. Figure 5.1 depicts this analogy.

When the feasibility analysis is complete, you should be able to determine whether the conditions are right for you to go forward with the business concept. If conditions are not favorable, you will need to review the areas you tested to see whether another approach might make the concept viable. For example, suppose you have a concept for a new type of wheelchair that is better suited to people with active lives. Through your analysis, you may have determined that the cost to execute the concept (set up a factory, purchase equipment, etc.) is well beyond your means and would probably not be of interest to major investors because it's not a high technology, high-growth concept. All it may take to make the concept feasible is to consider outsourcing the expensive aspects like product development and manufacturing to an existing company. Immediately, your direct costs are reduced and you don't have to invest in expense equipment and a manufacturing facility. Or you may decide that licensing your patent to a wheelchair manufacturer is a low-cost, low-risk way to bring your product to market.

The point is that many concepts can achieve feasibility if the right conditions are in place. The real question is, are you, the entrepreneur, convinced of the concept's feasibility and confident enough to put the time, money, and effort into its execution. Has your analysis provided you with enough supporting evidence that you're willing to take a calculated risk and begin to plan the launch?

An Overview of the Feasibility Tests

Table 5.2 provides an overview of the feasibility tests, the questions to be addressed by each test, and the chapter that discusses that aspect of the feasibility analysis and how to accomplish it in detail. In this section, you'll find a brief discussion of each of the tests so that you can get a big-picture view of the process.

Identifying Industry Risks and Benefits

The broadest level of analysis is an in-depth understanding of an industry, and it typically precedes the development of a concept, which is why we addressed how to conduct an industry analysis in the previous chapter (Chapter 4). A well-constructed industry analysis will point up strengths and weaknesses in the industry, provide an understanding of how the industry operates, and identify where your business might fit in. It also gives you clues to your competitors' strategies.

Analyzing Market/Customer Risks and Benefits

Testing the market and primary customer for the business concept is perhaps the most important test of all, because it indicates whether there is sufficient demand from customers for the product or service. The information you gather from primary and secondary research lets you develop a comprehensive customer profile, which will help you with product/service design and marketing. An effective

TABLE 5.2

Feasibility Analysis

Area to Be Analyzed and Questions to Ask

Industry (Chapter 4)
1. What are the demographics, trends, patterns of change, life cycle stage of the industry?
2. Are there any barriers to entry? If so, what are they?
3. What is the status of technology and R&D expenditures?
4. What are typical profit margins in the industry?
5. What are distributors, competitors, retailers, and so on saying about the industry?

Market/Customer (Chapter 6)
6. What are the demographics of the target market?
7. What is the customer profile? Who is the customer?
8. Have you talked with customers?
9. Who are your competitors, and how are you differentiated from them?

Product/Service (Chapter 7)
10. What are the features and benefits of the product or service?
11. What product development tasks must be undertaken, and what is the timeline for completion?
12. Is there potential for intellectual property rights?
13. How is the product or service differentiated from others in the market?

Founding Team (Chapter 8)
14. What experience and expertise does the team have?
15. What are the gaps and how will you fill them?

Finance (Chapter 8)
16. What are your start-up capital requirements?
17. What are your working capital requirements?
18. What are your fixed cost requirements?
19. How long will it take to achieve a positive cash flow?
20. What is the break-even point for the business?

Value Chain Analysis (Chapter 9)
21. What does your value chain look like?
22. Which distribution channel alternatives are available and which customers will be served by them?
23. Are there ways to innovate in the distribution channel?

market/customer analysis will demonstrate a demand for the product or service and prove that the customer is willing to purchase from your company. If it doesn't demonstrate sufficient demand, then you will need to revisit the concept based on the feedback you get. One entrepreneur had a concept to deliver on-demand interactive media through a set box on the customer's TV. His customers were the cable TV companies that wanted to use content in a new way. So he was able to show in his feasibility study that customers wanted what he had to offer. What he failed to do was prove that they would buy from him. And, in fact, that was the fatal flaw. He was a young entrepreneur with no experience in the industry and no credible management team, so the cable TV companies did not trust that he could deliver on his promise and, consequently, were unwilling to sign contracts with him.

Analyzing Product/Service Risks and Benefits

In this test, you will be developing the business concept and considering issues like intellectual property protection, product development, and prototyping. Your goal will be to establish the unique features and benefits of your products and services and to develop your bundle of competitive advantages. Heather Howitt is the founder of Oregon Chai, a producer of the milky tea drink that has become so popular as an alternative to lattes. The company's competitive advantage—the spice added to the traditional flavor and the ease for servers of making the drink—succeeded in getting Oregon Chai a coveted introduction through Starbucks' stores, which then led to shelf space in supermarkets and natural foods stores. Creating a bundle of competitive advantages ensures that you aren't putting all your eggs in one basket.

Evaluating the Founding Team

The founding team is what most investors and other interested parties look at first, because no matter how good the concept is, it won't get anywhere without a founding team that can execute the concept. In many cases, having a strong team becomes the deciding factor in whether the entrepreneur takes the risk associated with the new concept or not. And where the team lacks either expertise or experience, you must show that you have identified people you can tap to fill the gaps.

Analyzing Financial Risks and Requirements

In feasibility analysis, you start to consider money after you've determined that you have customers who will buy from you and a great team to execute the concept. The financial analysis focuses on the capital requirements for launching the business. Through forecasts of potential sales and expenses, as well as working capital and equipment requirements, the entrepreneur gains a sense of whether or not it's financially feasible to move forward with the business concept.

Analyzing the Value Chain

There are many ways to deliver a benefit to the customer: directly (by mail, the Internet, a manufacturer's outlet), through a distributor, or through a retailer, to name a few. The value chain is the distribution channel through which products and services flow from the producer to the end-user. At each point along the channel, intermediaries add value through the services they provide. Today, more than ever before, businesses can create a competitive advantage by looking at ways to streamline the value chain or bring products and services to customers in new ways. In this section of the feasibility analysis, it's important to justify your choice of the method of delivery of the benefit to the customer. In a world where technology and the Internet are regularly shortening value chains, it's vital to examine and justify your value chain for investors and others with a stake in your business.

Presenting the Feasibility Study

If you are doing feasibility analysis purely to convince yourself that you have a feasible business concept, you will probably not need to do a formal report. But, if you are planning to use your feasibility analysis to seek funding, attract management or other expertise to your team, or seek a credit line from your banker, you will want to convey the results of the analysis in a report form. An outline for an effective layout of the report can be found in Table 5.3.

In general, the report should be structured in such a way that the key questions (Table 5.2) are clearly answered and evidence for feasibility sufficiently amassed so that there is no doubt in the reader's mind that the business concept has the potential for market success. In other words, you have anticipated questions the reader might have and answered them with supporting evidence, building a strong case for feasibility.

As in any good report, numerical data are most effectively presented through bullets, tables, or graphs. In the case of tables and graphs, do not assume that the reader is able to spot the most salient points. Instead, these points should be highlighted and discussed. In the case of financial spreadsheets, make sure they are readable. Use breakout sheets, which detail items under a major heading like "Manufacturing Expenses," rather than clutter up the spreadsheet with more information than is necessary.

Remember that the primary purpose of a feasibility analysis is to assure yourself that you want to launch this new venture. If your research has indicated that the conditions are favorable and you feel passionate about it, your chances of enjoying a successful start-up increase.

TABLE 5.3

Feasibility Analysis Outline

Cover for the Feasibility Study

Executive Summary
- Include most important points from all sections of the feasibility study. *Do not exceed two pages.*
- Make sure the first sentence captures the reader's attention and the first paragraph presents the business concept.

Title Page (Name of Company, Feasibility Study, Genesis Team Members' Names)

Table of Contents

Feasibility Decision
- The decision regarding the conditions under which the entrepreneur is willing to go forward with the business concept

The Business Concept
- What is the business?
- Who is the customer?
- What is the value proposition or benefit(s) being delivered to the customer?
- How will the benefit be delivered (distribution)?
- What is the potential for growth and spin-offs?

Industry/Market Analysis
- Industry analysis
- Target market analysis (customer grid)
- Niche
- Competitor analysis and competitive advantages (competitive grid)
- Customer profile
- Distribution channels (alternatives and risks/benefits)

- Entry strategies (initial market penetration—first customer)

Genesis (or Founding) Team
- Qualifications of genesis team
- How critical tasks will be accomplished
- Gap analysis (professional advisers, board of directors, independent contractors)

Product/Service Development Plan
- Detailed description and unique features of product/service
- Current status of product development
- Tasks and timeline to completion
- Intellectual property acquisition (if relevant)
- Plan for prototyping and testing

Financial Plan
- Summary of key points on which financial feasibility is based
- Assumptions or premises for resource needs assessment
- Resource needs assessment
- Pro forma income statement (1–3 years) by month or quarter
- Break-even analysis

TImeline to Launch
- Tasks that will need to be accomplished up to the date of launch in the order of their completion

Bibliography or Endnotes (footnotes may be substituted)

Appendix (A, B, C, etc.)
- Questionnaires, maps, forms, resumes, etc.

NEW VENTURE CHECKLIST

Have you:

- ☐ Developed a clear and concise business concept that contains the product/service, customer, value proposition, and distribution?
- ☐ Done a quick test of your business concept to see whether it's worthy of a feasibility analysis?
- ☐ Conducted a full feasibility analysis beginning with a thorough understanding of the industry?
- ☐ Answered the key questions for every feasibility test?
- ☐ Determined the conditions under which you are willing to go forward with the concept?

ISSUES TO CONSIDER

1. Are there instances where a feasibility study is not warranted or can be reduced in scope?

2. Why are the purposes for a feasibility study and a business plan different?

3. How can a feasibility study be made more effective as a medium to persuade a potential investor?

EXPERIENCING ENTREPRENEURSHIP

1. Define a concept for a new venture using the four components discussed in the chapter: product/service, customer, benefit, and distribution. Quick test on some potential customers through a focus group, interviews, or a survey. Did you get enough information to move forward to a feasibility study? Why or why not?

2. Using a business concept that you develop, identify the key arguments that will have to be supported in the feasibility study.

ADDITIONAL SOURCES OF INFORMATION

Boyce, B., and S.D. Messner (2001). *Analyzing Real Estate Opportunities: Market and Feasibility Studies.* Cincinnati: South-Western.

McQuarrie, E.F. (1996). *The Market Research Toolbox: A Concise Guide for Beginners.* Thousand Oaks, CA: Sage Publications.

Miller, J.P. (2000). *Millennium Intelligence.* Medford, NJ: CyberAge Books.

Ruggles, R. (Ed.) (1997). *Knowledge Management Tools.* Woburn, MA: Butterworth-Heinemann.

INTERNET RESOURCES

CEO Express
http://www.ceoexpress.com
A guide to business resources on the Internet.

Lowe Foundation Resources
http://216.202.194.32/fmpro?-db=library.fp5&-
  format=generic.htm&title=startup&-find
Articles and ideas on a number of issues related to
  feasibility analysis.

EntreWorld.org
http://www.entreworld.org/Default.cfm
Articles and help on issues related to evaluating a
  business opportunity.

RELEVANT CASE STUDIES

Case 6   Highland Dragon

Case 7   Roland International Freight Service

Analyzing the Market and the Customer

Because its purpose is to create a customer, the business enterprise has two—and only these two—basic functions: marketing and innovation. Marketing and innovation produce results; all the rest are "costs."
Peter F. Drucker

Overview

Characterizing the target market

Forecasting new product/service demand

Getting the product/service to the customer

Preliminary conclusions as to feasibility

Build a Business by Knowing the Customer

There was a time when music labels like Motown were brand names, even bigger than any individual artists the labels represented. Today music labels as a brand have fallen to the background, with the exception of Rhino Records, which has a cult following of people who enjoy its retro, eclectic content in compilations and box sets. When Richard Foos and Harold Bronson set out to start a company in a very difficult industry, they decided to do it by breaking all the traditional rules. In the recording industry, everything is driven by market research, which essentially looks at the past. The goal is to replicate hits. Foos and Bronson took a different approach; they decided to create products that they would buy: CDs, videos, and books creatively packaged in collections of material from the past. In other words, they thought like customers. To make it work, they hired employees who felt the same way they did. If they found an artist they used to like who had never produced a "best of" album, Rhino Records took on the task with gusto and prospered. In fact, the name Rhino Records came from the fact that Foos started the business with no business plan, no financing; he just opened the doors and charged ahead.

The business started as a small shop in Westwood in 1973, an area of Los Angeles next to the UCLA campus, and it became known for its crazy promotions and crazier record collectors who came there looking for their favorite "oldies." In 1978, Foos sold the store to go into the recording business on a full-time basis. With his new partner, Bronson, they achieved their first hit, an all-kazoo version of Led Zeppelin's "Whole Lotta Love." It was a novelty tune, and the company grossed $60,000 in 1978 alone.

As the company grew, Foos and Bronson kept the overhead down and continued to focus on thinking like the customer. It was fortunate they did, for the market for the novelty tunes they were creating died in 1979. As part of the baby-boom generation, the undaunted pair saw demand increasing for compilations of past records. At the time, these songs, called reissues, were at the bottom of the food chain in the recording industry. But the partners took a fresh approach by creatively packaging these songs in themed collections. Their customer-focus strategy worked: 90 percent of their products today are profitable in an industry where only 10 percent of the records produced make a profit.

Today, Rhino is a music phenomenon that has taken its brand to new levels. In 1997, for example, Rhino introduced its Rhino Musical Aptitude Test, an open-book, 305-question music trivia test, which has now become an international event. It also serves to remind people of music they have forgotten that they can find among Rhino's compilations. Partnerships are another marketing strategy with which Rhino has found success. It joined Nabisco to link Breath Savers mints with its Cool Blast Music Trivia at the candystand.com site. Among additional co-

branders is Discovery Communications (Discovery Channel, Learning Channel, Animal Planet, Travel Channel), which figured out that music was a great complement to its cable TV lineup. It has also inked deals with Viacom's Nickelodeon kids channel and Time Warner's Cartoon Network to release soundtracks from the shows.

In January 2001, Rhino introduced its latest brand, Rhino Internet Solutions, www.rhinointernet.com, which contains case studies, a map of the Rhino process, and a client extranet that lets Rhino clients check on the status of their projects. Rhino also has another arm, Staging and Event Solutions, which provides labor for major events.

Foos and Bronson have deep roots in their Los Angeles communities and their philanthropic values have influenced their employees as well. In 1989, a group of Rhino employees formed the Social and Environmental Responsibility Team (SERT) that became the basis for a human resource policy that has all employees performing 16 hours of community service a week, which gives them a week of paid vacation between Christmas and New Year. The goodwill that Rhino employees generate in the community is worth far more than any advertising the company could do.

Today, it seems that everyone is interested in the reissue business, but Foos and Bronson aren't worried. Their customers like them and are like them, and Rhino Records isn't likely to go away any time soon.

SOURCES: Michael Warshaw, "Master the Future," *Success,* October 1996, pp. 28–30; http://www.rhino.com; http://www.rhinointernet.com; Mike Beirne, "Brand on the Run," *Brandweek,* October 30, 2000; T.L. Stanley, "Rhino's New Biz Safari," *Brandweek,* July 13, 1998; "Rhino Launches Redesign of Its Internet Solutions Web Site, Reveals New Brand," *Business Wire,* Tempe, Arizona, January 15, 2001; Anni Layne, "Give It Away, Now," *Fast Company,* http://www.fastcompany.com/feature/action/rhino.html.

Identification of the primary customer is one of the most important tasks the entrepreneur must undertake in analyzing the feasibility of a business concept. In broad terms, the definition of the customer begins with an analysis of the target market—that segment of the marketplace that will most likely purchase the product or service, in other words, the primary market. The secondary market, by contrast, consists of those customers outside the initial target market. These are customers the company will target after the primary market has been exhausted or the company has at least established a firm foothold.

How do you identify the primary customer in the first place? Most often by recognizing a need in the marketplace. Gus Conrades and his partner Bryan Murphy saw a need for a central online place where people and businesses could purchase auto parts and car-care products. In the highly fragmented auto products market, customers had a difficult time finding what they needed. Conrades and Murphy launched Wrenchead.com to remedy that situation and they now sell millions of auto parts and brand-name accessories around the world to people who love cars.

Identifying a need in the market is only part of the battle. Unfortunately, many entrepreneurs don't place enough emphasis on in-depth market analysis to support the need they have discovered. Instead they assume levels of need and demand without any evidence to support them. As a result, they tend to overestimate their market forecasts for demand by as much as 60 percent. And that kind of error can be devastating to a start-up venture that is relying on a certain level of sales to survive.

Characterizing the Target Market

No matter what the size of the target market, it is crucial that the entrepreneur know as much as possible about the customer. Sumerset Custom Houseboats really understands the customers for whom it builds customized houseboats. It has accomplished a long-term relationship between builders and owners by building an on-line community where customers can visually track the progress of their boat on a day-to-day basis. Sumerset posts pictures of each customer's boat and its progress; this is particularly important for customers in distant parts of the world. And the company has made the site interactive so it can get constant feedback from its customers; this saves its managers time and travel, which is particularly important when dealing with the firm's celebrity customers. (See www.sumerset.com.)

In the beginning stages of market analysis, you will probably have a fairly loose description of the target market. This description will be refined and may even change fairly substantially as you talk to target customers during field research. It is easy to become overwhelmed by the amount of information available about your target market, so it's important to keep in mind the key questions you will be attempting to answer.

▶ Who is most likely to purchase my product or service at market introduction?

▶ What do these customers typically buy, how do they buy it, and how do they hear about it?

▶ How often do they buy? What is their buying pattern?

▶ How can the new venture meet the customers' needs?

● Researching the Target Market

Target market research provides some of the most important data you need to decide whether the new venture is feasible. But data are only as good as the research methods used to collect them. To ensure that useful and correct conclusions can be drawn from the data collected, you must use sound research methods. A four-step process will ensure that the information needed to make this crucial decision is gathered and used correctly. (See Table 6.1.)

TABLE 6.1

Steps in Market Research

Assess your information needs.	• How will the data be used? • What data need to be collected? • What methods of analysis will be used?
Research secondary sources first.	• What are the demographics of the customer? • What are the psychographics of the customer (i.e., buying habits)? • How large is the market? • Is the market growing? • Is the market affected by geography? • How can you reach your market? • How do your competitors reach the market? • What market strategies have been successful with these customers?
Measure the target market with primary research.	• What are the demographics of your customer? • Would they purchase your product or service? Why? • How much would they purchase? • When would they purchase? • How would they like to find the product or service? • What do they like about your competitors' products and services?
Forecast demand for the product or service.	• What do substitute products/services tell you about demand for your product/service? • What do customers, end-users, and intermediaries predict the demand will be? • Can you do a limited production or test market for your product or service?

● *Assessing Information Needs*

Before you can begin to collect market data, you must determine how that data will be used in the market analysis. Will it demonstrate a demand for the product or service? Will it describe the target customer? You may be wondering how you can decide how data will be used and analyzed when it hasn't yet been collected.

This is precisely the point. A good researcher first decides what needs to be accomplished with the research, so that the correct types of data are gathered. Nothing is more discouraging than finding out that a crucial piece of information is missing after all the data have been collected.

Also, once you know what you want to determine with the data, it will be easier to choose a particular type of analysis that will lead to the desired result. For example, if one of your research goals is to refine the description of the target market—in other words, craft a more precise customer definition—you may decide to seek the most common characteristics or demographics (the statistical mode) of the customer, that is, the most common age, education level, income, and so on of the potential customers you tested. To do this, you will need to gather numerical data. Granted, this is a rather simple and obvious example; however, others are not so apparent.

Suppose, for example, you wish to calculate demand for the product or service by using a statistical forecasting technique. The type of technique you choose will dictate the kind of data you must collect. For example, if the technique requires continuous numerical data (i.e., all values for an answer are possible), you would not gather data or design a questionnaire that would give you "yes-no" answers. Fortunately, the market research most entrepreneurs conduct yields simple, descriptive statistics.

Recall that you want to collect both primary and secondary market data. It is important, however, to gather the secondary data first, so that you have a better understanding of the market and what others have reported about the target market prior to designing a sampling plan and doing the field research.

Researching Secondary Sources

The Internet is a good starting point for gathering secondary data. Many of the traditional resources found in libraries are now available in online versions; for example, U.S. census data can be found at www.census.gov. This data allows you to define your market by region of the country, major metropolitan area, city, or even neighborhood and look at demographic information such as age, education, and income. Using it, you can determine whether the geographic area you have defined is growing or declining, whether its population is aging or getting younger, or whether the available work force is mostly skilled or unskilled, along with many other trends.

Some demographics (data on age, income, race, occupation, and education) help identify the likelihood that a person will choose to buy a product.[1] Demographic data also allow you to segment the target market into subgroups that are estimably different from one another. For example, if the target market is retired people over age 60, their buying habits (such as product requirements and quantity or frequency of purchase) may vary by geographic region or by income level.

Finally, census data can be used to arrive at an estimate of how many target customers live within the geographic boundaries of the target market. Then, within any geographic area, those who meet the particular demographic requirements of the product or service can be segmented out.

It is not only consumer markets that are described by demographic data. Business markets can also be described by their size, revenue levels, number of employees, and so forth. Information about business demographics is found at sites like Economy.com's "The Dismal Scientist" at http://www.economy.com/dismal/ and the Census Bureau at http://www.census.gov.

Online sources are not the only sources of secondary market data. Most communities have economic development departments or Chambers of Commerce that keep statistics on local population trends and other economic issues. Some communities have Small Business Development Centers (SBDCs), branches of the Small Business Administration that contain a wealth of useful information, as well as services, for small and growing businesses. Other sources available in the library are reference books and trade journals on all types of industries (many of these are also available online). Apart from the library, useful information can be obtained from trade associations like the National Association of Manufacturers, commercial research firms, and financial institutions. These resources will assist you in determining the size and characteristics of the target market.

Measuring the Market with Primary Data

The most important data you collect on potential customers is primary data from observation, mail surveys, phone surveys, interviews, and focus groups, to name a few techniques. Each has advantages and disadvantages over the others, and a decision to use one or more of them is usually based on time and money. The first three techniques require drawing a representative sample from the population of customers you're interested in. The sample should be selected with great care, for it will determine the validity of the results. In general, you want to choose a random sample, that is, one in which you have as little control as possible over who will be selected to participate. You don't want to bias what respondents tell you.

Most entrepreneurs, because of limitations on cost and time, choose to use what is called a convenience sample. This means that not everyone in the defined target market has a chance of being chosen to participate. Instead, the entrepreneur may, for example, choose to select the sample from people who happen to be at the airport on a particular day. Clearly, the entrepreneur will not be reaching all possible customers at the airport, but if the target customer is typically found at airports, there's a good chance of achieving at least a representative sample, from which results can be derived fairly confidently.

Even if a convenience sample is used, there are ways to ensure the randomness of selection of the participants. Using the airport example, you can decide in advance to survey every fifth person who walks by. In this way, the person is not chosen on the basis of attractiveness or lack of it—or for any other reason, for that matter. A random number generator on a computer can select names from a telephone book. Whatever system is employed, the key point is to make an effort not to bias the selection. Often you will hear potential entrepreneurs say that they took a sample of friends and relatives who loved the new product idea. Friends and relatives may be able to give you some initial feedback, but they are not the best source of unbiased information. Remember, one of the reasons you are doing a feasibility study and ultimately a business plan is to convince others about the viability of the new venture concept. The credibility of your market research results will be measured by the quality of the sample you select.

While it is true that you are trying to collect information and data when you do surveys of any type, you should also be aware that the people you question are forming beliefs about your company based on how you handle the survey or interview, how you will use the information, and how you will protect the respondents' privacy.[2]

Primary Research Techniques

The following are some of the research techniques you can use to study your customers. Each has advantages and disadvantages, so choose the method or methods most appropriate to your business and its potential customers.

Mail Surveys.   Surveys are a common method for collecting data from a large sample and many entrepreneurs mistakenly believe that they can throw together a questionnaire and get all the information they need. But surveys are prone to many types of error including sampling errors, which occur during extrapolation of findings from the sample to the entire population, and nonsampling errors, which are due to problems in data collection and analysis.[3] Doing a mail survey entails designing a survey instrument, usually a questionnaire that, once filled out, provides the desired information. Questionnaire design is not a simple matter of putting some questions on a piece of paper. There are, in fact, proven methods of constructing questionnaires to help ensure unbiased responses. It is not within the scope of this text to present all the techniques for questionnaire construction; however, a few key points should be remembered.

- Keep the questionnaire short, with lots of white space, so that the respondent is not intimidated by the task at the outset.

- Be careful not to ask leading or biased questions.

- Ask easy questions first, leading up to the more complex ones.

- Ask demographic questions (age, sex, income) last, when the respondent's attention span has waned. These questions can be answered very quickly.

▶ For questions people generally hesitate to answer (about age and income, for instance), group possible responses in ranges (25–35 for age, $35,000–$45,000 for income) so the respondent doesn't feel he or she is disclosing very private information.

▶ Keep in mind that people generally increase their income classification one class and decrease their age one class.

▶ Mail surveys are a relatively easy way to reach a great many people in the target market, and they take less time than many other methods. However, mail surveys do have a few weaknesses.

   a. The response rate is generally very low, usually around 15 percent, which means that about 85 of every 100 persons sampled do not respond. Consequently, the potential for nonresponse bias makes it difficult to feel very comfortable about the reliability of the results.
   b. Mail surveys lack the benefit of nonverbal communication (body language) that would be available from an interview. This is significant when you consider that at least 85 percent of all communication is nonverbal.
   c. The entrepreneur has no way of questioning or clarifying a response.
   d. There is no control over the accuracy of the information given.

▶ Normally, a second, follow-up mailing is necessary to achieve the desired response rate.

Phone Surveys.   Like mail surveys, phone surveys use questionnaires, which offer the benefit of consistency in the questions asked. However, phone surveys have two particular advantages over mail surveys: they allow for explanation and clarification of questions and responses, and the response rate is higher. On the other hand, phone surveys take more time to accomplish and are more prone to surveyor bias; that is, there is more opportunity for the person conducting the survey to bias the results by the tone in his or her voice or by unscripted comments. In addition, phone surveys do not offer the opportunity to observe nonverbal communication.

Internet Surveys.   The Internet has made it easy for small businesses to conduct valuable market research without having to enlist the help of expensive market research firms.[4] Internet surveys are relatively inexpensive compared to traditional surveys and the response time is greatly reduced. It's easier to include global respondents seamlessly. Surveys posted on the Internet are a convenient way to conduct research if your primary customer is an Internet user. The survey can be posted in user groups, sent via e-mail to targeted customers, or placed on your web site as long as the people you want to respond to the survey have a way of knowing that it's there.

You need to be aware, however, of the negative aspects of Internet surveys. People who use the Internet are typically bombarded by data-gathering mechanisms and may resist filling out another survey, so the response rate may be low.[5] Remember that Internet surveys are only as good as the representative sample they seek to survey. If your customers aren't all Internet users, the Internet may not provide a true indication of demand for your product or service. Other methods may be more appropriate. Furthermore, it's difficult to target your sample effectively, and there are often technical problems that may cause some of the data to be lost.

Interviews. Although personal interviews are more costly and time-consuming than mail or phone surveys, they have many advantages.

▶ They provide more opportunity for clarification and discussion.

▶ They offer the advantages of nonverbal communication. The entrepreneur will be better able to discern the veracity of what the interviewee is saying.

▶ The response rate is high.

▶ Interviews permit open-ended questions that can lead to more in-depth information.

▶ They provide an opportunity to network and develop valuable contacts in the industry.

Where time and money permit, interviews are probably the best source of valuable information from customers, suppliers, distributors, and anyone else who can help the new venture. It is also possible, however, to use a combination of techniques. For example, you may start with phone surveys to obtain basic information and follow up with interviews with the most useful sources.

Focus Groups. One more efficient way to gain valuable information before investing substantial capital in production and marketing is to conduct a **focus group,** in which you bring together a representative sample of potential customers for a presentation and discussion session. Assuming that the new venture involves a consumer product, you may choose to introduce the new product in concert with other products to test the unsolicited response to the product when presented with its competition. For example, suppose your product is a new type of nonalcoholic beverage. You might serve the new beverage along with several competitors' beverages in glasses labeled with numbers, and then solicit feedback on aroma, color, taste, aftertaste, and so on.

Some products and services do not easily lend themselves to blind studies like the one just described. In those instances, the product can simply be presented to the focus group members and their opinions and feedback solicited. It is important to ensure that the person leading the focus group has some knowledge of group dynamics and will be able to keep the group on track. Many times these focus group sessions are videotaped so that the entrepreneur can spend more time later analyzing the nuances of what occurred. Thus, in many ways, focus groups can prevent the entrepreneur from making the costly error of offering a product or service in which there is little or no interest.

The Customer Profile

Out of your primary research will come a complete profile of your customer. You will be able to describe the primary customer, whether a consumer or a business, in great detail. The profile is critically important to your marketing strategy because it provides the information you need to determine your distribution channels for feasibility analysis and create a marketing plan when it comes time to do a business plan. Here is a list of some of the information that goes into a profile of a consumer or a business.

- age
- income level
- education
- buying habits—when, where, how much
- where customers typically find your types of products and services
- how they would like to purchase

The list will contain other data as well, depending on whether you're dealing with a consumer or a business. Sandy Gooch is one of the leaders in the health food industry. When she was preparing to open her first store, she had a complete picture of her target customer: a 45–50-year-old professional woman who was well educated, a life-long learner, into physical fitness, and who read labels when she shopped. She was a regular shopper, coming in several times a week on her way home from work. That level of description creates a clear image of who this customer is.

You can read more about Sandy Gooch in the case study, "Mrs. Gooch's," at the end of the book. Certainly, not everyone who shopped at Mrs. Gooch's was a 45–50-year-old professional woman, but that was the customer most likely to purchase when she started the business: her primary customer. Knowing so much about her customer allowed Gooch to tailor her advertising. Mrs. Gooch's ads always contained a lot of information, for instance, because she knew her customers wanted to learn something from each ad.

If you're dealing with a business customer, think of describing that customer in the same way Sandy Gooch described her customer, for example, a small to mid-sized construction company with annual revenues of $5 million that makes purchases quarterly, buys primarily over the Internet, and pays within sixty days. The customer profile will be an important piece in the marketing plan you develop in Chapter 15.

Forecasting New Product/Service Demand

One of the most difficult tasks facing the entrepreneur is forecasting the demand for the new product or service, particularly if that product/service has never existed previously in the marketplace. Adding to this difficulty is the tendency for most entrepreneurs to do their own research, because they generally don't have sufficient resources prior to start-up to hire professional market research firms. However, doing your own market research does have the advantage of giving you a clearer sense of your target market and its needs. It is helpful to triangulate demand from three different points of view: historical analogy, prospective end-users and intermediaries, and your own point of view, gleaned from going into limited production or doing a formal test market. A number of different techniques can assist you in arriving at a realistic forecast of demand.

● Use Historical Analogy or Substitute Products

If the new product is an extension of a previously existing product, it may be possible to extrapolate from that product's demand to yours. For example, the demand for compact disks was derived from the historical demand for cassette tapes and records. In other cases it may be possible to substitute another product in the same industry to give an indication of demand potential, assuming the same target market.

● Interview Prospective End-Users and Intermediaries

No one knows the market better than the men and women who work in it every day. They are typically very astute at predicting trends and patterns of buyer behavior. Spending time in the field talking with customers, intermediaries (distributors or wholesalers, sometimes referred to as "middlemen"), retailers, and the like can provide a fairly good estimate of demand.

● Go into Limited Production

Sometimes the only way to test the reaction of potential customers is to produce a small number of products and put them in the hands of people to test. This is also an appropriate next step if the first two techniques have produced positive results. Not only will limited testing of the product gauge customer satisfaction; it may suggest possible modifications to improve the product. These samples of the product are called prototypes. Prototypes are generally associated with product companies, but, in fact, service businesses must also develop a prototype of the operation or procedures involved in delivering the service. Prototyping permits the testing of a product or service in the actual environment in which it will be used. It is difficult to conduct meaningful market research without a working prototype, as most potential customers need to see and use the actual product before they can become enthusiastic about it. Construction of a prototype will also facilitate estimates of the costs to actually produce the product later on. We will discuss prototyping in more depth in Chapter 7, which focuses on product development.

● Do a Formal Test Market

When a product is fairly complex and expensive to produce, a formal test market in a selected geographic area can provide valuable information about demand for and acceptance of the product before you spend substantial capital for a major product roll-out. The movie industry regularly introduces new movies with a "limited release" in a few strategic theaters. In this way, film companies can gauge audiences' reactions and make changes based on them before releasing the film nationwide. Major product companies like Procter & Gamble will put a new product into certain geographic test markets like Denver, Colorado, to get feedback from customers. (Many a new product has met an early death as a result of these test market studies.)

● The Cost/Benefit of Market Research

Market research is undoubtedly one of the more expensive aspects of starting a business, and it is time-consuming as well. For these reasons, and because many entrepreneurs don't know how to conduct market research or believe their product or service is so good that customers will automatically desire it, the market analysis section is probably the least well-researched and least well-written section of the business plan. Yet good market research answers the question "Is there a demand for my product or service?" Surely that is the most crucial question an entrepreneur can answer.

Despite the importance of market research, you need to weigh the cost of doing certain types of market research against the benefits of getting the product/service into the market quickly. In today's dynamic business environment, this is a real concern. Spending too much time on market research can cost you a window of opportunity for entering the market. By understanding your industry (see Chapter 4) you will be able to balance the amount of time you spend in doing market research with the amount of time you have to get to market.

Getting the Product/Service to the Customer

With a well-defined target market and sufficient demand estimated to exist, the entrepreneur next faces the important task of deciding how to get the product or service to the customer. A distribution channel, quite simply, is the route a product takes from the manufacturer to the customer or end-user.

Depending on the type of new venture, there are many distribution choices available. Each choice will have distinct advantages, disadvantages, and consequences for the customer and will to some extent dictate the kind of organization the new venture becomes. Today your distribution strategy is as important as every other aspect of your business. Many new businesses are using distribution strategy as their competitive advantage. Kiyonna Clothing is the brainchild of young entrepreneur Kim Camarella and her partners who wanted to solve the problem of plus-size young women who were unable to find stylish clothing. Kiyonna Clothing is now earning over 30 percent of its revenues from sales made on its web site, kiyonna.com.

Each of the different methods of getting the product to the customer—the channels of distribution—puts you in a different kind of business. For example, if you want to sell direct to customers, you're in the retail business if you deal with consumers and in the wholesale business if you deal with business customers. By contrast, if you're a manufacturer, you usually don't deal with end-users but rather find intermediaries like distributors to set up retail channels for you. These intermediaries are your customers. The channel of distribution also determines to some extent your product's cost, the potential for loss or damage through transit, and the speed with which the product reaches the customer. Finding the most efficient and effective channel can provide a new venture with a distinct competitive advantage.

The subject of distribution channels is discussed in detail in Chapter 10, but for now we'll simply consider the distribution channel as the method for getting the product or service to the customer. One useful way to summarize and analyze the different customers and distribution channels available to you is to create a customer grid. The customer grid (see Table 6.2) outlines the customer, the benefit, and the distribution strategy. It can help you make sure that you're differentiating among customers and giving them exactly what they need, in the way they need it.

The grid in Table 6.2 highlights three potential customers for Rhino Records. Now you have to make a choice. Which of these three customers do you go after first? Notice the different benefits and distribution strategies for each customer. In effect, we have three different businesses here: a retail outlet, a whole-

TABLE 6.2

Initial Customer Grid for Rhino Records

Customer	Distribution	Benefit
Baby boomers	Convenience and economy: Can find compilations of their favorite songs without having to buy multiple one-artist albums.	Retail outlet
Record stores	Provides unique compilations of hard-to-find great hits of the past to satisfy the Baby Boomer segment of their market.	Wholesale to record store
The busy professional	Convenience: Can shop any time of the day or night and have all the information at their fingertips.	Internet store for online purchasing

sale distributorship, and an Internet business. The choice of where to go first is a function of the size of the market, customer demand, and resources. For example, owning a retail outlet is potentially the most costly in terms of facility, inventory, and marketing expenses, while the Internet may be the least costly. Take a look at Figure 6.1, which depicts the relationship between the location of your business in the distribution channel and time commitment and risk. Also read Profile 6.1 to learn more about Rhino Records.

You can make a customer grid as simple or as complex as you like, but it's an important tool for looking at your customer options.

Preliminary Conclusions as to Feasibility

Once the market study has been completed, you are in a good position to answer this question: Is there sufficient demand for the product or service the new venture will offer? If you have personally conducted the research and done all the work to this point, you not only will have important information to help make the decision; you will also have an intuitive or "gut" feeling as to whether or not the new venture concept is viable. If market indicators are positive, it is time to consider other aspects of feasibility and proceed to test the business concept further.

Many entrepreneurs find it difficult to abandon an idea with which they have fallen in love, even in the face of market data indicating that demand for the

FIGURE 6.1

The Commitment Pyramid

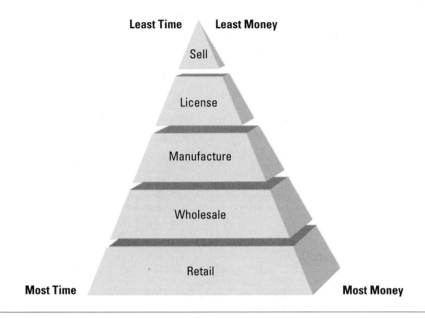

new product or service is weak. When this happens, it is important to remember that without customers there is no business. It is far better to abandon a business concept at this point than to venture ahead to the more costly aspects of a business start-up and ultimately fail.

NEW VENTURE CHECKLIST

Have you:
- ☐ Defined the target market for your product or service?
- ☐ Identified direct, indirect, and emerging competitors?
- ☐ Described your product or service's competitive advantage?
- ☐ Listed the information you will need in order to do the market analysis?
- ☐ Researched secondary data sources such as census data on demographics?
- ☐ Determined the most effective method for gathering primary data on your target market?
- ☐ Estimated demand for the product or service?

ISSUES TO CONSIDER

1. What is the value of defining a market niche?

2. Why is it important to do secondary market research before primary market research?

3. What advantages do interviews have over other data collection methods?

4. Suppose you are introducing a new type of exercise equipment to the fitness industry. What types of research methods would you use to forecast demand, and why?

5. Market research can be an expensive, time-consuming process. What can you do to minimize the costs while still achieving your goals?

EXPERIENCING ENTREPRENEURSHIP

1. Develop a business concept for either a new theme restaurant or an enterprise software application to manage the operations of small business owners. Create a customer grid similar to that in Table 6.2. Add at least one more column of information than what is given. Which customer would you seek out first, and why?

2. Pick a product or service and formulate a plan for researching the customer. Identify what information you need to collect and how you will collect it. Justify your plan.

ADDITIONAL SOURCES OF INFORMATION

Day, G.S. (1999). *Market Driven Strategy: Processes for Creating Value.* New York: Free Press.

Hague, P., and P. Jackson (1999). *Market Research: A Guide to Planning, Methodology and Research.* London: Kogen Page.

Levinson, J.C. (1984). *Guerrilla Marketing.* Boston: Houghton Mifflin.

McQuarrie, E.F. (1998). *Customer Visits: Building a Better Market Focus.* Thousand Oaks, CA: Sage Publications.

INTERNET RESOURCES

American Demographics/Marketing Tools
http://www.demographics.com/directory
This site will help you learn how to target your marketing efforts.

American Marketing Association
http://www.ama.org
Focuses on the services of this organization.

Quirks Marketing Research Review
http://www.quirks.com/
One-stop source for information on marketing research. Includes case studies

You Are Where You Live
http://yaw/claritas.com
Demographic information by zip code.

Research Info.com
http://www.researchinfo.com/
A source of free resources on market research topics.

Understanding Your Market
http://www.sbaonline.sba.gov
From the Small Business Administration; helps you go through the process of understanding your customers.

RELEVANT CASE STUDIES

Case 4   Beanos Ice Cream Shoppe

Case 5   Earthlink.net: The Journey to Recognizing an Opportunity

Case 8   Alcoholes de Centroamerica, S.A. de C.V.

7

Analyzing Product/Service Risks and Benefits

Innovation . . . endows resources with a
new capacity to create wealth.
Peter F. Drucker

Overview

The nature of product/process development

Entrepreneurial product/service development

The product development cycle

Intellectual property development

PROFILE 7.1

Prior Art Has Its Day

As recently as five years ago, the term intellectual property *was something only attorneys found interesting. It was certainly never seen as a source of wealth for a company. How times have changed. Today, even major companies like IBM are conducting scavenger hunts through their patent archives to extract hidden value. In fact, IBM has been so successful at it that it has increased its annual patent-licensing royalties a phenomenal 3,300%, from $30 million in 1990 to over $1 billion today.*

And IBM is not alone. Microsoft, Dell, Dow Chemical, and many others have all come to realize that competitive value is now found in ideas and innovation, not markets and raw materials. They are finding new and innovative ways to sell, license, and create from old technology that they thought had seen its day.

Finding new value in intellectual property is also the principle behind Bounty-Quest, an innovate web site that actually sets bounties—cash awards—for evidence leading to the resolution of intellectual property disputes. The idea is that many current patent applications are actually based on existing prior art that no one knows about. BountyQuest encourages scientists, engineers, academics, and others to find that prior art and challenge the new patent.

People have actually won money in this contest of the minds. In February 2001, BountyQuest announced four successes out of nineteen attempts. The four who won did not rely on traditional online resources; in fact, two put forth "leaps of logic" that reflected their expertise in the area. The patents they challenged were in the areas of online music, alterable event tickets, single-chip network routers, and databases. One winner, Perry Leopold, was stunned to discover that someone had patented downloadable digital audio in 1996. He had actually invented the technology in the late 1980s. It should be noted that winners on BountyQuest's web site don't automatically invalidate the patents they challenged, but they certainly are in a position to take that information to court.

The bottom line is that intellectual property has reached a new level of importance in the marketplace and will continue to do so for the foreseeable future.

SOURCES: Lisa Moskowitz, "Flimsy Patents Beware: There's a Bounty on Your Head," *MIT Technology Review,* February 2, 2001; Kevin G. Rivette and David Kline, "Discovering New Value in Intellectual Property," *Harvard Business Review,* January/February 2000.

Putting the customer at the center of the business is a persistent theme throughout this book. And that's particularly true when you're in the process of conceiving and developing a new product or service. Every business large or small, product or service, is involved in product/service development at every stage of its life cycle. Each time you introduce a new product or service or an improvement on an existing product or service, you will go through a design and development process. When you develop a new product or service, you are creating an asset for your business that you will need to protect, so it's also critically important to understand the process of protecting the intellectual property you develop.

On a sleepless night in 1957, Gordon Gould conceived the idea for the laser. He wrote down all his thoughts, sketched the design and its components, and forecasted future uses. Then he had a notary witness and date his notebook. It was at that point that he made a critical mistake. Thinking that he had to build a working model of the laser before filing for a patent, he went to work for Technical Research Group Inc. (TRG) to begin development of laser applications. In the meantime, a pair of scientists, Charles Townes and Arthur Schawlow, had filed for a patent on the optical maser (it used microwave energy instead of light as Gould's did), and it would be considered the true laser patent for many years. Gould spent the next 30 years of his life battling the Patent and Trademark Office to finally lay claim to one of the most important inventions of all time. His laser applications are used in 80 percent of the industrial, commercial, and medical applications of lasers. Had Gordon Gould understood the patent process, he might have saved himself years of struggle.

Product development and intellectual property development are closely intertwined. In addition to detailing the product/service development process, this chapter will look at how to protect the various assets you create from the process: patents, copyrights, trademarks, and trade secrets.

The Nature of Product/Process Development

The processes, techniques, and timelines of product development in the United States have undergone profound change in the last decade, largely brought about by four factors:

- International competition
- Sophisticated customers in fragmented markets
- Widely diversified and changing technologies[1]
- Shrinking cycle times

International Competition

Since the 1980s, the number of companies competing in the global marketplace has increased enormously. Couple that with the fact that most new products are derivatives of something that already exists, and you have the makings of an intensely competitive arena for product development. United States companies find they are no longer competing simply with other U.S. firms; now, they must also compete with companies from diverse regions of the world who put their own stamp on processes and products. This volatile environment actually is good news for entrepreneurs who realize that the most innovative new products emerge when there is high uncertainty, risk, and ambiguity.[2] In these environments small companies often shine because of their high degree of flexibility, which lets them respond quickly.

Sophisticated Customers in Fragmented Markets

Today's customers can differentiate products on a very subtle level and demand products that reflect their individual lifestyles and value systems. That makes it incumbent upon product developers to create offerings that differentiate themselves on many levels in the marketplace. Whereas product performance and price were the main competitive measures in the past, today these two factors are givens. Superior performance and value-based pricing must be present for a company to even begin to be competitive. This means that a manufacturing company can never stop improving its design and manufacturing processes if it wishes to remain competitive, and a service company must continually find ways to improve its delivery methods.

Widely Diversified and Changing Technologies

Certainly, technology is essential to product/service development, and today the marginal cost of added technological capability is small. Yet a growing business cannot build its competitive advantage around technology alone. Customers are primarily interested in a product that will meet a need or desire; they are not necessarily interested in the technology or technological processes that produced it. Often a customer is not willing to pay for extra technology just because it's easily available.

A company operating in a technology-based industry like electronics must keep up with changing consumer demand as well as with the technological innovations of its competitors. You can build a competitive advantage around a line of market-differentiated products, but it must be enhanced by proprietary processes. A new product must not only create value for the customer but also must be difficult for someone else to produce at the same quality level and for the same cost.

Shrinking Cycle Times

Technology has also shortened product life cycles. Whereas 50 years ago a new tool product or a game or toy had a life cycle of 18 or 16 years respectively, today those life cycles have shrunk to five years.[3] Consequently, companies must constantly be researching and developing new products and improving existing ones to stay ahead of the competition. The same can be said of service companies. New products often create the need for new services to support them. Even fundamental services like advertising, consulting, and food services are affected by shrinking product development life cycles. Customers expect service entrepreneurs to provide new and innovative services at faster speeds and lower costs. It is in this environment that we take up the topic of product/service development and look at the effects of the new business environment on the way we develop new products and services.

Entrepreneurial Product/Service Development

Most large corporations have separate departments responsible for research and development, engineering, and testing. In many cases, the budgets for these particular departments are astronomical, since new-product development and the continual improvement of existing products and processes are considered to be among the most important and challenging tasks of high-performing, world-class businesses.

In the case of start-up ventures, the task is equally challenging; however, most new ventures, unlike large corporations, have very limited or nonexistent budgets for product development. Most investors consider research and development, engineering, and testing to be the highest-risk stages for new companies; consequently, funding for these activities is difficult, if not impossible, to secure. Entrepreneurs are left with a dilemma: how to perform the R&D that will result in a high-quality, engineered prototype as quickly and as inexpensively as possible. In that context, it is not surprising, perhaps, that many good product ideas fail to achieve market introduction.

Still, there are ways for entrepreneurial firms to effectively compete in the area of product development. In fact, the new environment for product development is uniquely suited to smaller companies that are often better able to adapt to change and move quickly in a new direction. Here we look at three fundamental strategies that should be incorporated into any product development program to enhance your chances of competing.

● Designing Right the First Time

Today, more than ever before, it's important to design the new product, process, or service right the first time. Redesign, which calls for re-engineering, new drawings, and a reworking of the prototype, can be more costly than creating the original design, not just in monetary terms but in terms of the costs of missing a window of opportunity if you are working in a dynamic market. Product design accounts for only about 8 percent of the total budget for developing the product, but it determines fully 80 percent of the final cost of the product because design controls the type and quantity of components needed, as well as the required labor, manufacturing, and assembly. Design also influences the marketability, quality, reliability, and serviceability of the product. Moreover, the length of time to launch and the cost to produce are also determined by product design.

Realistically, it will be difficult for any entrepreneur to design the product or services so perfectly that no changes are necessary, but that should be the goal. One of the best ways to increase the chances of getting the design right the first time is to prototype early in the design process. Many service entrepreneurs fail to see the importance of designing a prototype for their businesses. But a prototype, whether physical in the form of a model, virtual in the form of a computer simulation, or simply drawn on a piece of paper, can resolve a number of potential problems before you're actually in business. For example, the food service industry is one that benefits enormously from a well-crafted design. Restaurateurs would be well advised to prototype not only the kitchen, serving, and eating areas, but all the foods and beverages that are the products of the business. Internet entrepreneurs typically design and prototype their business sites offline, then test the functionality online with a few trusted customers before making the site available to the general public.

Time-to-Market

One of the most critical aspects of effective product development today is time-to-market. If an entrepreneur takes too long to introduce a new product or service, the market may have changed just enough to force a redesign, which will not only lengthen the process but also hurt the company in terms of lost opportunities and higher costs. By contrast, the closer the designing of the product or service is to market introduction, the more likely it will meet customers' needs at that moment. It is estimated that a six-month jump on competitors in a market accustomed to eighteen- to twenty-four-month design lives can translate into as much as three times the profit over the market life of the design.[4]

The biggest gains in shortening the time-to-market come from:

1. Reducing wait time between design and production tasks

2. Using off-the-shelf components where possible

3. Overlapping tasks where possible

4. Avoiding redesign by designing right the first time

Outsourcing Product Development

It is becoming more and more common for entrepreneurs with both large and small companies to **outsource** all or part of their product development to third parties. The decision is due in large part to today's requirements for fast-paced innovation with shorter windows of opportunity. Most start-up companies don't have the resources to do adequate product development in-house. And there is no reason why it should be done this way when it is possible to reduce risk, lower costs, and decrease cycle times by factors of 60–90 percent through outsourcing product development?[5] Outsourcing provides a young firm with a network of expertise that it couldn't afford to hire in-house.

Some of the areas of product development that require engineering analysis, design, and expertise include:

- Component design
- Materials specifications
- Machinery to process
- Ergonomic design
- Packaging design
- Assembly drawings and specifications
- Parts and material sourcing (suppliers)
- Operator's and owner's manuals

All these areas are suitable for outsourcing.

When using other companies to do part or all of your product development, you need to understand that your company is only one of many these companies work with, so you will not likely be a high priority for them. That's why it's important to plan well in advance and allow extra time for delays that strategic partners might cause in the time-to-market plan. If time-to-market is the most critical factor in your business's success, you may want to consider doing tasks that could delay the process in-house rather than outsourcing them and being dependent on the time schedule of someone else. It's also a good idea to help your suppliers and **original equipment manufacturers (OEMs)** understand that the partnership will be a win-win relationship, so they have a vested interested in seeing you succeed. Draw up contracts with every consultant, original equipment manufacturer, or vendor with whom you do business, so there are no misunderstandings as to what you expect and what they need from you. During the process, stay in touch and make yourself available to answer questions as they come up.

The Product Development Cycle

Entrepreneurs who develop products usually go through a process much like that shown in Figure 7.1. The product development cycle consists of a series of tasks leading to introduction of the product in the marketplace. That linear

FIGURE 7.1

The Product Development Cycle

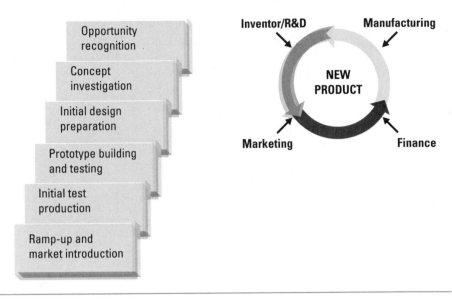

process has been a standard for decades. But, as the second graphic shows, because of the need for speed and flexibility, product development is no longer a linear process, but rather a team effort during which many tasks go on simultaneously. Recall that this process is equally applicable to service businesses. See Profile 7.1 for an example of how a service company might take advantage of the product development cycle. We will now consider each task in more detail.

Opportunity Recognition

Recall from Chapter 3 that the first stage in the development of a business concept is opportunity recognition: identifying a niche that has not been served, detecting an improvement in an existing product, or seeing an opportunity for a breakthrough product. Often inventors (who are not always entrepreneurs and vice versa) have an idea for a product or a technology without any thought to who might use the invention and in what manner. Recall the example of Gordon Gould, who understood the value of turning an invention idea (the laser) into an opportunity by identifying the practical uses for the invention. As you will learn in a later section, identifying the utility of an invention is also a critical requirement of a patent application. Once you have identified the opportunity, you will need to move quickly in its investigation.

Concept Investigation

Concept investigation is simply doing some preliminary research to determine whether the product or service idea currently exists, whether there is a potential market, how much it will cost to produce the product, and how much time it will take. This last piece of information is crucial, because an enforced shorter development cycle allows the company to have a first-mover advantage, better meet its customers' needs, lower the costs of production, and cut off the entrepreneur or inventor's natural tendency to keep "improving the product" instead of getting it out into the market. For technology-based products, technical feasibility is important because you want to determine, before you go too far, whether the concept you have designed on paper can actually function as you intended. Some of this feasibility work can be done with modeling software; the real technical feasibility comes after you have constructed a primitive prototype.

Initial Design Preparation

The first stages of design preparation go hand in hand with concept investigation because you normally need some preliminary working drawings of the product to estimate costs and manufacturing processes. These preliminary drawings are also used to apply for a patent if the product is patentable. However, once it has been determined that the product has real potential, it is time to bring in the design engineers and the other members of the functional team—marketing, operations, and finance—to put together accurate drawings of the product and initial specifications.

Prototype Building and Field Testing

From the initial engineered drawings will come the **prototype** or model of the product. Often the first prototype does not closely resemble the final product in appearance, but it usually does in function. In fact, today it's important to reach the physical stage of prototyping as quickly as possible, because the crucial involvement of key functional team members is much less expensive at this early stage. It is far less costly to discover from the marketing expert *now* that the customer will not like the ergonomics of the product, or from the operations and finance experts that the equipment to produce the product is beyond the current budget. With little money invested, team members are free to simulate the use of the product and discover potential problems as they work toward the best version of the prototype. In addition, physical prototypes are helpful in the following ways.

▶ Communicating the form, fit, and function of the device.

▶ Providing an example to a vendor for quotation.

▶ Facilitating quick changes in a design.

▶ Designing the correct tooling (devices that hold a product component in place during manufacturing and assembly).

Technology has entered the prototyping stage of product development in the form of rapid prototyping (RP), solid modeling, and virtual design. Today you can purchase a device that, working from information in your computer, will cut and shape raw materials into three-dimensional parts. In this way, you can design a part on the computer screen and then cut it into a real prototype instantly in your office. The obvious advantage is avoiding the need to ship two-dimensional drawings to a parts manufacturer and wait for the part to be made. Rapid prototyping can dramatically accelerate getting the right product to market faster. Rapid prototyping machines vary in price from $75,000 to over $800,000 depending on quality.[6] If you intend to do a lot of product development involving rapid prototyping, it makes sense to purchase the technology. For most entrepreneurs in the early stages of their ventures, however, it pays to outsource to specialized service bureaus. You can find a directory of these bureaus at http://home.att.net/~castleisland/sb_ci.htm.

Solid modeling is another way to produce three-dimensional models from a two-dimensional design. A part or device is designed on a computer screen as a solid, which makes it easier for non-technical personnel to understand the device. Using a computer and solid modeling software, you can describe the exterior and interior of a part or device in three dimensions and give it density, weight, and mass. All this is information you can't easily get from a two-dimensional design, and it helps engineers create higher-quality products much faster and more accurately.

Many companies like Boeing Company, Ford Motor Company, and Deere & Company are using virtual reality (VR) systems to analyze and test parts or complete assemblies of models in the digital world. VR is a way to create a prototype on a computer using stereoscopic eyewear and a 3-D input device such as a data glove and test it without ever building a physical prototype. For some types of business, this is an asset because physical prototypes would be prohibitively expensive to develop. For example, building a prototype of a car takes eight to twelve weeks and costs between $150,000 and $800,000. By doing the prototype virtually, you can reduce the cost by 60–70 percent. Smaller companies can often justify the cost of the VR system by comparing it to the cost of building physical prototypes.[7]

With a prototype it is also easier to acquire more accurate target-market demand information, better cost estimates, and a clearer sense of whether the product will work as proposed in the design phase. Eliminating features that do not create value in the mind of the customer can reduce manufacturing costs 25–40 percent. Moreover, field-testing the prototype with potential users allows adjustments and modifications to be made, leading to a production-quality prototype: in essence, the final product.

You can employ various kinds of engineers to take the crude prototype or breadboard version and identify the best assembly design, the types of materials to use, the most effective components, the required suppliers, and any other subcontractors needed to make the product ready for production. From the engineered assembly drawings, parts lists, and specifications, you can assemble the production-quality prototype. Small engineering firms or solo engineers who support entrepreneurs and inventors; small job shops; and machine shops or model builders may be used to complete the prototype. These sources are normally quicker and less expensive than the larger, better-known firms. When seeking an engineer or a model builder, you must use caution. It's important to check out their qualifications, experience, and references relative to the task you want them to do. A good source of referrals is a major university engineering department; so are other engineers.

Businesses that do not manufacture products—service, retail, wholesale, and so forth—still need to design a prototype, but the prototype in this case will not always be physical. Instead it will be a design or flowchart for how the business will provide a service or product to its customer, maintain and control inventories, hire employees, and guarantee quality and satisfaction. For example, a restaurant entrepreneur will design the layout of the restaurant and kitchen with an eye to how customers and servers move through the restaurant. The food preparation area will need to be laid out efficiently so the chef and his or her cooks can work quickly and not have to move great distances to retrieve cooking utensils and food items. Every activity the restaurant undertakes should be prototyped to ensure there is no duplication of effort and that each task occurs as efficiently and effectively as possible.

One of the time-consuming aspects of the prototyping stage of product development is sourcing the components and raw materials for the product. Deciding which switch to use, who should mold the plastic, or which vendors provide the best materials at the lowest prices requires a lot of legwork. Of course, you could leave these decisions to the design engineers, but at $150 or more an hour, it doesn't make sense to have the engineer searching for and comparing all the parts and materials. The engineer may offer suggestions based on experience but will generally prefer that you and your team do the actual legwork. What the engineer does is ensure that the product meets **Occupational Safety and Health Administration (OSHA)** standards (assuming that it needs to) and suggest warning labels that may be required on the product.

Initial Production Run

Once you have a working prototype of near production quality, you will want to field test it with potential users in typical environments where the product will be used. For example, when Gentech Corporation finished the product development of its PowerSource machine, which supplies both electrical and air power to run a variety of tools, it gave several of the machines to contractors and utility companies to use in their daily jobs. In this way, the company could get feedback based on actual use in real-life situations.

The number of prototypes used in the field-testing stage is normally limited, because the cost per unit is much higher (as much as ten times higher) than it will be when the company is in normal production. Usually the company has not yet met the supplier's volume level for discounts, so the cost to produce a single unit is very high. After conducting a small initial test production run in a limited market, you can go back and hone the product to completion and market-ready status. This is also the first opportunity for you to test the manufacturing and assembly processes and determine accurate costs of production at varying levels of volume.

Product Market Introduction and Ramp-Up

The achievement of a **production quality prototype,** one that has specifications that can be replicated in a manufacturing and assembly process, is a major milestone in the feasibility analysis process. You now have a product that you can sell in the marketplace. During the final phases of developing this production-quality product, you have probably been completing other aspects of your feasibility analysis. Now it will be important to consider manufacturing and assembly needs and whether you intend to manufacture in-house or outsource. You will need to prepare a marketing plan (Chapter 15) and an operations plan (Chapter 13) and complete financial projections (Chapter 16). Before you ever introduce a new product to the market, you must be prepared to meet customer demand. Failure to deliver products for which you have customers could damage the company for a long time to come. See Table 7.1 for a checklist for new product.

You must also be prepared to protect what you have created during product development, which is the subject of the next section.

Intellectual Property Development

When you develop a new product, you create an asset that must be protected. If you have developed a unique device, a unique process or service, or another type of proprietary item, you may qualify to apply for **intellectual property rights** under the law. Intellectual property pertains to the group of legal rights associated with patents, trademarks, copyrights, and trade secrets. Every business, no matter how small, has intellectual property rights associated with it. You may trademark the name of the business or a product name, copyright a presentation, patent a device you invented, or protect a trade secret such as the customer list.

Why would you want to take advantage of intellectual property rights? Suppose you have trademarked the name of your new product and have spent a lot of time and money to build a large customer following for your brand. Then a competitor comes along and copies your packaging and trademark, which

TABLE 7.1

New Product Checklist

The Market	Yes	No	Perhaps
Is there an existing need for this product in the marketplace?	___	___	___
Will I be first in the marketplace with this product?	___	___	___
Can I protect the product legally?	___	___	___
Can I erect entry barriers?	___	___	___
SWOT Analysis (Strengths, Weaknesses, Opportunities, and Threats)			
Do the strengths of this product exceed any weaknesses?	___	___	___
Are there various opportunities for commercializing this product?	___	___	___
Do any significant threats exist to the development of this product?	___	___	___
Design/Development/Manufacturing			
Is the product innovative?	___	___	___
Can it be developed quickly to market-ready state?	___	___	___
Can it be easily manufactured?	___	___	___
Do I have the resources to manufacture the product?	___	___	___
Is it more practical to subcontract the manufacturing?	___	___	___
Is there a possibility for spin-off products?	___	___	___
Financial			
Is the return on this investment sufficient to justify the effort?	___	___	___
Are the development costs within reason?	___	___	___
Can the manufacturing investment be minimized while still maintaining quality and control through outsourcing?	___	___	___
Is the money needed to produce the product available?	___	___	___

confuses customers. That's an infringement of your trademark rights that could cost you customers.

In the growing knowledge economy, the recognition and protection of intellectual property rights are gaining increasing importance. Any entrepreneur needs to understand what those rights are, not only to protect his or her property but also to avoid infringing on another's rights. In the next sections, we will look at the various rights under intellectual property law and how you can use them to your competitive advantage.

● *Patents*

If your new venture opportunity relies on a product or device of some sort, it is especially important that you investigate applying for a **patent,** which is the primary means of protecting an original invention. A patent grants an inventor the *right to exclude others from making, using, or selling the invention during the term of the patent.* In other words, a patent does not give you the right to make and distribute your invention, only the right to exclude others from doing so. The USPTO makes that fine distinction because it does not want to be in any way liable for the commercialization aspect of the invention. A patent gives the patent holder the right to defend the patent against others who would attempt to manufacture and sell the invention during the period of the patent. More importantly, patent law says that you *must* defend your patent against infringers or risk losing the patent. At the end of the patent life, the patent is placed in public domain, which means that anyone can use any aspect of the device the inventor created in their own invention without paying royalties to the inventor.

The U.S. patent system was designed 200 years ago by Thomas Jefferson. Its purpose was to provide a brief legal monopoly to give the inventor an opportunity to get the invention into the market and recoup development costs before competitors entered the market. Since the first patent was issued in 1790, more than five million U.S. patents have been granted.

Today, although most inventors work in the research departments of large corporations and 80 percent of all patents come from large companies, the basic legal tenets of patent law still protect the interests of the independent inventor. And in cases where large corporations have infringed upon those interests, the courts have generally sided with the independent inventor. In a further effort to support the small inventor, the Patent Office recently created the Office of the Independent Inventor to better serve the 20 percent of patents submitted by independent inventors. (Refer to Additional Sources of Information.)

Is the Invention Patentable?

You have created a device that you believe to be unique. Before you file for a patent, you need·to determine the patentability of the invention. The USPTO specifies four basic criteria for patentability of most inventions:

1. It must fit into one of the five classes established by Congress:

    1. Machine or something with moving parts or circuitry (fax, rocket, photocopier, laser, electronic circuit)
    2. Process or method for producing a useful and tangible result (chemical reaction, method for producing products, business model)
    3. Article of manufacture (furniture, transistor, diskette, toy)
    4. Composition of matter (gasoline, food additive, drug, genetically altered lifeform)
    5. A new use or improvement for one of the above

Many inventions can be classified into more than one category. That does not present a problem, however, since the inventor does not have to decide into which category the invention fits. In fact, the Supreme Court of the United States has stated that "anything under the sun that is made by man" falls into the statutory subject matter (*Diamond v. Chakrabarty,* 1980).[8]

With this definition, it may appear that anything can receive a patent, but, in fact, there are some exclusions. Laws and phenomena of nature, naturally occurring substances, abstract mathematical formulas, and mere ideas are not eligible to be patented. However, alterations to something found in nature, such as genetically enhanced corn, can be considered for a patent. In *Diamond v. Chakrabarty,* Chakrabarty engineered a bacterium that broke down components of crude oil. No such bacterium existed in nature; thus, the Court ruled that this bacterium was the product of human ingenuity and could be patented.

2. It must have **utility;** in other words, it must be useful. This is not usually a problem unless you have invented something like an unsafe drug or something purely "whimsical," although the USPTO has been known to issue patents on some fairly strange inventions, such as a laser beam to motivate cats to exercise (Patent No. 5,443,036, Aug. 22, 1995). The utility must be a reality, not merely speculation, and that utility must be described in the patent application.

3. It must not contain **prior art,** that is, it must be new or novel in some important way. Prior art is knowledge that is publicly available or published prior to the date of the invention—that is, before the filing of the patent application. This means that an invention can't be patented if it was known or used by others, patented, or described in a printed publication before a patent was applied for. Accordingly, it is important to document everything that is done during the creation of the invention. You must also follow the "one-year rule," which says the invention must not become public or available for sale more than one year prior to filing the patent application. This rule is meant to ensure that the invention is still novel at the time of application. Novelty consists of physical differences, new combinations of components, or new uses. There are two levels of challenge to novelty: **statutory** and **anticipation.** If the invention is published or

used in an unconcealed manner either in the United States or in another country, the inventor is statutorily barred from seeking a patent. Furthermore, if the patent is substantially similar to an existing patent, the inventor may not seek a patent because in this case the patent was anticipated.

4. The invention must not be obvious to someone with ordinary skills in the field. This is a tricky criterion, but it has been further explained by the USPTO as meaning that the invention must contain "new and unexpected results." That is, the invention should not be the next logical step for someone knowledgable in the field. Lack of nonobviousness is one of the most common reasons that patent applications are rejected.

If you have met all the requirements for patentability, you need to consider which type of patent is most appropriate for your invention. You will choose from three basic types: utility, design, and plant.

Utility Patents.   **Utility patents** are the most common type. They protect the functional part of machines or processes. Some examples are toys, film processing, protective coatings, tools, and cleaning implements. Software qualifies for patent protection if it produces a useful and tangible result. For example, you can't get a utility patent on a mathematical formula used in space navigation, but you can get one on software that translates equations and makes a rocket go.[9] (Copyrights, discussed in a later section, are commonly used for software programs that don't qualify for a patent.) A utility patent is valid for 20 years from the date of application.

Design Patents.   **Design patents** protect new, original ornamental designs for manufactured articles. A design patent protects only the appearance of an article, not its structure or utilitarian features.[10] The design must be nonfunctional and part of the tangible item for which it is designed. It cannot be hidden or offensive or simulate a well-known or naturally occurring object or person. Some examples of items that can receive design patents are gilding, an item of apparel, and jewelry. Design patents are valid for fourteen years from date of issuance.

Plant Patents.   **Plant patents** protect new and distinct varieties of asexually reproducing plants. The plant must be clearly different from those existing in nature. The patent is good for twenty years from the date of application.

Business Method Patents

The 1990s saw the advent of the **business method patent,** which arose out of the need of Internet companies to protect their ways of doing business. The rush to patent business methods all started with one click—that is, the single click of a mouse that allows a user to order a book from Amazon.com. That one click tells Amazon to charge the purchase, take the book from its warehouse shelves, and send it to the purchaser. Jeff Bezos, Amazon's founder, thought the concept was so original that he decided to patent it. And in September 1999, the PTO granted him U.S. Patent No. 5,960,411, "method and system for placing a purchase order via a communications network." Bezos followed that success with a lawsuit in U.S. District Court in Seattle for patent infringement against Barnes & Noble (*Amazon.com v. Barnesandnoble.com,* 73F. Supp. 2 1228 [W.D. Wash. 1999]). In December 1999, a federal judge issued an injunction against Barnes and Noble to stop it from using its version of the "One-Click" process, but in February 2001, a federal appeals court overturned the lower court's ruling because it "raised substantial questions as to the validity" of Amazon.com's patent.[11] In fact, the prior art discovered suggests that both Barnesandnoble.com and Amazon.com may be entangled in litigation for some time to come.

While the Amazon case opened the floodgates for business method patents, it was actually *State Street Bank & Trust Co. v. Signature Financial Group,* 149 F.3d 1360, which first allowed patents for business models in 1998. Priceline.com quickly followed in the wake of Amazon, filing a patent for its reverse-auction process. Since that time much controversy has surrounded the method patent. In fact, one online company, BountyQuest (http://www.bountyquest.com/), was founded for the purpose of offering rewards to anyone who can find prior art on certain patents. You can read about it in Profile 7.1.

Business method is actually a generic term to describe a variety of process claims, and to this date the courts have not yet defined what differentiates a business method claim from a process claim. Thus business method claims are treated like any other process claim.[12] On March 29, 2000, the Patent Office issued a statement that the business method patent will only cover fundamentally different ways of doing business, and that the embedded process must produce a useful, tangible, and concrete result.[13] This was part of an effort to do a more thorough job on prior art searches related to business method patents.

The process for applying for any of these patents is well-defined by the USPTO and is discussed in the next section.

The Patent Process

Although the USPTO has described the process clearly on its web site (www.uspto.gov), you are always well advised to seek the counsel of an intellectual property attorney. An attorney specializing in intellectual property understands the complex organization and system of the USPTO and can increase your chances of successfully moving through the application process. The following sections outline that process as an introduction and guide.

File a Disclosure Document

One very important way that inventors protect their inventions at the earliest stages of conceptualization is to take advantage of the USPTO's **Disclosure Document** Program. The purpose of a disclosure document is to serve as evidence of the date of conception of an invention. This statement is crucial in the event that two inventors are working on the same idea at the same time. The one who files the disclosure document first has the right to file for a patent. However, filing a disclosure statement does not in any way "diminish the value of the conventional, witnessed, permanently bound, and page-numbered laboratory notebook or notarized records as evidence of conception of an invention."[14] Furthermore, a disclosure document is not a patent application, so the date of its receipt at the USPTO will not be the effective filing date of any patent application an inventor might subsequently file.[15]

The disclosure document contains a detailed description of the invention and its uses and may include sketches and photos such that a person of "ordinary knowledge in the field of the invention" could make and use the invention.[16] The USPTO will keep the document in confidence for two years, and the inventor has that two-year period in which to file a patent application but must demonstrate diligence in completing the invention and filing the application to maintain the right to first filing for a patent.

Many people are under the mistaken impression that mailing a dated description of the invention to themselves by certified mail is as good as a disclosure document. Do not use this tactic, as it has no value to the Patent Office.

File a Provisional Patent

A **provisional patent** is a way for inventors to undertake a first patent filing in the United States at a lower cost than a formal patent application. It is legally more powerful than a disclosure document, allows the inventor to use the term *patent pending,* and is designed to protect the small inventor while he or she speaks with manufacturers about producing the invention. A provisional patent also puts U.S. applicants on a par with foreign applicants under the General Agreement on Tariffs and Trade (GATT) Uruguay Round Agreements (see discussion under Foreign Patents). The provisional patent does not, however, take the place of a formal patent application, which is discussed in the next section.

The term of the provisional patent is twelve months from the date of filing, and it cannot be extended. This means that the inventor must file a nonprovisional (formal) patent application during the twelve-month period. The twelve-month period does not count toward the twenty-year term for a nonprovisional patent. Since the twenty-year clock starts with the filing of the formal patent application, the provisional patent effectively extends patent protection by one year.

The invention disclosure in the provisional patent application should clearly and completely describe the invention so that someone with knowledge of invention could make and use it. Be aware that you can't file a provisional application for a design patent, but you can file multiple provisional applications and consolidate them in a single nonprovisional application for patent. If you do not file a nonprovisional application within the twelve-month period, the provisional application is considered abandoned, and you lose the ability to claim the nonprovisional date of application as the date of invention.

File a Nonprovisional Patent Application

The **nonprovisional patent** application is required for any patent whether or not you previously filed a provisional patent application, and it extends for twenty years from the date of filing. The patent application contains a complete description of the invention, what it does, how it is uniquely different from anything currently existing (including prior art), and its scope. It also includes detailed drawings, explanations, and engineering specifications such that a person of ordinary skill in the same field could build the invention from the information provided.

The **claims** section of the application specifies the parts of the invention on which the inventor wants patents and must include at least one claim that attests to its novelty, utility, and nonobviousness. The claim serves to define the scope of patent protection; whether or not the USPTO grants the patent is largely determined by the wording of the claims. The claims must be specific enough to demonstrate the invention's uniqueness but broad enough to make it difficult for others to circumvent the patent, that is, to modify the invention slightly without violating the patent and then duplicate the product.

For example, suppose you are attempting to patent a new type of rapid prototyping device. If your patent application defines the invention for use in prototyping of machine components, that would be a narrow definition. Another inventor could conceivably patent your invention for a new use, creating artificial bone, for example. That's why it's important to define your claims as broadly as possible to include as many potential applications as you can identify. Drafting a claim is an art, so it's a good idea to hire an intellectual property attorney to work with you on this.

The total cost of filing a patent application depends on the type and complexity of the patent. You can find a fee schedule on the USPTO web site (http://www.uspto.gov). Small inventors are entitled to lower fees as long as they can prove they are not inventing inside a large corporation. Patent application fees do not include the costs of engineered designs and drawings, which must accompany the application and vary significantly from product to product. Nor do the USPTO fees include attorney fees, of course. The more complex the application, the higher the patent attorney fees.

Once it has received the application, the USPTO will conduct a search of its patent records. The requested patent's status during this time period is described as "patent applied for," which establishes the inventor's claim and dates relative to prior art. An invention can stay in the patent-applied-for stage for up to two years, during which the public does not have access to the patent application and drawings, which might allow someone else the chance to design around the patent.

The Patent Office contacts the inventor and states that it either accepts or denies the claims in the application and gives the inventor a period of time to appeal or modify them. It is not uncommon for the original claims to be rejected in their entirety by the USPTO, usually due to the existence of prior art, but often because of lack of nonobviousness. It will then be the job of the inventor's attorney to rewrite the claims and resubmit the revised application to the USPTO for another review.

If and when the Patent Office accepts the modified claims, the invention enters the patent-pending stage, that is, awaiting the issuance of the patent. The inventor may market and sell the product during this period but must clearly label it "patent pending." Once the patent has been issued, the original application and the patent itself become public record.

If the patent examiner rejects the modified claims again, the inventor has the right to appeal to a Board of Patent Appeals within the Patent Office. Failing to find agreement at this point, the inventor may appeal to the U.S. Court of Appeals for the Federal Circuit. This appeals process may take years.

One thing that many inventors fail to realize is that there are maintenance fees on utility patents that occur at 3½, 7½, and 11½ years from the date the patent is granted. Failure to pay these fees can result in expiration of the patent. You can find a fee schedule on the USPTO web site.

Patent Infringement

Once issued, a patent is a powerful document that gives the holder the right to enforce the patent against infringement in federal court. If such a lawsuit is successful, the court may issue an injunction preventing the infringer from any further use and award the patent holder a reasonable royalty from the infringer; if the infringer refuses to pay, the patent holder can enjoin or close down the operation of the infringer. Alternatively, the court may mediate an agreement between the parties under which the infringing party would pay agreed on royalties to the patent holder in exchange for permission to use the patented invention.

Infringement of patent rights occurs when someone other than the inventor (patent holder) or licensee makes and sells a product that contains every one of the elements of a claim. The Patent Office also protects inventors from infringers who would violate a patent by making small, insignificant changes in the claims. This policy is called the *doctrine of equivalents*. If you had a patent on a three-

PROFILE 7.2

The Importance of Proprietary Rights

Bob Kearns was tired of windshield wipers that operated either too slowly or too fast. He wondered why they couldn't function like an eyelid and literally blink. Kearns had a damaged eye, the result of being hit with a champagne cork on his wedding night, and had great difficulty seeing while driving one night in a severe rainstorm. That's when the inspiration for intermittent windshield wipers came to him.

For Kearns, generating ideas for products that solved problems was a way of life. His first invention was a comb that distributed hair tonic, and then came an amplifier for people who had undergone laryngectomies, followed by an innovative type of weather balloon. Most of the ideas never went beyond the model stage, which is not atypical for inventors. Kearns, who had a master's degree in mechanical engineering, began working on the prototype of the intermittent wiper blade in 1963. When he had a working prototype, which he installed in his car, he arranged to show it to engineers at Ford. They encouraged him to field test it to see if it would achieve three million cycles. When it did, he again approached Ford, which suddenly didn't seem interested anymore. He then went to a friend who owned a mid-sized manufacturing firm that supplied parts to the auto industry. Kearns assigned the rights to the patent to his friend in exchange for his friend's paying the costs of getting the patents and paying Kearns royalties plus $1,000 a month to continue research and development.

Then, surprisingly, in 1969, Ford came out with an intermittent wiper blade that used the Kearns design. GM followed suit in 1974 and Chrysler in 1977, along with several foreign car companies. Kearns, who by that time had reacquired his patent rights, filed suit against Ford in 1978 for patent infringement and later against Chrysler. It took twelve years of intense work (Kearns represented himself) for the first case to come to trial. In the first suit, Ford agreed to settle for $30 million after the jury found in Kearns's favor, but he turned that down (he was seeking $1.6 billion). In a second trial, Kearns was awarded $5.2 million. Ultimately Ford and Kearns settled for $10.2 million. The Chrysler case, which concluded in June 1992, gave Kearns an additional $11.5 million, but he was still unhappy because the jury didn't find that the automaker had been willful in the infringement. Still, Kearns stands as a role model to other inventors who regularly face patent infringement by large corporations.

Source: Mike Hofman, "Patent Fending," *Inc.* Magazine, December 1, 1997.

---

legged wooden chair and the infringer made the exact same chair but gave it three metal legs, that person would be violating your patent under the doctrine of equivalents.

Patent infringement actions are costly and difficult to prosecute. Many times the alleged infringer will defend him- or herself by attempting to prove that the patent is invalid, that is, that the USPTO mistakenly issued the patent. Today, unfortunately, a number of companies regularly challenge their competitors' patents in the courts as a business strategy. The story of Bob Kearns in Profile 7.2 is a good example of the persistence of an inventor who knew his rights.

• *Foreign Patents*

It's important to remember that the patent rights granted to you extend only to the borders of the United States. They have no effect in any foreign country. Because every country has different laws regarding intellectual property, patent attorneys face a real challenge when assisting their clients in applying for or defending foreign patents. However, several international agreements have clarified many issues. For example, the Paris Convention of 1967 stopped the clock for a year if the inventor files a patent application in any member country.[17] That means that the second country in which an inventor files for a patent will treat that application as though it were filed on the date of the initial application.

The Patent Cooperation Treaty (PCT) of 1970 allows an inventor to file a PCT document or blanket application in his or her home country and designate in which countries a patent is desired.[18] The inventor can do a preliminary prior art search but within thirty months must begin the process of formal patent application in each country listed in the PCT according to their respective laws. Another way to file a blanket application is to use the European Patent Convention (EPC), which covers member European countries. While the EPC grants rights in all member countries, enforcement is on a country-by-country basis.

Two important differences exist between international and U.S. procedures in the areas of first-to-file and novelty.[19] First, the EPC grants patent rights to the first person to file for the patent, whether or not that person is the original inventor. By contrast, in the United States, only the original inventor has the first right to file an application. Second, in the United States, an inventor can sell an invention up to one year before filing a patent application. That is not true in other countries, where publication of any kind before the date of filing will bar the right to a patent. Furthermore, most countries require that the invention be manufactured in the country within three years of the issuance of the foreign patent.

When considering foreign patents, be sure to consult with an intellectual property attorney who specializes in this area. Because of the high cost and effort in obtaining foreign patents, you must also be sure that you will make a reasonable profit from them. Often, it's more valuable to seek solid strategic alliances in other countries to provide good distribution channels through which to export your products, than to spend the time and money seeking patents in every country in which you will do business. Understanding your industry and market, as well as consulting with a good attorney, will help you make that decision.

• *Trademarks*

Trademarks have become nearly as popular as patents as intellectual property assets. A trademark is a symbol, logo, word, sound, color, design, or other device that is used to identify a business or a product in commerce. The term *trademark* is regularly used to refer to both trademarks and servicemarks, which identify services or intangible activities "performed by one person for the benefit of a person or persons other than himself, either for pay or otherwise."[20] There are other, less commonly used classifications of trademarks. You can find them at the PTO web site.

Here are some examples of trademarked items:

- Logo: McDonald's double arches
  http://www.mcdonalds.com/

- Slogans: Xerox's "The Document Company"
  http://www.xerox.com/

- Container shape: Coca-Cola's classic beverage bottle
  http://www.coca-cola.com/

In the 1995 Supreme Court case *Qualitex Co. v. Jacobson Products Co.,* 115 S.Ct. 1300 (1995), the Court held that the green-gold color of a dry cleaning press pad can be trademarked. To do so, the applicant must be able to demonstrate that the color has a secondary meaning, that is, that people associate the color with the product. For example, pink has been associated with insulation even though the color has nothing to do with the insulation's function. Colors that are functional in nature cannot be trademarked.

A trademark—with certain conditions—has a longer life than a patent. A business has the exclusive right to a trademark for as long as it is actively using it. However, if the trademark becomes part of the generic language, like *aspirin* and *thermos*, it can no longer be trademarked. Furthermore, a trademark cannot be registered until it is actually in use. You have undoubtedly seen the symbol ®, which means "registered trademark." Before the trademark is registered, the entrepreneur should file an intent-to-use application and place ™ (or ℠ for services) after the name until the trademark has been registered. This is an important point because trademarks cannot be stockpiled and then sold to potential users. They must be in use in the market to be protected.

Registering a Trademark

To register a trademark, you can use one of three methods:

1. If the mark has already been in use, you can file a use application requesting registration and ownership of the mark. You will also have to submit three specimens showing actual use of the mark.

2. If the mark has not yet been in use, you can file an intent-to-use application. After the mark has been used, you must submit three specimens showing actual use before receiving registration.

3. Depending on international agreements with a specific country, you can file on the basis of having a trademark in another country.

To apply, you need to submit USPTO Form 1478 with a drawing of the mark and the appropriate fee, which starts at $325 for each class of product or service in which you want to use the trademark. To give you an idea of the scope of categories, here are the first few categories from the USPTO web site.

▶ 01   Celestial bodies, natural phenomena, geographical maps

▶ 02   Human beings

▶ 03   Animals

▶ 04   Supernatural beings, mythological or legendary beings

▶ 05   Plants

▶ 08   Foodstuff

▶ 09   Textiles

The USPTO does not require a search for potentially conflicting marks prior to filing the application. However, it is probably wise to do a search, since it isn't difficult and it can save you some time and effort later. You can conduct a search in the USPTO public search library at www.uspto.gov or in a patent and depository library, or you can hire a specialist to search for you. The USPTO determines whether your mark may be registered and notifies you. If the USPTO rejects the application, you have six months to respond.

Marks that cannot be trademarked include:

▶ Anything immoral or deceptive

▶ Anything that uses official symbols of the United States or any state or municipality, like the flag

▶ Anything that uses a person's name or likeness without permission

Trademark Infringement, Counterfeiting, and Dilution

Like patents, trademarks can suffer from infringement, counterfeiting, or misappropriation. Infringement is found if a mark is likely to cause confusion with a trademark already existing in the marketplace. The deliberate copying of a mark (counterfeiting) is subject to civil and criminal penalties.

From Cybersquatters to Typosquatters

From the moment that people realized what a domain name was, it didn't take long for some creative and opportunistic person to realize that it might be lucrative to register domain names for major corporations and organizations and then sell those domain names back to them for substantial fees. But just as quickly as cybersquatting came into being, it was cut short by the application of the Lanham Act to say that corporations with trademarked names were being infringed upon by these cybersquatters. Network Solutions (NSI), the designated registration site for domain names at the time, ultimately began suspending domain names that were under litigation from trademark holders. In fact, NSI was also under attack from victims of cybersquatting who thought that it should be liable for registering infringing names. As a result, trademark holders began taking domain names from their original owners in retaliation.

With no place to go, cybersquatters found a new form of infringement—typosquatting. Here, typosquatters look for domain names that attract the most traffic and then register the name changing perhaps only one letter, usually the letter that is most often mistyped. For example, "silliconvalley.com" would take you to the typosquatter's web site.

Just remember that if you trademark a name, you are in a better position to protect it and its associated domain name.

Trademarks are also subject to dilution, which occurs when the value of the mark is substantially reduced through competition or the likelihood of confusion from another mark. For example, American Express was able to prove that it suffered dilution when a limousine service used the American Express trademark for its business even though the two companies were in different businesses.[21]

Trademarks and the Internet

The biggest disputes on the Internet are over domain names, the addresses for web sites. The reason is that trademark laws and rules for domain name protection have not been congruent. Under federal trademark law it is possible for similar businesses to use similar names if they do business in different geographic regions (15 U.S.C. sec. 1057c, 111565-6). But registering a domain does not constitute use under the Lanham Act, which prevents trademark uses that cause confusion in the marketplace.[22] Still, the global nature of the Internet precludes any geographic boundaries. As an example, under trademark law, General Mills, General Tire, and General Foods can all exist legally because they are in different types of businesses—different industries. But under the Domain Name System (DNS), only one *general.com* can exist. By the same token, generic terms can be registered as domain names even when the USPTO will not grant a trademark, such as *cavities.com*.

International Protection

The World Trade Organization (WTO) was established in 1995 as a result of the GATT to provide intellectual property rights to its members. Under GATT and a number of other treaties, the United States assumed obligations for registering trademarks internationally under Section 44(b) of the Trademark Act 15 U.S.C. sec.1126. As a result U.S. trademarks are respected in all countries party to the agreements. You can find these agreements on the PTO web site.

● Trade Secrets

A **trade secret** consists of a formula, device, idea, process, pattern, or compilation of information that gives the owner a competitive advantage in the marketplace, is novel in the sense that it is not common knowledge, and is kept in a confidential state. Some examples of trade secrets include the recipe for Mrs. Field's cookies, survey methods used by professional pollsters, customer lists, source codes for computer chips, customer discounts, and inventions for which no patent will be applied.

Many companies like Hewlett-Packard (HP) choose not to patent some of their inventions but rather keep them for internal use only, as trade secrets. The reason is that once a patent has been issued, anyone can look up the patent on the USPTO web site and see how the device is made. Some of HP's inventions are devices used in the manufacture of its computers and peripherals, and they give the firm a significant competitive advantage that it would lose if they got into the hands of competitors. With the patent in hand, the competitor could build that device and use it to improve its own manufacturing processes. As long as the competitor is not selling the device in the market, it would require a court to decide whether the firm is actually infringing on HP's patent.

There are no legal means under patent and trademark law to protect trade secrets. The only way to protect them is to have all employees sign an employment contract that specifically details what is considered trade secret information, both at the time the employee is hired and during his or her tenure as an employee. Then, should a current or former employee use or reveal a specified trade secret, the company can use legal remedies, such as an injunction or suing for damages.

● Copyrights

It has been said over and over again that we live in an information economy. Certainly information-based products and services have been growing at a breathless pace, propelled by technology and the Internet. But with the proliferation of digital works comes the difficult task of finding ways to protect all the intellectual property that is being accessed, duplicated, transmitted, and published in digital form. **Copyrights** are the form of protection that comes into play here.

Copyrights protect original works of authors, composers, screenwriters, and computer programmers. A copyright does not protect the idea itself but only the form in which it appears, which cannot be copied without the express permission of the copyright holder. For example, a computer programmer can copyright the written program for a particular type of word processing software but cannot copyright the idea of word processing. This is why several companies can produce word processing software without violating a copyright. What they really are protecting is the unique programming code of their software.

A copyright lasts for the life of the holder plus seventy years, after which it goes into public domain; however, under the Sonny Bono Copyright Extension Act of 1998, no expired copyrights will enter the public domain until 2019. Works for hire and works published anonymously now have copyrights of ninety-five years.

The first copyright statute was enacted in 1793, but it has been successfully adapted for over 200 years. The courts have said, "the purpose of the copyright law is to create the most efficient and productive balance between protection (incentive) and dissemination of information, to promote learning, culture, and development."[23] Certainly copyright law is undergoing its most strenuous test in the information economy.

The Digital Millennium Copyright Act.   One of the problems associated with delivering products over the Internet is the ease with which a person can infringe on another's rights. In October 1998, President Clinton signed into law the Digital Millennium Copyright Act (DMCA), which prohibits the falsification, alteration, or removal of copyright management data on digital copies. The law contains a **safe harbor clause** to protect service providers from monetary damages if they unknowingly infringe on someone's rights, either by transmitting or storing infringing material, or by linking users to web sites containing infringing material. This law clears the way to licensing intellectual property for a fee over the Internet. You will learn more about licensing in Chapter 18.

The Special Case of Software.   For entrepreneurs who publish software, federal copyright protection (absent the ability to patent) is the most important legal protection available. But just as with patents, if someone infringes on your copyright, it's your job to file a lawsuit and plead your case against the infringer. And you can't file the lawsuit unless you have registered your copyright, so it's a good idea to register the copyright when your product is ready to go to market. Another benefit of registering early (before you face infringement) is that if you win a lawsuit against an infringer, you may be entitled to recover attorney fees, court costs, and statutory damages up to $100,000 without having to establish the actual cost of damages to you, which is not easy to do.

Obtaining Copyright Protection.   To qualify for federal copyright protection, the work must be in a fixed and tangible form—that is, you must be able to see or hear it. It should contain a copyright notice (although this is no longer required by law) so that a potential violator cannot claim innocence because there was no notice. The notice should use the word *copyright* or the symbol (c) and should provide the year and the complete name of the person responsible for the work as in *Copyright © 2001 by Stephen Barry.*

Though it is not required, registration at the Copyright Office at the Library of Congress in Washington, D.C., is important in order to obtain full protection under the law. Along with the application and a fee of approximately $30 per copyright request, you must submit a complete copy of an unpublished work or two complete copies of a published work. Copyright registration is effective on the date it is received at the Library of Congress.

International Protection.   Fortunately, copyright protection laws are fairly consistent across countries because of a number of international copyright treaties, the most important of which is the Berne Convention. Under this treaty, which includes more than one hundred nations, a country must give copyright protection to authors who are nationals of any member country for at least the life of the author plus fifty years.

Some Final Words on Intellectual Property

In this chapter you saw how important it is to your business strategy to protect the assets you create. In Chapter 18, you'll learn more about how to create revenue streams from these intellectual property assets. The key point to remember about intellectual property rights is that they can't stop someone from infringing on your rights. What they can do is provide you with offensive rights—that is, the right to sue in a court of law, a long and costly process (remember the story of Gordon Gould at the beginning of the chapter). Consequently, intellectual property rights should never be the sole competitive advantage a business possesses, but rather one of a bundle of strategies that includes customer relationships and organizational culture.

There are risks and benefits associated with the products and services you develop. Part of the goal of feasibility analysis is to address those risks and benefits so that you will be able to make an informed decision as to whether or not you want to go forward with a new business concept.

NEW VENTURE CHECKLIST

Have you:
- ☐ Found ways to incorporate customer input into the design of your products, processes, and services?
- ☐ Found independent contractors who can help you build your prototype?

☐ Determined which aspects of your product, service, or business can be protected from infringement?

☐ Filed a notice of disclosure if your product is patentable?

☐ Consulted with an intellectual property attorney?

ISSUES TO CONSIDER

1. How has the environment for product development changed in the last decade, and what does that mean to you as an entrepreneur starting a new business?

2. Suppose you are going to develop and market a new device for tracking calories consumed during the day. What will your product development strategy be, and why?

3. In what ways should you protect your invention from its earliest conception?

4. Suppose you have an idea for a new type of sunless tanning lotion. What procedures would you follow to protect your idea?

EXPERIENCING ENTREPRENEURSHIP

1. Interview an entrepreneur who has developed a product. What was the entrepreneur's product development strategy, and was the entrepreneur satisfied with its effectiveness?

2. Visit your local patent office or the U.S. Patent Office on the Internet, http://www.uspto.gov. Pick a patented product that interests you and do a search to find the patent for the product. How many patents have been filed that closely match your product?

ADDITIONAL SOURCES OF INFORMATION

Cohen, I. (1995). *Quality Function Deployment: How to Make QFD Work for You.* Upper Saddle River, NJ: Prentice Hall.

Cooper, R.G. (2000). *Product Leadership: Creating and Launching Superior New Products.* Cambridge, MA: Perseus Publishing.

Kahin, B., and H.R. Varian (2000). *Internet Publishing and Beyond: The Economics of Digital Information and Intellectual Property.* Cambridge, MA: MIT Press.

Maskus, K.E., and C.F. Bergsten (2000). *Intellectual Property Rights in the Global Economy.* Washington, DC: Institute for International Economics.

Mosely Jr., T.E. (1992). *Marketing Your Invention.* Dover, NH: Upstart Publishing.

Pine II, J. (1993). *Mass Customization.* Boston: Harvard Business School Press.

Ulrich, K.T., and S.D. Eppinger (1999). *Product Design and Development.* New York: McGraw-Hill.

Wheelwright, S.C., and K.B. Clark (1992). *Revolutionizing Product Development.* New York: Free Press.

INTERNET RESOURCES

European Patent Office
http://www.epo.co.at/epo

Japan Patent Office
http://patent-jp.com

The Digital Dilemma: Intellectual Property in the Information Age
http://www.nap.edu/books/0309064996/html/
A free online book that presents comprehensive information on protecting digital property.

The National Technology Transfer Center
http://www.nttc.edu
This organization helps companies work with federal laboratories to turn their work into technology that businesses can use and sell.

KuesterLaw
http://www.kuesterlaw.com/
The technology law resource guide

SBA Office of Technology (SBIR)
http://www.sbaonline.sba.gov/sbir

U.S. Copyright Office
http://lcweb.loc.gov/copyright

U.S. Patent and Trademark Office
http://www.uspto.gov

Worldwide Rapid Prototyping Service Bureau
http://home.att.net/~castleisland/sb_ci.htm
An up-to-date directory of over 525 locations where RP capability is available.

RELEVANT CASE STUDIES

Case 4   Beanos Ice Cream Shoppe

Case 6   Highland Dragon

Case 8   Alcoholes de Centroamerica, S.A. de C.V.

The Founding Team

The people who get on in this world are the people who get up and look for the circumstances they want, and, if they can't find them, make them.
George Bernard Shaw

Overview

The founding team

Professional advisers

Board of directors

Outsourcing with independent contractors

PROFILE 8.1

Testing the Entrepreneurial Waters with a Corporate Team

Today, more than ever before, we are seeing start-up companies emerging out of very large corporations at an increasing rate. It's called "corporate venturing," and it stems from the need of these large organizations to be able to compete with faster, more flexible entrepreneurial companies who do a better job of introducing new technology.

But, once in a while, a very large company like Nortel Networks, the Canadian telecommunications equipment giant, supports the launch of a start-up venture that is only on the fringe of its core competency. In 1996, Gord Larose and David Allan were employees of the Ottawa office of Nortel Networks. One day they were playing around with ideas and came up with an interesting concept: renting software over the Internet. Their concept would let people try out sample programs by using one of three methods: 1) using a free trial offer, 2) paying for several hours of use, or 3) renting to own.

The average entrepreneur with an exciting concept finds a way to bring together the resources needed to make the concept work on his or her own. But Larose and Allan were not ready to leave Nortel; moreover, they didn't believe they had the experience to start a business on their own. So they went to their boss and explained the concept. He liked the concept enough to authorize a skunk-works project to test it.

Nortel is very encouraging of corporate entrepreneurs, and has created an in-house incubator called the Business Ventures Group to assist its entrepreneur employees to develop the next great innovation. Larose and Allan knew that with Nortel's resources behind them, they had a much better chance of developing a successful venture. Nortel already had all the equipment they needed and as investors in the new venture, Nortel was far more patient than an external investor would have been. Furthermore, Nortel's brand was an enormous asset in opening doors to the fledgling venture—Channelware.

The Nortel VP who runs the Business Ventures Group claims that most of the proposals submitted for consideration lack a great team that is willing to devote all their efforts to the new venture. Larose knew that he was best at the technical side of things, so he brought on Jeff Dodge, who could better relate with customers. The core technology was developed over a two-year period by a team of talented engineers.

Channelware, now called NetActive, was spun off as a separate company in the summer of 1999 and is now an independent, privately held company with several offices. Some of its clients include Barnes & Noble, Sega Enterprises, and Sprint Communications.

SOURCES: Ron Lieber, "Startups—The Inside Stories," *Fast Company,* March 2000; http://www.netactive.com/Home/default.asp; http://www.nortelnetworks.com/index.html.

In the past, entrepreneurs in their quest for independence often attempted a new venture as soloists. In this way they could retain sole ownership, make all the key decisions, and not have to share the profits. This approach to starting a business is still common in small firms and in the craft or artisan areas. However, in today's global, complex, and fast-changing environment, most entrepreneurs find it necessary to start their ventures with a team.

Teams have a much greater chance for success than solo efforts for a variety of reasons.[1]

▶ The intense effort required of a start-up can be shared.

▶ Should any one team member leave, it is less likely to result in the abandonment of the start-up.

▶ With a founding team whose expertise covers major functional areas—marketing, finance, operations—the new venture can proceed further before it will need to hire additional personnel.

▶ A skilled founding team lends credibility to the new venture in the eyes of lenders, investors, and others.

▶ The entrepreneur's ability to analyze information and make decisions is improved because he or she benefits from the varied expertise of the team; in this way ideas may be viewed from several perspectives.

The reality is that entrepreneurs never start businesses all on their own. Recall the start-up team of NetActive, discussed in Profile 8.1. Researchers have learned that entrepreneurs are "embedded in a social context, channeled and facilitated, or constrained and inhibited, by their positions in social networks."[2] Successful ventures take advantage of social networks to grow and maintain loyal customers. For example, building a community was online auction company eBay's goal from the start, and it has been one of the most important reasons why eBay has survived where others have not. Its customers manage the site—rating the quality of trading experiences with buyers and sellers, forming neighborhood watch groups to protect users against fraud and abuse, and providing input to the company on web site design. eBay has become the place where people go to network with others who share their interests. eBay's CEO describes eBay as "of the people, by the people, for the people."[3]

The team that comes together to recognize and develop the opportunity is usually called the **founding team** or *genesis team*. But team building reaches far beyond the founders, who will need to form strategic partnerships with professional advisers, industry players, and others who help devise and execute an effective business strategy. The extended networks of entrepreneurs are critical to the entire entrepreneurial process.[4] Extended networks consist of "the relations between owners, managers, and employees, as they are structured by patterns of coordination and control."[5] Furthermore, when the entrepreneurial firm interacts

FIGURE 8.1

The Entrepreneur's Team

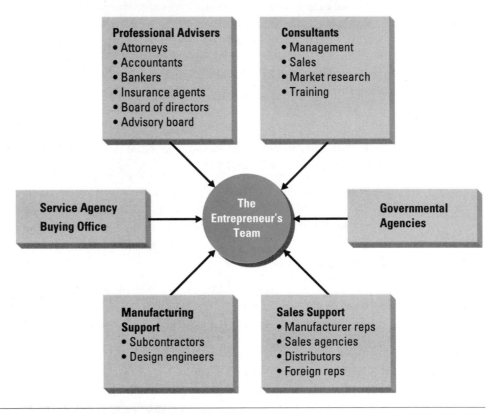

with other firms in its industry, it creates additional extended networks. At the hub of this network, or agile web as it's often called, is the founding team that has the vision and dedication to coordinate the efforts of all the partners toward a common goal. See Figure 8.1 for an overview of the entrepreneurial team.

The Founding Team

Choosing partners to start a new venture is one of the most difficult and important tasks that the entrepreneur must undertake. It is difficult because you can't always be sure that you've made the right decisions until well after you have begun working with someone on the venture. Even if you have chosen to work with people you know, you don't always know how they will react in the stressful environment of a start-up venture. Everyone from investors to bankers to potential customers looks at the founding team of the new venture to determine whether its members have the ability to execute their plans. So, it is vital to choose partners who complement your skills and experience and who do not have a history that might be a detriment to the company.

Finding partners with complementary skills means making sure that your team is not overloaded with people who all have the same expertise. For example, if you happen to have education and experience as an engineer, you might consider adding partners who have expertise in such areas as marketing and finance.

There's another advantage to forming a multifunctional team. Because its members invest not only their time but often their money as well, they share the burden of gathering resources. The lead entrepreneur also gains access to the network of contacts of the other members, in addition to his or her own. This vastly increases the information and resources available to the new venture and allows it to grow more rapidly.

Of course, it isn't always possible or necessary to put together the "perfect" team from the start. You may not have found the right person yet to fill a particular need—or you may have found the right person, but he or she is too expensive to bring on board during start-up. No matter. Talk to that person anyway about joining the team at a later date, and keep him or her up to date on what the company is doing. You may be surprised to know how many times an aggressive start-up company has wooed an experienced person away from a major corporation.

The issue of whether to use family and friends on the team is always of concern because family and close friends bring personal experiences to the business that most business partners don't have. See the Sidebar "Rules for Friends and Families" to help you make a decision that's right for your business.

Also, whenever you have a business relationship with partners, it's important to have a written agreement that details all the terms of the partnership. That subject will be discussed in Chapter 12, "Analyzing Legal Risks and Benefits."

● *A Benchmark for an Effective Team*

While there are no perfect founding teams and no fail-safe rules for forming them, there are some good rules of thumb to consider.

▶ Try to achieve a team whose expertise covers the key functional areas of the business: finance, marketing, and operations.

▶ Make sure that someone on the founding team has experience in the industry in which you are doing business.

▶ Make sure that the team members have good credit ratings. This will be important when you seek financing.

▶ Choose partners who have solid industry contacts with sources of capital.

Rules for Friends and Families

Turning to friends and family is certainly the easiest and quickest way to find partners to help you start your venture, but it may not be the best decision for your business. If you are starting a small business with no intentions of seeking outside financing, having all family on the founding team may not be a problem if you work well with them. But if you are planning to grow your venture significantly and will need to seek outside investors or potentially do a public offering, a founding team of family members may not be an attractive asset. Here are some things to think about before you make the decision to take on a family member or close friend as a partner.

- Friends or family members should possess real skills and expertise your business needs to be successful.
- They should have the same work ethic you do. If you are a workaholic and love it and the family member is a slacker, you will have problems.
- If you do have family members on the start-up team, make sure you put outsiders on the advisory board and/or board of directors, so that you have the benefit of objective input to the business.
- When working with family and friends, treat the relationship like a business relationship. Spell out responsibilities and duties and how disagreements will be settled. And try not to bring the business home at night.

> ▶ Choose team members who are passionate about your business concept and will work as hard as you do to make it happen.

> ▶ Choose people who are free to spend the time it takes and endure the financial constraints of a typical start-up.

● *Special Issues for High-Tech and Internet Teams*

New ventures in the high-tech arena and fast-start Internet companies—both of which are frequently funded by angel or venture capital—face different issues in the formation of their founding teams. Very often, the founding team consists of scientists, technologists, or in the case of Internet start-ups, very young entrepreneurs with little market experience. Investors understand clearly that these kinds of teams are not the most effective for overseeing the rapid and successful execution of the business strategy. A high-tech venture with significant up-front funding and the potential for exponential growth early on requires a professional management team with experience and an excellent track record in the industry. Usually, the investors will help the entrepreneurs locate the right people for the job. Bringing on professional management at start-up ensures that there will be no glitches when rapid growth begins, and it also leaves the creative founders the time they need to continue to develop the product and/or service.

Professional Advisers

When a new venture is in the infancy stage, it generally doesn't have the resources to hire in-house professional help such as an attorney or an accountant. Instead, it must rely on building relationships with professionals on an "as-needed" basis. These professionals provide information and services not normally within the scope of expertise of most entrepreneurs, and they can play devil's advocate for the entrepreneur, pointing out potential flaws in the business concept. They provide the new venture—and the entrepreneurial team in love with its own concept—a reality check that is invaluable. There are a number of these professional advisers that you will need to rely on at various times in your venture's life.

● ### *Attorneys*

Attorneys are professionals who specialize in one area of the law: tax, real estate, business, patents. Therefore, it is important to select an attorney who specializes in the particular area you need. Attorneys can provide a wealth of support for the new venture. Within their particular area of expertise, attorneys can:

▶ Advise the entrepreneur in the selection of the correct legal organizational structure—that is, sole proprietorship, partnership, LLC, or corporation.

▶ Advise and prepare documents for intellectual property rights acquisition and licensing agreements.

▶ Negotiate and prepare contracts for the entrepreneur, who may be buying, selling, contracting, or leasing.

▶ Advise the entrepreneur on compliance with regulations related to financing and credit.

▶ Keep the entrepreneur apprised of the latest tax reform legislation and help minimize the venture's tax burden.

▶ Assist the entrepreneur in complying with federal, state, or local laws.

▶ Represent the entrepreneur in any legal actions as advocates.

Choosing a good attorney is a time-consuming but vital task that should be accomplished prior to start-up. Decisions about such things as the legal form of the business or contracts made at inception may affect the venture for years to come; hence, the need for good legal advice. A few tips may facilitate the search.

▶ Ask accountants, bankers, and other business people for recommendations of attorneys who are familiar with the challenges facing start-ups, particularly those in your industry.

▶ Retain an experienced attorney who is competent to do what you want. For example, if you have an e-commerce business, find an attorney who is experienced in the new laws evolving in cyberspace.

▶ Look for an attorney who is willing to listen, has time for you, and will be flexible about fees while the business is in the start-up phase.

▶ Check out the firm by phone first. You can learn a lot about the law firm by noting who answers the phone and with what tone of voice. If the attorney answers his or her office phone directly, that might suggest that this is a very small firm with limited resources. Does the person with whom you're speaking sound genuinely interested in helping you?

▶ Confirm that the attorney carries malpractice insurance.

● *Accountants*

Your lawyer is your advocate, but your accountant is bound by rules and ethics that do not permit advocacy. Therefore, while your attorney is bound to represent you no matter what you do, your accountant, who is bound by the accounting industry's **GAAP** (Generally Accepted Accounting Principles), cannot defend you should you choose to do something that violates the GAAP.

Accounting is a fairly complex form of communication that the entrepreneur needs to understand at least well enough to be able to communicate with accountants, auditors, lenders, bankers, and investors, in addition to internal and external stakeholders. In the beginning of the business, the accountant may set up the company's books and maintain them on a periodic basis, or—as is often the case—the entrepreneur may hire a bookkeeper to do the day-to-day recording of transactions; the entrepreneur then can go to the accountant only at tax time. The accountant will also set up control systems for operations as well as payroll. A growing business has to do the following:

▶ Verify and post bills

▶ Write checks

▶ Issue invoices

▶ Make collections

▶ Get suppliers to cooperate

▶ Balance the checkbook

▶ Prepare financial statements

▶ Establish inventory controls

▶ File yearly tax returns

▶ Prepare budgets

▶ Prepare stockholder reports

▶ Make payroll tax deposits

▶ Secure insurance benefits

▶ Keep employee records

The accountant can assist in all these areas. Once the new venture is beyond the start-up phase and growing consistently, it's a good idea to do an annual audit to determine whether your company's accounting and control procedures are adequate. The auditors may also require a physical inventory. If everything is in order, they will issue a certified statement, which is important should the entrepreneur ever decide to take the company public on one of the stock exchanges.

Accountants are also a rich networking source in the entrepreneur's search for additional members of the new venture team. Like attorneys, accountants tend to specialize, so finding one who is used to working with young, growing businesses will be an advantage. It is highly likely that the accountant who takes your business through start-up and early growth will not be the person to take care of the company's needs when it reaches the next level of growth. As the financial and record keeping needs of the business increase and become more complex, the entrepreneur may need to consider a larger firm with expertise in several areas.

● Bankers

There is a saying that all banks are alike until you need a loan. Today that phrase is even truer, so having a qualified banker on the advisory team will put the new venture in a better position to seek a line of credit for operating capital or a loan to purchase equipment. Bankers offer a variety of valuable services, and you should think of a banker as a business partner who can contribute in these ways:

- ▶ Be a source of information and networking
- ▶ Help you make decisions regarding capital needs
- ▶ Assist you in preparing pro forma operations and cash flow analyses and evaluate projections you have made
- ▶ Assist you in all facets of procuring financing

You should choose a bank as carefully as you select an attorney or accountant. To narrow the search for a banker, you need to develop a list of criteria that define the banking needs of the new venture. You should also talk with other entrepreneurs in the same industry to identify a bank that works well with the type of venture planned. Asking an accountant or attorney to suggest the best bank for the new venture is another way to find a good banker.

When choosing a banker, seek out an officer with a rank of assistant vice president or higher, as these officers are trained to work with new and growing businesses and have a sufficient level of authority to quickly make decisions that affect the new venture. Today many of the largest banks have moved their lending facilities to a central location, so it's difficult to establish a relationship with the person who has responsibility for approving your request. That's why many entrepreneurs seek out community banks that have a vested interest in supporting local businesses.

● **_Insurance Agents_**

Many entrepreneurs overlook the value of a relationship with a competent insurance agent, but a growing venture will require several types of insurance.

- Property and casualty
- Medical
- Errors and omissions
- Life on key management
- Workers' compensation

- Unemployment
- Auto on firm's vehicles
- Liability (product and personal)
- Bonding

Major insurance firms often can handle all types of insurance vehicles, but many times you will need to seek out specialists for certain kinds of protection such as **bonding** (which is common in the construction industry to protect against a contractor's not completing a project), product liability insurance, and **errors and omissions** (which protects the business against liability from unintentional mistakes in advertising). The new venture's insurance needs will change over its life, and a good insurance agent will help the entrepreneur determine the needed coverage at the appropriate times.

Board of Directors

The decision to have a **board of directors** is influenced by the legal form of the business. If the new venture is a corporation, a board of directors is required. If the business needs venture capital, a board will be necessary and the venture capitalist will probably demand a seat on it. Boards of directors serve a valuable purpose: if chosen correctly, they provide expertise that will benefit the new venture. In that capacity they act as advisers. They also assist in establishing corporate strategy and philosophy. They do not have the power to sign contracts or commit the corporation legally. Instead, they elect the officers of the corporation who are responsible for the day-to-day operations of the corporation.

It is important to distinguish between boards of privately owned corporations and those of publicly owned corporations. In a privately owned corporation, the entrepreneurial team owns all or the majority of the stock, so directors serve at the pleasure of the entrepreneur, who has effective control of the company. On the other hand, directors of publicly traded companies have legitimate power to control the activities of the company and liability for what they do or fail to do. They are elected by the shareholders and represent their interests in the company.

Boards can be comprised of inside or outside members or a combination of the two. An inside board member is one who is a founder, employee, family member, or retired manager of the firm, while an outside board member is

Functions of a Board of Directors

In general most boards of directors perform the following duties and functions:

1. Select and hire or fire the CEO
2. Approve the selection, hiring, and termination of senior management
3. Nominate other directors, who are then voted upon by the shareholders
4. Audit the company's records in accordance with GAAP
5. Review the performance of the company against projections
6. Prepare and monitor the strategic plan for the company
7. Approve the sale of company assets, major acquisitions, and investments
8. Approve major policy changes
9. Monitor compliance on legal, ethical, and environmental issues
10. Declare dividends
11. Step in in times of crisis

Source: Grant Thornton, "Changing Roles for Boards of Directors in Entrepreneurial Companies," GT Online: *Assurance and Governance,* 1996 (http://www.gt.com/gtonline/assuranc/changec.html).

someone with no direct connection to the business. Which type of board member is better is a matter of opinion and circumstance, as research has not provided any clear results on this issue. In general, however, outside directors are beneficial for succession planning and capital raising. They can often bring a fresh point of view to the strategic planning process, along with expertise that the founders may not possess.

Insiders have the advantage of complete knowledge about the business; they are generally more available and have demonstrated their effectiveness in the particular positions they have in the business. Often the company CEO, Chief Financial Officer (CFO), and in-house attorney sit on the board. But, there are political ramifications when the board members report to the CEO; insiders may not always be objective and independent. They also may not have the broad expertise from outside the company that is necessary to effectively guide the growth of the business.

Consider carefully whether the new venture requires a working board, that is, one that directs the strategy of the business. Most working boards are used for their expertise, for strategic planning, for auditing the actions of the firm, and for arbitrating differences. These activities are not as crucial in the start-up phase, when the entrepreneurial team is gathering resources and raising capital. However, a board of directors can assist the entrepreneurial team in those functions and can network with key people who can help the new venture. At this juncture in the new venture, some potential directors will ask to be included on the board so that they can monitor their investment in the company. This is common among large private investors, bankers, and even accountants. To ensure getting only the best people on the board, standards for membership should be set in advance and strictly adhered to.

The size and complexity of your business will determine how many directors serve on the board. There is no research consensus on the relationship between the size of the board and the performance of the company, although some research has found that a large board encourages laziness on the part of some members[6] and consequently an inability to initiate strategic actions.[7] Moreover, larger boards tend to develop factions and coalitions that often lead to conflict. The general recommendation is to have no fewer than five and no more than fifteen board members. In the earliest stages of a new venture, the board will often consist of the founders, though that should quickly change as the company begins to grow and needs to tap the expertise of people who have managed growth in their own companies.

When choosing people to serve on the board of directors, you should consider those who have:

- The necessary technical skill related to the business
- Significant, successful experience in the industry
- Experience running a company at the level you want to grow to next
- Important contacts in the industry
- Expertise in finance, capital acquisition, and possibly IPOs
- A personality compatible with the rest of the board
- Good problem-solving skills
- Honesty and integrity, to engender a sense of mutual trust

If the entrepreneurial team is not careful, it may learn too late that a director it has appointed to the board considers the position an appointment for life, much like being appointed to the Supreme Court. To prevent such a situation from occurring and to bring a fresh point of view to the board, ask directors to serve on a rotating basis for a specified period of time.

The board is headed by the Chairman, who, in a new, private venture, is typically the lead entrepreneur. The entrepreneur will also, most probably, be the President and CEO. The current trend is for the CEO and perhaps the Chief Operating Officer (COO) to be the only inside members on the board.

Boards normally meet an average of five times a year, depending on the type of business. How often the board meets will be largely a function of how active it is at any point in time. Directors typically spend about nine to ten days a year on duties related to the business and are usually paid a retainer plus a per-meeting fee, with their expenses also reimbursed. The compensation can take the form of cash, stock, or other perquisites.

Today it is more difficult to get people to serve as directors because in some cases they can be held personally liable for the actions of the firm, and the frequency with which boards are being sued is increasing. For this reason, potential directors will require that the business carry directors' and officers' (D & O) liability insurance. The expense of this insurance is often prohibitive for a growing company, but it is essential in getting good people to serve. Additional expenses related to the development of a board of directors include meeting rooms, travel, and food. Because of the expense of a formal board of directors, many entrepreneurs with new ventures maintain a small insider board of directors and rely heavily on their informal advisory board for a more objective perspective.

● *Advisory Board*

The advisory board is an informal panel of experts and other people who are interested in seeing the new venture succeed. Advisory boards can range from those that meet once or twice a year and do not get paid, to those that meet more regularly and are compensated.

Advisory boards are often used when a board of directors is not required or in the start-up phase when the board of directors consists of the founders only. An effective advisory board can provide the new venture with needed expertise, without the significant costs and loss of control associated with a board of directors. In a wholly owned or closely held corporation (in which the entrepreneur or team holds all the stock), there really is no distinction between the functions of a board of directors and those of a board of advisers, because in either case control remains in the hands of the entrepreneurial team. The advisory board is not subject to the same scrutiny as the board of directors since its actions are not binding on the company.

Entrepreneurs tend to resist the idea of having outside advisers because of the founders' intense desire to be independent and to maintain some secrecy about the business. Entrepreneurs also tend to believe that an outsider could never understand the business.[8] Although many business owners may reject a formal board, they risk developing tunnel vision unless they consider using an advisory board. An advisory board is a step in the direction of creating a more professional organization, one that researcher Donald R. Jonovic asserts is comprised of three elements:

1. Shareholder harmony, achieved through shareholder agreements and buy-sell agreements

2. Effective management that has a vision and goals for the company

3. Efficient internal communication, achieved through shareholder meetings, advisory board meetings, and management meetings.[9]

● *Mistakes to Avoid with Boards*

Putting together the extended founding team is a serious undertaking that, if unsuccessful, could have severe ramifications for the future of the business. Several common mistakes in forming the team should be avoided:

▶ Forming the team casually or by chance—that is, without careful consideration of the experience and qualifications each person brings to the team.

▶ Putting together a team whose members have different goals; this could impede the growth of the company.

▶ Using only insiders for the board of directors—that is, friends and family members instead of the people most qualified to advise the business.

▶ Using family members or friends as attorney and accountant for the business. Because these professional advisers must remain objective at all times to best represent and assist the entrepreneur, choosing relatives can cause unnecessary problems.

▶ Giving the founding team stock in lieu of salary. The lead entrepreneur does not want significant shares of stock in the hands of people who may later leave the company if things don't work out. The use of a buy-sell agreement to prevent this problem is discussed in Chapter 12.

● *The Mentor Board*

Every entrepreneur should have a personal board of mentors, the members of which serve as sounding boards for ideas and coaches to raise your spirits and tell you when you're headed down a wrong path. The people on your personal board usually are your role models, people who have businesses and lifestyles like the one you want to create. Your mentors are a safe place for you to take your fears, concerns, hopes, and dreams.

Outsourcing with Independent Contractors

A new business typically does not have the resources to pay for all the management staff that may be necessary to keep it running. In fact, most entrepreneurs try to avoid hiring employees as long as possible because employees are the single biggest expense in the business. But how does a new venture survive with as few employees as possible and still grow?

The solution lies in **outsourcing,** which means using **independent contractors.** Independent contractors (ICs) own their own businesses and are hired by the entrepreneur to do a specific job. They are under the control of the entrepreneur only for the result of the work they do and not for the means by which that result is accomplished. Some examples of independent contractors that entrepreneurs use on a regular basis are consultants, manufacturers, distributors, and employee leasing firms (note that professional advisers are also independent contractors). The popularity of outsourcing can be seen in the fact that companies outsource about one-third of their information technology, human resources, and marketing and sales, and one-fifth of their financial activities.[10] One of the most popular areas to outsource is information technology because of its expense. It's difficult for most companies to keep up with changes in technology, and the vendors to which they outsource can provide the same service and better performance at a lower cost.

Entrepreneurs seek out independent contractors for their expertise in specific areas needed by the new venture. Using an independent contractor means that the new venture doesn't have to supply medical and retirement benefits, unemployment insurance, or withhold income and Social Security tax. These are costly benefits that can amount to more than 32 percent of an employee's base salary.

But there are hidden costs to outsourcing that you should be aware of.[11]

- ▶ The cost of searching for and contracting with an independent contractor. The best way to reduce this cost is to get referrals from people you know who have had a successful experience with the IC.

- ▶ Transferring your activities to the IC. Getting your IC up to speed on your business takes time and human resources. You can reduce your transfer costs by knowing up front what you want the IC to handle.

- ▶ Managing the independent contractor. This is one of those cases where experience counts. The first IC contract takes the longest and costs the most. The best IC relationships occur when communication is an ongoing process so that the IC becomes a real part of the business.

- ▶ Bringing the activity in-house. Many companies eventually bring in-house activities that they once outsourced. This may occur because the company has grown to the point where it needs and can afford in-house staff for the activity or because the company wants more control over the activity. One way to reduce the transition cost is to have the person who manages the IC relationship learn enough about the activity to be able to ease the company through the transition.

Here are some suggested ways to reduce the hidden costs of using independent contractors.

- ▶ Avoid outsourcing critical activities or those that are idiosyncratic or unique to your business.

> ◗ Research vendors carefully and get referrals from people you know.

> ◗ Work with legal people who have experience in independent contractor law to draft well-written contracts.

The IRS and Independent Contractors

The IRS has very strict rules for the use of independent contractors. The Law of Agency defines the terms *employee* and *independent contractor*.[12] It states, "While an employee acts under the direction and control of the employer, an independent contractor contracts to produce a certain result and has full control over the means and methods that shall be used in producing the result." If you don't follow the rules regulating classification of workers as independent contractors, they can be considered your employees for tax purposes and you can be held liable for all back taxes plus penalties and interest, which can amount to a substantial sum.

To ensure compliance with IRS regulations, entrepreneurs using independent contractors should

> ◗ Consult an attorney.

> ◗ Draw up a contract with each independent contractor, specifying that the contractor will not be treated as an employee for state and federal tax purposes.

> ◗ Be careful not to indicate the time or manner in which the work will be performed, only the desired result.

> ◗ Verify that the independent contractor carries workers' compensation insurance.

> ◗ Verify that the independent contractor possesses the necessary licenses.

More specifically, the IRS uses a 20-point test for classifying workers. (See Table 8.1.) Even if you follow all the IRS rules, however, there is no guarantee that the IRS won't challenge your position. Therefore, it is important to document the relationship with an independent contractor through a legal agreement that explicitly demonstrates that the independent contractor owns his or her own business. The IRS can decide that a worker is an employee even if only one of the 20 points is true.

On the plus side, independent contractors can make the very small start-up venture look like an established corporation to anyone on the outside. A large corporation will generally have vice presidents for departments of operations, sales, marketing, and finance. It is possible to replicate these large-corporate functions by using independent contractors, thereby lowering costs and remain-

TABLE 8.1

The 20-Point Test for Independent Contractors

A worker is an employee if he or she
1. Must follow the employer's instructions about how to do the work.
2. Receives training from the employer.
3. Provides services that are integrated into the business.
4. Provides services that must be rendered personally.
5. Cannot hire, supervise, and pay his or her own assistants.
6. Has a continuing relationship with the employer.
7. Must follow set hours of work.
8. Works full-time for an employer.
9. Does the work on the employer's premises.
10. Must do the work in a sequence set by the employer.
11. Must submit regular reports to the employer.
12. Is paid regularly for time worked.
13. Receives reimbursements for expenses.
14. Relies on the tools and materials of the employer.
15. Has no major investment in facilities to perform the service.
16. Cannot make a profit or suffer a loss.
17. Works for one employer at a time.
18. Does not offer his or her services to the general public.
19. Can be fired at will by the employer.
20. May quit work at any time without incurring liability.

ing more flexible. Figure 8.2 shows how a growing entrepreneurial venture can imitate the strength, stability, and expertise of a much larger, more established company through the use of independent contractors. The concept is called the "virtual corporation" and will be discussed at length in Chapter 10.

Types of Independent Contractors

Many types of independent contractors operate behind the scenes of the new venture but make a valuable contribution nonetheless. Here we discuss a few of them.

Consultants

The consulting industry is one of the fastest growing industries in the United States, and it can provide a variety of services for the new venture.

- Train the sales staff and/or management

- Conduct market research

FIGURE 8.2

The Virtual Entrepreneurial Company

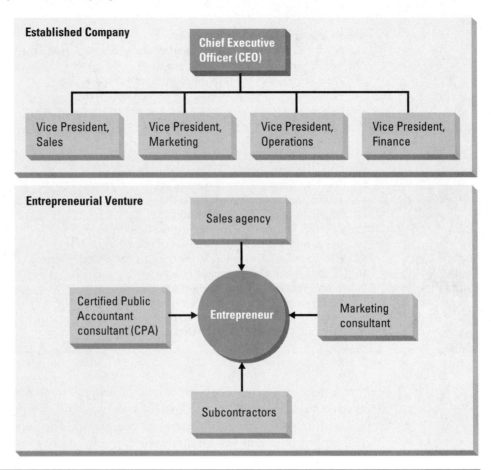

- ▶ Prepare policy manuals
- ▶ Solve problems
- ▶ Act as temporary key management
- ▶ Recommend market strategy
- ▶ Design and engineer product
- ▶ Design a plant layout and equipment
- ▶ Conduct research and development
- ▶ Recommend operational and financial controls

Since they tend to be fairly expensive, consultants are best used for critical one-time advising or problem-solving assignments. In that capacity, they are typically more cost effective than employees because they are accustomed to working quickly within the constraints of a fixed budget.

Consultants are generally paid in one of three different ways:

▶ Monthly retainer, which pays for a specified amount of time per month

▶ Hourly rate

▶ Project fee

More recently, consultants have also been known to ask for stock options or some other form of equity stake in the companies for which they consult. Some entrepreneurs have chosen to go this route when cash is in short supply. But you should consult with an attorney before giving up any equity in your company.

Staff

Leasing the staff is a way for a new business to enjoy the advantages of major corporations without incurring the expense. A leasing company assumes the payroll and human resource functions for the business for a fee that generally ranges from 3 to 5 percent of gross payroll. Each pay period, the new venture pays the leasing company a lump sum to cover payroll plus the fee. The National Staff Leasing Association reports that there are about one million leased employees in the United States and that the industry is growing at an annual rate of 30 percent.

Manufacturing Support

Even those new ventures that involve manufacturing a product can avail themselves of the benefits of independent contractors. Because the cost of building and equipping a new manufacturing plant is immense by any standards, many entrepreneurs choose to subcontract the work to an established manufacturer. In fact, it is possible for the entrepreneur with a new-product idea to subcontract the design of the product to an engineering firm, the production of components to various manufacturing firms, the assembly of the product to another firm, and the distribution to yet another.

Sales Support

Hiring sales staff can be an expensive proposition for any new venture, not only from the standpoint of benefits but because salespeople must be trained as well. As new high-growth ventures seek a geographically broad market, even a global one, it is vital to consider manufacturer's representatives (reps) and foreign reps who know those markets and can act as the entrepreneur's representative. Using distributors allows the entrepreneur to reach the target market without having to deal with the complex retail market. In addition, sales agencies can provide fully trained sales persons to the new venture in much the same manner as temporary services supply clerical help. Some can also provide advertising and public relations.

Application Service Providers (ASP)

A very recent phenomenon is the **application service provider** or ASP, which arose out of the need for businesses to take advantage of new technology that they couldn't afford to own. Under this scenario the company leases the use of, for example, an enterprise software application to manage the operations of the business. The entrepreneurial team accesses that application through the Internet, and the ASP maintains the application, runs the system, and stores and backs up the files for the business. This service saves the growing company time and money.

Service Agencies

With many established firms downsizing and contracting out for services, some entrepreneurs have seen an opportunity to provide those services and have built highly successful, high-growth businesses. As a result, it is now possible for a new venture to subcontract for payroll services, technology support, and temporary help, to name a few. The service firm employs the individual and provides the benefits while the entrepreneur pays a fee for the services.

Buying Offices

When the entrepreneur is ready to consider a global market, he or she may opt to use either an import/export agency or broker or the international department of a major bank. These people understand the laws, customs, and currency exchange rules in the countries with which the entrepreneur will deal.

Governmental Agencies

Many agencies at the federal, state, and local levels offer various services to new ventures. Notable among them are the Small Business Administration, which provides education, loans, and grants to small business; the Department of Commerce, which can assist the entrepreneur on issues of trade; and state and local economic development corporations.

By taking advantage of the many services available, an entrepreneur can literally start a business from home to reduce start-up capital requirements yet still operate like a major corporation. This is not to suggest that a company can always avoid hiring employees and still grow. That will depend on the type of business started. However, it does suggest that in the start-up phase of a new venture, the use of independent contractors can help ensure that the business survives long enough and generates enough revenues to hire employees.

NEW VENTURE CHECKLIST

Have you:

- ☐ Identified the members of the founding team or at least the expertise needed to start the venture?
- ☐ Begun asking questions about potential professional advisers such as an attorney or accountant?
- ☐ Determined if you will need a board of directors or advisory board or both?
- ☐ Identified at least one type of independent contractor the new venture could use?
- ☐ Determined what expertise is missing from the management team and how you will take care of it?

ISSUES TO CONSIDER

1. For what kinds of businesses is starting as a solo entrepreneur sufficient? Are there advantages to starting even these types of businesses with a team?

2. What should an entrepreneur's strategy be for bringing on a personal board, an advisory board, and a board of directors?

3. Attorneys are considered advocates; accountants are not. Why is this important for the entrepreneur to know?

4. How can you ensure that you are using independent contractors correctly and in accordance with the law?

5. Suppose you are starting a technology consulting firm that does custom programming. What kinds of independent contractors can help you start this venture?

EXPERIENCING ENTREPRENEURSHIP

1. Interview an entrepreneur who started a venture as a soloist; then visit an entrepreneurial venture started by a team (two or more people). Based on your interviews, what are the advantages and disadvantages of each approach?

2. Choose a lawyer, accountant, or banker to interview as a potential professional adviser to your business. What information will you need to get from him or her to make your decision?

ADDITIONAL SOURCES OF INFORMATION

Ford, R.H. (1992). *Boards of Directors and the Privately Owned Firm.* New York: Quorum Books.

Lipnack, J., and J. Stamps (1997). *Virtual Teams: Reaching Across Space, Time, and Organizations With Technology.* New York: John Wiley.

Robbins, H., and M. Finley (2000). *Why Teams Don't Work: What Goes Wrong and How to Make It Right.* San Francisco: Berrett-Koehler.

Ward, J. (1991). *Creating Effective Boards for Private Enterprise.* San Francisco: Jossey-Bass.

INTERNET RESOURCES

EntreWorld
http://www.entreworld.com
Excellent source of information on team building as well as other start-up issues.

Lawyer.com
http://www.lawyer.com
Learn how to choose an attorney among many other legal guides.

National Association of Corporate Directors
http://www.nacdonline.org/
The premier educational, publishing, and consulting organization in board leadership and the only membership association for boards, directors, director-candidates, and board advisers.

Putting Together an Entrepreneurial Team
http://www.entreworld.com/audio/id66.ram
This is an audio article on the ins and outs of designing an entrepreneurial team.

RELEVANT CASE STUDIES

Case 3   Overnite Express

Case 4   Beanos Ice Cream Shoppe

Case 6   Highland Dragon

Case 7   Roland International Freight Service

Analyzing Start-up Financial Risks and Benefits

Finance is the art of passing currency from hand to hand until it finally disappears.
Robert W. Sarnoff,
Former president NBC/RCA

Overview

Finding the right numbers

Estimating sales and expenditures

Preparing the pro forma income statement

How much start-up money is needed?

PROFILE 9.1

How Do You Explain a "No-Profit" Strategy? Revisiting the Internet Business Model

Investors expect that most new ventures will not show a profit for a time. What they don't expect to see is a strategy stating explicitly that the company doesn't expect to make money for a long time. Yet that's exactly the tactic Jeffrey Bezos used with investors in his online store, Amazon.com. Bezos fervently extolled the necessity for growing as fast as possible and that meant profits were not in the foreseeable future.

When Bezos first conceived the idea for Amazon in 1994, his vision for online retailing was so clear in his head and so attractive to customers that from the first day in business, Amazon became the standard for retailers online.

Bezos was not crazy. His publicly held company saw its stock rise from $18 to $23.50 at close on the first day of trading in May 1997, so his investors appeared to have confidence in his strategy. Venture capitalists Kleiner Perkins Caufield & Byer bet $8 million on Amazon, the biggest single placement ever at that time, for 15 percent of the company. They also brought in the professional management and top-flight programming talent needed to scale out quickly.

In 1994, Bezos was a rising senior vice president with a successful Wall Street hedge fund when he saw a huge opportunity in online commerce. After he considered a number of different types of businesses to start and various products to sell online, he finally settled on books because there are so many of them, and unlike the music industry (his other choice) there are no "800-pound gorillas" in book publishing and distribution. Even the Goliath-sized Barnes & Noble holds less than 12 percent of the market. From a garage in the Seattle area, he built a multimillion-dollar virtual company that sold its first book in July 1995. What made the Amazon brand so powerful was its simplicity (customer-centered) and its devotion to scale. In the first twenty-four months of its life, Amazon grew at 6 percent per week, faster than any business at the time, while building a loyal community of customers and strategic partners.

Bezos' goal is to be the "world's most customer-centric company." He wants people to come to Amazon to find virtually anything they need. With that in mind, Amazon has expanded to include everything from music and software to garden tools and cars. It has also entered the auction market to bring its 8.4 million buyers a larger selection. As of this writing, Amazon has more than 16 million different items to be purchased. As much as products, Amazon sells information about its products in the form of reviews, customer feedback, and discussion.

However, the jury is still out on whether Amazon will succeed over the long term. On January 4, 2000 Amazon's stock climbed to a fifty-two-week high of 91.50, but by December 2000 it had plummeted to 14.875, an 84 percent decline in valua-

tion. As of February 3, 2002, the stock sat at 13.730, but the company succeeded in showing its first profitable quarter. Whatever the final outcome, Amazon pioneered e-commerce and built a major brand, while simultaneously changing the face of venture capital.

SOURCES: Michael H. Martin, "The Next Big Thing: A Bookstore?" *Fortune,* December 9, 1996, p. 169; "Q&A with Amazon's Jeff Bezos," *Businessweek Online,* May 14, 2001; Udayan Gupta, *Done Deals.* Boston: Harvard Business School Press, 2000.

Once you have determined that a market exists for your new venture concept, it's time to consider the financial conditions under which you would be willing to go forward knowing that the venture has the potential to be profitable and generate a sustainable positive cash flow. No matter how many financial tools entrepreneurs use or how many complex analyses are constructed, the bottom line for any new venture is cash. Income statements and balance sheets can make a company look good on paper—these are accounting measures—but cash pays the bills and allows the company to grow. A new venture's health is measured by its cash flow. In the late 1990s, Internet companies were spending huge amounts of money as fast as possible to see whether they had a concept that would work. You began to hear talk of "fume" dates and "flameout" dates, indicating when the company would be operating purely on fumes and when it would finally run out of cash. Neither situation has anything to recommend it and neither should be considered an effective entrepreneurial strategy. It was also a time when we learned that having a lot of cash at start-up doesn't always result in wise management decisions, and that achieving a positive cash flow is essential to success. Look at Profile 9.1 to read about Amazon.com, one of the major Internet companies that is dealing with the dilemma of how to grow rapidly and maintain a positive cash flow. Only time will tell if it will succeed.

So in making the decision to go forward with a new venture concept, you will want to estimate your cash needs for starting and operating the business until it can produce a positive cash flow from the revenues it generates. To do this requires a cash flow projection, a profit and loss projection, and a break-even analysis. We will deal with other types of financial analyses (balance sheet, ratio analysis, and the like) in Chapter 16 where they are more appropriately associated with the financial plan portion of the business plan. Before we consider how to do a cash needs assessment, however, you need to gather the necessary data.

Finding the Right Numbers

Estimating revenues, expenses, and start-up costs at the feasibility stage is a daunting task at best for an entrepreneur with a new business concept. At this stage the concept is still fluid, and in the case of a new product in the design phase, the numbers you gather relative to the cost of producing that product may be quite different from the final numbers achieved when the business plan is complete. We should say at this point that even the numbers you arrive at for the business plan will change when the business is in operation and the real world throws unexpected curves your way. There are many reasons why the numbers you use to determine feasibility will probably change when you move to the business plan.

1. If you are a manufacturer or are outsourcing to a manufacturer, it will be nearly impossible for you to estimate parts and manufacturing costs accurately without a production-quality product in place. For this reason, it's important to get to a physical prototype stage early, so as to have a better idea of the parts, components, and types of materials you'll need, as well as labor.

2. For many new-product companies, product development may take several months to several years, depending on the nature of the product—and the costs for prototyping are always substantially higher than the ultimate production cost will be. Therefore, it's difficult to determine true feasibility from an economic perspective before you have a physical prototype.

3. For service companies, the actual costs to deliver a service must be based initially on information gathered from other companies in the industry. This is difficult to achieve without "inside information," that is, without the benefit of knowing someone who works in that type of company. Your estimates for the cost of delivery of the service will be more accurate if you do an "alpha" test and prototype the service under a variety of the most common scenarios. For example, a restaurant owner might want to calculate how long it takes to completely serve a customer from the time of arrival to the time of departure. The owner would need to look at the number of tables planned, hours of operation, and number of servers and cooks needed. Peak and slow periods and other aspects of serving customers would also be factored in. The more variables you can account for, the better your estimates will be.

4. As you grow in knowledge of your industry, you naturally gather better information because you know whom to talk with and where to find the best industry intelligence. Since getting inside an industry is a difficult and time-consuming task, many entrepreneurs choose to start ventures in industries with which they're familiar or in which they have experience.

Table 9.1 presents some sample expenditures for various types of businesses. With an understanding of the inherent difficulties in forecasting numbers for a potential new business, let's consider an overall strategy that will at the very least give you a higher probability of arriving at some numbers that make sense. The process is called triangulation, which means that you will attack the problem from three angles: your own knowledge, the industry, and the market/customer.

TABLE 9.1

Expenditures for Various Types of Businesses

Sample Manufacturing or Construction Expenses List

Manager's Salary	Paid Employees' Salaries
Payroll Taxes	Vehicle Lease and Maintenance
Related Travel	Packaging Costs
Supplies	Depreciation on Owned Equipment

Sample Distribution and Warehouse Expenses List

Manager's Salary	Employees' Salaries
Drivers' Salaries	Payroll Taxes
Vehicle Lease and Maintenance	Warehouse Loading Vehicles
Lease/Maintenance	Depreciation on Owned Equipment
Freight Expenses	Supplies

Sample List of Selling Expenses

Sales Manager's Salary	Inside Sales Salaries
Inside Sales Commissions	Telephone Sales Salaries
Telephone Sales Commissions	Field Sales Salaries
Field Sales Commissions	Payroll Taxes for Sales Employees
Sales Vehicles Lease and Maintenance	Sales-Related Travel
Advertising and Promotion	Depreciation on Owned Equipment

Sample List of General, Selling, and Administrative Expenses

Advertising	Rent
Salaries and Wages	Utilities
Office Supplies	Insurance
Office Equipment	Business Taxes
Payroll	Taxes

● *Your Knowledge and Experience*

The knowledge and experience you bring to the business will also be helpful in forecasting sales. If you've worked in the industry for a while before starting a business (and it's highly recommended), you may already have a sense of the volume of sales you can expect. Remember, though, that since your venture is new, it probably won't be able to generate the level of sales of others in the industry for a time. Also your knowledge and experience come from the personal network of people you trust or seek out when you need objective opinions.

While they may not have the exact answers you seek, they have a circle of contacts as well that you can tap through them.

It's always wise to do a lot of homework and build up your knowledge base before you talk to people in the industry or potential customers. That way you will be able to ask more specific, higher level questions and not waste their time on basic information you could have found quite easily. Refer to Chapter 4 where the issue of researching an industry was discussed. In addition to consulting the online sources mentioned there, consider taking a finance course at the college level or check into workshops provided by the Small Business Administration (SBA) or Service Core of Retired Executives (SCORE) in your community.

● *The Industry*

The importance of understanding how an industry works cannot be stressed enough. You need to get out and talk with suppliers, vendors, manufacturers, distributors, and industry experts. You also need to read industry trade journals and other periodicals written by experts in the field. Merely going to a similar or even a competing business to ask how they forecast sales is not going to work. For the most part, private business owners consider these figures to be proprietary—part of their competitive strategy—so they're unlikely to reveal them to you. However, you may find others in the industry, such as distributors, to be more forthcoming. Public company reports are readily available on the Internet, but these figures should be used with caution. Sales patterns in public companies rarely match those in new, private companies, but they're a start. Go shopping and talk to wholesalers and retailers of products similar to yours to get a feel for how much volume they're doing on a monthly basis. If you're in a service business, find out how many clients your business can reasonably serve in a month or over a specific period of time. Remember, you need to collect as much information as reasonably possible from a variety of good sources in the industry to complete this important leg of the triangle.

● *The Market/Customer*

Another critical source is the customer. Customers are far more likely than a competing business to give you useful information. From customers you will learn what they buy, how often, in what quantities, and on what terms. One good technique is using field observation of your customers in their "normal habitat." That is, go to a place where they're likely to purchase what you have to offer and observe the buying ritual. Notice how many customers come into a location over a specific period of time and determine how many of them actually purchase something. What did they buy and how much did it cost? You can gain considerable valuable information by spending time away from your desk and out in the field.

From your customers, you'll also learn what gaps exist in your competitors' relationships with their customers. Furthermore, you can also extrapolate from competitors' numbers to your customers if they are similar in nature. The customer should be at the core of every aspect of your business, and that includes efforts to predict sales. Don't rely on what others say about customers. Get out and talk to them yourself.

While there are companies that will conduct market research for you, it's always a wise idea to talk to the customer yourself. No one knows your business concept better than you, so you're often in a better position to elicit useful information in a process called triangulation.

Using all three sources of information—industry, market/customer, and your own knowledge—you should arrive at three estimates of sales volume that are fairly close together. You will then need to make a judgment call as to whether to choose one of those numbers as the most probable estimate or whether to average them to arrive at an estimate. Remember that estimating sales is more art than science in a new venture. The important thing at this point is to get as close as you can—a best estimate. This will allow you to calculate the financial feasibility of the venture and figure how much money you'll need to start and operate the business to a positive cash flow.

Estimating Sales and Expenditures

The sales forecast should be calculated first because sales affect the expenditures of the business. With a new product that is either a line extension or the next generation of an established product, you can rely on historical data showing monthly sales volume over a period of time that will help ensure a more accurate estimate. With a brand new or breakthrough product, however, you are left to rely on market data that was gathered by others, comparison of similar products, and the opinions of market experts, which are often found in trade journals.

Therefore, to improve the estimate, use the triangulation process discussed in the previous section; in addition to calculating a variety of scenarios triggered by predictable events, that will cover about 90 percent of all the possible sales results. Some examples of predictable events are seasonality (some products sell better at certain times of the year or month), a general economic downturn or upturn, and unexpected high demand by customers.

You can do this type of analysis (called **sensitivity analysis**) by

1. Identifying events that could trigger a change in your estimate at any point in time.

2. Calculating the impact of the change on your estimate. Will it cause sales to go up? Down? Remain stable?

3. Figuring the probability that the event will occur. Is there a 50 percent chance it will occur? 20 percent? The percentage you choose is based on the information you gathered during the triangulation process. It is your best estimate.

By testing the effects of various events on sales, you will learn more about the highest and lowest levels of sales you can expect as well as the most common level of sales. This information will be important not only in calculating start-up costs but in considering how and when expenditures should be incurred. In the next two sections, we'll deal with some common differences in forecasting for consumer products/services and industrial products.

Forecasting Sales for Consumer Products and Services

If the product or service being offered does not currently exist in the market, you must find a competing product or service that is similar or is a substitute product to study. The information needed includes the volume of **"sell-in"** to the retailer and the volume of **"sell-through"** to the customer—that is, the amount of product that is sold by the manufacturer or distributor to the retailer and the amount of that product that is ultimately sold to the customer. Naturally, since a service business generally operates with direct channels of distribution, it concerns itself only with the sell-through volume. In addition, you'll want to determine whether there is any seasonality in the market that would affect the volume of sales during any particular period of time.

The mistake made by many companies that sell to retailers is focusing on how much product they are selling to the retailer or wholesaler, as the case may be, and structuring their production and/or inventory accordingly. They do not carefully monitor retail sales to the customer (sell-through). Consequently, when consumer buying slows and the retailer cannot move sufficient product, the manufacturer or producer is left with excess inventory. The entrepreneur with a new product or service, therefore, should monitor retail sales of competing products to consumers in the same category to arrive at an estimate of sales demand. One word of caution: when choosing competing companies for comparison purposes, be aware that if the company is publicly held or well-established, your new venture probably will not achieve the same level of sales for some time. Therefore, the sales figures you gather serve merely as an upper limit as you determine how much below that figure your sales level will be. The percentage increase in your sales over a three- to five-year period will depend on these factors:

▶ Growth rates in the market segment of the product or service

▶ The innovations offered that will make your product/service more attractive to the consumer, even at a higher price

▶ The technological innovations employed that permit you to produce the product or service at a lower cost than your competitors, thus making it more accessible and enticing to the consumer

Forecasting Sales for Industrial Products

With industrial products, which are generally sold business to business, it is important to understand the needs of the customer and the buying cycles of the industry. Again, talking with experts (e.g., distributors) in the field, getting sales figures from noncompeting product manufacturers in the same industry, and generally determining the size of the market niches you intend to enter all help in arriving at an estimate of sales demand. The rate at which sales increase is a function of the same three factors listed for consumer products and services.

Forecasting Expenditures

Once sales have been forecast, predicting expenditures becomes a much easier task, particularly if expenditures vary with sales as in the case of the cost of goods sold and commissions. In wholesale businesses, for example, after you have determined the sales forecast, you can apply the figures for inventory purchases as a percentage of sales and forecast from that. So if inventory cost is 25 percent of sales, you can apply that percentage to sales as they increase to forecast increases in the volume of inventory. Be aware, however, that in some industries, volume discounts on raw materials or inventory may actually reduce costs over time. This is an important piece of information that is gathered during your research.

In manufacturing businesses, forecasting expenditures is a bit more complex because you must first derive the **cost of goods sold** (COGS), which usually consists of direct labor, cost of materials, and direct factory overhead. Looking at the sales forecast in terms of units produced to arrive at a dollar figure for COGS and then applying COGS as a percentage of sales will probably suffice for purposes of pro forma statements (see p. 195) for the feasibility stage. Month-by-month analysis of outcomes and use of a cost accounting model that considers raw materials inventory, work-in-process inventory, finished-goods inventory, total inventory, factory overhead, work-in-process flow in units, and weighted-average cost per unit will give a more accurate estimate as the business grows.

In service businesses, the COGS is equivalent to the time expended for the service. The rate at which you bill the service, say $100 an hour, is comprised of the actual expenses incurred in providing the service, a contribution to overhead, and a reasonable profit. The actual expenses incurred are the cost of goods sold equivalent.

General, Selling, and Administrative Expenses

The expenses of running the business, or general, selling, and administrative (G,S&A) expenses, are considered fixed because they do not vary with the volume of sales. They should be forecast separately in a detailed breakout statement. This is so because some of these items may vary over a 12-month period, while others remain stable. For example, rent is normally fixed during a 12-month period while utilities will vary based on use and commissions will vary based on sales. Therefore, do not use a percentage of sales figure for G,S&A expenses. To make the financial statements clearer and more concise, use only the totals of G,S&A expenses for each month in the financial statements, with a footnote directing the reader to the G,S&A breakout statement. Selling expenses, which include advertising, travel, sales salaries, commissions, and promotional supplies, should be handled in the same manner, with a breakout statement, and totals only in the financial statements. Table 9.1 depicts sample lists of manufacturing or construction expenses, distribution and warehouse expenses, and selling expenses. Keep your financial spreadsheets as clean as possible—avoid cluttering them with minute details that are better attached as a breakout statement.

Taxes

The last item to forecast is taxes, which includes such things as payroll taxes and federal, state, and local income taxes. You can find the various rates for those taxes and when they must be paid by consulting the IRS web site at http://www.irs.gov/ and your state franchise tax board or local governmental agency. To calculate your business tax liability, you will need to do a **pro forma income statement,** which is discussed in the following section.

Preparing the Pro Forma Income Statement

The income statement, also known as a profit and loss statement, gives information regarding the profit or loss status of the business for a specified period of time. **Profit** and **loss** are accounting terms that refer to how much your business earned or lost after you deduct all expenses. Figure 9.1 displays an example of an income statement for a corporation. It is normally the first financial statement you calculate so that you can determine your business's income tax liability. The taxes owed—your income tax liability—are based on the profit made by the company and they appear on the cash flow statement (which records the cash inflows and outflows to the business) when they are paid. Because income taxes vary from state to state, the financial statements presented here are not indicative of tax rates in every state. Furthermore, whether your company pays the taxes or you pay the taxes at your personal rate is a function of the type of legal entity you choose for your business. The legal form of organization, discussed in Chapter 12, is an important decision during the development of the business plan.

FIGURE 9.1

New Venture Inc.—Pro Forma Income Statement, 1st Year

(in thousands)

	Premise	Start-up 0	Month 1	Month 2	Month 3	Month 4	Month 5	Month 6	Month 7	Month 8	Month 9	Month 10	Month 11	Month 12	Total
Sales Forecast			0.0	20.0	25.0	35.0	50.0	65.0	85.0	100.0	120.0	130.0	150.0	160.0	940.0
Total Revenues		0	0.0	20.0	25.0	35.0	50.0	65.0	85.0	100.0	120.0	130.0	150.0	160.0	940.0
Cost of Goods Sold															
Material Costs	35% of sales		0.0	7.0	8.8	12.3	17.5	22.8	29.8	35.0	42.0	45.5	52.5	56.0	329.0
Gross Profit		0.0	0.0	13.0	16.3	22.8	32.5	42.3	55.3	65.0	78.0	84.5	97.5	104.0	611.0
Start-up Expenses															
Deposits—legal, utilities		2.0													2.0
Lease Deposit	1 month in advance	4.5													4.5
Employee Training		7.0													7.0
Equipment Purchase	1 mo. Salary	50.0													50.0
Total Start-up Expenses		63.5	0.0	0.0	0.0	0.0	0.0	0.0	0.0	0.0	0.0	0.0	0.0	0.0	63.5
Operating Expenses															
Salaries—Principal (including tax)	3K per month		3.0	3.0	3.0	3.0	3.0	3.0	3.0						21.0
Salaries (including tax)	6K @ 100K in Sales									6.0	6.0	6.0	6.0	6.0	30.0
	3 employees		7.0	7.0	7.0	7.0	7.0	7.0	7.0	7.0	7.0	7.0	7.0	7.0	84.0
	Additional employees					3.5	3.5	7.0	7.0	7.0	7.0	7.0	7.0	7.0	56.0
Bookkeeper Salary	1000 per month		1.0	1.0	1.0	1.0	1.0	1.0	1.0	1.0	1.0	1.0	1.0	1.0	12.0
Building Rent	Per 1 year lease		4.5	4.5	4.5	4.5	4.5	4.5	4.5	4.5	4.5	4.5	4.5	4.5	54.0
Insurance			0.4	0.4	0.4	0.4	0.4	0.4	0.4	0.4	0.4	0.4	0.4	0.4	4.8
Advertising			0.5	0.5	0.5	0.5	0.5	0.5	0.5	0.5	0.5	0.5	0.5	0.5	6.0
General & Administrative			3.0	3.5	4.0	4.6	5.2	6.0	6.9	8.0	9.2	10.6	12.1	14.0	87.0
Equipment Lease Payment	3K per mo + 15% growth		0.5	0.5	0.5	0.5	0.5	0.5	0.5	0.5	0.5	0.5	0.5	0.5	6.0
Total Operating Expenses			19.9	20.4	20.9	25.0	25.6	29.9	30.8	34.9	36.1	37.5	39.0	40.9	360.8
Depreciation	Straightline 3 years		1.4	1.4	1.4	1.4	1.4	1.4	1.4	1.4	1.4	1.4	1.4	1.4	16.8
Net Income Before Taxes		(63.5)	(21.3)	(8.8)	(6.0)	(3.6)	5.5	10.9	23.0	28.7	40.5	45.6	57.1	61.7	169.9
			(84.8)	(93.6)	(99.6)	(103.2)	(97.7)	(86.8)	(63.8)	(35.1)	5.4	51.1	108.2	169.9	169.9

It is important to note that revenues and expenses are recorded in the income statement when the transaction occurs in the case of sales, and when the debt is incurred in the case of expenses, whether or not money has been received or expended. If a sale occurs in March, it is recorded as a sale in March even if the money is not received until May. In the interim that money becomes an account receivable.

● ***Preparing the Income Statement***

The first section of the income statement details the revenues coming into the business from a variety of sources, but typically from sales. A product-oriented business will then show a *cost of goods produced or sold,* which is a calculation of all the costs directly related to making the product or purchasing the goods to be sold. Refer to the discussion of cost of goods sold in the previous section. A service business does not typically calculate a COGS.

The difference between COGS and revenues is **gross profit.** This is an important figure because gross profit divided by sales gives the **gross margin,** which is a figure often used to describe the room that businesses have to make financial mistakes. For example, suppose a company sees revenues of $500,000 in Year One and the COGS equals $350,000. Subtracting the COGS from revenues gives a gross profit of $150,000. Then the gross margin is 30 percent, which means that out of every dollar the company earns, it has 30 cents left to pay its general, administrative, and selling expenses. See below.

Revenue $500,000
COGS   ($350,000)
Gross Profit $150,000
Gross Margin = $150,000/$500,000 or 30%

The next major section of the income statement is operating expenses, which details all the expenditures of the business. A typical income statement might have the following expenses:

Selling expenses
Advertising and promotion
Salaries and wages
Office supplies
Rent
Utilities
Insurance
Payroll taxes
Interest on loans
Depreciation
Miscellaneous

Consult with your accountant as to the most appropriate approach for your business. Subtracting operating expenses from gross profit gives net profit before taxes (income taxes). This is your taxable income. Subtracting your company's tax liability gives net profit. Most entrepreneurs project profit and loss out three years. The farther out you go with projections, the less reliable they are, so it's better to stay within three to five years.

● Providing Assumptions

The income statement should also contain footnotes for each item to refer the reader to supporting material in the "Notes to Financial Statements" or "Assumptions." Any unusual major expenses, such as the cost of participating in a trade show, should be footnoted separately and explained. The examples in this chapter have a column of premises or assumptions in the statements. Normally, these would be accompanied by more detailed explanation in a separate assumptions page.

It is not uncommon for a new business to show no profit in its first year. Whether you show a profit is really a function of the type of business and the cost of start-up. In particular, high technology and manufacturing start-ups are capital intensive due to a heavy investment in R&D, equipment, and facility. They generally take longer to realize a profit than service businesses. In the example of New Venture Inc. (see Figure 9.1), the company projected ending the year with a cumulative net profit before taxes of $169,900.

How Much Start-up Money Is Needed?

Probably the key question to be answered when you're developing the financial plan for the new business is how much money will be needed to start the business and keep it operating until a positive cash flow has been achieved. The first thing to understand is that the best estimates of the start-up total are just that—estimates. There is no way to guarantee that you have figured correctly. Through the careful collection of information about both potential revenues and expenses, however, you can achieve figures that will prevent the business from dying before it has a chance to succeed.

This section starts with a summary of start-up costs, and then moves to constructing the pro forma cash flow statement, at which point there will be enough information to calculate the total start-up funds needed to keep the business running until a positive cash flow has been achieved.

● Calculating Start-up Costs

The bulk of expenses in the first year of a new business are probably incurred prior to the business's opening its doors for the first time. The costs of purchasing furniture, equipment, start-up inventory, and supplies can quickly add up to a substantial amount. Add to that deposits for leases and utilities and you may have used up the first year's profits, assuming there would have been profits. A manufacturing start-up might also include product development costs, a plant lease deposit, and raw materials costs. Start-ups with new products typically ac- crue heavy pre–start-up development costs that include engineering, prototyp- ing, and patent assessment and application. These are one-time expenses to get the business started.

For accounting purposes, some of these initial costs like equipment must be depreciated or discounted over a period of time on the income statement; oth- ers, such as organizational and formation expenses, must be amortized or spread out over time as start-up costs. You should check with your accountant to learn the correct method for depreciating and amortizing certain expenses for your type of business. For determining start-up funding requirements, however, we will treat these costs as a lump sum. Be sure to keep careful records of any ex- penses related to the business and do not commingle business expenses with your personal expenses.

● *Forecasting Cash Flow*

The **cash flow statement** is the entrepreneur's most important financial state- ment, because it depicts the cash position of the company at specified points in time and lets the entrepreneur know when the company is expected to generate a positive cash flow based on sales—in other words, the company's liquidity po- sition. It is important to others (bankers and investors) because it reflects the company's ability to generate future positive cash flow, meet its obligations, and pay dividends (assuming a corporate structure).

To begin to forecast cash flow in an effort to determine how much start-up capital is needed, you must obtain a good estimate of potential sales. As you learned earlier in this chapter, this is no easy task. However, the market research you conducted certainly has given you a sense of the demand for your product or service.

Figure 9.2 gives an example of a cash flow statement for New Venture Inc. As with all financial statements, each item on the statement should be footnoted in the "Notes to Financial Statements" to explain what the assumptions were and how the figures were derived.

The first section of the statement, cash inflows or receipts, records all the sources of cash that come into the business when they are received. This is an important point to remember about a cash flow statement: it records cash in- flows and outflows when they occur. Therefore, if a sale is made in March, for example, but payment is not received until April, the sale is counted in April on the statement. Recall that the income statement differs from the cash flow state- ment in this regard. The next section records operating cash outflows or dis- bursements. Notice that since this is a start-up venture, we have included a

FIGURE 9.2

New Venture Inc.—Pro Forma Unfunded Cash Flow, Year 1

(in thousands)

	Premise	Start-up 0	Month 1	Month 2	Month 3	Month 4	Month 5	Month 6	Month 7	Month 8	Month 9	Month 10	Month 11	Month 12	Total
Cash Inflows	Actual Sales	0.0	0.0	20.0	25.0	35.0	50.0	65.0	85.0	100.0	120.0	130.0	150.0	160.0	940.0
	Collection in 30 days		0.0	0.0	20.0	25.0	35.0	50.0	65.0	85.0	100.0	120.0	130.0	150.0	780.0
															0.0
Total Cash Inflows		0.0	0.0	0.0	20.0	25.0	35.0	50.0	65.0	85.0	100.0	120.0	130.0	150.0	780.0
Cash Outflows															
Upfront Cash															
Deposits—legal, utilities		2.0													2.0
Rent Lease Deposit	1 month in advance	4.5													4.5
Employee Training	1 mo. salary	7.0													7.0
Equipment Purchase		50.0													
Total Upfront Cash		63.5	0.0	0.0	0.0	0.0	0.0	0.0	0.0	0.0	0.0	0.0	0.0	0.0	13.5
Variable Cost															
Material Costs	25% of sales	0.0	0.0	5.0	6.3	8.8	12.5	16.3	21.3	25.0	30.0	32.5	37.5	40.0	235.0
Total Variable Cost		0.0	0.0	5.0	6.3	8.8	12.5	16.3	21.3	25.0	30.0	32.5	37.5	40.0	235.0
Fixed Expenses															
Salaries—Principal	3K per month		3.0	3.0	3.0	3.0	3.0	3.0	3.0						21.0
Salaries (including tax)	6K @100K in Sales									6.0	6.0	6.0	6.0	6.0	30.0
	3 employees	7.0	7.0	7.0	7.0	7.0	7.0	7.0	7.0	7.0	7.0	7.0	7.0	7.0	84.0
	Additional employees					3.5	3.5	7.0	7.0	7.0	7.0	7.0	7.0	7.0	56.0
Bookkeeper Salary		1.0	1.0	1.0	1.0	1.0	1.0	1.0	1.0	1.0	1.0	1.0	1.0	1.0	12.0
Building Rent	Per 1 year lease	4.5	4.5	4.5	4.5	4.5	4.5	4.5	4.5	4.5	4.5	4.5	4.5	4.5	54.0
Insurance		0.4	0.4	0.4	0.4	0.4	0.4	0.4	0.4	0.4	0.4	0.4	0.4	0.4	4.8
Advertising		0.5	0.5	0.5	0.5	0.5	0.5	0.5	0.5	0.5	0.5	0.5	0.5	0.5	6.0
General & Administrative		3.0	3.0	3.5	4.0	4.6	5.2	6.0	6.9	8.0	9.2	10.6	12.1	14.0	87.0
Equipment Lease Payment	3K per mo + 15% growth	0.5	0.5	0.5	0.5	0.5	0.5	0.5	0.5	0.5	0.5	0.5	0.5	0.5	6.0
Total Fixed Expenses		19.9	19.9	20.4	20.9	25.0	25.6	29.9	30.8	34.9	36.1	37.5	39.0	40.9	360.8
Total Cash Expenditures		63.5	19.9	25.4	27.1	33.7	38.1	46.2	52.1	59.9	66.1	70.0	76.5	80.9	609.3
Net Cash In/Out Per Mo		(63.5)	(19.9)	(25.4)	(7.1)	(8.7)	(3.1)	3.8	12.9	25.1	33.9	50.0	53.5	69.1	170.7
Cash Balance: Beg of Mo		0.0	(63.5)	(83.4)	(108.8)	(115.9)	(124.6)	(127.7)	(123.9)	(111.0)	(85.9)	(52.0)	(1.9)	51.6	120.7
Net Cash In / Out Per Mo		(63.5)	(19.9)	(25.4)	(7.1)	(8.7)	(3.1)	3.8	12.9	25.1	33.9	50.0	53.5	69.1	120.7
Cash Balance		(63.5)	(83.4)	(108.8)	(115.9)	(124.6)	(127.7)	(123.9)	(111.0)	(85.9)	(52.0)	(1.9)	51.6	120.7	120.7

Month Zero to account for up-front expenses that occur before the business is in operation. Other expenses could include such things as cost of goods sold, general and administrative expenses, selling expenses, and other expenses of running the business. Recall that only the totals of G&A and selling expenses should be reported on the cash flow statement. Longer lists of expenses should be reported in a separate, detailed breakout statement prepared to present the individual expenditures.

The final section gives crucial information to the entrepreneur: the net change in cash flow—in other words, whether the business had a positive or a negative cash flow in that month. Note that in each month, the net cash flow reflects only the cash inflows and outflows for that month, assuming no start-up capital.

With the net change computed for each month of Year One, it is now possible to calculate how much total cash is needed to start the business. There are several ways to do this. One simple approach is to use the ending balance for the year and add to that the start-up costs (if they were not already included in the balance). This amount will take you to a positive cash flow. You can verify this by inserting the total capital requirements you have calculated in the spreadsheet and seeing the effect on cash flow.

Another way to estimate cash needs is to identify the highest cumulative negative cash balance on the cash flow statement. This amount, $127,700 on the cash flow statement in Figure 9.2, is the amount it would take for you to feel confident that you could go forward with the venture. The highest negative in our example occurs in Month Five, but for some businesses, the highest negative may occur at any time in the first three years.

Figure 9.3 presents a breakout of the start-up capital requirements of $127,700. Hard costs (equipment) and soft costs (deposits, wages) are separated out so that you can readily see the categories of expenditures. Notice that the total of these items is equal to the total capital requirement of $127,700. Working capital covers such things as accounts receivable, inventory, and materials and is the difference between the highest cash need from the cash flow statement and the sum of the up-front cash (hard and soft costs). It's important to also calculate a safety factor. Remember, these capital requirements are estimates and minimums. Any unexpected deviation from them could cause real problems for the new business, so you should add a cushion to at least make sure your fixed costs are covered. Since every industry and every business is different, deciding on a safety factor requires understanding the nature of the business. You might decide you need an additional amount to cover six months of fixed costs in case of changes in your estimates; if your business has significant seasonal fluctuations, you may need a greater amount. In any case, it's essential to look ahead and predict any possible deviations from your original estimates as carefully as you can.

From doing this cash needs assessment, you now know that you will need a minimum of $127,700 (and $217,900 with the safety factor) to start and operate

FIGURE 9.3

Breakout of Start-up Capital Requirements

New Venture Cash Needs Assessment	
Hard Costs (Equipment)	50.0
Soft Costs (Deposits & Training)	13.5
Working Capital	64.2
Minimum Start-up Capital (highest negative of cumulative cash flow)	127.7
Safety Factor based on average three months of fixed expenses	90.2
Total Start-up Capital	**217.9**

this business until it generates a positive cash flow and makes a profit on its own. By breaking out this amount in hard, soft, and working capital categories, you may find ways to lower that amount, at least initially. For example, instead of investing $50,000 in cash up front for equipment and software, you may be able to lease the equipment, thereby reducing your initial cash outlay significantly. Your accounts receivable is determined by when you are able to collect on sales. If you're in a business where you can collect COD, your working capital needs will decline significantly. If, on the other hand, your customers typically pay in sixty days, you'll need working capital to cover your expenses during that period.

Analyzing the financial risks and benefits of a new venture is a difficult and challenging exercise, but it must be done so that two fundamental questions can be answered:

1. Do the start-up capital requirements make sense? (In other words, is the business feasible?)

2. If we look at the capital investment and the profit possibilities, is there enough money in this opportunity to make the effort worthwhile?

Unfortunately, many businesses are feasible—they can be made to work financially—but the return on the initial investment is so low that the entrepreneur would be better off putting that investment in the stock market. New businesses take an extraordinary amount of work, which entrepreneurs frequently fail to put a value on. All too often the business is running and making a profit, but the entrepreneur is making less than he or she would have made working for someone else. The feasibility stage, when the investment has been minimal, is the time to look seriously at the financial feasibility and potential of the venture to ascertain exactly what the risks and benefits are.

The financial calculations and projections you made in this chapter will help you make the decision of whether or not to go forward with the business. You will, however, need to do many more financial calculations before you ever open the doors to your new business. You will also need a complete financial plan—Chapter 16 will take you through that process.

✓ NEW VENTURE CHECKLIST

Have you:
- ☐ Gathered the numbers you need for performing your financial analysis?
- ☐ Gathered sales forecast data through triangulation?
- ☐ Calculated a pro forma income statement for three years?
- ☐ Created a cash flow statement for three years?
- ☐ Performed a cash needs assessment to determine how much capital you'll need to start the business?

ISSUES TO CONSIDER

1. Why is the cash flow statement the most important statement for the entrepreneur?

2. What are some ways to effectively forecast sales for a retail business? A manufacturer? A service business?

3. How is forecasting sales for consumer products different from forecasting sales for industrial products?

4. What are the three basic types of money found in the cash needs assessment and how are they used to control how much money is needed to start the business?

EXPERIENCING ENTREPRENEURSHIP

1. Interview a banker and an accountant about the key financial statements that entrepreneurs need to understand to run their businesses. Ask about the biggest mistakes business owners make in preparing their financial statements. Compare and contrast the responses of the banker and the accountant. Are their views of the financials different? Why?

2. Interview an entrepreneur who has been in business no longer than five years to find out how he or she calculated how much money was needed to start the venture. Did it turn out to be enough? Why or why not? What would you have advised the entrepreneur to do differently?

ADDITIONAL SOURCES OF INFORMATION

Kolb, R.W., and R.J. Rodriguez (1996). *Financial Management.* 2d ed. Cambridge, MA: Blackwell.

Burton, E.J. and S.M. Bragg (2000). *Accounting and Finance for Your Small Business.* New York: John Wiley.

Stickney, C.P. (1997). *Financial Reporting and Statement Analysis: A Strategic Perspective.* New York: Dryden.

Vaughn, D.E. (1997). *Financial Planning for the Entrepreneur.* Upper Saddle River, N.J.: Prentice-Hall.

INTERNET RESOURCES

AccountingNet
http://www.accountingnet.com
A general source of accounting information for business owners.

Browse the Federal Tax Code—Tax Regs in Plain English
http://www.irs.gov/tax_regs/
Here you can search for specific words and phrases.

Glossary of Insurance and Financial Planning Terms
http://www.ucalgary.ca/MG/inrm/glossary/index.htm
A handy web site that is simple to use.

Internal Revenue Service—The Digital Daily
http://www.irs.ustreas.gov/prod/
This web site is full of free information about the IRS and tax-related issues.

Office.com
http://www.office.com/
Good place to find help on creating financial statements.

Teach Me Finance
http://www.teachmefinance.com
A great web site for learning the basic financial concepts.

RELEVANT CASE STUDIES

Case 4 Beanos Ice Cream Shoppe

Analyzing the Value Chain: Distribution Channels

The ability to learn faster than your competitors may be the only sustainable competitive advantage.
Arie P. de Geus,
Dutch/Shell

Overview

Distribution as a competitive strategy

Distribution channel options

Creating a distribution strategy

PROFILE 10.1

An Unlikely Internet Candidate

Who would have thought that a used-car auction service could become a billion-dollar winner on the Internet? Not Dennis Berry, publisher of the Atlanta Journal-Constitution *when he was trying to persuade used car dealers to advertise in his paper. But when he became president and CEO of Manheim Auctions Inc., he found himself having to work with the dealers and that was a whole new ballgame.*

Manheim is the world's largest used-car auctioning service and under Berry's leadership, it became the leading wholesale seller of used cars on the Internet. In 1996, Manheim sold only sixty-two cars on the Internet, but in 1999, that number exceeded $615 million worth of cars.

Manheim's advantage in the marketplace was its loyal customer base of over 80,000 dealers, which represents 90 percent of all dealers in the United States. Its goal was to help dealers succeed.

Manheim's strategic advantage over a pure dot com company like AutoByTel was that it recognized that used car auctions aren't simply marketplaces. They are a ritual, a culture that has existed for decades. Dealers come not only to purchase autos but also to socialize with other dealers. Manheim clearly loves dealers and provides additional services that no pure dot com can claim. Its goal is to make life easier for dealers so it has linked its web site to all its bricks-and-mortar auction sites. Its 160 acres of parking lot holds more than 15,000 cars. That's what gives Manheim a competitive advantage over its dot com counterparts, because dealers that have cars coming back in off of leases need a place to store them. Most small dealers can't afford to let the cars sit on a lot and depreciate. So Manheim solves the problem for them.

To make dealers aware of this new distribution channel and get them to buy in to using it, Manheim set up kiosks and hired technology specialists who would teach dealers how to use the Internet and also how it would benefit them. As soon as dealers understood the benefits, they signed up in droves because Manheim's dealer-to-dealer transactions gave them the option to sell cars without bringing them to the auction.

But Manheim also realizes that only 30 percent of all cars on a used-car lot come from auctions. The rest come from dealer-to-dealer transactions, consumer trade-ins, and banks. Manheim believes that its web site will give these small used-car dealers wider access to other dealers. And it has boosted its relationship with dealers by also providing them with its proprietary Tracker software that lets them manage inventory, track buying patterns, calculate commissions, and even find financing.

SOURCES: Cheryl Dahle, "Used Cars, New Models," *Fast Company,* July 2000; http://www.manheim.com.

While **distribution** has always been an important part of the marketing process, it has been a rather dull subject when compared to the more exciting areas of advertising and sales. At its core, distribution is the means by which products and services move from the producer to the end-user. This movement usually entails a system of intermediaries (middlemen), a series of activities known as logistics, and relationships with the intermediaries, called channels of distribution. The distribution industry (those businesses concerned with all aspects of distribution) is comprised of two principal activities: transaction accomplishment and physical logistics.[1] The transaction aspect is comprised of all the information required to bring buyers and sellers together in the marketplace to develop and consummate a deal, transfer title and payment, and provide any after-sales service. The logistics side of distribution is concerned with the physical storage, movement, and delivery of product.

With the advent of the Internet and the dot com retailer debacle of December, 1999 when thousands of online customers did not receive their orders in time for Christmas, distribution—specifically fulfillment—became the subject on everyone's mind. Fulfillment is about stocking, filling orders, and shipping to customers. This "back-end" function suddenly took center stage as business owners realized that getting customers is only half the marketing equation. You also have to be able to fill orders in a timely fashion.

Today distribution has taken its place among the most important competitive strategies a successful company can have. For proof of that, look at Profile 10.1 to see what entrepreneur Dennis Berry learned about distribution. This chapter will look at distribution from a strategic point of view and consider how it can create a competitive advantage for a new and growing company.

Distribution as a Competitive Strategy

It's important to understand how we reached a point where distribution strategies can now make or break a business because recognizing patterns of change is a key ingredient in entrepreneurial success. The precipitating forces for change derive from two principal sources—digital technology and the Internet. Each has made irreversible changes in the way business is conducted and the way industries function. We'll talk about each of them in more detail.

Digitization

The ability to convert information to a series of 0's and 1's called **binary code** has revolutionized the way we obtain, share, and act on information. Because of digital technology "text, sound, video—can be put into a digital form that any computer can store, process, and forward."[2] That has made information a more valuable product, and for any company that produces information in any of its forms—books, music, software, art, film, and so forth—two significant production costs have been reduced: reproduction and distribution.[3] Digital technology reduces the cost of reproduction to pennies, so the direct costs of producing an information product lie in the development and prototyping phases. Furthermore, digital technology allows information products to be distributed easily and quickly, particularly over the Internet. What is unique about this is that previous technologies created one or the other benefit, but not both simultaneously in the manner that digital technology does.

A good example of this phenomenon is a VHS recording of a concert. VHS tape is an inexpensive way to get copies of the concert, but it costs as much to distribute the copied tapes as the original. So, in essence, you have reduced the cost to copy, but you still have expensive distribution costs. Recording the concert in a digital format and sending the file over the Internet reduces those distribution costs to zero.

The Internet

The Internet is the most disruptive technology to come about in the past decade. It has not only affected the way business is transacted but has also caused societal changes that can be seen in education, entertainment, communication, and even relationships, to name just a few. The Internet has taken on a life of its own and given Internet businesses a life cycle of their own. Internet years are counted like dog years, so an Internet business that is one year old looks and acts like a business that has been around for seven years.[4]

The Internet has the potential to be an extremely efficient channel because it is widely available, relatively inexpensive, and relatively fast. Although it can provide most of the required functions for an effective channel, it must often rely on offline intermediaries in channels that move tangible products. For example, software, because of its digital nature, can be produced, warehoused, shipped, purchased, negotiated, warranted, and financed completely in the e-commerce channel with no intermediaries. On the other hand, apparel cannot be produced and distributed through the e-commerce channel as effectively because it requires offline manufacture, warehousing, and shipping. Only marketing, purchasing, and the actual transaction (placing the order and paying) take place on the Internet.

We now consider in detail how the Internet as a distribution channel has reduced transaction costs and facilitated disintermediation.

Transaction Costs

Suppose one day you find that you've run out of toner for your printer. Assuming that, like most businesses, you keep an inventory of supplies on hand, you will merely go retrieve a new cartridge. You no doubt consider carrying costs when you track the inventory of your products for sale that are on hand, but you probably have not considered the cost of carrying supplies on hand. You carry those supplies as a convenience to your employees, so they don't have to spend the time to go out and buy them when they run out. Going out to purchase a new cartridge is a cost of using a printer that you have saved.

Of course, this is a very simple example. But extrapolate for a moment to a manufacturer that purchases raw materials from a supplier and must negotiate terms, conditions, and all sorts of legal issues as part of the purchase. That's a much bigger transaction cost, and that kind of cost often propels a manufacturer to vertically integrate, in other words, acquire its supplier to bring all those expensive processes in-house and reduce transaction costs.

The Internet has made firms and markets more efficient and thereby reduced transaction costs. Your office supply company is now linked electronically to your supply inventory, so you don't even have to think about stocking printer cartridges. It knows your usage record and restocks just in time, saving you time and money. It is no wonder then that most companies use the Internet to manage their supply and distribution chains.

Disintermediation

The second major impact of the Internet is to reduce the value chain by getting rid of intermediaries. Most products are part of a distribution channel that includes one or more intermediaries. The function of intermediaries is to reduce the transaction costs for manufacturers in areas that are outside their core competency. They do that by providing added value services like warehousing, shipping, and distribution to retail outlets. They are valuable to the manufacturer as long as the cost of using them is less than those services might cost in the open market. And that's where the Internet comes in. The Internet brings buyers and sellers together in a way that makes many of the services of the intermediaries unnecessary. The process is called **disintermediation.** If a manufacturer can easily sell directly to the customer over the Internet and ship directly from the manufacturing plant, it has reduced its transaction costs and made a higher profit on each transaction.

Many industries were not prepared for the disintermediation impact of the Internet. The auto industry never believed that people would make such an expensive purchase online, but companies like AutoByTel can help consumers make purchase decisions and even route them to a qualified dealer who will provide a binding quote within 24 hours. The banking industry was also slow to react to the Internet effect and watched as consumers were willing to set up online checking accounts with Internet banks that seemed to appear out of nowhere. In nearly every industry, the Internet has begun to reduce costs, make supply chains more efficient, and generally change the way the industry operates.

Distance does not affect the cost for services or products that can be digitized, online businesses are always open, and web businesses can be operated from anywhere in the world. For this reason, the "Internet effect" has been characterized as a move from marketplace to market space.[5] Businesses that operate in market space differ from conventional businesses in terms of what the buyer purchases, the circumstances in which the purchase occurs, and what the firm needs to do business. The typical Internet business, like Amazon.com, is selling information as much as it's selling books, through a computer screen from a database housed in a server. This is quite different from buying books off shelves in a bookstore.

But the critical difference between the Internet as a distribution channel and traditional channels is that the Internet is interactive rather than merely a passive conduit for products. Consequently, it has the ability to create virtual marketplaces like eBay (www.ebay.com). However, one interesting effect of the Internet is that it has taken us back to mass marketing and commoditization (competing on price) because it reduces the marketer's ability to differentiate the product or service, and the only differentiating factor becomes price. The more efficient channels become, the more opportunity for commoditization.[6]

● ***Distribution Trends***

In his book *Value Migration,* Adrian J. Slywotzky identified four new distribution patterns that entrepreneurs should be aware of.[7]

1. *The collapse of the middle.* In many industries a shift from routine product sales to a customized bundling of price, distribution, support, and information has occurred. These product/service bundles are referred to as value-added business solutions. Intuit sells more than its popular accounting software. It provides information through its web site, support, and distribution of upgrades and add-ons over the Internet.

2. *Emergence of new customer groups.* As important as it is to identify current customers, it is equally important to recognize emerging customers. These emerging customers represent new niches in the market and, potentially, new distribution strategies. For example, in the airline industry, deregulation resulted in a whole new class of leisure travelers who were price conscious, so airlines began to offer packages that delivered this benefit.

3. *Migration within the value chain.* The most successful companies are aware of the differing importance of individual steps in the value chain and concentrate on particular activities that allow them to capture maximum value at a particular step. On the computer value chain, for example, suppliers Microsoft and Intel followed a strategy to dominate key upstream activities—operating systems and processors—while companies like EDS and Hewlett-Packard captured key downstream activities—the delivery of computing solutions to end-users in the form of software and printers.

4. *Redefinition of the product/service.* **Value migration** has occurred in many products and services. This means that customers now find new and different value in existing products because of the way entrepreneurial

companies have positioned them. Starbucks, for instance, changed the way customers thought about coffee. The company transformed the product from a daily grind to an affordable luxury, from a beverage to an experience.

In addition to these four trends observed by Slywotzky, we are also seeing, particularly in the business-to-business arena, powerful intermediaries that are consolidating mom-and-pop distributors to reduce or eliminate channel costs.[8] **Consolidation** in an industry distribution channel comes about when a small number of companies control a majority of the market share in a relatively short period of time.

This trend is particularly important to manufacturing entrepreneurs. Faced with a potential consolidation of its distribution channel that will reduce competition and likely increase prices, the manufacturer has four choices.[9]

▶ Enter a partnership with the potential winners of the distribution consolidation. This will ensure that the manufacturer can choose the consolidator that makes the most sense for his or her business.

▶ Invest in independent distributors in the channel to avoid being tied to a major consolidator. In effect the manufacturer creates a consortium of independent distributors dedicated to distributing its products.

▶ Create an alternative route to the market by forward integration, a tactic whereby the manufacturer will try to acquire distributors and retailers in an effort to own the channel and not be subject to the dictates of the consolidator.

▶ Make a stronger effort to build the company's brand recognition in the channel so that the company will be in a better position to negotiate with consolidators.

Consolidation is not necessarily a negative outcome for a small business. For many business owners with mom-and-pop businesses, putting the business under the umbrella of the consolidator provides a way for the owner to eventually cash out the wealth created in the business when the umbrella company goes public. Typically, the small business owner will stay on in a management position and help the consolidator build a region.

From a strategic perspective, distribution channels offer many options to the entrepreneur. In the next section, we'll consider those options.

Distribution Channel Options

Recall that a distribution channel is, quite simply, the route a product takes from the manufacturer to the customer or end-user. There are a number of choices available, depending on the nature of the venture, and each choice will offer ad-

FIGURE 10.1

Direct and Indirect Channels

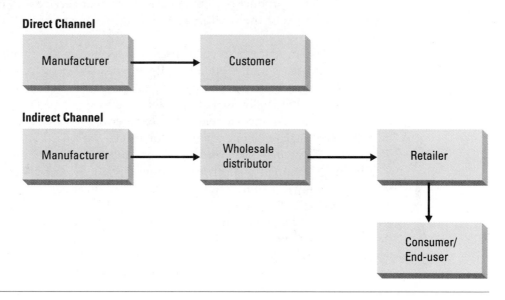

vantages, disadvantages, and consequences. Where you locate your business in the distribution channel will have an important impact on the kind of business you create in the sense that it will determine who your customer is, whether or not you need showplace facility because customers will come to your site, and generally how expensive it will be to start the business.

There are two basic types of distribution channels: direct and indirect. See Figure 10.1 for examples of both.

In a **direct channel of distribution**, the product or service moves from the manufacturer or producer directly to the customer with no intermediaries. Service businesses generally operate in this fashion. For example, when you call a plumber to fix a pipe, or call your accountant to do your taxes, the work is handled directly by the company you called; no one else is involved. Selling through mail order is another way of using a direct channel. When manufacturers sell to the customer through one of their manufacturer's outlets, they are also using a direct channel. Newer examples of direct channels include the Internet and cable TV programming like Home Shopping Network.

An **indirect channel of distribution** has one or more **intermediaries** (middlemen), people who move products from the manufacturer or producer to the end-user. They include wholesalers, retailers, distributors, brokers, and agents. For example, suppose you are producing paper products such as cups, plates, and so on. When the product leaves the production facility, it may go to a wholesaler who will then secure retailers. The retailer's job is to advertise in order to find customers who will buy the product. Each channel intermediary adds value to the product by providing its particular service and can therefore mark up the price of the product to the next intermediary and ultimately the consumer.

We said earlier that where your business is located in the channel has an impact on the business itself. Certainly, it determines who your customer is. Recall that the customer is the person or entity that pays you; the end-user is the person or entity that actually uses the product or service. If you're a wholesaler or distributor, your customer can either be a retailer or end-user/consumer. By contrast, if you're a manufacturer, your customer may be a distributor, and if you're a producer of raw materials, your customer may be a manufacturer.

Channel location also affects the amount of capital you have to put into your facility. Certainly a manufacturer can outsource a lot of tasks and operate virtually, and a distributor can locate a warehouse on less expensive real estate, but a bricks-and-mortar retail business will need an attractive facility in a location where retail customers typically shop. The cost-per-square-foot for a retail location is generally substantially higher than for a distribution or manufacturing site and that adds to the overall higher cost for staffing a retail operation and dealing directly with consumers.

Certainly, when choosing a distribution channel, it would be important to consider the effectiveness of the channel.

What Defines an Effective Channel?

An effective distribution channel will have several characteristics.[10]

Inventory

At various points along the channel, inventory must be warehoused and ready to be shipped where needed, whether it is raw materials to the manufacturer or finished goods to the consumer.

Ownership

It is important to distinguish between who owns the goods and who has possession of them. As goods move through the channel, ownership typically changes hands at the point of purchase but possession may occur at various points. For example, when a fulfillment house agrees to warehouse and ship for a company, it takes possession of the goods but does not purchase them and therefore does not own them. Information as an intangible product presents some unique challenges with regard to ownership and can result in illegitimate channels being formed to move the product through the channel. We see this in the pirating of software and music.

Negotiation

Many channels that deal in expensive items like automobiles, industrial equipment, and so forth, function primarily as price negotiators. Prices are set merely as a starting point for negotiation with the final customer. So for these channels to be effective, they must provide the ability to negotiate.

Gathering of Market Information

The Internet has facilitated the gathering of market intelligence by companies and industries of all sizes, which is critical to successful product development and business planning, so it has also become a characteristic of a successful channel.

Financing and Payment

Credit is an essential element of an effective channel because it smoothes out the fluctuations in cash experienced by purchasers. Methods for collecting payments for purchases have been enhanced by technology.

Risk Management

Movement of products through channels entails some level of risk for which third-party insurance is required. Examples of such risk are product loss or breakage during shipping, product liability, and failure to collect payment for goods. In addition, manufacturers take on responsibility for risk to the customer via warranty programs and after-sale service agreements.

Member Power

Effective channels often produce channel members who gain the power to control aspects of the channel. A channel member gains power if 1) other members rely on it for their primary needs, 2) it controls financial resources, 3) it plays a critical role in the value chain, 4) it has no substitute, or 5) it has information that reduces uncertainty.[11] For example, Wal-Mart is well known for its strong-arm tactics to exact the lowest prices possible from its suppliers. Since it is the world's largest retailer, it is well aware that smaller suppliers cannot afford to lose such a huge customer. Strong retailers can also force manufacturers to adopt new systems, as was the case in the 1980s when retailers forced manufacturers to provide UPC symbols on packages so the retailers could scan them for inventory and sales tracking.

In an effective channel, strong members include other members in the decision-making process; they share information and often provide concessions when a new policy or technology is costly to a member.[12] One excellent example of channel collaboration comes out of the apparel industry where DuPont, a fiber producer; Milliken & Co., a textile mill; Robinson Mfg., an apparel manufacturer;

and JC Penney, a retailer, joined forces to identify customer needs and develop a new line of clothing.

Creating a Distribution Strategy

Distributors, retailers, and other outlets are one means through which manufacturers and other producers communicate to the customer, so they are very much partners with the organization, particularly in a virtual company. Their goal is to gather information from the customer so that the manufacturer or producer can revise and improve its offerings, thereby providing them with products to sell what customers want. Finding good, loyal outlets is competitively difficult. In fact, distribution, once a mundane, routine occupation, has become the glamour stock of the business world with "channel surfer" entrepreneurs constantly seeking the most productive channel.

The following are just a few examples of companies that have found innovative distribution strategies.

▶ Snap-on Tools differentiates itself in its market by stocking mobile trucks with its products and sending them to sites where buyers of tools are likely to be.

▶ Jet Blast Corporation found its most effective distribution channel in TV shopping channels like Home Shopping Network and QVC for products like the Pro-Jet 2000, which converts ordinary garden hose pressure into high-velocity water flow. For inventors with single products, TV shopping channels afford a means of competition against major companies.

▶ McAfee Associates produces and distributes security tools, in particular Virus-Scan, a program that detects and destroys computer viruses. Its strategy was to post virus fixes on computer bulletin boards and ask anyone who downloaded its software to pay what they thought it was worth. That strategy made John McAfee $5 million in his first year. And the company continues to offer many of its products for free in the form of computer downloads.

Before choosing a strategy, it's always wise to look at the various distribution channels that similar companies in your industry are using. That gives you an indication of customer expectation about time and place of delivery and it helps you spot opportunity gaps—innovative distribution strategies that might allow you to capture a group of customers that is not currently being served.

● Comparing Channel Options

Every product or service has more than one channel option, so it's a good idea to depict your distribution options graphically so you can compare their ef-

FIGURE 10.2

Information Provided by a Channel Graphic

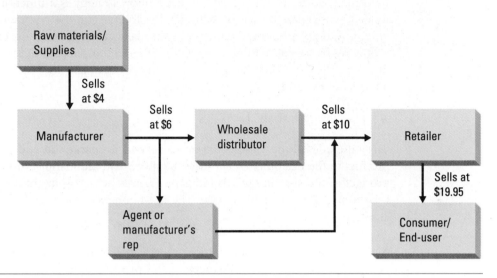

fectiveness. Graphing your distribution channel will help you see more clearly how to:

▶ Measure the time from manufacturing to customer on the basis of the lead time needed by each channel member.

▶ Determine the ultimate retail price, based on the markups required by the intermediaries.

▶ Figure the total costs of marketing the product. For example, manufacturers have to market to distributors, but to support their distributors they may also market to retailers and even end-users or consumers

Refer to Figure 10.2, which depicts a complex distribution channel and the **markups** along the channel. The raw materials product charges the manufacturer $4 per unit; the manufacturer turns the raw material into product and sells it to the distributor for $6.00. Alternatively, the manufacturer can use an independent sales representative (sales rep) who will find outlets and receive a commission on sales made. Notice that the retailer typically doubles (or more) the price to the consumer. This is known as **keystoning.** Also notice that markups typically increase the farther down the channel you go. This occurs because the cost of doing business increases down the channel, as does the risk.

● *Factors Affecting the Choice of Strategy*

In very broad terms, the choice of distribution strategy is a function of desirability (will customers be happy with it?), feasibility (can the channel do what you want it to do?), and profitability (can you make money using this channel?). The following factors should be considered when attempting to determine the most effective distribution strategy: costs, market coverage, level of control, speed and reliability, and type of intermediary.

Costs

Costs include all the various expenses related to marketing and distributing the product to the customer or end-user. Suppose you are manufacturing a consumer product in the sporting goods industry. Here is how you might compare the distribution options available to you. The most common route to the customer is:

Supplier → Manufacturer → Wholesaler → Retailer → Customer

At each stage, the channel member adds value to the product by performing a service that increases the chances of the product's reaching its intended customer (see Figure 10.2). The wholesaler seeks appropriate retail outlets, and the retailer advertises and promotes the product to its customers. The value created allows each channel member to increase the price of the product to the next channel member. For example, the manufacturer charges the wholesaler a price that covers the costs of producing the product plus an amount for overhead and profit. The wholesaler, in turn, adds an amount to cover the cost of the goods purchased and his or her overhead and profit. The retailer does the same and charges the final price to the customer. That price can typically be 4 to 5 times what it cost to manufacture the product (labor and materials).

Suppose you decide to bypass the wholesaler and sell directly to retailers:

Manufacturer → Retailer

It appears on the surface that the final retail price could be substantially lower, perhaps even the rate at which the wholesaler sold to the retailer in the first example. However, there is a flaw in this reasoning. The wholesaler performed a valuable service. He or she made it possible for the manufacturer to focus on producing the product and not incur the cost of maintaining a larger marketing department, a sales force, additional warehouses, and a more complex shipping department. All these activities now become a cost to the manufacturer of doing business with retailers and must be factored into the price charged the customer as well as the decision to choose this distribution channel. This is not to say that it never makes sense for manufacturers to sell direct to retailers. However, it is important for the entrepreneur to consider all the costs, advantages, disadvantages, and consequences of choosing a particular market channel to reach the customer.

Other aspects of starting the new venture can be examined by studying the distribution channel options. For example, where you locate your business and how you transport products to the customer are affected by your channel option. Suppose you have chosen the following channel:

Manufacturer → Retailer

In this instance it may be advantageous to locate the manufacturing plant near major transportation networks to hold down shipping costs. Now consider the following channel:

Manufacturer → Wholesaler → Retailer → Customer

Here it is not important for the manufacturer to be located conveniently near the retailer. Having a location that minimizes shipping costs to the wholesaler becomes a more relevant issue.

If the entrepreneur is a retailer (or wholesaler), he or she looks at the distribution channel from both directions. The customer will be reached directly, but looking back down the distribution channel, the retailer is also concerned with finding a good distributor who represents quality manufacturers. The cost of a distribution channel will directly affect the company's ability to make a profit.

Market Coverage

With a start-up company, it's often advantageous to use intermediaries because it allows you to enter a larger market more quickly. Selling your product to just five distributors can give you access to hundreds of wholesale and retail outlets without increasing your marketing efforts or sales staff. This is important when you have very limited resources.

Control of Distribution

The choice of distribution strategy will affect the level of control you exert over what happens to your product once it leaves your hands. If your product is such that it requires unique or unusual marketing tactics to entice the customer, you may not want to put it with an intermediary that is carrying competing lines or a variety of other products, as your product may not get the attention it requires to achieve the sales level you need. In this case, a direct channel may be more appropriate.

Speed and Reliability

The Internet creates the impression that business is moving much faster than before, and in some cases it is. Customers expect products and services to be available more quickly and they want instant access to information. If speed is essential to the successful distribution of your product or service, then any channel you consider must meet that criterion to allow your company to be successful. Likewise, if a reliable channel is essential to your distribution strategy, then many channels will be screened out of the selection process on that point alone.

● *The Functions of Intermediaries*

Recall that intermediaries are available in most channels of distribution to take on some of the activities that aren't part of the core competency of the producer or the manufacturer. Intermediaries serve both the producing end of the channel and the end-user end because they make it easier for customers to find products when and where they expect to find them. You will need to evaluate intermediaries carefully to see whether they fit the overall distribution strategy. Stern and El-Ansary argue that intermediaries and distribution channels have three broad purposes for existing.[13]

1. They support economies of scope by adjusting the large volume of a small variety of goods to small quantities of a large variety of goods to meet the needs of customers.

2. They minimize the cost of distribution by creating routines for handling distribution tasks, standardizing a variety of tasks such that they can be automated using state-of-the-art distribution facilitating technology.

3. They organize the information needed by manufacturers and customers and provide a place for them to come together.

More specifically, and in addition to assuming the risk of distribution, intermediaries do the following:

1. **Aggregate heterogeneous goods into a line of goods under a single retail or wholesale category.** For example, a small producer of a sports accessory like Gregg Levin's Perfectcurve™, which maintains the curve in baseball caps, would look for a distributor of sports equipment and accessories so that potential retailers could find everything they need from one distributor.

2. **Break bulk.** Some distributors buy from manufacturers in huge volume and then break that bulk into quantities that their customers typically purchase. That way they can get the cost advantage of a bulk purchase but customize it to their customers' needs.

3. **Provide customer/market information to the producer/manufacturer.** This information will help the producer/manufacturer price products more effectively and also better control production to avoid under- or over-producing.

Agents and Manufacturer's Reps

Manufacturers and producers often retain **agents**—brokers or manufacturer's reps—to find suitable outlets for their products. These agents arrange agreements with wholesalers and retailers for the manufacturer. Agents usually do not buy or hold an inventory of goods from the manufacturer; instead, they bring manufacturers and distributors or retailers together to establish the most efficient distribution channel. The manufacturer or producer shares the cost with other manufacturers represented by the agent and pays a commission only on what the agent sells.

Manufacturer's reps are essentially independent salespeople who handle the manufacturer's business in specific territories and are paid on commission. Unlike agents who bring buyers and sellers together for individual transactions, reps work with a specific manufacturer on a continuing basis, receiving a commission per product sold. Reps may also provide warehousing in a territory and handle shipping the product to the retailer.

Logistics

Although you can't avoid making decisions about your distribution channel, you may be able to get help on logistics and fulfillment. **Logistics** is the transportation, storage, and materials handling of goods in the distribution channel. Recall that fulfillment is handling orders that come into the company by storing, packing, and shipping products for the company. Sometimes these two functions—fulfillment and logistics—are combined in one firm.

It takes a long time before a new venture can justify having its own distribution center. Consequently, many growing companies are outsourcing their packaging, warehousing, inventory control, and trucking requirements to third-party fulfillment and logistics firms. In addition to other services, logistics firms can negotiate the best deals and the most efficient carriers, potentially saving the growing venture thousands of dollars.

The Internet has made it easy to find major carriers online using such sites as iShip (www.iship.com) and Consolidated Delivery and Logistics (www.edl.net). Companies like Dotcom Distribution (www.dotcomdist.com/) and Quality Fulfillment Services (www.qfsinc.com/) provide a variety of services such as the following:

▶ Receipt and warehousing of inventory

▶ Inventory management and control including full Internet-based inventory and order visibility

▶ Product assembly and packaging

▶ Offer and promotion management

▶ Automated, paperless order processing including picking, packing, and shipping

▶ Complete receivables management including turnkey billing; credit; cash collections (cash, credit card, check or electronic check [ECP]); cash applications; and customer payment deductions, to name just a few

▶ Mailing list management (both traditional and email lists)

▶ Customer service and care (phone and web based)

▶ Returns processing and reverse logistics

When you're ready to decide on a logistics or fulfillment firm, make sure it meets the following requirements:

▶ It can provide the services you need when you need them.

▶ Its prices compare favorably with the industry.

▶ It currently deals with similar products.

▶ It provides strong guarantees to protect your goods during shipment.

Distribution has become a critical component of feasibility for any company and should be considered as vital as building a great product or service and delivering value to the customer.

NEW VENTURE CHECKLIST

Have you:
- ☐ Determined the most effective channel of distribution to get your product or service to the customer?
- ☐ Planned how you will get information about the members of your distribution channel so you can choose the best people to serve your business?
- ☐ Figured the costs associated with the distribution channel you have chosen?
- ☐ Determined the length of time it will take to get your product to the customer?

ISSUES TO CONSIDER

1. How do digitization and the Internet affect the service industry? The manufacturing industry?

2. How might the four trends in distribution discussed on page 209 affect the retailer of consumer electronics?

3. How does direct selling in the consumer and industrial channels of distribution differ?

4. What kinds of companies may be involved in both consumer and industrial channels?

5. What are the advantages of using intermediaries? What are some potential disadvantages?

6. How does a distribution channel affect the price of the product or service?

EXPERIENCING ENTREPRENEURSHIP

1. Surf the Internet and come up with five products or services that are using the Internet as a new distribution channel, not just as an advertising medium. How are they accomplishing this?

2. Pick a product in the consumer marketplace and trace it back through the value chain to its origins. Show where value is added at each point. Are there effective ways to shorten the value chain?

ADDITIONAL SOURCES OF INFORMATION

American Logistics Management Association, 2000 Santa Cruz Street, Anaheim, CA 92805. Tel. (714) 937-8970; fax (714) 937-0402.

Bovet, D., J. Martha, Mercer Management Consulting, and A.J. Slywotsky (2000). *Value Nets: Breaking the Supply Chain to Unlock Hidden Profits.* New York: John Wiley.

Inbound Logistics, 5 Penn Plaza, Eighth Floor, New York, NY 10001.

Lambert, D.M., J.R. Stock, and L.M. Ellram (1997). *Fundamentals of Logistics Management.* New York: McGraw-Hill.

Martin, C. (1999). *Logistics and Supply Chain Management.* Upper Saddle River, NJ: Prentice-Hall.

North American Logistics Association, 1300 W. Higgins Road, Suite 111, Park Ridge, IL 60068. Tel. (708) 292-1891; fax (708) 292-1896.

Transportation and Distribution Magazine, 100 Superior Avenue, Cleveland, OH 44114. Tel. (216) 696-7000; fax (216) 696-4135.

INTERNET RESOURCES

Council of Logistics Management
http://www.clm1.org/
Monthly feature articles and case studies on logistics.

EXPOguide
http://www.expoguide.com
A large list of trade shows and conferences.

Industrial Distribution
http://www.manufacturing.net/magazine/id/
Supply chain news and distribution technology.

Transportation and Logistics Directory
http://www.cargolog.com/
Offers a way to submit a rate inquiry to a group of freight forwarders.

RELEVANT CASE STUDIES

Case 5 Earthlink.net: The Journey to Recognizing an Opportunity

Case 6 Highland Dragon

Case 7 Roland International Freight Service

Case 9 Wizards of the Coast

PART THREE

Building a Company: The Business Plan

11

The Business Plan

When all is said and done, the journey
is the reward. There is nothing else.
Randy Komisar,
The Monk and the Riddle

Overview

From feasible concept to business plan

Types of business plans

The business plan components—an overview

Putting the business plan together

Visual presentation of the business plan

Oral presentation of the business plan

PROFILE 11.1

Anatomy of a New Business Failure

Stories of great successes can be inspiring, but entrepreneurs can often learn much more and avoid fatal mistakes by doing a postmortem on a failed business. David Blackburn learned that lesson when his entrepreneurial venture, nTrusted, an application service provider to employers, insurers, and health-benefit administrators, met an untimely death less than two years after its founding. nTrusted's primary application was MyLifeTracker, which stored health-benefits information.

The Opportunity

Health-care administrators and the like are burdened by the paperwork load and liability of maintaining health care information on their members. Blackburn defined the benefits of his application to his customers after careful study of the industry. Employers would benefit from being able to communicate the value of health benefits offered to employees and dependents. Human resources departments would see reduced costs from fewer phone calls. Insurance administrators would benefit from reduced paperwork and mailings. Blackburn was able to prove a need in the market and acquire three paying customers in hand.

Experience of the Founders

Blackburn was the principal founder. He had two years of experience as a venture capitalist, during which time he reviewed the business plans of others. He also spent one year as the manager of an e-health technology company. It was at that company that he had the opportunity to test a version of his business concept.

How the Business Makes Money

nTrusted's revenue model was based on an annual license fee from employers, insurers, and health-benefit administrators. The fee was on a sliding scale depending on the number of members in the health care plan. The problem with this model is that it depends on outside financing to cover customers' payments until they come in. This model also requires a fast scale-out and strategic partners.

Timing Is Everything

With a need for backing, Blackburn began searching for venture funds in April 2000, just one week before the technology crash on the stock market. Investors who had been interested now backed away. In addition to their nervousness about the market, they were also concerned by the potential slow rate of adoption once the application was commercially available. As a result, even with three customers in hand, Blackburn could not raise the money to fully test the concept. In the on-line world, speed and scale are the names of the game. To achieve both requires substantial resources, which he was unable to secure. Though the concept made sense from a value proposition point of view, the timing of his market entry was challenged by forces beyond his control—namely, the downward slide of Internet-based businesses. In retrospect, Blackburn would spend more time planning and making sure that the business model is the correct one for the times. As of January 2002, nTrust.com's domain name was available for sale.

SOURCE: David Blackburn, "Healthy Model in an Ailing Market," *Entrepreneur's Byline,* Entreworld. www.entreworld.org/Content/EntreByline.cfm?ColumnID=259. Jan. 28, 2002.

You wouldn't build a home without a plan; neither would you design or develop a new product without a plan. Yet, many entrepreneurs believe that they can start something as complex as a new business without a plan, and they point to successful entrepreneurs who have done just that. But, today's fast-moving, global, and technologically driven environment requires an in-depth understanding of the complexity of inputs and outputs any business will face. In other words, today, more than any time previously, entrepreneurs must do their homework before entering the market with a new business.

When Jennifer Lawton started Net Daemons Associates in 1992, she didn't have a plan. At the time the economy was in recession, so as an independent contractor providing computer networking services to companies without in-house staff, she had plenty of business. It was not until several years into the business in more competitive times and with fifteen associates that she and her management team realized that it would be easier to concentrate on strategy and explain where the business was going if they had a plan.[1]

While building a comprehensive business plan is no guarantee of success (see Profile 11.1 for proof of that), it goes a long way toward strengthening the new venture's chances of survival. The process of completing a business plan prepares the entrepreneur to understand how the new business operates and interacts with its environment. Furthermore, drafting a business plan is one way to gain more knowledge about the business and gives the entrepreneur credibility in the eyes of others. It reduces risk and helps keep the entrepreneur on target as the business starts operations.

This chapter explores the differences between a business plan and a feasibility study and then discusses how to create an effective plan that will give you an edge in the marketplace.

From Feasible Concept to Business Plan

Chapters 1 through 10 dealt with analyzing the feasibility of a new venture concept. You started by recognizing an opportunity and developing a clear and concise concept: the product/service, customer, value proposition or benefit, and distribution. This concept was designed to be tested in the market through feasibility analysis. In feasibility analysis, you looked at the role of the industry, the market, the customer, and the founding team. You analyzed the risks and benefits of the product or service, the customer, the value proposition, and the distribution channel. Then you calculated how much capital it would take to start the business and operate to a positive cash flow. In short, the feasibility analysis helped to determine the conditions under which you would be willing to go forward and design a plan for execution of the concept. Now it's time to build an infrastructure that will help you execute that concept.

Feasibility versus Business Planning

What is the difference between a feasibility study and a business plan? A feasibility study provides a way to test a new concept in the marketplace. By contrast, a business plan is a more comprehensive analysis designed to help the entrepreneur build a company to execute the feasible business concept. Simply stated, feasibility is about the business idea; the business plan is about the company that will bring that idea to market. The business plan serves three purposes:

> It serves as a reality check.

> It is a living guide to the business.

> It is a statement of intent for interested third parties.

The Reality Check

There is more to a successful venture than a feasible concept. The business plan serves to get the entrepreneur to think about ways to introduce the concept to the market.

In fact, the process of doing the business plan helps the entrepreneur understand more clearly the nature of all aspects of the business: Researching costs, preparing forecasts, and strategizing about operating procedures sometimes reveal potential problems previously unrecognized. Very often the business planning process will reveal strong negatives or difficulties that can lead to a decision not to proceed. To reach the business plan stage and decide not to go forward is not a failure for the entrepreneur. It merely indicates the value of doing a business plan in the first place. It is certainly preferable to halt the effort at that point than to go forward and possibly fail farther down the road when significant time and money have been expended.

The Living Guide to the Business

The business plan is a blueprint for the start-up and growth of the new venture. It is a complete and comprehensive picture of the business. It's called a living document because it's subject to an ever-changing environment. The original business plan for a new business contains estimates and assumptions for what the entrepreneur expects will happen when the business starts, and it is often prepared with subjective data. Consequently, it is difficult to find an entrepreneur whose business plan—particularly the financial projections—is right on the mark once the business has started. Entrepreneurs typically re-evaluate their plans and update them periodically during the first year, then annually thereafter. This process compares the goals and projections from the original business plan with the actual achievements of the firm during the period under investigation. If significant differences in figures are observed, the entrepreneur attempts to learn what may have caused the differences and adjusts projections for the next period to account for any changes. In this way the business plan always reflects what the business is actually doing, thereby improving and refining projections for the future.

Statement of Intent for Third Parties

In addition to the entrepreneur, it may be necessary to induce others to become interested in the new venture. These third parties include:

▶ Investors

▶ Bankers/lenders

▶ Potential management

▶ Strategic partners

Each of these groups looks at the business plan from a different perspective.

Investors

Investors review closely both the factors that predict growth and the qualifications and track record of the management team. They do so because they want to ensure that their investment will increase in value over the period of time during which they are involved in the business and that it is in capable and experienced hands. They look at the **deal structure;** that is, what their investment will buy them in terms of an equity interest and subsequent ownership rights in the company. They also want to know how they will be able to liquidate their investment at some future date.

Bankers/Lenders

Bankers/lenders are primarily interested in the company's margins and cash flow projections because they are concerned about how their loans or credit lines to the business will be repaid. The **margins** indicate how much room there is for error between the cost to produce the product or deliver the service and the selling price. If margins are tight and the business finds itself having to lower prices to compete, the firm may not be able to pay off its loans as consistently and quickly as the bank would like. Similarly, bankers look at cash flow projections to see whether the business can pay all its expenses and still have money left over at the end of each month. Bankers also look at the qualifications and track record of the management team and may require personal guarantees of the principals.

Potential Management

At start-up or some later date, the entrepreneur may want to attract qualified personnel to the key management team to fill the gaps in experience. The business plan provides these people with a complete picture of the business and the role they could potentially play in its start-up and growth.

Strategic Partners

Some entrepreneurs, particularly those who intend to manufacture a product, choose to form a strategic alliance with a larger company so that they don't have to incur the tremendous costs of purchasing equipment for a manufacturing plant. They may, for example, license another firm to manufacture and assemble the product and supply it to the entrepreneur to market and distribute. Alternatively, they may enter into an agreement with a supplier to provide necessary raw materials in exchange for an equity interest in the start-up venture.

Strategic partners like this want to review the growth plans of the company and the market strategy, as these plans indicate how much business the strategic partner may get. They are also interested in the new venture's ability to pay them for their work. Knowing in advance what these third parties are looking for will prompt you to address their specific needs in your business plan, facilitating your ability to achieve the goals of the business.

● A Reflection of Your Passion for the Business

A business plan is more than a blueprint for you and others on how the business is going to work. It must also be a document that, in one entrepreneur's words, "engages your heart as well as your head."[2] When it was time for Keith Walton to go to his banker for a $50,000 line of credit for his business that supplies retailers with vintage and contemporary fixtures, it was his passion for the business that won the banker over. Yes, he had all the numbers in place and built a credible case for his request, but in the end the passion with which he delivered his plan secured the line of credit.

Passion is simply what drives you to start your business. In Walton's case, it was his love for antiques and the firm belief that he should start a business to do something he really enjoyed doing so that it wouldn't seem like work. The business plan should reflect that passion and your values and beliefs.

Types of Business Plans

Just as there are many different readers of business plans, there are different types of plans depending on the business and the needs of the target audience for the plan. In this section, we'll discuss two basic types of plans: the traditional plan and the plan for an e-commerce company. These two represent the two extremes in style, although it must be noted that, in general, the length of business plans has shortened considerably from plans written ten years ago. Investors and others who read a lot of business plans don't want to peruse pages of lengthy discourse. They are looking for concise plans that hit the most important points clearly and effectively.

● *The Traditional Plan*

Most businesses will follow the traditional plan, which is about twenty pages in length plus appendices. A sample outline for a traditional business plan can be found in Table 16.2 (p. 385) and we will review its major sections later in this chapter. This plan takes a justification or inductive approach to convincing the reader that this is a great business opportunity; that is, it states the opportunity at the outset in the Business Concept section and then proceeds to provide evidence to support the concept. This is the type of plan that most readers are used to seeing, and unless your readers tell you otherwise, it is the type you should choose.

● *The e-Commerce Business Plan*

The dot com, B2B, or other e-commerce business plan is no different from the traditional plan in the fundamentals. The plan still has to demonstrate that the business is creating value, has customers, and will make a profit. Investors are scrutinizing Internet business plans with far more care and discernment than they were in the dot com craze of 1999 and early 2000 when entrepreneurs merely had to tell a great story and show how the business could scale. It is now rare for a concept to be funded on a compelling story alone.

In addition to demonstrating the concept's compelling story and the ability to scale up to a size that is attractive to investors, the e-commerce plan must show how value is created and profits are made. In other words, it must have a solid business model. Other important elements that distinguish this type of plan from the traditional are[3]

▶ A timeline to launch and trigger points for the growth of the venture. Certainly a traditional business plan will also have a timeline to launch and identify trigger points for action, but because of the nature of the Internet environment, e-commerce companies have the potential to grow much faster than traditional businesses and be global from the first day. Consequently, trigger points to identify when an action should be taken (hire more employees, acquire more space) will come earlier and be spaced more closely together. You will also want to show how your venture will create value at various points in its growth cycle. See the section "What Every Business Plan Needs" to learn more about the factors that create value.

▶ The technology standards you will employ. It's important to use standards that can be accessed by the majority of online customers. For example, if you are using Flash technology, you may also want to offer the alternative of basic html to customers so as not to exclude those who don't have the latest technology. You will also need to show that your standard works with the bandwidth available to the average customer and addresses security standards including firewall security.

▶ The software and hardware needed to operate the business and how you will acquire it. What are the development tools you will use? Are you developing some of it in-house and outsourcing the rest? Are you licensing technology from a third party?

▶ The Internet service provider you will use to connect the business to the Internet. It is important to find one as close to the Internet backbone as possible with 24/7 support, redundancy, and backup and recovery capabilities.

▶ A storyboard of the product or service you are offering, so the reader of the plan can visualize the concept. You will also want to demonstrate that the product or service can operate across a variety of platforms (e.g., Windows, Linux).

Depending on the requirements of the investor or other reader for the plan, the e-commerce business plan can range from as few as seven pages to the more typical fifteen to twenty pages.

● *What Every Business Plan Needs*

Every business plan—no matter what type of business—needs to answer the following fundamental questions:

▶ *What need is being served? In other words, is there really an opportunity here?*
Support for the answer to this question will come from the market research section of the business plan. It should tell you whether there really is a market for this opportunity and how much of a market. It should also convey that the company is customer driven, that it is solving a real need that

customers have.[4] In addition, the plan should provide a detailed profile of the most likely customer and evidence that you have talked with customers and perhaps even have a first customer in hand.

▶ *Do you have a team that can serve that need?*
Can you show that you have a team with experience and skills in the various areas required by your business? Do they have their own money invested in this concept? It's easy to spend other people's money or to consider "sweat" equity as equivalent to cash—but it's not equivalent in the eyes of investors, who figure you won't give up easily if you have invested your own money in the deal. Does your team have passion and the drive to make this business a success? Passion and drive are difficult to measure but are reflected in the level of work that was put into the business plan—particularly in the market research. How many people did you talk to—industry experts, customers, and so forth?

▶ *Why is now the right time to launch this business concept?*
What makes your concept so valuable right now? If no one else is doing it, ask yourself why. Has anyone tried this before and failed? If so, why? What makes the current environment right for your venture?

▶ *Can you make money at it?*
The most important financial statement is the cash flow statement. It's easy to make the company look successful on paper with revenue projections. It's more difficult to accurately predict expenses and actual income. Can you support all the numbers you present in your financials?

The business plan must also indicate how value is being created at various points in the proposed life of the business. According to business valuation consultant Rock Hankin, at every stage in the life of a business value is created when the business has

▶ Adequate capitalization

▶ Highly regarded investors

▶ An experienced management team

▶ A unique technology or service

▶ The ability to innovate

▶ A rapidly expanding market.[5]

Once the new venture has passed the start-up stage, additional value is created by its position in the market, significant customers, effective operating systems, a strong gross margin, positive cash flow, and a high return on equity.

Since business plans are most often used to raise capital, the questions they answer are often those things that will most interest an investor or lender. Some of the questions to consider include

⬧ What opportunity or problem will the concept address?

⬧ How much money is needed to address this opportunity or problem?

⬧ How will capital be allocated (i.e., increase sales, profits, or the value of the company)?

⬧ How will the business provide a superior return on investment (ROI)?

⬧ What level of equity is being offered to investors?

⬧ Which exit strategies are possible?

Take a look at Profile 11.1 to see an example of one business plan that failed because it didn't answer all the questions.

The Business Plan Components—An Overview

Every business plan has some major sections in common. Here, you'll see a review of those sections. Remember that these sections and the outline in the appendix are merely guides. You will want to customize your business plan to meet your needs and the needs of those who will read it.

● The Business Concept

The business concept—product/service, customer, value proposition, and distribution—should be stated clearly and concisely. Then elaborate a bit on each of the components so that the reader has a clear understanding of the opportunity. You should also include a discussion of the business model—how the business will make money. Refer to Chapter 5 for a discussion of the business concept. This section should also include a discussion of the development of the prototype for the product or service. Where are you in that development process? What still needs to be done to achieve a commercially ready product or service? What intellectual property rights can you gain and how will they help you create a competitive advantage. Refer to Chapter 7 for additional help.

● The Industry/Market Analysis

In this section, you will discuss the nature of the industry in which your company will do business. Does the industry support a new entrant? Where is the industry in the life cycle? Who are your primary competitors? You will also discuss the results of your market analysis of the customer. Precisely, who is the customer? What do you know about the customer? Will the customer buy from you? How big is the market? This is one of the most important sections of the business plan and the most persuasive argument you need to build to convince investors. A unique resource base will set your company apart from competitors.[6] See Chapters 4 and 6 for more information.

The Founding Team

This section needs to provide evidence that you have a team with the necessary skills and experience to successfully execute the business plan. Everything depends on a great team. If the founding team is lacking in some area of expertise or experience, make sure you have closed that gap with a member of your board of directors, additional management you intend to hire, or a strategic partner. See Chapter 8 for more about building a founding team.

Operational Analysis

In this section of the business plan, a detailed description of the business operations is presented. The status of product/service development is addressed in more detail than was presented in the Business Concept section, as well as additional steps that must be taken before the product/service is ready to sell to the public. The time and cost requirements of completing the development tasks are also included. In addition, this section contains a discussion of the distribution channels used to move the product or service from the producer to the end-user. Block and Macmillan suggest milestone planning.[7] This process includes ten milestones or performance points at which the entrepreneur must make choices that will have a significant impact on the success of the company. See Table 11.1 for these milestones.

A major portion of this section is devoted to a description of how the business will operate, where it will get its raw materials, how the product will be manufactured and/or assembled, and what type and quantity of labor will be required to operate the business. This is best represented in a process flow chart, which is discussed in Chapter 13.

Organization Plan

The organization plan focuses on issues related to how the company will be structured and includes such things as the philosophy of management and company culture, the legal structure, key management, compensation, and key policies. The issues that need to be addressed in the organization plan are dealt with in Chapter 13.

TABLE 11.1

Product Development Milestones

1. Completion of concept and product testing
2. Completion of prototype
3. First financing
4. Completion of initial plant tests (pilot or beta test)
5. Market testing
6. Production start-up
7. Bellwether sale (first substantial sale)
8. First competitive action
9. First redesign or redirection
10. First significant price change

Technology Plan

This section describes how the entrepreneur intends to use technology to create a competitive advantage. Whether technology is the product of the business or an enabler of business goals, it is an important component of a competitive strategy. You can learn more about the technology plan in Chapter 13.

Marketing Plan

The marketing plan is something quite distinct from market analysis. Market analysis gives the entrepreneur the information about the customer that will be used to create a marketing plan, which is the strategy for making the customer aware of the product/service. The marketing plan includes a discussion of the plan's purpose, the market niche, the business's identity, the tools that will be used to reach the customer, a media plan for specific marketing tools, and a marketing budget. The marketing plan is discussed in Chapter 15.

Financial Plan

The financial plan presents the entrepreneur's forecasts for the future of the business. Generally these forecasts are in the form of financial statements broken out by month in the first year or two, and then annually for the next two to five years. This section demonstrates the financial viability of the venture and the assumptions made by the entrepreneur in doing the forecasts. It is designed to show that all the claims about the product, sales, marketing strategy, and operational strategy can work financially to create a business that can survive and grow over the long term. This section also includes a cash needs assessment of the capital required to start the business. A complete discussion of financial analysis related to the business plan is found in Chapter 16.

Contingency Plan

The contingency plan is simply a way of recognizing that sometimes the "best laid plans" don't work the way you intended. It presents potential scenarios, usually dealing with situations like unexpected high or low growth or changing economic conditions and then suggests a plan to minimize the impact on the new business. The contingency plan is discussed in Chapter 19.

Growth Plan

The growth plan discusses how the entrepreneur plans to take the business from start-up through growth. It looks at the strategy that will be used to ensure that the business continues to grow over its life. This may mean looking at new products and services or acquiring other businesses. It's important that this section reassure an investor or lender that the company has a future. Growth is the subject of Chapter 17.

Deal Structure

The deal structure section presents the offering to potential investors, including how much capital is required, in what form (equity, debt, or a combination), return on investment, and a plan for harvesting the investment at a later date. This section should be written from the investor's point of view and present the benefits to the investor of putting money into the new venture. See Chapter 17 for more on deal structure.

Executive Summary

The executive summary, although discussed last here because it should be written last, is probably the most important part of the business plan and appears at the beginning. It is the primary means of stimulating an investor, banker, or other interested party to read the full business plan. The executive summary should be no more than two pages and should contain the most important points from all the sections of the business plan.

It is vital that the executive summary capture the reader's attention instantly in the first sentence by using a key selling point or benefit of the business. One way to do this is by introducing a problem and countering with the opportunity the company has to alleviate the problem. Another way is by using a provocative statement or statistics to entice the reader. In any case, the first paragraph

TABLE 11.2

Business Plan Checklist

1. Does the executive summary grab the reader's attention and highlight the major points of the business plan?
2. Does the business product/service plan clearly describe the purpose of the business, the customer, the benefit to the customer, and the distribution channel?
3. Does the management team section persuade the reader that the team could successfully implement the business concept?
4. Does the market analysis support acceptance for the business concept in the marketplace?
5. Does the operations plan prove that the product or service could be produced and distributed efficiently and effectively?
6. Does the management and organization section assure the reader that an effective infrastructure is in place to facilitate the goals and operations of the company?
7. Does the marketing plan successfully demonstrate how the company will effectively create customer awareness in the target market?
8. Does the technology plan demonstrate how the company will use technology to create a competitive advantage?
9. Does the financial plan convince the reader that the company has long-term growth potential and will provide a superior return on investment for the investor and sufficient cash flow to repay loans to potential lenders?

should contain a clear and concise statement of the business concept, including the product/service, customer, value proposition, and distribution, so that the reader instantly knows the nature of the business. In addition, you should emphasize the business model, the profitability potential of the company, and the potential for growth. For some business plans, particularly e-commerce plans, a proof of concept is used. This is simply a one-page executive summary that condenses the key persuasive arguments.

Remember, you have only about thirty seconds to capture the attention of an investor, banker, or venture capitalist, who probably sees many business plans a month. Use the checklist in Table 11.2 as a guide to preparing your executive summary.

Undertaking a feasibility study and completing a business plan are certainly daunting tasks, but they are absolutely essential exercises that help the entrepreneur understand more clearly every aspect of the new venture and how all the pieces fit together. Even successful entrepreneurs who have started businesses without a written plan have had to write business plans when they needed growth capital or a credit line from the bank. Those starting high-growth global ventures will find they need outside capital and resources fairly quickly.

Putting the Business Plan Together

This book was designed to carry you through the business planning process in a logical progression. Following this progression may be the ideal way to go about preparing a business plan, but, frankly, business plans aren't often handled in such an orderly fashion. Typically, information for the various parts of the business plan is gathered at various points in time, usually at the convenience of the entrepreneur. You may talk with a distributor in the industry seeking a sense of market demand for the proposed product and wind up getting, in addition, an understanding of typical gross margins in the industry—information that will not be needed until after it has been determined that there is a market for the product. From talking with suppliers during market research, you may become concerned that the cost to produce the product is too great, so you will quickly calculate the cost to produce and the probable selling price, based on preliminary information, to see whether there will be enough money left to pay overhead and eventually make a profit. If it looks as though there isn't enough profit in it to make the effort worthwhile, you may decide to abandon the concept even before finishing the market research.

As you can see, business planning is a fluid and dynamic process. One way to gain a measure of control over the information gathered over time is to set up files for each of the major sections of the business plan. As you collect each piece of information, file it in the appropriate folder. When it's time to analyze and prepare that section of the business plan, all the information you need to do it will be there.

It appears that many entrepreneurs choose to use business plan software, judging by the speed at which that software leaves the retailers' shelves. A word of caution here about products that claim to make the business planning process a snap: for the most part, these programs don't deliver on their promises. The reality is that no fancy software can make up for a poorly conceived business concept. Furthermore, because these programs typically produce generic business plans, they may actually hurt your chances when you present the plan to an investor who can spot these standardized versions instantly. Jake Holmes, founder of Stowe Canoe Company, in Stowe, Vermont, created his business plan with word processing software and a spreadsheet. It reflected his personality, his background, and, most importantly to investors, the fact that he had invested his own money in the business.[8] As a result, he was able to prove his credibility to those who were risking their capital on his venture.

If you do choose to use business planning software, find a program that gives you a lot of freedom to modify the template so that your business plan reflects you, the character of your business, and the information you believe to be vital to your plan, not simply your ability to fill in blanks in a software template.

● *Organizing to Write the Plan*

No one will deny that writing a business plan is a chore, but if you organize the information in advance and plan for the time it takes to actually do the writing, it can be accomplished with a minimum of pain and frustration. Be realistic. This is not a job that can be completed in a marathon weekend, but one that you as the lead entrepreneur and the key members of your founding team must tackle seriously if you are to ensure the best chance for achieving the goals of the business. Plan on taking several months to do it properly.

Too often entrepreneurs approach the writing of the business plan with a "what do I need to know" approach, without considering the reader's interests. It is important to know prior to writing the plan that different readers have different needs, which must be addressed. How is it possible to write one business plan for several different audiences? It isn't. You may need to have more than one version of the plan to appropriately address the specific needs and requirements of various audiences. For example, a business plan written with venture capitalists in mind would focus on growth and high return on investment but might be considered too risky by a banker, who is more interested in how the bank's loan will be repaid. Likewise, a plan written to meet the needs of the banker will not capture the attention of a venture capitalist, because generally it is too conservative in its projections.

● *Understanding the Audience for High Growth Business Plans*

In an earlier section, we addressed the needs of various third parties to a traditional business plan. Here we look at the potential audience for a high growth business or Internet business: investors and venture capitalists, bankers or lenders, strategic alliances, customers and suppliers, and key management. We will look at some specific needs of these parties.

Investors and Venture Capitalists

Anyone investing in the new venture has four principal concerns: rate of growth, return on investment, degree of risk, and protection. Investors are generally betting that the value of their ownership interest in the business will increase over time at a rate greater than that of another type of investment or of a bank account. They want to know how fast the business is projected to grow, when that growth will take place, and what will ensure that the growth actually occurs as predicted. For this reason, they tend to look for market-driven companies as opposed to product or technology-driven companies because they're interested in such things as short payback periods for customers.[9] They expect that predictions will be based on solid evidence in the marketplace and a thorough knowledge of the target market.[10] Investors are naturally concerned about when and how the principal portion of their investment will be repaid and how much gain on that investment will accrue over the time they are invested in the company. The answers to these concerns are largely a function of the structure of the investment deal, whether that be a limited or general partnership, or preferred or common stock, and so forth. Consequently, investors want to understand what the entrepreneur intends as far as deal structure, knowing full well that the investor will at some point have some input into how the deal is ultimately structured.

Investors want to thoroughly understand the risks they face in investing in the new venture; principally, how their original equity will be protected. They expect the entrepreneur to present the potential dangers facing the new venture, along with a plan for mitigating or dealing with them to protect the investors against loss. Finally, investors want to know how their equity will be protected if the business fails and how the business will protect its assets from seizure by creditors.

There are some typical errors that entrepreneurs make when writing the business plan for investors or venture capitalists: This list may help you avoid them.

- ▶ **Projected rapid growth beyond the capabilities of the founding team.** This is a common problem. The new venture shows potential for rapidly increasing demand, sales doubling or tripling on an annual basis in the first few years. The entrepreneur believes this will be very attractive to investors. What he or she doesn't realize is that there is no evidence in the business plan to prove that the founding team can manage and control this type of growth, and this is cause for great concern on the part of the investors. Too often they have seen a business fail during rapid growth because management didn't have the systems in place to deal with it. You should be careful to project controlled growth and have a plan for bringing on the necessary personnel at the point at which the company is ready for more rapid growth. The other danger in projecting too high a level of success is that you increase your chances of not being able to achieve it. It is better to project a little more conservatively and try to exceed those projections.

- ▶ **The three-ring circus with only one ringleader.** Many entrepreneurs pride themselves on being a "jack of all trades." They claim to have expertise in all the functional areas of the new venture. What they really have is general knowledge of all the functional areas and maybe a real expertise in only one. Investors are very nervous about relying on solo entrepreneurs to lead world-class ventures. They much prefer a team of founders with at least one person specializing in each of the functional areas.[11]

- ▶ **Performance in some or all areas that exceeds industry averages.** While it is possible for a new venture to exceed industry averages in a particular area, it is not likely. Most averages, such as those for receivables turnover and bad debt losses, have come about as a result of economies of scale, which the new venture is not likely to achieve for some time. It is better for the business plan to initially indicate performance measures at or slightly below industry averages with a plan for how to exceed those averages at some point in the future.

▶ **Underestimated need for capital.** Investors need to know that the business plan projects sufficient capital infusion to grow the company until internal cash flows can carry the load and then provide for an additional infusion of capital when the company is ready for rapid expansion. If the entrepreneur underestimates the amount of capital needed, most savvy investors will recognize this and attribute the error to naiveté on the part of the entrepreneur, or, conversely, they will rely on the figures presented in the plan and ultimately suffer the potential loss of their investment as a result. Every estimate for capital should contain an additional amount for contingencies.

▶ **Strategy mistaken for tactics.** It is much easier to develop tactics than to develop strategies. Strategies define the overall focus of the business; tactics are the methods by which those strategies will be achieved. When an investor asks what the entrepreneur's strategy is for achieving a projected market share by Year Three and the entrepreneur responds with "attending trade shows and advertising in trade journals," the entrepreneur loses the confidence of the investor by responding with tactics. This mistake is often made, as many entrepreneurs focus too much attention on tactics, often to the exclusion of identifying the overall strategy those tactics will support. The strategy for achieving the market share may be to become the first mover in a market niche.

▶ **Price as a market strategy for a product or service.** Using price as a strategy is similar to projecting performance above industry averages. It is rarely possible for a new venture with a product or service that currently exists in the marketplace to enter on the basis of a lower price than that of its competitors. Established companies have achieved economies of scale that the new venture usually cannot, and they will no doubt easily match the price set by a new entrant into the market. Furthermore, this strategy does not impress investors. They are more interested in how the new venture will differentiate itself in terms of product, process, distribution, or service.

▶ **Entrepreneur has not invested in the business.** Investors are more comfortable investing in a new venture where the entrepreneur has contributed a substantial amount of the start-up capital. That signals to the investors a level of commitment necessary to achieve the goals of the company.

Bankers or Lenders

Like investors, bankers or lenders want to know they are going to get their money back. When considering a business plan and an entrepreneur for a loan, lenders have several concerns:

▶ **The amount of money the entrepreneur needs.** Lenders are looking for a specific amount that can be justified with accurate calculations and data.

▶ **The kind of positive impact the loan will have on the business.** Lenders would like to know that the money they are lending is not going to pay off old debt or pay salaries, but rather improve the business's financial position, particularly with regard to cash flow.

▶ **The kinds of assets the business has for collateral.** Not all assets are created equal. Some assets have no value outside the business because they are custom-made or specific to that business and therefore cannot be sold on the open market. Lenders prefer to see industry-standard equipment and facilities that can easily be converted to another use.

▶ **How the business will repay the loan.** Lenders are interested in the earnings potential of the business over the life of the loan, but, more important, they want to know that the business generates sufficient cash flow to service the debt. While fixed expenses are fairly easy to predict, variable expenses—those related to the production of the product or service—present a more difficult problem. That is why lenders are also interested in the market research section of the business plan, which tells them what the demand for the product/service is, and the marketing plan, which tells them how the entrepreneur plans to reach the customer.

▶ **How the bank will be protected if the business doesn't meet its projections.** Lenders want to know that the entrepreneur has a contingency plan for situations where major assumptions prove to be wrong. They want to ensure they are paid out of cash flow, not by liquidating the assets of the business.

▶ **The entrepreneur's stake in the business.** Like investors, lenders feel more confident about lending to a business in which the entrepreneur has a substantial monetary investment. Such an investment reduces the likelihood that the entrepreneur will walk away from the business, leaving the lender stranded.

Strategic Alliances

Strategic alliances may take the form of formal partnership agreements with major corporations or simply an informal agreement such as a large purchase contract. In either case, the larger company that is allying itself with the new venture is usually looking for new products, processes, or technology that complement its current line of products or services. Accordingly, it will search for a new venture management team that has some large corporate experience so that the relationship will be smoother. Larger companies are also interested in strategic issues like the marketing and growth strategies of the new venture.

Major Customers and Suppliers

Major customers and suppliers are concerned with the new venture's performance record dating back to when the company was founded. Because it takes some time to establish a stable performance record, these third-party readers of the business plan will probably not be interested in seeing the plan until the business is up and running and beginning to demonstrate that its predictions for sales are fairly accurate.

Key Management

Key management that the founding team wishes to attract during the growth phase of the new venture will also be concerned about how precisely and accurately the entrepreneur has forecasted demand for the product or service. Many of these targeted key management people will leave other jobs to join the new venture, so they will want to feel confident that the business will not fail and has strong potential for growth. More than any other group mentioned, potential key management will be interested in the details of the operations of the company.

Visual Presentation of the Business Plan

The appearance of the business plan is the first step in getting the plan read. The trick, however, is to have the plan look professional without being too slick, for instance, in a hard-bound, full-color, textbook-style format. Besides, a hard-bound plan suggests it's not subject to change anytime soon, which is not an impression you want to convey. Here are some suggestions for ways to make the business plan stand out from the crowd.

▶ The plan should be bound in such a way that it lies flat when you read it. A spiral-type binding or binder works well.

▶ Use index tabs to separate major sections and make it easier for the reader to find something.

▶ Use a 12-point type font and a font style like Times Roman, for readability.

▶ Use bold subheadings and bullets generously, again to facilitate finding information.

▶ If you have a logo, use it at the top of every page.

▶ Make sure your writing is focused and concise. Prune excess words with a vengeance.

▶ Revise and rewrite several times.

▶ Ask several people to edit the plan.

▶ Make sure all claims are supported by solid evidence.

▶ Do not use fill-in-the-blanks computer programs to write the plan. The result will not reflect the personality of your business.

▶ Number each copy of the business plan and include with it a Statement of Confidentiality that the reader should sign. Keep track of who has which copy of the plan.

▶ Place a statement on the cover page prohibiting copying of the plan.

● *Physically Organizing the Business Plan*

While there are no hard and fast rules about all the items to include in a business plan and where to put them, most business plans contain the items discussed below.

The Cover Page for the Bound Document

Like any other document designed to sell something, the business plan is attempting to convince various third parties—and the entrepreneur—of the viability of the new venture. Therefore, the cover page should convey in an attractive, professional manner the confidence and creativity of the entrepreneur. Dozens of business plans cross the desks of most venture capitalists and lenders every day, so it is important to make your plan stand out. Appearance may be only skin deep, but positive first impressions go a long way toward attracting the attention of a potential financial source. The typical information to have on the cover page is

▶ The name of the company

▶ The words *Business Plan*

▶ The name of the contact person for the new venture and the address and phone number of the business

Some ways to make the business plan stand out are to use color on the cover, the business's logo with the name, or a design that reflects the personality of the business.

Between the executive summary and the table of contents for the business plan, it is useful to put another cover page containing the name of the business and the words *Business Plan* to separate the executive summary from the body of the business plan. Consider the executive summary as a stand-alone document that is not part of the main business plan. In this way, you can hand it out to interested parties, particularly in situations where you don't want to release the complete business plan.

The Body of the Business Plan

The body of the business plan contains all the major sections of information that were discussed earlier in the chapter.

Business plans contain a lot of private information, some of which you may not want to share with everyone who reads the plan. This is a reason for having several different versions of the plan so that you can give the appropriate version to the appropriate person. A section like "Deal Structure," for example, probably should not be included in a plan being given to a lender or potential management employee but usually is needed when dealing with investors or venture capitalists.

Supporting Documents—The Appendices

Many items that might be important to the reader but would clutter the body of the business plan and make it more difficult to read quickly can be placed in appendices after the body of the plan. Some items that typically go in an appendix include

- Complete financial statements (A summary goes in the body of the plan)
- Media plan
- Résumés of the founding team
- Job descriptions
- Lease agreements
- License agreements
- Contracts
- Letters of intent
- Incorporation agreements or partnership agreements
- Evidence of patents
- Designs, architectural or product
- Personal financial statement (only where required, typically by a lender or investor)

Oral Presentation of the Business Plan

It is not uncommon, particularly if the plan is being used to seek capital, for the entrepreneur to be asked to do a presentation of the business concept, highlighting the key points of the business plan. Usually this occurs after the potential funders have read the executive summary and perhaps done a cursory reading of the complete business plan. In any case, they feel it is worth their time to hear from the entrepreneur and the founding team to see whether they measure up to expectations. While this presentation should not be confused with a formal speech, it does share with a speech many common elements. The presentation of the business plan should

- ▶ *Answer the fundamental questions as discussed in the preceding section on the Business Plan Components.*

- ▶ *Be under a half hour.* That is plenty of time to present the key elements. Questions and discussion will probably follow the presentation.

- ▶ *Catch the audience's attention in the first sixty seconds.* Let them know you're happy to be there and immediately get them involved in the presentation by showing concern, for example, about whether or not they can easily see the presentation slides.

Here are some additional tips that will help you create a winning presentation.

- ▶ *Stand without using a podium.* It will give you better command of the situation and make it easier to use gestures and visual aids.

- ▶ *Move around but don't pace.* It is deadly to stand constantly in one place, but it is equally annoying to pace back and forth with no purpose. Moving helps reduce stress and livens up the presentation.

- ▶ *Maintain eye contact with everyone.* Talk to the audience, not over their heads.

- ▶ *Use visual aids.* Color slides or overheads help keep the presentation on track and focused on key points. Be careful not to dazzle the audience with too many overheads, however, as listeners may find themselves more interested in the rhythm of the motions you subconsciously develop as you flip through the slides than in what you say. Keep the slides simple—no more than five lines per slide—big enough to read, and professional-looking.

- ▶ *Make sure the key members of the founding team are involved in the presentation.*

- ▶ *Do a demonstration of the product or service where possible.* It helps generate excitement for the concept.

▶ *Practice the presentation in advance for a small group of friends or colleagues who will critique it, or videotape the practice session so that the founding team can critique themselves.*

▶ *Test the technology you are using for the presentation BEFORE the presentation, so you're sure it's working correctly.*

▶ *Anticipate questions that may be asked by funders and determine how they should be answered.*

If the founding team has successfully made it through the presentation, it has cleared the first hurdle. The second hurdle, however, is harder: answering questions from the funders. One thing to learn about funders is that they generally like to ask questions to which they already know the answers; this is a test to see whether the founding team knows what it's talking about. Furthermore, funders will ask questions that either require an impossibly precise answer or are so broad as to make the entrepreneur wonder what the questioner is looking for.

Another type of question typically asked is "What are the implications of . . . ?" With this question, funders are looking for an answer that addresses their needs and concerns relative to the request for capital. Finally, the type of question that poses the most problems for the founding team is the inordinately complex one that contains several underlying assumptions. For example, "If I were to analyze your new venture in terms of its market share before and after this potential investment, how would the market strategy have changed and how much of the budget should be allotted to changing that strategy?"

The first thing you should do when faced with such a complicated question is to ask that it be repeated, to ensure nothing has been missed that might cause you to make an incorrect assumption. Alternatively, you can restate the question and confirm that you have understood it correctly. Then ask for a few minutes to formulate your answer. You may feel comfortable answering only part of it; for example, you may have evidence you could present to support a change in market share as a result of the capital infusion. On the other hand, you probably don't want to commit to any course of action or any budget amount without having had time to consider it further and gather more facts. Saying this in response to the question will no doubt gain you a measure of respect, for you will have demonstrated that you don't make important decisions precipitously, without considering all the facts.

If you are asked a factual question for which you do not know the answer (usually these are tangential to the business plan and are asked to see how you will respond), admit that you don't have that answer off the top of your head but will be happy to find it after the meeting is over and get back to the questioner. If the presentation or anything the team has proposed is criticized (a likely possibility), be careful not to be defensive or turn the criticism in any way on the audience, or you will lose your chance with them immediately and may never regain it. Remember, you are playing in their ballpark. They make the rules. If it appears that they will be difficult people to deal with as investors or lenders, you don't have to use them. Chalk up the presentation to practice and go on to the next one.

Preparing and presenting the business plan is the culmination of months of work. The business plan represents the heart and soul of the new venture, and if it has been researched and written well, it can enhance the chances of starting a successful high-growth venture. Entrepreneurs should understand, however, that a business plan is not just for those starting new businesses, but for the growing company as well. The business plan lets you benchmark your progress toward company goals. It establishes the purpose, values, and goals of the company that will guide its decision making throughout its life. No entrepreneur plans to fail, but many fail to plan and end up reacting to situations in the environment instead of proactively dealing with a changing environment.

NEW VENTURE CHECKLIST

Have you:
- ☐ Determined the conditions under which you are willing to go forward?
- ☐ Gathered all the information necessary to complete the business plan?
- ☐ Determined the focus of the plan and who the potential readers are?
- ☐ Decided the presentation format for the business plan?

ISSUES TO CONSIDER

1. Why is the business planning process an excellent exercise for any entrepreneur contemplating the start-up of a new venture?

2. What is the difference between a feasibility study and a business plan?

3. How might the business plan change if the reader were an investor versus a potential management hire?

4. How do traditional business plans differ from e-commerce plans?

5. When might you need to include a personal financial statement in the appendix?

6. What are three key elements of a successful business plan presentation?

EXPERIENCING ENTREPRENEURSHIP

1. Interview an "angel," someone who invests in small businesses, about what they look for in a business plan. Based on your discussion, what will you need to remember when you write your business plan?

2. Go to http://www.bplans.com/ and select a business plan to review. Using the guidelines for an effective plan from this chapter, evaluate the plan. What were its strengths and weaknesses?

ADDITIONAL SOURCES OF INFORMATION

Covello, J., and B.J. Hazelgren (1998). *Your First Business Plan.* 3rd ed. Naperville, IL: Sourcebooks Trade.

Hoff, R. (1992). *I Can See You Naked.* Kansas City, MO: Andrew and McMeel.

Pinson, L., and J. Jinnett (1999). *Anatomy of a Business Plan.* 4th ed. Chicago: Dearborn Publishing.

INTERNET RESOURCES

BizPlanit
http://www.bizplanit.com/vplan.htm
Helps entrepreneurs create, evaluate, and improve business plans.

Build a Strong Business Plan, Section by Section
http://www.inc.com/guide/item/0,7462,
    CHL1_GDE66,00.html
Inc. Magazine's guide to writing business plans.

Business Plan Templates
http://www.vfinance.com/
Business plan templates that can be downloaded and viewed in Microsoft Word.

RELEVANT CASE STUDIES

Case 3   Overnite Express

Analyzing Legal Risks and Benefits

It will not injure you to know enough of law to keep out of it.
The Old Farmer's Almanac (1851)

Overview

PROFILE 12.1

Which Form Is Best?

Deciding on the best legal form for your business is no longer a simple task; you have more choices than ever before. Yet many new business owners are making the decision without adequate expert advice. Mark Kalish is the co-owner and vice president of EnviroTech Coating Systems, Inc. of Eau Claire, Wisconsin. His company paints products ranging from motorcycles to musical instruments, using an electrostatic process known as powder coating. In trying to determine which legal form made sense, Kalish and his business partner John Berthold focused on three key issues: legal liability, tax ramifications, and cost of creation. Kalish and his partner didn't want and couldn't afford the personal liability for any potential losses or problems occurring from the operation of the business. This meant that they could not consider the sole proprietor and partnership forms, as both result in personal liability for the owner.

The next consideration was the ability to minimize tax liability. Corporations have more options in regard to this but are subject to "double taxation"; that is, income is taxed at the corporate level and again when dividends are distributed. However, Kalish learned that his company might benefit from the Limited Liability Company (LLC) form of organization, which passes profits and losses through to the owner to be taxed at the personal income tax rate. In addition, the losses that businesses typically face in the early years can be used to reduce the owners' personal tax liability.

The next issue to consider was the cost of formation and maintenance of the chosen form. Kalish learned about the high cost in time and money of record keeping and paperwork associated with a corporation, as well as the higher initial costs of incorporating.

His conclusion was that the sole proprietorship certainly was the best option in terms of cost, assuming that the business owner had a substantial umbrella insurance policy for protection against liability. Unfortunately, for several reasons Kalish could not avail himself of that option. He had intentions of growing the business by issuing and selling additional shares of stock. The corporate form makes this relatively easy to do as does the LLC with its membership interests. He also wanted to ensure that the business survived his death, and both the corporation and the LLC would do that.

The decision about the legal form of the business should be made with careful consideration to the type of business you have and your personal goals for that business. Most important, get legal advice from a competent attorney before making the final decision.

When it's time to form a company, you have several choices about its legal structure. The choice of structure is one of the most important decisions to be made about your business because it carries with it ramifications for many of the things you will do going forward, including how much tax you pay and the cost of maintaining the structure. For example, if your business entails any degree of risk, such as product liability, you will want to choose a legal form that protects your personal assets from being attached as the result of a lawsuit, in addition to carrying the appropriate insurance. In order to make an informed decision about the legal form of your business, you must understand all the risks and benefits associated with the form you choose. See Profile 12.1 to learn how one business made its choice of legal form. This chapter will look at the major forms of organization and give you a good start in thinking about a form that will help you achieve your business goals.

The Legal Form of the New Venture

All businesses operate under one of four broad legal structures—sole proprietorship, partnership, limited liability company, or corporation— or under a variation of one of these. The legal structure of a new venture has both legal and tax ramifications for the entrepreneur and any investors; consequently, entrepreneurs must carefully consider the advantages and disadvantages of each form. Also, since businesses change over time, it's quite possible a business might change its legal form sometime during its lifetime, usually for financial, tax, or liability reasons. We will discuss these situations as we consider each legal form. Table 12.1 presents a summary comparison chart of all the forms. We will consider each in detail in the next sections.

Sole Proprietorship

Nearly 76 percent of all businesses in the United States are **sole proprietorships,** most probably because the sole proprietorship is the easiest form to create. In a sole proprietorship, the owner is the only person responsible for the activities of the business. Likewise, the owner is the only one to enjoy the profits and suffer the losses.

To operate as a sole proprietor requires nothing more than a DBA if the entrepreneur does not use his or her name as the name for the business. A **DBA** is a "Certificate of Doing Business under an Assumed Name" and can be obtained by filing an application with the appropriate local government agency. The certificate, sometimes referred to as a "fictitious business name statement," ensures that yours is the only business in the area (usually a county) using the name you have chosen and provides a public record of business ownership for liability purposes. For example, Jennifer Brooks Associates does not require a DBA if the entrepreneur's name is Jennifer Brooks, but Corporate Consultants does.

TABLE 12.1

Comparison of Legal Forms of Ownership

Issues	Sole Proprietorship	Partnership	Limited Liability Company	C-Corporation
Number of Owners	One	No limit	No limit. Most states require minimum of two members.	No limit on shareholders
Start-up Costs	Filing fees for DBA and business license	Filing fees for DBA. Attorney fees for partnership agreement	Attorney fees for organization, documents, filing fees	Attorney fees for incorporation documents, filing fees
Liability	Owner liable for claims against business, but with insurance can overcome liability.	General partners liable for all claims. Limited partners only liable to amount of investment.	Members liable as in partnerships.	Shareholders liable to amount invested. Officers may be personally liable.
Taxation	Pass-through taxation	Pass-through taxation	Pass-through taxation	Tax-paying entity. Taxed on dividends distributed
Continuity of Life of Business	Dissolution on the death of the owner	Dissolution on the death or separation of a partner unless otherwise specified in the agreement. Not so in the case of limited partners	Most states allow perpetual existence. Unless otherwise stated in articles of organization, existence terminates on death or withdrawal of member.	Continuity of life
Transferability of Interest	Owner free to sell. Assets transferred to estate upon death with valid will.	General partner requires consent of other generals to sell interest. Limited partners' ability to transfer subject to agreement.	Permission of majority of members needed to transfer interest.	Shareholders free to sell unless restricted by agreement.
Distribution of Profits	Profits go to owner.	Profits shared based on partnership agreement.	Profits shared based on member agreement/Articles of Organization	Paid to shareholders as dividends according to agreement and shareholder status.
Management Control	Owner has full control.	Absent an agreement to the contrary, partners have equal voting rights.	Rests with management committee.	Rests with the board of directors appointed by the shareholders.

● *Advantages*

Sole proprietorships have several advantages.

▶ They are easy and inexpensive to create. If you're using your own name, you won't even have to fill out any forms. You may, however, be required to apply for a business license in your city.

▶ They give the owner 100 percent of the company and 100 percent of the profits.

▶ They give the owner complete authority to make decisions about the direction of the business.

▶ The income from the business is taxed only once, at the owner's personal income tax rate.

▶ There are no major reporting requirements as you have with corporations.

● *Disadvantages*

There are, however, some distinct disadvantages that deserve serious consideration.

▶ The sole proprietor has unlimited liability for all claims against the business; that is, any debts incurred must be paid from the owner's assets. Therefore, the sole proprietor puts at risk his or her home, bank accounts, and any other assets. In the current litigious environment, exposure to lawsuits is substantial. To help mitigate this liability, a sole proprietor should obtain business liability insurance, including errors and omissions coverage.

▶ It is more difficult to raise debt capital because often the owner's financial statement alone may not qualify for the amount needed.

▶ The sole proprietor usually relies on his or her skills alone to manage the business. Of course, employees with specific skills can be hired to complement the skills of the owner.

▶ The business's ability to survive is dependent on the owner, and, therefore, the death or incapacitation of the owner can be catastrophic for the business.

Often small businesses such as pizza parlors and boutiques are run as sole proprietorships. This is not to say that a high-growth venture cannot be started as a sole proprietorship—many are—but it will in all likelihood not remain a sole proprietorship for long, as the entrepreneur will typically want the protections and prestige a corporation affords. If you know your business will need to take a corporate or limited liability form, it's probably better to either start that way or move to that form once the business has started to grow because your record keeping will be more consistent, and you'll probably enjoy more clout in your industry as a corporation.

Patti Glick knew that most of all she wanted to be a mom and raise her kids right. A nurse by trade, she discovered that she had a passion for feet and a desire to help people in her Silicon Valley community take better care of theirs. She envisioned starting a business that would allow her to be home when her children arrived from school. With the full support of her family, Glick started Foot Nurse (www.footnurse.com/), and in her first year as a sole proprietor she conducted twenty-four presentations for major companies like Cisco. Demand was escalating and in Year Two she did forty-six presentations. Now she is finding ways to leverage her new-found celebrity with foot-care products and a web site. She prefers the life of a soloist, saying that she would rather charge more than have to hire someone to do what she does.[1]

Partnership

When two or more people agree to share the assets, liabilities, and profits of a business, the legal structure is termed a **partnership.** The partnership form is an improvement over the sole proprietorship from the standpoint that the business can draw on the skills, knowledge, and financial resources of more than one person. This is an advantage not only in operating the business, but in seeking bank loans and the like. Like the sole proprietorship, however, the partnership requires a DBA when the last names of the partners are not used in naming the business. Professionals like lawyers, doctors, and accountants frequently employ this legal structure.

In terms of its advantages and its treatment of income, expenses, and taxes, a partnership is essentially a sole proprietorship consisting of more than one person. However, where liability is concerned, there is a significant difference. In a partnership, each partner is liable for the obligations another partner incurs in the course of doing business. For example, if one partner signs a contract with a supplier in the name of the partnership, the other partners are also bound by the terms of the contract. This is known as the **doctrine of ostensible authority.** Creditors of an individual partner, on the other hand, can attach only the assets of that individual partner, including his or her interest in the partnership.

Partners also have specific property rights. For example, each partner owns and has use of the property acquired by the partnership unless otherwise stated in the Partnership Agreement. Each partner has a right to share in the profits and losses, and each may participate in the management of the partnership. Furthermore, all elections such as depreciation and accounting methods are made at the partnership level and apply to all partners.

Structuring an Effective Partnership Agreement

An effective partnership agreement, formal or informal, between individuals or companies, should address several critical issues.

- The legal name of the partnership
- The nature of the business
- The duration of the partnership
- Contributions of the partners
- Sales, loans, and leases to the partnership

- Withdrawals and salaries
- Responsibility and authority of the partners
- Dissolution of the partnership
- Arbitration

Remember that in the absence of a partnership agreement, all partners are considered equal. In any case, an attorney should oversee the development of the partnership agreement.

● *Advantages*

Partnerships have all the advantages of sole proprietorships in addition to the following advantages unique to partnerships:

▶ Partners share the risk of the doing business.

▶ Partnerships have the clout of more than one partner and, therefore, more than one financial statement.

▶ Partners can share ideas, expertise, and decision making.

▶ Partnerships enjoy pass-through earnings and losses to the individual partners to be taxed at their personal tax rate.

▶ Unless a buy-sell agreement is included in the partnership agreement, the partnership dissolves when a partner either leaves or dies. See the next section.

● *Disadvantages*

Partnerships have several disadvantages that should be considered carefully before using this form.

▶ Partners are personally liable for all business debts and obligations.

▶ Individual partners can bind the partnership to a contract or other business deal.

▶ Individual partners can be sued for the full amount of any partnership debt. If that happens the partner must sue the other partners to recover their shares of the debt.[2]

● *Partnership Agreement*

Though the law does not require it, it is extremely wise for a partnership to draw up a written partnership agreement, based on the **Uniform Partnership Act** that spells out business responsibilities, profit sharing, and transfer of interest. This is advisable because partnerships are inherently fraught with problems that arise from the different personalities and goals of the people involved. A written document executed at the beginning of the partnership will reduce the eventual disagreements and provide for an orderly dissolution should irreconcilable differences arise. Partnerships are burdened by the same disadvantages as sole proprietorships, with the additional encumbrance of personal conflicts, usually over power and authority, which can result in the dissolution of the partnership. Many partnerships have solved these problems by assigning specific responsibilities to each of the partners in the partnership agreement.

● *Types of Partnerships*

There are two types of partnerships: general and limited. In a general partnership, all the partners assume unlimited personal liability and responsibility for the management of the business. In a limited partnership, by contrast, the general partners have unlimited liability and they seek investors whose liability is limited to their monetary investment; that is, if a limited partner invests $25,000 in the business, the most he or she can lose if the business fails is $25,000. It is important to note, however, that limited partners have no say in the management of the business. In fact, they are restricted by law from imposing their will on the business. The penalty for participating in the management of the business is the loss of their limited liability status.

● *Protective Measures in Partnerships*

Issues arise when one or more of the partners in a partnership leaves, either voluntarily or through death. To protect the remaining partners, the partnership should have in place a buy-sell agreement and key person life insurance.

Buy-Sell Agreement

A **buy-sell agreement** is a binding contract between the partners and contains three primary clauses that govern[3]:

1. Who is entitled to purchase a departing partner's share of the business, whether another partner or an outsider.

2. What events can trigger a buyout. Typically, those events include a death, disability, or other form of incapacity; a divorce; or an offer from the outside to buyout the partner.

3. What price will be paid for the partner's interest.

Having this formula in place from the beginning prevents disagreements and legal battles with the departing partner or with the estate of a deceased partner.

It is unfortunate that many entrepreneurs fail to take the precaution of creating a partnership agreement with a buy-sell clause. The consequences can be critical for the business. For example, one partner dies and the partnership, absent a buy-sell agreement, is forced to work with the spouse or family member of the deceased who may not be qualified to run the business. With no partnership agreement, one partner can sell his or her interest to a stranger without the consent of the other partners. If you choose a partnership form of organization, you must have a partnership agreement.

Key Person Insurance

Key person life insurance is a policy on the life of principal members of the partnership, usually the senior partners. Upon the death of a partner, the insurance proceeds can be used to keep the business going or to buy out the deceased partner's interest under a buy-sell agreement.

David and Steve are friends who met during their MBA studies at the University of Southern California in Los Angeles. They wanted to find a way to provide a funding source for many of the students they saw who were trying to start businesses. They chose the partnership form of organization to start their venture because it gave them flexibility, was relatively easy to start, and wouldn't cost a lot of money. With this form they can now bring in limited partners to contribute to their seed fund. They are also looking at moving to an LLC form in the near future, which gives the advantages of a partnership as well as those of a corporation. They know that big money sources prefer forms based on the corporate model and if they intend to grow their fund, this will be important. Despite the fact that they have been friends for many years, their attorney advised them to draw up a partnership agreement with a buy-sell clause to protect their respective interests in the partnership.

If you are looking for more protection from liability and easier access to formal sources of capital, then you may want to consider the next legal form: the corporation.

Corporation

Only about 17 percent of all U.S. businesses are corporations, but they account for 87 percent of all sales transactions. A corporation is different from the pre-

Incorporation Checklist

1. Determine in which state to incorporate. This should be done first as it will affect many of the other tasks in the checklist.
2. Select the name of the corporation.
3. Find a registered agent who will receive legal service for the business in another state, if necessary.
4. Fill out a certificate of incorporation and file with the secretary of state with filing fees.
5. Hold a meeting to elect directors and transact necessary business.
6. During the first organizational meeting of the board of directors, select the corporate seal and stock certificates, issue shares, elect corporate officers (CEO, president, etc., as necessary).
7. Open bank accounts and apply for an Employer Identification Number.
8. Choose the corporation's fiscal year.
9. If necessary, file a DBA certificate.
10. Fill out applications to do business in other states if necessary.
11. Apply for required state and local licenses or permits.
12. If appropriate, elect an S-corporation status.

ceding two forms in that it is a legal entity in and of itself. The U.S. Supreme Court has defined the corporation as "an artificial being, invisible, intangible, and existing only in contemplation of the law." It is chartered or registered by a state and can survive the death or separation of the owner(s) from the business. Therefore, it can sue, be sued, acquire and sell real property, and lend money. The owners of the corporation are its stockholders who invest capital in the corporation in exchange for shares of ownership. Like limited partners, stockholders are not liable for the debts of the corporation and can lose only the money they have invested.

Most businesses form what is known as a **closely held corporation;** that is, the corporate stock is owned privately by a few individuals and is not traded publicly on a securities exchange such as the New York Stock Exchange. This chapter will focus on such private corporations. The issue of "going public" typically arises after the business is established and desires to raise substantial capital for growth by issuing stock (shares of ownership in the corporation) through an initial public offering (IPO). The IPO and public corporations in general are the subject of Chapter 18.

A corporation is created by filing a certificate of incorporation with the state in which the company will do business and issue stock. This is called a **domestic corporation.** A **foreign corporation,** by contrast, is one that is chartered in a state other than in the one in which it will do business. A corporation requires the establishment of a board of directors, which meets periodically to make strategic policy decisions for the business. The regular documentation of these meetings is crucial to maintaining the corporation's limited liability status. The board also hires the officers who will run the business on a day-to-day basis.

There are two corporate forms from which to choose: the C-corporation and the S-corporation. Their purpose and advantages and disadvantages are discussed in the next sections.

● C-Corporation

It would be difficult to claim that the Pennsylvania Railroad Corporation of the 1950s resembles in any way the General Electric Corporation of today, let alone the Business.com Corporation spawned by the Internet phenomenon. Even the most traditional of legal forms has evolved over time. Yet the corporation retains its aura as the most commonly chosen form for a growing company that seeks outside capital in the form of equity or debt.

Advantages

The C-corporate form has several important advantages. It enjoys limited liability in that its owners are liable for its debts and obligations only to the limit of their investment. The only exception to this protection is payroll taxes that may have been withheld from employees' paychecks but not paid to the Internal Revenue Service.

Capital can be raised through the sale of stock up to the amount authorized in the corporate charter; however, be aware that the sale of stock is heavily regulated by federal and state governments. A corporation can create different classes of stock to meet the various needs of its investors. For example, it may issue nonvoting preferred stock to conservative investors who, in the event the corporation must liquidate its assets, will be first in line to recoup their investment. Common stock is more risky because holders of it are paid only after the preferred stockholders. Common stockholders are, however, entitled to vote at stockholders' meetings and divide the profits remaining after the preferred holders are paid their dividends, assuming that these profits are not retained by the corporation to fund growth.

Ownership is easily transferred. This is at once an advantage and a disadvantage, as the entrepreneur will want to be careful, particularly in the start-up phase, that stock does not land in the hands of undesirable parties such as competitors. This problem is normally handled through a buy-sell clause in the stockholders' agreement that states that stock must first be offered to the corporation at a specified price before being offered to someone outside the corporation.

Because it is a legal entity, the corporation can enter into contracts, sue, and be sued without the signature of the owners. In a start-up or young company, bankers, creditors, and such will likely require that majority stockholders or officers personally guarantee loans to ensure that they are protected against the potential failure of the corporation by having the ability to pursue the assets of the owners.

Corporations typically enjoy more status and deference in business circles than do other legal forms, principally because they are a legal entity that cannot be destroyed by the death of one of or even all the principal shareholders. Moreover, to enter the public equity markets, a business must be incorporated and will, consequently, be subjected to greater scrutiny from governmental agencies. The reason for this scrutiny is the fact that the assets of the corporation are separate from the assets of the individual owner/shareholders. So the owners may take risks that they wouldn't take with their personal assets.

Corporations can take advantage of the benefits of retirement funds, Keogh and defined-contribution plans, profit-sharing, and stock option plans for their employees. These fringe benefits are deductible to the corporation as an expense and not taxable to the employee.

Finally, the entrepreneur can hold certain assets such as real estate in his or her own name and lease the use of the assets to the corporation.

Disadvantages

Corporations do, however, have disadvantages that must be carefully considered. They are certainly more complex, subject to more governmental regulation, and cost more to create than sole proprietorships or partnerships. While it is possible to incorporate without the aid of an attorney, it is not recommended. In too many cases, businesses ultimately failed or endured significant financial hardship because they did not incorporate properly at the start of the business.

A more cumbersome disadvantage derives from the fact that the corporation is literally a person for tax purposes. Consequently, if it makes a profit, it must pay a tax whether or not those profits were distributed as dividends to the stockholders. And unlike partners or sole proprietors, stockholders of C-corporations do not receive the benefit of losses (the S-corporation does enjoy these benefits and will be discussed in the next section). In a C-corporation those losses, if they can't be applied in the year they are incurred, must be saved to be applied against future profits. Accordingly, C-corporations pay taxes on the profits they earn, and their owners (stockholders) pay taxes on the dividends they receive; hence, the drawback of "double taxation." It is principally for this reason that many entrepreneurs who operate alone or with a partner do not employ this form. However, if the entrepreneur draws a salary from the corporation, that salary is expensed by the corporation, effectively reducing the company's net income subject to taxes. The entrepreneur will be taxed at his or her personal income tax rate.

By creating a corporation and issuing stock, the entrepreneur is giving up a measure of control to the board of directors. But for privately held corporations, the entrepreneur largely determines who will be on the board. Entrepreneurs who seek outside venture funding in the early stages of their venture may find that they have to give up the majority of the stock to the investors. The choice is between hanging onto the equity and watching the business stall because you can't secure funding, and giving up control so that you can own a smaller piece of something successful. It is not always necessary, however, that the entrepreneur retain 51 percent of the stock to maintain effective control. As long as the entrepreneur's skills and vision are vital to the success of the venture and as long as most of the shareholders share that vision, the entrepreneur will have effective control of the organization, no matter how much stock has been given up. With a corporate form, unlike the sole proprietorship or partnership, the entrepreneur is accountable principally to the stockholders and secondarily to anyone else. If the corporation is privately held, the board usually serves at the pleasure of the entrepreneur, who is accountable to himself or herself and any investors.

A corporation must endeavor in all ways to act as an entity separate from its owners. It must keep personal finances completely separate from corporate finances, hold directors' meetings, maintain minutes, and not take on any financial liability without having sufficient resources to back it up. Failing to do any of these things can result in what is known as "piercing the corporate veil," which leaves the officers and owners open to personal liability.

● *Where to Incorporate*

Apart from legal considerations, where to incorporate is also an important issue. It is normally advantageous to incorporate in the state in which the entrepreneur intends to locate the business, so that it is not under the regulatory powers of two states (the state in which it is incorporated and the state in which it must file an application to do business as an out-of-state corporation).

Normally, however, a corporation will not have to qualify as a "foreign" corporation doing business in another state if it is simply holding directors'/shareholders' meetings in the state, or holding bank accounts, using independent contractors, or marketing to potential customers whose transactions will be completed in the corporation's home state. It has often been said that you should incorporate in Delaware because it has laws that are favorable toward corporations. If you don't intend to seek venture capital or do a substantial amount of business in Delaware, however, the cost and hassle of qualifying in another state as well may outweigh the benefit of being a Delaware incorporation. Also consider the favorableness of the tax laws governing corporations in the state chosen. Some states, like California, have a required, minimum annual corporate income tax, whether or not the business has a taxable income.

● *S-Corporation*

An **S-corporation**, unlike the C-corporation, is not a tax-paying entity. It is merely a financial vehicle that passes the profits and losses of the corporation to the stockholders. It is treated much like the sole proprietorship and the partnership in the sense that if the business earns a profit, that profit becomes the income of the owners/stockholders, and it is the owners who pay the tax on that profit at their individual tax rates.

The rules for election of the S-corporation option are very specific.

▶ The business must first be incorporated.

▶ It can have no more than 75 stockholders.

▶ Shareholders must be U.S. citizens or residents (partnerships and corporations cannot be shareholders). It is important that the shareholder agreement protect shareholders against termination of the S-corporation election through transference of shares to an unqualified person or entity.

▶ It can have only one class of stock issued and outstanding; that is, either preferred or common. But within that class of stock, it can issue voting and nonvoting shares.

▶ No more than 25 percent of the corporate income can be derived from passive investments, such as dividends, rent, and capital gains.

▶ The S-corporation cannot be a financial institution, a foreign corporation, or a subsidiary of a parent corporation.

It is always wise to check with an attorney to make certain the election of S-corporation status is valid. If a C-corporation elects to become an S-corporation and then reverts back to C-corporation status, it cannot re-elect S-corporation status for five years.

The S-corporation is different from the C-corporation in several ways.

▶ In most states, the S-corporation is not a tax paying entity like a C-corporation. If the S-corporation is owned by more than one person, however, it will need to file an informational tax return, similar to a partnership or LLC. Check with the tax division of your state's treasury department to find out how S-corporations are treated in your state.

▶ The entrepreneur is taxed on corporate earnings whether they are distributed as dividends or retained in the corporation.

▶ Any losses incurred by the S-corporation can be used as a deduction on the entrepreneur's personal income tax up to the amount invested in the corporation. If there is more than one shareholder, the loss is shared according to the percentage of ownership.

▶ If the entrepreneur sells the assets of the business, the shareholder pays a tax on the amount of appreciation. With a C-corporation, the gain is taxable to the corporation, and the balance paid to the stockholder is also taxed.

Advantages

The S-corporation lets you pass business losses through to be taxed at your personal tax rate. This offers a significant benefit to people who need to offset income from other sources. The businesses that benefit most from an S-corporation structure are those that don't have a need to retain earnings. In an S-corporation, if the entrepreneur decides to retain, say, $100,000 of profit to invest in new equipment, the stockholders must still pay taxes on that profit as if it had been distributed.

The S-corporation is a valuable financial tool when personal tax rates are significantly lower than corporate rates. However, as top personal rates increase, a C-corporation might be preferable at higher profit levels. For some small businesses, however, the S-corporation may still be less costly in the long run because it avoids double taxation of income. A good tax attorney or certified public accountant (CPA) should advise the entrepreneur on the best course of action.

Ventures that typically benefit from election of the S-corporation status include service businesses with low capital asset requirements, real estate investment firms during times when property values are increasing, and start-ups that are projecting a loss in the early years.

Disadvantages

Entrepreneurs should probably not elect the S-corporation option if they want to retain earnings for expansion or diversification, or if there are significant passive losses from investments such as real estate. Furthermore, while most deductions and expenses are allowed, S-corporations cannot take advantage of deductions based on medical reimbursements or health insurance plans. Another consideration is that unless the business has regular positive cash flow, it could face a situation in which profit is passed through to the owners to be taxed at their personal rate, but the firm has generated insufficient cash to pay those taxes, so it must come out of the pockets of the shareholders.

One young entrepreneur from Massachusetts finally realized her dream of opening a restaurant catering to people who dined as much for the atmosphere and service as for the great food she served. She wanted the protection of a corporate form but didn't want the double taxation of a corporation. She also knew that restaurants generate a lot of cash, so her attorney advised her to consider the S-corporation. That way her company's earnings would be taxed at her personal tax rate and her restaurant would generate enough cash to pay the tax liability on the profits. She could also have as many as 75 investors if she wanted.

Legal forms of organization evolve over time to meet the changing needs of business. In the next section, you'll learn about the newest legal structure: the limited liability company.

Limited Liability Company

A new legal structure is now available in most states. It is known as a **limited liability company (LLC)** and, like the S-corporation, it enjoys the pass-through tax benefits of partnerships in addition to the limited liability of a C-corporation. It is, however, far more flexible in its treatment of certain ownership issues. Only privately held companies can become LLCs, and they must be formed in accordance with very strict guidelines. LLC statutes vary from state to state, so in addition to meeting the partnership requirements of the Internal Revenue Code, you must also file with the state in which you intend to do business and follow its requirements as well.

An LLC is formed via filing articles of organization, which resemble articles of incorporation. You can now form an LLC with only one person in every state that allows this form except for Massachusetts and the District of Columbia, which require two people. The owners of an LLC are called "members" and their share of ownership is known as "interests." The members can undertake the management of the company or hire other people to manage it. Managers, officers, and members are not personally liable for the company's debts or liabilities except when they have personally guaranteed these debts or liabilities. The members create an "operating agreement," which is very similar to a partnership agreement that spells out rights and obligations of the members.

● *Advantages*

Most LLCs will be organized for tax purposes like partnerships, so that income tax benefits and liabilities will pass through to the members. In New York and California, however, the LLCs will also be subject to state franchise taxes or fees. Under the Internal Revenue Code, an LLC maintains all four characteristics of a corporation—limited liability, continuity of life, centralized management, and free transferability of interests—and still can be treated as a partner for tax purposes without fear of being reclassified as a corporation. This enhances the attractiveness of the LLC, already the fastest growing legal form.

The LLC is most often thought of as a combination of a limited partnership and an S-corporation. However, there are differences. In a limited partnership, one or more people (the general partners) agree to assume personal liability for the actions of the partnership while the limited partners may not take part in the management of the partnership without losing their limited liability status. This is not the case with an LLC. Unlike a limited partnership, in an LLC a member does not have to forfeit the right to participate in the management of the organization in order to retain his or her limited liability status.

Moreover, in an LLC, unlike in an S-corporation, there are no limitations on the number of members or on their status. LLCs permit corporations, pension plans, and nonresident aliens as members. Also, while S-corporations can't own

80 percent or more of the stock of another corporation, an LLC may actually possess wholly owned subsidiary corporations. LLCs are not limited to one class of stock, and in some ways they receive more favorable tax treatment. For example, unlike an S-corporation shareholder, the LLC member can deduct losses in amounts that reflect the member's allocable share of the debt of the company.

If at a later date the entrepreneur decides to go public, the LLC can become a C-corporation by transferring the LLC assets to the new corporation. It is, however, a bit more difficult to go the other way, as you must pay capital gains tax on the appreciation.

● *Disadvantages*

While the LLC does offer a lot of flexibility over other forms, it does have a few disadvantages that you should consider.

▶ Unlike a partnership or sole proprietorship, you must pay a filing fee when you form the LLC.

▶ It is probably not a good form if you will have a large number of members as it will be difficult to reach consensus among the owners, who may also be the managers of the LLC.

▶ It is not a separate tax paying entity. Earnings and losses are passed through to the members to be taxed at their individual tax rate, so members must make quarterly estimated tax payments to the IRS.

▶ If all the members do not elect to actively manage the LLC, the LLC ownership interests may be treated like securities by your state and the Securities and Exchange Commission (SEC). This means that if you don't qualify for an exemption (and most small LLCs do), you must register the sale of your member interests with the SEC. You can find out the requirements for an exemption by visiting the SEC web site at www.sec.gov/smbus/qasbsec. htm#eod6.

LLCs are also becoming a popular vehicle for companies that may have global investors, because the S-corporation does not permit foreign ownership. You should consult an attorney to find out whether this form is available in your state. The attorney can help you understand and abide by the requirements associated with the LLC.

One ambitious entrepreneur knew that she wanted her furniture importing business to be global in all its aspects. She even intended to bring in investors from among her business acquaintances around the world because that would help her find the important contacts she needed to be successful. As an importer, she needed liability protection but did not want the high tax rates she would have with a corporation. Friends had told her about the S-corporation that would solve the tax problem, but her attorney advised her to consider the LLC as her choice of legal form because it would allow her to have foreign investors.

Professional Corporations

State laws permit certain professionals such as health care professionals, engineers, accountants, and lawyers to form corporations called professional service corporations. Anyone who holds shares in the corporation must be licensed to provide the service it offers.

The LLC form of organization is also available to professions, but in a special form known as a professional limited liability company (PLLC). Under this form, the member is only liable for his or her own malpractice, not that of other members. Some states also offer the limited liability partnership (LLP), which protects you from the malpractice claims of your partners but not from other partnership debts.

The Nonprofit Corporation

It is not outside the realm of possibility for a nonprofit corporation to be a high-growth, world-class company; however, it is not generally started with that goal in mind. A nonprofit corporation is a corporation established for charitable, public (e.g., scientific, literary, or educational), religious, or mutual benefit (e.g., trade associations, tennis clubs) purposes as recognized by federal and state laws. Some additional examples of typical nonprofits are

- Child care centers
- Schools
- Religious organizations
- Hospitals
- Museums
- Shelters
- Community health care facilities

Like the C-corporation, the nonprofit corporation is a legal entity and offers its shareholders and officers the benefit of limited liability. There is a common misconception that nonprofit corporations are not allowed to make a profit. As long as the business is not set up to benefit a single person and is organized for a nonprofit purpose, it can make a profit on which it is not taxed if it has also met the IRS test for a tax-exempt status. However, income derived from for-profit activities is subject to income tax.

There are two distinct hurdles that nonprofit corporations must overcome if they want to operate as a nonprofit corporation and have tax-exempt status:

1. Meeting the state requirements for being designated a nonprofit corporation that can operate as such in a given state, and

2. Meeting the federal and state requirements for exemption from paying taxes (IRS 501(c)(3)) by forming a corporation that falls within the IRS's narrowly defined categories.

● *Advantages*

Nonprofit organizations offer many advantages to entrepreneurs seeking to be socially responsible or just start a business from something they love doing that helps others.

▶ The nonprofit with tax-exempt status is attractive to corporate donors who can deduct their donations as a business expense.

▶ You can seek cash and in-kind contributions of equipment, supplies, and personnel.

▶ You can apply for grants from government agencies and private foundations.

▶ You may qualify for tax-exempt status, which means that your nonprofit is free from paying taxes on income generated from nonprofit activities.

In forming the nonprofit corporation, the entrepreneur gives up proprietary interest in the corporation and dedicates all the assets and resources of the corporation to tax-exempt activities. If a nonprofit corporation is ever dissolved, its assets must be distributed to another tax-exempt organization.

● *Disadvantages*

There are few disadvantages to a nonprofit organization. For example,

▶ You cannot distribute any profits earned by the corporation.

▶ You cannot contribute money to political campaigns or engage in lobbying.

▶ Nonprofits do not have shareholders or owners but simply members.

▶ You do not own your nonprofit, so you can't sell it. If your directors decide to dissolve it, they must distribute all the remaining assets after paying all debts to another tax-exempt nonprofit.

▶ The nonprofit cannot make substantial profits from unrelated activities and it must pay taxes on the profits it does make.

You might not think of musical theater companies as nonprofit organizations, but James Blackman had no doubt that this was the form of choice for the Civic Light Opera of South Bay Cities in California, one of the top musical theater companies on the West Coast. The nonprofit form would allow Blackman to receive donations from corporations and grants from foundations to support his efforts in the community with the physically challenged. It would also allow him to sell tickets to performances and make a profit, as long as that profit was not distributed but remained in the company. More importantly, he would meet the requirements for tax exemption and that would allow him to keep more money in the business to help it grow.

Making the Decision

Now that you have a good grounding in the different legal forms, you're in a better position to make a decision about what's right for your business. Before doing that, however, ask yourself several very important questions.

1. Do you and your team have all the skills needed to run this venture?

2. Do you have the capital required to start the business alone or must you raise it through cash or credit?

3. Will you be able to run the business and cover your living expenses for the first year?

4. Are you willing and able to assume personal liability for any claims against your business?

5. Do you wish to have complete control over the operation of the business?

6. Do you expect to have initial losses or will the business be profitable almost from the beginning?

7. Do you expect to sell your business some day?

The answers to these questions will narrow your choices. Then it's always wise to get the advice of an attorney and/or accountant. For example, if you expect to have initial losses, say, in the first year due to product development or other large start-up costs (question #6), you may want to choose a form that allows those losses to pass through to be taxed at your personal income rate. Since your company is not yet generating income, by doing this you will be able to shelter your other personal income from a tax liability. Sole proprietorships, partnerships, S-corporations, and limited liability companies all permit pass-through earnings and losses.

It's also good to know where you plan to take your business in the future because you will want to choose either a form that you won't have to change or one that you can easily shift to when the time is right. For example, suppose you plan to offer shares of stock in your company at some point in the future. To accomplish that, your company will need to become a corporation or LLC, so if you started as a sole proprietor, you will need to file incorporation or LLC papers in the state in which you will be doing business. The next section considers the issues of evolving from one form to another.

Evolving from One Legal Form to Another

As is clear from the previous sections, growing businesses often move from one legal form to another as their needs change. Consider the following example.

Suppose your spouse is a highly paid executive for a major corporation, making it possible to develop a product you've been playing around with. You decide to set up a small business with a shop near your home. You are not worried about medical insurance because you are already covered by your spouse's company. However, you need to limit your liability, because you and your spouse have acquired a number of valuable assets and you don't want those to be in danger should things go badly. You realize that in any business dealing with products, some liability issues crop up and you want to make sure you're covered.

In the beginning, you expect losses as you purchase equipment, build your prototypes, and test them in the market. Once you launch your product, you probably will have continuing losses because you're promoting your business, finding space outside your home to lease, and hiring new employees, and that takes a lot of money. But you have big plans for this business; in fact, within a year of introducing the product, you expect to need venture capital to be able to grow as fast as the market demands. You also see an IPO in your future. What is the best legal strategy given these circumstances?

In the beginning, during product development, it often doesn't make sense to use a more formal form such as a corporation. A simple sole proprietorship or partnership (if there's more than one person involved) will solve both needs. In this case, the liability to your family assets would be small. But the minute you grow out of the home environment and take on the responsibilities of a lease and employees, you must consider either being heavily insured or moving to a legal form with limited liability. In our example, you were moving the business to a leased location and hiring employees. Since there would still be losses and you would want to use them to shelter other income, you might consider either the S-corporation or the LLC, depending on the degree of flexibility you need. In any case, at the point at which you decided to seek venture capital and/or an IPO, you would need to convert to a C-corporation.

As you can see, the legal form of an organization is not a static decision, but rather one based on the needs of the company at the time of formation and into the future. Choosing the legal structure of the new venture is one of the most important decisions an entrepreneur can make, for it affects the tax strategy of the company for years to come. The correct selection depends on the type of venture the entrepreneur is starting, the profits the venture generates, the personal tax bracket of the entrepreneur, the assets used by the business, its potential for growth, and state laws. Again, particularly in the case of corporations and LLCs, it is important that an attorney review the documents to ensure that you have followed the rules and will receive all of the benefits to which the business is entitled.

NEW VENTURE CHECKLIST

Have you:
- ☐ Decided on the legal form that will best suit your business?
- ☐ Completed the necessary agreements for the legal form you have chosen (partnership agreement, articles of incorporation, and so forth)?
- ☐ Met the test for tax exemptions under IRC 501(c)(3) if you are founding a nonprofit corporation?

ISSUES TO CONSIDER

1. Assuming you were running a successful business as a sole proprietorship, what would induce you to change the legal form to a corporation?

2. Why would you choose an LLC form over a partnership or an S-corporation?

3. What kinds of businesses are well suited to the nonprofit legal structure?

EXPERIENCING ENTREPRENEURSHIP

1. Interview an attorney about the various forms of legal ownership. Using a business that you might want to start, get his or her advice about the best form to use for your type of business.

2. Visit an entrepreneur whose business is set up as a partnership. What kind of experience has setting up the business been for the partners? How have they divided up the duties and responsibilities? What key issues have they covered in their partnership agreement?

ADDITIONAL SOURCES OF INFORMATION

Bagley, C.E., and C.E. Dauchy (1998). *The Entrepreneur's Guide to Business Law.* Mason, OH: Southwestern Publishing.

Clifford, D., and R.E. Warner (1997). *The Partnership Book.* Berkeley, CA: Nolo Press.

Diamond, M.R., and J.L. Williams (2000). *How to Incorporate: A Handbook for Entrepreneurs and Professionals.* New York: John Wiley.

Warda, M. (2000). *How to Form a Non-Profit Corporation.* Newington, CT: Sphinx Press.

Whitman, M.N. (1999). *New World, New Rules: The Changing Role of the American Corporation.* Boston: Harvard Business School Press.

INTERNET RESOURCES

Biz Filings Incorporated
http://www.bizfilings.com/index.html

A web site that provides information and guidance in determining a legal form of organization as well as the ability to create that form online.

Findlaw
http://www.findlaw.com/

Provides a wealth of resources on the law, including cases, codes, and forms.

Internet Legal Resource Guide
http://www.ilrg.com/

A comprehensive web site containing information on the law and attorneys.

NOLO Law for All
http://www.nolo.com/index.html

A comprehensive web site with legal information and tools.

RELEVANT CASE STUDIES

Case 1   Mrs. Gooch's

Case 2   Franchising a Dying Business

13

Management and Operations Strategy

*Until someone has a small business,
they have no comprehension of how
hard it is. People who start businesses
from scratch, if they survive, are the
toughest people on the face of the earth.*
Sue Szymczak, Safeway Sling

Overview

Organization: The way the business works

Location: Finding the appropriate business site

People: Organizing the start-up team

PROFILE 13.1

You Won't Find This Fender on a Car

If your company and its products achieve the enviable position of being the brand in the industry, be prepared for an uproar if you ever make major changes. Fender Musical Instruments can attest to that. Its clients, who range from Bruce Springsteen to Eric Clapton and Travis Tritt, love their Fender guitars because "they're as close to perfection as anything gets." And that has been true for fifty years. Actually, in the 1950s Leo Fender revolutionized the music industry when he introduced his solid-body electric guitars—the Telecaster and the Stratocaster—to the music industry in a market niche and soon set the standard.

In the late 1970s, however, a recession hit, interest rates soared, and Fender's famous quality began to take a precipitous slide. William Schultz, then an executive for CBS, organized a buyout and in 1985 acquired the name and distribution, taking the company private. At that point Fender was manufacturing only twelve guitars a day, as musicians were becoming entranced with music synthesizers. Schultz, however, succeeded in implementing a total quality management plan that would make Fender profitable every year from 1985 on. Fender now produces more than 335,000 guitars annually, all presold.

Schultz's plan revisited the organization of his business and focused on five areas that needed improvement.

1. **The management team.** *Schultz put together a group of people who had musical backgrounds and were as passionate about Fender as he. As a team, they would carry the vision.*

2. **Location.** *He moved the guitar factory from Orange County, California, eastward to less pricey Corona in Riverside County. This allowed the company to focus its resources on production and quality.*

3. **Quality.** *Schultz invested in state-of-the-art woodworking machines, so that quality would be consistent. He also trained every worker in quality control procedures and efficiency and incorporated inspecting for quality into the manufacturing process, so that every guitar would be defect-free.*

4. **Customization.** *Schultz created a separate custom shop to meet the needs of customers requesting guitars designed and hand-built to their exact specifications. These customers have a wait of up to one year and pay between $1,500 and $50,000.*

5. **Core competency.** *One of the outstanding things Schultz did was return Fender to what it had been doing best when it was the industry leader in the late 1950s*

and 1960s. To win back loyal customers, he reissued some of the original designs and updated 1940s low-tech vacuum-tube amps that were preferred by professional musicians.

Today, Fender Musical Instruments has come of age and is creating the best guitars possible, using Silicon Graphics Indy workstations; blending science, music, and computer technology; and reducing time-to-market and material costs.

From this company that has successfully reinvented itself, the lesson for entrepreneurs is to maintain the vision at all costs, make sure your employees hold the vision as well, choose your business location carefully, focus on what you do best, and do it the best way you can.

SOURCES: Bob Spitz, "And on the Lead Guitar . . ." *Sky,* August 1996, p. 55; Fender Musical Instruments Corporation, "SiliconWorks Success Stories" (http://www.sgi.com/Works/SuccessStories/fender.html); http://www.fender.com/.

Once you know you have a feasible business concept, the process of developing a business plan will help you design and create a company to execute that concept. In the business plan, you will address the infrastructure, processes, and systems by which you will take the business from idea to reality. Therefore, it becomes important to consider how to organize the business effectively and profitably. Understanding how your business works—how information flows through the business—is critical to making decisions about business location, number of employees, management expertise required, and technology needed to facilitate business goals, to name just a few.

Three components make up the entrepreneurial organization: formal processes, people, and culture. Formal processes include the planning system, control mechanisms, compensation and reward policies, and other processes that make the organization run more efficiently and effectively. These processes are not independent units, but rather are linked to all functions of the organization that require them. For example, quality control mechanisms are not solely the purview of a single department, but flow from product development through manufacturing, to distribution, and throughout all the support functions needed to facilitate the process of getting the product to the customer.

People who work in market-oriented, entrepreneurial companies must think not only of their individual tasks but also of the product and company as a whole. People required to make the business work need to have team-building skills as well as the ability to make decisions and implement them with very little input from top management or the CEO. In new ventures those teams may consist of independent contractors whose skills are being "rented" on an as-needed basis. Informal networks create flexibility and speed up operations. They also have the advantage of managing the personal issues not easily handled through policies and structure.

Culture is fundamentally the personality of the organization, the reflection of the company's vision and goals. The culture that you want to create in your organization forms the basis for all the other activities that your company conducts. It is also the view of the company that customers see. An effective company culture enhances customer relationships, reduces employee turnover, and serves as a formidable competitive advantage for your company.

In this chapter you will learn some strategies for organizing the business and its many processes, finding an appropriate location, and organizing the start-up team that will implement all those processes.

Organization: The Way the Business Works

Organizing the business is a critical part of a plan to execute the business concept you created and tested during feasibility analysis. Fortunately, technology has facilitated new kinds of structures that allow businesses to compete more effectively in a rapidly changing, dynamic environment.[1] To help convey the essence of an organizational structure more effectively than a definition might, we will use one of the most commonly employed metaphors—improvisational jazz.[2] Jazz is distinguished from other forms of music by the way in which its musicians improvise on the core structure of the music. When the musician improvises, he or she changes the rhythms, alters the harmonies, and manipulates the melody, while preserving the core of the music. In other words, the musicians play around the structure; they do not play with it directly.[3] This is why jazz is so creative.

Because of limited resources and a creative and opportunistic mindset, entrepreneurs are naturals at improvisation—they are the jazz musicians of the business world—they can find ways to work around even the most rigid structure of a traditional bricks-and-mortar business model. For entrepreneurs, the jazz metaphor appropriately describes the kind of organizational structure that is probably most compatible with the new environment. What this means in organizational strategy terms is that improvisation is critical to success. Because entrepreneurial organizations reflect a fine balance between structure and chaos, they are innovative and creative. In that environment, entrepreneurs give free rein to new ideas and space to allow them to grow. Entrepreneurs in dynamic environments need to retain internally what the company does best and outsource the rest. In other words, focus on your core competencies until the company has established itself in the market. Then begin to look outside core competencies for new opportunities. You also need to look for ways to keep overhead—non–revenue-producing plant and equipment—to a minimum. Again, outsourcing and operating as a virtual enterprise will facilitate this. You will learn more about the virtual organization in a later section.

In Chapter 2, you learned about the importance of establishing a vision and goals for your business. We reiterate here that having goals in place is critical to all the decisions you will make about your organizational structure and the activities your business conducts. With these goals in mind, you can begin the process of identifying all the business processes or tasks and activities that will occur in your business on a daily basis. Knowledge of your business processes will help you make decisions about facility, equipment, and personnel as well as help you see how to streamline processes so that your business runs as efficiently and effectively as possible.

Identify Your Business Processes

One of the most eye-opening experiences you will have as an entrepreneur is identifying all the processes (activities, tasks, etc.) that occur in your business. Even more eye opening and revealing of how the business works is a process map that details how information flows through the business. To create such a map and make the job of defining the operations, information flow, and requirements of the business easier, take an imaginary tour of the business during a single day listing all the functions, people, equipment, supplies, and space required to run the business as you go. For example, as you enter the imaginary door of the business, ask yourself several questions:

1. Who does the work in this business?

2. Where do they work?

3. What do they need to do the work?

4. What information is being generated?

5. Where does that information go?

Then begin making lists of tasks, equipment, and people needed to complete a particular process or activity. This information will also be useful when you need to figure expenses for financial projections later on and when you determine what kind of personnel you need to hire to perform those tasks. You will learn more about how to find appropriate personnel in a later section of the chapter.

For example, suppose you have a packaging solutions business. When a customer approaches the site, what is the first thing he or she sees? The sign for business? A display window? When customers enter, is there a counter with someone who will answer their questions? What equipment does that person use to do his or her job? As you can see, you've already amassed quite a list of items and you have just entered the door of the business. The imaginary tour is one of the best ways to begin to detail the processes in your business. Take a look at Figure 13.1 for a graphic of one such imaginary tour of a service business. Understanding how your business works should help to clarify whether

FIGURE 13.1

Simple Business Process Flowchart for a Service Business

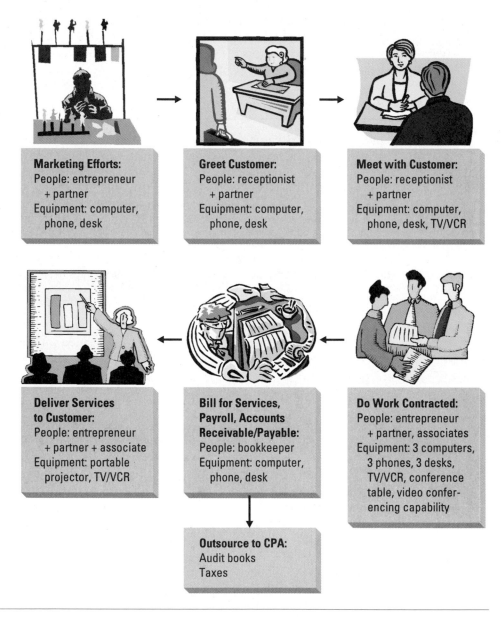

Marketing Efforts:
People: entrepreneur
  + partner
Equipment: computer,
  phone, desk

Greet Customer:
People: receptionist
  + partner
Equipment: computer,
  phone, desk

Meet with Customer:
People: receptionist
  + partner
Equipment: computer,
  phone, desk, TV/VCR

**Deliver Services
to Customer:**
People: entrepreneur
  + partner + associate
Equipment: portable
  projector, TV/VCR

**Bill for Services,
Payroll, Accounts
Receivable/Payable:**
People: bookkeeper
Equipment: computer,
  phone, desk

Do Work Contracted:
People: entrepreneur
  + partner, associates
Equipment: 3 computers,
  3 phones, 3 desks,
  TV/VCR, conference
  table, video confer-
  encing capability

Outsource to CPA:
Audit books
Taxes

you can employ a virtual organization structure or whether a traditional organizational structure is more appropriate.

The Virtual Organization

In the early 1990s, the virtual organization was a relatively new concept and certainly had yet to benefit from the technology of the Internet, which didn't reach the business sector in any significant way until 1995. The term **virtual enterprise** was borrowed from the science of virtual reality, which allows a person to become an integral part of a computer-generated, three-dimensional world. In business, a "virtual enterprise" has much the same purpose. The entrepreneur builds a company that to the rest of the world looks like any other company, but it is a business without walls where the entrepreneur does not incur the risk of acquiring employees, costly equipment, and enormous overhead. A virtual company makes it possible to operate the business from virtually anywhere—a home, car, or vacation cabin. The goal of the virtual enterprise is to deliver to the customer the highest-quality product at the lowest possible cost in a timely manner. To do this requires the participation and management of the entire distribution channel from producer to customer through a series of strategic alliances. Traditionally this was accomplished by building the business to the point where it could afford to buy out its suppliers and/or distributors, giving the company more control over quality and delivery. This strategy is known as vertical integration. Today that same goal can be accomplished through strategic partnerships with other companies in the value chain. Verifone was one of the first companies to employ the virtual organization structure (or lack of it). In 1982, when it launched its first credit authorization box, it had five people in four different locations, few resources, and huge competitors like AT&T and GTE.[4] Verifone quickly discovered that the very bigness and centralization of these companies worked in Verifone's favor because it was agile and flexible and could make changes rapidly. That virtual strategy turned out to be the secret of its success as Verifone garnered 70 percent of its market. In the next few sections, we'll consider aspects of the virtual organization in more detail.

Outsourcing in a Virtual World

Today it is much more difficult for a new venture to accomplish total in-house control of its value chain. The global marketplace is more complex, time-to-market has decreased, and it is difficult for any one company to have the necessary expertise for mastering all the functional levels of the distribution channel. Today a growing company is more likely to increase its flexibility by choosing one function to concentrate on, its core competency, and subcontracting functions it does not want to handle. The general rule is, if the resources to manufacture, assemble, and distribute the product effectively already exist in the market in which you wish to do business, don't duplicate the process. Outsource it. Often a business whose competitive advantage lies in proprietary rights to its product will choose to maintain control of strategic functions and outsource such things as warehousing, transportation, and some aspects of marketing. A retailer may outsource administrative functions like payroll, accounting, and inventory management and may even lease its employees from an employee leasing company while operating the company in the virtual world of the Internet. Becoming a virtual company lets the new venture be more innovative, closer to the customer, and quicker to market. Today many companies outsource aspects of their business processes, but virtual organizations outsource everything except their core management function. To their customers, they look like any other company, but behind the public image lies a very different kind of organization—one where the entrepreneur is basically a ringmaster in a three-ring circus.

Forming a Network of Strategic Alliances

Yet another way that virtual companies become more flexible and responsive is by forming strategic alliances or teams of businesses to share resources and reduce costs. These alliances are more than simply sources of capability for the entrepreneurial venture; they are the glue that holds the venture together. Strategic alliances are more like true partnerships. They may purchase major equipment jointly, or share the costs of research and development and of training. Particularly in the area of R&D, it is very difficult for any one small company to manage the expense alone. Networking and business alliances allow smaller businesses to bid successfully against large companies. They offer the convenience and savings of one source for everything, shared quality standards, and coordination of vendors. The key to successfully managing a small-business alliance is being willing to share internal information such as manufacturing processes, quality control practices, and product information for the good of all. Strategic alliances as funding sources are discussed in Chapter 17.

Building a virtual company and dealing with strategic alliances is not without problems. For the entrepreneurial team that wants to maintain control of every aspect of the growing venture, it is frustrating to have to give up some of that control to other companies. Getting virtual partners to meet entrepreneurs' demands for quality, timeliness, and efficiency can also be a long and difficult process. Consequently, it is important that the entrepreneur and the virtual partner come to written agreement on their duties and responsibilities and that they both enjoy the benefits of the relationship. Many entrepreneurs have found that the benefits of virtual partners far outweigh the problems and that the virtual corporation is the most efficient and effective way to get the venture off the ground.

Technology has contributed to helping start-up ventures perform like major corporations for relatively little money. Computer networks, user-friendly software, and the Internet allow new ventures to do things that previously required experts. Electronic networks make it easier to communicate with strategic alliance partners and to access commercial information databases around the world. Computerizing control systems on machine tools permits growing entrepreneurial manufacturers to compete with major companies. But don't make the mistake of thinking that becoming a virtual company is as easy as purchasing the right technology. On the contrary, there are management issues unique to this type of business, and they must be understood. Look at Profile 13.2 and the next section to learn what these management challenges are and how to solve them.

Keeping Virtual Employees and Partners Linked

One of the important challenges of virtual organization strategy is keeping everyone connected and in touch when they're geographically separated. A virtual company may be a great way to keep overhead down and flexibility up, but it is no substitute for human contact and face-to-face communication. Even in a virtual environment it's important to

- Conduct a face-to-face meeting at least once every three to six months. Arrange for employees and partners in specific geographic regions to meet regularly in between company-wide meetings.

- Create a discussion area on your company's Intranet and encourage everyone to share important information and discussion points.

- Set up a regular conference call once a week to stay in touch.

- Investigate videoconferencing. There are companies like Kinkos that rent video time to companies and individuals. You can determine if such an option makes economic sense for your company.

Online Help for Virtual Companies

With virtual companies growing by leaps and bounds, online companies have sprung up to provide services and products these businesses might need. Here are some examples (you can find resources in these areas at the end of the chapter):

- *Management team:* Many web sites aggregate independent professionals and help you find experienced financial management on a small budget.

- *Workers:* At several online sites, you can accomplish your public relations, marketing, direct mail, and even market research for far less than it would cost you to hire a marketing firm.

- *Supply chain management:* Online companies will do everything from order management to assembly, configuration, and packaging, to e-commerce fulfillment and collaboration.

PROFILE 13.2

Gizmos Well Suited to a Virtual World

What does it feel like to be a one-man floating corporation in the San Francisco Bay. Ask Timothy Simon, and he'll tell you it's a lot of fun. Simon designs unusual products for companies like Sharper Image and Brookstone from his sixty-foot sailboat. Instead of putting his money into office rent, he puts it into technology. To manufacture his gizmos, he works with independent contractors and manufacturers over the Internet. The products range from motorized tie racks to snore abatement devices—no rocket science here, but this unusual tinkerer claims over $7 million in annual revenues.

By choosing to operate his business as a virtual corporation, he has reduced the stress of overhead and has been able to balance his life by living the lifestyle he wants to. Of course, working with virtual partners requires some due diligence. To avoid problems when working with other companies in strategic alliances or in independent contractor relationships, be sure to do the following:

• Investigate the company's track record and assure yourself that it is trustworthy. This can be accomplished by checking with its customers, vendors, and distributors.

• Always remember that the contracting company doesn't know your customers' needs the way you do, and it is more worried about keeping all its own customers happy than about yours. Let contractors know specifically what your customers need.

• Make sure your subcontractors and partners understand the big picture. Otherwise, outsourcing all of your business's activities can be a coordination nightmare. Explain how the whole process works.

• Educate subcontractors and partners as to how your business works and what you must do to satisfy your customers.

• Create a situation where contractors have a vested interest in seeing your business succeed. Usually this will happen if you can demonstrate to them that your company holds the potential to provide them with a new, untapped market.

Source: Tom Post, "Floating Design Palace," *Forbes,* December 14, 1998; Courtney H. Price and Kathleen Allen, *Tips and Traps for Entrepreneurs; Real-Life Ideas and Solutions for the Toughest Problems Facing Entrepreneurs,* 1998, McGraw-Hill Publishing.

● *The Traditional Bricks-and-Mortar Enterprise*

Perhaps the two biggest differences that separate bricks-and-mortar (B&M) businesses from virtual ones are flexibility and cost. B&M businesses by their very nature are not as flexible as virtual businesses. They are confined to a physical location that defines much of the success of the business. That physical location also contributes to their relatively higher cost to operate so B&M businesses must make more sales to achieve the same level of profit as a virtual company. While B&M businesses may outsource some of their activities, the majority of their processes are conducted in-house. Because of that fact, location and facility have an important impact on the way the business operates. In the next sections you will learn how to choose an appropriate site for your type of business.

Location: Finding the Appropriate Business Site

A significant part of the organizing process is finding an appropriate site for doing business. You may already be familiar with the three key factors for determining value in real estate: "location, location, location." The location of the business has a serious impact on its success. Location determines who will see the business, how easily they can find it and access it (Is the business at ground-floor level and easily seen? Or out of sight in a multi-story building?), and whether or not they will want to access it (Is the neighborhood safe? Is parking available?). Even businesses like manufacturing, where the customer doesn't come to the site, benefit from a location near major sources of transportation. Since many business owners view their business site as permanent, selecting the best site becomes one of the most crucial decisions to make, one that will need to be justified to the readers of the business plan. Site decisions begin at a macro level with the state or region of the country and work their way down to the parcel on which the facility is located.

● *Choosing the Region or State and Community*

Locating a site for a new business normally begins with identifying the area of the country that seems best suited to the type of business being started. "Best suited" may mean that firms in your industry tend to congregate in a particular region, such as the high-tech firms that gravitate to Route 128 in Massachusetts or to Silicon Valley in California. For some businesses "best suited" may mean that a state is offering special financial and other incentives for businesses to locate there. In other cases, "best suited" means a manufacturer's choosing to locate near major suppliers. Often the entrepreneur starts the business in a particular region because that's where he or she happens to live. This may be fine during the incubation period, but the area must be considered carefully for what it contributes to the potential success of the business.

Of course, there is another important factor that must be included in the decision mix, and that is the entrepreneur's desire for a certain lifestyle. Sometimes the desire to maintain a particular lifestyle in a particular location far outweighs the potential negative effects of locating the business in a less than optimal location. Mo Siegal, founder of Celestial Seasonings, was one such entrepreneur. He was adamant about remaining in his beloved Colorado when he started his now enormously successful venture. Doing business there may have cost more and may not have been as convenient for shipping purposes, but the ability to run his business from his hometown was more important. In fact, as it turns out, the image of Colorado with its Rockies, cool streams, and beautiful blue skies depicted on the packaging actually enhanced the perception of his herbal teas. On the other hand, Heidi Lang started her business, Transatlantic Marketing Group (TMG), in Toronto, Canada in 1995 when her husband was transferred there.

Her product was private-label frames, which she sold to retailers, but she soon discovered that the majority of her customers were in the United States. Tired of traveling, she decided to move the business to Jacksonville, Florida, because she loved the ocean. But the move also made business sense because she wanted to make major changes in her personnel and moving the business made that job easier. In 2000, she was on track to grow 55 percent.[5]

Economic Base

The **economic base** of a region or community is simply the major source of income for the area. Communities are viewed as primarily industrial, agricultural, or service-oriented. In general, industrial communities export more goods out of the community than they import into it. For example, suppose the community's principal income is derived from farming and the associated products it ships to other communities. This activity brings money into the community. Now suppose the citizens of the community must travel to another community to do major shopping. This activity takes money out of the community. The important thing to learn about the community is whether the money brought in from farming exceeds the money leaving for shopping. If it does, the community appears to have a growing economic base, which is a favorable factor for new businesses.

You can learn more about the economic base of any community in which you are interested by contacting the state or regional economic development agency in the area. These organizations exist to bring new business into the region, so they have to stay on top of what is going on. They can give you all the statistics you will need on the economic condition of the region as well as estimate the cost of doing business there. Also check the U.S. Department of Commerce web site at www.doc.gov.

Financial Incentives

Most community governments are faced with cash needs that go well beyond the tax tolerance level of their citizens; consequently, they work diligently with economic development agencies to attract new businesses and the accompanying tax revenues into the community. One of the ways they attract businesses is by offering incentives such as lower taxes, cheaper land, and employee training programs. Some communities have enterprise zones, which give the businesses that locate in them favorable tax treatment from the state based on the number of jobs created, as well as lower land costs and rental rates. They also expedite permit processes and help in any way they can to make the move easier.

Look carefully, however, at communities that offer up-front cash in compensation for the community's lack of up-to-date infrastructure. They may be hiding a high corporate tax rate or some other disincentive that could hurt your business's chances of success. In general, the larger the incentives, the more careful you should be in doing your homework.

● *Demographics*

In addition to studying the economic base and the community's attitude toward new business, look carefully at the population base. Is it growing or shrinking? Is it aging or getting younger? Is it culturally diverse? The level and quantity of disposable income in the community will indicate whether there is enough money to purchase whatever you are offering.

Demographic information is usually based on the U.S. census, which tracks changes in population size and characteristics. The United States is divided into **Standard Metropolitan Statistical Areas** (SMSAs), which are geographic areas that include a major metropolitan area like Los Angeles or Houston. These are further divided into census tracts, which contain approximately 4,000–5,000 people, and neighborhood blocks. With this information you can readily determine, for example, if the city in which you want to locate a new software development firm has enough people with sufficient technical and educational skills to support it. Population data also indicate the number of people available to work. Demographic data is easily obtained from the economic development agency, the public library, the Internet, or the post office, which tracks populations by zip code.

● *Choosing a Retail Site*

With a retail business, the entrepreneur is dealing directly with the consumer, so naturally, one of the first considerations is being near the customers. Since a retail business lives or dies based on the number of consumers who have access to the business, it is important to locate where there are suitable concentrations of consumers.

The Trade Area

The **trade area** is the region from which the entrepreneur expects to draw customers. The type of business will determine to a large extent the size of the trade area. For example, if the business sells general merchandise that can be found almost anywhere, the trade area is much smaller, as customers will not travel great distances to purchase common goods. Yet a specialty outlet—for example, a clothing boutique with unusual apparel—may draw people from other communities as well.

Once the location within the community is identified, you can calculate the trade area. With a map of the community, designate the site for the business; then, using a compass, place the point of the compass on the proposed site and draw a circle that represents the distance (the radius) you expect people to drive to reach the site. Within the circle is the trade area, which can now be studied in more detail. Using the demographics and a census tract map, identify census tracts within the trade area and look at the census data to determine how many people reside within the boundaries of the trade area. (See Figure 13.2.) The

FIGURE 13.2

Sample of a Trade Area

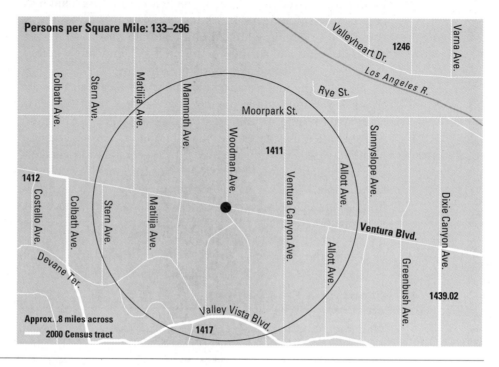

Source: www.census.gov.

demographic information will also describe these people in terms of education level, income level, average number of children, and so forth.

Competition and Character

Within the trade area, you can also identify the competition. To do this, drive or walk through the area (assuming it is not too large) and spot competing businesses. Note their size and number, and also gauge how busy they are at various times of the day by observing their parking lots or actually entering the business. If competitors are located in shopping malls or strip centers, look for clusters of stores similar to yours and low vacancy rates. This would indicate a strong attraction for the site. Look at the stores near your proposed site to check for compatibility. Often, locating near a competitor is a wise choice because it encourages comparison shopping. Observe the character of the area. Does it appear to be successful and well maintained? Remember that the character of the area will have an impact on your business.

Accessibility

It is important to identify the routes your customers might take to reach the proposed site: highways, streets, and public transportation routes. If the site is difficult to locate and hard to reach, you can be certain potential customers will not expend the effort to find you. Also check the parking situation. Most communities require a sufficient amount of parking space for new construction, through either lots or garages; however, in some older areas, street parking is the only available option. If parking is hard to find or too expensive, you will lose customers.

Do a foot and car traffic count for your proposed site to determine how busy the area is. Remember, retail businesses rely heavily on traffic for customers. Whether or not you need a high volume of foot traffic is a function of the type of business. Obviously, a coffee house benefits immensely from a high volume of foot traffic, whereas it may not be as vital for a warehouse hardware store. A traffic count is easily accomplished by positioning yourself near the targeted site and tallying the customers going by and into the business. City planning departments and transportation departments maintain auto traffic counts for major arterials in the city.

● Choosing the Service/Wholesale Site

If a service or wholesale business has customers who come to the place of business, the needs for a site will parallel those of the retailer in some respects. Accessibility, attractiveness, and a trade area of sufficient size are all key factors in the selection of a site. The entrepreneur does not, however, need to choose from the more expensive commercial sites, as the expectations of the customers may not be as great for a wholesale outlet that sells to the public, for example. Customers going to these types of businesses usually want to save money, so they don't expect the Cadillac version of a business site. Some service businesses, on the other hand, require attractive office space that is easily accessible. These are usually professional businesses—lawyers, accountants, consultants, and so forth. The image they present through the location and appearance of their offices is crucial to the success of the business.

● Choosing the Manufacturing Site

For the manufacturer, the location choices narrow significantly. Communities have zoning laws that limit manufacturing companies to certain designated areas away from residential, retail, and office commercial sites so as to reduce the chance of noise, odor, and pollutants affecting the citizens. Often these areas are known as industrial parks, and they usually are equipped with electrical power and sewage plants appropriate to manufacturing. By locating in one of these parks, the new business may also benefit from the synergy of other manufacturing nearby. Opportunities for networking and sharing resources and costs are enhanced.

Another common location for manufacturing is **enterprise zones,** which are public–private partnerships designed to bring jobs to inner cities, downtown areas, and rural areas suffering from the shift of jobs and population to the suburbs. The draw for businesses is tax incentives, regulatory relief, and employee training programs. Tom Hursman of Spectrum MedSystems Corporation in Irvine, California wanted to launch a new line of business—a manufacturing plant that produced a plastic insert for work boots. Through some investigation, he learned that if he relocated this new business to an economic-development zone in Syracuse, New York he would save a lot of money, qualify for low-interest rate loans, get free land from the city, and qualify for discounted electricity. Logistically, the site was closer to his customers as well.

However, the enterprise or economic development zone program is not without its critics. The principal criticism is that there is no net economic gain for the community. Since businesses often move from one area of town to the enterprise zone simply to take advantage of tax breaks, no new jobs are created. Still another criticism comes from established businesses in the area that complain that the zones are nothing but incubators for competitors. In spite of these criticisms, enterprise zones are likely to continue as one method for creating jobs and rebuilding decaying inner cities. You can find out where the empowerment zones are in your state by going to the U.S. Housing and Urban Development Agency web site at www.hud.gov/ezec/locator/.

Wherever you look for a manufacturing site, you are concerned with four key factors: access to suppliers, cost of labor, access to transportation, and cost of utilities. These factors may not be equally weighted. Depending on the type of manufacturer, one or more factors may have greater importance in evaluating a site.

Access to Suppliers

Manufacturers and processors usually try to locate within a reasonable distance of their major suppliers to cut shipping time and save transportation costs. Certainly a food processor attempts to set up business near the growing fields, so that the food is as fresh as possible when it arrives at the processing plant. Similarly, a manufacturer that uses steel as one of its main raw materials might want to locate in the same region of the country as the steel mills to save the high costs of trucking heavy steel great distances.

Cost of Labor

Today many manufacturers choose a location on the basis of the cost of labor, rather than proximity to suppliers, since labor is generally the single highest cost in the production of goods. Wages and laws relating to workers, such as workers' compensation, vary from state to state, and sometimes from city to city. For example, California laws and cost of living tend to make it a more expensive place to hire employees than those same employees might cost in Missouri.

Some labor-intensive businesses have found that the only way they can compete is by having plants in Mexico or China, where labor costs are a fraction of those in the United States, and where laborers are not protected by as many laws. Mattel Toy Company, for example, has a plant in China to produce the hundreds of different toys it markets every year. The bottom line is that the entrepreneur must weigh carefully the costs in terms of access to labor when considering a particular location for a manufacturing plant.

Access to Transportation

Most manufacturers prefer to locate near major transportation networks: railways, major highways, airports, and ports of call. The reasoning is obvious: the greater the distance between the plant and a major transportation network, the higher the cost to the company and ultimately, to the customer. Also, the more transportation people who handle the product, the greater the cost. Thus, in terms of simple economics, to remain competitive, manufacturers must consider the cost benefit of locating away from a major transportation network. Higher transportation costs will result in a smaller profit margin for the company or higher costs for the customers. Either way, you lose.

Cost of Utilities

Utility rates vary from state to state, and usually from city to city within a given state. If the new venture is heavily dependent on electricity, gas, or coal, this factor could be a significant variable in the cost of producing a product and therefore you should examine it carefully.

● The Building: The Lease-Build-Buy Decision

The land and location are only part of the equation. You must also carefully consider the type of building on the site. If the site contains an existing building, the question becomes whether to lease or buy. If the site is bare land, building a facility is the only choice. Because a significant portion of a new venture's start-up costs is contained in a facility, we will look at each of these scenarios in more detail. Also look at Table 13.1 for an overview of the broad criteria for the lease-build-buy decision.

The Existing Building

Finding an existing building on a site is probably the most common scenario. However, no matter how attractive the building and site, you must examine it carefully with the following considerations in mind:

  ▶ Is the building of sufficient size to meet current and reasonable future needs?

  ▶ Do the building and site allow for future expansion?

TABLE 13.1

The Lease-Build-Buy Decision

Stage of Business	Lease	Build	Buy
Start-up	A short-term lease will give the business a chance to determine its long-term requirements	At start-up, use this approach only when there is no facility available to meet the needs of the business because this approach takes capital and time.	Not recommended at start-up unless it is the only option and the company is sufficiently capitalized.
Rapid Growth at Start-up or Shortly Thereafter	A short-term lease will allow you to move to larger facilities to meet the growing demands of the business.	Resist building during rapid growth as it will use up precious cash needed for growth	Rapid growth is not the time to buy a facility unless the company has received a large infusion of cash from investors that more than meets its operational needs.
Stable Growth	If the location is appropriate to the growth needs of the company, a long-term lease will provide more stability.	With stable growth and positive cash flow, the company can afford to spend the time, effort, and capital to build a facility that specifically meets its needs.	Buying a building that allows for expansion is appropriate when company growth stabilizes and the company has matured with a loyal base of customers. It is also appropriate when the company needs to show a sizeable asset on its balance sheet. If the company needs cash for a new period of growth, it can sell the building to an investor and lease it back, providing an instant infusion of capital.

▶ Is there sufficient parking?

▶ Is there space for customers, storage, inventory, office space, and rest rooms?

Allowing for future growth is essential. Avoiding the extraordinarily high costs of moving and the potential for lost sales and time away from the fundamental work of the business while the business is in transition often offsets the initial higher cost of a larger building.

When examining an existing building, begin with the exterior and ask the following questions:

1. Does the building have curbside appeal, assuming customers will come to the site?

2. Is the building compatible with its surroundings?

3. Does it have enough windows of sufficient size?

4. Is the entrance inviting?

5. Is the signage attractive, and does it satisfy the local regulations?

6. Is the parking adequate to meet customer and employee demand and satisfy local building codes?

7. Does the interior of the building meet your needs in terms of walls, floors, and ceilings?

8. Are there sufficient lighting fixtures and outlets, and is there enough power to run equipment?

These are just a few of the questions to ask before finalizing a decision on a building. Most entrepreneurs can answer these eight questions to their own satisfaction, but to be certain the building is not hiding anything that could come back to haunt you and be costly for the business, it is wise to hire a licensed contractor or inspector to examine the building for structural soundness. In addition, it may be prudent to work with a real estate broker who regularly deals with these types of buildings.

Leasing a Building

The speed of change, innovation, and technological advancement has shortened and will continue to shorten product and service life cycles, and this has an impact on the facilities in which businesses operate. Also, buildings have long physical lives and typically are very expensive to refurbish and remodel. Both of these factors affect the decision to lease a building. Most entrepreneurs with start-up ventures will probably seek short leases of five years or less. In this way you do not tie up precious capital that you may not be able to recover should you need to expand to another facility or close the business in the event of failure. Although the short-term lease has the advantage of flexibility, it also carries some serious disadvantages.

▶ Rents are escalated more frequently, due to short-term renewal. Many a business has found itself in this awkward position. Demand for the product or service has been successful beyond initial predictions, so the business needs to remain in its current location beyond the terms of the lease. When the entrepreneur goes to renegotiate the lease terms, he or she inevitably finds that the landlord intends to raise the rent for a new lease. This is usually justified by increasing market rents; however, at the same time, the landlord is aware that it would be costly for the tenant to relocate. The business would have little time to do so and still maintain its current production rate. Furthermore, the potential for having to replace employees and create new logistics for suppliers and buyers is daunting. All these factors puts the entrepreneur in a very weak position to negotiate a new lease.

▶ To strengthen your position, negotiate up front a clause that permits the option to renew at a specified rate and an escape clause in case the business must be closed. These two clauses may cost a bit more initially but can yield long-term savings.

▶ It will be more difficult to remodel mid-term. If you have a short-term lease, the landlord will be less likely to approve any substantial tenant improvements if they do not increase the value of the building to future tenants.

▶ When the lease is first negotiated, come prepared with a five-year plan for the facility and be able to demonstrate the benefits to the landlord of allowing the remodeling of the building.

▶ You will not be able to show a substantial asset on the balance sheet. Therefore, it will not be a good vehicle for raising capital.

If you own the building, by contrast, you can later sell it to raise needed capital and lease it back, thereby avoiding moving costs and providing the new landlord with an instant tenant, a factor that increases the value of the building to the new owner.

The cost of leasing a building is a function of the demand in the marketplace for rentals as well as a number of other factors.

▶ Buildings that are newer, suitable for a variety of uses, and well located generally enjoy higher lease rates, as do buildings in short supply.

▶ Since rent is normally based on square footage of space, the larger the space, the more costly the lease.

▶ Retail and service business sites are generally more expensive than industrial sites.

▶ A retail site in a regional mall will likely be the most expensive.

Be aware, though, that while manufacturing sites enjoy low rental rates, manufacturers usually pay higher amounts for water, power, and sewerage. That is why it is worthwhile to consider all the costs related to leasing a facility. Not including the cost of expensive utilities or a common-use area fee could spell disaster to the business's cash flow.

Businesses face three basic types of leases.

1. **Gross lease.** You pay a fixed rate per month, with the landlord covering the cost (and getting the benefit) of insurance, taxes, and building operating expenses such as outdoor lighting, security, and so forth.

2. **Net lease** (also known as triple net). You pay a fixed monthly rate plus taxes and operating expenses—essentially everything but the mortgage and the building insurance, which the landlord pays.

3. **Percentage lease.** You may pay a percentage of your business's net income or a flat rate plus a percentage of the business's gross revenues. The latter is very common in retail operations. This is the most complicated of all the lease types because it has several variations.

Remember first and foremost that leases are written from the landlord's point of view and, therefore, are negotiable. The fact that something appears in printed form does not mean it is true or that you have to agree to it. A lease represents a significant portion of a business's overhead, and you will most likely have to live with it for a long time, so make sure it's what you really want. Leases are a great way for start-up businesses to get into the marketplace, but don't let your enthusiasm for starting the business blind you to the potentially disastrous terms of a poorly written lease. The best advice is to seek the assistance of an attorney who can represent your interests.

Buying a Building

If you have the resources, buying a building has some advantages. A valuable asset is immediately created on the balance sheet, which can be leveraged later on when growth capital is needed. For example, the building could be sold and leased back (called a **sale-leaseback**), withdrawing equity for other uses and negotiating favorable long-term lease terms. Sale-leasebacks are attractive options for investors, so these buildings generally sell quickly. Of course when you sell the building, you effectively lose control of it, so be certain to negotiate terms that allow you to remodel and extend the lease should you wish to do so.

One advantage of owning a building is that it can be traded in a **tax-deferred exchange** for other property you need. For example, suppose you own an office building but need a distribution warehouse to support a new direction your business is taking. You might take advantage of a tax-deferred exchange by trading the office building for the warehouse. The exchange would defer capital gains tax on the sale of the office, and you would have the warehouse you need.

Buying a building requires a contract, much like a lease agreement. It spells out the terms of the purchase and the items included and excluded from the purchase agreement. As always, read it carefully to make sure that what you agreed to verbally has been translated correctly on paper. It would be wise to hire a due diligence team (inspector, contractor, CPA, attorney) to inspect the building and the agreement so that your interests are protected.

Building the Facility

When you can't find the type of building in the location you want, building the facility from the ground up becomes the only option. This will entail an architect, permits, possibly zoning variances, a construction bidding process, off-site improvements (curbs, gutters, water and power lines, roads), and a lengthy building and inspection process. This option should not be undertaken without the aid of a licensed general contractor. Be sure to check the reputation of any contractor you are considering. This is important should the contractor have a dispute with any of the subcontractors hired for the various aspects of the job. The subcontractors have a right to lien the property you own. You will then have to sue the contractor to resolve the issue and remove the lien (you cannot receive a Certificate of Occupancy if any liens are present), and this is a time-consuming and costly process.

Constructing a building is no doubt the most complex option; however, you will end up with a building that completely meets your needs. This option is most suitable when the needs for the building and/or the location are unique, when you have the time to wait, and when you intend to remain in the facility long term.

● Alternatives to Conventional Facilities

Today business owners have a variety of alternatives to conventional business locations. These alternatives lower the cost of overhead and make it easier for a business to change its mind should the location not work out. We'll consider four of these alternative sites: incubators, shared space, mobile locations, and temporary tenant agreements.

Incubators

Some entrepreneurs find it helpful to start their new venture's life in a business incubator, which has the same purpose as an incubator for an infant—to create a controlled environment that will enhance the chances that the business will survive the start-up phase. Private and state-sponsored incubators can be found in nearly every region of the country for almost any type of business. Incubators offer space at a lower-than-market rate to several businesses, which may then share common support functions like receptionist, copy machine, and conference room. The incubator may even offer business courses and training to help new entrepreneurs with the myriad details involved in running the business. After about three to five years, depending on the incubator, the young business is helped to move into its own site elsewhere in the community.

Some incubators cater only to high-tech firms or to service firms. Others, like the Entrepreneur Partnership Program at the Mall of America in Bloomington, Minnesota, help entrepreneurs determine whether their retail or service businesses are suited to the demands of a major mall. This particular program helps the entrepreneur formulate a business plan and open a store. It also provides incentives such as waiving the costs of improving the store space and consulting in marketing and operations.

When considering an incubator, look at its track record and make sure it provides critical higher order needs like a network of contacts, access to expertise and capital, professional resources, and access to customers.

Shared Space

Another choice is to locate the company within the facilities of a larger company. As the largest of the chain stores continue to downsize, opportunities to take excess space arise. A variation on this theme is to lease a location that has enough space for you to sublease to a complementary business. For example, a copy service might lease excess space to a new computer graphics company or one that is seeking a new location. If you decide on a location that's good for your business, approach a complementary business in the area to see whether that company is interested in a shared arrangement.

Mobile Locations

One of the more interesting ways to introduce new businesses and new products/services to the marketplace is through the use of pushcarts and kiosks. This was the strategy of Bill Sanderson, president of CalCorn, Inc., which owned Popcorn Palace, a chain of boutique-type gourmet popcorn stores, before it was sold to Orville Redenbacher. The store's typical location is a high-traffic site in an upscale regional mall. This type of space is one of the most expensive in the mall; therefore, to test the potential viability of a new site, Sanderson often started with a pushcart location on that site before making a commitment to a long-term lease. Pushcarts and their more fixed alternative, the kiosk—a small booth—also allow a company to expand to many new locations without the high overhead of a conventional retail storefront.

Temporary Tenant Agreements

Some landlords have found that rather than sit on an empty space until the new tenant moves in, they can rent the space on a temporary basis so that their cash flow is not interrupted. In fact, the concept of the temporary tenant has grown so rapidly that there are now leasing agents who specialize in that area. The most successful of these temporary tenants have the following characteristics that seem to draw customers to them:

▶ Personalized merchandise

▶ Opportunities to sample the product

▶ Products that can be demonstrated

▶ Products that can be used for entertaining the customers.[6]

For the temporary concept to work, significant foot traffic and high customer turnover is required. This is an excellent alternative for retail businesses that want to test a location before making a major commitment.

Relying on experts to select a site is probably the best way to ensure a good decision. Armed with the information from the preceding sections, you can find the appropriate consultant for the type of business location you're seeking. The advantage to using consultants is that they have a duty of confidentiality, they generally are unbiased and take an objective view, and they take a broader view of the needs of the business than, say, a real estate broker who is representing specific properties.

People: Organizing the Start-up Team

While the organization of the business processes and the site for the business are critical aspects of the operational plan, it is people who implement those processes and use the company facility on a daily basis. The roles and responsibilities of people in the organization are typically depicted in an organizational chart. Compare in Figure 13.3 the traditional organizational chart, which tends to have layers or a hierarchy, with the distinctive entrepreneurial start-up, which is very flat structurally. The entrepreneur and the founding team often perform all the functions when the business is just starting and much of the work is accomplished through an informal organization or network of relationships. Informal networks of people consist of those who tend to gravitate toward each other in an effort to accomplish tasks in a more efficient and effective manner than may be dictated by the organizational chart. These networks form the shadow organizational structure that brings the business through an unexpected crisis, an impossible deadline, or a formidable impasse. They are social links that form the real power base in the organization. Metaphorically speaking, the organizational chart may be thought of as the skeleton of the body, while the informal network constitutes the arteries and veins that push information and activity throughout the organization—in other words, the lifeblood of the organization.

Research has found three types of informal networks: the advice network, which includes those people who are the problem solvers in the organization; the trust network, where political information is shared; and the communication

FIGURE 13.3

Traditional Line and Staff Organizational Chart for a Simple Manufacturing Plant

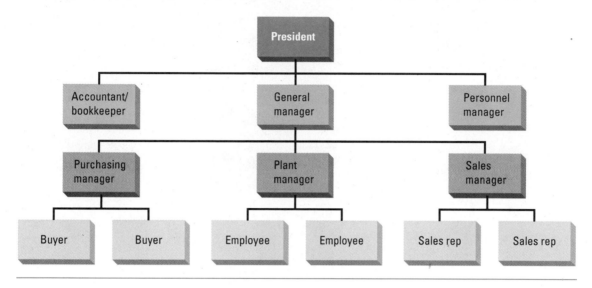

network, which consists of employees who discuss work-related issues on a frequent basis.[7] Often the people in these networks come from various functional areas in the organization that don't typically deal with each other on a daily basis. For example, the trust network might include the bookkeeper, a sales representative, and a plant employee.

Entrepreneurs seem to have recognized intuitively the value of informal networks in the organizational structure and often the most successful new ventures adopt a team-based approach with a flatter structure. Figure 13.4 depicts the nature of this structure. The lead entrepreneur is the driving force for the entrepreneurial team, which normally consists of people with expertise in at least one of the three functional areas of a new venture: marketing, operations, and finance. The organization consists of interactive, integrated teams. In the new venture, these are rarely "departments" in the traditional sense, but rather functions, tasks, or activities. The statistics reflect this pattern. Fifty-one percent of the growing companies that have made it to the *Inc. 500* list do not have a marketing director, while 61 percent have neither a COO nor a personnel director. Thirty-two percent do not have a CFO, and an astounding 67 percent have no one to manage information systems in their companies.[8]

What is the explanation for this? For one thing, entrepreneurs are usually too creative and flexible to be bound by the strictures of a formal organizational structure. They are more comfortable bringing together resources and people as a team and making decisions on the spot without having to go through layers of

FIGURE 13.4

An Entrepreneurial Organization

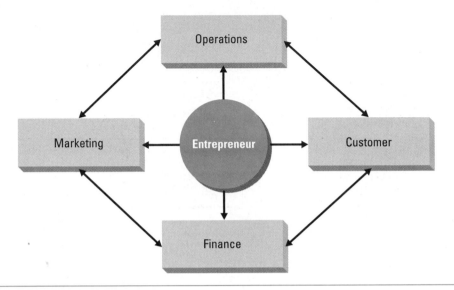

management. Another reason is that growing new ventures must be able to adapt quickly as they muscle their way into the market. Uncertainty and instability are a way of life for young ventures, and a rigid, formalized, bureaucratic structure would unduly burden a new venture both financially and operationally.

Teams come in many varieties: self-directed work teams, problem-solving teams, quality teams, cross-functional teams. Essentially they serve the same underlying purpose: "A team is a small number of people with complementary skills who are committed to a common purpose, set of performance goals, and approach for which they hold themselves mutually accountable.[9] What makes the entrepreneur's situation unique is that—at least when the venture is in the start-up or initial growing phases and capital resources are limited—the team the entrepreneur develops will most likely consist of several people outside the organization: namely, independent contractors. For example, you may decide to subcontract the manufacturing of a product to an established company. This means that you need to understand how that subcontractor works and will, of necessity, become a part of that company's team in the production of the product. Your marketing, sales, operations, and finance people must also be able to work with the manufacturing subcontractor to ensure that the goals of the new venture are met with the timeliness and level of quality desired. This requires the team to have skills not normally learned in school, skills such as diplomacy in the management of intra- and inter-team relationships, problem-solving skills, and the ability to take responsibility for innovative changes on the spot, often without your direct approval.

Hiring the Right Team

Today, with more employees suing their bosses for wrongful discharge, sexual harassment, and racial/gender/age discrimination, it is increasingly important that the entrepreneur understand how to hire. Hiring, however, is not a simple matter of placing a help-wanted ad in the newspaper, receiving résumés, and then holding interviews to select the best candidate. The bulk of the work of hiring comes before the person is actually needed.

Functions to Fill

Part of organizing the business is determining what positions are needed for the required tasks of the business. You did that when you created the flowchart of your business processes. If you have a start-up venture, you probably noticed that you are doing the biggest share of the work yourself, but at some point you will have to hire employees, even if just a receptionist or administrative assistant. Preparing profiles and job descriptions for all the functions of the business ahead of time ensures that you have them when you need them. Typically when entrepreneurs (and managers) develop job descriptions, they focus entirely on the duties and responsibilities of a particular job. While this is important, it is equally important to develop behavioral profiles of these jobs; in other words, what behavioral traits are typical of and vital to a particular position. An effective bookkeeper, for example, may require the following attributes: has detail orientation, is focused, can work alone, is responsible and organized. In addition to looking at desired behavioral traits for each position, the entrepreneur must have a good sense of the business culture. Even though a job candidate may have the education and experience required by the job description and display some of the behavioral traits necessary for success in the position, the candidate's chemistry may not fit in well with the culture of the organization. This is an important distinction because while education and experience can be achieved and behaviors can in most cases be taught, the right chemistry—which allows the new hire to fit in with the company culture—must already be present. In today's business environment, your company's culture is a competitive advantage, so hiring people to fit it becomes the most important goal with regard to hiring.

The Employee Search

The first and best place to look for an employee is among your current employees, subcontractors, or professional advisers. Referrals from people you know and trust who know the business have a greater likelihood of producing a successful hire. Therefore, if you can induce a key management person to leave an organization and join your business, that person might induce someone else you need later on to come as well. Even during start-up, be constantly on the look-out for good people who might come on board as the business grows.

Executive search firms are good sources for management positions, and on-line resources have become a good starting place for hiring, particularly with technically oriented positions. Companies like Monster.com (www.monster.com), Guru.com (www.guru.com), and MSN Job Hunt (http://content.jobhunt.careers.msn.com/) are places where qualified people post their resumes and it's easy to search for the particular skills you need.

The most important thing to know about any résumé you receive is that it is a selling document. The person is attempting to convince you to give him or her an interview. Therefore, expect most résumés to exaggerate a person's impor-tance somewhat. If a résumé indicates that a person has had a number of jobs in a relatively short period of time or a number of "very important" positions—vice president of this company and president of that company—it may mean that this person truly is in demand and has been wooed away from several companies, or it may mean that this person can't hold a job. Consequently, you need to think of the résumé as a screening tool to see whether the candidate has the requisite skills and experience. The more important information will be gained in the interview.

Interviews

Most entrepreneurs dread interviewing job candidates, primarily because they don't know what to say and don't understand that they should ask questions that get at the person's personality—how he or she might react in certain situa-tions. This can be accomplished in part by asking open-ended questions, ques-tions that call for more than "yes-no" answers. For example,

▶ What is your greatest strength?

▶ How would you handle the following hypothetical situation?

While the person is answering the questions, be careful to note the nonverbal communication being sent through body language. Does the person appear con-fident, at ease with what is being discussed? Does the person look at you directly? Does the person sit with a very closed posture (arms crossed as if to protect) or in a more open, relaxed manner? It is said that 90 percent of com-munication is nonverbal, so if you don't trust what a person is saying verbally, check to see whether the nonverbal signals match the verbal ones. This topic could cover an entire book in itself, so if you want to do a better job of inter-viewing, seek the advice of a human resources consultant who will guide you in the process.

Entrepreneurs should know that certain questions should never be asked in an interview situation because they are illegal and leave you open to potential lawsuits. Under the laws administered by the **Equal Employment Opportunity Commission** (EEOC), before the point of hire you may not ask about a person's

▶ Religion or religious background

▶ Nation of origin

▶ Living arrangements or lifestyle choice

▶ Plans for pregnancy

▶ Age (to avoid discrimination against people over 40 or under 21)

▶ Criminal arrest record (You may ask only "Have you ever been convicted of a crime?")

▶ Military record

Screening Potential Employees

In an effort to screen potential employees for drugs, criminal records, false information, and workers' compensation history, some entrepreneurs are hiring firms that do background checks. Whether or not you need to run a background check is a function of the type of job for which you are hiring. A receptionist position probably does not require more than contacting previous employers to verify information on the résumé. But hiring a bookkeeper or a CFO may call for checking for a criminal record. Likewise, a truck driver position may require verifying a clean driving record.

Some companies are requiring drug tests as well, and those jobs with physical requirements may call for medical exams. In addition, many companies are using integrity tests, which are psychological tests that measure whether a candidate is more or less likely to steal, take drugs, or be violent. Still others use personality assessment tests to see how a person matches a job profile or fits in with the company culture. Since psychological tests can be wrong, however, it is important to give them as only one part of a comprehensive interview and hiring process. To avoid the possibility of a discrimination suit, all these tests should be given *only after a job offer has been made.*

Human Resource Leasing

If you're not ready to make a firm, long-term commitment to a position in your company, or you need to remain flexible because your business environment is volatile and unpredictable, you may want to consider leasing or temporary services. When you lease an employee, he or she is not legally your employee, but rather the employee of the lessor organization. That firm is responsible for all employment taxes and benefits. You simply receive a bill for the person's services.

Employee leasing is a rapidly growing industry, now known as the **professional employer organization** (PEO) industry (www.peo.com/peo/). More and more business owners are finding it advantageous to have a third party manage their human resources. In effect, the PEO becomes a co-employer, taking on the responsibility of payroll, taxes, benefits, Workers' Compensation, labor law compliance, and risk management.

● *Planning for Ownership and Compensation*

Two of the most perplexing management issues facing an entrepreneur with a new corporation are how much of the company to sell to potential stockholders and how much to pay key management. There is a tendency on the part of small, privately held companies to use minority shares as an incentive to entice investors and to pay key management, primarily because new companies do not have the cash flow to provide attractive compensation packages. The prevailing wisdom is that providing stock in the new company will increase commitment, cause management to be more cost conscious, reduce cash outlay for salaries, and induce loyalty to the company in the long term. But studies have found this is not always the case.[10] More often than not, the person to whom you have given stock in good faith will ultimately leave the company, possibly taking the stock with him with the potential for future harm to the business. During the dot com craze of the late 1990s and into 2000, stock options were the most attractive benefit to potential employees and many candidates would forego large salaries in favor of more stock options. But after the dot com crash in April 2000 and the subsequent decline in valuation of technology stocks in general, stock options took second place to salaries.

In the initial growth stage of a new venture, it is difficult to determine with any degree of accuracy what long-term role a particular person may play in the organization. Due to limited resources, you are usually not able to attract the best person to take the company beyond the start-up phase, so you will likely hire a person with fewer qualifications for little salary plus a minority ownership in the company. In this scenario, you are literally betting on the potential contribution of this person, an eventuality that usually doesn't pay off. Later, when your company can afford to hire the person it needs, you have to deal with a minority shareholder who has developed territorial "rights." Therefore, when minority ownership is an important issue to a potential employee, it is important to make clear to that person what it means. There are few legal and managerial rights associated with a minority position; thus, for all practical purposes, minority ownership is simply the unmarketable right to appreciated stock value that has no defined payoff period and certainly no guarantee of value.

Founder's Stock

Founder's stock (144 stock) is stock issued to the first shareholders of the corporation or assigned to key management as part of a compensation package.

The payoff on this stock comes when the company goes public or is sold. Assuming the company is successful, founder's stock at issuance is probably valued at the lowest level it will ever be, relative to an investor's stock value. Consequently, one tax problem that arises as a result occurs when private investors provide seed or working capital to the new venture. Often the value of the stock the investors hold makes it very obvious that the founder's stock was a bargain and not the true value of the stock. According to Internal Revenue Code (IRC) §83, the amount of the difference between the founder's price and the investor's price is taxable as compensation income.

One way to avoid this problem is to issue common stock to founders and key management, and convertible preferred stock to investors. The preference upon liquidation should be high enough to cover the book value of the corporation so the common stockholders would receive nothing. This action would effectively decrease the value of the common stock so it would no longer appear to be a bargain for tax purposes and subject the founders to an immediate tax liability.

Founder's stock is restricted, and the SEC rules (Rule 144) state that the restriction refers to stock that has not been registered with the SEC (private placement) and stock owned by the controlling officers and shareholders of the company (those with at least 10 percent ownership). If a stockholder has owned the stock for at least three years and public information about the company exists, Rule 144 can be avoided in the sale of the stock. If the stockholder has held the stock for less than three years, the rules must be strictly complied with. It is not the intent of this chapter to discuss the details of Rule 144. It suffices to say that the rule is complex and the appropriate attorney or tax specialist should be consulted.

Compensating with Stock

Giving someone ownership rights in the company is a serious decision that should receive very careful consideration. There are several things to contemplate before taking on an equity partner, whether an investor or key management.

1. Anyone brought in as an investor/shareholder or partner with the entrepreneur does not have to be an equal partner. An investor can hold whatever share of stock you have determined is warranted based on what that partner will contribute to the business.

2. Never bring someone in as a partner/investor if you can hire that person to provide the same service, no matter what you may feel the urgency of the situation is. The most advantageous way to hire someone for a new venture is to hire the person as an independent contractor.

3. Do not lock yourself into future compensation promises like stock options. Use cash as bonuses whenever possible.

4. Establish the company as yours before taking on partners, unless, of course, you have founded the company as a team.

5. Consider having employees work for the company at least two years before they are vested and given stock or stock options.

Issuing Stock When the Company Is Capitalized

The number of shares you authorize when you form the corporation is purely arbitrary. Suppose you decide there will be one million **authorized shares** in the new venture. This means you have one million shares available to be issued to potential stockholders. If you value each share of stock at $1 and capitalize $100,000, you will have 100,000 **issued shares;** if each share is valued at $10, you will have 10,000 issued shares. The value you place on each share is arbitrary; for psychological reasons you may wish to value a share at $1, so a shareholder who contributes $10,000 to the business can say that he or she owns 10,000 shares of stock as opposed to 1,000 shares at $10/share. In short, the number of shares issued depends on the initial capitalization and the price per share.

Now suppose that you, the entrepreneur, will initially be contributing $250,000 in cash and $300,000 in assets (equipment, furniture, etc.) to the company. At $1 a share, you issue yourself 550,000 shares of stock and own a 100 percent interest in the company because you have issued only 550,000 shares total. At a later date you issue 29,000 additional shares at $5 a share to an investor. Your minority shareholder has therefore contributed $145,000 to the company and owns a 5 percent interest in the company (29,000/579,000 issued stock). The investor will require that the current value or future additional income of the company be sufficient to justify the increase in price per share. You can see that as additional shares are issued, the original stockholder's percentage ownership in the company declines. However, the founder's shares will not go below 55 percent (550,000/1,000,000) unless the company authorizes additional shares and issues a portion or all of those additional shares.

The type of stock you will be issuing is **common stock,** which is a basic ownership interest in the company. This means that holders of common stock share in both the successes and the failures of the business and benefit through dividends and the appreciating value of the company. Once common stock is issued, a company can issue **preferred stock,** whose holders are paid first if the company is liquidated. Preferred stockholders, however, must accept a fixed dividend amount, no matter how much profit the company makes. If you form a sub-chapter S-corporation, you may issue only one type of stock.

One form of stock you may want to offer investors as an inducement is called IRC Sec. 1244 stock, which permits a shareholder of a corporation with capital and paid-in surplus of $1 million or less to treat a portion of any loss on the disposition of the stock as an ordinary loss, rather than a capital loss. The amount the shareholder can take as a loss is limited to the shareholder's original investment.

Perks for Entrepreneurial Ventures

Most entrepreneurs can't afford to provide their management and employees with expensive perks. Yet there are many other ways to show appreciation and provide incentives for employees. BMC Software Inc., a Houston, Texas company, provides its employees with on-site car washes and oil changes as well as a hair and nail salon and dry cleaner.

Here are some ways you can provide valuable benefits at very little cost.

1. Provide flexible schedules so that employees who commute don't have to come in every day.
2. Offer a casual dress code as long as the employee can quickly switch to business attire if necessary.
3. Share the perks of your industry. For example, Hot Topic, a chain of music-related apparel and accessories based in Pomona, California, reimburses its employees for tickets to rock concerts. In return the employees must report on the apparel of the artists and offer some merchandising ideas.
4. Do the unexpected. One entrepreneur periodically rents a bus and takes his staff to a Mariners baseball game or to play laser tag.
5. Feed your employees.

Of course, the most effective benefit of all is recognition for a job well done.

Sources: Nancy Einhart, "Extreme Perks," *Fast Company,* Issue 42, January, 2001, p. 80; Christopher Caggiano, "Perks You Can Afford," *Inc. Magazine,* November, 1997, p. 107.

Alternatives to Equity Incentives

There are other ways to compensate key management that will not require the entrepreneur to give up equity in the company. The following are a few of those alternatives. Check with your accountant to help you structure the most effective plan for your business.

Deferred Compensation Plans. In a **deferred compensation plan,** the entrepreneur can specify that awards and bonuses be linked to profits and performance of both the individual and the company, with the lion's share being on the individual's performance. The employee does not pay taxes on this award until it is actually paid out at some specified date.

Bonus Plans. With a bonus plan, a series of goals are set by the company with input from the employee, and as the employee reaches each goal, the bonus is given. This method is often used with sales personnel and others who have a direct impact on the profitability of the company. The key to success with bonus plans is to specify measurable objectives.

Capital Appreciation Rights. **Capital appreciation** rights give employees the right to participate in the profits of the company at a specified percentage, while not being full shareholders with voting rights. Capital appreciation rights, or "phantom stock," provide for long-term compensation incentives whose value is based on the increase in the value of the business. The phantom stock will look, act, and reward like real stock, but will have no voting rights and will limit the employee's obligation should the business fail. Typically the employee has to be with the company for a period of three to five years to be considered vested, but otherwise employees do not have to pay for these rights.

Profit-Sharing Plans.   **Profit-sharing plans** are distinct from the previously discussed plans in that they are subject to the ERISA rules for employee retirement programs. These plans must include all employees without regard to individual contribution to profit or performance. They are different from pensions in that owners are not required to contribute in any year and employees are not "entitled" to them.

Organizing business processes, location, and people is an important and difficult task that requires thought and planning. Decisions made in the earliest stages of the new venture can seriously—and often negatively—affect the new firm's ability to grow and be successful in the future. This chapter highlighted many critical organizational considerations and offered suggestions for addressing them. However, you will also want to consult with people who specialize in these functions to make sure that you are making the right decisions for your company.

NEW VENTURE CHECKLIST

Have you:
- ☐ Identified the processes and information flow in your business?
- ☐ Found ways to operate like a virtual enterprise?
- ☐ Located a site for the business?
- ☐ Decided whether to lease, buy, or build the facility?
- ☐ Determined the personnel required to run the business at start-up and over the next three to five years?
- ☐ Created job profiles for positions in the business?
- ☐ Determined the ownership and compensation requirements of the business?
- ☐ Formulated a plan to find the best candidates for positions in the company?

ISSUES TO CONSIDER

1. What are the advantages and the disadvantages of a virtual company?

2. What is the purpose of the imaginary tour of the business?

3. Which important factors in choosing a retail site would not be relevant to a manufacturing site—and vice versa?

4. Explain two disadvantages of short-term leasing.

5. What are the advantages and disadvantages of using stock as compensation and incentives?

6. How can the entrepreneur improve the chances of choosing the best job candidate?

7. List three alternatives to equity incentives for key management.

EXPERIENCING ENTREPRENEURSHIP

1. Choose an industry in which you have an interest. Find a business in that industry and do a flowchart of the business process, based on visiting the site and talking with key personnel. Did you find any inefficiencies that if corrected could improve the process flow?

2. Interview an entrepreneur about his or her hiring practices. How successful have those practices been in getting and retaining good employees?

ADDITIONAL SOURCES OF INFORMATION

Berger, L.A., and D.R. Berger (1999). *The Compensation Handbook*. New York: McGraw-Hill.

Bruce, S.D. (1993). *How to Write Your Employee Handbook*. Madison, CT: Business & Legal Reports.

Lipnack, J., and J. Stamps (2000). *Virtual Teams: People Working Across Boundaries with Technology*. New York: John Wiley.

Nobile, R.J. (1995). *Guide to Employee Handbooks*. Boston: Warren Gorham Lamont.

Small Business Association. *Using Census Data to Select a Store Site*. SBA Pub. No. MA2.023. Washington, DC.

Yate, M. (1997). *Hiring the Best: A Manager's Guide to Effective Interviewing*. Avon, MA: Adams Media Corporation.

Zankel, M.I. (2000). *Negotiating Commercial Real Estate Leases*. Fort Worth, TX: Mesa House Publishing.

Bureau of Labor Statistics
http://stats.bls.gov/

Census Bureau
http://www.census.gov
Demographic information useful for identifying and analyzing the trade area.

Digital Work
http://www.digitalwork.com
A web site where you can do a variety of marketing tasks and market research for less than it costs to hire a marketing firm.

EntreWorld
http://www.Entreworld.org
A source of information and articles on all aspects of starting and building a company.

Guru.com
http://www.guru.com
Here you will find independent professionals and financial management.

HUD Empowerment Zones and Enterprise Communities
http://www.hud.gov/ezec/locator/
At this web site, you can locate the empowerment zones in your state.

Institute of Management and Administration Business Pages
http://www.ioma.com/
Sample articles about things like employee benefits and handling receivables. Hundreds of links to other web sites.

ILogistix
http://www.ilogistix.com
Handle all of your logisitics needs from order management to assembly and packaging.

PEO Community Web Site
http://www.peo.com/splash/
Clearinghouse for information on professional employer organizations.

U.S. Workers' Compensation Law
http://www.law.cornell.edu/topics/workers_compensation.html

Case 7   Roland International Freight Service

Case 9   Wizards of the Coast

14

Producing Products and Services

One way to increase productivity is to do whatever we are doing now, but faster . . . There is a second way. We can change the nature of the work we do, not how fast we do it.

Andrew S. Grove, CEO, Intel Corp.

Overview

The components of production

Preparing to produce products and services

Calculating production costs

Maintaining and warranting production processes

Keeping America's Companies Clean

Most people might think that a company producing industrial detergent would be pretty mundane. (After all, how difficult is it to produce a cleaning agent?) To ChemStation in Dayton, Ohio, industrial cleaners are as varied and unique as the customers, and the company mass-customizes its products to the specific needs of each customer.

Customers of the nineteen-year-old company range from car wash companies to the U.S. Air Force. In 1983 ChemStation was delivering its industrial detergent in its own 55-gallon drum, but at about that time the cost of plastic, gasoline, and drivers went up drastically. CEO George Homan soon found himself spending more for packaging than for making the detergent. In a moment of creativity and daring, he began a new delivery system based on permanent reusable containers, tanks half the size of the originals. They were half-sized because he was now delivering concentrate, letting the customer add the water on site. During the process of installing permanent tanks at customer sites, he discovered that his detergent reacted differently in different environments. In other words, it cleaned better in some environments than in others. Homan was determined to meet his customers' cleaning needs, but accomplishing this would require adopting the latest technology and training his salespeople to collect the required information from the customer.

The process of collecting this information became very important. Chem-Station's salespeople go out to the customer sites to learn firsthand what kind of dirt, grease, or grime a customer is dealing with and what type of cleaner is needed. Information collected in the field is stored in a database called the Tank Management System, or TMS, which is linked by modem to the ChemStation main lab and each of the over forty-three plants nationwide. The plants contain the computer-driven machines that mix the customer's formula, machines that George Homan developed. When the plant receives a request for a particular type of detergent, the worker simply touches the number of the correct detergent formula; the machine then adds the selected raw materials and mixes the formula. Then a driver takes the mixture to the customer's site and fills the reusable tank. This process is based on the just-in-time system, so ChemStation monitors the usage of detergent at each site. In the beginning the salesperson will check the site periodically and call in an order when the tank is low. Over time, however, usage patterns develop and the salesperson doesn't have to check the tank. Homan is working on a device attached to the customer's tank that will dial the TMS when the tank is low and order a new batch.

Homan claims that using the mass customization technique has saved the company a tremendous amount of money. The company began franchising in 1984, and since 1985 its gross profit margin per customer has jumped about 50 percent, while the cost per customer has dropped 25 percent. In fact, because of technology, ChemStation now can manufacture the custom product as cheaply as the company was able to manufacture a standardized product.

SOURCES: Sarah Schafer, "Have It Your Way," *Inc. Technology,* November, 1997, p. 56; http://www.chemstation.com/.

One of the topics that is rarely covered in entrepreneur texts is the manufacturing process, yet today, most new ventures produce a product of some sort, even if they define themselves as service businesses. The reality is that today every business is a service business and nearly every business produces a product; in other words, the boundaries between these two types of businesses have blurred if not disappeared altogether. Consequently, every entrepreneur should understand production processes and apply those concepts to his or her venture.

In simple terms, production is about managing the flow of material and information from raw materials to finished goods.[1] Think of manufacturing equipment as hardware, and the people and information needed to run the machines as software. If you do that, you'll see why it's possible for two companies to have the same equipment, yet produce significantly different outcomes. The difference lies in the software driving the machinery—in other words, information and people.

Many high-growth ventures market innovative new products. The operational plan for the business in this case consists of a fairly complex analysis that includes product development, prototyping, production processes, and inventory control mechanisms. The depth of analysis is a function of the type of product offered, the technological newness of the product, and the number of different ways the product can be produced. The more complex the product, the deeper the analysis.

Certainly ChemStation's development of a sophisticated process to serve customer needs resulted in enormous growth and substantially higher gross margins than its competitors because it involved the customer every step of the way. (See Profile 14.1.)

This chapter will look at the way products and services are produced. Recall that the product development aspect of the production process was discussed in Chapter 7.

The Components of Production

Production is comprised of four primary components: the customer, state-of-the-art technology, superior resources and processes, and continuous improvement. The absence of any one of them will result in a reduction in the overall productivity and effectiveness of the company.

The Customer

The customer is considered the driving force and the foundation on which all the other functions are based. You can achieve superior performance as a manufacturer or producer only when your customer is involved in the process. Today, when customers expect superior levels of quality, service, and response time, manufacturers and producers cannot afford to be rigidly structured, cumbersome in size, and bureaucratic in their decision making. Instead, they must be small, flexible, fast, organizationally flat, and simple in design. This is good news for entrepreneurs, whose businesses generally reflect these characteristics.

Technology

Probably no single factor has had more of an impact on manufacturing processes for entrepreneurs than technology. Technology has made it possible for entrepreneurs to focus on their core competencies—what they do best—and outsource to other manufacturers those tasks that the other manufacturers do best. **Network technology** enables entrepreneurs to stay in touch with the companies to which they outsource and to decrease their set-up and wait times. In fact, in some industries, small companies are elaborately linked to provide a type of "one-stop shopping" experience for a much larger company. Certainly this is the case in the film industry, where many smaller companies (special effects artists, graphics artists, sound editors, etc.) work together on a single project for a much larger film production and distribution company. In addition to private networks, the Internet has added a new dimension to manufacturing processes by causing manufacturers to rethink their relationships with suppliers and customers.[2] To accomplish this, manufacturers need to agree on business practices and be willing to share information. Accenture, a supply-chain management enabler, has identified six processes that benefit from collaborative manufacturing: 1) planning and scheduling, 2) product design, 3) new product introduction, 4) order management, 5) sourcing, and 6) order management.[3] Had Dave and Dan Hanlon (Profile 14.2) outsourced the production of their innovative motorcycle, they might have avoided the need to purchase capital-intensive equipment that sent their company into a tailspin.

Superior Resources and Processes

Manufacturing is a process that uses the inputs supplied by procedures, people, and information to produce something tangible. So the job of manufacturing is to keep the process moving along by coordinating all the activities and keeping records of procedures to ensure quality control. It also includes resource planning and demand flow.

Total quality management (TQM) refers to a framework or system for integrating superior quality into all aspects of a business. For manufacturers this

It May Not Be a Harley, But ...

Sometimes you just have to have another choice. At least that's what Dave and Dan Hanlon believed when they decided to go head to head with the mythic motorcycle giant Harley-Davidson Corporation. Both had grown up in a farming community in Minnesota and had spent many pleasurable hours on motorcycles of one sort or another. For these two, biking was not a hobby; it was a way of life. And so it seemed natural that they would decide to start a manufacturing company and compete with the $1.2 billion icon known as Harley-Davidson.

They were not the stereotypical entrepreneurs, however; they had no contacts, no money, and knew nothing about manufacturing and the motorcycle business. But they knew that had to compete with Harley on its own terms with the Excelsior-Henderson motorcycle, a historic name that would resonate with bikers. In fact, the original Excelsior was the first bike to break the 100-mile-per-hour speed barrier. When the Hanlons discovered that the original trademark on the Excelsior had lapsed, they knew they were in business.

To raise money, they sought out executives, CEOs, and founders of manufacturing firms and by 1996 had raised $15 million. A public offering in 1997 brought in $27.6 million. To build their state-of-the-art factory, they sought professionals. Enticing the engineering manager at Triumph, a competitor, to come on board was a real coup. They were able to launch their first running prototypes at the Daytona Speedway in 1997. By 1998, their dealer network had reached eighty throughout the United States. Their first production bike, the Super X, rolled off the line and into their museum in 1998. By 1999, they had started shipping motorcycles to their dealers and were officially in business.

But the cost of their state-of-the-art manufacturing facility and other costs related to marketing of their new product were more than the enterprising duo could manage on their own. After a relatively brief term in Chapter 11 reorganization to restructure their financial situation, the company emerged under new owners, E.H. Partners, Inc., in September 2000. Professional management was brought in to reposition the company for market re-entry in 2002.

This is not an uncommon story in entrepreneurial manufacturing. The costs of building and tooling a state-of-the-art factory are enormous and can quickly exhaust the capital raised early in the venture. Furthermore, as the Hanlons quickly learned, passion for your product and a great product can only take you so far; you need the right people to manage the business side of the enterprise, which is fairly complex. Perhaps after a false start, the Hanlons will finally see their dream realized.

Sources: Excelsior-Henderson Motorcycle Manufacturing Company, http://www.excelsior-henderson.com/index01.html; Marc Ballon, "Anatomy of a Start-Up: Born to Be Wild," *Inc. Magazine,* November 1, 1997.

means designing processes that include continuous improvement, total quality control, self-directed teams, automation, computer-integrated manufacturing, and just-in-time production and inventory control. For service providers it means designing processes that include continuous improvement, total quality control, and self-directed teams, but also methods for acquiring feedback from customers on additional services and potential products that might satisfy their needs. We will consider those TQM activities that product and service businesses have in common.

● **Continuous Improvement**

Under the principle of **continuous improvement,** everything a company does is a process, and every element of that process is held under a microscope to see whether it can be improved upon. Continuous improvement can be accomplished through a process known as PDCA, which stands for *plan, do, check, act.* It is a way of analyzing a process problem (for example, a problem in judging quality against a standard), then planning for a change in the current process and monitoring the results of that change.

● **Total Quality Control**

The goal of **total quality control** (TQC) is to eliminate all defects at all stages of the process; in other words, to achieve perfection. The basic principles of TQC include 1) customer satisfaction as the fundamental goal of any organization; 2) the use of quality circles or some process by which employees are brought together frequently to discuss issues and plans; 3) policy deployment or a planning and review tool that consists of annual objectives and strategies; and 4) foolproof solutions to problems, so that they don't occur again. TQC is discussed in more detail on page 324.

● **Self-Managed Teams**

Like quality circles, **self-managed teams** (SMTs) give employees more input into what they do for the company and result in higher levels of productivity and quality. They also improve flexibility and responsiveness to changing market conditions because decisions are made more quickly and changes are implemented with fewer problems. In manufacturing, this may mean putting a team in charge of the production of a particular product or a particular portion of a more complex product. They have responsibility and authority to make decisions related to quality issues. Similarly, in a service company, it may mean putting associates in charge of projects and making them accountable for the outcomes.

Preparing to Produce Products and Services

Building a complex production system while the company is in start-up or later while it's rapidly growing is a recipe for disaster. If you are fortunate enough to have a product that enjoys mass-market acceptance early on, you must be prepared in advance to meet market demand. Many a company has lost customer loyalty and significant revenues by its inability to meet demand because of a lack of effective systems and controls that allow the firm to produce and deliver products to customers in a timely fashion. Once lost, that customer base is nearly

PROFILE 14.3

Using Technology to Produce Success

Building relationships with customers, vendors, and partners based on shared intelligence is a powerful competitive advantage in a fast-moving world. One company that has taken relationship building to new levels of effectiveness is MicroStrategy Inc., the Virginia-based company that converts information into intelligence that strengthens customer, supplier, and partner relationships, then distributes it anywhere their customers want through wireless devices. It is one of the fastest growing software manufacturing companies in the world, and its customers need real-time intelligence. If inventory levels drop below a trigger point, the firm wants to know instantly so it can act on that information before it has a negative impact on the company.

MicroStrategy understands that need and the need to move beyond its core data mining business. It put substantial resources into a personal-intelligence network being developed by its spin-off company, Strategy.com, whose software can respond to a set of predefined conditions and send an alert to a customer's pager, fax machine, or cell phone. Strategy.com has its own president and board of directors.

To achieve its lofty goal, Strategy.com has acquired more than fifty strategic partners like Ameritrade, USAToday.com, and EarthLink Network Inc. Shared intelligence has made it possible for MicroStrategy to reach new customer markets and collaborate more effectively with their partners.

MicroStrategy attributes a good share of its success to what it calls "information transparency." Information throughout the entire organization is shared through a central information portal called the Enterprise Solutions, a company Intranet. There, employees can find anything they need to know about the company and share their experiences about their jobs, customers, and even the last conference they attended.

Like most technology companies, MicroStrategy has spent the last couple years revitalizing their brand and making sure they continue to be a profitable, value-added, conservative-growth company.

Sources: Lewis Perelman, "Anything, Anywhere, Anytime—Any Questions?" *Fast Company,* April, 1997, Issue 8, p. 50; Chuck Salter, "People and Technology—Microstrategy Inc.," *Fast Company,* April, 2000, Issue 33, p. 190; Microstrategy, www.microstrategy.com; Strategy.com, www.strategy.com; Michael Saylor, "Michael Saylor on MicroStrategy's Wild Ride," *BusinessWeek Online,* February 21, 2001.

impossible to regain in time to fend off competing companies and save the company from failure.

One of the best ways to understand how the production process touches customers and affects your bottom line is to follow an order through the company and document where the order flow gets bogged down, is duplicated, or is hindered in some manner. Any slowdown or duplication of effort means higher production costs and slower response to the customer. Suppose you have a market research firm that provides customized reports to companies to allow them to judge their markets for new products and services. This is an example of what would typically be called a service firm, yet notice that the service firm produces a product—a market research report. Now suppose that in the process of gathering the research and analyzing it, there is no plan for who should do a particular area of the research. Duplication of effort could easily occur, and it's possible that you will overlook covering something important like an emerging competitor. Duplicating effort and having to go back to recover something you missed is costly and slows down the process and threatens to cause you to miss your customer's deadline.

For any product or project, It's important to track all the components, raw materials (parts), or data. Here are some things to look for:

▶ Costs to purchase from the supplier and inspect for quality

▶ How long it sits in your inventory before you use it in your production process

▶ How many people handle the part or data before it becomes part of the product or project

▶ How many set-ups (i.e., adjusting machinery to do a particular task) before you can assemble it

▶ How much time a product or project spends in production

▶ How many times you have errors during the process

▶ How effective your delivery process is

Each one of these points in the process can be a source of delay and cost for the company, so the production process needs to make each one as efficient and effective as possible. One of the best ways to do that is to inspect for quality in product and process at every point of activity along the production line and keep the tolerance levels for error or variance very high. This avoids failures in the product after it's in the hands of the customer. Pelco, Inc., a leader in the video surveillance industry, has designed quality control into every process in its company. Any worker can stop production for a defect, so that by the time the product reaches the end of the production line, it is defect free. They would rather take the time to look for errors before the product reaches the customer than to have the customer find them. Contrast this approach with that of the software industry, which regularly launches products with "bugs" that they expect their customers to find and report.

● *The Production Process*

A typical manufacturing plant has five functional areas—purchasing, materials management and production scheduling, production and assembly, quality control, and maintenance—as depicted in Figure 14.1. Each has measurable components that should be tested for effectiveness; that is, there are ways to measure the efficiency and effectiveness of every aspect of the production process. In general, manufacturing and production firms are organized as product-focused

FIGURE 14.1

The Production Process

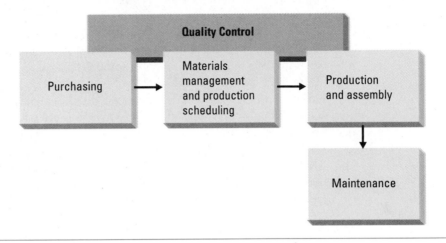

or process-focused organizations. Product or **project-focused organizations** generally are highly decentralized, so that they can respond better to market demands. Each product or project group acts essentially like a separate company, a profit center. This type of organization is well suited to products or projects that don't require huge economies of scale or capital-intensive technologies. **Process-focused organizations,** on the other hand, are common among manufacturers with capital-intensive processes such as those seen in the semiconductor industry and among service companies such as advertising firms. These organizations are highly centralized in order to control all the functions of the organization. Whether the company is product- or process-focused, it must be able to extend its control beyond the five functional areas, so that it is not at the mercy of its suppliers at one end and its distributors at the other. This control is usually accomplished through strategic alliances.

As discussed in Chapter 10, the **virtual enterprise,** consisting of strategic alliances between all links in the value chain, is one way to achieve control of the entire process from raw materials to distribution, while still keeping the firm small and flexible enough to meet changing needs and demands. This model is similar to the **Japanese *keiretsu,*** which links banks, suppliers, electronics, and auto firms together through a series of cross-ownerships. The United States model leaves ownership in the hands of the individual owners but links the organizations into a virtual entity that acts as a team with a common goal. Wal-Mart is probably the best example of this type of partnership and integration. It has established point-of-sale linkups with its suppliers and has given its manufacturers the responsibility for handling inventory. The ultimate goal is to construct one organization with a common purpose that encompasses the entire supply chain from raw materials supplier to retailer, with each link along the chain performing the task that it does best. Establishing this type of network takes time. A start-up company can't expect to quickly achieve the level of integration and control that a Wal-Mart has taken years to accomplish. Instead, start-up companies need to build relationships slowly, starting with key independent contractors to whom they may be outsourcing some tasks.

The Internet has been a valuable tool for streamlining distribution and supply channels in many industries, and even small, growing businesses can take advantage of its power. For example, suppose you are sourcing parts for a product you're building, that is, you're trying to find out where to find the best parts at the best prices. Before the Internet, it could have taken months of phone calls and faxes to find the best vendors. Now you can quickly compare them online, whether you're a large company or a small start-up.

In the next sections, we'll look more closely at the five functions of production.

Materials Requirements

Any business that purchases raw materials or parts for production of goods for resale must carefully consider the quality, quantity, and timing of those purchases. Quality goods are those that meet specific needs. Quality varies considerably among vendors, so if you've established certain quality standards for your products, you must find vendors who will consistently supply that precise level of quality because your customers will expect it. The quantity of raw materials or parts that you purchase is a function of 1) demand by the customer, 2) your manufacturing capability, and 3) your company's storage capability; consequently, timing of purchases is very important. You must plan your purchases so that capital and warehouse space are not tied up any longer than necessary. Because materials account for approximately 50 percent of total production cost, it is crucial to balance these three factors carefully.

Vendor Issues

Locating vendors to sell you raw materials or goods for resale is not difficult, but finding the best vendors for your purposes is another matter entirely, as you learned in Chapter 10. The issue of vendor relationships has become increasingly important in markets that demand that companies reduce costs and maintain effective relationships. Research has found that these relationships rely on factors such as trust or commitment,[4] uncertainty and dependence[5] and the effect of these on performance.[6]

Furthermore, buyers and sellers are connected in an increasing number of ways: through information sharing that improves the quality of the product produced[7] or brings about new product development[8]; operational linkages like computerized inventory, order replenishment systems, and just-in-time delivery;

legal bonds such as binding contractual agreements; cooperative norms; and relationship adaptations where vendors modify their products to meet the needs of the customer.

Given the importance of the vendor-customer relationship,[9] should you buy from one vendor or more than one? Obviously, if a single vendor cannot supply all your needs, that decision is made. There are several advantages to using a single vendor where possible:

▶ You will probably get more individual attention and better service.

▶ Your orders will be consolidated, so you may be able to get a discount based on quantity purchased.

However, the principal disadvantage of using just one vendor is that should that vendor suffer a catastrophe (i.e., its facility burns to the ground, like the Japanese company that was the prime supplier of RAM chips several years ago), it may be difficult or impossible to find an alternate source in a short period of time. To guard against this contingency, you may want to follow the general rule of using one supplier for about 70 to 80 percent of your needs, and one or more additional suppliers for the rest.

When considering a specific vendor as your source, ask yourself several questions:

1. Can the vendor deliver enough of what you need when you need it?

2. What is the cost of transportation using the vendor you are considering? If the vendor is located far away, costs will be higher and it may be more difficult to get the service you require.

3. What services is the vendor offering you? For example, how often will sales representatives call on you?

4. Is the vendor knowledgeable about the product line?

5. What are the vendor's maintenance and return policies?

It is also important to shop vendors to compare prices, just as you would if you were purchasing equipment. Check for trade discounts and quantity discounts that may make a particular vendor's deal more enticing.

Computer technology has made materials planning more of a science than ever before. Information systems can now provide you or the person doing your purchasing with detailed feedback on supplier performance, delivery reliability, and quality control results, which facilitates supplier comparisons. Comparing results across suppliers gives you more leverage when it's time to renegotiate the annual contracts with suppliers. Check Profile 14.3 to see what one company does to build vendor and customer relationships.

Inventory Requirements

Today, businesses that hold inventories of raw materials or goods for resale have found that they must reduce these inventories significantly to remain competitive. Instead of purchasing large quantities and receiving them on a monthly basis, businesses are purchasing daily or weekly in an effort to avoid costly inventories. Of course, some inventory of finished goods must be maintained to meet delivery deadlines; therefore, a delicate balance must be achieved between goods coming into the business, work in progress, and goods leaving the business to be sold.

In the past, inventories were built up on the basis of the state of the economy or in reaction to problems in an inventory control system. If times were good, producers increased stocks of inventory to meet expected demand. Then, when the economy slowed, they usually had shelves of leftover stock. Reductions in inventory succeeded in exposing typical problems: equipment imbalances, paperwork backlog, excessively long set-ups, vendor problems, and problems with purchase lead-time.

Newer systems, like just-in-time (JIT), help manufacturers and producers maintain better control of their inventories by eliminating production and inventory problems, then reducing inventory to only that which is needed.

Just-in-Time

The **just-in-time system** of materials and inventory management is fundamentally different from other inventory systems. Coming originally from Japan, JIT took hold in the United States. The philosophy behind JIT is to produce the minimum number of units in the smallest possible quantities at the latest possible time. A well-devised and implemented JIT system can do the following things.

- Increase direct and indirect labor productivity
- Increase equipment capacity
- Reduce manufacturing lead-time
- Reduce the cost of failure
- Reduce the cost of purchased materials
- Reduce inventories
- Reduce space requirements

In essence, the goal of JIT is to eliminate waste in the manufacturing process. Consequently, to implement JIT it is necessary to look beyond mere inventory to all other aspects of the manufacturing process as well. Starting with the last operation, which is usually the customer requirement, work backward through the manufacturing process. Customer demand determines how many products are produced. The number of products to be produced determines the production capability requirements, which in turn determine the amount of raw materials needed. In general, a JIT firm maintains an inventory no larger than needed to support one day of production. To do this, it has to have the cooperation of its suppliers and its distributors, with severe penalties for not being on time—that is, for being either too early or late. This, of necessity, reduces the number of suppliers a JIT firm typically deals with. JIT also requires strict quality control, because with minimal inventories there is no excess inventory to cover rejects.

A traditional factory is laid out by functional department, usually based on a particular process or technology. The result is that products are produced in batches. This is the antithesis of JIT, which specifies that the plant be laid out by product. With JIT the equipment is positioned in the order in which it is used to produce a particular product or family of related products. It is also important to plan production so as to produce only enough to meet demand. For example, suppose you expect to sell a total of 100 units of your product next month. Then:

100/20 work days = 5 units a day
5/8 work hours = .63 unit per hour
or 1 unit every hour and a half

This calculation must be reworked every month as demand changes.

One way suppliers are meeting the needs of a company using JIT is by involving independent contractors specializing in "time-sensitive" deliveries. For example, one company has installed two-way satellite communication on its trucks so that shipments can be tracked in real time. Other businesses, like American Cargo Systems, help businesses that need to ship to retailers. They stock merchandise in their warehouses, process orders, make deliveries, and handle billing. In that way retailers don't incur the costs associated with a backup supply of items. Avoiding too much inventory seems to be a continuing trend for the next decade. However, to work effectively, it requires careful coordination and cooperation of all members of the supply chain.

● *Production Requirements*

The lifeblood of any business is its production function. Decisions made about production directly affect output level, product quality, and costs. Planning for production, therefore, is key to manufacturing efficiency and effectiveness. Most manufacturers and producers begin by scheduling; that is, by identifying and describing each activity that must be completed to produce the product, and the amount of time it takes to complete each activity. Two methods traditionally used to aid the scheduling process are Gantt Charts and PERT Diagrams.

FIGURE 14.2

Gantt Chart

——— Scheduled time   ---- Actual progress

Order Number	Order Quantity	September 6-9	12-16	19-23	26-30	October 3-7	10-14	17-21	24-28	November 1-5	7-11	14-18	21-25
5348	1,000	———————————————————											
5349	1,500			———————————————————————									
5350	500						———————————————————————						

Gantt Charts

Gantt Charts are a way to depict the tasks to be performed and the time required for each. Consider Figure 14.2. The task to be completed is outlined (in this case, fulfilling customer orders) on the vertical axis, with the time to completion on the horizontal. Notice that the solid line represents your plan for completion, while the dashed line depicts where you are in the process toward completion. Gantt Charts are best for simple projects that are independent of each other.

PERT Diagrams

PERT is an acronym for Program Evaluation and Review Technique. This method is helpful when the production being scheduled is more complex and subject to the interdependence of several activities going on either simultaneously or in sequence. In other words, some tasks cannot be started until others have been completed. To begin, you must identify the major activities involved in producing the product and arrange them in the order in which they occur. Be sure to identify any activities that must occur in sequence; that is, one activity cannot occur until another is finished.

Construct a pictorial network that describes the process. Then estimate the time to complete each activity and note it on the chart. This is usually done three times, and the answers are given as most optimistic, most likely, and most pessimistic. The statistics of analyzing the network are beyond the scope of this book but essentially consist of 1) identifying the critical path, which is the longest path and is important because a delay in any of the activities along the critical

FIGURE 14.3

PERT Diagram

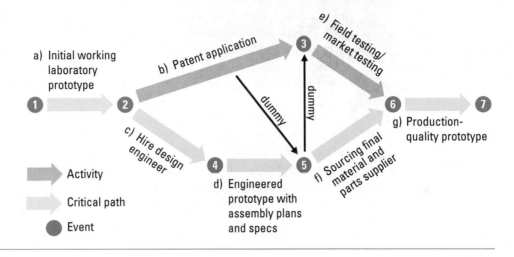

path can delay the entire project; 2) computing slack time on all events and activities (difference between latest and earliest times); and 3) calculating the probability of completion within the time allotted.

The numbered nodes on the diagram (Figure 14.3) refer to the start and completion points for each event. The dummy line was placed in the diagram to account for the completion of event e's being preceded by events b and d. Both must be completed before event g can start.

There are several popular software products on the market, such as Micro Planner X-Pert and Microsoft Project that can help entrepreneurs schedule their production capacity. Like any new technique, however, you will need to invest the time to learn the system, but it is time well spent. Tracking production from the outset of the business allows you to make more realistic strategic decisions about growth and expansion.

Identifying all the tasks in the production process makes it easier to determine what equipment and supplies are needed for completing the tasks. If you determine that the equipment necessary to produce the product is beyond your start-up resources, it may be time to consider outsourcing part or all of production to a manufacturer who has excess capacity with the needed equipment.

After the production tasks have been identified, you can create a preliminary layout of the plant to estimate floor space requirements for production, offices, and services. It may be beneficial to consult with an expert in plant layout to ensure that you make the most efficient use of the limited space you have.

● *Quality Control*

Quality control is the process of reconciling product or project output with the standards set for that product or project. More specifically, it is "an effective system for integrating the quality-development, quality-maintenance, and quality-improvement efforts of the various groups in an organization so as to enable marketing, engineering, production, and service at the most economical levels, which allow for full customer satisfaction."[10] In this sense quality does not necessarily mean "best," it means "best for certain customer requirements," which consists of the features and benefits of the product or service and its selling price.[11] It is said that one thing manufacturers and producers learn from history is that "the primary objective of the company is to put the quality of the product ahead of every other consideration. A profit or loss notwithstanding, the emphasis will always be on quality."[12] Today thousands of manufacturers and producers have embraced the philosophy of quality first but have focused principally on equipment and processes rather than on the human element. Both must be considered in order for total quality control to permeate every aspect of the organization. Over the past twenty years, manufacturers have invested heavily in quality improvements. Concepts like lean manufacturing and Six Sigma have helped companies lower production costs, produce less scrap, experience fewer defects, and reduce warranty expense.[13]

When you produce products for the medical industry, quality is not simply a desired outcome, but an essential one. When Corinna Lathan decided to produce devices to help disabled children enjoy their physical therapy exercises, she knew her products had to be perfect. Therapeutic devices are costly—nearly ten times the price of a high-tech toy for able-bodied children. Lathan, a Ph.D. in neuroscience and a professor of biomedical engineering, recognized that while she had the ability to take the product through the primitive prototype phase, she needed a major partner to get the product to the projected $2 billion market. To cut the cost of her JesterBot to a retail price of $100 and ensure consistent quality, she is working on a licensing agreement with Toytech Creations to mass-produce the robot for her.[14]

Quality is a strategic issue that is designed to bring about business profitability and positive cash flow. Effective total quality programs result in "improved levels of customer satisfaction, reduced operating costs, reduced operating losses and field service costs, and improved utilization of resources."[15]

The Inspection Process

One way manufacturers and producers control quality is through a regular inspection process that takes place during several stages of the production process. Often, primarily due to cost, a random sample of products or project outcomes is chosen for the inspection. This method catches potential defects early in the process, before the products become finished goods. Whether each item produced is checked, or a random sampling is conducted, is a function of what is being produced, the cost, and whether the inspection process will destroy the item. For example, if you are producing an expensive piece of machinery, it may be prudent to subject each item to the inspection process, because the cost of inspection is more than offset by the price of the item. But if you are producing a food product, once it is inspected it cannot be sold, so you can't afford to inspect more than a representative random sample of each batch.

Entrepreneurs who want to achieve total quality will probably set a no-defect goal for product manufacturing. In Chapter 7 we discussed the importance of designing right the first time and designing for producibility. Superior design is the first step in achieving defect-free production. Another step is giving work teams the power to stop production in order to resolve a quality issue. Recall the example of Pelco earlier in the chapter.

Six Sigma

Six Sigma is a quality initiative that Motorola introduced in the 1980s. The program identifies quality levels that predict the likelihood that defects will occur—the higher the level, the lower the probability of a defect. Six Sigma relies on statistical tools and specific processes to achieve the measurable goals of fewer defects, increased productivity, reduced waste, and superior products and processes.[16]

While large companies like GE and Allied Signal are known for their Six Sigma programs, small companies like Technically, Inc., a Boston-area provider of contract laboratory services and manufacturing to the chemical industry, have also benefited from the program. Technically, Inc.'s founder, Debra Saez, left Dupont to start the company in 1985 and brought with her the Six Sigma skills that now give her company a rigorous approach to refining industrial processes. For example, the statistical technique ANOVA or analysis of variance is used to optimize weak processes so that they can be performed with less labor and raw materials and in about half the time.[17]

Quality Circles

Quality circles are groups of employees who regularly work together on some aspect of the production process. They meet several times a month with the help of an outside facilitator to discuss problems and ideas related to their work environment. They often come up with new solutions to problems, solutions that are then put into effect, thus improving the efficiency and effectiveness of the manufacturing process and the product as well. Quality circles give employees a vested interest in what they are producing; consequently, they are more likely to pay close attention to improving the way their task is completed.

The real success or failure of the quality control effort is dependent on the human element in the process: customers, employees, and management. Quality begins with satisfying the needs of the customers, and that cannot be accomplished unless those needs and requirements are communicated to management and employees. As an entrepreneur with a new venture, you have a unique opportunity to create a philosophy of quality from the very birth of the business, in the way the business is run and in the employees hired. In this sense you have the advantage of creating new habits and patterns of behavior instead of having to change old ones.

Using Customers for Quality Control

The philosophy that a company produces what the customer needs, when he or she needs it is fundamental to quality control. Customers, by their demands for reliability and performance in a highly competitive market, establish the standards that must be met when the product is designed and produced. If customers perceive that the product does not meet their needs or does not meet them as well as another product could, lost sales result.

Using Employees for Quality Control

If you want employees to buy into the notion of quality control at every level, they must be given the responsibility and authority to make changes that will improve the process and product at every level. If you are going to install new technology to improve the process, the employees need to be trained not only in how to use it but also in how to look for potential problems that would affect quality. The continual use of awareness and training programs will help employees understand their importance in the whole manufacturing process.

Using Management for Quality Control

For total quality management to work, key management must be "on the floor," learning every aspect of production and supporting the efforts of employees. It is their job to bring the requirements of customers to the people who will satisfy those requirements. It is also management's job to establish company-wide, measurable quality goals. Too often management focuses more on productivity goals than on quality goals. Ultimately it is quality, not productivity, that will sell the product.

In an increasingly global market, it is not surprising that the need for international quality standards has arisen. ISO 9000, developed by the International Organization for Standardization in Geneva, Switzerland, is a series of international quality standards and certification that makes it easier for a product to enter the export market. Adopted by thousands of companies in over 100 countries, the standards apply to both manufacturing and service businesses and certify quality control procedures. The ISO standards are too detailed for presentation here, but the broad areas covered include the following requirements:

- System
- Management

▶ Resource

▶ Realization or deliverables

▶ Remedial processes

Look at the resources at the end of the chapter to find an online site with more information about these standards.

The purpose of ISO is to provide a single set of standards internationally that everyone agrees on. To meet ISO standards, you will need to develop a quality management system. That process starts by doing a gap analysis—comparing where your company is now with the ISO requirements. Then complete the following steps:

1. Fill the gaps between where your company is and where it needs to be for ISO requirements.

2. Conduct an internal audit to ensure that you have met the requirements.

3. Secure a registrar to audit the effectiveness of your system. They will issue an official certificate.

4. Advertise that your products and services are ISO 9000 certified.

Registration is not a requirement for ISO. You can certainly comply with the requirements without formally registering, but customers are more likely to put faith in what you claim if there is an independent auditor behind it.

Putting effective production processes in place is only half the battle. Maintaining them is equally important as you'll see in the next section.

Calculating Production Costs

In Chapter 7, which focuses on product development, we discussed the need to source raw materials and parts for the product prototype. Once you have accomplished this and defined your assembly process, including labor requirements, it is possible to calculate the total investment required to start the business and the per-unit cost of manufacturing the product. To be sure, the initial units produced will cost significantly more to manufacture and assemble because the volume will usually not be sufficient to achieve industry discounts on raw materials and parts, and the plant and equipment will not be used to full capacity. Consequently, gross margins may be extremely small in the early stages until a sufficient increase in volume allows an economy of scale that reduces the per-unit cost. Similarly, you will need to itemize the materials, supplies, and labor required to provide your company's service. Service entrepreneurs often fail to realize that time and materials are the production costs associated with providing a service. They tend to think only in terms of hourly rates. The service process must be itemized in the same manner as the manufacturing process.

The calculation of the up-front investment in plant, office, and equipment, coupled with the high per-unit cost of production, has resulted in many entrepreneurs deciding to outsource manufacturing to an established manufacturing firm. Some products that consist of off-the-shelf components from **original equipment manufacturers** (OEMs) can give the entrepreneur the option to set up an assembly operation, which is far less costly than a manufacturing plant. In any case, the process of outlining all the costs of setting up a product company is invaluable in making the final decisions about how the business will operate.

Entrepreneurs who wish to manufacture products have many options today. It is still possible in most industries to manufacture domestically and be able to compete if you refine your processes and build quality into every step. If it is too costly to do all your manufacturing in-house, consider outsourcing the capabilities that are not your strengths, or outsource everything and play a coordination role until the company is producing a healthy cash flow. Many entrepreneurs learned this lesson the hard way when they tried to start car companies—Preston Tucker with The Tucker in 1946, Henry J. Kaiser with the Henry J. in 1952, and John DeLorean with the gull-wing DeLorean in 1982. Robert Lutz intends to learn from their mistakes. As a thirty-five-year veteran of the auto industry, he recently started Cunningham Motor Company to produce a sports coupe, the Cunningham C-7. Industry analysts say that he has a chance to succeed because he is outsourcing design, engineering, and production and employing just twenty people for his "virtually integrated" car company.[18] The reality is that many successful companies today are outsourcing production. Compaq Computer produces only about 10 percent of the computers it sells, while Coca-Cola Company outsources its machinery-intensive bottling work to third parties, but often holds an equity stake in those companies to control quality.

In some industries, particularly labor-intensive ones, the only way to achieve competitive costs is to manufacture in a country where labor costs are low; Mexico and China are two examples. Look at what other firms in your industry are doing. Be aware, though, that customers are not always looking for the lowest cost; rather, they're looking for the highest quality at a competitive price. If the products you produce are innovative and meet the specific needs of your target customer, you will be able to manufacture domestically in a successful way.

Maintaining and Warranting Production Processes

Maintenance, in the production process, refers both to the maintenance of plant and equipment used to produce a product or project outcome and the maintenance or servicing of the product or project outcome after it is sold.

● Process Maintenance

At some point any machine or process will break down, which can mean lost sales and costly repairs and redesign. There are three ways to prevent unexpected breakdowns from disrupting the production process. The process can be organized so that when one machine is down, the work can be shifted to another. Another way is to build up inventories at each stage of the production process so that machines can keep working as long as the inventory lasts. (This method, however, will probably not work in a company that has chosen a JIT system of inventory management.) The third, and perhaps the best, approach is to regularly undertake preventive maintenance by checking and fixing the machines before they break down. The advantage of this approach is that you control when the downtime occurs.

Service processes can also break down when a key person on a project becomes ill or leaves the company. Similar to a manufacturing process, you will want to cross-train your personnel so that someone else can immediately step into the absent person's position and keep the process moving along.

Product Maintenance

The entrepreneur who subscribes to total quality management will likely wish to provide warranties with products and services, so as to protect against potential liability and to demonstrate that the company stands behind what it produces and the work that it does. Today product/service warranties have also become a competitive marketing tool.

Some of the decisions to be made regarding warranties include:

▶ *Length of warranty.* This depends on industry standards.

▶ *Covered components of the product or aspects of the service.* Some components may come from other manufacturers who have their own warranties. In this case, it is important to have your use of that component on the product certified by the OEM so that you don't inadvertently invalidate the warranty. Then, if a warranted component from that manufacturer becomes defective, you can return it to the OEM. However, it is probably good business practice to have customers return the product directly to you or your distributors for service, repair, or exchange under your warranty, which covers the whole product. Warranties on services cover satisfaction with work completed. For example, your company may conduct ISO 9000 certification workshops for companies and warrant that if a company goes through your workshops and implements your suggestions, it will receive certification. If, for some reason, the client does not receive certification, there is no way to return a workshop in the way that you would a product, but you can offer the client a fact-finding audit to discover what went wrong or you can simply refund their money (a less satisfactory solution for the client).

▶ *Product/process scope.* Will the warranty cover one or all products in a line or will there be separate warranties? Generally, for services, a warranty covers the service as a whole, unless there are products involved as well.

▶ *Market scope.* Will the same warranty apply in all markets? This will be a function of local laws.

▶ *Conditions of the warranty that the customer must fulfill.* Is there anything the customer must do to keep the warranty in force, such as servicing or replacing disposable parts? These conditions should not include registering the product via a postcard. Today a product is covered by warranty from the moment it is purchased, whether or not the purchaser returns a postcard stating when and where it was purchased and answering a short, informational questionnaire. What many companies do to get the postcard information is offer update notification and potential discounts on future products in exchange for the information.

▶ *Who executes the warranty?* You must decide who will handle warranty claims (manufacturer, dealers, distributors, your company), recognizing that customers do not like to mail products back to the manufacturer.

▶ *How the public will be educated about the warranty.* What are your plans for advertising and promotion relative to the warranty?

▶ *Policies for refunds and returns, and shipping and handling costs.* A return policy is a function of the entrepreneur's philosophy about doing business. A customer-oriented company would probably offer a generous return policy and pay for the cost of returns.

Providing a warranty incurs a cost for the manufacturer; however, that cost must be weighed against the potential loss of business if no warranty is provided. In the case of a new business with a new product or service, it is difficult to anticipate the number of problems that might occur as the product or service gets into the marketplace. Careful and adequate field testing prior to market entry will go a long way toward eliminating many potential problems and the possibility of a recall (in the case of a product), which is very costly for any firm, let alone a growing new business. Recall the recent recall of Firestone tires and the disastrous financial and public relations impact it had on Firestone and its customer, Ford Motor Company.

Production is a critical component of any business. The fastest way to increase profits is to reduce the cost of production by becoming more efficient—purchasing the right materials and supplies at the right time and in the right quantities, inspecting for quality during the production process to avoid costly returns, and providing warranties that ensure customer loyalty.

NEW VENTURE CHECKLIST

Have you:
- ☐ Outlined the production process for your business?
- ☐ Found suppliers for your materials and supply requirements?
- ☐ Determined how inventory will be handled?
- ☐ Developed quality control measures?
- ☐ Itemized and calculated your production costs?
- ☐ Determined the product/process maintenance requirements?

ISSUES TO CONSIDER

1. Why is it important to consider your manufacturing plan in the earliest stages of your new venture?

2. What are three factors that should be taken into consideration when choosing vendors to meet materials requirements?

3. Suppose you had a new advertising firm. How could you use just-in-time scheduling to create more efficiencies in your operations.

4. In what ways can the human resources of the business help control quality in all areas of the organization?

EXPERIENCING ENTREPRENEURSHIP

1. Visit a manufacturing facility that is using technology and develop a flow chart of the manufacturing process. Can you see any ways to improve the process?

2. Interview a manufacturing entrepreneur about his or her views on quality. How is this entrepreneur implementing quality control in his or her organization.

ADDITIONAL SOURCES OF INFORMATION

Clark, K., and T. Fujimoto (1991). *Product Development Performance.* Boston: Harvard Business School Press.

Conner, G. (2001). *Lean Manufacturing for the Small Shop.* Dearborn, MI: Society of Manufacturing Engineers.

Dobler, D.W., and D.N. Burt (1995). *Purchasing and Supply Management.* New York: McGraw-Hill.

Griffin, A., and J.R. Hauser (1993). "The Voice of the Customer." *Marketing Science,* 12 (1):1.

Juran, J.M. (1998). *Juran's Quality Handbook.* New York: McGraw-Hill.

Laraia, A.C., P.E. Moody, and R.W. Hall (1999). *The Kaizen Blitz: Accelerating Breakthroughs in Productivity and Performance.* New York: John Wiley.

Miller, W.B., and V.L. Schenk (2000). *All I Need to Know About Manufacturing I Learned in Joe's Garage.* Bayrock Press.

Pande, P.S., R.P. Neuman, and R.R. Cavanagh (2000). *The Six Sigma Way: How GE, Motorola, and Other Top Companies Are Honing Their Performance.* New York: McGraw-Hill.

Shores, R. (1994). *Reengineering the Factory: A Primer for World-Class Manufacturing.* Milwaukee, WI: ASQC Quality Press.

Williams, B.R. (1995). *Manufacturing for Survival.* Boston: Addison-Wesley.

INTERNET RESOURCES

Form-Net: Manufacturing Forms
http://www.entrepreneur.com/Home/HM_Static/
1,1845,formnet_manufacturing,00.html
Find production schedules, routing sheets, and progress charts to help track manufacturing processes.

ISO Online
http://www.iso.ch
The International Organization for Standardization web site, which explains their work and the standards for quality management and assurance.

ISO 9000 in Plain English
http://praxiom.com/iso-intro.htm
The ISO is a worldwide federation of national standards bodies from some 140 countries, one from each country.

Manufacturing.net
http://www.manufacturing.net/
Clearinghouse for information and resources in manufacturing.

National Center for Manufacturing Sciences
http://www.ncms.org/
Center for collaborative research on manufacturing techniques.

Supply Chain Management Solutions
http://www.research.ibm.com/pdtr/scm.html
IBM gives you step-by-step instructions for building cost-effective business processes.

Technology Transfer Information Center
http://www.nal.usda.gov/ttic
A good web site to help turn federally funded research into profits.

RELEVANT CASE STUDIES

Case 7   Roland International Freight Service

Case 9   Wizards of the Coast

15

The Marketing Plan

Don't forget that it [your product or service] is not differentiated until the customer understands the difference.
Tom Peters, Thriving on Chaos

Overview

Relationship marketing

The marketing plan

Product/service promotion

Online marketing

PROFILE 15.1

Doing All the Right Things

What company can boast that its stock over the three years from 1995 to 1997 far outpaced in growth the stock of industry giants Intel, Microsoft, Cisco Systems, and Compaq? Only Dell Computer Corporation can; its stock went from a split-adjusted low of $.39 a share in 1990 to $80 a share in 1997—not bad for a company started in 1983 in Michael Dell's dorm room at the University of Texas at Austin with $1,000. Although Dell suffered along with the rest of the industry during the technology stock volatility of 2000/2001, analysts appear to be bullish about its future. Its fifty-two-week high on April 6, 2000, prior to the dot com crash, was 56.875. It ended the year at a low of 16.25 on December 21, but recovered in the third quarter of 2001 to reach $22.76 a share. The fact that it can continue to show double-digit growth and solid operating margins in the range of 7 percent demonstrates the effectiveness of the Dell model.

The secret of Dell's enduring success? Superior execution and low-cost, direct sales, not just to consumers but to businesses like Ford, Boeing, and the mammoth Deutsche Bank. Fueling its contined growth is its foray into enterprise computing systems, geographic expansion, and added services. In 1999, Dell's very successful web site accounted for $6 million in daily sales. Dell has learned that some of its sales are made completely online and that customers who first go online and then call are twice as likely to buy.

Dell's success cannot be attributed solely to its products—state-of-the-art computers that have virtually become commodities in an industry where, to the customer, price is everything. Instead, it's a result of superior execution of its founder's production and marketing strategies, along with a very clear understanding of how the business should work. At its Austin, Texas factory, loading docks are labeled by the type of part being unloaded: CD-ROMs, cases, power supplies, and so forth. More than 1,500 workers inside the assembly plant construct PCs according to the customer's specifications. The whole process (assembly, configuration, testing, and packaging) takes about five hours. Dell has been known as one of the earliest proponents of mass customization.

Michael Dell personally spends a great deal of time with customers and has even been known to participate in sales presentations to senior executives. He believes that it's vital to stay in touch with the market and that talking directly with customers is the best way to do that. He created a web site that allows customers to configure their own computers and see the price on the spot. His business customers such as Boeing, which buys about 160 computers a day, have a dedicated Dell sales representative working inside their company.

In the computer industry, no market position is ever guaranteed, since the environment is so dynamic. In the early 1990s Dell Computer was growing so fast—

that's where the focus was—that it was in danger of falling apart for lack of systems and controls. On the management side, Dell brought in experienced Motorola executive Mort Topfer to contribute maturity to the decision making. In addition, the company implemented some very controversial strategies that ran counter to industry trends. First, instead of instigating a price war to increase sales, Dell Computer focused on high-margin customers like Boeing. Second, it used direct marketing to these customers, bypassing retail and the burgeoning home PC market. Dell began to concentrate on what it does best—achieving on-time, rapid delivery of customized PCs to a market that orders via phone and fax. Today the mission of the company includes not only growth but liquidity and profitability, and competitors such as Compaq are considering imitating Michael Dell's strategy.

Intel and Microsoft technologies dominate the industry. For Dell, this is a positive, because their customers will get those technologies via Dell computers in the most effective and least costly way possible.

Michael Dell has learned some important lessons about growth: focus on what you do best and give the customers what they want. Those lessons seem to be paying off.

SOURCES: Bob Sechler, "Dell: Pricing Is Competitive, but Within Expectations," *Wall Street Journal Interactive,* October 4, 2001; Richard Murphy, "Michael Dell," *Success,* January, 1999; Donna Fuscaldo, "Merrill Says Dell May Beat Views in Fiscal 1Q," *The Wall Street Journal,* March 28, 2001; Dell Computer Corporation, Company Research, *The Wall Street Journal,* March 30, 2001; Andrew E. Serwer, "Michael Dell Turns the PC World Inside Out," *Fortune,* September 9, 1997, p. 76; Michael Dell, "Michael Dell's Plan for the Rest of the Decade," *Fortune,* June 9, 1997 (http://pathfinder.com/fortune/digitalwatch/0609dig2.html); Rahul Jacob and Rajiv M. Rao, "The Resurrection of Michael Dell," *Fortune,* September 18, 1995.

Marketing includes all the strategies, tactics, and techniques used to raise customer awareness, to promote a product, service, or business, and to build long-term customer relationships. You can think of marketing as a bundle of benefits your company is providing to customers. These benefits reflect the core values of your company. For example, one of Southwest Airline's core values is that the customer's needs are paramount. How does that translate to customer benefits? Southwest provides some of the lowest fares in the industry to destinations that their customers go to most often. And their flight crews make the passengers feel right at home with their unabashed passion for their work as well as their nonstop sense of humor. (See Profile 15.2.)

Traditionally, marketing was described by the "5 P's"—people, product, price, place, and promotion. It consisted of a **push strategy,** whereby a customer who did not necessarily express a need for or interest in a company's product or service was persuaded to purchase it through selling techniques. In other words, the focus of the traditional marketing effort was the product, not the customer. Most entrepreneurs understand that a business cannot exist without customers and so rather than push a marketing strategy on potential customers—a very costly approach—entrepreneurs, who typically have limited resources in the early stages of their ventures, prefer to invest in relationship marketing. In relationship marketing, the primary focus is on the customer. If the product or service is designed with the customer's needs in mind, much of the "selling" that would otherwise have to be done has been taken care of by giving customers what they want, when they want it, and in the way they want it. As you saw in Profile 15.1, Michael Dell learned early the value of knowing the customer, which accounts in large part for the success of Dell Computer.

Marketing in times of change means that you can't always use the same methods you have been using for years. When you consider that unique products and services are now competitive for a much shorter time, your challenge is to rise above the crowd and build a competitive brand that is sustainable.[1] It is a fact that too many entrepreneurs underestimate the strength of their competitors, discount the impact of the global market, and develop products for a general rather than a specific and unique niche market. This chapter is based on marketing for a changing environment predicated on the need to reinvent, to acquire technological competence, and to build relationships with customers, strategic partners and even competitors.

It is not the intent of this chapter to review marketing fundamentals but to explore marketing from an entrepreneurial perspective and discuss how to create a marketing plan that will help you build long-term relationships with your customers. This chapter builds on the market research strategies and tactics in Chapter 6 that were used to conduct the feasibility analysis. You can now apply the market/customer information gathered during market research to the business plan in the form of a marketing plan.

Relationship Marketing

The essence of relationship or **one-to-one marketing** is building trust, satisfying customers, producing shared customer and company goals, communicating with customers, and making customers part of the team. Don Peppers and Martha Rogers, in their book *The One to One Future,* call this trend "share of customer."[2] **Relationship marketing** is about developing a learning environment where customer and company learn from each other with the goal of achieving a mutually beneficial life-long relationship. Relationship marketing is also about providing a bundle of benefits that the customer sees as valuable. In today's Internet environment where many products and services quickly become commodities, that is, price becomes the key differentiating factor, strong, loyal, lifetime customer relationships can allow a company to break out of the commodity bracket. Table 15.1 displays the differences between traditional transaction marketing and relationship marketing.

Relationship marketing changes not only the company's philosophy but the very way the company does business. Using interactive databases, companies can effectively focus on one customer at a time, with the goal of supplying as

TABLE 15.1

Transaction versus Relationship Marketing

Transaction Marketing	Relationship Marketing
Concerned with the single sale	Concerned with maintaining a long-term relationship
Focus on product/service features	Focus on benefits to customer
Customer service is an afterthought	Customer service is everything
Limited commitment to customer	Total customer commitment
Moderate customer contact	Continual customer contact
Quality is responsibility of production	Quality is everyone's business

many individual needs as possible. However, one-to-one marketing is not just about collecting information from the customer. For example, merely asking customers where and how they bought your product doesn't produce an answer to the question "How do customers *want* to buy the product?" It only tells you which of the purchasing methods you made available they chose. It doesn't tell you which purchasing method they would prefer.

Relationship marketing is about carrying on a dialogue with the customer over time in a market niche that you have created and defined. That means that market share per se is no longer a major goal because in your market niche, you have the potential to serve 100 percent of the market. For example, suppose through primary market research you have learned that today many professionals are commuting into major metropolitan areas from other cities and even other states to spend three or four days out of every week at their work and then fly back to their homes and families. While they are in the major city, they need a regular place to stay that is less costly than a hotel and makes more sense than maintaining an apartment full-time. You decide to satisfy that need with your business concept, which creates a niche market so you can enter the very competitive hotel and apartment markets with a group of customers who aren't presently being served. So your concern is not getting your share of the larger market but rather attracting all the potential customers in the niche you've defined and making them loyal customers. Retaining loyal customers and selling more to them is more cost efficient than constantly striving for more and more customers in a much larger market. Once you have established your company in the niche, you'll be in a better position to expand to new customer segments.

There is a side benefit to the creation of customer relationships. If a problem occurs, a customer who has spent time building a relationship with the company won't automatically shift loyalty to a competitor. Often that loyalty is actually strengthened after a problem-solving session with the company results in a satisfying conclusion. All too often, however, customers have had negative experiences with companies where the problem is not resolved satisfactorily. In those situations, the customer never forgets. Today, customers have a multitude of platforms from which to air their grievances, and one problem aired on national television can cause a public relations nightmare from which the company may never recover. A case in point is the classic story of the public relations disaster the Cunard cruise line experienced when, in what could only be described as a moment of insanity on the part of management, it decided to launch its expensive Christmas cruise of the renovated *Queen Elizabeth II* despite having a ship full of builders who hadn't yet finished their work. Apparently Cunard believed the customers would overlook the mess! This is not the way to build long-term customer relationships.

Perhaps the most important benefit to a company of establishing life-long customer relationships is that over time, the full value of customers is revealed. Customers no longer are viewed as a series of transactions but as bona fide, contributing members of the team who bring value to the bottom line. The more the company learns from its customers, the better the company becomes, and the more difficult it will be for a competitor to adversely affect the business.

● *Identifying and Rewarding the Best Customers*

It is not uncommon for a company to find that as few as 24 percent of its customers account for 95 percent of its revenues. That 24 percent are the customers the company needs to know well and keep happy because these are the customers that will readily try new products and services and refer the company to others. After a company has been in business for a while, it becomes easier to identify the most valuable customers. One way to do this is to calculate the **lifetime customer value** as a series of transactions over the life of the relationship.[3] A statistical method for doing this calculates the present value of future purchases, using an appropriate discount rate and period of time for the relationship. Add to that the value of customer referrals and subtract the cost of maintaining the relationship (advertising, promotions, letters, questionnaires, 800 numbers). The result will be the customer's lifetime value. Another, nonstatistical, method is to simply carry on a dialogue with customers about their buying intentions. The more you interact with your customers, the better your company will know them and the more valuable and reliable their feedback will be.

Frequency Programs

There are a variety of ways companies can provide special programs, incentives, and rewards for their best customers.

The airlines have used frequency programs with great success. The people who fly the most frequently with the airlines receive free tickets, VIP service, and upgrades. Rewards increase with use; therefore, the customer is given a vested interest in using a particular airline over and over.

Frequency programs have also yielded good results for other businesses. Cosmetics companies, for instance, issue cards that give customers a free product after a certain number of purchases. Similarly, small entertainment centers like miniature golf and water parks often offer discounts for season passes purchased by customers who use the service the most.

Setting up a club or membership makes customers feel special, because they have input into the company and receive special privileges for being a member; examples of these privileges include informational newsletters, discounts, and other special programs. Some companies offer their best customers next-day delivery as well as access to a special unlisted toll-free number.[4] For your company, frequency programs derive their benefit from the repeat purchases they inspire. The more a customer buys from you, the higher the probability that he or she will buy repeatedly and the lower the cost to your company of each repeat purchase. In establishing one-to-one relationships, it's essential to single out the best customers for special treatment.

Just-in-Time Marketing

Customer wants are often tied to major events or rites of passage such as birthdays, marriage, purchase of a home, pregnancy, and relocation. Keeping track of dates that are important to customers gives the company an opportunity to contact the customer on a special occasion, such as a birthday, to remind the customer of the need to purchase something or to notify a customer of an impending sale of an item he or she typically buys. This is known as just-in-time marketing. Amazon.com has made **just-in-time marketing** a critical component of its overall marketing strategy. Not only does Amazon welcome you back to its web site with the latest books and gadgets based on your interests, but it also notifies you by e-mail of new books or videos in areas you have selected.

Complaint Marketing

A dissatisfied customer will probably tell at least nine other people about the problem he or she faced with a company. (And of course those nine people will tell their friends as well!) It's easy to see how quickly even one unhappy customer can damage a company's reputation. Consequently, you ought to think of complaints not as something to avoid dealing with, but as opportunities for continual improvement. Make it easy for your customer to register a complaint and carry on a dialogue with a human being who listens and attempts to understand. Nothing is more frustrating than to have to leave a complaint on a voice mail message. Pizza Hut provides a toll-free number for customers. When you call to complain, you talk with a trained representative (Pizza Hut contracts this service out) who then communicates the nature of the complaint via e-mail to the manager of the appropriate store. The manager is then required to call you within forty-eight hours and resolve the issue.[5]

Some companies have used bulletin board services on the Internet to let customers communicate complaints, but this method, though effective, attracts more complaints than other methods. Companies using bulletin boards have found, in fact, that this system works almost too well, since customers feel free to vent their frustrations more angrily online than when they are hearing a soothing, caring voice at the other end of a phone line. Moreover, since anyone with access to the Internet can read the angry messages, a strong complaint can build momentum and create more problems than necessary.

One way to stem complaints at the source is to provide satisfaction surveys at every point of contact with the customer, so that you can cope with problems quickly, at the outset, before the customer becomes so angry that resolution and satisfaction will be nearly impossible. Following are several suggestions for effective handling of complaints.

▶ Recognize that the customer is a human being and treat him or her as such, never as a number, never as someone without a name or feelings.

▶ Let the customer completely explain the complaint without interruption. In this way, you are acknowledging that the complaint is important and worthy of attention.

▶ To find out what the customer really wants, ask the most important question: *"What is one thing we can do to make this better?"*

▶ Defuse the anger of the customer by sincerely taking his or her side on the issue; then move the customer from a problem focus to a solution focus. Get the customer to agree on a solution.

▶ Contact the customer one week later to find out whether he or she is still satisfied with the solution and express the company's desire for a continued relationship.

The most important message you can send to your customers through your marketing efforts is that the customer is the most important part of the organization and you will do whatever it takes to keep good customers satisfied. While it's certainly true that a young, growing company needs to build a customer base by continually adding new customers, it will reap the greatest returns from investing in the customers it currently has.

The Marketing Plan

For any company, an effective marketing strategy begins with a marketing plan. The marketing plan for an entrepreneurial company is a living guide to how the company plans to build customer relationships over its life in order to fulfill the mission statement in the business plan. It details the strategies and tactics that will create awareness on the part of the customer and build a loyal customer base. Marketing plans are written at many points in the life of a business. The original business plan will contain a marketing plan for introducing the company and its products and services to the marketplace. Later you may develop a marketing plan to introduce new products and services, and to grow the business, perhaps in a new direction.

A few important steps taken before the actual writing of the marketing plan ensure that the plan is on target and is one you can live with for a long time. Saying you must live with the plan for a long time may sound inconsistent with the entrepreneur's need to remain flexible and adapt to change in the marketplace, but one of the biggest problems with most marketing plans is that they are not followed long enough to achieve the desired results.

Typically, the business owner does not see immediate results from the marketing effort and decides it must not be working—so he or she changes it and starts the cycle all over again. Changing the plan on impulse is the wrong thing to do. It takes time to make customers aware of the product or service. It takes time for a particular marketing strategy to take hold and build confidence in the customer. From the first time a customer sees an ad, for example, to the point at which the customer actually buys the product may be weeks or even months. In fact, on average, the customer will see an ad fifteen to twenty times before actually purchasing a product. Therefore, just like a good stock market investor, you must think of the marketing plan as an investment in the future of the business, and realize that any investment takes time to mature. Reaping the benefits of a well-structured marketing plan requires persistence and unwavering dedication until the plan has an opportunity to perform.

Remember that the initial mission you chose for your company and your core values will set the tone for the marketing plan that you develop. There are several steps to take prior to writing a marketing plan.

1. *Define your approach to the market.* Think of your approach to the market as the bridge between strategy and execution. It includes such things as the message, differentiation tactics, channel strategies, and performance goals. Choosing the wrong approach can result in your customers not understanding the benefits you're providing. Choosing the same approach for all customers will mean that you won't be satisfying everyone. To identify the most effective approach to the market, you need to return to your market research (see Chapter 6) and make sure you correctly understand your customers' needs.

2. *Make a list of the options.* To even begin to know which marketing options should be considered, you need to talk to other business owners, customers, and suppliers. Read some books and articles on marketing

strategies for entrepreneurs, like those suggested at the end of this chapter. This process will produce a list of possibilities for you to consider that may range from sponsoring a business conference to advertising in a national trade publication. Determining which strategies are the most effective, or even feasible, can be left for later.

3. *Think like a customer.* Imagine the business from the customer's point of view. What would entice *you* to enter that store, buy that product, avail yourself of that service?

4. *Study the competition.* Take a look at the businesses that will be competing with yours and determine what makes them successful or unsuccessful. What marketing strategies do they seem to employ, and are those effective? How could you improve on what your competitors are doing? Refer to the competitive analysis you did in Chapter 4.

5. *Analyze the options and rank them.* Eliminate first those that either don't meet the needs of the target market or simply are not feasible at this time (usually for budgetary reasons). Then rank the top ten choices. You are now ready to begin writing the marketing plan.

● The Marketing Plan in One Paragraph

Many experienced marketers suggest that the first step in creating the marketing plan is to condense all the ideas about marketing strategy into a single paragraph that says it all. Impossible? Not at all. A single well-written paragraph will force you to focus carefully on the central point of the overall marketing strategy. The paragraph should include:

▶ The purpose of the marketing plan.
  What will the marketing plan accomplish?

▶ The benefits of the product/service.
  How will the product/service help the customer or satisfy a need?

▶ The target market.
  Who is the primary buyer?

▶ The market niche.
  Where do you fit in the industry or market? How do you differentiate yourself?

▶ The marketing tactics to be used.
  What specific marketing tools will be employed?

> ❱ The company's convictions, its identity.
> *How will the customers define the company?*

> ❱ The percentage of sales the marketing budget will represent.
> *How much money will you be allocating to the marketing plan?*

Here is an example of an effective one-paragraph statement of the marketing plan for a product/service business.

> TradePartners enables qualified importers and exporters from a variety of countries to find trading partners through an Internet-based, business to business network. The **purpose** of the marketing plan is to create awareness and name recognition for TradePartners in the market space. The **target customer** is the small exporter who needs to find buyers in another country or find a buyer for excess inventory, and the importer who wants to find new sources for products to import. TradePartners provides the **benefits** of reduced time and risk in finding new customers or suppliers. The company has defined a **niche** targeting smaller companies that want access to the same opportunities as large companies worldwide. **Customers will view** TradePartners as a professional, innovative, and customer-focused company. Initial **marketing tactics** include personal selling at industry events, strategic alliances with complementary companies and providing free workshops on import/export. TradePartners will spend an average of **40 percent of sales** to implement the marketing strategy in the initial stages.

With your paragraph in hand and the focus established, you can now create a more detailed marketing plan.

Overview of Marketing Plan Components

Every marketing plan incorporates the traditional 5 P's of marketing: people, product, price, place, and promotion, which are discussed in any marketing text. Once you have dealt with these aspects of the plan, you can move on to the creative aspects such as the advertising goals. You will also develop a media plan that details what media will be used, when they will be used, and how much they will cost. Here is an outline of the major issues that should be addressed in the marketing plan. You may also want to refer to the "Business Plan Outline" in the Appendix for additional items that should be included in the marketing plan.

Marketing Plan Outline

Keep in mind that the following topics are only suggested sections to include in your marketing plan, and they apply to most types of businesses. Depending on the type of business you have, you may want to include additional sections.

One-Paragraph Marketing Plan

This is the paragraph you created earlier in this section and is an excellent opening summary for the marketing plan.

Key Marketing Issues That Will Affect the Success of the Company

Identify issues your company faces that will affect the way you can market your products and services to customers. For example, your company may not be located near your customers, so you will have to figure out creative ways to create those important personal relationships.

Launch Objectives

These are your key objectives for your marketing campaign. What do you want to accomplish and how do you intend to do it?

Milestones

It's a good idea to take out a calendar and plan the timeline to achieve your marketing objectives. Marking milestones for advertising, promotional events, and trade shows gives some direction to your marketing plan.

Strategic Alliances

Many businesses today form partnerships with other companies in compatible markets to promote each other's products and services. Which companies and other partners will you use in your marketing campaign?

Metrics

Measuring the effectiveness of marketing efforts is critical to avoid wasting precious company resources. For example, match your sales forecasts to specific marketing tactics and assign responsibility for measuring the outcome to a specific person. One way entrepreneurs measure success in a marketing effort is to ask customers how they heard about the company or the product/service.

Strategic Alignment

Strategies deal with the needs of the market and what you're offering to satisfy those needs. Tactics are the media, channels, and delivery mechanisms you use to reach the customer. Are your goals, strategies and tactics in alignment? If your business's goal is to emphasize reliability and customer satisfaction, for example, does your marketing plan have strategies and tactics for achieving that, like customer feedback mechanisms and training in the use of your products?

● **Strategies for Pricing**

Pricing a product or service is as much a part of a marketing strategy as it is part of the financial strategy because it is one of the many features associated with your product or service. Pricing, in fact, is a key aspect of your marketing plan and becomes the central selling point when your product or service is a commodity; that is, when the only feature differentiating your product or service from your competitors' is price. Some examples of commodities are basic food products like milk and most electronics categories that have been in the market for some time like desktop computers and printers. Entrepreneurs can price new technology higher because it offers features and benefits not currently in the market, but it quickly becomes a commodity item as competitors introduce their versions of the new technology.

How you price your product or service is a function of your company's goals. Is your goal to

> ▶ *Increase sales?* This may entail lowering prices to raise the volume sold.

> ▶ *Increase market share?* Again, lowering prices may increase volume, thus increasing market share.

> ▶ *Maximize cash flow?* Increasing cash flow can be achieved several ways, including raising prices and reducing direct costs and overhead.

> ▶ *Maximize profit?* Similar to maximizing cash flow, this can be accomplished several ways, including raising prices, lowering prices and increasing volume, or decreasing overhead.

> ▶ *Set up entry barriers to competition?* Lowering prices on the basis of using efficient production methods, achieving economies of scale, and keeping overhead low can often set up entry barriers to companies that can't compete on that scale.

> ▶ *Define an image?* Setting a higher price based on higher perceived and/ or actual quality is one way of establishing a particular image in an industry.

> ▶ *Control demand?* Where a company does not have the resources to meet demand, prices can be set at a level that discourages sales to a particular degree.

Knowing what a pricing strategy is supposed to accomplish in advance of setting a price will ensure compatibility with the company's goals. Once you have established a pricing strategy, you will want to consider the various components of an effective strategy.

Cost-Based Pricing

In this pricing strategy you add the cost of producing the product, the related costs of running the business, and a profit margin to arrive at a market price.

Demand-Based Pricing

Demand pricing is based on finding out what customers are willing to pay for the product, then pricing it accordingly. For new products or services with no direct comparison, a combination of this approach and cost-based pricing is often used to arrive at a satisfactory price. In general, customers recognize several prices for any one product: the standard price, which is the price normally paid for the item; the sale price; the price paid for specials; and the relative price, which is the price of the item compared to a substitute product. For some products, customers may have to add to the normal cost of shipping, handling, or installation in their comparison with other like products.

Competition-Based Pricing

Where the product has direct competition, you can look at competitors' pricing strategy and price the product or service in line with theirs—higher if it is determined that the product has added value or lower if competing on price.

Psychological Pricing

Using an odd-even strategy can suggest a pricing position in the market, an odd number ($12.99) to suggest a bargain, an even number ($40.00) to suggest quality, or higher than average pricing to suggest exclusivity.

Distribution Channel Pricing

The channel of distribution through which you choose to move your product or service will affect the ultimate price to the customer, as you must allow for each intermediary in the channel to make a certain percentage of profit.

Extrapolating from Other Industries

It is important to look at the pricing strategies of businesses in other industries. The fact that your industry does not seem to employ a particular strategy does not mean that the strategy won't work. Staying competitive on price means always looking for new methods of pricing products.

Product/Service Promotion

For many entrepreneurs, putting a lot of money into advertising and promotion doesn't make sense; they don't have the resources of a General Motors, so their money is better spent on more effective ways of reaching very specific cus-

Permission Marketing

One of the latest buzz words in the marketing world is **"permission marketing,"** coined by Internet marketer and entrepreneur Seth Godin, whose company, Yoyodyne Entertainment, is designed to teach the new marketing lessons for a new world.

Godin claims that mass marketing is a problem for consumers because to get their attention, mass marketers have to interrupt them with commercials, newspaper ads, and so forth. That style of marketing worked in the 1950s and 1960s when people weren't so bombarded by information in the form of marketing. But today the challenge is to get customers to voluntarily pay attention to what you're trying to say. And considering that the average consumer sees or hears about one million marketing messages a day, this is no small task, but not new either. Certainly it is the basis of relationship marketing touted by Peppers and Rogers and others who believe that having loyal, life-long customers is the secret to business success. The approach that Godin takes is to get the customer involved in a game show, contest, or sweepstakes. His company, Yoyodyne, a direct marketing firm, develops games and contests that people play via e-mail. He is turning dull corporate web sites into attractive places to spend some time. He is telling potential customers what's in it for them.

For example, one of Godin's clients, H&R Block, was interested in introducing a concept called Premium Tax, aimed at upper-income customers.

To do that, H&R Block had to get their attention, since those customers typically had their own accountants. Yoyodyne put banner ads on a variety of appropriate web sites that announced, "We'll pay your taxes sweepstakes." More than 50,000 people responded giving their e-mail addresses. By participating in the sweepstakes, these potential customers were giving H&R Block permission to tell them about their new service.

Is Godin's strategy successful? In a word, yes. The company now receives more e-mail than any company in the world. In 1998 Web portal Yahoo acquired the direct marketer for about $29.6 million in stock. Here are four questions that Godin suggests you ask yourself about your relationships with customers:

1. Do all of your marketing efforts encourage the customer to communicate with you?
2. Do you keep track of people who have given you permission to communicate with them?
3. Do you know what you would say to customers once they have given you permission?
4. Once you have someone as a customer, how do you work to keep that customer?

Sources: William C. Taylor, "Permission Marketing," *Fast Company,* April, 1998; "Seth Godin: Feeding the Gorilla," *BackTalk, CIO Web Business Magazine,* August 1, 1999; www.yoyo.com; www.permission.com; Sandeep Junnarkar and Jim Hu, "Yahoo to Buy Yoyodyne," CNET News.com, October 12, 1998.

tomers. Amilya Antonetti, the founder of SoapWorks, a manufacturer of hypoallergenic soap products, has built a large customer base on a fairly small advertising budget.[6] She does it by interacting constantly with her current and prospective customers; and many of her female customers, who are tired of all the advertising hype directed at them, gravitate to her all-natural products and more personal approach. She also uses her web site (www.soapworks.com) to make it more convenient for her customers to purchase her products.

Antonetti takes many of the calls that come into her company daily and personally hands out samples of her products at hospitals and women's shelters. Her customers regularly share their problems and needs with her and spread the word about her company to others they meet. Antonetti has found an effective way to promote her business directly to the people she wants to serve.

Entrepreneurs approach marketing from a point of view distinctly different from that of the traditional marketer. While they may employ some of the same techniques as a large corporate marketer, they also will take advantage of many other marketing opportunities, ones that the corporate marketer may ignore. Jay Conrad Levinson has called the entrepreneurial marketing approach **guerrilla marketing,** which is an alternative to traditional, expensive marketing tactics.[7] Given that entrepreneurs don't have the time or money for elaborate, high-profile marketing strategies, they essentially mimic what the big companies do, but for much less money, in more creative ways, and for a shorter period of time. Guerrilla marketing is a do-it-yourself approach to marketing for entrepreneurs. Throughout this chapter you will find guerrilla-type tactics that you can quickly employ in your business to more effectively reach and keep customers. For example, the tactics in an earlier section—just-in-time marketing, frequency programs, and complaint marketing—are big-company tactics with a guerrilla twist to them. And you'll find additional resources at the end of the chapter.

A new business requires two promotional plans: one for opening the business and making customers aware of its existence and the other, for growing the business. The opening plan establishes the identity or philosophy of the business. Remember that identity and philosophy are quite different from image. An *image* is what you may aspire to be, whereas your business character and philosophy define who you are in reality.

There are many ways to effectively promote your company and its products and services. In this section, we'll look at a variety of promotional tactics from an entrepreneurial perspective.

● *Taking Advantage of Publicity*

Publicity and word-of-mouth or referrals are two of the most effective entrepreneurial marketing tools around because they don't cost the company any money. What they do require is a compelling story that will attract attention. When you write a concept statement for your business or an executive summary for your business plan, the reader or listener needs to understand the plan. Why should they be interested in your company and its products or services? In other words, what is your compelling story? Perhaps you have noticed that people have to shop around for nutritional supplements. They can't find all the best items in one location, so they're spending a lot of time and money shopping. Suppose, like Mike Minsky, a young entrepreneur from the Chicago area, you decide to provide a one-stop shopping experience online for the very best nutritional supplements and advice from a leading expert, Bonnie Minsky (http://www.nutritionalconcepts.com/). By doing this, you are solving a compelling problem for consumers—you are saving them time and money by giving them one central location, Nutritional Concepts, for all their supplement needs. And that's newsworthy.

Or perhaps, like Kim Camarella, you learned from a close friend that larger-sized young women are having trouble finding stylish clothing and feeling good about themselves. You design a line of clothing created to make these women look wonderful and you let them buy online as well as in boutiques, so they can also experience shopping in the privacy of their homes (www.kyonnakloth-ing.com). When you can tell a compelling story about your business and solve a problem, it's easier to get customers' and media attention.

Getting Publicity

If the business or product is newsworthy, there are several ways to get some publicity. Write to a reporter or editor to tease him or her with an idea, and follow up with a phone call. Whenever possible, get to know people in the media on a first-name basis and even take them to lunch. This gives you instant clout when you need free publicity. Issue a press release answering the who, what, where, when, and why of the business and include a press kit containing the press release, bios and photos of the key people in the story, any necessary background information, and copies of any other articles written about the company. The idea is to make it as easy as possible for the reporter to write or tell the story. The media are always looking for news and appreciate the effort to give them something newsworthy. When an article is written about the business, use reprints in future advertising and brochures to get even more value for the effort.

Constructing an Effective Press Release

An effective news release should contain the following:

- ▶ The date, your name, and a phone number
- ▶ The release date (for immediate release, or after a certain date)
- ▶ An appropriate headline
- ▶ The release information typed double-spaced with wide margins
- ▶ The who, what, where, when, and why at the very beginning of the press release
- ▶ A photo if appropriate
- ▶ A note explaining briefly why you sent the release

There are also several publishing services that can be used to gather and distribute information about the business. For example PR Newswire is the leading source for press releases on companies (http://www.prnewswire.com/).

Getting Customers to Talk about You

The best customers you will ever have will be the result of referrals from satisfied current customers. So how can you get customers to tell more people about your business? Here are several suggestions from entrepreneur trainer and author Kimberley Stansell.[8]:

▶ Start a referral service and enroll everyone who shops at your business. Give them business cards to distribute to people they know.

▶ Provide incentives for your referral program. Give them a commission for bringing in new leads (this works well in professional service businesses like consulting) or a discount on their next purchase.

▶ Offer a big prize—a trip, cash, lottery tickets, etc.—to the customer who brought in the most referrals during the year.

▶ Get feedback from your customers on referral tactics and incentives.

Most of all, do something big that gets your customers excited about referring business to you. It will be far less expensive than advertising.

● *Giving It Away*

While it is often true that you get what you pay for, today it's also true that you may get what you don't pay for. More and more entrepreneurs are using the tactic that Netscape and Microsoft used— they gave their browsers away to rapidly grow their markets. Giving customers something for free makes sense in an environment where it's hard to even get the customer's attention in the first place. But you have to know when giving something away will help the business or simply cost money you can't afford to lose.[9] Consider giving away information, consulting, or samples of your product when

▶ You believe you will see this customer again.

▶ The cost to you for each additional item is low, that is, margins are high.

▶ Customers need to try the product or service in order to risk the money to buy it, especially if it's unproven technology. Consider offering the product or service to a well-known customer who will testify to his or her satisfaction with it.

▶ You can provide samples of your product or service at a large event like a conference or tradeshow, so that you can generate a lot of interest inexpensively.

On the other hand, don't give away your product or service when it's something like financial expertise that relies on credibility, because customers may be wary and question it's quality. Don't give away expensive items or commodity items, especially when your probability of retaining those customers is low.

● ### Advertising

Advertising is promotion that costs your company money. Advertising media generally fall into two categories: print and broadcast. The following sections examine the various types of media and their uses. It is not the purpose of this book to provide all the information needed to use each medium presented, only to create awareness of how and when each is used, so that you can make a decision about which media will best serve the business.

Print Media

The Newspaper   The purpose of a newspaper is to distribute the news in a direct, to-the-point fashion. Today that doesn't mean just the town gazette. Most cities have one or more major newspapers in addition to business newspapers, shopper newspapers, ethnic newspapers, and national newspapers, which often have regional editions as well. How does an entrepreneur know which is most appropriate for the product or service being sold? With businesses spending nearly one-third of their advertising dollars on newspaper ads, this question becomes crucial.

Newspaper advertising offers these advantages:

▶ Broad coverage in a selected geographic area

▶ Flexibility and speed in bringing an ad to print and changing it along the way

▶ Quickness in generating sales

▶ Relatively low cost

Newspapers have disadvantages as well. Broad coverage means you are paying to reach people who may not be part of the target market. Furthermore, since newspapers carry hundreds of ads every day, it is not easy (short of taking a full page) to attract the attention of the reader. Then, too, a newspaper has a very short life. A person may read it with breakfast and throw it out before leaving for work. Even an ad that was noticed may be forgotten by the end of the day. Therefore, you may want to consider a specialized newspaper that will better reach the customer you want.

Here are some tips for using newspaper advertising.

▶ Determine which newspaper is best for your business by placing ads in all the papers in your target region the first time. If appropriate for your business, include in the ad a coupon or toll-free number so that the potential customer will either bring the coupon into your place of business or call on a special line. In either case, ask the person who responds where he or she heard about the business. Ads in the papers with the highest response rates should be continued and all others dropped. Once you have done this in one or two geographic regions, you can safely assume that a similar type of newspaper in another part of the country will give similar results.

▶ Be sure you or someone you have paid designs the ad so that it doesn't look like every other one on the page. Often a distinctive border will make the ad stand out.

▶ Create a basic design for advertising that reflects the philosophy of the business and use that design consistently in all advertising. Customers will eventually recognize that the ad is for your company before they even read it.

▶ The best location for the ad (because it is the most visible) is a right-hand page, above the fold of the newspaper, but it is often the most costly.

▶ Keep track of the results of your ads by asking a sample of customers who contact the business how they found the business and what they thought of the ad, particularly if you are experimenting with size and design.

▶ A national newspaper like *USA Today* offers a good opportunity to do national advertising for less money and a broader reach than a magazine.

Magazines   A number of national magazines offer businesses the opportunity to advertise to certain broad-based target markets. Magazines like *People, Newsweek, Business Week,* and *Time* reach hundreds of thousands of people every week. In addition, there are specialty magazines like *Sports Illustrated, Modern Maturity, Rolling Stone,* and *Road & Track* that focus on specific interests. These magazines are useful for businesses that are targeting a particular interest like cars and car accessories or senior citizen issues. There are also a great number of trade magazines that reflect the needs of specific trade organizations, like *Advertising Age* and *Variety.* Magazine advertising, however, is more costly and the time lag for printing is generally six to eight weeks, so it lacks the flexibility of newspaper advertising. These things must be weighed against the fact that you may be doing a better job of reaching the target market and more than one person generally reads a single issue of a magazine, which is a benefit over newspapers.

Magazines also offer the entrepreneur one thing newspapers can't: credibility. According to Jay Levinson, author of *Guerrilla Marketing* and many other books, "A properly produced magazine ad, preferably of the full-page variety, gives a small business more credibility than any other mass marketing medium."[10] Obviously, you would want to run the ad more than once; but it is possible to run the ad one time and order reprints at a fraction of the original cost to use in direct mail campaigns and in brochures.

Here are some tips for magazine advertising.

▶ If the magazine has a regional edition, such as *Time,* run the ad in the region you are targeting. This makes more sense economically because you will be more effective in reaching the people you need to reach.

▶ Use a media buying service to gain real cost advantages. A buying service purchases a lot of ad space in bulk, so they get it at rates that you as a single company cannot get.

▶ Ask the magazine whether you can buy a split-run ad; that is, run one headline in half the magazines that go to one geographic area and another in the other half. Be sure to code them so you can keep track of responses.

▶ Code all ads to reflect publication, date, run, and ad size so you can figure out which is more effective. Then be sure to do that sample of customers mentioned earlier to check their reaction to the publication.

▶ Use color effectively and take advantage of the fact that you can provide more information in a magazine ad than in a newspaper ad, because the reader generally spends more time with a magazine ad.

▶ Always give a phone number, web address, or mail-in coupon in the ad to encourage people to contact you for a full brochure or a video so that you have the opportunity to begin a relationship.

▶ Check on "remnant space," leftover space that must be filled before the magazine goes to print. It will be a fraction of the original cost of an ad. Call the advertising manager for the publication to inquire about timing for remnant space.

The Yellow Pages   Many businesses can benefit from placing ads in the Yellow Pages of their telephone directory. If you are in the retail business or offer a service not considered a professional service (that is, you are not a consultant, lawyer, accountant), there is a good chance people will look in the Yellow Pages for what you offer. However, remember that the Yellow Pages is fairly expensive advertising space and targets only the local market for your product or service, so it should not be considered a major advertising resource, particularly if you market nationally or globally.

Signs   Signs are a relatively inexpensive way to expose a lot of people to the business. They also encourage impulse buying of consumer products. Naturally, signs play the most important role in retail businesses where they become part of the total advertising campaign. In other types of businesses, the sign is merely a feature to help someone locate the business. Signs for sales or special events do, however, outlive their usefulness fairly quickly. If a sale sign is left in a window too long, people will tune it out and it will have lost its value.

What's in a Name?

Even the name of your business should be part of the overall marketing plan because it's the first point of identity you establish with the customer. It should be easily remembered and should relate to what you are selling. "Useful Products," the name of one California company, would not win any prizes for originality and style, but "Higher Ground," an Oregon coffee company, might.

Direct Marketing

Direct marketing includes direct mail, mail order, coupons, telemarketing, door-to-door, and TV shopping networks. The essence of direct marketing is that the entrepreneur attempts to close a sale at the moment the advertising takes place. Direct marketing also permits coverage of a wide geographic area while, at the same time, targeting specific customers; therefore, more sales can be generated with fewer dollars. Much more information can be provided in a direct-response brochure than in other types of advertising; in other words, the brochure can answer all the customer's questions so that he or she can make an immediate decision. Consequently, direct mail has the highest response rate of any type of advertising, and the responses you receive from a purchased mailing list can become the basis of your business's own direct mailing list. Another way to create a personalized mailing list is to have people who walk in to the place of business fill out a database card and suggest other people who may be interested in the product or service.

The average response rate for direct mail is 2 percent. That rate can be increased 50 to 100 percent if you include a toll-free number in the advertising, which is easier for many customers than filling out an order form. That response rate, in turn, can be increased 100 to 700 percent by following up the mailing with a phone call—a method known as telemarketing—within seventy-two hours. When you use telemarketing as a tactic, be sure that you understand the Telephone Consumer Protection Act (47 USC 227), which requires that you maintain a "do-not-call" list and bans unsolicited advertising via fax machines. You can find out more about this act at www.the-dma.org/library/guidelines/tcpa.shtml.

It's important for a small, growing company to consider the staff resources available and to control mailings to the number you can reasonably follow up on within the seventy-two hours. To get the highest possible response rate, you have to do several repeat mailings and repeat the telemarketing effort. For catalogs, four times a year is typical. Also, since most customers have a tendency to throw out direct, unsolicited mail before reading it, it is important to put the central selling point on the envelope as well. Customers must be enticed to open the envelope. A tag line that suggests that what is contained in the envelope will bring the customer something he or she values will certainly encourage people to see what you have to offer. Be sure to continuously update your mailing list and refine it so that the number of nonresponses declines.

Success with direct mail depends on using a good mailing list, offering something the customer wants, and being creative in the marketing of the product or service. If you use a targeted mailing list, offer a real benefit to the customer, and send that offer in a business envelope with no return address, the chances of getting a response climb significantly. This occurs because customers are bombarded every day by advertising campaigns of one sort or another. So, if they see that the return address is a consumer product or service company, they may not bother to open the envelope at all. You are offering a real value to your customers, so you have to get their attention and overcome the negative effects of companies that have not offered value.

Not all products are suitable for direct mail, however. Those that do not require repeat orders, are not easily shipped, are readily available in stores, or are seasonal or short-lived (like fad items) are not good bets.

If you are dealing in a consumer item, you may also want to consider interactive TV shopping shows or infomercials to sell the product. The interactive version where the viewer can see the product and order it immediately is in place in several test markets and will eventually be accessible to anyone who wishes it. Interactive TV allows you access to the consumer you seek, defined by sex, age, special interests, occupation, and so forth. This is definitely a growing market for direct market sales.

Broadcast Media

Radio   Radio is an excellent medium for local or regional advertising, because the audience can be targeted geographically and generally by age group. Radio stations keep extensive records on the demographics of their listening audience to help determine whether this audience will be interested in a particular product or service. It is useful to advertise on more than one station to saturate your market. Recently many companies have been able to gain a national presence by sponsoring a national radio program. When dealing in radio advertising it is important to understand that the ad can't be a one-shot ad. Because radio listeners are fickle and tend to change stations often, the ad needs to be played several times a day, several days a week to achieve an impact. Keep track of the responses received from the ad in the same manner as suggested for print media so you will know where it has made the greatest impact.

A general rule of thumb is that prime radio time is during commuting hours in the morning and late afternoon. The cost will be higher at those times, but you will reach the most people. Be sure to provide finished recorded commercials to the station so you can maintain quality and consistency in your advertising. Don't rely on the radio station personnel to give your ad the energy and professionalism it needs. Here are a few more tips for radio advertising.

‣ Stick to shorter spots. You can usually achieve just as much in a well-designed thirty-second ad as you can in a one-minute ad.

‣ Use music and sound effects to set the tone for the commercial. Both can be rented from most radio stations for a modest amount.

‣ Be sure to design the commercial to catch the listener's attention in the first few seconds.

‣ Run your ads three weeks out of every four for good coverage at less cost.

Television   Many businesses spend one quarter of their advertising dollars on television; consequently, it is the second-most-popular form of advertising for consumer products (after newspapers). With television, people can see as well as hear about the product or service, and the audience can be targeted at the national, regional, or even local level as well as by interest group by using cable channels. However, television advertising is expensive, with high costs not only for the actual on-air time but also for the preparation and filming of the commercial.

When using television, seek the help of a media buying service. These services are the equivalent of buying health insurance through group pools, and they can get your media time much more cheaply than you can because they buy millions of dollars' worth every month.

While learning how to produce a television spot fills a book by itself, here are two pieces of advice: 1) Write the script yourself and let the television studio provide the product equipment and expertise and 2) do not appear in the commercial unless you are a professional actor.

Miscellaneous Advertising   Many simple advertising tactics have been very successful for new and growing consumer products or service businesses. Offering T-shirts and baseball caps with the company's name emblazoned on them for sale (or as a giveaway) has been a very successful tactic. Using searchlights to attract people to your business site is an attention getter. Couponing has certainly been an advertising staple, and there are many coupon magazines in which you can buy space. These magazines are distributed to households across the country and have been an excellent source of new customers for businesses. Look for any and all opportunities to demonstrate the product free to potential customers. One southern California entrepreneur who developed a successful, easy-to-use cleaner for silk plants reports his sales always increase when he does demonstrations in stores. Creating a videotape of the product in action is another useful technique, especially where the product is not easily transported.

● *Personal Selling*

Traditional selling techniques just don't meet the needs of today's customers. They expect a quality product at a fair price with good service. That's a given. If you start with this in mind, you will find that the way you sell your products and promote your business is quite different from the traditional approach. Today, a business distinguishes itself in the marketplace by identifying and meeting specific customer needs. So even if you are selling a commodity, you need to figure out some way to add value to the product.

A good example of a company that adds value to a product is a small manufacturer of molded plastic parts in Massachusetts. Its largest account is a major acoustic speaker manufacturer, also in Massachusetts. The speaker company asked the plastics company to assign a full-time salesperson to its plant, which would help it eliminate some of the costs of buyers and planners and at the same time let the plastics plant concentrate on service rather than on trying to acquire new accounts. As a result, the plastic company's sales have increased nearly 40 percent per year.

Becoming a value-added company by tailoring products to meet customers' needs requires that everyone in the company become service oriented, a time-consuming task that necessitates training and educating employees. It also demands an opportunity mindset, rather than a selling mindset. It is a more lengthy process; however, the returns are potentially greater. Working more closely with customers can translate into reduced selling and marketing costs.

Improving Personal Selling Skills

Here are some tips to improve your personal selling skills.

- Do your homework before you try to sell. In other words, know what your customers want from the sale and give them what they want. Your first meeting with the customer should be designed to gather as much information about his or her needs as possible.

- Build credibility with the customer before you try to sell anything and do a lot of listening to understand your customer's needs.

- Position yourself as a solution provider in the mind of your customer.

- Make sure you grab the customer's interest immediately.

- Be sure to let the customer use the product (if this is possible) so they understand it and appreciate it.

- Always stand in front of the customer, not to the side. You want to see his or her facial expressions as you explain the benefits.

- Don't waste your customer's time, or yours. Get to the point as quickly as possible. If the customer seems to balk at making a decision, ask him or her to explain why.

- If the customer says no, maintain your sense of humor, then ask why. Repeat the value you are providing and ask the prospect to contact two of your existing customers.

▶ If the customer buys from someone else, find out who and determine how you could have done a more effective job of presenting your case.

One of the most difficult issues an entrepreneur faces with regard to selling is compensation—what and how to pay sales representatives. The possibilities are endless: incentives can be tied to profit or gross margins, contract size, the number of new accounts acquired, company goals, and so on. You can also choose to pay salespeople a straight salary or a salary plus a percentage of the profits.

Yet another issue is how to compensate those who provide service to customers. Service is the key to customer retention, and the people who provide that service are becoming increasingly more important to a firm's success. Studying the compensation practices in your industry as well as those of other industries will help you decide which method is best for your business.

Trade Shows and Exhibits

For entrepreneurs in many industries like electronics, industrial equipment, gift items, and so forth, trade shows, fairs, and exhibits are a primary way to expose their products. Trade shows are a good way to find out who the competitors are and what marketing techniques they are using. It is also the place to meet and negotiate with sales representatives and to get names for a mailing list. But the primary reason to display your products at a trade show is to eventually sell more product. To accomplish this, you should do the following:

1. Rent booth space. Hire a display designer to design and produce a quality display booth that will attract attention. Visiting several trade shows prior to doing your own will give you some ideas as to what works and what doesn't. You may also be able to work out a deal with a company that has compatible products to share a booth and combine resources.

2. Hire a professional model or sales person to distribute an information sheet that invites people to stop by the booth. Save the expensive brochures to hand out to potential customers who actually come to the booth. Also be sure to ask for business cards so you can follow up with people who took the brochure.

3. Have enough knowledgeable, personable people in the booth so that potential customers are not kept waiting to talk with someone. Stagger breaks to keep the booth staffed at all times.

4. Consider renting a hospitality suite in the hotel where the trade show is located, to entertain key people in your industry.

5. Offer something free at your booth: a sample or a contest.

6. Follow up with letters to anyone whose business card was collected and phone calls to all serious prospects.

Dealing with Information Overload

One of the biggest problems entrepreneurs have when using databases to keep track of customer information is how to control the massive amounts of information they amass. Here are a few tips for dealing with information overload.

1. Be careful about what you choose to store in your database. Make sure it's really useful, not just another piece of minutia you'll have cluttering up the file.
2. Rank your customers as to their importance to the company so that as you enter more information, you can make better decisions about whether or not to keep it.
3. Keep careful track of customers who have given you permission to contact them to pro-

vide further information about your products and services.
4. Think carefully about how to enter names and key words so that you can easily find things again. If, for example, a company is known by its corporate initials, as in AAA, don't file it under American Automobile Association.
5. Keep only your best customers in the main database. Archive older or lost customers for future reference if needed.
6. To make a database work, you must regularly enter data; in other words, keep it current.
7. Make the interface to the database user-friendly so that the appropriate people can access its contents easily.

Marketing to Industrial Customers

When the target market you are trying to reach is other businesses, the marketing strategy is somewhat different in terms of advertising and promotion. Consumer products and services require a considerable amount of high-profile advertising and promotion to entice customers away from numerous other possible choices. With industrial products and services, the focus is on letting the targeted businesses know that the product or service is available and what it can do for the business.

In general, producers of industrial products and services do not use broadcast media or most popular print media. Instead, they rely heavily on direct mail, personal selling, trade shows, and articles and advertisements in trade journals. Because most industrial product manufacturers distribute their products through wholesalers, it becomes the wholesalers' job to market to and locate retail outlets. If you are dealing with industrial customers, investigate how products and services are marketed in your particular industry. Today, many industries do much of their supply-chain transacting on the Internet through companies like VerticalNet and Oracle. It has saved them time and money as well as making it possible for employees to make purchases from their desktops.

One of the newest and most rapidly growing areas of marketing is customer relationship management or CRM. It is a critical component of any successful marketing plan.

● **Customer Relationship Management (CRM)**

Customer relationship management (CRM), formerly known as database marketing (DBM), is a combination of technology, training, and business strategy that results in a system for gathering and using information on customers and prospects with the goal of increasing profitability. It has been a mainstay of large corporations and until only a few years ago was out of reach for smaller companies. Today, however, affordable database software with sample templates makes it easy to set up a useful database in a relatively short period of time. A good CRM system can generate better sales leads, allow rapid responses to changing customer needs, and ensure that everyone who needs customer information has it when they need it in the form they need.

A well-constructed database will contain names, addresses, and attributes of people who are likely to purchase what the company has to offer. It will help the entrepreneur define a trading area, reach new customers in the marketplace, select specific target audiences, and survey current customers.

CRM is not merely a way to reach customers by mail more easily. Today retaining and maintaining current customers is more important than spending money to find new customers. It has been reported that 65 percent of a company's business comes from current customers. In fact, it costs five to ten times more to go after a new customer than to serve an existing one.[11] With good customer profiles, an entrepreneur can match demographic information about current customers with demographic data in the geographic area of interest to find prospects more effectively. Information contained in the database can be used in advertising, sales promotion, public relations, direct mail, and personal selling.

The competitive advantages of CRM are many. Customer relationship management helps entrepreneurs increase their response rates, aids in the development of new products, helps in the forecasting of sales, and improves mass marketing decisions. Database marketing also allows the company to personalize advertising, cross-sell related products, and increase customer loyalty. For example, an entrepreneur with a combination book, video, and CD outlet can begin to track customers by offering a frequent buyer card that entitles the customer to free items once they have achieved a certain level of purchases with the company. To receive the card, the customer fills out an information form. Every time the customer purchases something, the item is recorded in the customer's database record. Over time, the entrepreneur can detect patterns in the kinds of items this customer buys and also buying patterns in terms of frequency. Then the entrepreneur can begin suggesting purchases to the customer that match those patterns.

CRM is really an overall approach to doing business, an approach that requires the total commitment of everyone in the organization. As in any marketing effort, the payoff to this approach takes time, and many frustrated entrepreneurs will give up before seeing the results of the efforts. To successfully implement CRM, you must be patient and continually monitor customer feedback to make sure it's producing the results you want. American CRM provides a customer relationship management directory at its web site to make it easier to locate CRM solutions (http://www.american-crm-directory.com/).

Online Marketing

The big challenge in online marketing is to give customers what they want instead of what marketers think they want. Although users want the ability to sign up for free samples online, the ability to receive coupons and offers online, and the opportunity to learn about community events, online marketers overwhelmingly tend to give them only product and company information and advertising.

EMarketer, a New York–based market research firm, reports that 22 percent of the e-mail an average person receives is marketing related.[12] About half of those are the result of the person giving the company permission to send the e-mail. Emarketer further estimates that by 2003, about 29.7 percent of the marketing mail a person receives will be unsolicited—junk mail. Because people are tired of receiving so much unsolicited mail, the click-through rates, or the rate at which users click on ad banners to get more information, on banner ads have dropped from 10 percent to 5 percent. Part of the reason for all this unwanted mail is the fact that online marketers sell their customer lists to other marketers who were not originally given permission to send e-mails. As a result, chances are that e-mail marketing campaigns could go the way of banner ads in effectiveness.

There is also a misconception that advertising on the Internet is cheap and/or free. Actually, any method of acquiring new customers on the Internet carries an acquisition cost that can be quite high. AOL spends about $90 to acquire a customer.[13] The only reason it can justify that cost (you couldn't for a one-time sale) is that the company is selling a subscription, so it is building a relationship with the customer for the long term. Here's another example. If you understand how key-word search engines work, you can creatively insert key words in your home page that will bring up your web site ahead of others. But this will take a lot of time; you will have to cover all the major search engines, or you will have to pay thousands of dollars to hire an expert to do it for you.

Fortunately, there are easier ways to effectively use online marketing. You can find research about Internet trends and usage at web sites like Cyber Atlas (www.cyberatlas.com) and Emarketer (www.emarketer.com). For general Internet statistics, try Mediamark (www.mediamark.com) and IDC (www.idc.com).

Any marketing strategy should be anticipated, personal, and relevant. Potential customers don't want to be surprised by your tactics. They want to know that your marketing is about them, and they want to know that it's about things they're interested in. The reason most online marketing campaigns (and offline ones as well) are unsuccessful is that they are unanticipated, impersonal, and

PROFILE 15.2

On Equal Footing

Success, even in the Internet world, can come when you find a market that isn't being served. Angie Kim, Jim Fox, and Aaron Martin started their company, EqualFooting.com, after a strategizing session in June 1999 (one year prior to the dot com bust) where they came to the conclusion that small construction and manufacturing companies needed a virtual purchasing agent to find industrial products (MRO: maintenance, repair, and operating supplies) that ranged from front-end loaders to staple removers. They also saw a need to help small businesses arrange loans and enjoy discounted shipping like their much larger counterparts.

Three aspects of the industry made this concept the right choice at the time:

1. MRO was ready for consolidation because it was a highly fragmented industry. One of the largest companies, W.W. Grainger, held only 2 percent of the market with 1999 sales of $4.5 billion. Most other companies in the industry were much smaller.
2. Distributors were forced to take on one of two strategies: they could offer only the most popular products or they could offer a narrow range of products but from all the different vendors.

3. Business-to-business exchanges were very popular and all reports indicated that they would continue to grow rapidly.
4. Small businesses were not being served because they didn't purchase in large enough quantities.

The trio saw as their differentiation point the fact that they wanted to be the small business owner's purchasing agent for everything that owner might need and that goal became the focus of their promotional campaign. Benefits to the small business customer included the ability to choose from a much wider variety of goods and services than they would have found individually and their purchases were automated, so the small business owner and his or her employees were free to do more important tasks. Moreover, EqualFooting's exchange service was user-friendly.

But EqualFooting, which started as a way to serve small businesses, actually ended up hurting the very companies it intended to help. Its suppliers already had difficulty serving their existing customers in a highly competitive market. The EqualFooting exchange now forced them to compete on price instead of things like superior service, customer relationships, and leading-edge products, which were the primary ways these

irrelevant. We discuss two effective online strategies in the next two sections, and a third in the sidebar "Permission Marketing" on page 347.

● *Viral Marketing*

Viral marketing was born of the Internet's ability to replicate and distribute information quickly and efficiently. Its offline counterparts are "word-of-mouth" and "network marketing." While the name has negative connotations, viral marketing has been accepted as the term of art for a marketing strategy that entices customers to pass on the marketing message to others. For example, Hotmail.com,

companies differentiated themselves from their competitors. Exchanges like EqualFooting tend to encourage small businesses to focus on getting the lowest price.

To avoid the commodity syndrome and keep its suppliers and customers happy, EqualFooting began diversifying its offerings to provide more value and entice them to become part of the exchange. It offered these services through partners for such things as accounting and customer relationship management. Cross-promotional alliances were also prominent in EqualFooting's marketing plan. For example, through an agreement with PurchasePro.com, a leader in B2B e-commerce solutions, that company would promote EqualFooting as its preferred provider of MRO supplies and equipment, while EqualFooting would promote PurchasePro as the preferred e-commerce solution provider. This strategic alliance would give EqualFooting's customers the most advanced procurement solution at their desktops.

In a public relations effort, EqualFooting was also working to raise awareness of the impact of small business on the economy and the ways in which the Internet was empowering small business. It developed two online courses related to purchasing to help small business owners and, in particular, women business owners improve their purchasing skills.

In February 2001, EqualFooting announced yet another important alliance, this time with Virtual Compliance, a leading provider of outsourced regulatory compliance solutions, so now the bundle of benefits to EqualFooting's customers included all relevant product information, particularly on hazardous materials, so they could make better decisions.

For all its marketing savvy, EqualFooting had a fight ahead to build its business. With multiple competitors, major distributors creating their own online stores, and small business customers unsure if they were receiving the value that was being touted, EqualFooting needed to continually revisit and revise its marketing plan. By March 2001, the company realized that the procurement side of its business was not going to be profitable and discontinued it. By November 2001, the company, under its new name, Equidity, filed for Chapter 11 bankruptcy protection. In January 2002, the assets of Equidity were acquired by Sanchez Computer Associates.

Sources: Steve Ulfelder, "Market Muscles," *CIO Magazine*, November 15, 2000; www.equalfooting.com July 2001; "EqualFooting.com President Releases SBA State Award Winner Survey Findings," *Business Wire*, May 24, 2000; Susan Avery, "The Bricks Fight for Clicks," *Purchasing*, May 3, 2001; "EqualFooting.com Designated Preferred Provider of MRO Equipment on PurchasePro.com," *Business Wire*, July 6, 2000; Sean Madigan, "EqualFooting Lays Off 120, Will Sell Unit," *Washington Business Journal*, March 9, 2001.

the highly successful free e-mail service, provides its users with free e-mail addresses but carefully includes a tagline on each message the user sends: "Get your private, free e-mail at www.hotmail.com." Hotmail is betting that when users send messages to friends, they will sign up as well, taking its services to an ever-widening audience. If the strategy is well-developed, it will spread very rapidly.

Another example is Adobe Acrobat. Adobe, the successful software company, gives away free its proprietary software that lets people share documents across multiple platforms in a form called PDF, which retains the original formatting but can't be manipulated. Adobe puts a link in the document that sends the person to the Adobe web site to download the required Adobe Reader. That gives Adobe an opportunity to let the user know about its other software products available for sale. The strategy has been so successful that it is now the de facto standard for sending corporate documents.

Online greeting card companies like Blue Mountain Arts have become some of the most popular sites online. Although Blue Mountain Arts doesn't sell much (mostly advertising), it receives so many hits on its web site that it was acquired by Excite for over a billion dollars, just to gain access to all those customers.

While there is no one way to craft a viral strategy, most successful viral marketers do the following:

▶ **Provide free products and services.** Good marketers know that "free" is the most powerful word in any language, and online marketers know that if they generate enough "eyeballs" through a viral marketing campaign, somewhere down the road, they will also achieve a level of profit.

▶ **Make it easy to pass on the message.** There is nothing easier than clicking on a button and forwarding an e-mail to someone. For example, online magazines have made it easy for you to forward an article to someone by simply clicking on a button that brings up an e-mail message into which you enter the person's address.

▶ **Make sure that the mail server can handle the traffic.** There is nothing worse than starting a viral campaign that ultimately annihilates its host. Remember that viral marketing spreads your message extremely rapidly, so plan ahead for additional server capacity.

▶ **Take advantage of existing social networks.** Just as in the offline world, people in cyberspace create networks of people and information that they tap regularly. Place your message into one of those networks and its diffusion is accelerated exponentially.

▶ **Use other people's web sites.** Find compatible web sites and arrange to place your message on them. In that way, you are tapping into another network and increasing the scope of your own.

● *Affiliate Programs*

One way to increase the traffic on your web site is to use **affiliate programs,** which are basically strategic partnerships with other companies that offer complementary products and services. Banner exchange programs are one example of an affiliate program. After signing up with the banner exchange, you post some HTML code containing your message on your web page and the banner exchange that you use posts the banner on other web sites. You can find a free banner exchange mega list at www.bxmegalist.com/. A great example of effective banners can be found at Eyescream Interactive www.eyescream.com/. You can generate your own banner at www.3dtextmaker.com/. There may be costs associated with posting a banner or you may be able to negotiate a barter exchange if your web site is compatible with the other web site on which you want to place your banner.

But getting your banner on a web site may be the easiest part of the challenge. Convincing people to click through and buy your product or service is quite another thing. Here are some tips to help you attract customers to your web site.

▶ Assure them that you will not give or sell their name and e-mail address to anyone. And mean it.

▶ Give them something free to entice them to discover more.

▶ Offer them more, beyond the free information, that they will have to pay for.

▶ Use electronic gift certificates as a way of getting customers to try your products or services.

▶ Provide a toll-free number for people who need to hear a human voice to overcome resistance.

▶ Offer to accept as many ways as possible to pay for items: credit cards, checks, debit cards, etc.

Know the Consumer

Consumers buy benefits, not features. They want to know how a product or service will save them time, make them wealthy, healthy, and sexy, or give them something they need. Consumers who use the Internet to purchase items do so for several reasons.

▶ It's convenient. They don't have to deal with traffic (unless a web site has too many people trying to access it at the same time), crowds, and parking.

▶ It's easy to compare prices. They can click on web sites like www.msn.com that will find the best prices on any product they're looking for.

▶ They have immediate access to a greater variety of stores than they have in their own community. They can literally shop around the world.

▶ They might actually pay less online.

▶ It's entertaining.

At the same time, entrepreneurs who choose to market online should also be aware of the challenges for customers and look for ways to overcome them.

▶ There is a time lag between purchasing the product and receiving it. No instant gratification here.

▶ The buyer cannot test or try on the product.

▶ It can be risky dealing with a retailer you don't know.

● ## Privacy Issues

Although companies have collected consumer information for years and used it to target customers and sell more products and services, with the advent of e-commerce, consumers are more aware of privacy issues. When Jane Consumer goes online to purchase a hand-made doll for her collection, she soon finds that she is inundated with advertisements for gifts, collectibles, and anything else remotely related to her doll collection. This is the power of the Internet at work as it magnifies anything done in the offline world.[14] The retailer who sold her the doll probably sold her information to catalog companies and others who are looking to target the same customer. Amazon.com ran afoul of the Federal Trade Commission (FTC), which claimed that the company's practices were deceptive. Amazon did not make it clear to customers that it was selling their information to other companies. In fact, an FTC survey estimates that 97 percent of all e-commerce web sites collect information that is personally identifiable.[15] Therefore, companies must now do more to assure their customers that their privacy is respected. Customer-focused companies inform their customers about how the information collected will be used. The most successful companies, like L.L. Bean, maintain policies against selling customer information. But if you do have a privacy policy, you must not violate it or you risk reprisal from the FTC. Even Excite@Home, a company in bankruptcy, declined seven-figure offers in order to comply with its privacy policy, which requires permission from the customer before information can be shared. Other firms seek seals of approval by online auditing companies such as TrustE, BBBOnlines, and PricewaterhouseCoopers LLP, but these audits can be expensive, costing up to tens of thousands of dollars. The best rule of thumb is to get your customer's permission before using their information for any purpose. Any effective marketing strategy, whether online or offline, should target the appropriate customers and address their specific needs, including those of privacy.

NEW VENTURE CHECKLIST

Have you:
- ☐ Analyzed the marketing options and ranked them?
- ☐ Written a clear, concise, one-paragraph statement of the marketing plan?
- ☐ Developed an advertising, publicity, and promotion strategy?
- ☐ Discovered your business's compelling story?
- ☐ Created some innovative ways to promote your business online?

ISSUES TO CONSIDER

1. What are the differences between an entrepreneurial marketing strategy and a large corporation's marketing strategy?

2. Why is it important to stick with your marketing plan even if it isn't returning immediate results?

3. Why should an entrepreneurial venture not engage in image positioning like large corporations often do?

4. Suppose you have invented a new product and you're trying to determine an appropriate price. What should you consider when setting your initial price?

5. How does the promotion strategy for consumer-oriented businesses differ from that of industrial businesses?

EXPERIENCING ENTREPRENEURSHIP

1. Compare and contrast the marketing strategies of two companies in the same industry in terms of the points in the marketing plan on pages 340–346.

2. Find an entrepreneurial company that is using relationship marketing strategies; interview the entrepreneur or the person in charge of implementing their marketing strategy to discuss how they build effective customer relationships.

ADDITIONAL SOURCES OF INFORMATION

Bangs, D.H. (1998). *The Market Planning Guide.* 5th ed. Dover, NH: Upstart Publishing.

Hoyer, W.D., and D.J. MacInnis (1997). *Consumer Behavior.* Boston: Houghton Mifflin.

Koehn, N.F. (2001). *Brand New: How Entrepreneurs Earned Consumers' Trust from Wedgwood to Dell.* Boston: Harvard Business School Press.

Levinson, J.C. (1993). *Guerrilla Marketing.* Boston: Houghton Mifflin.

———. (1993). *Guerrilla Marketing Excellence.* Boston: Houghton Mifflin.

Seybold, P.B., R.T. Marshak, and J.M. Lewis (2001). *The Customer Revolution.* New York: Crown.

Treacy, M., and F. Wiersema (1995). *The Discipline of Market Leaders: Choose Your Customers, Narrow Your Focus, Dominate Your Market.* Reading, MA: Addison-Wesley.

INTERNET RESOURCES

AdvertisingAge
http://www.adage.com
This is the online version of the magazine that focuses on the advertising industry.

American Demographics/Marketing Tools
http://www.marketingtools.com
This web site will help you learn how to target your marketing efforts.

American Marketing Association
http://www.ama.org
Focuses on the services of this organization.

CEO Express
http://www.ceoexpress.com/
A one-stop source for all business information.

Online Marketing
http://www.marketing.haynet.com/
Online journal for marketers.

PR Week
http://www.prweekus.com/us/index.htm
This online journal provides all the latest news in the public relations industry.

Sales Marketing Network
http://www.info-now.com/SMN/
    default.asp?source=SMN
A source of articles and meetings related to marketing issues.

Success with Internet Marketing and Promotion
http://www.satcom.net.au/success/
    tips-tricks-tools.html
Contains tips, tricks, tools, and techniques for marketing on the Internet.

Synergyx
http://www.synergyx.com/cgi-bin/sgx/
    d.cgi?S1137
This is an integrated shopping cart, affiliate program, and delivery system for digital products.

RELEVANT CASE STUDIES

Case 1   Mrs. Gooch's

Case 8   Alcoholes de Centroamerica, S.A. de C.V.

Case 9   Wizards of the Coast

16

The Financial Plan

The wise man understands equity; the
small man understands only profits.
Confucius (c. 551–c. 479 B.C.),
Analects

Overview

Estimating sales and capital expenditures

Preparing the pro forma income statement

Preparing the pro forma cash flow statement

Preparing the pro forma balance sheet

Ratios to describe the business

PROFILE 16.1

How to Save a Lot of Money

If you keep scanning the environment, you can often see signs of impending problems that might adversely affect your business's cash flow. In 1996, the management of Hi-Shear Technology, a Torrance, California aerospace subcontractor, recognized signs of a recession on the horizon. They noticed that federal dollars were no longer flowing to military and space projects and their own customers, the big aerospace manufacturers, were slowing their orders. Hi-Shear was on the verge of a cash crunch.

Something had to be done immediately. Understanding that the quickest route to increasing profits is to cut costs, Hi-Shear's management began to take a hard look at their fixed costs and found to their surprise that water costs, for example, had increased 50 percent. Gas and electricity were also on the rise. The source of much of the problem was leaky pipes and inefficient lighting. Once these were repaired, utility costs declined immediately. Those results encouraged management to look at other areas of the company, such as long-distance rates and insurance rates. More importantly, they got everyone involved in finding ways to cut costs.

Today, the $14 million company reviews its utility bills quarterly and its insurance policies annually. It shuts off the air conditioning at night and no longer heats or cools storage areas. Its new production capabilities and manufacturing techniques have lowered the cost of production while increasing its speed. Savings techniques like these have helped the company offset times when sales volume is lower or contract awards are delayed.

Several warning signs will help business owners determine whether they are about to face a cash flow problem.

- ▶ *Liquidity ratios decline.*

- ▶ *Working capital is running out.*

- ▶ *Inventory turnover is higher than the industry average.*

- ▶ *There is too much short-term debt.*

- ▶ *The firm is not taking advantage of early payment discounts from vendors.*

- ▶ *Receivables are increasing, and collections are slow.*

- ▶ *Fixed costs are rising.*

SOURCES: Ilan Mochari, "A Simple Little System," *Inc. Magazine,* October 1, 1998 and Hi-Shear Technology, http://www.hstc.com/; David H. Bangs Jr. and Michael Pellecchia, "Five Severe Warning Signs of Cash Flow Problems," *Inc Magazine,* August 15, 1999.

The financial plan for the new business is a way for investors and others to learn if the entrepreneur really understands how the business works. It is based on a clear understanding of the operations of the business, demand from the customer, and the milestones that need to be met to move the business forward. Doing a financial plan is a valuable exercise critical to creating a growth strategy that translates business objectives into achievable financial results. Recall that in Chapter 9 we looked at the financials from the point of view of a feasibility analysis; that is, we wanted to know how much money it would take to launch the business and carry it to a positive cash flow. In this chapter, we take the perspective that we now have a feasible business concept and we need to develop a financial plan for the next three to five years.

There is no better way to gain an understanding of how your business works than to prepare a financial plan and pro forma statements, even if they're just the first draft and are passed on to the bookkeeper or accountant. However, don't just turn the books over to that bookkeeper; you must monitor them yourself. And a few words of caution about spreadsheets are in order. If you have formulated your own spreadsheets to prepare the pro forma financials, check them over carefully, especially the formulas in the cells. Spreadsheets work so fast that it's easy to make a mistake and not detect it.

In Chapter 9 you learned how to create pro forma cash flow and income statements for a new venture in order to calculate the start-up capital requirements. This chapter looks at the financial statements that are found in the typical business plan. The financial plan for the new business is based on growth strategies you establish, milestones you expect to achieve, as well as on the market research you've done to determine demand. While this book has promoted creativity in all aspects of developing the business concept, originality should not be reflected in the design of your financial statements. Financial statements must follow **GAAP,** the "generally accepted accounting principles" of the accounting profession, so that the reader of the business plan recognizes standard terms and sees items in their normal order of presentation. This familiarity instills confidence in the reader. Furthermore, every assumption made in constructing the statements must be justified with supporting evidence, because with a new venture, you are forecasting not on the basis of historical performance but on your belief as to how the new venture will perform into the future. Industry expertise, test marketing, and/or experience with a similar business goes a long way toward imbuing the reader with a sense of trust. In addition, having your accountant prepare and/or review the financials also adds credibility. Look at Figure 16.1 for an overview of the financial planning process. Note that it begins with some basic information that must be on hand to start the planning process. That basic information consists of

FIGURE 16.1

Steps in Preparing the Financial Plan

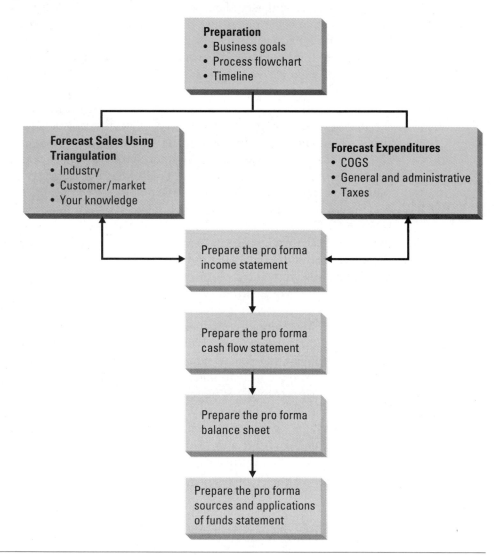

▶ *The business goals.* Where are you planning to take the business? What will the business look like in three to five years?

▶ *The business flowchart.* Create a flowchart that depicts how the business works: all the activities of the business, the personnel required to conduct those activities, and the equipment needed to carry out the activities. This information was part of the feasibility analysis, but you no doubt have more and better information as you have been preparing the business plan. Incorporate that new information and update the financial estimates.

▶ *The business timeline.* Every business has milestones on its growth path. Think in terms of 1) the first customer, 2) multiple customers, 3) multiple products and services. Each of these stages brings with it different financial requirements that must be taken into consideration in the financial plan. When do you plan to hire the first employee? When will you begin to take a salary from the business? These are scenarios that you will be able to analyze and test via the financial statements.

Estimating Sales and Capital Expenditures

Forecasting for a new venture is a difficult task at best. An example will make the challenge clear. Gentech Corporation is a company manufacturing a technology-based industrial machine. It had to purchase motors and other parts from its suppliers. In the start-up phase, the company did not have enough sales to buy parts in sufficient volume to warrant the maximum discount from the supplier, so initially material costs were high. To compensate, the founders subcontracted some of the work, performed the assembly themselves, and sold products with little or no gross margin. The question then became "When will the business generate enough sales to buy in adequate volume, thereby reducing costs and increasing profit?" At the same time, once the volume was attained, the business would likely need to purchase additional equipment, perhaps expand facilities, and add employees. At what point should the founders do this, and how much should they spend?

This is the dilemma of the new venture. To answer these difficult questions, the entrepreneur must gain a great deal of knowledge about the industry and how similar businesses operate within it, then extrapolate from that until the business has been in operation for a while and has developed some patterns of its own that better define it.

The information needed to complete the pro forma financial statements includes demand, cost, and operating figures. The goal is to forecast the financial condition of the new venture for the next three to five years on the basis of the information collected. These pro forma statements reflect your best estimate of how the company will perform and what the associated expenses will be. You should also consider that you may want to acquire credit and take on debt at some later date and that event will affect those estimates. Estimates are always subject to change based on the more accurate information gained when the business actually begins operating. This is why you will probably reevaluate the financial statements on a monthly basis for the first year.

● *The Importance of Assumptions*

Financial statements are only as valuable as the assumptions or premises that support them. Numbers in a cash flow or income statement have no meaning if the reader doesn't know how you calculated them—what the premises were that led to those numbers. Every line item in a financial statement should have a note to describe where that number came from. In particular, the sales forecast requires substantiation. Too many entrepreneurs forecast annual sales based on a wing and a prayer, instead of actual facts. To improve the chances of arriving at believable and realistic sales forecasts, you need to do several things.

▶ Convert your expectations to numbers. What is the annual growth rate expected based on your knowledge of the industry and your research with industry participants and customers.

▶ Ask good questions and be sure to get answers. It is common to find people in the industry who are willing to toss around statistics with no validation. Be sure that you demand the source of the statistics and the basis on which they were determined.

▶ Once all the homework has been done and you have the results, accept them, whether you like them or not. If the results are negative, explain why and how you are going to deal with them.

● *Preparing the Operating Budget*

The operating budget helps the entrepreneur consider the sources of revenues to the company as well as the expenses associated with specific tasks the company undertakes. The first step is to forecast sales. Use the forecast generated in Chapter 9. Remember, those sales figures need to make sense when looked at from the point of view of how many units or how many hours of service they represent. When Ben Cohen and Jerry Greenfield of Ben & Jerry's Homemade, Inc. had to forecast sales on an application for an SBA loan, they forecasted they would do $90,000 in the first year. That may not sound like a lot of money, but it translates to a lot of ice cream cones per hour.

The next step is forecasting the expenses of the company. For nonmanufacturing businesses, this means forecasting purchases and beginning and ending inventories based on sales projections. For manufacturing businesses, the operating budget is a bit more complex. You need to create a production budget, a materials purchase budget, and a direct labor budget to meet the projected sales demand. The production budget details the number of units the company needs to produce to meet its sales forecast for a particular month. To this number, add the number of units to be left in ending inventory as a buffer for the month. This becomes the total inventory for the month. In the next month, add the ending inventory (unsold) from the previous month to the number of units demanded in that month. Once the production budget has been determined, you can figure the materials and labor requirement needed to produce the forecasted units each month.

The last step is to calculate the fixed and variable operating expenses by month. Recall that fixed costs are those that do not change month to month, for example, rent and depreciation. Variable costs change with operating activities, in particular, sales and production volume.

Preparing the Pro Forma Income Statement

The income statement reflects the profit and loss status of the business at the end of a specified period, normally one fiscal year. It contains the sources of revenues to the company as well as the company's expenditures. The income statement should also contain footnotes for each item to refer the reader to supporting material in the "Notes to Financial Statements." Any unusual major expenses like the cost of participating in a trade show should be footnoted separately and explained. The income statement is often prepared first because it gives you the profit/loss figures needed to figure taxes for the cash flow statement. Recall that the income statement differs from the cash flow statement in that revenues and expenses are recorded when the transaction occurs whether or not money was received or expended, while in the cash flow statement, revenues and expenses are recorded when money goes in or out of the business. Refer to the income statement you prepared in Chapter 9 to help you judge start-up capital requirements.

Look at Figure 16.2 to see a hypothetical example of an income statement for New Venture Inc. The company is planning to purchase equipment for $50,000. For purposes of this example, the equipment is depreciated over three years on a straightline basis. For your own business, you will need to check with your accountant as to the preferred method of depreciating a particular asset.

Preparing the Pro Forma Cash Flow Statement

No matter how many financial tools entrepreneurs use or how many complex analyses are constructed, the bottom line for any new venture is cash. Income statements and balance sheets can make a company look good—these are accounting measures—but cash pays the bills and allows the company to grow. Cash is the lifeblood of the business and so the cash flow statement is the most important statement of all.

The cash flow statement records all the cash inflows and outflows of the business. Figure 16.3 gives an example of the cash flow statement for New Venture Inc. showing monthly for Year One. As with all other financial statements,

FIGURE 16.2

New Venture Inc. Pro Forma Income Statement (in 1000s)

	Premise	Start-up 0	Month 1	Month 2	Month 3	Month 4	Month 5	Month 6	Month 7	Month 8	Month 9	Month 10	Month 11	Month 12	Total
Sales Forecast		0.0	0.0	20.0	25.0	35.0	50.0	65.0	85.0	100.0	120.0	130.0	150.0	160.0	940.0
Total Revenues		**0**	**0.0**	**20.0**	**25.0**	**35.0**	**50.0**	**65.0**	**85.0**	**100.0**	**120.0**	**130.0**	**150.0**	**160.0**	**940.0**
Cost of Goods Sold															
Material Costs	35% of sales	0.0	0.0	7.0	8.8	12.3	17.5	22.8	29.8	35.0	42.0	45.5	52.5	56.0	329.0
Gross Profit		**0.0**	**0.0**	**13.0**	**16.3**	**22.8**	**32.5**	**42.3**	**55.3**	**65.0**	**78.0**	**84.5**	**97.5**	**104.0**	**611.0**
Start-up Expenses															
Deposits - legal, utilities		2.0													2.0
Rent Lease Deposit	1 month in advance	4.5													4.5
Employee Training	1 mo. Salary	7.0													7.0
Equipment Purchase		50.0													50.0
Total Start-up Expenses		**63.5**	**0.0**	**0.0**	**0.0**	**0.0**	**0.0**	**0.0**	**0.0**	**0.0**	**0.0**	**0.0**	**0.0**	**0.0**	**63.5**
Operating Expenses															
Salaries - Principal (including tax)	3K per month		3.0	3.0	3.0	3.0	3.0	3.0	3.0						21.0
Salaries (including tax)	6K @ 100K in Sales									6.0	6.0	6.0	6.0	6.0	30.0
	3 employees		7.0	7.0	7.0	7.0	7.0	7.0	7.0	7.0	7.0	7.0	7.0	7.0	84.0
	Additional employees					3.5	3.5	7.0	7.0	7.0	7.0	7.0	7.0	7.0	56.0
Bookkeeper salary	1000 per month		1.0	1.0	1.0	1.0	1.0	1.0	1.0	1.0	1.0	1.0	1.0	1.0	12.0
Building Rent	Per 1 year lease		4.5	4.5	4.5	4.5	4.5	4.5	4.5	4.5	4.5	4.5	4.5	4.5	54.0
Insurance			0.4	0.4	0.4	0.4	0.4	0.4	0.4	0.4	0.4	0.4	0.4	0.4	4.8
Advertising			0.5	0.5	0.5	0.5	0.5	0.5	0.5	0.5	0.5	0.5	0.5	0.5	6.0
General & Administrative	3K per mo + 15% growth		3.0	3.5	4.0	4.6	5.2	6.0	6.9	8.0	9.2	10.6	12.1	14.0	87.0
Equipment Lease Payment			0.5	0.5	0.5	0.5	0.5	0.5	0.5	0.5	0.5	0.5	0.5	0.5	6.0
Total Operating Expenses			**19.9**	**20.4**	**20.9**	**25.0**	**25.6**	**29.9**	**30.8**	**34.9**	**36.1**	**37.5**	**39.0**	**40.9**	**360.8**
Depreciation	Straightline 3 years		1.4	1.4	1.4	1.4	1.4	1.4	1.4	1.4	1.4	1.4	1.4	1.4	16.8
Net Income Before Taxes		**(63.5)**	**(21.3)**	**(8.8)**	**(6.0)**	**(3.6)**	**5.5**	**10.9**	**23.0**	**28.7**	**40.5**	**45.6**	**57.1**	**61.7**	**169.9**
			(84.8)	(93.6)	(99.6)	(103.2)	(97.7)	(86.8)	(63.8)	(35.1)	5.4	51.1	108.2	169.9	169.9

FIGURE 16.3

New Venture Inc. Pro Forma Cash Flow Statement (in 1000s)

	Premise	Start-up 0	Month 1	Month 2	Month 3	Month 4	Month 5	Month 6	Month 7	Month 8	Month 9	Month 10	Month 11	Month 12	Total
Cash Inflows															
Actual Sales		0.0	0.0	20.0	25.0	35.0	50.0	65.0	85.0	100.0	120.0	130.0	150.0	160.0	940.0
Collection in 30 days		0.0	0.0	0.0	20.0	25.0	35.0	50.0	65.0	85.0	100.0	120.0	130.0	150.0	780.0
Investment Capital		217.9													217.9
Total Cash Inflows		217.9	0.0	0.0	20.0	25.0	35.0	50.0	65.0	85.0	100.0	120.0	130.0	150.0	997.9
Cash Outflows															
Upfront Cash Expenditures															
Deposits - legal, utilities		2.0										—			2.0
Rent Lease Deposit	1 month in advance	4.5										—			4.5
Employee Training	1 mo. Salary	7.0													7.0
Equipment Purchase		50.0													50.0
Total Upfront Cash		63.5													63.5
Variable Cost															
Material Costs	25% of sales	0.0	0.0	5.0	6.3	8.8	12.5	16.3	21.3	25.0	30.0	32.5	37.5	40.0	235.0
Total Variable Cost		0.0	0.0	5.0	6.3	8.8	12.5	16.3	21.3	25.0	30.0	32.5	37.5	40.0	235.0
Fixed Expenses															
Salaries - Principal	3K per month		3.0	3.0	3.0	3.0	3.0	3.0	3.0						21.0
Salaries (including tax)	6K @ 100K in Sales; 3 employees; Additional employees		7.0	7.0	7.0	7.0	7.0	7.0	7.0	7.0	7.0	7.0	7.0	7.0	84.0
Bookkeeper Salary			1.0	1.0	1.0	1.0	1.0	1.0	1.0	1.0	1.0	1.0	1.0	1.0	12.0
Building Rent	Per 1 year lease		4.5	4.5	4.5	4.5	4.5	4.5	4.5	4.5	4.5	4.5	4.5	4.5	54.0
Insurance			0.4	0.4	0.4	0.4	0.4	0.4	0.4	0.4	0.4	0.4	0.4	0.4	4.8
Advertising			0.5	0.5	0.5	0.5	0.5	0.5	0.5	0.5	0.5	0.5	0.5	0.5	6.0
General & Administrative	3K per mo + 15% growth		3.0	3.5	4.0	4.6	5.2	6.0	6.9	8.0	9.2	10.6	12.1	14.0	87.0
Equipment Lease Payment			0.5	0.5	0.5	0.5	0.5	0.5	0.5	0.5	0.5	0.5	0.5	0.5	6.0
Total Fixed Expenses		0.0	19.9	20.4	20.9	25.0	25.6	29.9	30.8	34.9	36.1	37.5	39.0	40.9	360.8
Total Cash Expenditures		63.5	19.9	25.4	27.1	33.7	38.1	46.2	52.1	59.9	66.1	70.0	76.5	80.9	659.3
Net Cash In/Out Per Mo		154.4	(19.9)	(25.4)	(7.1)	(8.7)	(3.1)	3.8	12.9	25.1	33.9	50.0	53.5	69.1	338.6
Cash Balance: Beg of Mo		0.0	154.4	134.5	109.2	102.0	93.3	90.2	94.0	160.9	132.0	165.9	216.0	269.5	338.6
Net Cash In/Out Per Mo		154.4	(19.9)	(25.4)	(7.1)	(8.7)	(3.1)	3.8	12.9	25.1	33.9	50.0	53.5	69.1	
Cumulative Cash Balance		154.4	134.5	109.2	102.0	93.3	90.2	94.0	106.9	132.0	165.9	216.0	269.5	338.6	

FIGURE 16.4

New Venture Balance Sheet as of January 1 and December 31, 200x

Assets	1/1/200x	12/31/200x	Liabilities & Equity	1/1/200x	12/31/200x
Current Assets			**Current Liabilities**		
Cash	217.9	338.6			0.0
Accounts Receivable	0.0	160.0			
Prepaid Assets	6.5	6.5			
Total Current Assets	224.4	505.1			
Fixed Assets			Total Current Liabilities	0.0	0.0
Equipment	50.0	50.0			
Less Depreciation		(16.8)			
Total Fixed Assets	50.0	33.2	**Equity**		
			Capital Stock	337.9	368.4
			Retained Earnings		
			Net Profit for period	(63.5)	169.9
			Total Equity	274.4	538.3
Total Assets	274.4	538.3	**Total Liabilities & Equity**	274.4	538.3

each item on the statement should be footnoted in the "Notes to Financial Statements" to explain what the assumptions were and how the figures were derived.

Notice that the cash flow statement includes the amount by which the new venture was capitalized. In Year One, New Venture received $217,900 in investment funding from the founders and a private investor. The company ended the year with a positive cash flow of $338,600, which will appear on the balance sheet (Figure 16.4) as a current asset. Use a spreadsheet program to set up the cash flow statement as well as the other financial statements. Because it is relatively easy to produce very detailed analyses, however, there is a tendency to overwhelm the potential reader of the business plan with page after page of financial statements. This will hurt rather than help. Instead, be concise and to the point, and be sure to understand and document how figures were calculated, so that you can explain them if asked.

Spreadsheets make it easier to consider various scenarios for the financial statements. Doing these sensitivity analyses is extremely valuable because they provide a range of capital needs based on different economic scenarios. For example, what effect will a sudden decrease in sales have on the overall picture? What would be the impact of delaying the development of the second product? Looking at the financial impact of various scenarios will help you refine the business strategy to respond to the more probable events.

The Consequences of Actions

Many entrepreneurs fail to realize that nearly every action they take has a financial consequence for the business, even when it comes to taking on a new customer. Suppose for a moment that your small, but growing, consulting company is looking to increase its customer base. You identify a series of different potential customers; you only have the resources to take on two and are not sure which are the best two to target. Here is the list of customers you have identified.

- A large and respected regional customer will give you a contract for $250,000 annually but typically doesn't pay for 120 days. You figure it would probably cost your company about $25,000 annually to serve this customer.
- A Fortune 500 global company will give you a contract for $50,000 annually.
- An e-commerce company can't afford more than $30,000 of your services annually, but it has substantial potential. It will cost you about $15,000 to upgrade your technology in order to take care of this customer.
- An existing customer wants to add an additional $10,000 a year to its account, already worth $25,000 to you.
- A large local company needs consulting for a year for a contract of about $150,000. There is probably no potential for additional work, and the company is not in the healthiest condition and tends to be slow in paying bills.

Which two customers would you choose? The existing customer will probably cost the least to serve because you know them, so there's no lag time in understanding what's needed. It's always less costly to sell more to existing customers. On the other hand, if the company is to grow, it needs to take a bit of risk and spend some money. Having name brands in the customer base is good for the company's reputation, so the Fortune 500 company may be a good choice. The e-commerce company presents a substantial risk because you will need to spend $15,000 before collecting any revenues from the customer, and with this type of company, you are betting on an upside that may never happen.

The large local company represents a big revenue stream for a year but then nothing, and the risk of problems collecting that money is fairly high. Still, it does represent a big contract that will help the company grow, so if you are able to collect the fees up front or in stages based on performance, it may be a good choice. On the other hand, it might be better to invest in an ongoing customer for the long term than to invest in a quick hit.

There are no right or wrong answers to this dilemma. What you must do is weigh the advantages and the risks, and calculate what it will cost to choose a particular customer.

Determining the amount of capital needed to start and run the business is certainly not the only use for the cash flow statement. Particularly during the first year of operation, you should compare the monthly cash flow statement against actual inflows and outflows of cash to determine where the estimates deviated from reality. Making adjustments to the remaining projections avoids any surprises later on. Essentially the cash flow statement becomes a budget for the business. As the business grows, it is also a good idea to put someone in charge of monitoring cash flow throughout all functions of the organization. That person should be familiar with all the operations of the business and their various cash needs and cycles; consequently, the accountant is often not the best choice for someone to manage cash flow at the operational level.

Preparing the Pro Forma Balance Sheet

The balance sheet shows the condition of the business in terms of its assets and liabilities and the net worth of its owners at the end of a specified period of time. Unlike the cash flow and income statements, which summarize operations for the entire accounting period, the balance sheet is prepared to reflect the condition of the business at the end of a defined period, usually a year. The balance sheet also provides a financial profile of the operating plans and it can be used to estimate financing that might be needed to support long-term goals for the company. Figure 16.4 displays a sample balance sheet for New Venture Inc. for the start of the business, Month Zero, and the end of the first year.

● ### Forecasting Assets

The first section of the balance sheet is the assets, everything of value the business owns. Assets are valued in terms of actual cost for the item. Current assets are those consumed in the operation of the business during the year, while fixed assets are tangible assets used over the long term.

Accounts receivable, which are current assets on the balance sheet, must be forecast based on the seasonality experienced by the business. If the business experiences no pronounced seasonality, you may be able to assume a certain percentage of sales that will not be paid in cash each month, based on industry averages or an accounts receivable turnover rate. Once the business is established, however, it develops its own pattern of receivables, and you can calculate a more accurate turnover rate. To account for the fact that some accounts receivable will not be collected, some entrepreneurs choose to subtract from receivables an allowance for bad debt, a small percentage (2–5 percent) based on typical bad debt figures for the industry. Again, your business will develop its own unique pattern over time, and it will be easier to predict more accurately what the bad debt rate will be.

Inventory turnover, another current asset, must also be forecast. The rate at which inventory is sold is described by the turnover rate or cost of sales/inventory. The desired level of inventory is then found by dividing the cost of goods sold by the inventory turnover rate. If the business experiences seasonality, it is not feasible to employ a constant turnover rate based on cost of goods sold. Inventory is a more complex issue for a manufacturing firm than accounts receivable, because at any time a business may have in inventory raw materials, work in process, and finished goods. In the beginning stages of the business, you will probably estimate the dollar amount of each of these stages and then use the year's total of the three as the estimate for the year-end balance sheet. As the business grows, however, a cost accounting model in which the three totals are shown separately on the balance sheet is preferred because it provides more detailed and accurate information that will help you do a better job of inventory management.

● *Forecasting Liabilities*

Liabilities are everything the business owes to its creditors. Those liabilities that are due within one period are called current liabilities. New ventures generally have to pay for materials and inventory with cash until they have established a line of credit with suppliers, so you need to show a separate schedule that depicts when you expect to begin to use credit. Indicate only the total of materials and inventory for the year on the balance sheet, however. If the business paid cash for the entire year, which is not uncommon for a start-up, there will be no accounts payable. The current portion of long-term debt is that portion owed in the coming year.

New Venture has no line of credit and has not taken out any loans against the business in the first year.

● *Owner's or Stockholder's Equity*

Owner's equity, also known as stockholder's equity in the corporate form, represents the excess after liabilities have been subtracted from assets and is the net worth of the business. Retained earnings means the profit (loss) from the business that was not distributed as dividends. In general, new ventures do not distribute dividends but retain those earnings to put back into the company for growth. In our example, New Venture retained earnings of $169,900 at the end of the first year.

When the balance sheet is completed, the total of the assets must equal the sum of the liabilities plus owners' equity. In other words, the balance sheet must balance! Understand that, should you decide to use venture capital, private investors, or bank financing, the party involved may want a say in the debt-to-equity ratio; therefore, as capital is raised, the balance sheet is subject to adjustment.

The financial statements presented as examples in this section do not contain all the elements that might be found in financials for a particular type of business. It is not within the scope of this book to delve too deeply into accounting issues. Therefore, it is always wise to consult an accountant to help you structure the pro forma financial statements. Also look at the resources at the end of the chapter.

Ratios to Describe the Business

Many tools are needed to completely analyze a company's financial picture. No one tool or technique can provide all the answers to a very complex situation. **Ratios** are a particularly good way to begin to interpret the information contained in the financial statements from a lender's or investor's perspective. What ratios do is to make comparisons of items in the financial statements and put them in relative terms so they can be compared to ratios in other periods. This facilitates looking for important changes in the company's position. It is possible to compute ratios for virtually all the items on the financial statements, but this would be a daunting and ineffective approach. A better approach is to select financial relationships that yield useful information about important aspects of the company. The three most common groups of ratios are 1) liquidity and activity ratios, 2) debt and financial risk ratios, and 3) profitability ratios. In discussing ratio analysis, we will turn to the example statements from New Venture and use the most important ratios in each category.

● *Liquidity and Activity Ratios*

Liquidity and **activity ratios** provide information about the company's ability to meet short-term obligations over time and to maintain normal operations. The more liquid the current assets, the more easily they are converted to cash to pay off short-term obligations and maintain operations, and, thus, the lower the risk for creditors.

Current ratio = total current assets/total current liabilities

New Venture's current ratio for end of Year One is \$505,100/0 = 0. Since New Venture has no liabilities, it is a very liquid firm. The higher the number, the more liquid the firm. Over time it would be important to look for increasing numbers signaling a trend toward greater liquidity, or decreasing numbers portending declining liquidity.

Acid test = (current assets – inventory)/current liabilities

This is yet another way to measure a company's ability to meet its current liabilities with its current assets, but the acid test is tougher because it removes inventory, which may be difficult to convert to cash because it is obsolete or, in the case of fraudulent practices, doesn't exist. This forces the current assets to be considered alone, which often means it's more difficult for them to be sufficient to meet current liabilities. Traditionally, the rule of thumb is a minimum of 1:1. All the liquidity ratios help the company find financial problems early so they can be more easily corrected.

● *Profitability Ratios*

The most commonly used measures of profitability are the profit margin, return on assets, and return on equity.

Operating profit margin (PM) = net income/net sales

The **profit margin ratio** uses net income before taxes from the income statement and net sales from the income statement to portray the amount of each dollar of sales remaining after all costs of normal operations are accounted for. The inverse of this percentage (100% – PM) equals the expense ratio or the portion of each sales dollar that is accounted for by expenses from normal operations. It is an important way to monitor costs. New Venture's profit margin for Year One = $169,900/$940,000 = .18.

Return on assets (ROA) or return on investment (ROI) = net income/total assets

Return on assets, also called return on investment, uses net income before taxes from the income statement and total assets from the balance sheet. It gives the percentage[2] that represents the number of dollars of income earned per dollar of invested capital. The greater the number, the greater the return. For New Venture, this ratio in Year One is $169,900/$538,300 = .32. About 32 percent was earned on every dollar of invested capital.

Return on equity = net income/owners' equity

Net income before taxes from the income statement and owners' equity from the balance sheet give a measure of the amount of net income earned per dollar of paid-in capital plus retained earnings. This result is called return on equity. It is a way to look at the efficiency and effectiveness of the use of investor capital. For New Venture in Year One, this ratio is $169,900/$538,300= .32, so $.32 is earned per dollar of paid-in capital plus retained earnings.

● Leverage Ratio

A **leverage ratio** expresses the degree to which the company relies on debt. In most cases, a higher number signals a riskier company because, whereas the firm's earnings will change, debt payments remain fixed.

Debt to asset = total debt/total assets

Debt to asset ratio is a balance sheet ratio that measures the percentage of the firm's assets that are covered by creditors against the percentage that is covered by the owners. That is, when you borrow money against the assets of your firm, the creditors have claim to those assets in the event that you default on the loan. For example, it is estimated that most manufacturing firms have debt to asset ratios between 0.30 and 0.70.[1] Recall that New Venture has no debt.

Ratios are important tools only when compared across time or when one company's ratios are compared with another's. When you look at ratios calculated by others, always verify how the ratio was calculated—what was included—and watch for ways in which some companies improve their appearance of liquidity, for example, by taking out a long-term loan just before the end of the fiscal year and repaying it at the start of the new year. The cash from the loan will strengthen the current ratio, but it doesn't reflect the true liquidity of the company.[2] When you are looking at the financial health of the company, the cash flow statement and its associated ratios are more reliable than balance sheet ratios, which are static, end-of-year figures.[3]

TABLE 16.1

Total Fixed Expenses

Operating Expense	Total for Year
Salaries—Principal (including taxes)	$ 51,000
Salaries (including taxes)	$140,000
Bookkeeper Salary	$ 12,000
Building Rent	$ 54,000
Insurance	$ 4,800
Advertising	$ 6,000
General and Administrative	$ 87,000
Equipment Lease Payment	$ 6,000
Total Operating Expenses	$360,800

● Break-even Analysis

You'll need to understand what volume of sales you have to achieve in order to make a profit; this number provides you with an important indicator of whether you're on target to reach your financial goals. **Break-even analysis** is a tool that will help you find that number. In short, break-even is the sales volume where all your fixed expenses are covered.

Start by identifying the fixed expenses on a monthly basis. These are the expenses that will be paid out of the gross profit. Table 16.1 shows the total first-year fixed expenses from the New Venture example.

The $360,800 must be covered by the gross profit. The gross profit margin for New Venture is 65 percent (gross profit/sales), and we want to know what volume of sales will be required to reach break-even. Simple algebra gives the answer.

$$\$360,800 = 65\%X$$

$$X = 360,800/.65 = \$555,076$$

What this means is that New Venture must sell $555,076 worth of product before it will begin to make a profit.

Clearly, the goal is to reduce the break-even number. That can be done in a number of ways

TABLE 16.2

Financial Plan Outline

Summary of Financial Plan Highlights
Sales (how forecast, trends)
Earnings (When does the company make a profit?)
Cash flow (When does the company achieve a positive cash flow?)
Total start-up cash requirements for new business (cash needs assessment)

Pro Forma Cash Flow Statements
Years 1–3, monthly years 1–2
Notes to cash flow statements

Pro Forma Income Statements
Years 1–3, monthly years 1–2
Notes to income statements

Pro Forma Balance Sheets
Years 1–3
Notes to balance sheets

Key Ratios

▶ Reduce direct costs, so the gross margin goes up. This is accomplished by more effectively purchasing materials, dealing with inventory, or getting more productivity out of your labor.

▶ Reduce the overhead (fixed) costs.

▶ Raise prices 4–5 percent. One word of warning on this technique: the fastest way to more profit is to reduce costs. Here's the proof. Suppose you have a sales price of $15,000 and direct costs of $10,500.

Raise prices by $750	**Lower costs by $750**
Sales price $15,750	$15,000
Direct costs $10,500	$ 9,750
Gross profit $ 5,250 (33%)	$ 5,250 (35%)

Don't forget that raising prices can reduce sales if customers don't tolerate the increase. An effective financial plan should include all the elements in Table 16.2. The number of years out that you forecast is dependent on the requirements of your investor or lender. In today's dynamic environment, three to five years is about as far out into the future as anyone is willing to bet on.

The financial plan represents your best estimate of the condition of the business at a particular point in time. Understanding the nature of the industry and the market in which you do business will ensure that those estimates come as close to reality as possible. The financial plan is also a tool that will guide you in the execution of the business's goals. It is only as good as the numbers and assumptions used to create it.

NEW VENTURE CHECKLIST

Have you:
- ☐ Collected all the operating cost data and sales volume estimates needed to construct the financial statements?
- ☐ Studied competitor products to learn about seasonality, sales volume, and market share?
- ☐ Developed some assumptions about such financial statement line items as sales and operating expenses?
- ☐ Studied your financial statements and pulled out the key numbers that will support the case for your business concept?

ISSUES TO CONSIDER

1. Why is the cash flow statement the most important statement for the entrepreneur?

2. Define an effective strategy for gathering the information required to complete the financial statements.

3. Why would you want to consider a variety of economic scenarios when developing your financial statements?

4. What is the role of ratio analysis in considering the financial condition of the business?

EXPERIENCING ENTREPRENEURSHIP

1. Interview an accountant familiar with the type of business you're interested in to learn some of the particular issues you need to consider when doing your financial statements.

2. Interview a banker about your business to learn the key financial ratios the bank looks for when it analyzes your business.

ADDITIONAL SOURCES OF INFORMATION

DeThomas, A. (1991). *Financial Management Techniques for Small Business.* Grants Pass, OR: Oasis Press.

Fraser, L.M., and A. Ormisten (2001). *Understanding Financial Statements.* Upper Saddle River, NJ: Prentice-Hall.

Kolb, R.W., and R.J. Rodriguez (1996). *Financial Management.* 2nd ed. Cambridge, MA: Blackwell.

Press, E. (1999). *Analyzing Financial Statements: 25 Keys to Understanding the Numbers.* New York: Lebhar-Freidman Books.

Stickney, C.P. (1990). *Financial Statement Analysis: A Strategic Perspective.* New York: Harcourt Brace.

INTERNET RESOURCES

AllBusiness.com
http://www.allbusiness.com
A general purpose source of financial information including how to do recordkeeping and example financial statements.

Internal Revenue Service—The Digital Daily
http://www.irs.ustreas.gov/prod
This web site is full of free information about the IRS and tax-related issues.

Pro2Net
http://accounting.pro2net.com/
A general source of accounting information for accountants, business owners, and students.

Teach Me Finance
http://teachmefinance.com/
Provides lessons in all aspects of finance.

RELEVANT CASE STUDIES

Case 4   Beanos Ice Cream Shoppe

Case 8   Alcoholes de Centroamerica, S.A. de C.V.

PART FOUR

Planning for Growth and Change

17

Planning for Growth

The entrepreneurial approach is not a sideline at 3M. It is the heart of our design for growth.
Lewis Lehr, Chairman, 3M Company

Overview

To grow or not to grow

Intensive growth strategies—growing within the current market

Integrative growth strategies—growing within the industry

Diversification growth strategies—growing outside the industry

Growing by going global

Some final thoughts on rapid growth

PROFILE 17.1

Preparing for Growth

If Dan Weinfurter seems undaunted by the astounding growth rate his company, Parson Group—a supplier of financial advice to big companies—has experienced, it's because he knew he wanted to grow his company and he prepared for it. In fact, he has become a growth expert. In the five years leading up to 2000, his company's revenues soared an astronomical 27,992 percent, which took his sales from $200,000 to $56 million and made his company the leader on the 2000 Inc. 500 Fastest Growing Private Companies list.

One of the lessons that Weinfurter learned along the way was the importance of a good accounting and financial-reporting system. In fact, it was the recognition that companies had nowhere to turn if they needed sophisticated assistance with budget analysis or a temporary controller. So he decided to offer experienced professionals who could provide not only high-level advice but management experience as well.

Through an associate at his previous job, Weinfurter was introduced to two venture capitalists who instantly liked what Weinfurter was proposing, and they appreciated his experience. They invested $7.2 million in the venture, which was then called Current Assets LLC, and Weinfurter added another $800,000 of his own capital. Fortunately for Weinfurter, these investors provided more than capital. They helped him develop a business plan and assemble a board of directors that got him his first customers.

Knowing that his concept was not rocket science and could easily be co-opted by someone else, Weinfurter decided that the company needed to expand quickly. In fact, he is positive that speed contributed to his success. But speed can also result in poor decisions. For example, it seemed to make sense to open a location near his home base, Chicago, so he chose Minneapolis and hired a manager from a newspaper ad. That turned out to be a mistake, so he changed his strategy to opening in a city where he had the right person for the job. As many other entrepreneurs have learned, people count more than location; in other words, if you can't find the right people in a particular location, it's a sign that maybe you need to look elsewhere. Recruiting is one of the toughest jobs any business owner undertakes, so you shouldn't make it harder by choosing the wrong location for the company.

After the company began to grow rapidly, one of the things that Parsons did right was to slow the company down for a year to return to profitability. Because growth costs a lot, many companies show losses for a time.

Growth often brings issues that the entrepreneur never foresaw when he or she started the business. As Weinfurter began opening locations in other states, he soon discovered that a staffing business in California was using the term current *assets in its promotional materials. As a result, Weinfurter changed the name of his business to Parson Group and broadened the scope of its offerings. Now the company is a consulting services business that also does mergers-and-acquisitions integration, risk management, and enterprise resource planning. Changing the company's focus is part of the natural evolution of any growing business if it wants to respond to its customers. Parson's clients continually ask the company to take on more and more tasks for them. Today about three-quarters of Parson's more than $100 million in revenues come from consulting.*

Parson will continue to grow at a 30–40 percent rate because it needs to if it wants to continue to attract top-flight talent. Moreover, an IPO is probably somewhere in its future, and any company contemplating going public should have a sustainable 40 percent growth rate at a minimum.

SOURCES: Edward O. Welles, "Growth: How Fast Is Too Fast?" *Inc. Magazine*, October 15, 2000; Susan Hansen, "Ready, Set, Grow," *Inc Magazine*, October 15, 2000; http://www.parsongroup.com/pages/careers.html.

Expansion is a natural by-product of a successful start-up. Growth helps a new business secure or maintain its competitive advantage and establish a firm foothold in the market. Growth is the result of a strong vision on the part of the entrepreneur and his or her team. Recall that one of the important tasks you need to undertake when you begin to put together a business plan is to have a vision for the company that becomes the guiding light for all your decision-making. If, for example, you want the company to be known as *the* customer-oriented company in the industry, you will probably choose a more controlled growth plan so that you can develop long-term customer relationships as the company grows. If, on the other hand, your vision is to be the largest company in the industry, you may choose a growth strategy focused more on rapid growth and acquisition. Some entrepreneurs shy away from growth because they are afraid of losing control. That fear is not unfounded; many businesses falter during rapid growth because of the enormous demands placed on the resources of the company. But with solid planning in place *before* growth occurs, you can avoid many of the pitfalls of rapid growth.

There is a misconception that if you want to grow rapidly, you must seek the support of venture capital. However, a review of the *Inc. 500* for the year 2000, indicates that 96 percent of the fastest growing private companies were not venture backed; that is, they were not funded by venture capital. In fact, in 2000, only about 4,000 companies in the United States received venture capital, so most companies grow through their own internal resources or with private investor money or debt.[1] Another misconception about growth is that a company can't be profitable while it's growing. The *Inc. 500* included 64 companies that were in some way related to the Internet, which was twice the number of those that landed on the list in 1999. These companies were not the no-profit models that went public almost from the outset. Of the twelve dot com companies on the 2000 *Inc. 500, two-thirds* were profitable in 1999. One example is Tech-Books, a technical publishing company that processes content for publishers that want online versions of their books. It had sales of $20 million in 1999 and was profitable during a period of rapid growth.

So, what do fast-growing ventures look like? The statistics about them reveal some interesting patterns. According to *Inc. Magazine's* annual survey of the 500 fastest growing private companies,[2] the most popular locations for high-growth ventures in 2001 were New York City, Washington, DC, Boston, San Francisco, and Chicago. The founder's median age was 41, and 93 percent of them were male. Over 81 percent were married and 54 percent had four-year college degrees. The median annual compensation of *Inc. 500* CEOs was $215,000; the average growth rate of the companies was 1,933 percent with average annual sales of $24,976,000. Most of the companies were in computer sales and services and related fields. But these businesses did not all start with a lot of money and expensive office space. The reality is that 56 percent of the 2001 class started from home and about half started with less than $20,000. You will find a profile of the company that made it to the #1 position on the *Inc. 500* for 2000, Parson Group LLC.

Contrary to the popular opinion that computer software firms dominate the high-growth sector of the economy, the fastest growing small companies come from a variety of industries including service, restaurants, product manufacturing, and clothing companies. So while some industries, like computers and telecommunications, provide a seemingly natural environment for high growth, a similar level of growth can occur in other industries as a result of the business strategy of the entrepreneur.

High-growth companies stand out from the crowd because they display some very distinct characteristics. Typically, they are

▶ First in a niche market they created and in which they became the leaders.

▶ Better at what they do than their competitors.

▶ Leaner in their operations.

▶ Unique in what they offer.

Being first in the market with a new product or service is one of the strongest competitive advantages there is. It provides a chance to establish brand recognition so that customers immediately think of *your* company when they think about a particular product or service, and it lets you set the standards for those who follow. This was certainly the strategy of Samuel Adams in the microbrewed beer industry and Microsoft in the operations and applications software industry. By combining a pioneering strategy with innovative processes, leaner operations, and a unique, innovate product or service, you can set up formidable barriers to competitors.

To Grow or Not to Grow

Some entrepreneurs make a conscious choice to control growth even in the face of extraordinary market demand. This is not to say that growth is slowed to single digits. Instead, the entrepreneur may choose to maintain a stable growth rate of 35 to 45 percent per year rather than subject the young venture to a roller coaster ride in the triple digits. In general, entrepreneurs who restrain growth do so because they are in the business for the long term; in other words, they're not in a hurry to harvest the wealth they create by selling the business or doing a public offering. They also typically don't like to take on a lot of debt or give up equity to grow. Consequently, they don't advertise heavily or aggressively seek new customers beyond their capabilities. They also diversify their product or service line from the beginning to make themselves independent of problems that may face their customers or their industries. By offering a diversified product/ service line, they have multiple streams of revenue that protect them from the loss of any one customer or market.

It is intoxicating for a new venture to realize that potential demand for its product or service is enormous, and that the company could grow well beyond industry averages. But "hyper-growth" has destroyed many companies that did not have the capacity, skills, or systems in place to meet demand. Recall the holiday season of 1999 when all the Internet retail businesses, like eToys, were not prepared for demand. They had little or no fulfillment systems in place and no plan for handling returns. These very companies are no longer in business today.

The growth phase of a new business can be one of the most exciting times for an entrepreneur. But if the entrepreneur has not prepared for growth with a coherent plan and a budget to match, it can be disastrous.

So, how do you decide whether to grow or not to grow? In many cases, it may not be your decision at all; demand for the product or service may compel you to keep up, or, by contrast, the market may not be big enough to allow the company to grow. Normally, by the time the company has reached a point where it is poised to grow to the next level, you will have a few employees and, of course, the founding team. To take that next step, you should consider some benchmarks for successful growth.

▶ Do you have leadership skills? When you started the business, you were involved in every one of the business's activities, but as the company began to grow, you found it necessary to delegate tasks to others. The more you delegated, the more you realized that your job had suddenly changed. Now you were not needed to do the tasks of the business; you were needed to lead the business, to make sure that the vision became reality. Everyone looked to you to ensure that the company survived. Leadership involves guiding the company and its people to achieve the company's goals. To accomplish that, you must have the ability to inspire people to action.

▶ Do you give your employees opportunities to learn and grow? A company can't successfully grow and change if its people don't grow and change with it. You need to encourage employees to stretch beyond what they knew when you hired them in the early days of the company, to learn more aspects of the business, and to give input into how the business is run.

▶ Does your company have a commitment to growth? With growth comes change—new ways to serve customers, new products and services, and new processes. Growing effectively requires the commitment of employees and customers. They have to see that growth is a good thing for them.

▶ Is everyone in your organization responsible and accountable for the success of the company? Everyone should understand what he or she contributes to the financial success of the company and everyone should have a stake in that financial success. Rapid growth requires teamwork, and for teams to operate effectively, they must be given responsibility and accountability for what they do.

There are times when saying "no" to growth makes sense for the business. That was the strategy that Bishop Partners took for its "growth" strategy.[3] The firm's managers learned early on to say no to clients that pulled their small executive search firm away from its core values and mission. Though the company was growing quickly, Susan Bishop, its founder, saw that its profit margin remained low and that, even as it took on more clients, the company's earnings remained flat. Bishop pulled her team together and started asking questions. To her amazement, she discovered that everyone had a different vision of the company and where it was going. It was no wonder that they had problems defining the right customer for the company. Once Bishop conveyed her vision to the employees, they worked together to define those customers and say no to those who didn't match their model. In the end, the company grew faster and remained healthy with a more focused strategy.

To comprehend the role of growth in a company's evolution, it is important to understand the factors that affect growth.

● *Factors That Affect Growth*

The degree and the rate at which a new venture grows are dependent on both the market and the management strategy. Market factors that affect a firm's ability to grow include the following:

▶ The size, characteristics, and buying power of the target market. If the niche market into which the company is entering is by nature small and relatively stable as to growth, it will of course be more difficult to achieve the spectacular growth and size of the fastest growing companies. On the other hand, if the product or service can expand to a global market, growth and size are more likely to be attained.

▶ The nature of the competition. Entering a market dominated by large companies is not in and of itself an automatic deterrent to growth. A small, well-organized company is often able to produce its product or service at a very competitive price while maintaining high quality standards, because it doesn't have the enormous overhead and management salaries of the larger companies. Moreover, if an industry is an old, established one, a firm entering with an innovative product in a niche market in that industry can experience rapid rates of growth.

▶ The degree of product innovation in the market. In some industries, like the computer industry, innovation is a given, so merely offering an innovative product is not in itself enough. In highly innovative industries, the key to rapid growth is the ability to design and produce a product more quickly than competitors. By contrast, in an industry that is stable and offers products and services that could be considered commodities, entering with an innovative product or process will provide a significant competitive advantage.

▶ The status of intellectual property (IP) rights like patents, copyrights, trademarks, and trade secrets. Intellectual property rights offer a competitive advantage to a new venture because they permit a grace period in which to introduce the product or service before anyone else can copy it. However, relying on proprietary rights alone is not wise. It is important to have a comprehensive marketing plan that allows the new business to secure a strong foothold in the market before someone attempts to reproduce the product and compete with it. True, an intellectual property owner has the right to take someone who infringes on their proprietary rights to court, but it is a time-consuming and costly process, one the typical small company can ill afford at a time when it needs all its excess capital for growth. See Chapter 7 for a complete discussion of intellectual property.

▶ The volatility of the industry. Some industries are by their very nature volatile; that is, it is difficult to predict what will happen for any length of time and with any degree of accuracy. The computer industry in the 1980s was such an industry; it has lately become somewhat more predictable as leading players have emerged. The young and dynamic telecommunications industry, however, is very volatile at this time. Consequently there are opportunities for extraordinary growth in new ventures and, at the same time, a higher risk of failure. A new entry into such an industry needs to maintain a constant awareness of potential government regulations, directions the industry is taking, and emerging competitors.

▶ The barriers to entry. Some industries, simply by their size and maturity, are difficult for a new venture to enter and difficult to penetrate with sufficient market share to make a profit. Other industries prohibit new entries because the cost of participating (plant and equipment or fees and regulations) is so high. Yet in the right industry, a new venture can erect barriers of its own to slow down the entry of competing companies. Patent rights on products, designs, or processes, for example, can effectively erect a temporary barrier to allow the new venture a window of opportunity to gain market share. When Gentech Corporation entered the old and established generator/compressor industries, it did so with three patents on its combination unit. Then, by creating a niche market in the construction industry, it could test its product in the market and establish itself before it had to compete against much larger companies.

Management factors that affect a firm's ability to grow include the following:

▶ The inertia of success. When the new company has survived and is successful, albeit as a small business, there is a tendency to believe that you must be doing everything right and should continue in the same way. That is a fatal error on the part of many entrepreneurs who don't recognize that change is a by-product of success. Many times it isn't until the venture is in crisis that the entrepreneur realizes the time has come to make a transition to professional management, which requires of the entrepreneur a fundamental change in attitudes and behaviors.[4]

▶ The entrepreneur's ability to move from controlling all aspects of the company to delegating authority and responsibility for major functions. Rapid growth requires different skills from start-up skills. In the beginning of a new venture, the entrepreneur has more time to take part in and even control all aspects of the business. But when rapid growth begins to occur, systems must be in place to handle the increased demand without sacrificing quality and service. Unless the entrepreneur is able to bring in key professional management with experience in high-growth companies, chances are the growth will falter, the window of opportunity will be lost, and the business may even fail needlessly. Many entrepreneurs have found that at some point in the business's growth, they must step down and allow experienced management to take over.

▶ The ability to encourage entrepreneurship in the entire venture team. Growing the business does not have to mean that the entrepreneurial spirit is lost, but rather that the entrepreneur must become very creative about maintaining that sense of smallness and flexibility while growing. Subcontracting some aspects of the business is one way to keep the number of employees down and retain team spirit. Developing self-managing teams is another way.

● ## *Stages of Growth in a New Venture*

Rates and stages of growth in a new venture vary by industry and business type; however, there appear to be some common issues that arise in the areas of strategic, administrative, and managerial problems. The importance of knowing when these issues will surface cannot be overstated, for it should be part of the entrepreneur's well-orchestrated plan to anticipate events and requirements before they occur.

Research has suggested that organizations progress sequentially through major stages in their life and development.[5] Still other studies have noted that at each stage of development, the business faces a unique set of problems.[6] For example, the start-up stage is characterized by marketing and financial problems, while the growth phase is associated with strategic, administrative, and managerial problems. One study looked at changes in the patterns of problems companies faced as they grew and found that the most significant changes from start-up to the growth stage were

1. the number of organizations that claimed their most difficult problem was obtaining financing declined from 17 percent at start-up to 1 percent in the growth phase and

2. the percentage of firms with human resource problems increased from 5 percent at start-up to 17 percent in the growth phase.[7]

The stages of growth (see Figure 17.1) can be described as four phases through which the business must pass: 1) start-up concerns of capital, customers, and distribution, 2) initial growth concerns of cash flow and marketing, 3) rapid growth concerns of resources, capital, and management, and 4) stable growth concerns of innovation and maintaining success.

Start-up Success

During start-up, the first stage, the entrepreneur's main concerns are to ensure sufficient start-up capital, seek customers, and design a way to deliver the product or service. At this point, the entrepreneur is a jack-of-all-trades, doing everything that needs to be done to get the business up and running. This includes securing suppliers, distributors, facilities, equipment, and labor. The very complexity of start-up with all of the various activities required is one reason that many new ventures fail. It also suggests that a team-based venture is better equipped to achieve a successful launch than a solo effort. If the company survives to achieve a positive cash flow from the revenues it generates, it is in a good position to grow and expand its market. If, however, revenues generated

FIGURE 17.1

Stages of Growth

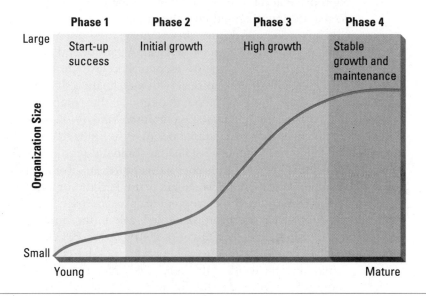

fail to cover company expenses, it will not be possible to grow without seeking outside capital in the form of equity or debt.

Initial Growth

If the new venture makes it through the first phase, it enters the second level of activity with a viable business that has enough customers to keep it running on the revenues it generates. Now the entrepreneur's concerns become more focused on the issue of cash flow. Can the business generate sufficient cash flow to pay all its expenses and at the same time support the growth of the company? At this point, the venture is usually relatively small, with few employees, and the entrepreneur is still playing an integral role. This is a crucial stage, for it is the decisions made here that will determine if the business will remain small or move to the next level, high growth, which entails some significant changes in organization and strategy. The entrepreneur and the team need to decide whether they are going to grow the business to a much larger revenue level or remain stable yet profitable.

Rapid Growth

If the decision is to grow, all the resources of the business have to be gathered together to finance the growth of the company. This is a very risky stage because growth is expensive, and there are no guarantees the entrepreneur will be successful at attempting to reach the next level. Planning and control systems must be in place and professional management hired because there will be no time to do that during the rapid growth period.

The problems during this stage center on maintaining control of rapid growth. They are solved by delegating control and accountability at various levels; failure usually is due to uncontrolled growth, lack of cash, and insufficient management expertise to deal with the situation. If growth is accomplished, it is in this stage that entrepreneurs often sell the company at a substantial profit. It is also at this stage that some entrepreneurs are displaced by their boards of directors, investors, or creditors because the skills that made them so important at start-up are not the same skills the company requires to grow to the next level. As a result, many entrepreneurial ventures reach their pinnacle of growth with an entirely different management team than the one that founded the company. To the extent that the entrepreneur is a vital part of the vision of the company and can identify an appropriate new role in the now larger company, he or she will remain the primary driver of the business. Bill Gates, Microsoft's co-founder, is one example of an entrepreneur who took his company from start-up to global corporate giant while at the helm. Only recently did he step out of the CEO position in favor of one of the founding team members, Steve Ballmer.

Stable Growth and Maintenance

Once the business has successfully passed through the rapid growth phase and is able to effectively manage the financial gains of growth, it will have reached Phase 4, stable growth and maintenance of market share. Here the business, which usually is now large, can remain in a fairly stable condition as long as it continues to be innovative, competitive, and flexible. If it does not, sooner or later it will begin to lose market share and could ultimately fail or revert to being a much smaller business. High-tech companies seem to be an exception to traditional growth patterns. Because they typically start with solid venture capital funding and a strong management team (dictated by the venture capitalists), they move out of Phases 1 and 2 very rapidly. During Phases 3 and 4, if the structure is effective and their technology is adopted in the mainstream market, they become hugely successful. If, on the other hand, the structure is weak and the technology is not readily adopted, they can fail rapidly.

● Problems with Growth

It is a sad fact that many entrepreneurial ventures that start with great concepts and experience early success eventually hit a wall. Growth stalls, or the firm can even die. Studies have found that among all the factors affecting growth, the most critical in a slowdown or failure appears to be inability to understand and respond to the business's environment.[8] That is, the entrepreneur did not recognize the opportunities and challenges developing outside the company and their potential to harm it.

For example, in its first eight years one manufacturer's representative firm with thirty highly trained salespeople grew to $20 million in sales and came to dominate its Midwestern market. But, at the eight-year point, the firm stopped growing and sales hit a plateau. Its founder thought the problem was an internal one, sales effectiveness. What really happened, however, was that the firm's competitors had changed their marketing and distribution strategies. One competitor had moved to a direct sales effort; another developed a strong telemarketing capability. The effect of these changes was to stall the sales of the entrepreneur's company in a matter of just months.[9] This entrepreneur had failed to recognize the changes in the environment and respond rapidly to them.

What this suggests to entrepreneurs is that they must continually

▶ Scan and assess their environment for changes and emerging competitors.

▶ Plan for growth.

▶ Hire for growth.

▶ Make growth part of the company culture.

Look at Table 17.1 for a framework for growing the business.

New business growth for the most part is a very positive thing. It does, however, bring with it some issues for which the entrepreneur must be prepared. For example, if the new venture is a retail business and you expand by opening additional stores, you need to decide whether or not to retain control of all functions in one main store or delegate the day-to-day management of each store and centrally control only marketing, accounting, finance, and purchasing. It may be necessary to establish a computer network to keep track of sales at all locations. For a manufacturing firm, expansion may entail significant capital investment in additional plant and equipment or developing new strategic alliances to keep production in line with demand. It may also mean locating additional distributors and even new channels of distribution. For a service business, growth may mean taking on additional associates or employees and investing in computer systems to manage information. And, of course, for the entrepreneur growth means giving up some control to others with the management skills to successfully guide the company.

● ***Growth Strategies***

This chapter looks at several strategies for growing the business:

▶ **Intensive growth strategies,** those that exploit opportunity in the current market

TABLE 17.1

A Framework for Growth

Strategy	Tactics
Scan and assess the environment	1. Analyze the environment a. Is the customer base growing or shrinking? Why? b. How are competitors doing? c. Is the market growing? d. How does your company compare technologically with others in the industry? 2. Do a SWOT analysis (strengths, weaknesses, opportunities, threats)
Plan the growth strategy	3. Determine the problem 4. Brainstorm solutions a. Don't limit yourself to what you know and have done in the past b. Choose 2–3 to test 5. Set a major goal for significant change in the organization 6. Set smaller, achievable goals that will put you on the path to achieve the major goal 7. Dedicate resources (funding and staff) toward the achievement of these goals
Hire for growth	8. Put someone in charge of the growth plan 9. Bring in key professional management with experience in growing companies 10. Provide education and training for employees to prepare them for growth and change
Create a growth culture	11. Involve everyone in the organization in the growth plan 12. Reward achievement of interim goals
Build a strategy advisory board	13. Invite key people from the industry who can keep you apprised of changes 14. Make them part of the planning process 15. Invite more outsiders than insiders

FIGURE 17.2

Growth Strategies for Entrepreneurs

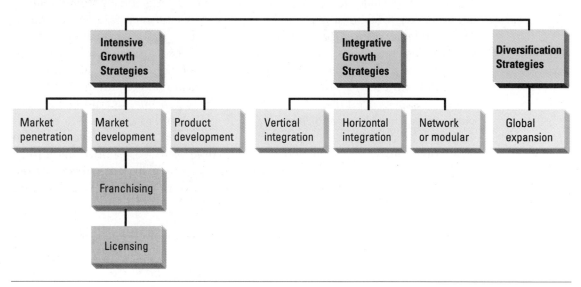

> ▶ **Integrative growth strategies,** those that take advantage of growth within the industry as a whole

> ▶ **Diversification strategies,** those that exploit opportunities outside the current market or industry

> ▶ **Global strategies,** those that take the business into the international arena

Figure 17.2 gives an overview of these strategies.

Intensive Growth Strategies—Growing within the Current Market

Intensive growth strategies focus on exploiting the current market fully; that is, expanding the market share to the greatest extent possible. This is accomplished by increasing the volume of sales to current customers and the number of customers in the target market. There are generally three methods for implementing an intensive growth strategy: market penetration, market development, and product development.

● Market Penetration

With market penetration, the entrepreneur attempts to increase sales by using more effective marketing strategies within the current target market. This is a common growth strategy for new ventures because it allows entrepreneurs to work in familiar territory and grow while they're getting their systems and controls firmly in place. Under this strategy you would move out gradually from the initial target market, whether it is a geographic area or a customer base. For example, the initial target market for the online travel guide might be travel agencies. You would focus your efforts and resources on getting those customers solidified, then gradually move on to other target customers like hotels and convention bureaus.

Additional uses for the product persuade customers to buy more. Arm & Hammer experienced that when its customers began buying baking soda not only for cooking but also for brushing their teeth and deodorizing their refrigerators. Yet another way to employ market penetration is to attract customers from your competitors by advertising product qualities, service, or price that distinguishes your product from others. A fourth way is to educate nonusers of the product or service as to its benefits, in an effort to increase the customer base.

● *Market Development*

Market development consists of taking the product or service to a broader geographic area. For example, if you have been marketing on the East Coast, you may decide to expand across the rest of the United States. One of the most popular ways to expand a market geographically is to franchise because it is generally less costly than setting up a national distribution system.

Franchising

Franchising allows the business to grow quickly in several geographic markets at once. The franchiser sells to the franchisee the right to do business under a particular name; the right to a product, process, or service; training and assistance in setting up the business, as well as ongoing marketing and quality control support once the business is established. The franchisee pays a fee and a royalty on sales, typically 3–8 percent. What the franchisee may get for the fee, depending on the business, are the following:

- A product or service that has a proven market.
- Trade names and/or trademarks.
- A patented design, process, or formula.
- An accounting and financial control system.
- A marketing plan.
- The benefit of volume purchasing and advertising.

Franchises generally come in three types: dealerships, service franchises, and product franchises. Dealerships allow manufacturers to distribute products without having to do the day-to-day work of retailing. Dealers benefit from combined marketing strength, but are often required to meet quotas. Service franchises provide customers with services such as tax preparation, temporary employees, payroll preparation, and real estate services. Often the business is already in operation before it applies to become a franchise member. The most popular type of franchise is one that offers a product, a brand name, and an operating model. Some examples are Kentucky Fried Chicken and Golf USA.

Though a popular vehicle for growth, franchising a business is not without its risks. It is virtually like creating a whole new business, because the entrepreneur must carefully document all processes and procedures in a manual that will be used to train the franchisees. Potential franchisees need to be scrutinized to ensure that they are qualified to assume the responsibilities of a franchise. Moreover, the cost of preparing a business to franchise is considerable and includes legal, accounting, consulting, and training expenses. Then, too, it may take quite a long time to show a profit, as many as three to five years.

The risk to franchisees who may have purchased the franchise as an entry into business ownership is also great. Franchisees will typically pay 2–10 percent of gross sales to the franchiser for monthly royalties and marketing fees, which means there is a tremendous challenge for the franchisees to control costs and get a return. The reason for failures of franchises is that they are typically found in retail industries (35–40 percent of retail sales come from franchised businesses),[10] primarily eating and drinking establishments, which have a pattern of high risk and low return. Other types of franchises in the recent past have been successful. For example, Handyman Connection (http://www.handymanconnection.com/) is a Cincinnati firm founded in 1990 to provide low-cost, residential home repairs and remodeling. The company began franchising in 1993 and as of 2000 had over 100 locations with plans to add another 40. Its revenues top $60 million.[11] Still many studies have found failure rates among franchisees to range from 38.1 percent to a high of 71.4 percent.[12] Bankruptcy of the parent company, the franchiser, should be another concern for potential franchisees, and it's not uncommon. In the past decade, dozens of franchises have experienced Chapter 11 bankruptcy, including 7-Eleven, Nutri-System, American Speedy Printing, Church's Fried Chicken, and Days Inns. Most have emerged intact, but not without some harm to the franchisees. During the bankruptcy, the franchisees are left essentially in limbo, without support or information, and wondering whether they'll have a viable business when it's all done. The association of the franchisee with the bankrupt parent is also a negative, since customers assume that if the parent has financial problems, so does the child. Furthermore, most franchisees have invested their life's savings in their businesses. Under the arbitration clauses in most franchise agreements, franchisees don't have the option of going to court to recoup their losses. Even if the company comes out of Chapter 11, its image is tarnished. It will have to cut back somewhere, and savvy consumers know this to be true.

Not all businesses are suitable for franchising as a growth strategy. A successful franchise system will need to have the following characteristics:

▶ A successful prototype store (or preferably stores) with proven profitability and a good reputation so that the potential franchisee will begin with instant recognition

▶ Registered trademarks and a consistent image and appearance for all outlets

▶ A business that can be systematized and easily replicated many times

▶ A product that can be sold in a variety of geographic regions

▶ Adequate funding, as establishing a successful franchise program can cost upwards of $150,000

▶ A well-documented prospectus that spells out the franchisee's rights, responsibilities, and risks

▶ An operations manual that details every aspect of running the business

▶ A training and support system for franchisees, both before they start the business and ongoing after start-up

▶ Site selection criteria and architectural standards

Developing a franchise program requires the assistance of an attorney and an accountant whose advice should be carefully considered before undertaking the effort. One of the things you will develop with the aid of your attorney is a franchise agreement. This document is often 40–60 pages in length and deals with a variety of legal issues. Some of the components of a franchise agreement are

▶ Rules by which the franchisor and franchisee will have to abide during the term of the franchise.

▶ Reference to the operations manual for the franchise to ensure that the franchisee adheres to the approved system for running the business.

▶ The term of the agreement. Remember that a franchise is like a lease. The franchisee is merely renting the business for the period of the franchise.

▶ Renewal provisions that include when notice must be given that the franchisee wishes to renew the agreement and what fees are to be paid.

▶ First right of refusal or option to take on additional franchises offered by the franchisor.

▶ The costs associated with purchasing the franchise. These may include an up-front fee, regular meeting expenses, and a percentage of the gross revenues to cover marketing and promotion costs.

▶ Rules related to the premises in which the franchise will be located. The franchisor may pay some of the costs of renovation and will often lease the property and grant a sublease to the franchisee.

▶ The stock of goods and materials needed to open the business and maintain a proper level of inventory.

▶ Intellectual property rights and who owns them.

▶ Whether you have the right to sell the franchise.

▶ How the franchise agreement can be terminated and what to do in case of disputes.

You can no doubt see why it's important to engage an attorney when structuring a franchise offering.

Licensing

Like franchising, **licensing** is a way to grow a company without investing large amounts of capital in plant, equipment, and employees. A license agreement is a grant to someone else to use intellectual property and exploit it in the marketplace by manufacturing, distributing, or using it to create a new product. For example, you may have developed a new patented process for taking rust off machinery. You could license that process to other companies to use on their equipment and receive a royalty. Conversely, you may have an idea for a new line of promotional products and want to license a famous name and likeness to use on them, to make them more attractive to consumers. This would entail seeking a license agreement from the owner of the name and likeness to use it commercially, for example, seeking a license from Paramount Pictures Corporation to use the Star Trek characters on a line of products.

But licensing is much more than this, and entrepreneurs need to understand fully the value of intellectual property and how it can provide income in a variety of different ways. For the purposes of this discussion, we'll state that anything that can be patented, copyrighted, or trademarked, or that is a trade secret, has the potential for licensing. If a company has intellectual property that someone else might pay to use or commercialize in some way, there are some steps that should be taken to ensure that both parties to the transaction win. Licensor and licensee depend on each other very much for the success of the agreement, so the outcomes must be worthwhile at both ends of the deal.

The following are steps licensors should take to ensure a successful transaction.

Step 1: Decide exactly what will be licensed. The license agreement can be for a product, the design for a product, a process, the right to market and distribute, the right to manufacture, or the right to use the licensed product in the production of yet another product. It will also be important to decide whether the licensee may only license the product as is or may modify it.

Step 2: Understand and define the benefits the buyer (licensee) will receive from the transaction. Why should the licensee license from your company? What makes the product, process, and so forth, unique and valuable? The licensee should clearly see that dealing with your company has many advantages and will be much more profitable than dealing with someone else.

Step 3: Conduct thorough market research to make sure the potential customer base is sufficient to ensure a good profit from the effort. Of course, the licensee too will have done market research, particularly if he or she approaches you with a proposal for a licensing agreement. But the latter situation is typical only with intellectual property that is well recognized in the marketplace: characters, for instance (Mickey Mouse, Batman, Harry Potter). A company with a new intellectual property that is unproven in the marketplace may need to seek out licensing agreements to get the property commercialized.

Step 4: Conduct due diligence on potential licensees. It's important to make certain any potential licensee has the resources to fulfill the terms and conditions of the license agreement, can properly commercialize the intellectual property, and has a sound reputation in the market. A license agreement is essentially a partnership and you want to choose your partners carefully.

Step 5: Determine the value of the license agreement. The value of a license agreement is determined by several factors: 1) the economic life of the intellectual property; that is, how long it will remain viable as a marketable product, process, and so on; 2) the potential that someone could design around the intellectual property and directly compete; 3) the potential for government legislation or regulation that could damage the marketability of the IP; 4) any changes in market conditions that could render the IP valueless.

Once you have determined the monetary value of the license based on these four factors, the license becomes negotiable. Generally, the licensor wants some money up front as a sign of good faith, then a running royalty for the life of the license agreement. The amount of this royalty will vary by industry and by how much the licensee must invest in terms of plant, equipment, and marketing to commercialize the license.

Step 6: Create a license agreement. With the help of an attorney who specializes in licenses, a license agreement or contract will be drawn up that will define the terms and conditions of the agreement between licensor and licensee. The following are just some of the clauses that are typically found in such license agreements.

▶ A **grant clause** specifies what is being delivered to the licensee and whether or not the license is exclusive (only the licensee has the right to this property) or nonexclusive (others also have a similar right).

▶ A performance clause specifies dates by which the licensee should achieve certain agreed-upon sales targets. This is important to prevent situations where the licensee ties up a technology through an exclusive agreement but never commercializes it, leaving the inventor without anything for his or her efforts.

▶ A secrecy clause or confidentiality clause spells out who may know the details of the intellectual property and for how long.

▶ A payment clause details the method by which payment will be made. If the license agreement deals with a foreign licensee, it will be important to designate the currency in which royalties will be paid. Normally, a U.S. licensor will want to take payment in U.S. dollars, but a combination of dollars and the licensee's currency is also used. Be aware that the value of any foreign currency will fluctuate over the life of the license agreement, so royalty payments will vary as well. This could mean more or less income for the licensor and higher or lower payments for the licensee.

▶ A **grantback clause,** or improvement clause, permits the licensee to improve on the product and grant back to the licensor the right to any improvements. Likewise, there may be a grantforward clause, which gives the licensee the right to use any improvements made by the licensor on the product.

▶ A definite term for the license agreement.

▶ A **sublicense clause** that specifies whether or not the licensee can sublicense the property or assign the right to another.

Being a licensee is also a way to grow your company without having to incur the expense of always developing new products. From the licensee's point of view, here are a few things to remember.

1. Search for a technology, product, logo, character, or other intellectual property that you want to license.

2. Be sure to prepare a business plan to present to the licensor, showing what you're proposing to develop and market with the licensor's intellectual property. The plan should include such things as estimated sales, the target market, the plan for penetrating the market, and how you intend to finance the agreement; that is, what resources you have for carrying out the agreement.

3. Conduct due diligence on the licensor to ensure that the company is reputable, the intellectual property is sound, and the company has the kind of people you want to work with over the period of the license. Remember, this is much like a partnership, so it's important to choose a partner carefully.

4. Try to negotiate favorable terms: conservative performance targets, lower royalties, little or no up-front capital, and so forth. Be aware, however, that if the intellectual property is well known or in great demand, there may not be much room to negotiate, so you'll probably pay a premium for the agreement.

Again, licensing is an excellent way to move more quickly in the marketplace with less capital investment than is needed for other forms of growth.

● *Product Development*

The third way to exploit the current market is to develop new products and services for existing customers or offer new versions of existing products. That is the tactic of software companies, which are constantly updating software with new versions their customers must buy if they want to enjoy all the latest features.

Savvy businesses get their best ideas for new products from their customers. These new ideas usually come in either of two forms: incremental changes in existing products or totally new products. Incremental products often come about serendipitously when engineers, sales personnel, and management spend time out in the marketplace with the customers, learning more about their needs. Bringing all these team members together on a weekly basis to discuss ideas helps the business to quickly zero in on those incremental products that are possible within the current operating structure and budget. The advantage of incremental products is that, because they are based on existing products, they can usually be designed and manufactured fairly quickly.

New or breakthrough products, on the other hand, have a much longer product development cycle and are therefore more costly to undertake. Breakthrough products cannot be planned for; instead, they usually come about through brainstorming, exercises in creativity, and problem-solving sessions. In other words, if the entrepreneur creates a business environment that encourages creative, "off-the-wall" thinking, the chances are greater that it will eventually come up with breakthrough products. The breakthrough environment, of necessity, has no budget or time constraints and does not run on a schedule. A combination of incremental and breakthrough products is probably the most effective way to go. The speed and cost efficiency of the incremental products keeps cash flowing into the business, cash that helps fund the more costly breakthrough products.

Branding

The most successful entrepreneurs recognize the power of a brand name; therefore, they strive to gain brand name recognition for their products and services as quickly as possible, so that they can use the recognition to create a family of related products and services under that name. A company that is able to establish brand recognition will find its marketing effort that much easier and its costs reduced. A brand name that reflects quality, service, and value is an asset that ultimately can generate huge profits for the business.

One example of the value of brand name recognition is the T-shirt industry. Companies like Mossimo and Nike buy basic T-shirts from an apparel manufacturer and print their own designs and logos on them. Customers will pay more for a T-shirt with the Mossimo name on it than they will for the same T-shirt with an unknown company name on it—that's brand recognition.

To establish brand recognition,

▶ Know what you're good at. List the strengths the company and its products possess. For example, do you offer a higher-quality product, a wider range of accessories or models, or exciting new colors?

▶ Educate customers about your strengths. Once core strengths have been identified, communicate them over and over again in all your marketing efforts, from brochures to signs to advertising. They should literally become a mantra for the customer. The minute customers think of your product, they should associate it with its strengths.

▶ Develop a set of rules for using the brand name. If you want the brand name to be associated only with wholesome things, you probably won't want to advertise during a television show containing violence, for example. How the brand name will be used also needs to be decided. Gentech Corporation, for instance, wanted the trade name for its product Power-Source always to be associated with the company name, so in all its advertising and promotion, the product is referred to as the Gentech Power-Source. In this way, when additional products are developed, the common thread will be the company name, Gentech.

▶ Get feedback on brand name recognition. To make sure the brand name is achieving the recognition level you are seeking, check periodically with the target customer. Ask them what their favorite brands are and how often they choose a product based on brand.

Once brand name recognition has been established, take advantage of it by developing related products under the same brand name. However, this works only when you are offering new benefits to your target market or taking the same benefits to a new market. If you take a new product to a new market, the brand recognition will not necessarily follow.

Integrative Growth Strategies—Growing within the Industry

Traditionally, when entrepreneurs have wanted to grow their businesses within their industries, they have looked to vertical and horizontal integration strategies, but now that it is important to be "lean and mean," they have been looking, more often than not, to a modular or network strategy. This section examines all three strategies—modular, vertical, and horizontal.

● *Vertical Integration Strategies*

An entrepreneurial venture can grow by moving backward or forward within the distribution channel. This is called **vertical integration.** With a backward strategy, the company either gains control of some or all of its suppliers or it becomes its own supplier by starting another business from scratch or acquiring an existing supplier that has a successful operation. This is a common strategy for businesses that have instituted a just-in-time inventory control system. By acquiring the core supplier(s), the entrepreneur can streamline the production process and cut costs. With a forward strategy, the company attempts to control the distribution of its products by either selling directly to the customer (that is, acquiring a retail outlet) or acquiring the distributors of its products. This strategy gives the business more control over how its products are marketed. In 1995, Eric Gift made a growth decision that increased his revenues by $1.5 million. Gift is the founder and CEO of A&B Books, a New York family-owned retail bookstore and distributor. When customers began asking how they could get their books published, he saw an opportunity and decided to move up the channel to take on the task of book publishing. To date, his company has published over 200 titles, bringing revenues to $3 million in 2000. Gift has found that by having control over who gets published and where the books are distributed, he can control pricing, marketing, and the people with whom he does business.[13]

● *Horizontal Integration Strategies*

Another way to grow the business within the current industry is to buy up competitors or start a competing business (sell the same product under another label). This is **horizontal integration.** For example, suppose you own a chain of sporting goods outlets. You could purchase a business that has complementary products, such as a batting cage business, so that your customers can buy their bats, balls, helmets, and so forth from the retail store and use them at the batting cage.

Another example of growing horizontally is to agree to manufacture your product under a different label. This strategy has been used frequently in the major appliance and grocery industries. Whirlpool, for example, produced

Sears's Kenmore washers and dryers for years. Likewise, major food producers put their brand name food items into packaging labeled with the name of a major grocery store.

● *Modular or Network Strategies*

The latest way to grow within an industry is to focus on what you do best and let others do the rest. If the core activities of the business include designing and developing new products for the consumer market, other companies can make the parts, assemble the products, and market and deliver them. In essence, your company with its core activities becomes the hub of the wheel, with the best suppliers and distributors as the spokes. This **modular** or **network strategy** helps the business grow more rapidly, keep unit costs down, and turn out new products more quickly. In addition, the capital saved by not having to invest in fixed assets can be directed to those activities that provide a competitive advantage. The electronics and apparel industries used this growth strategy long before it became trendy. Today many other industries are beginning to see the advantages of a modular approach. Even service businesses can benefit from outsourcing functions like accounting, payroll, and data processing, which require costly labor.

Outsourcing noncore functions can often help a company get products to market faster and in greater quantities, while at the same time spreading risk and delivering the capabilities of a much larger company without the expense. In fact, a Coopers & Lybrand survey of 400 fast-growing small companies found that two-thirds used outsourcing; their revenues, sales prospects, and growth rates far exceeded those of companies that did not.[14] Outsourcing permits small, growing companies to have noncore functions completed more efficiently at a lower cost and a higher level of quality than these companies could manage on their own. Innovative Medical Systems Inc., a New Hampshire–based manufacturer, outsources the manufacture of subassemblies, product design, computer networking, payroll administration, and direct mailing and advertising placement and handles in-house only final assembly, quality assurance, strategic marketing, and customer service.[15] As with anything else, there are some negatives to outsourcing. If most functions are outsourced, it becomes difficult to develop any kind of corporate culture that will bind workers together and make them loyal to the company. When "employees" are no longer employees, they may find it easier to leave on a moment's notice. They also will tend not to be as committed to the company's goals because they don't see a long-term role for themselves. These problems also apply to suppliers and distributors to whom you may outsource a capability. They must understand how they can also benefit from this relationship. That way, when your business begins to grow rapidly, they will be willing to ramp up to meet demand.

Diversification Growth Strategies—Growing Outside the Industry

When entrepreneurs expand their businesses by investing in or acquiring products or businesses outside their core competencies and industries, they are employing a diversification growth strategy. Usually, but not always, this strategy is used when the entrepreneur has exhausted all growth strategies within the current market and industry and now wants to make use of excess capacity or spare resources, adapt to the needs of customers, or change the direction of the company because of impending changes in the market or economy. One way to diversify is to use a synergistic strategy in which you attempt to locate new products or businesses technologically complementary to yours. For example, a food processor may acquire a restaurant chain that can serve as a showcase for the food. Another way to diversify is to employ a strategy whereby you acquire products or services that are unrelated to your core products or services. For example, a manufacturer of bicycle helmets may acquire an apparel manufacturer to make clothing with the company logo on it to sell to helmet customers. A final strategy for diversifying, **conglomerate diversification,** entails acquiring businesses that are not related in any way to what you are currently doing. An entrepreneur might use this strategy to gain control of a related function of doing business—for example, purchasing the building in which the business is housed and then leasing out excess space to other businesses to produce additional income and gain a depreciable asset. Many entrepreneurs whose work causes them to travel extensively find it advantageous to acquire a travel agency to reduce costs and provide greater convenience.

It doesn't matter where your business is located, there are ways to diversify to grow the business. Daffodil Harris started a tiny laundry business out of her boat in Admiralty Bay off a seven-square-mile island called Bequia near the Grenadines. She would travel from yacht to yacht picking up soiled clothing and returning them washed, dried, and folded. People loved the service. But Harris was not satisfied to be a one-person business. By 1999, she had grown the business into a multidivisional conglomerate that included a desalination plant, a marine service to rent moorings and dinghies and repair sails and equipment, a Chinese restaurant, and a grocery store. All of these businesses came out of asking customers what they wanted.[16]

A diversification strategy for growth is not something to undertake without careful consideration of all the factors and potential outcomes, particularly an acquisition. While it is true that the entrepreneur can find consultants who are experts in mergers and acquisitions to help smooth the path financially and operationally, what is difficult to predict with any degree of certainty is how the cultures of the two businesses will merge. Acquisitions and mergers cannot be successful on the basis of financial and operational synergy alone. Organizational styles and individual personalities of key management all come into play when an acquisition or a merger takes place. As a result, the human side of the two businesses must be analyzed and a plan developed for merging two potentially distinct cultures into one that can work effectively.

Many researchers have attempted to determine the most effective growth strategy for a new venture. In general, it has been found that horizontal integration, vertical integration, and synergistic diversification have been more successful than unrelated diversification. This is true whether the entrepreneur acquires an existing company or starts another company to achieve the goal. That is not to say that unrelated diversification should never be chosen as a growth strategy. If the potential gains are by comparison extraordinarily high, the risk may be worth the taking. It is also generally true that an acquired business has a better chance of success than a brand-new venture, for the obvious reason that it has usually already passed the crucial two stages of start-up and survival and is more likely to be poised to grow.

Growing by Going Global

Today the question for a growth-oriented company is not "Should we go global?" but "When should we go global?" There are many reasons why entrepreneurial ventures must consider the global market even as early as the development of their original business plan. Technology is hardly the sole province of the United States, and the United States can no longer ship its obsolete technology to other countries to extend its market life. Other countries now expect to receive the latest technology in the goods they purchase, and it may not always come with a United States label on it. In fact, the United States, while a huge market, represents less than half the total global market.[17]

Furthermore, due to rapidly changing technology, product lives are growing increasingly short. With R&D so expensive, companies are forced to enter several major markets at once to gain the maximum advantage from the window of opportunity. Entrepreneurs who attend world trade shows know their strongest competition may as easily come from a country in the Pacific Rim as from the company next door. Entrepreneurs also know they may have to rely on other countries for supplies, parts, and even fabrication to keep costs down and remain competitive.

With increasing competition and saturated markets in some industries, looking to global markets can add a new dimension to the entrepreneur's business. Many entrepreneurs have found new applications for their products in other countries or complementary products that help increase the sales of their products domestically. Several events have made exporting United States products to other countries more attractive than ever before.

▶ Relatively low United States interest rates have made it easier for businesses to finance the exporting of their products.

▶ The North American Free Trade Agreement (NAFTA) eliminated trade barriers among the United States, Mexico, and Canada, which makes exporting to those countries more attractive.

▶ The opening up and growth of untapped markets like China and Vietnam means more potential customers for U.S. products.

▶ The establishment of the first four Federal Export Assistance Centers gives businesses considering exporting a new source of help. The four centers are located in Baltimore, Long Beach, Miami, and Chicago.

▶ The Uruguay Round of GATT (General Agreement on Tariffs and Trade) reduced or eliminated tariffs among 117 countries in 1995. It also improved patent and copyright protection, which has been a problem for businesses exporting protected products to other countries where proprietary rights may not be recognized or protected.

While you should include a global strategy in any business planning, you may not be able to export until the business is somewhat established and offering a high-quality product or service at a competitive price. Still, we are seeing more and more "global start-ups"—companies like Logitech, the Swiss manufacturer of computer mouses—take a global strategy from the very inception of the business. Researchers have found that the number of global start-ups appears to be growing.[18] Oviatt and McDougal studied a dozen global start-ups and followed them over time. Four failed, for a variety of reasons, but in general those that failed had fewer of the success characteristics that Oviatt and McDougal found in those that survived. These success characteristics include

1. A global vision from the start.

2. Internationally experienced managers.

3. Strong international business networks.

4. Preemptive technology.

5. A unique intangible asset such as know-how.

6. Closely linked product or service extensions. (The company derives new and innovative products and services from its core technology.)

7. A closely coordinated organization on a world-wide basis.[19]

However, going global is also a risky proposition. Building a customer base and distribution is difficult in the domestic market; it is a colossal challenge in foreign markets.[20] Moreover, financing is more difficult when you enter global markets because of the inherent risks.

Those concerns are not unfounded. Many small entrepreneurial companies have made their first foray into the global marketplace via a single order from a potential customer in another country. If that one transaction goes smoothly, the entrepreneur may be under the misguided perception that doing business in another country is easy. One small computer component business learned that lesson the hard way. The company shipped a $10,000 replacement component to a customer in France. Six months later the owner was billed $2,500 for value-added tax, something he knew nothing about. He had no choice but to absorb the loss.

Whether or not you have a global start-up, exporting is a long-term commitment that may not pay off for some time. In the meantime you may have to adapt the product or service somewhat to meet the requirements of the importing country and develop good relationships with agents in the country. If you are dealing in consumer products, target countries that have disposable income and like U.S. products. If, however, you are dealing in basic or industrial products, look to developing countries that need equipment and services for building infrastructures and systems. One example is Mexico, which is taking on the enormous task of building bridges and roads as it positions itself as a major player in the world market.

● ### *Finding the Best Global Market*

Finding the best market for a product or service can be a daunting task, but there are some sources and tactics that help make the job easier. Start with the *International Trade Statistics Yearbook of the United States,* which is available in any major library or can be purchased online. With the **United Nations Standard Industrial Trade Classification (SITC) codes** found in this reference book, you can find information about international demand for your product or service in specific countries. The SITC system is a way of classifying commodities used in international trade. You should also be familiar with the Harmonized System of classification, which is a ten-digit system that puts the United States "in harmony" with most of the world in terms of commodity tracking systems. If your international shipment exceeds $2,500, you must know your HS number for documentation.

Consult additional sources of information like the district office or the Washington, D.C., office of the International Trade Administration and the Department of Commerce (DOC). The commerce department's online database links all the DOC International Trade Administration offices and provides a wealth of valuable research information.

The successful launch of a program of global growth should include a marketing plan and budget directed toward that goal in the business plan. You also need to bring someone onto the team who has international management experience or export experience. Depending on your budget, you may choose

PROFILE 17.2

Will Europeans Walk Around with Cardboard Coffee Cups?

The Starbucks empire stretches from Seattle to Boston to Shanghai and Dubai. The success of Howard Schultz in taking a commodity drink and turning it into an experience enjoyed world renown. But in March 2001, with 200 outlets already established in the United Kingdom, Starbucks opened its first outlet in Continental Europe in Zurich, Switzerland, with plans to open 650 more stores in neighboring countries by 2003. A daunting task anywhere, bringing U.S. coffee to Europe presents a new challenge for the growth-hungry entrepreneur. Europeans, for the most part, have their own coffee heritage with very particular tastes and a general aversion to U.S. commercialism. Moreover, the American coffee they have tasted to date has not lived up to their expectations. Europeans also resist the cookie-cutter approach to business that they've seen with major franchises like McDonalds and Burger King. They tend to prefer coffee houses that are quiet and cozy, quite the opposite of the utilitarian, no-nonsense atmosphere in a Starbucks that is focused on getting busy people in and out quickly. In fact, the whole concept of "take-away" coffee was unheard of in Europe until another American, Peter Joos, founded a chain of coffee shops called Frazer Coffee in Frankfurt, Germany.

Schultz looked hard at the European market and determined that Switzerland, with its French, German, and Italian cultures, was an excellent place to test the market. He also believed that the coffee culture of Europe was a natural for Star-bucks, and it appears he may have been right. The day the first store opened in Zurich, people lined up to be the first to enter. Starbucks is undertaking its European expansion with Swiss joint venture partner the Bon Appetite Group. By July 2001, the team also opened an outlet in Vienna, Austria, where traditional coffee houses are the norm, and in September 2001 announced a deal with a German retailer, Essen-based Karstadt Quelle department stores, to offer its coffee products in Germany.

Shultz's strategy is to capture the youth market in Europe, consumers ranging in age from 20 to 30 years old who might be looking for a different coffee experience. European Starbucks will be more suited to European tastes and provide soft seating, music, and American-style beverages. Starbucks is still not certain that Europeans will carry around coffee in cardboard cups like their U.S. counterparts.

As Schultz moves forward with his plans for more outlets, one hurdle remains: the price. Europeans are accustomed to spending thirty cents on a cup of coffee. It remains to be seen if they will be willing to pay Starbuck's premium prices for its coffee experience on a regular basis.

Sources: "Starbucks Moves into Austria," *Agra-Food-News,* July 19, 2001; Hans Greimel, "Starbucks' Final Frontier Is Winning European Palates," *Austin American Statesman,* March 9, 2001, p. 3B; "Starbucks in Deal with German Retailer," *DSN Retailing Today,* September 17, 2001; Kathy Mulady, "Switzerland, Meet Starbucks," *Seattle Post-Intelligencer,* March 7, 2001.

to hire a consultant who specializes in this area. It is also important to attend foreign trade shows to learn how businesses in the countries in which you are interested conduct business, who the major players are, and who the competition is.

Export Financing

To make a sale in the global market, requires funds to purchase the raw materials or inventory to fill the order. Unfortunately, many entrepreneurs assume that if they have a large enough order, getting financing will be no problem. Nothing could be further from the truth. Export lenders, like traditional lending sources, want to know that the entrepreneur has a sound business plan and has the resources to fill the orders. Entrepreneurs desiring to export can look for capital from several sources:

- Bank financing
- Internal cash flow from the business
- Venture capital or private investor capital
- Prepayment, down payment, or progress payments from the foreign company placing the order

A commercial bank is more interested in lending money to a small exporter if the entrepreneur has secured a guarantee of payment from a governmental agency such as the Import-Export Bank, which limits the risk undertaken by the commercial bank. Asking buyers to pay a deposit up-front, enough to cover the purchase of raw materials, can also be a real asset to a young company with limited cash flow.

Foreign Agents, Distributors, and Trading Companies

Every country has a number of sales representatives, agents, and distributors who specialize in importing U.S. goods. It is possible to find one agent who can handle an entire country or region, but if a country has several economic centers, it may be more effective to have a different agent for each center. Sales representatives work on commission; they do not buy and hold products. Consequently, the entrepreneur is still left with the job of collecting receivables, which, particularly when dealing with a foreign country, can be costly and time consuming.

Agents are a way to circumvent this problem. Agents purchase a product at a discount (generally very large) off list and then sell it and handle collections themselves. They solve the problem of cultural differences and the ensuing difficulties inherent in these transactions. Of course, with an agent you lose control over what happens to the product once it leaves your hands. You have no say over what the agent actually charges customers in his or her own country. If the agent charges too much in an effort to make more money for him- or herself, you may lose a customer.

If you are just starting to export or if you are exporting to areas not large enough to warrant an agent, consider putting an ad in U.S. trade journals that showcase U.S. products internationally. If you are producing a technical product, you may be able to find a manufacturer in the international region you are targeting that will let you sell your products through its company, thus giving you instant recognition in the foreign country. Ultimately, that manufacturer could also become a source of financing for your company.

Another option is to use an export trading company (ETC) that specializes in certain countries or regions where it has established a network of sales representatives. ETCs may also specialize in certain types of products. What often happens is that a sales representative may report to the ETC that a particular country is interested in a certain product. The ETC then locates a manufacturer, buys the product, and sells it in the foreign country. Trading companies are a particularly popular vehicle when dealing with Japan.

Choosing an Intermediary

Before deciding on an intermediary to handle the exporting of products,

1. Check the intermediary's current listing of products to see whether there is a good match with the kind of products you make.

2. Understand with whom you will be competing; that is, does the intermediary also handle your competitors?

3. Find out whether the intermediary has enough representatives in the foreign country to adequately handle the market.

4. Look at the sales volume of the intermediary. It should show a rather consistent level of growth.

5. Make sure the intermediary has sufficient warehouse space and up-to-date communication systems.

6. Examine the marketing plan.

7. If necessary, make sure the intermediary can handle servicing of your product.

Once you have decided on the intermediary, draft an agreement detailing the terms and conditions of the relationship. It is very much like a partnership agreement, so consult an attorney specializing in overseas contracts. The most important thing to remember about the contract is that it must be based on performance, so that you do not tie yourself up for many years with someone who is not moving enough product for you. Negotiate a one- or two-year contract with an option to renew should performance goals be met. This will probably not please the intermediary, as most want a five- to ten-year contract. Be firm; it is not in your best interests to have a longer-term contract until you know that the person is loyal and can perform.

Other issues that should be addressed in the agreement include the following:

▶ Your ability to use another distributor; in other words, negotiate for a non-exclusive contract so as to have some flexibility and control over distribution.

▶ The specific products the agent or distributor will represent. This is important, because as your company grows you may add or develop additional products and not want this agent to sell those products.

▶ The specific geographic territories for which the agent or distributor will be responsible.

▶ The specific duties and responsibilities of the agent or distributor.

▶ A statement of agreed-upon sales quotas.

▶ A statement of the jurisdiction in which any dispute would be litigated. This will protect you from having to go to a foreign country to handle a dispute.

Choosing a Freight Forwarder

The **freight forwarder's** job is to handle all aspects of delivering the product to the customer. The method by which you ship a product has a significant impact on the product's cost or the price to the customer, depending on how the deal is structured, so consider the choice of a freight forwarder carefully. The ability to fill a shipping container to capacity is crucial to reducing costs. Freight forwarders, who can present shipping documents to your bank for collection, prepare the shipping documents, which include a bill of lading (the contract between the shipper and the carrier) and an exporter declaration form detailing the contents of the shipment. You, however, are responsible for knowing whether any items being shipped require special licenses or certificates, as in the case of hazardous materials or certain food substances.

Global Franchising

The first franchisers on the global scene were primarily the large food franchises such as McDonald's, Kentucky Fried Chicken, and Burger King. Today even smaller franchisers like Popcorn Palace are going global. Foreign governments generally welcome franchisers, because they bring to the country not only a product but also a way of doing business, which provides jobs for the citizens of the country. Those who have chosen to try their luck in developing countries or the old Eastern Bloc countries have consistently found the cost of doing business there much higher. In addition, they may have to deal with unstable governments, volatile currencies, and a general lack of understanding of competitive market systems. Many international franchisers have discovered that having a local partner is one of the keys to a successful global effort because it allows them to acquire an understanding of the business and consumer culture in the country. Franchisers also tend to try to establish master franchise agreements, which give the franchisee the rights to the entire country or region because they will only have to deal with one franchisee in a particular region.

One of the challenges facing international franchisers is achieving the same level of productivity and service they offer in the United States. In some countries relatively low productivity is the norm, and changing old habits can require hours of training. One source of help for potential international franchisers is the International Franchise Association (IFA) located in Washington, D.C. This organization has established a code of ethics and, through its Franchisee Advisory Council, provides dispute resolution for both franchisees and franchisers.

Some Final Thoughts on Rapid Growth

In 1999, *Fortune* magazine looked at its annual list of fast-growing companies to see why they were so successful and so profitable.[22] *Fortune* discovered some very similar characteristics across all the companies. Here are some of them.

- ▶ They deliver on time. The ability to deliver products on schedule is critical to successful growth. Rainforest Café, a chain of jungle-themed restaurants, saw its share price drop 40 percent annually over three years, even with growing revenues, because it experienced delays in opening its restaurants.

- ▶ They promise only what they can deliver. There is a lot of pressure to keep setting higher benchmarks on earnings, sales figures, and so forth. But growth is a hungry animal that needs to be fed, so retaining earnings to invest in growth is often the better strategy. That has been the strategy of MiniMed, the California-based manufacturer of insulin pumps. The company's growth has been impressive, but not as impressive as it could have been because its founder and chairman, Dr. Alfred Mann, believes in investing heavily in research for the future sustainability of the company.

- ▶ They pay attention to the details. When Qualcomm manufactured its first generation of cellular phones, it took sixty workers three hours to build each phone. When Qualcomm's engineers saw that, they got to work redesigning—eliminating ball bearings, springs, and pins—so that sixteen workers could build a phone in fifteen minutes.

- ▶ They protect their business with barriers to entry. That's the reason that MiniMed puts significant money into research and patents. It builds a barrier around the company that competitors can't easily penetrate.

Growth can be an exciting time. And while a company's growth rate won't resemble a hockey stick for long, strong growth can be sustained over time if entrepreneurs plan for it and keep scanning the horizon for changes.

NEW VENTURE CHECKLIST

Have you:
- ☐ Identified market factors that may affect the growth of the business?
- ☐ Determined which growth strategy is most appropriate?
- ☐ Identified potential international markets for the product or service?
- ☐ Developed a plan for globalization of the company at some point in the future?

ISSUES TO CONSIDER

1. What are four characteristics of high-growth companies?

2. How can both market and management factors affect the growth of a new venture?

3. What questions should you ask at each level of the new venture's growth?

4. What advantages do intensive growth strategies have over integrative and diversification strategies?

5. Why is it important to start a growth-oriented business with a plan for globalization from the beginning?

6. What are the differences among foreign agents, distributors, and export trading companies in terms of the services they provide?

EXPERIENCING ENTREPRENEURSHIP

1. Visit an export center in your area and talk to a Department of Commerce trade specialist who can advise you on how to become prepared to export. What did you learn that you hadn't learned from reading this text?

2. Interview an entrepreneur in the early stages of his or her venture and question him or her about the growth strategy for the business. Can you identify the type of strategy being used?

ADDITIONAL SOURCES OF INFORMATION

Catlin, K., and J. Matthews (2001). *Leading at the Speed of Growth: Journey from Entrepreneur to CEO.* Chicago: Hungry Minds.

Hill, C.W.L. (2000). *International Business: Competing in the Global Marketplace: Postscript 2001.* New York: Irwin.

McKnight, L.W., P.M. Vaaler, and R.L. Katz (2001). *Creative Destruction: Business Survival Strategies in the Global Internet Economy.* Cambridge: MIT Press.

Trade Information Center. Tel. (800) USA-TRADE or (800) 872-8723. Ask for an industry desk officer who specializes in your industry.

Whiteley, R., and D. Hessan (1996). *Customer-Centered Growth.* Reading, MA: Addison-Wesley.

Wolf, J.S. (1992). *Export Profits.* Dover, NH: Upstart Publishing.

Woznick, A., and E.G. Hinkelman (2000). *A Basic Guide to Exporting.* 3rd ed. Novato, CA: World Trade Press.

INTERNET RESOURCES

Global Business Online
http://www.exporttoday.com
Tips for businesses that want to trade internationally.

International Business Forum
http://www.ibf.com
Geared toward entrepreneurs who want to get into the international marketplace. Contains lists of resources in various countries, opportunities, and associations.

The International Trade Desk
http://members.aol.com/tradedesk/
A screening web site for key trade information.

The Internationalist
http://www.internationalist.com
An excellent source for information on a wide range of international issues including business, investment, and travel.

International Trade Administration
http://www.ita.doc.gov
A division of the Department of Commerce. Offers help to companies that wish to export.

RELEVANT CASE STUDIES

Case 1   Mrs. Gooch's

Case 3   Overnite Express

Financing Start-up and Growth

Money is the seed of money, and the first guinea is sometimes more difficult to acquire than the second million.

Jean Jacques Rousseau

Overview

PROFILE 18.1

Persistence Is the Key Ingredient

When it's time to seek funding for a new or growing venture, one of the key ingredients to a successful experience is persistence, not average persistence but dedicated persistence. When C.J. Comu and John Potter decided to raise growth capital of about $5 million for their indoor air-purification equipment company, they had no idea how difficult that task would become. If someone had told them up-front that they would have to pitch their concept to 500 people and not take any pay for two years, they might never have grown Airtech, their Dallas-based company, beyond its small beginnings.

In 1997, the partners invested $550,000 of their own money and $6 million in friendly money to develop a working prototype of their air-purification equipment. But then they had no more cash left to manufacture and distribute the product, so they put together a business plan and hit the road. People loved the concept, but no one was buying. After flying all over the country and approaching more than 500 people in offices and coffee shops, they finally met a Denver investment banker who connected them with West End Capital LLC, a venture capital firm based in New York City. Their persistence paid off. They received their $5 million in one check. Today their company includes customers like Southwest Airlines and T.G.I. Fridays.

Michael Stern could identify with the tenacity of Comu and Potter. He too had a rather unusual experience attempting to raise seed capital for his new company, Information Markets Corporation, located in New York's Silicon Alley. Stern first tried to raise money by appearing on the cable TV program Win Ben Stein's Money, *but he didn't do well and returned to New York to continue his search. Actually, with Stern's background as a Harvard graduate with experience in a New York investment-banking firm, it should have been relatively easy for him to tap the money markets. But that wasn't the case. Like Comu and Potter, Stern struggled. For four months he telephoned everyone he knew who could possibly help him start his Internet business. Infomarkets.com was a way for people to get information from experts by paying for it. If you needed information on the market for your air-purification device in Tokyo, you could post the offer and an expert in that market would respond.*

Finally after four months of persistence, Stern managed to acquire commitments from forty "angels" for $2.1 million. Then, flush from his first success, he raised a second round of $6 million from America Online, Inc. and Bulldog Capital Management.

The lesson for entrepreneurs? If you believe in your concept and you've proven the market, the money is out there. It's a matter of persistence and finding the right investor.

SOURCES: Juan Hovey, "Marathon Men," *Fortune Small Business,* April 16, 2001; Juan Hovey, "The Power of Persistence," *Fortune Small Business,* April 16, 2001; http://www.airtechenv. com/; http://www.infomarkets.com/servlet/HomePage.

"How can I fund my new business?" Probably no question is more on the minds of entrepreneurs with new venture ideas. Everyone believes that money is the driver of successful new ventures. If you have enough money, you can make any business concept a success. Unfortunately, that reasoning doesn't always hold true. In fact, reality may be quite the opposite. Throwing money at a bad idea doesn't change the quality of the idea; it just delays the inevitable failure. Moreover, having more money than you need often results in poor decisions made quickly because there's plenty of money to allow for mistakes.

Alternatively, you may wonder, "I've got an idea for a business and I need to find venture capital." This assumption springs from a lack of understanding of start-up ventures and the nature of financial markets.

Because start-up companies are inherently risky investments, the number of sources for financing them is more limited. Once a business has survived start-up and achieved a successful track record, however, multiple new sources of financing are available to help the business grow. Still, funding opportunities is a difficult process because of information asymmetry; entrepreneurs have more information about themselves and their ventures than do the people from whom they seek funding.[1] The entrepreneur understands the value of his or her concept, but can that value be successfully conveyed to the investor market? So how does an entrepreneur improve his or her chances of securing venture funding? Research points to the importance of the entrepreneur's social network and reputation in increasing the chances of securing funding.[2] But that is only the beginning. This chapter will look at sources of financing for both start-up and growing companies to better prepare you for finding the right funding from the right source at the appropriate time. Not all of the sources and strategies discussed in this chapter will be suitable for every business, but it's important to understand all of the options so that you can make wiser choices.

Starting with a Plan

The first rule in funding a new venture or financing the growth of an existing business is that you must start with strategies for targeting the right amount of money from the right sources. It's important to raise only what you actually need, not what you think is possible in the current economic environment. But, with that in mind, you want to look ahead and plan carefully so that you don't have to seek financing too often, because looking for money costs money, as we'll see shortly.

Start by identifying the stages of growth your business will experience. Every business is a bit different, but in general, each will reach certain milestones that suggest it's time to grow to the next level. For example, look at Figure 18.1 where the typical funding stages are presented. In Phase 1, start-up funds are required. These will typically come from the founders and other "friendly money." Once the company is up and running and has achieved success in a small market, it's time to grow the company to reach a wider audience.

At Phase 2, the company may be unable to grow rapidly enough using internal cash flows and instead will require outside capital from a private investor or venture capitalist (VC). Now suppose the company is once again successful at growing the business using private investor or venture capital money and would like to achieve a substantial size and give its investors the opportunity to harvest the wealth that has been created. The entrepreneurial team may decide to make a public offering, which will give them access to the capital markets from which it is easier to raise large amounts of money. A public offering takes a lot of planning and funding. Consequently, in Phase 3, they will require a different type of money, called **mezzanine or bridge financing,** to provide them with the capital they need to get through an initial public offering where they will perhaps raise millions of dollars. As you can see, there are different types of money for different stages of the venture. In general, the milestones a business achieves create more value for the business and as a result allow it to seek greater and greater amounts of capital in the form of equity or debt.

In addition, entrepreneurs who are successful at raising capital consistently do three things:

▶ Create value for their businesses by establishing long-term, loyal customer relationships and superior products.

▶ Run businesses that are profitable, something the dot coms didn't understand.

▶ Make sure their businesses operate with a positive cash flow.

Planning for a Traditional Business

Traditional businesses display fairly predictable stages of growth, as you saw in Figure 18.1. In Phase 1, you're seeking seed capital for start-up—to finish product development and prepare to launch the business. This capital is typically planned to take the business from launch through a positive cash flow that results from the generation of sufficient revenues to cover all the expenses of the business. By the second phase, the business is requiring capital to grow based on a proven concept. In fact, customers may have demanded that the company grow, a point that most entrepreneurs look forward to. Phase 3, rapid growth, can come relatively early in the venture's life cycle or very late. For some businesses, particularly lifestyle businesses, rapid growth may never be part of their evolution. They may instead enjoy slow, steady growth. If a business survives over the long term it will likely reach a mature phase where it ideally maintains

FIGURE 18.1

Stages of Growth

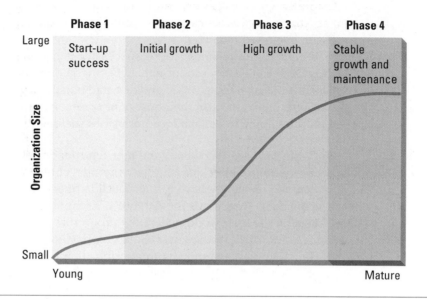

a stable revenue stream with a loyal customer base. In today's dynamic environment, however, stability is rarely an enduring state. To continue to be profitable, a mature business must punctuate its equilibrium with new products and services and new markets so that it can remain competitive. Typically, in the third or fourth phase, the founder, if he or she chooses to, is able to reap the rewards of years of effort by harvesting his or her investment through a buyout (sale of the company), public offering, or merger.

While the length of time a business spends in each stage varies, most entrepreneurial businesses follow this pattern. E-commerce and high technology businesses display different characteristics and they are discussed in the following sections.

● *Planning for an E-Commerce Business*

At the start of the new millennium e-commerce businesses fell into disfavor with funding sources for good reason. Most had not demonstrated that they could create real value—they were merely concepts with no solid business model behind them. Still, any pure Internet business or one that is substantially based on the e-commerce model will have a financial strategy that is part formula and part artistic achievement. For example, Drugstore.com (www.drugstore.com) received its initial funding on its concept alone; funders really liked the idea of buying pharmaceuticals over the Internet and could readily see the benefits to customers. On the other hand, a provider of web-based audience analysis, Web-SideStory (www.websidestory.com) had to prove its business model would work online, that is, prove that customers would buy, before it could secure any funding from interested investors.

For an Internet business to be successful it needs to scale out relatively quickly and that means a lot of expensive marketing and customer acquisition dollars at the earliest stages. So, unlike a traditional business, e-commerce businesses often have to raise the equivalent of second-stage funding at start-up. Several rules apply to e-commerce businesses seeking funding.

▶ *Find smart money.* While funding from friends and family may work fine for a traditional business, it isn't the best choice for an Internet concept that will ultimately have to seek outside financing from angels or venture capitalists. Who funds the venture is as important as the venture concept itself in the web world, where the group that is backing your concept can make or break the business. Smart money is investors that bring more to the table than just money; they bring such things as expertise, contacts, and help finding professional management for the company.

▶ *Ask one of your business advisors to introduce you to funding sources.* It's easier to get the attention of a funder through an introduction than a cold call.

▶ *Don't grab the first term sheet you receive.* Venture capitalists use term sheets to define the negotiating terms of an agreement. They include such things as the amount being invested, the term of the investment, the rate of return, the number of board seats required, and so forth. There is still a lot of money out there for a good Internet venture, so it is possible that more than one funding source may be interested in your venture. Moreover, you should take a deal that moves the company to the next stage of growth or development and involves people you can work with.

▶ *Purchase the best management team possible.* Most investors invest in the team more than anything else. If you can't afford the management you need, consider a strategic alliance with a company whose management you can leverage. Many small companies team with larger companies to benefit from their mutual core competencies.

Planning for the High-Tech Venture

High-tech ventures introducing **break-through** or **disruptive technologies,** like a new drug or a device like the fax machine that changes the way we do things, tend to follow a pattern discussed in the works of Geoffrey Moore.* Early

---

*See *Crossing the Chasm* (1999). New York: HarperBusiness, and *Inside the Tornado* (1999), New York: HarperCollins.

seed funding supports a long period of product development. Often this money comes from government grants or foundations. It is a rare venture capital firm that will invest during the product development phase of a high-tech venture. Once the product is market ready, however, it moves into a phase known as the "early adopter" stage where technically oriented users, who regularly purchase leading edge technology, begin to use it. The company will require marketing and educational dollars to capture enough niches in the market to cause the product to be drawn into what Moore refers to as the "tornado," a period of mass adoption of the new technology where it typically becomes the standard in the industry. During this frenzied period, the business focuses solely on producing and delivering product to meet extraordinary demand. Later when demand tapers off, money needs to be devoted to building loyal customer relationships and developing new applications for the core technology over the long term. High technology ventures have longer development times but generally move through the product and business evolution cycle much faster than other types of businesses. Of course, their products often have shorter life cycles as well.

See Figure 18.2 for an overview of the various stages of funding for a new venture.

Financing Start-ups

Most start-up ventures begin with a patchwork of funding sources that include credit cards, savings, friends, family, borrowing, and bartering or trading products and services. **Bootstrapping** refers to techniques for creative financing, getting by on as few resources as possible and using other peoples' resources whenever feasible. It involves begging, borrowing, or leasing everything needed to start a venture and is the antithesis of the "big money model" espoused by many when they talk about entrepreneurial ventures.[3] More often than not, bootstrapping is a model for starting a business without money—or at least without any money beyond that provided by the entrepreneur's personal resources.

This section looks at the various sources of funding for start-up ventures.

● *Entrepreneur Resources*

Most entrepreneurs start their ventures with their own resources. These resources include savings, credit cards, mortgages, stock market accounts, and friends and family. The Department of Commerce reports that 67 percent of all businesses were started without borrowed money. Enita Nordick liquidated her stocks and sold her home to contribute the required capital to start Unity Forest Products, which remanufactures lumber blanks into such things as siding and paneling and sells them to retailers (http://www.unityforest.com/).[4] Fawcette Technical Publications was started in 1991 in Palo Alto on no capital. By 1997 it was doing $24 million a year in revenues (http://www.fawcette.com/).[5] These entrepreneurs comprise the rule, not the exception; typically, only close friends and

FIGURE 18.2

Stages of Financing for Ventures

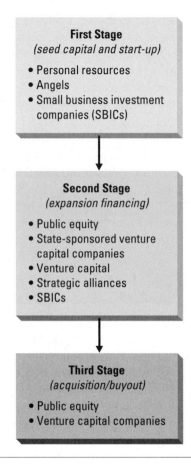

family will fund the risk of a new venture. This is the case because the new venture has several things going against it:

1. New ventures by definition have no track record, so all their estimates of sales and profits are pure speculation.

2. An enormous number of new ventures fail, so the risk for an outside investor is usually high.

3. Many new ventures have no proprietary rights that would give them a competitive advantage.

4. The founders often do not have a significant track record of success.

5. Too many new ventures are "me too" versions of something that already exists, so they have no competitive advantages.

In addition to the personal resources already mentioned, entrepreneurs can tap the equity in their brokerage accounts, which is, in effect, another source of credit. When interest rates in general fall below those of the typical credit card, this source of funds becomes very attractive. The security in your brokerage account is pledged as collateral for the money borrowed, just like pledging the equity in your home against a second mortgage. You can still trade the collateralized security (buy or sell), but you cannot take possession of it until the loan is repaid.

Using friendly money from family and friends is both an advantage and a disadvantage. The benefit is that you may not have to give up as much of the company as you would with an outside investor. But, as the story goes, the downside is that friendly money is "money you pay for the rest of your life."

Here are some bootstrapping tips for financing the launch of a new venture.

Hire as Few Employees as Possible

Normally the greatest single expense a business has is its payroll (including taxes and benefits). Subcontracting work to other firms, using temporary help, or hiring independent contractors can help keep the number of employees and their consequent costs down. But you need to be careful. One California company, a maker of heart catheters, found out the hard way that if you don't follow the rules, it can cost you a lot. Some of this company's independent contractors were working forty hours a week exclusively for the high-tech company and getting paid by the hour, all of which suggests to the IRS that they were really employees. This misclassification cost the company $25,000 in penalties and interest. The rules for using independent contractors and leasing employees are discussed in Chapter 8.

Lease or Share Everything

Virtually all new ventures at some point need to acquire equipment, furnishings, and facilities. By leasing rather than purchasing major equipment and facilities, you can avoid tying up precious capital at a time when it is badly needed to keep the new venture afloat. With a lease, there usually is no down payment, and the payments are spread over time. A word of caution, however. Be careful about leasing new and rapidly changing technology for long periods of time or you may soon find yourself with obsolete equipment but a continuing obligation.

Some entrepreneurs have shared space with established companies not only to save money on overhead but to give their fledgling ventures the aura of a successful, established company.

Other People's Money

Another key to bootstrapping success is getting customers to pay quickly and suppliers to allow more time for payment. Entrepreneurs must be willing to stay on top of receivables. Sometimes that means walking an invoice through the channels of a major corporation in person or locating the person who can adjust the computer code that determines when a government agency pays its bills.

Suppliers are an important asset of the business and should be taken care of. If you establish a good relationship with your major suppliers, you may be able to arrange favorable payment terms. After all, the supplier also has an interest in seeing the new venture succeed. Use several suppliers to establish credit. Often a young company can't get sufficient credit from one supplier, so it is a good idea to seek smaller amounts of credit from several reputable suppliers. In this way, when you can qualify for a larger credit line, you will know which supplier is the best source.

If possible, sell wholesale rather than retail. Dealing with wholesale distributors makes your life easier because they are the experts at working with the customers. They have already set up the consumer and industrial channels you may need for expanding your market.

Bootstrapping Ethics

Ethical issues arise whenever bootstrapping tactics are employed to let a new venture survive long enough to use other sources of financing. When an entrepreneur bootstraps, by definition he or she is making the new venture appear much more successful than it is to gain some credibility in the market. But the entrepreneur must be careful, because that image, if it is ill-gotten, comes at a tremendous price to the business. Lying to survive will return to haunt the business at some future time. Intuit, a very successful software manufacturer, spent several start-up years bootstrapping, during which it quickly became clear to the company that trust is an essential element to long-term success. It has been a common practice in the software industry to use promotional schemes to load dealers with excess product in the belief that the dealer will then push that product to get rid of it before taking on a competitor's product. Intuit refused to participate in this scheme and preferred to communicate expectations for sales honestly to the dealers. In this way, the dealers were not burdened with excess inventory, and Intuit kept its manufacturing facilities operating at an even keel rather than in costly boom-and-bust cycles. Look at Figure 18.3 for a profile of a typical bootstrapper.

● *Financing with Equity*

When someone invests money in a venture, it is normally done to gain an ownership share in the business. This ownership share is termed **equity.** It is distin-

FIGURE 18.3

The Bootstrapper Profile

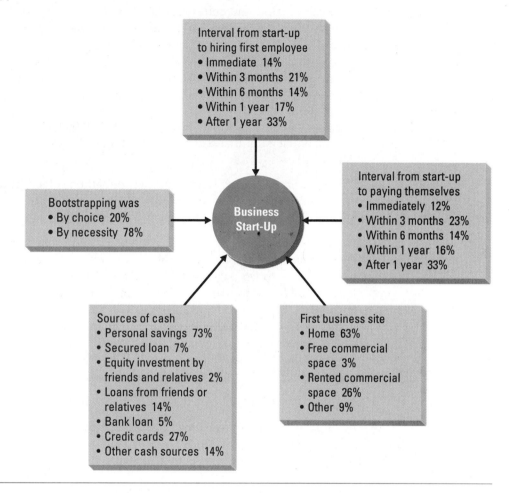

guished from debt in that the equity investor puts his or her capital at risk; usually there is no guaranteed return and no protection against loss. For this reason, most entrepreneurs with start-up ventures seek investment capital from people they know who believe in them. There are a variety of sources of equity financing, including personal resources, angels, private placement, and venture capital. (Since fewer than 1 percent of all new ventures are funded with venture capital at the start-up stage, we'll discuss venture capital in the growth funding section of this chapter.)[6]

Private Investors—Angels

The most popular follow-up source of capital for new ventures is private investors, typically people the entrepreneur knows or has met through business acquaintances. These investors, called **angels,** are part of the informal risk-capital market—the largest pool of risk capital in the United States. They can't be found in a phone book, and they don't advertise. In fact, their intentions as investors are often well hidden until they decide to make themselves known. They do, however, have several definable characteristics:

▶ They normally invest between $10,000 and $500,000 and usually focus on first-stage financing; that is, start-up funding or funding of firms younger than five years.

▶ They are well educated, often entrepreneurs themselves, and tend to invest within a relatively short distance from home, as they like to be actively involved in their investment.

▶ They tend to prefer manufacturing, energy and resources, and service businesses. Retail ventures are less desirable because of their inordinately high rate of failure. Today angels are also investing in high technology firms. [7] They typically look to reap the rewards of their investment within three to seven years. The risk/reward ratio is a function of the age of the firm at the time of investment. Angels may want to earn as much as ten times their original investment if the venture is a start-up, and as much as five times their investment if the venture has been up and running for a couple of years.

▶ They find their deals principally through referrals from business associates.

▶ They tend to make an investment decision more quickly than other capital sources, and their requirements as to documentation, business plan, and due diligence may be lower. Due diligence is discussed on page 448.

Today many angels have joined forces to create larger pools of capital. These "bands" of angels have strict rules about how much their members must invest each year and how much time they must spend in exercising due diligence over other members' deals. In some cases, these angel groups look and act like professional venture capitalists; as venture capital pools have grown in size to where the deals are much larger, angels have stepped in to take the deals formerly funded by VCs.

In general, angels are an excellent source of seed or start-up capital. The secret to finding these elusive investors is networking—getting involved in the business community—so you come into contact with sources of private capital or people who know these sources—lawyers, bankers, accountants, and other business people. Developing these contacts takes time; you can't wait until you need the capital to look for it. Of course, taking on an investor means giving up some of the ownership of the company. Therefore, it is probably wise to plan at the outset for a way to let the investor exit. Including a buyout provision in the investment contract with a no-fault separation agreement will ensure that the entrepreneur doesn't have to wait for a criminal act like fraud to end the relationship. Structuring the buyout to be paid out of earnings over time will avoid jeopardizing the financial health of the business. Above all, avoid using your personal assets as collateral to protect an angel's investment.

Private Placement

Private placement is a way of raising capital from private investors by selling securities in a private corporation or partnership. Securities are common, stock, preferred stock, notes, bonds, debentures, voting-trust certificates, certificates of deposit, warrants, options, subscription rights, limited partnership shares, and undivided oil or gas interests. The investors you solicit via a private placement memorandum must be aware of the rules of private placement, which are stated in the Securities and Exchange Commission's **Regulation D.** Regulation D was designed to simplify the private offering process and allow the entrepreneur to seek funding from private investors who met the rule's requirements. Doing a private placement memorandum requires first completing a business plan and a prospectus detailing the risks of the investment.

As with any complex legal document, it is crucial to consult an attorney well versed in the preparation of the private placement memorandum and disclosure of information about the company and its principals. Problems don't usually arise if the business is successful; however, if the venture fails and the investors uncover a security violation, you and other principal equity holders may lose your protection under the corporate shield and become personally liable in the event of a lawsuit. Security violations have been dealt with severely by the courts, and there is no statute of limitations on the filing of such a suit.

Private placement is a less costly, less time-consuming process than a public offering, and many states now offer standardized, easy-to-fill-out disclosure statements and offering documents.

The advantages of a private offering are many. The growing venture is not required to have a great many assets or credit references, which it would need for bank financing, or a lengthy track record. The entrepreneurs also don't have to file with the Securities and Exchange Commission (SEC). They do, however, have to qualify under the rules of Federal Regulation D, which makes it easier and less expensive for smaller companies to sell stock. Not all states recognize the exemptions under Regulation D in their "Blue Sky" laws (laws that protect investors from fraud), so the issuer of a private placement memorandum may have to register with the state.

The burden is on the issuer to document that the exemption from registration requirements has been met. Therefore, the "sophistication" of all offerees should be examined closely and the reasons why they qualify carefully documented. A sophisticated investor is one who has a net worth of at least $1 million and has taken investment risk in the past. The issuer should number each private placement memorandum and keep a record of who has looked at the memorandum or discussed the offering with the issuer. The memorandum should have a qualifying statement on it that the contents must not be copied or disclosed to anyone other than the offeree. If an offeree becomes an investor, the issuer should document when and where the offeree examined the books and records of the company. When the offering is complete, the issuer should place in the offering log a memo stating that only those persons listed in the log have been approached regarding the offering.

Even if the offering qualifies as exempt from registration, it is still subject to the antifraud and civil liability provisions of federal securities laws and state Blue Sky securities laws. Many states have adopted the Small Corporate Offering Registration Form, also called **SCOR U-7,** which makes the registration process much simpler by providing fifty fill-in-the-blank questions that ask for the basic financial, management, and marketing information for the company. Your lawyer should be consulted, as some of the adopting states have restrictions as to who can use Form U-7.

Within the structure of the corporate private placement, the entrepreneur can sell preferred and common stock, **convertible debentures** (debt that can be converted to equity), and debt securities with warrants (similar to convertible debentures). Recall that preferred stock has dividend and liquidation preference over common stock, in addition to antidilution protection and other rights as may be specified in a stockholder agreement. Common stock, on the other hand, carries with it voting rights and preserves the right of the corporation to elect S-corporation status. Convertible debentures are secured or unsecured debt instruments that can be converted to equity at a later date as specified in the agreement. In its debenture form, however, it provides for a fixed rate of return (interest), which can be deducted by the corporation. Debt securities with warrants give the holder the right to purchase stock at a fixed price for a specified term. Purchasing common stock under this instrument does not invalidate the preferred position of the debt holder as creditor.

Strategic Alliances

A partnership with another business—whether formal or informal—is a **strategic alliance.** Through strategic alliances, entrepreneurs can structure deals with suppliers or customers that will help reduce expenditures for marketing, raw materials, or R&D. Reducing expenditures increases cash flow, providing capital that wouldn't have otherwise been available. Tim Gocher founded his Internet consulting and e-commerce company in 1995. By 1998, he knew that he needed to raise outside capital in order to provide his customers with a one-stop shop operation. During his search for $5–10 million, he realized that a strategic partner might be a better way to go. Gocher hired an investment banker who helped him find SenseNet, a much larger Internet-systems company. The two companies ended up merging in a stock swap.[8]

One type of strategic alliance is the **R&D limited partnership.** This vehicle is useful for entrepreneurs starting high-tech ventures that carry significant risk due to the expense of research and development. The limited partnership contracts with the new venture to provide the funding for the R&D to develop a market technology that will ultimately be profitable for the partnership. This is advantageous for both the limited partner and the new venture. Limited partners are able to deduct their investment in the R&D contract and enjoy the tax advantages of losses in the early years on their personal tax returns; they also share in any future profits. In the R&D limited partnership, the new venture acts as a general partner to develop the technology, then structures a license agreement with the R&D partner whereby the venture can use the technology to develop other products. Often the limited partnership's interest becomes stock in a new corporation formed to commercialize the new technology.

An alternative to this arrangement is an agreement to pay royalties to the partnership. Yet another vehicle is the formation of a joint venture, which allows the entrepreneur to purchase the joint venture interest after a specific period of time or when the company reaches a certain volume in sales. As in the private placement, you should work through an attorney. The new venture may incur significant costs in creating the partnership, a process that could take up to a year. In addition, giving up sole ownership of the technology may be too high a price to pay if the partnership does not survive.

Small Business Investment Company (SBIC)

Small business investment companies are actually privately managed venture capital firms licensed by the Small Business Administration. They get financing at very favorable rates, in partnership with the federal government, to invest through equity (generally preferred stock or debt with warrants) and long-term debt in small and growing businesses.

Companies that qualify for SBIC financing should have a net worth under $18 million and average after-tax earnings of less than $6 million during the past two years. The typical deal involves a loan with options to buy equity, a convertible debenture (debt that can be converted to equity). Preferred stock, which pays the investor back first in the event of a failure, is sometimes used for first-round financing.

Grants

The **Small Business Innovation Development Act of 1982** was designed to stimulate technological innovation by small businesses in the United States. It requires that all federal agencies with research and development budgets in excess of $100 million give a portion of their budgets to technology-based small businesses in the form of grants. Small businesses find out about these grants by checking the published solicitations by the agencies to see whether they can qualify by providing what the agency needs.

The grants have three phases:

1. Phase I is the concept stage and feasibility phase, which provides $50,000 to $100,000 for an initial feasibility study to determine the scientific merit of the proposed idea. This amount is for six months. If results are promising, the company is eligible for Phase II funding.

2. Phase II provides up to an additional $200,000 to $750,000 for two years to pursue the innovation and develop a well-defined product or process.

3. Phase III brings in private sector funds to commercialize the new technology.

To qualify for an SBIR grant, the company must employ fewer than 500 people, be at least 51 percent independently owned by a U.S. citizen, be technology-based, be organized for profit, and not be dominant in its field. The grant holder must perform two-thirds of the Phase I effort and one-half of the Phase II effort. At least half the principal investigator's time must be spent working in the small business.

Venture Capital Institutes and Networks

Many areas of the country offer access to venture capital networks through institutes established on the campuses of major universities. The university acts as a conduit through which the entrepreneurs and investors are matched and assumes no liability for nor has any ownership interest in either the new venture or the investor's company. The entrepreneur typically pays a fee, in the $200 to $500 range, and submits a business plan to the institute. The plan is then matched to the needs of private investors in the database who subscribe to the service. If an investor is interested in the business concept, he or she contacts the entrepreneur. In general, venture capital networks are a way for entrepreneurs to gain access to investors they may not be able to find through other channels. Furthermore, the investors in the database are there voluntarily, so they are actually looking for potential investments.

● Financing with Debt

When an entrepreneur chooses a debt instrument to finance a portion of the start-up expenses, he or she typically provides a business or personal asset as collateral in exchange for a loan bearing a market rate of interest. The asset could be equipment, inventory, real estate, or the entrepreneur's house or car.

While it is important to avoid making your personal assets collateral for a loan, it's sometimes unavoidable as banks generally require first-time entrepreneurs to personally guarantee loans. There are several sources of debt financing.

Commercial Banks

Banks are not normally a readily available source of either working capital or seed capital to fund a start-up venture. Banks are highly regulated; their loan portfolios are scrutinized carefully, and they are told in no uncertain terms not to make loans that have any significant degree of risk. Banks like to see a track record of positive cash flow because this is how their loan will be repaid. Unfortunately, new ventures don't have a track record, so an unsecured loan is probably not possible.

Generally, banks make loans on the basis of what is termed "the five C's": character, capacity, capital, collateral, and condition. In the case of the entrepreneur, the first two—character and capacity—become the leading consideration because the new business's performance is based purely on forecasts. Therefore, the bank will probably consider the entrepreneur's personal history carefully. However difficult, it is important for the new venture to establish a lending relationship with a bank. This may mean starting with a very small, secured loan and demonstrating the ability to repay in a timely fashion. Bankers also look more favorably on ventures with hard assets that are readily convertible to cash.

Commercial Finance Companies

As banks have tightened their lending requirements, commercial finance companies have stepped in to fill the gap. They are able to do this because they are not as heavily regulated and they base their decisions on the quality of the assets of the business. Thus, they are often termed asset-based lenders or hard asset lenders. They do, however, charge more than banks, as much as 5 percent over prime at rates more similar to credit cards. Therefore, the entrepreneur must weigh the costs and benefits of taking on such an expensive loan. Of course, if it means the difference between starting the business or not starting it, or surviving in the short term or not, the cost may not seem so great.

Factoring is a particular type of receivable financing wherein the lender, called the factor, takes ownership of the receivable at a discount and then lends against the receivable.

Small Business Administration

When a traditional commercial bank loan does not appear to be a viable option, the entrepreneur may want to consider an SBA guaranteed loan. In 2000 alone, the SBA backed more than $12.3 billion in loans to small businesses. With an SBA guaranteed loan, you apply for a loan from your bank and the SBA guarantees to repay up to 90 percent of the loan to the commercial lender (generally a bank) should the business default. This guarantee increases your chances of getting a loan that you might not have gotten otherwise. A further incentive to banks is that SBA-funded ventures tend to be growth-oriented and have a higher survival rate than other start-ups. Of course, since the government backs these loans, the documentation and paperwork are extensive, and interest rates are usually no different than with a conventional loan.

The Small Business Administration also has a program called the micro loan that makes it easier for entrepreneurs with limited access to capital to borrow small amounts (up to $25,000). Instead of using banks as in their guarantee program, the SBA uses nonprofit community development corporations.

State-Funded Venture Capital

Many states provide a range of services to help new and growing ventures. From venture capital funds to tax incentives, states such as Massachusetts, New York, and Oregon are seeing the value of establishing business development programs. They usually receive their funding from the state government, which enables them to seek larger investment amounts from private sources. In states where equity funding is not available, there is typically a loan program aimed at new ventures. For example, in Massachusetts favorable debt financing is often exchanged for warrants to purchase stock in the new company. Pennsylvania was the first to create a funding program aimed at minority-owned businesses.

Incubators

There is no doubt that after the dot com debacles and subsequent drop in technology stocks, the incubators that spawned a rash of Internet businesses have fallen on hard times. **Incubators** are places where start-up ventures can get space and support for the early stages of start-up. Because of the dot com implosion, the term *incubator* has developed such a negative connotation that Idealab, one of the first companies to popularize the for-profit incubator concept, has stopped referring to itself as an incubator.[9] Not only is the name under attack, but the very concept of an incubator is as well. In the beginning, incubators were nonprofit organizations designed to help nascent businesses get up and running so their chances of survival in the marketplace would be enhanced. But the new for-profit incubators seem designed to produce concept deals rather than technology deals with real value. Moreover, many of the new incubators were founded by former New Economy entrepreneurs who had become successful and believed that they had the credentials to make other entrepreneurs successful. One example is e-Companies, founded by Earthlink founder Sky Dayton and Disney executive Jake Winebaum. You can read more about them in the case study at the end of the book.

Some incubators, like Idealab in Pasadena, California, are giving birth to companies that appear to be surviving, although Idealab has cut its overhead substantially in an effort to stay afloat itself. One of Idealab's companies is DotTV, which bought the domain suffix dot-tv from the small island nation of Tuvalu for $50 million. To date, more than 50,000 companies have leased dot-tv domain extensions from the company.[10]

For entrepreneurs starting new businesses—Internet or otherwise—incubators should be examined with caution. See Chapter 13 where we discuss start-up organizational strategies for some suggestions on what to look for in an incubator.

Customers and Suppliers

Many entrepreneurs neglect to consider one of the largest and most accessible sources of funding—their customers and suppliers. The reason they are more accessible than many other types of financing is that they are colleagues in your industry; they understand your business and have a vested interest in seeing you succeed. Suppliers and customers can provide extended payment terms or special terms favorable to your business. In return, your business can provide such things as faster delivery, price breaks and other benefits they might need.

Financing Growth

The natural by-product of a successful start-up is growth. But growth is costly and often puts an enormous strain on the already tight resources of the young venture. Typically, to meet significant demand, the new company will need additional capital beyond any internal cash flows. Growth capital, or second-round financing, refers to those funds needed to take the venture out of the start-up phase and move it toward becoming a market presence. To the extent that the entrepreneur has met the sales and earnings targets estimated in the start-up business plan, available financing choices increase substantially when growth financing, or second-round financing, is sought.

The fact that more choices are available is important because, normally, the amount of money needed to grow the business is significantly larger than that required to start the business. One exception is high-tech companies that incur considerable R&D costs prior to start-up. This type of company may spend millions of dollars and accrue several years of losses before its first sale.

Most venture capital today is still going to the biotechnology, software, and other high technology ventures, but in general the best companies in any industry have the easiest time finding capital from any source. Being one of the "best" companies requires having an excellent track record (however short), a sound management team, a potential for high growth, and a plan for investor exit with an excellent rate of return on the money invested. Investors in growth companies typically will not go into a situation where their new money is paying off old debt or where cash flow is poor. They want to know that the infrastructure is in place, sales are increasing, and the growing venture needs capital only to take it to the next stage.

● *The Cost and Process of Raising Capital*

Make no mistake about it, raising growth capital is a time-consuming and costly process. For this reason, many entrepreneurs opt instead for growing slowly, depending exclusively on internal cash flow to fund growth. They have a basic fear of debt and of giving up any control or equity of the company to investors. Unfortunately, they may act so conservatively as to actually stifle growth.

Raising Money Takes Time

It's important to understand the nature of raising money so that your expectations will not be unreasonable. The first thing to understand about raising growth capital (or any capital, for that matter) is that it will invariably take at least twice as long as expected to actually have the money in the company's bank account. If you are attempting to raise a substantial amount of money—several million dollars, for instance—you can expect to spend up to several months finding the financing, wait several more months for the potential investor or lender to do due diligence and say yes, and then wait up to six more months to receive the money. In other words, if you don't look for funding until you need it, it will be too late. Moreover, as this search for capital can take you away from the business when you are needed most, it is helpful to use financial advisers who have experience in raising money, and to have a good management team in place so that you don't have to worry about the business while you're out raising capital.

The second thing to understand about raising growth capital is that the chosen financial source may not complete the deal, even after months of courting and negotiations. It's essential, therefore, to continue to look for investors who may become backups if the original investor fails to materialize.

Another point about second-round investors is that they often request a buy-out of the first-round funding sources, who could be friends or family, because they feel the first round has nothing more to contribute to the business and they no longer want to deal with them. This can be a very awkward situation, since the second-round funder has nothing to lose by demanding the buy-out and can certainly walk away from the deal; there are thousands more out there.

It Takes Money to Make Money

It truly does take money to make money. The costs incurred before the money is received must be paid up-front by the entrepreneur, while the costs of maintaining the capital (accounting, legal) can often be paid from the proceeds of the loan, or in the case of investment capital, from the proceeds of a sale or internally generated cash flow.

If the business plan and financial statements have been kept up-to-date after the start of the business, you have taken the first step in preparing the company for presentation to a funding source and saved some money in the process. If you are seeking capital in the millions, however, growth capital funding sources prefer that financials have the approval of a financial consultant or investment banker, someone who regularly works with investors. This person is expert in preparing loan and investment packages that are attractive to potential funding sources. Your CPA will prepare the business's financial statements and work closely with the financial consultant. All these activities result in costs to the entrepreneur. In addition, if you are seeking equity capital, you need a prospectus or offering document, which requires legal expertise and often has significant printing costs. Then there are the expenses of marketing the offering: such needs as advertising, travel, and brochures can become quite costly.

In addition to the up-front costs of seeking growth capital, there are "back-end" costs when the entrepreneur seeks capital by selling securities (shares of stock in the corporation). These costs can include investment banking fees, legal fees, marketing costs, brokerage fees, and various other fees charged by state and federal authorities. The total cost of raising equity capital can go as high as 25 percent of the total amount of money sought. Add that to the interest or return on investment paid to the funding source(s) and it's easy to see why it definitely costs money to raise money.

The Venture Capital Market

Private venture capital companies have been the bedrock of many high-growth ventures, particularly in the computer, software, biotechnology, and telecommunications industries. Since venture capitalists rarely invest in start-up ventures outside the high-tech arena, the growth stage of a new venture is where most entrepreneurs consider approaching them. Waiting until this stage is advantageous to the entrepreneur because using venture capital in the start-up phase can mean giving up significant control.

Private venture capital is, quite simply, a pool of money managed by professionals. These professionals usually assume the role of general partner and are paid a management fee plus a percentage of the gain from the investment by their investors. The venture capital firm takes an equity position through ownership of stock in the company. It also normally requires a seat on the board of directors and brings its professional management skills to the new venture in an advisory capacity.

The Venture Capital Sequence of Events

To determine whether venture capital is the right type of funding for the growing venture, the entrepreneur must understand the goals and motivations of venture capitalists, for they dictate the potential success or failure of the attempt. The venture capital company invests in a growing business through the use of debt and equity instruments to gain long-term appreciation on the investment

FIGURE 18.4

Risk versus Rate of Return

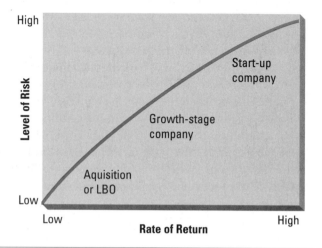

within a specified period of time, typically five years. By definition, this goal is often different from that of the entrepreneur, who usually looks at the business in a much longer frame of reference. The venture capitalist also seeks varying rates of return, depending on the risk involved. An early-stage investment, for example, characteristically demands a higher rate of return, as much as 50 percent or more, whereas a later-stage investment demands a lower rate of return, perhaps 30 percent. Very simply, as the level of risk increases, so does the demand for a higher rate of return, as depicted in Figure 18.4. This relationship is not surprising. Older, more established companies have a longer track record on which to make predictions about the future, so normal business cycles and sales patterns have been identified, and the company is usually in a better position to respond through experience to a dynamic environment. Consequently, investing in a mature firm does not command the high rate of return that investing in a high-growth start-up does.

Usually the first thing venture capitalists look at when scrutinizing a potential investment candidate is the management team, to see whether experienced people with a good track record are in place and able to take the company to the next level of growth. In addition to experience, venture capitalists are looking for commitment to the company and to growth because they recognize that growing a company requires an enormous amount of time and effort on the part of the management team. Once they have determined that the management team is solid, they look at the product and the market to see whether the opportunity is substantial and whether the product holds a unique or innovative position in the marketplace. Product uniqueness, especially if protected through intellectual property rights, helps create entry barriers in the market, commands higher prices, and adds value to the business.

The other major factor is the potential for significant growth and the amount of growth possible, because it is from the consequent appreciation in the value of the business that the venture capitalist will derive the required return on investment. The venture capitalist weighs that potential for growth against the risk of failure and the cost of achieving the growth projected. Therefore, when negotiating with venture capitalists, you should have a good sense of the value of the business, a topic we discuss at the end of this chapter.

Armed with an understanding of what venture capitalists are looking for, you are prepared to begin the search for the company that meets your needs. As the venture capital community is fairly close-knit, at least within regions of the country, it is wise not to "shop" the business plan around looking for the best deal. First do some research on the venture capital firms in your state to see whether any specialize in your particular industry or type of business. Get recommendations from attorneys and accountants who regularly deal with business investments. In fact, the best way to approach venture capitalists is through a referral from someone who knows the VC.

Once a venture capital company has been chosen, it is preferable to stay with that company unless and until you are certain the deal will not work. Under no circumstances should you be talking with two companies at once after a firm has been chosen. The venture capital community is small and everyone knows what everyone else is doing. If you are seriously negotiating with two firms at once, it will eventually get out and you may be left with no firm wanting to invest in your company.

The venture capital company will no doubt ask for a copy of the business plan with an executive summary. The executive summary is a screening device— if it can't be immediately determined that the entrepreneurial team's qualifications are outstanding, the product concept innovative, and the projections of growth and return on investment realistic, the company officials will not bother to read the rest of the business plan.

On the other hand, if after studying the plan they like what they see, they will probably call for a meeting to determine whether the entrepreneurial team can deliver what they project. This may or may not call for a formal presentation of the business by the entrepreneur. During this meeting, the initial terms of an agreement may also be discussed; however, you should not be too eager to discuss issues like owner compensation until the venture capitalist indicates a deal is imminent. It is also very important that you not hype the business concept or make claims that cannot be substantiated. Venture capitalists have literally seen it all and readily recognize when an entrepreneur is puffing. You should, however, disclose any potential negative aspects of the business and propose ways to deal with them.

If the meeting goes well, the next step is due diligence—that is, the venture capital firm has its own team of experts check out the entrepreneurial team and the business thoroughly. If the venture capitalists are still sold on the business, they draw up legal documents to detail the nature and terms of the investment and declare "the check is in the mail." Don't spend the money, however, because it may take some time to receive it. Some venture capitalists wait until they know they have a satisfactory investment before putting together a partnership to actually fund the investment. Others just have a lengthy process for releasing money from the firm.

You should not be surprised if the money is released in stages based on agreed-upon goals. Also realize that the venture capital firm will continue to monitor the progress of the new venture and probably will want a seat or several seats on the board of directors, depending on its equity stake in the company, to have a say in the direction the new venture takes.

Capital Structure

It may seem that the entrepreneur is totally at the mercy of the venture capitalist. That, unfortunately, is true if the entrepreneur enters the negotiation from a weak position, desperately needing the money to keep the business alive. A better approach is to go into the negotiation from a position of strength. True, venture capitalists have hundreds of deals presented to them on a regular basis, but most of those deals are not big hits; in other words, the return on the investment is not worth their effort. They are always looking for that one business that will achieve high growth and return enough on their investment to make up for all the average- or mediocre-performing investments in their portfolio. If the entrepreneur enters the negotiation with a business that has a solid record of growth and performance, he or she is in a good position to call many of the shots.

Any investment deal has four components:

1. The amount of money to be invested

2. The timing and use of the investment moneys

3. The return on investment to investors

4. The level of risk involved

The way these components are defined will affect the new venture for a long time, not only in constructing its growth strategy but also in formulating an exit strategy for the investors.

Venture capitalists often want both equity and debt—equity because it gives them an ownership interest in the business, and debt because they will be paid back more quickly. Consequently, they tend to want redeemable preferred stock or debentures so that if the company does well, they can convert to common stock, and if the company does poorly or fails, they will be the first to be repaid their investment because they have preferred stock. If you have entered the negotiation from a position of strength, you will more likely be able to convince them to take common stock, which makes things much easier for you. In another scenario, the venture capitalists may want a combination of debentures (debt) and warrants, which allows them to purchase common stock at a nominal rate later on. If this strategy is carried out correctly, they can conceivably receive their entire investment back when the debt portion is repaid and still enjoy the appreciation in the value of the business as stockholders.

There are several other provisions venture capitalists often request to protect their investment. One is an antidilution provision, which ensures that the selling of stock at a later date will not decrease the economic value of the venture capitalist's investment. In other words, the price of stock sold at a later date should be equal to or greater than the price at which the venture capitalist could buy the common stock on a conversion from a warrant or debenture.

In addition, to guard against having paid too much for an interest in the company, the VC may often request a forfeiture provision. This means that if the company does not achieve its projected performance goals, the founders may be required to give up some of their stock as a penalty to the VC.[11] The forfeited stock increases the VC's equity in the company and may even be given to new management that the VC brings on board to steer the company in a new direction. Entrepreneurs should never accept these terms unless they are confident of their abilities and commitment to the venture. One way to mitigate this situation is for the entrepreneur to request stock bonuses as a reward for meeting or exceeding performance projections.

Using venture capital is certainly an important source for the entrepreneur with a high-growth venture. It is, however, only one source, and with the advice of experts, the entrepreneur should consider all other possible avenues. The best choice is one that gives the new venture the chance to reach its potential and the investors or financial backers an excellent return on investment.

● *The Initial Public Offering (IPO)*

Making the **initial public offering,** or "going public," is the goal in many companies because it is an exciting way to raise money for growth. However, deciding whether or not to do a public offering is difficult at best, because once the decision has been made to go ahead with the offering, a series of events is set in motion that will change the business and the relationship of the entrepreneur to the business forever. Moreover, returning to private status once the company has been a public company is an almost insurmountable task.

An initial public offering is simply a more complex version of a private offering, in which the founders and equity shareholders of the company agree to sell a portion of the company (via previously unissued stocks and bonds) to the public by filing with the Securities and Exchange Commission and listing their stock on one of the stock exchanges. All the proceeds of the IPO go to the company in a primary offering. If the owners of the company subsequently sell their shares of stock, the proceeds go to the owners in what is termed a *secondary distribution*. Often there is a combination of the two events; however, an offering is far less attractive when a large percentage of the proceeds is destined for the owners, as that clearly signals a lack of commitment on the part of the owners to the future success of the business.

Advantages and Disadvantages of Going Public

The principal advantage of a public offering is that it provides the offering company with a tremendous source of interest-free capital for growth and expansion, paying off debt, or product development. With the IPO comes the future option of additional offerings once the company is well known and has a positive track record. A public company has more prestige and clout in the marketplace, so it becomes easier to form alliances and negotiate deals with suppliers, customers, and creditors. It is also easier for the founders to harvest the rewards of their efforts by selling off a portion of their stock as needed or borrowing against it. In addition, public stock and stock options can be used to attract new employees and reward existing employees.

There are, however, some serious disadvantages to the public offering. Of the 3,186 firms that went public in the 1980s, only 58 percent are still listed on one of the three major exchanges today. Moreover, in 1993 the stock of only one-third of these firms was selling above its issue price.[12] A public offering is a very expensive process. Whereas a private offering can cost about $100,000, a public offering can run well over $300,000, a figure that does not include a 7–10 percent commission to the underwriter, which compensates the investment bank that sells the securities. One way to prevent a financial disaster should the offering fail is to ask for stop-loss statements from lawyers, accountants, consultants, and investment bankers. The stop-loss statement is essentially a promise not to charge the full fee if the offering fails.

Going public is an enormously time-consuming process. Entrepreneurs report that they spend the better part of every week on issues related to the offering over a four- to six-month period. Part of this time is devoted to learning about the process, which is much more complex than this chapter can express. One way many entrepreneurs deal with the knowledge gap is by spending the year prior to the offering preparing for it by talking with others who have gone through the process, reading, and putting together the team that will see the company through it. Another way to speed up the process is to start running the private corporation like a public corporation from the beginning; that is, doing audited financial statements and keeping good records.

A public offering means that everything the company does or has becomes public information subject to the scrutiny of anyone interested in the company.

The CEO of a public company is now responsible primarily to the shareholders and only secondarily to anyone else. The entrepreneur, who before the offering probably owned the lion's share of the stock, may no longer have the controlling stock (if he or she agreed to an offering that resulted in the loss of control), and the stock that he or she does own can lose value if the company's value on the stock exchange drops, an event that can occur through no fault of the company's performance. World events and domestic economic policy can adversely (or positively) affect a company's stock regardless of what the company does.

A public company faces intense pressure to perform in the short term. Though an entrepreneur in a wholly owned corporation can afford the luxury of long-term goals and controlled growth, the CEO of a public company is pressured by stockholders to show almost immediate gains in revenues and earnings, which will translate into higher stock prices and dividends to the stockholders. Last but not least of the disadvantages, the SEC reporting requirements for public companies are very strict, time-consuming, and therefore costly.

The Public Offering Process

There are several steps in the IPO process, as depicted in Figure 18.5. The first is to choose an underwriter, or investment banker. This is the firm that sells the securities and guides the corporation through the IPO process. Some of the most prestigious investment banking firms handle only well-established companies because they feel smaller companies will not attract sufficient attention among major institutional investors. Consequently, you should contact anyone you know who either has gone public or has a connection with an investment bank to gain entry.

The importance of investigating the reputation and track record of any underwriter cannot be stressed enough. Investment banking has become a very competitive industry, with the lure of large fees from IPOs attracting some firms of questionable character. The entrepreneur should also examine the investment mix of the bank. Some underwriters focus solely on institutional investors, others on retail customers or private investors. It is often useful to have a mix of shareholders, because private investors tend to be less fickle and more stable than institutional investors. The investment bank should also be able to support your IPO after the offering in the way of giving financial advice, help in buying and selling stock, and help in creating and maintaining interest in the stock over the long term.

Once chosen, the underwriter draws up a letter of intent, which outlines the terms and conditions of the agreement between the underwriter and the entrepreneur/selling stockholder. It normally specifies a price range for the stock, which is a tricky issue at best. Typically, underwriters estimate the price at which the stock will be sold by using a price/earnings multiple that is common for companies within the same industry as the IPO. That multiple is then applied to the IPO's earnings per share. This is only a rough estimate; the actual going-out

FIGURE 18.5

The IPO Process Simplified

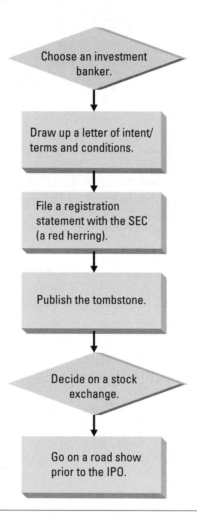

price will not be determined until the night before the offering. If the entrepreneur is unhappy with the final price, the only choice is to cancel the offering, an action that is highly unattractive after months of work and expense.

A registration statement must be filed with the SEC. This document is known as a **"red herring,"** or prospectus, because it discusses all the potential risks of investing in the IPO. This prospectus is given to anyone interested in investing in the IPO. Following the registration statement, an advertisement called a "tombstone" announces the offering in the financial press. The prospectus is valid for nine months; after that the information becomes outdated and cannot be used except by officially amending the registration statement.

Another major decision to make is where to list the offering—that is, on which exchange. In the past, smaller IPOs automatically listed on the American Stock Exchange (AMEX) or National Association of Securities Dealers Automated Quotation (NASDAQ) only because they couldn't meet the qualifications of the New York Stock Exchange (NYSE). Today, however, with companies like Microsoft and Netscape, NASDAQ is the fastest-growing exchange in the nation.

There is a difference between the way the NASDAQ and the other exchanges operate. The NYSE and AMEX are auction markets with securities traded on the floor of the exchange, enabling investors to trade directly with one another. The NASDAQ, on the other hand, is a floorless exchange that trades on the National Market System through a system of broker-dealers from respected securities firms that compete for orders. In addition to these three, there are regional exchanges like the Pacific and Boston stock exchanges that are less costly alternatives for a small, growing company.

The high point of the IPO process is the road show, generally a two-week whirlwind tour of all the major institutional investors by the entrepreneur and the IPO team to market the offering. This is done so that once the registration statement has met all the SEC requirements and the stock is priced, the offering can virtually be sold in a day before the stock has the chance to fluctuate in the market. The coming-out price determines the amount of proceeds to the IPO company, but those holding stock prior to the IPO often see the value of their stock increase substantially immediately after the IPO.

On the other hand, many IPOs reach the final stage only to be withdrawn at the last minute. One Houston, Texas company had revenues of $50 million in January 1998 when it decided to raise $35 million in an IPO to support its growth strategy of acquiring small companies in a highly fragmented industry. Unfortunately, the underwriter pulled the offering because of negative market conditions. The offering was launched again in the summer of 1998 and once more the underwriter pulled it for bad market conditions. An IPO can help a company grow much faster than it otherwise might, but the market dictates whether or not you can successfully execute the IPO. After the dot com bust, many companies had to pull their plans for an initial public offering because institutional investors were backing away from the public markets. If you are considering doing an IPO, you should look at the condition of the market and very carefully weigh the pros and cons of becoming a public company as discussed in the previous section.

Strategic Alliances to Grow

Earlier in the chapter we discussed how to use strategic alliances to create the virtual company or grow the business. Strategic alliances with larger companies are also an excellent source of growth capital for young companies. Sometimes the partnership results in major financial and equity investments in the growing venture. Such was the case for United Parcel Service of America, which acquired a 9.5 percent ownership interest in Mail Boxes Etc. for $11.3 million. This gave Mail Boxes Etc. capital to grow and UPS additional pick-up and drop-off outlets.

Growing companies that link with established companies usually get a better deal than they would have gotten from a venture capitalist. In addition, they derive some associated benefits that give them more credibility in the marketplace. The large investing partner is, at a minimum, looking for a return of the cost of capital, but in general a return of at least 10 percent on the investment.

Strategic alliances are every bit as tricky as partnerships, so you must evaluate the potential partner carefully as well as performing due diligence on the company. That means that you need to carefully investigate the company to make sure that it is everything it claims to be. You should examine its business practices, talk to its customers and value chain members, and make sure that this company will make your company look good. It is also crucial not to focus on one potential partner but instead to consider several before making a final decision. For the partnership to really work, the benefits should flow in both directions; that is, both partners should derive cost savings and/or revenue enhancement from the relationship. It probably is best not to form a partnership that requires one of the partners (usually the smaller company) to be too heavily dependent on the other for a substantial portion of its revenue-generating capability. This is a dangerous position to be in, should the partnership dissolve for any reason.

Valuing the Business

A key component of any financial strategy is determining the value of the company, since a realistic value figure is needed no matter which avenue is undertaken to raise growth capital. Today the already difficult task of valuation is exacerbated by the fact that most of the valuable assets that companies hold are intangible. That is, instead of plant and equipment, companies find their competitive assets in patents, knowledge, and people.[13] For example, Macromedia Inc., a software company with over 550 employees, calculates value based on how close its relationships with its customers are. People are the firm's most important asset and one of the core drivers of value in its business.

Calculating value is challenging at best because value is a subjective term with many meanings. In fact, at least six different definitions of value are in common use. Summarized, they are as follows:

▶ **Fair Market Value**—the price at which a willing seller would sell and a willing buyer would buy in an arm's-length transaction. By this definition, every sale would ultimately constitute a fair market value sale.

▶ **Intrinsic Value**—perceived value arrived at by interpreting balance sheet and income statements through the use of ratios, discounting cash flow projections, and calculating liquidated asset value.

▶ **Investment Value**—the worth of the business to an investor based on his or her individual requirements as to risk, return, tax benefits, and so forth.

▶ **Going Concern Value**—the current financial status of the business as measured by financial statements, debt load, and economic environmental factors such as government regulation that may affect its long-term continuation.

▶ **Liquidation Value**—the amount that could be recovered from selling off all the company's assets.

▶ **Book Value**—an accounting measure of value that refers to the difference between total assets and total liability. It is essentially equivalent to shareholders' or owners' equity.

In today's economy, those who finance ventures also use some new, nonfinancial yardsticks to measure value.

▶ The experience level of the management team.

▶ The innovative level of the firm's distribution channels.

▶ The nature of its relationships in the industry and with customers.

▶ The company's ability to be fast and flexible.

▶ The amount and kind of its intellectual property.

Methods for Valuing a Business

In this section, we examine some financial measures for business valuation. The first thing to know about valuation is that nearly all techniques rely on the analysis of the future market for the company's products. With that in mind, book or liquidation value is not a satisfactory method except to establish a residual value to use in a discounted cash flow method. Moreover, with more and more new businesses relying on intangible assets, book value does not make sense.

Market multiples such as price/earnings (P/E) ratios are often used by venture capitalists, but their use is speculative at best because they are based on public companies in the industry and on the bet that the new company will go public in three to five years. The discounted cash flow (DCF) method is probably the most commonly used technique to account for the going concern value of a business. We discuss both the multiples technique and the DCF in the following sections.

Multiple of Earnings

Using a price/earnings ratio (P/E) to value a business is a common method among publicly owned companies because it's simple and direct. It consists of dividing the market price of the common stock by the earnings per share. For example, if a company has 200,000 shares of common stock and its net income is $250,000, earnings per share is 200,000/$250,000, or $.80 per share. If the price per share rises to $3.00, the price/earnings ratio is $3/$.80, or 3.75. The business would now be valued at $750,000 (200,000 shares ¥ 3.75).

Another method, which typically results in a higher valuation, is using a year's worth of after-tax earnings and multiplying it by the industry average multiple based on the P/E ratio of public companies in the industry. This method must be considered with care. To say that a young private company with earnings of $250,000 in an industry where the average P/E is 12 should be valued at $3 million is probably overstating the case. It has been suggested that public firms have a premium value of about 25–35 percent over closely held companies because they are more highly regarded by the financial community. Remember that public companies are held to more scrutiny than private companies and therefore any P/E multiple used should be discounted to reflect that premium.[14] That would mean that our private company now has a value of $2,250,000 ($250,000 ¥ 9). Even with discounting, the variation in ways a company can calculate earnings and the difficulty in finding a public company that is comparable often make this a dubious measure at best for purposes of valuation.

Discounting Cash Flows

If valuing the business by its potential earning power is the goal, the most common measure—and the one that gives more accurate results—is future cash flows, because only cash or cash equivalents are used in the calculations. The method is called **discounted cash flow analysis,** or capitalization of future cash flows to the present value. This simply means calculating how much an investor would pay today to have a cash flow stream of X dollars for X number of years into the future.

There are four components of the DCF that must be addressed:[15]

1. **The assumptions.** Assumptions define the model for conducting the business and take into account sales, R&D, manufacturing costs, selling and general and administrative costs. These should be benchmarked against the growth of other successful companies in the industry.

2. **Forecast period.** Typically the forecast period is three to five years and reflects the length of time that investors intend to have a stake in the venture.

3. **Terminal value.** Terminal value is the going-concern value at the end of the projection period, assuming that the company will continue in opera-

tion into the foreseeable future (in perpetuity). It may be thought of as a perpetuity, which assumes no growth and constant earnings (annual payment/cost of money), or as a growth in perpetuity, which estimates a growth rate and profitability.

4. **Discount rate.** The discount rate determines the present value of the projected cash flows and is, in reality, the expected rate of return for the investor.

For this analysis, the entrepreneur uses pro forma cash flow statements for the business and determines a forecast period. Refer to Chapters 9 and 16 for discussions of pro forma cash flows and methods for forecasting sales and expenses. The entrepreneur must also understand the length and nature of business cycles in the industry in order to decide whether the forecast period goes from trough to trough or from peak to peak. In other words, the forecast period must include at least one complete business cycle in order to give a fair representation of the effect of that cycle on cash flow. (See Figure 18.6.)

Once the forecast period has been defined and the cash flow projections prepared, a discount rate must be chosen. This is not a purely arbitrary exercise. The buyer's or investor's point of view must be considered, and that viewpoint will often include the opportunity cost of investing in or buying this business. It has been suggested that the decision should be based on three factors:

FIGURE 18.6

Business Cycles and the Forecast Period

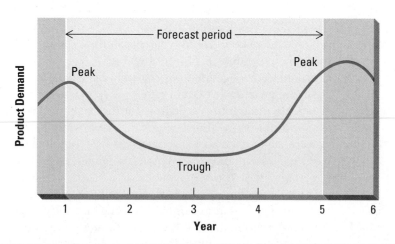

1. The rate achievable in a risk-free investment such as U.S. Treasury notes over a comparable time period. For example, for a five-year forecast, the current rate on a five-year note is appropriate.

2. A risk factor based on the type of business and the industry, which should be added to the interest rate in #1. Several precedents for determining what these factors are have been established over years of study. One accepted standard is that offered by James H. Schilt[16] in the form of six categories of business. Note that even within each category there is room for degrees of risk.

   a. Category 1: Established businesses with good market share, excellent management, and a stable history of earnings: 6–10 percent
   b. Category 2: Established businesses in more competitive industries, still with good market share, excellent management, and a stable earnings history: 11–15 percent
   c. Category 3: Growing businesses in very competitive industries, with little capital investment, average management team, and a stable earnings history: 16–20 percent
   d. Category 4: Small businesses dependent on the entrepreneur or larger businesses in very volatile industries; also the lack of a predictable earnings picture: 21–25 percent
   e. Category 5: Small service businesses operating as sole proprietorships: 26–30 percent

3. The life expectancy of the business. Discounting is typically based on this factor.

The example in Table 18.1 will illustrate this valuation method. Assuming that the current rate on a ten-year Treasury note is 6 percent and the business is a Category 2 business with a 14 percent risk factor, the adjusted discount rate becomes 20 percent. Using a calculator or a present value table, we can calculate the present value of the five-year cash flow stream. What this example shows is that this hypothetical business will generate $1,575,000 of positive cash flow over five years. Hence, a buyer would be willing to pay $875,700 today for that business, given the discount rate.

Create three future scenarios for the firm: success, survival, and liquidation. You will then have three values for the business. Then assign a probability of occurrence to each scenario based on how probable you think it is that the scenario will occur, and multiply the discounted cash flow by that probability to arrive at an adjusted present value.

Once a mathematical estimate of value has been achieved, other factors will come into play that are difficult to put into the equation and are more rightly points of negotiation. All the projections used in the valuation of the business are based on assumptions, and the buyer/investor will likely question them and perhaps discount the value of the business even further.

TABLE 18.1

One Method for Discounting Cash Flows

Assume:	6% risk-free rate
	+14% risk factor (Category 2 business)
	20% discount rate
Discount the Cash Flow	

End of Year	Cash Flow ($000)	Factor (20%)	Present Value
1	200	.8333	166.7
2	250	.6944	173.6
3	300	.5787	173.6
4	375	.4823	180.9
5	450	.4019	180.9
Totals	$1,575		$875.7

Another factor affecting the final valuation is the degree of legitimate control the owner has in the business. This is typically measured by the amount of stock the owner holds. Buying out an owner who holds the majority of the stock is more valuable than buying out one who does not hold a majority interest because you will control more of the business. A company in which you can control the majority of the stock is more valuable to you than one in which you hold only a minority interest. Finally, intangibles like a loyal customer list, intellectual property, and the like will also create additional value for the business. The "real" value or market value of the business will ultimately be determined through negotiation with investors, lenders, or underwriters. However, doing the calculations just discussed provides an excellent jumping-off point for the negotiations.

Valuation is by its very nature an incremental process of bringing together key pieces of information that give some insight into the health and future of the business. In all discussions of value, you should be clear about whose definition of value is being used. In general, what a willing buyer and seller can agree on under normal market conditions is the real value of the company at a particular point in time.

With a new venture there are many financing options. However, creating a capital structure that works depends in large part on creativity and persistence in securing the capital needed at the right price to successfully launch the venture.

Recall from Chapter 1 that entrepreneurs work with a vision of where they see their companies going and what they will look like when they get there.

That vision sustains them through the ups and downs of start-up and the breathless speed of growth when the company finally takes off. It also supports them in the difficult search for capital to feed that growth and ensure that the business will remain successful. The growth period of a world-class venture can be an extraordinarily exciting time for everyone involved if the entrepreneurial team has prepared for growth by doing the following:

▶ Networking, researching, and lining up potential capital sources well in advance of need.

▶ Determining at least three years in advance whether the company will go public at the most appropriate window of opportunity. This early planning allows the company to begin, if it hasn't already, to regularly prepare audited financial statements using a nationally recognized accounting firm, and to put in place the financial and control systems required of a public company.

▶ Updating the comprehensive business plan to reflect the most current information you have about your business.

NEW VENTURE CHECKLIST

Have you:
- ☐ Considered how many personal resources you have to help fund the new venture?
- ☐ Determined ways to bootstrap the start-up of the new venture?
- ☐ Networked to come in contact with potential "angels"?
- ☐ Identified an attorney who can help structure a private placement agreement if needed?
- ☐ Investigated the sources of debt financing in the community?
- ☐ Determined how much growth capital will be needed?
- ☐ Developed a strategy for seeking growth capital?
- ☐ Established a value for the business?

ISSUES TO CONSIDER

1. How does bootstrap financing fit into the strategic plan of a new venture?

2. What is the role of angels as a source of new venture funding?

3. At what stage of venture development do venture capitalists typically become involved, and why?

4. Why are commercial banks not usually a reliable source of new venture financing?

5. Why should a private offering be used as a capital-raising vehicle before a public offering is used?

6. For what kind of business would private venture capital be a logical financial strategy for growth? Why?

7. How can strategic alliances be used to help grow the business?

8. What are some things that should be done to prepare for a public offering before the year of "going public"?

9. In approaching a venture capitalist, how can the entrepreneurial team deal from a position of strength?

10. What are the key components in valuing a new or growing venture?

EXPERIENCING ENTREPRENEURSHIP

1. Define a venture concept that interests you. Then develop a timeline and financial strategy for the venture.

2. Interview a venture capitalist or an angel (preferably both) to learn their expectations when they are reviewing business plans for new ventures.

ADDITIONAL SOURCES OF INFORMATION

Bartlett, J. W. (1999). *Fundamentals of Venture Capital.* New York: Madison Books.

Boer, P. (1999). *The Valuation of Technology.* New York: John Wiley.

Koller, T., J. Murrin, T. Copeland, and W. Foote (2000). *Valuation: Measuring and Managing the Value of Companies.* 3rd ed. New York: John Wiley.

Long, M. (2000). *Financing the New Venture.* Holbrook, MA: Adams Media Corporation.

Moore, G. (1999). *Crossing the Chasm: Marketing and Selling High-Technology Products.* New York: HarperBusiness.

Moore, G. (1999). *Inside the Tornado: Marketing Strategies from Silicon Valley's Cutting Edge.* New York: HarperCollins.

Robinson, R. J., and M. Van Osnabrugge (2000). *Angel Investing: Matching Startup Funds with Startup Companies.* New York: Jossey-Bass.

Tuller, L. W. (1994). *Small Business Valuation Book.* Holbrook, MA: Bob Adams.

INTERNET RESOURCES

Capital Growth Interactive
http://www.capitalgrowth.com/
A journal dedicated to private capital and growth company financing.

Foundation Center
http://fdncenter.org
A nonprofit organization designed to help individuals and organizations find funding from foundations and philanthropists.

Small Business Administration
http://www.sba.gov
Source of information on SBA loans.

VCAOnline
http://www.vcaonline.com/
A marketplace for venture capital and private equity.

Vfinance.com
http://www.vfinance.com/
Portal for private ventures seeking funding.

RELEVANT CASE STUDIES

Case 2   Franchising a Dying Business

Case 3   Overnite Express

Case 5   Earthlink.net: The Journey to Recognizing an Opportunity

Case 8   Alcoholes de Centroamerica, S.A. de C.V.

Case 9   Wizards of the Coast

Planning for Change

We know not yet what we have done, still less what we are doing. Wait till evening and other parts of our day's work will shine than we had thought at noon, and we shall discover the real purport of our toil.
Henry D. Thoreau

Overview

PROFILE 19.1

Persistence Is the Secret to Surviving Change

One way to get attention at a trade show with 2,000 other booths is by creating a little magic. That's what Doumar Products Inc. did at the International Housewares Show in January 1998. Mark Foley, the company's marketing director, wowed the audience by using Doumar's product, un-du, to separate duct tape from single-ply toilet paper without doing any damage to either. As if that weren't enough, he went on to show the audience that after a few seconds, the duct tape became sticky again.

This was not Doumar's first trade show. Actually, the company had spent the previous two years in market tests, trade shows, and appearances on QVC's home shopping program and was just beginning to see some commercial success.

Doumar was founded in 1995 by a former salesman, Mark Foley (who had experience in the unlikely combination of liquor, apparel, chocolate, and medical sales), and a real estate agent, Douglas Farley, who was the man behind Milton Bradley's party game Twister®. It was Foley's father, Charles, who invented un-du. With $6,000 of start-up money, Foley and Farley started Doumar and acquired the right to distribute un-du for a period of two years. They soon realized they needed more money. A lawyer who had helped them incorporate introduced them to a Mr. Reichling, who, despite the holes he saw in the business plan, agreed to invest $75,000 in 1996 with the agreement that Doumar would acquire permanent distribution rights for un-du.

As the founders set up their network of sales representatives and did the trade show route, 1996 was a busy year. In June of that year they won the "best new product" award at the Business Product Industry Association show, and later that year Reichling became the CEO. Their first year ended with $38,000 in revenues and $400,000 in expenses. The second year brought sales of $800,000 but more investment in facilities, equipment, and employees.

The founders had a sense of relief when they managed to acquire a few nationwide retailers like Walgreens and Staples. But that relief was short-lived; they learned that these major retailers paid in ninety days. Doumar's own suppliers were requiring payment in sixty days. According to Foley, retailers have enormous power in the market to determine which products consumers can purchase. Unfortunately, retailers often choose products based on how much money they can make versus offering the best quality products to the consumer. This is particularly true when a small start-up business goes into a market dominated by name brands. Retailers may not give the upstart a chance to get shelf space, because the name brand is paying them a lot of money to dominate that space. Furthermore, you can't be a one-product company and succeed. Retailers will pay more attention if you have a dozen skus (product numbers) than one, even if that one is a great product.

Doumar's has a single product with multiple applications, so you may find it in the hobby section, in the kitchen section, or the office section of a retailer. To succeed in that kind of environment, entrepreneurs have to be persistent and never quit, even when daily challenges are thrown their way.

Then came the biggest challenge to date: Mark and Doug discovered that the Magic American Corporation, a Cleveland-based producer of specialty cleaners with $30 million in revenues, had asked the Consumer Product Safety Commission to investigate Doumar's labeling of its flammable product. Although no evidence of wrongdoing was found, the situation distracted the founders from their work. And as if to add insult to injury, Magic American announced that it would be offering a lower-priced version of un-du under the very popular GooGone brand name. When Magic American's product came out, Doumar was discouraged to find that the packaging resembled that of un-du but was different enough that Doumar had no cause for legal action. Even though the product did not have some of the benefits of un-du, Doumar now had to mount a national campaign for name recognition of its own product.

Foley's persistence has paid off. Doumar has certainly achieved name recognition. Its products are found in major retail chains like Lowes, Linens n' Things, and Office Max. The hobby and craft industry voted it the most innovative product of 1998. Foley believes that, besides persistence, one of the keys to operating in a changing environment is to hire people who can do what you can't. If you leave your ego out of the decision making, your company will have a chance to achieve what you wanted it to achieve.

SOURCES: Barnaby J. Feder, "Good Product, Sound Plans, No Sure Thing," *New York Times,* January 18, 1998; Un-du web site, http://www.un-du.com/;" Buss, Dale D., "Embracing Speed," *Nation's Business,* June 1999.

There is no crystal ball that will tell an entrepreneur what the future holds for a new venture. Many an entrepreneur has started a business with a plan in mind for where that business would go but found along the way that things changed. Forces beyond the control of the entrepreneur pushed the venture into new directions, and a new set of plans had to be constructed. That was certainly true of Doumar and its battle with Magic American (Profile 19.1).

Consider the highly volatile technology market during the first two years of the new millennium. How many entrepreneurs with business plans for new e-commerce ventures who were seeking capital in early 2000 knew that their window of opportunity to secure those investments was but a few months long? In April of that year the stock market declined precipitously, foreshadowing an enormous shakeout in the dot com world and the end of "money for nothing." During that time, hundreds of potential new e-commerce ventures failed to make it to the marketplace.

Some would argue that the signs were there all along, but the easy availability of venture capital inspired the notion that all you needed was a great idea that could scale out to a huge market. In any case, most entrepreneurs were not prepared for the change and certainly had no contingency plans in place.

It is a sad fact that most entrepreneurs with growing ventures do not have time for contingency planning; they are just too busy keeping the business alive. But planning is essential. In the absence of planning, the business will find itself in a reactionary mode, virtually at the whim of the environment in which it operates. Instead of dealing from a position of strength, entrepreneurs may find themselves reacting in panic and without information to situations for which they are not prepared. As a result, the quality of decision making is reduced and the business suffers.

This chapter will look at the contingency plan, alternatives for harvesting the wealth of your venture, and alternatives should your venture fail.

The Contingency Plan

By forcing entrepreneurs to consider multiple outcomes and possibilities, contingency plans help a growing business deal with downturns and upturns in the economy, new regulations, changes in customer tastes and preferences, and many other events that regularly, and often without much warning, disrupt the equilibrium of the firm. For example, the reason many businesses fail during a recession is that they haven't prepared for it by forecasting the potential impact on demand when signs of a recession appear and calculating how they can adjust and still maintain a positive cash position.

Recessions do not happen overnight. There are signs, even within specific industries, that signal a slowdown. Since the government began compiling indices on the economy after World War II, some consistent trends have appeared. For example, the Leading Index of Economic Indicators, which consists of such items as the Producer Price Index, the Consumer Confidence Index, and the Manufacturers' Orders for Durable Goods, typically declines for nine months prior to the onset of a recession. The **coincident-lagging index,** which is a ratio of the coincident index (employment, personal income, industrial production) to the lagging index (Consumer Price Index, interest rates, unemployment), declines for thirteen months prior to the onset of a recession.

Recognizing the signs of recession before they affect the business gives the entrepreneur a chance to prepare in many ways, including maintaining a higher degree of liquidity. In recessionary times it is more difficult to raise capital from either bankers or private sources, so being liquid opens up opportunities that become available only during recessions. For example, the entrepreneur may be able to purchase a building that in good economic times was beyond reach, or he or she may be able to negotiate more favorable terms from suppliers just to keep the business moving forward. Look at Profile 19.2 to see how two restaurants managed change and remained vital.

Tradition Comes of Age

Most entrepreneurs accept change as a way of life; many look forward to it—even seek it—because they know that with change comes opportunity. Still, tradition has its place as well, so when change and tradition are juxtaposed, it makes for some exciting contrasts and can breathe new life into a potentially stagnant business. Such is the case with two very old, established, respected members of the New Orleans restaurant community that have decided that change is good. Antoine's Restaurant was founded by Antoine Alciatore in 1840 when it began the tradition of great dining in New Orleans. Antoine's is home to one of the great culinary creations of all time—Oysters Rockefeller, the recipe for which is a closely guarded secret. Through the Civil War, two world wars, Prohibition, and the Great Depression, this family restaurant has persisted.

Galatoire's Restaurant was founded in 1905 by Jean Galatoire, who came to the United States from France. Like Antoine's, this restaurant has also experienced major environmental changes, but it thrives today as one of the leaders in Creole cuisine. Both restaurants are highly successful family businesses that have seen the New Orleans restaurant scene change dramatically over the past twenty years. Even fifteen years ago, there were only a handful of really first-rate restaurants with very high-profile chefs. Today, the New Orleans restaurant market is home to celebrity entrepreneurs, like Paul Prudhomme and Emeril Lagasse, among others. The market has changed; expectations are higher and competition fiercer.

All this forced Antoine's and Galatoire's to look at themselves with a critical eye. How could they enter the twenty-first century, yet maintain the traditions that their customers expected? One of the first things Antoine's did was set up a web site with an online reservation system. Although the owners have resisted modernizing the restaurant itself because they're afraid of destroying the mystique, using electronics to advertise seems to work.

Galatoire's also uses the Internet and e-mails menus to customers who request them. To improve marketing strategy, the restaurant hired a public relations firm. At the firm's recommendation, Galatoire's began issuing personal charge cards to customers with accounts at the restaurant and now tracks accounts via a computer database. Though a few customers have complained about seeing a computer in the dining room, most find the changes positive.

Both restaurants have realized that to keep your customers coming back in the face of changing market conditions, you have to keep up with the times and at the same time maintain the traditions that have come to be associated with your business.

SOURCES: Sarah P. Jones, "Restaurants Put Change on Menu," *Inc. Online Local Business News,* November 10, 1997; James Slaton, "Technology Mingles with Tradition in Two Bastions of Fine Dining," *New Orleans CityBusiness Online,* Vol. 18, Issue 18, p. 15; http://www.antoines.com/menu.html; http://www.galatoires.com/.

Growing entrepreneurial ventures need to engage in both short- and long-range planning. Short-range planning sets quantitative goals for the coming year and develops a plan for achieving them. If a business does any planning, it is usually short-range. Long-range plans, by contrast, are based on the business's mission and focus on the direction it will take, accounting for potential changes in the environment in which it operates. It certainly is not possible to account for all contingencies, but there are some key crisis issues that seem to occur for all ventures.

• Taxes and Regulations

Government regulations and regulatory paperwork are severe problems for growing ventures, and the cost of compliance is rising to the point that entrepreneurs are looking for ways to avoid coming under the purview of some of the regulations. The Family Leave Act now has a threshold firm size of fifty employees, so many small businesses fight to stay below that number, because in a small, growing company, the protracted absence of an employee who cannot be replaced can affect operations severely.

The cost of hiring an employee is becoming so prohibitive that many companies are solving the problem by subcontracting work and leasing employees. Take the hypothetical example of a growing manufacturing company with fewer than fifty employees. On an hourly basis, per employee:

▶ Base pay is $11.00 an hour.

▶ Health coverage costs about $3.00 an hour.

▶ Social security, Medicare, and unemployment insurance are about $1.50 an hour.

▶ Workers' compensation is $1.00 an hour, for a total hourly cost of $16.50.

If you then factor in profit sharing, bonuses, and retirement plans, you can easily reach $20.00 an hour as the actual cost of hiring that employee. It is no wonder that many business owners prefer to work with independent contractors. However, the government is cracking down on businesses that incorrectly categorize people as independent contractors, so IRS rules must be carefully followed. (See Chapter 8.)

• Product Liability

If you manufacture a product, the chances are fairly good that your company will at some point face a product liability suit. The states with the heaviest concentration of industry naturally have the highest number of claims, with Pennsylvania, Ohio, Texas, and New York leading the list. More and more of the risk of product-related injuries has been shifted to manufacturers, creating a legal minefield that could prove disastrous to a growing company.

Even if a company carefully designs and manufactures a product and covers it with warnings and detailed instructions, that company still is vulnerable to the misuse of and consequent injury from the product. For a company to be legally liable, the product must be defective and an injury must have occurred. But in a litigious society, those requirements don't stop people from suing. Most product liability insurance covers the costs of defense, personal injury, or property damage, but not lost sales and the cost of product redesign. Moreover, if your insurance company must pay on a claim, your premiums will, no doubt, increase.

A growing company must plan for potential litigation from the very inception of the business. One proven method is to establish a formal safety panel that includes people from all the major functional areas of the business. During the start-up phase, that panel may consist of only the entrepreneur and one or two outside advisers with experience in the area. It is the job of the safety panel to review safety requirements on a regular basis, establish new ones when necessary, and document any injuries or claims made against the product.

Prior to product introduction in the marketplace, the panel should see that careful records of all decisions regarding final product design, testing, and evaluation procedures are maintained. Advertising regarding the product should contain no exaggerated claims or implied promises that may give customers the impression you are claiming more safety features than the product actually has. Implied promises can be used against you in a court of law. Instruction manuals should be easy to follow and should point out potential hazards. They should also include guidelines for when and how to service the product, which components made by other manufacturers are not covered by your warranty (unless pass-through warranties have been negotiated), and statements that the warranty is invalidated by misuse, mis-assembly, or modification and is valid only if the specified maintenance procedures are followed. Of course, the best insurance is to keep in contact with your customers so that if a problem occurs, you will be given the opportunity to fix it before legal action is taken.

Early in the operation of the business, identify a qualified attorney familiar with your industry to handle any potential product liability claims. This attorney should handle the first case with which the business is faced. Thereafter, if other suits arise in various parts of the country, you can save money by hiring a "local attorney" in the jurisdiction of the claim. Then let the primary attorney brief the local attorney on the precedent-setting cases related to the claim and assist while the local attorney carries the case to court. In this way, you do not have to send the primary attorney on the road, incurring significant travel and time expenses.

● *Loss of Key Employees—Succession Planning*

Even less today than in the past can anyone count on having the same management team over the life of the business—or even after the start-up phase. The demand for top-notch management personnel, particularly in some industries like high-tech, means that other companies will constantly be trying to woo the best people away from the best firms. Losing a CEO in times of high turnover, not to mention physical risk, is not uncommon. In 2001, companies like Yahoo, Maytag, Hershey Foods, Gateway, and GE changed CEOs. Succession planning then becomes an important part of the contingency plan, so that you identify people who can take over key company positions in an emergency. Ideally that person or persons will come from within the company, but in the case of a growing entrepreneurial company that has been operating in a "lean and mean" mode, that may not be possible, so outsiders must be found. To prepare for the eventuality that a key employee will be lost, the entrepreneur must have shared his or her vision for the company with others both inside and outside the company. It's also a good idea to purchase "key-person insurance" to cover the cost of suddenly having to replace someone.

Bringing in a consultant to guide the management team in succession planning is a valuable exercise for any growing venture. Often consultants are even hired temporarily to take over a vacant position for a specified period of time during which they train a permanent successor. Another solution is to cross-train people in key positions so that someone can step in, at least for the short term, in the event of an emergency. Cross-training is generally an integral part of a team-based approach to organizational management.

Succession Planning in Family-Owned Businesses

Entrepreneurs who head family-owned companies face special problems because they tend to look to a son, daughter, or other family member to succeed them. Succession in a family-owned business will not happen unless you plan for it, however. In fact, over half of family-owned businesses don't continue into the second generation [1] This is due in part to the fact that you must deal not only with business issues related to succession—ownership, management, strategic planning—but you must also deal with the unexpected, such as a death and relationship issues with family members, a much more difficult task. Succession planning tends to expose family issues that may have been kept in the background but have been building over time. For example, the daughter whom you planned would take over the business has no interest in doing so but may never have told you. Or, by contrast, the child may believe him or herself capable of simply stepping in and assuming a managerial role with no previous experience. If you have created a plan for succession, a problem like this may be solved by making it a requirement that a child or potential successor work for another company for several years to gain some business savvy and learn whether he or she wants to take over the family business. Robert Bradford is the CEO of the Center for Simplified Strategic Planning in Ann Arbor, Michigan. He believes that you need to think about succession planning very early in the growth of your business because finding the right person to succeed you in the business is not an easy task.[2] CEOs act as visionaries and also play functional roles, balancing finance, marketing, and operations. A person you have chosen to succeed you must be given the time to understand those roles; it's not something that will happen overnight. Bradford planned for succession by evaluating his current human resources and also the company's ability to evaluate a potential candidate. He wrote his own job description and then began looking at people inside his firm for signs of leadership skills. Once he had narrowed the field to a few potential candidates, he asked them to do a self-assessment and then he compared the gaps between what skills they believed they had and his own job description. In fact, Bradford did this himself before he succeeded his father in the business.

To start the process of succession planning, put all the active family members on a committee to explore the options. Some of the questions you will want to examine are

- Is the next generation being sufficiently prepared to take over the business when the time comes?

- What is the second generation's expectations for the future of the business and is it congruent with the company's vision?

- What skills and experience does the second generation need to acquire?

- What would the ideal succession plan look like?

Then, with the help of an attorney, develop buy-sell agreements to ensure that heirs receive a fair price for their interest in the business upon a partner's death and to protect against a shareholder's permanent disability by buying out the disabled partner's interest. An estate planning professional can help you evaluate the impact of any changes in the business on your personal assets.

Given that most privately owned businesses in the United States are family-owned businesses, this succession planning strategy is useful for any business that wants to be prepared for the loss or retirement of its leader.

Decline in Sales

When sales decline and positive cash flow starts looking like a memory, entrepreneurs often go into a period of denial. They start paying their suppliers more slowly to preserve cash, they lay people off, they stop answering the phone, and they insulate themselves against the demands of their creditors. Their panic frequently causes them to make poor decisions about how to spend the precious cash they have. They figure that if they can just hold on long enough, things will turn around. Unfortunately, this attitude only makes the problem worse, effectively propelling the business toward its ultimate demise. How can an entrepreneur lose touch with the business and the market so much that he or she puts the business at risk? What often happens is that entrepreneurs get so tied up with the day-to-day operations of the business that they don't have time to contemplate the "big picture" or stay in tune with their customers. Consequently, all too often they don't see a potential crisis coming until it's too late.

When sales decline, the solution isn't necessarily to lower prices. If you have educated customers about the value of your product or service, the sudden discounting will confuse them. When there is a decline in sales, it is especially important to look at all possible sources, not just the economy. You may have been lax about checking the credit status of customers and distributors, or the inventory turnover rate may have changed. You may have failed to notice an emerging competitor offering a product or service more in line with current tastes and preferences.

When a growing business first notices a dip in sales, it is time to find the cause and make the necessary changes. This will be easier if the business has a contingency plan in place. If, however, those changes cannot be made in time to forestall a cash-flow problem, it is time to consult a debt negotiation company, a crisis management consultant, or a bankruptcy attorney who is willing to work through the problem without going to court. These experts can help you work with creditors until the problem is resolved. To prepare the best defense against a cash-flow crisis, you must be continually committed to

▶ Producing exceptional-quality products.

▶ Controlling the cost of overhead, particularly where that overhead does not contribute directly to revenue generation (expensive cars, travel, excessive commissions).

▶ Controlling production costs through subcontracting and being frugal about facilities.

▶ Making liquidity and positive cash flow the prime directive, so the company can ride out temporary periods of declining demand.

▶ Having a contingency plan in place.

The Harvest Plan

Many first-time entrepreneurs have questioned the need for an exit plan, or harvest plan, since they are more concerned with launching the business and making it a success than they are with thinking about how they're going to get out. But, while some entrepreneurs stay with their new ventures for the long term, the majority enjoy the challenge of start-up and the excitement of growth and abhor the custodial role of manager of a stable, mature company. Consequently, exiting the business does not necessarily mean exiting the role of entrepreneur. It may in fact mean taking the financial rewards of having grown a successful business and investing them in a new venture.

There are entrepreneurs who do that very thing over and over again throughout their lives, and in the recent past we have seen more and more of this phenomenon as entrepreneurs build businesses to "flip," that is, to take public or sell to a larger firm. Other entrepreneurs find that when the venture reaches a

Making a Graceful Exit

Entrepreneurs need to think of their companies as part of an ongoing career path. So says Jerome Katz, director of the Jefferson Smufit Center for Entrepreneurial Studies in St. Louis. He has been studying the career paths of entrepreneurs and finds that there are four major types.

1. *Growth entrepreneurs.* These are entrepreneurs who measure their success by the size of their company. They tend not to have an exit plan because they're always striving for bigger, better, faster.
2. *Habitual entrepreneurs.* These are people who love to *start* businesses and may start and run several at once. They are probably even less likely to have an exit plan because there are always new opportunities out there.
3. *Harvest entrepreneurs.* These entrepreneurs start and build a venture for the purpose of

selling it. Some of these owners will start, build, and harvest many companies during a career.

4. *Spiral, or helical, entrepreneurs.* Women entrepreneurs often fall into this category. These entrepreneurs are driven by what is going on in their personal lives, so their entrepreneurial tendencies occur in spurts. At times they may appear stagnant as they deal with family issues.

Katz believes it's never too early to begin to think about an endgame strategy, so that your exit will be graceful rather than "feet first."

SOURCE: Jerome A. Katz, "Which Track Are You On?," *Inc. Magazine,* October 1995, p. 27.

certain size, the business needs professional management skills that the entrepreneur often does not possess. In fact, the entrepreneur may actually be holding the company back without realizing it. Whether or not you intend to exit the business at that point, you should have a plan for harvesting the rewards of having started the business in the first place. There are several methods by which you can achieve a rewarding harvest.

● *Selling the Business*

Selling the business outright to another company or an individual may be the goal if you are ready to move on to something else and want to be financially and mentally free to do so. Unfortunately, however, selling a business is a life-changing event. For several years, you have probably devoted the majority of your time and attention to growing the business, and it played an important role in structuring your life. When the business has been sold, you may experience a sense of loss, much like what accompanies the death of a loved one. If you have not prepared for this change in your life, emotional stress could be the consequence. There are several alternatives to selling the business outright that will be discussed in the next section. For now, let's just say that before selling the business, you should plan for what will happen after the business is no longer part of your life.

The best way to sell a business is to know almost from the beginning that selling is what you want to do. In this case you will make decisions for the business that will place it in the best position for a sale several years later. For one thing, you will maintain audited financial statements that give the business forecasts more credibility. Your tax strategy will not be to minimize taxes by showing low profits, but to show actual profits and pay the taxes on them, because you will probably more than make up for the expense at the time of sale. Higher recorded profits will likely help the business be worth more. You will keep the business expenses and activity totally separate from your personal expenses. You will also plan for the time it will take to sell the business and wait to sell until the window of opportunity has opened.

Smaller businesses for sale often use the services of business brokers; however, a high-growth venture will more likely employ the services of an investment banking firm that has experience with the industry. Investment banks normally want a retainer to ensure the seriousness of your commitment to sell, but that retainer will be applied against the final fee on the sale, which averages 5 percent of the purchase price. It is recommended, however, that a third party with no vested interest in the sale be employed to judge the fair market value of the business. This "appraiser" can also prepare financial projections based on the history of the company and the appraiser's independent market research.

When a business is sold, the entrepreneur does not have to sell all the assets. For example, the building could be held out of the sale and leased back to the business purchaser, with the original owner staying on as landlord.

While the potential purchaser is conducting due diligence on the entrepreneur and the business, the entrepreneur needs to do the same with the purchaser. The purchasing firm or individual should be thoroughly checked out against a list of criteria the entrepreneur has developed. The purchaser should have the resources necessary to continue the growth of the business, be familiar with the industry and the type of business being purchased, have a good reputation in the industry, and offer skills and contacts that will ensure that the business continues in a positive direction. It is often helpful to make a complete list of criteria and then weight them by importance to fairly compare one potential buyer with another.

● *Cashing Out But Staying In*

Sometimes entrepreneurs reach the point where they would like to take the bulk of their investment and gain out of the business but are not yet ready to cut the cord entirely. They may want to continue to run the business or at least retain a minority interest. There are several mechanisms by which this can occur.

Selling Stock

If the company is still privately owned, the remaining shareholders may want to purchase your stock at current market rates so that control doesn't end up in

FIGURE 19.1

Restructuring the Business

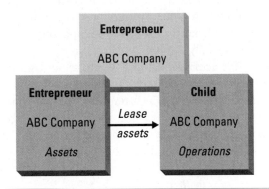

other hands. In fact, the shareholders' agreement that was drafted when you set up the corporation may have specified that you must first offer the stock to the company before offering it to anyone else.

If the company is publicly traded, the task of selling the stock is much simpler; however, if you own a substantial portion of the issued stock, you must follow strict guidelines set out by the SEC in the liquidation of your interests. If the company had a successful IPO, your founders' stock will have increased substantially in value, which presents a tax liability you should not ignore. That is why many entrepreneurs in such situations cash out only what they need to support whatever goals they have. This strategy, of course, is based on the presumption that the company stock will continue its upward trend for the foreseeable future.

Restructuring

Entrepreneurs who want to cash out a significant portion of their investment and turn over the reins of business to a son, daughter, or other individual can do so by splitting the business into two firms, with the entrepreneur owning the firm that has all the assets (plant, equipment, vehicles) and the child owning the operating aspect of the business while leasing the assets from the parent's company. See Figure 19.1.

A Phased Sale

Some entrepreneurs want to soften the emotional blow of selling the business, not to mention the tax consequences, by agreeing with the buyer—an individual or another firm—to sell in two phases. During the first phase the entrepreneur sells a percentage of the company but remains in control of operations and can continue to grow the company to the point at which the buyer has agreed to complete the purchase. This approach gives the entrepreneur the ability to cash out a portion of his or her investment and still manage the business for an agreed-upon time, during which the new owner will likely be learning the business and phasing in. In the second phase, the business is sold at a prearranged price, usually a multiple of earnings.

This approach is fairly complex and should always be conducted by an attorney experienced in acquisitions and **buy-sell agreements.** The buy-sell agreement, which spells out the terms of the purchase, specifies the amount of control the new owner can exert over the business before the sale has been completed and the amount of proprietary information that will be shared with the buyer between Phases 1 and 2.

Joining a Roll-up

In recent times the **consolidation** play, or the Pac-Man strategy, has become a way for many small business owners to realize the wealth they have created in their businesses. This is how it works. A large, established company finds a fragmented industry with a lot of mom-and-pop–type businesses. The consolidator buys them up and puts them under one umbrella to create economies of scale in the industry. The local management team often stays in power, while the parent company begins to build a national brand presence. The payoff for the entrepreneur comes when the consolidator takes the company public and buys out all the independent owners.

It is important to conduct due diligence on any consolidator, because your ability to cash out will be a function of the consolidator's ability to grow the company and take it public.

Dealing with Failure: Bankruptcy

It is an unfortunate fact of life that some entrepreneurs must exit their businesses through liquidation. For whatever reasons, the business could not pay its obligations and was unable to secure capital to float the business until it could. Certainly no entrepreneur starts a high-growth venture with liquidation in mind as the exit strategy, but sometimes the forces working against the business are so great that the entrepreneur must have an exit vehicle so he or she can move on to do something else. What forces a corporation into bankruptcy is difficult to pinpoint. The immediately precipitating cause is the failure to pay debt; however, myriad other events led up to that cause. They include economic and business cycles, excessive debt, surplus overhead, shifts in demand, excessive expenses, poor dividend policies, union problems, supplier problems, and poor financial management. Of course, the common denominator for all these factors is poor management. Over 95 percent of all bankruptcy filings are nonbusiness

---

Strategies for Avoiding Bankruptcy

- Avoid relying on one major customer or industry for revenue generation.
- Keep overhead costs to essentials that directly contribute to the generation of revenues.

- Maintain a degree of liquidity equal to about several months of overhead expense.
- Maintain current and honest relationships with bankers, creditors, and suppliers.

---

or consumer filings.[3] In October 2001, Congress was stalled in dealing with a major bankruptcy reform act that principally dealt with consumer debt. Entrepreneurs should keep a watchful eye out for the eventual passage of the reform act as it will have particular impact on businesses that deal with consumers.

Not all businesses can file for bankruptcy protection. Those that are exempt include savings and loan associations, banks, insurance companies, and foreign companies. Furthermore, a bankruptcy filing cannot occur where the intent has been to defraud, and a company may file only once every six years.

The Bankruptcy Reform Act of 1978 and Public Law 95-958 provide for more than just liquidation of the business. Therefore, you should have a clear understanding of the bankruptcy mechanisms available if you are faced with financial adversity. The bankruptcy code consists of several chapters, but two chapters are relevant to an entrepreneurial business:

▶ Chapter 7 discusses liquidation.

▶ Chapter 11 handles reorganization of businesses.

The two chapters pertinent to the entrepreneur are Chapter 7 and Chapter 11.

Chapter 11

Chapter 11 reorganization under the bankruptcy code is really not a bankruptcy in the commonly used sense of the word. It is simply a reorganization of the finances of the business so it can continue to operate and begin to pay its debts. Only in the case where the creditors believe the management is unable to carry out the terms of the reorganization plan will a trustee be appointed to run the company until the debt has been repaid. Otherwise, the entrepreneur remains in control of the business while in a Chapter 11 position. If the entrepreneur has aggregate noncontingent liquidated secured and unsecured debts that do not exceed $2 million (11 U.S.C. Sec. §101[51C]), he or she qualifies to be considered a small business owner, which puts the case on a fast track and doesn't require a creditors' committee. After filing for reorganization, the entrepreneur and the creditors must meet within 30 days to discuss the status and organiza-

A Little Magic

If you need a magician to wave a magic wand and turn your flagging business into a roaring success, a turnaround consultant may be just the ticket. Turnaround consultants are good at putting an unhealthy business on a diet, setting small, achievable goals, and making sure you stay on track until you're in the black.

But when the business cannot be turned around, you can still turn a bad situation into a more positive one by doing the following:

• Talk to other entrepreneurs who have been in a similar situation and listen carefully to what they learned.
• If your business is going to fail, end the business quickly before it affects your personal life. The business may have failed, but you did not. Set a hard deadline for when the business must be profitable or generate a positive cash flow; if it doesn't, close it. When the numbers don't add up, you must limit the time you are willing to devote to making the business work.

• Do not under any circumstances commingle personal and business funds or other assets. If you lend money to your corporation, you will simply be another creditor in line to receive funds from the bankruptcy. And, in fact, you may be required to return any funds you received in repayment of the loan for one year prior to a bankruptcy.
• Don't ignore the government. You may risk your personal assets and accrue a debt for life if you borrow funds from your payroll-tax and sales-tax accounts.
• Begin looking for opportunity. Do not wallow in failure. Sometimes the best opportunities are found when you're willing to leave a failing business behind.
• Do whatever you can to pay back investors. While it is true that they took a calculated risk investing in your business, if you find a way to pay them back—even if it takes a long time— they will respect you and be there when that next opportunity comes along.

tion of the business. The court then appoints a committee, which usually consists of the seven largest unsecured creditors, to develop a plan for the business with the entrepreneur. That plan must be submitted within 120 days, and acceptance of the plan must come within 60 days of submittal. Of the total number of creditors affected by the plan, representing at least two-thirds of the total dollar amount, at least one-half must accept the plan. Once the court has approved the reorganization plan, the entrepreneur is relieved of any debts with the exception of those specified in the plan.

● Chapter 7

The filing of a petition under Chapter 7 of the bankruptcy code constitutes an Order for Relief and is usually chosen when the business does not have sufficient resources to pay creditors while continuing to operate. It is essentially the liquidation of the assets of the business and the discharge of most types of debt. The debtor files a petition and several required schedules of assets and liabilities with the bankruptcy court serving the area in which he or she lives. A trustee is appointed to manage the disposition of the business and a meeting of the creditors is held twenty to forty days after the petition is filed.

The goal of the bankruptcy is to reduce it to cash and distribute the cash to the creditors where authorized. After exemptions, the monies derived from liquidation go first to secured creditors and then to priority claimants such as those owed wages, salaries, and contributions to employee benefit plans.

Any surplus funds remaining after this distribution go to the entrepreneur. Prior to distribution, the entrepreneur has the right to certain exempt property. If the business is a corporation, those exemptions are minimal:

▶ Interest in any accrued dividends up to a specified maximum

▶ The right to social security benefits, unemployment compensation, public assistance, veterans' benefits, and disability benefits

▶ The right to stock bonuses, pensions, profit sharing, or similar plan

Lest it seem as though the entrepreneur is at the mercy of the creditors in a bankruptcy situation, it should be made clear that in either type of bankruptcy petition, Chapter 7 or Chapter 11, the business owner has a great deal of power and control over the process. This power comes from the natural desire of the creditors for a quick and equitable resolution to the problem, and the protections inherent in the bankruptcy law. Often the creditors are better served by negotiating a restructuring of debt while the company is still operating and prior to Chapter 7 liquidation, where they are not likely to receive as great a portion of what is owed them, if anything. There are, however, certain things the entrepreneur will not be permitted to do within a certain period of time before the filing of a bankruptcy petition:

▶ Hide assets or liabilities

▶ Give preferential treatment to certain creditors ninety days prior to filing the petitions

▶ Make any potentially fraudulent conveyances up to one year prior to the filing of the petition

The court may recoup any of the above transactions during the bankruptcy proceedings.

Entrepreneurs can take advantage of a relatively new vehicle under Chapter 11. Known as a "prepackaged bankruptcy," it requires the entrepreneur to present the creditors and equity owners with a reorganization plan *before* the bankruptcy filing actually goes to court. If the entrepreneur can achieve the required number of votes agreeing to the plan (more than half the total creditors and two-thirds within each class of creditors), the prepackaged plan can then go forward expeditiously. This process generally takes just four to nine months to complete rather than the typical nine months to two years.

The entrepreneur gains an obvious advantage from using this approach. Under the traditional Chapter 11 process, the creditors and everyone else learn of the company's problems only at the filing. With a prepackaged plan, by contrast, an approved plan is already in place at the point at which the public becomes aware of the problem, and the creditors thus may experience a greater sense of confidence in the entrepreneur. Moreover, the prepackaged plan ties up far less time in legal processes. For this approach to succeed, however, the statement of disclosure for the creditors about the positive and negative aspects of the business must be carefully constructed to give the creditors all the information they need in order to consider the plan and protect their interests.

Before considering bankruptcy as an option to either exit a troubled business or restructure the business in an effort to survive, you should seek advice from your attorney and/or a specialist in turnarounds in your industry. With the aid of an accountant, you need to audit your assets and liabilities to see whether the business can qualify for and benefit from Chapter 11 reorganization. Often, seeking help before filing a bankruptcy petition can lead to alternative, less difficult solutions that are more beneficial to the entrepreneur and creditors alike.

In the end, knowing what your goals are relative to your business and how you intend to harvest the wealth the business has created can help you structure a growth plan that will get you there. Preparing for the unexpected—contingency planning—will go a long way toward ensuring that you stay on the path to your goals.

Becoming a World-Class Start-up Venture

This chapter ends a long journey through the mind and behavior of the entrepreneur preparing for the start-up of a new venture. By now, it should be clear that the mindset of the entrepreneur is distinctly different from that of the manager and even from that of the small business owner, so it is no wonder that the ventures they launch will look different as well. A world-class start-up venture is not defined by size, number of employees, revenues, or any of the other traditional measures of business success typically attributed to large companies. While a large, bureaucratic company may have the financial resources and clout to become world-class, and many have, it will more often succumb to the inertia of its own success and fail to radically innovate and change itself to meet the dynamic needs of the times. By contrast, a start-up entrepreneurial venture reinvents itself continuously to remain flexible enough to change when market conditions change.

What does it take to be a successful start-up today? Here are the enduring characteristics and the signature of a world-class start-up venture.

1. *Customers are the heart of the business.* World-class entrepreneurs are fanatical about their customers. Customers decide what is produced, when, in what manner, how much, at what price, and where it can be purchased and serviced. Fanatical customer attention means that everyone in the business spends time with the customer and everyone knows what he or she contributes to the customer's satisfaction.

2. *People are the soul of the business.* Venture capitalists know it; customers know it; value chain partners know it—people beat products every time. The success of your business will be due primarily to the success of the relationships you have with people.

3. *Creating new value is the engine that drives the business.* New value comes from continual innovation punctuated periodically by radical innovation that stretches the business in new directions. It is innovation that builds sustainable companies today, innovation in every aspect of the business.

4. *Recognizing big opportunities positions the business for long-term growth.* It takes as much effort to start a business that has no potential for growth as it does to start one that has huge potential for growth over the long term. Big opportunities—those with potential for growth domestically and globally—provide the entrepreneur with more options, access to more resources, more chances to create wealth for the company, the entrepreneur, the employees, and stakeholders. They also excite more people to get involved and help the entrepreneur enjoy the ride.

5. *Entrepreneurial passion and persistence translate into a higher probability of success.* When entrepreneurs do what they're passionate about, they generally do it very well. The result is a successful business with the potential for super-normal profits and sustainability. The passion of the entrepreneur comes from the satisfaction of being in charge of his or her own destiny and the belief that anything is possible.

If you constantly pursue excellence in your life and you are a person who is passionate about what you do, you can become a world-class entrepreneur, one of those intrepid people who say not only "I can," but "I will"—and who envision their success long before they achieve it.

NEW VENTURE CHECKLIST

Have you:
- ☐ Identified the issues that could affect your business at various points in the future?
- ☐ Developed a contingency plan for all the various scenarios that may affect the business at some future date?
- ☐ Determined your goals for the business relative to an exit strategy?

ISSUES TO CONSIDER

1. Contingency planning is not foolproof. How can you ensure that the contingent plans you devise will keep your business on the path to its goals?

2. How can the entrepreneur prepare for potential product liability litigation, both to minimize the chance of occurrence and to give the company the best chance of prevailing against a product liability claim?

3. How can the entrepreneur prepare for a potential decline in sales?

4. You have built your business successfully over several years and now have the opportunity to start another business compatible to your current one. How can you leave your original business yet stay involved?

5. In what ways can bankruptcy law be a tool for the entrepreneur?

EXPERIENCING ENTREPRENEURSHIP

1. Interview an entrepreneur in an industry of your choice to learn what his or her harvest strategy is. What is this entrepreneur doing to ensure that the strategy will be achieved?

2. Interview a turnaround consultant about some ways to recognize problems that could lead to business failure. From this interview, devise a list of do's and don'ts that will help you avoid business failure.

ADDITIONAL SOURCES OF INFORMATION

Altman, E.I. (1993). *Corporate Financial Distress and Bankruptcy.* 2nd ed. New York: John Wiley.

Bradford, R.W., J.P. Duncan, P. Duncan, and B. Tarcy (1999). *Simplified Strategic Planning.* Worcester, MA: Chandler House Press.

Dinapoli, D. (1999). *Workouts and Turnarounds II: Global Restructuring Strategies for the Next Century.* New York: John Wiley.

Staubus, M., R. Bernstein, D. Binns, and M. Hyman (2001). *Transitioning Ownership in the Private Company: The ESOP Solution.* La Jolla, CA: Foundation for Enterprise Development.

INTERNET RESOURCES

Business Owner's Toolkit
http://www.toolkit.cch.com/
Everything you ever wanted to know about running a business.

Entreworld
http://www.entreworld.org/
A resource for business strategy from start-up through growth and harvest.

Findlaw.com
http://www.findlaw.com
Good source of legal information in a variety of areas.

Research Institute for Small and Emerging Business, Inc.
http://www.riseb.org/
Provides corporations, policymakers, and business or trade associations serving the small and emerging business sector with substantive research on issues impacting the formation and growth of small and emerging businesses.

RELEVANT CASE STUDIES

Case 1   Mrs. Gooch's

Case 5   Earthlink.net: The Journey to Recognizing an Opportunity

Case 6   Highland Dragon

Mrs. Gooch's

Entrepreneurs start businesses for many reasons, but not many do it because they want to save their lives. Sandy Gooch was one such entrepreneur. In 1974, she was a wife, mother, teacher, and full-time home-maker who, like millions of other Americans, often relied on convenience foods even though she knew they contained potentially harmful chemicals. One day she woke up with persistent sniffles for which the doctor prescribed tetracycline. A few days later, however, she thought she was having a heart attack. She was rushed to the hospital. The doctors could not find the cause of her symptoms. Two weeks later she developed an eye infection and was again given tetracycline. This time her "attack" lasted three days, and she nearly died. Her father, a biologist/chemist, began what was to be a year of research into food manufacturing practices. He found that Gooch was allergic to chemicals and additives commonly found in food. They affected her body in such a way that it was unable to fight off disease.

From the information her father had gathered, Gooch decided a natural diet was her best weapon, and she proceeded to get rid of everything that was not natural in her kitchen. Within a period of about three months, she was feeling better, and within nine months she was healthier than she had been for years. As she began to study nutrition and whole foods, Gooch found others who shared her problem. Like Gooch, these people had to travel from health food store to health food store, along with shopping at grocery stores, to find the natural foods they needed.

The Birth of Mrs. Gooch's

Gooch felt frustrated. Coming from a family that had always helped people in the community, it was natural that she began to explore ways to make life easier for people who wanted to eat healthy foods. There were lots of things she could do—start a newsletter, form a co-op, give seminars—but the only idea that would allow her to make a real impact on people's lives was the idea of a natural foods store that would carry only things that were good for them. Excited by the possibilities, Gooch began to consult with herbalists, chemists, biologists, cosmetologists, and physicians to gather all the information she could about diet, wholesome foods, and food allergies.

Armed with a wealth of nutritional knowledge, Gooch realized that all the knowledge in the world about food could not compensate for lack of experience in business. She would need to take on a partner. Fortunately, she had a friend who was managing a health food store in the San Fernando Valley, and she succeeded in getting him to help.

They had to find a store location that was accessible and in a good area of town. After much driving around and consulting newspapers, they found a market on the west side of Los Angeles that had gone out of business. It was obvious that the owners had run it into the ground, but to Gooch it couldn't have been more perfect. Using her teacher retirement money and all her savings, she opened her first natural foods market on this site in 1977. The store was an overnight success in spite of her having done no location studies or psychographic studies. She was not simply lucky, however. She had correctly determined that there were a great many people who shared her problems with unnatural foods. In other words, she had innocently and intuitively found a niche in the market. Customers lined up and kept her at the register for six hours straight without a break on the first day.

Early Problems

High demand for what you have to offer has its obvious pluses and its not-so-obvious minuses. One of the problems Gooch faced early on was a shortage of cash. Often cash flow problems are the result of poor management, but in Gooch's case, it was caused by the need to stock sufficient inventory to meet tremendous demand. That required a lot of capital, which she and her business partner didn't have. Banks were unwilling to take a chance on a woman in the grocery business, even though she could point to lines of customers extending out the door of the store. Undaunted, Gooch moved ahead by keeping overhead costs down and scrimping anywhere that didn't affect the customer. This strategy allowed her to keep up with demand fairly well.

Growing the Business

Gooch's passion for her business, her need to help people, and the tremendous demand for what she was offering led to the opening of a second store within a year. To finance this store, Gooch offered limited partnerships to raise $125,000. From then on, through the use of internal cash flows, five more stores followed over a period of fifteen years, with each store reflecting Sandy Gooch's philosophy and mission for the business.

Mrs. Gooch's was committed to offering the highest-quality natural foods, related products, service, and information that optimize and enrich the health and well-being of the individual as well as the planet. The mission guided all the decisions she made about the stores. Accordingly, Gooch required that her suppliers guarantee the quality of their products and be able to furnish laboratory analyses or signed affidavits if requested. The products she carried could not contain chemicals, white flour, sugar, preservatives, artificial colors or flavors, caffeine, chocolate, hydrogenated vegetable oil, or irradiated food. Her mission also gave her a way to expand the product line to include, in addition to food, nutritional supplements and body care products. To increase efficiency as the company grew, she opened a produce/grocery distribution center, a food commissary for the preparation of deli and bakery foods, a design studio to create store decor, and a construction shop to build the displays.

Former teacher Sandy Gooch's love of education found its way into her business. To help achieve her mission, her 800 employees were carefully trained to be knowledgeable about the products she carried. Gooch believed strongly that her product was really knowledge and information. That belief formed the basis of her marketing strategy. She knew that an informed consumer would be an advocate for the type of nutritional lifestyle she was proposing. As

advocates, her customers would return again and again to purchase her products and gain more knowledge. She promoted health awareness by offering seminars, producing a newsletter, and giving her customers free brochures on nutrition and tasty recipes. A mini bookstore in each store contained all the latest books and research on foods and their relationship to the body. Even the ads that appeared in newspapers were educational in nature.

Looking to the Future

Gooch incorporated the business early in its development and set up a board of directors, which included herself, her partner, a general manager, and their attorney. As this privately held company began to grow, Gooch wondered if she had made the correct decision putting only "insiders" on the board and giving up so much equity to them. Would they continue to share her mission for the business? Already, in the early 1990s, she was beginning to see some dissention and a desire on the part of some board members to broaden the scope of the products they offered, even introducing items, like alcohol, that did not fit in with the vision of Mrs. Gooch's. Board meetings became stressful, and Gooch began asking herself if she really wanted to continue in this negative environment. Would she be able to maintain her vision in the face of such challenges?

In September 1993, Gooch had the opportunity to sell her company to Whole Foods Markets, Inc., a publicly traded company, for $63 million (Mrs. Gooch's was generating $90 million in annual revenues and had 830 employees). Like so many entrepreneurs before her, she recognized that she had taken the company as far as she could and it was time to pass the baton. It was not easy leaving Mrs. Gooch's behind. Before her seven stores were renamed Whole Foods Markets, she found it difficult returning to them to purchase groceries. Her loyal employees missed her and complained about all the changes that Gooch would not have approved of. It was like seeing a child you had raised but knowing that the child was no longer yours.

The Recovering Entrepreneur

It was time to enter a new phase of her life and put the wealth she had created to good use. One of her first forays into business after the sale of Mrs. Gooch's was a chain of bagel stores in the Midwest. She thought that her experience in the food industry made this a natural next venture to invest in. However, after many unexpected events conspired against the stores, including long-term construction near their first store that made it impossible for customers to get to the store, she decided to close that venture, take her losses, and move on. With her husband, Harry Lederman, she formed Sandy Gooch Enterprises and, taking advantage of her innate talent for design, began building and refurbishing estate homes incorporating pro-environmental features including energy efficiency, water purification, and conservation protective landscaping as well as the use of natural rather than synthetic products.

Always a socially responsible entrepreneur, Gooch took her efforts related to environmental and health issues to a much broader market. Beginning with the development of the Healthy School Meals Program in 1995, which educates high school students, food service directors, and school administrators about diet and nutrition, she then wrote a book, *If You Love Me, Don't Feed Me Junk!* to spread her holistic approach to nutrition to an even wider audience. In 2001, not old enough to retire and too entrepreneurial to sit passively on the sidelines, Sandy Gooch was looking for the best way to leverage her knowledge and experience. Where should she look for opportunity? How could she best use her skills and experience to help others? Was there a niche out there deserving of a new business?

DISCUSSION QUESTIONS

1. Why is Mrs. Gooch's considered an entrepreneurial venture?

2. How did the mission of Mrs. Gooch affect the decisions she made as the business grew?

3. What intellectual property rights could she acquire?

4. What other kinds of businesses could Sandy Gooch have started, given her philosophy?

5. What potential effect could there be from using insiders on the board of directors? What could she have done to remedy the situation?

Franchising a Dying Business

If you had told Vidal Herrera back in the 1960s that someday he would be known as "El Muerto," king of the private autopsy business, he probably would have laughed. For in the 1960s in East Los Angeles, this self-described hippie raised in a tough environment was working in a pizza joint, just trying to keep money in his pocket. Today he presides over a rapidly growing industry that he created. Autopsy/Post-Services fills a niche in the market for private autopsies created by cutbacks in funding for hospitals and coroner's offices. In addition to providing these services to families, law enforcement, and such high-profile attorneys as Johnny Cochrane, Autopsy/Post-Services also promotes and handles organ and tissue donations, does postmortem biopsy diagnosis, DNA (paternity) analysis, toxicology, and serology. Herrera has also done TV and movie production consultation.

The Birth of the Company

In 1975, Vidal Herrera decided that he had to find a career with a future. He began volunteering four days a week for two and a half years at the Los Angeles County morgue, training to become a qualified autopsy technician. He was then given a job there as a way to earn a living while going to school. It was on-the-job training all the way, from transporting bodies to assisting pathologists at autopsies. He learned about medical photography, lifting, and labeling. He learned to eviscerate, to excise, and to dissect tissue. He also learned how to harvest tissue and clean crime scenes. He worked on such high-profile cases as the Hillside Strangler and the Nightstalker; at the crime scene of the latter, he discovered a fingerprint that ultimately led to the identification of Richard Ramirez as the Nightstalker. But in 1984, while moving a cadaver, he suffered a back injury that put him out of business for over four years. During that time he had trouble finding another job and things got tough. Finally, in 1988, his former boss, one-time Los Angeles County Coroner

Thomas Noguchi, who by then was in private practice, hired Herrera to help with an autopsy and passed the word of Herrera's skills to others in the industry. As a result, the VA Medical Center in West Los Angeles hired him as an autopsy technician on a contract basis to fill the gap in the availability of trained technicians. Herrera discovered that other hospitals and mortuaries were experiencing the same problem; soon he was able to establish a network of contracts, and his business got off the ground.

It wasn't until 1993 that the business really began to take off. One day as he was watching TV, he noticed ads for 1-800-DENTIST and 1-800-LAWYER. He quickly checked with the telephone company to see if 1-800-AUTOPSY was available, and it was. He now had the hook for his business. He purchased a van and painted 1-800-AUTOPSY on the side panels. This attracted a lot of attention for his growing business. Soon families began calling him for second opinions on suspicious deaths or to exhume bodies for re-autopsy. Today, the majority of his customers are still attorneys seeking evidence for malpractice actions or criminal defense cases. Whereas a coroner's office would charge $2,854 for a private autopsy (if it even had the time or manpower to perform it), Herrera charges $2,000, and the results that the coroner's office takes nearly 120 days to produce, Herrera produces in 10 days.

Autopsies, by law, must be performed by a doctor, but Herrera assists the nine doctors who work with him. In addition, he has two full-time autopsy technicians who do about 60 percent of the physical work of opening a body and dissecting and weighing the organs.

Autopsy/Post-Services offers a variety of services including:

▶ Forensic autopsies
▶ Private autopsies
▶ Partial, limited, and re-autopsies
▶ Toxicology and serology analysis
▶ Exhumation/disinterment autopsies
▶ Consulting as a medical malpractice and wrongful death specialist

---

This case is intended to be used as the basis for class discussion rather than as an illustration of either effective or ineffective handling of the situation.

▶ Tissue and organ procurement / retrieval
▶ Postmortem neurological diagnosis (e.g., Alzheimer's disease, multiple sclerosis, amyotrophic lateral sclerosis disease (ALS or Lou Gehrig's disease), Down syndrome, Tourette's syndrome, schizophrenia, acquired immune deficiency syndrome (AIDS))
▶ Postmortem HIV and AIDS diagnosis
▶ Postmortem genetic DNA (deoxyribonucleic acid) banking
▶ Postmortem asbestos procurement/analysis
▶ Postmortem DNA (paternity) analysis
▶ Postmortem radiation detection
▶ Hospital autopsy support services
▶ Contract autopsy services available
▶ Medical photography and video services
▶ Medical appliance recycling (e.g., eyeglasses, hearing aids, pacemakers, wheelchairs, prosthesis, etc.)
▶ Autopsy report and medical records review
▶ Off-site laboratory-morgue facility available
▶ Posttraumatic (decomposition) clean-up services

Its customers include families (next of kin), funeral directors, cremationists, hospitals, attorneys, transplant institutions, cadaver-tissue research investigators, and other related organizations.

The Industry

The death care industry is an $8 billion a year industry that is expected to grow to $20 billion by the year 2010, due principally to aging baby boomers. But the reality is that the practice of autopsy is a dying science. Thirty years ago, hospitals performed autopsies on about 50 percent of patients who died in the hospital. Today teaching hospitals autopsy only 10–20 percent of deaths. In most communities without teaching hospitals, the rate dips to below 5 percent.[1] This is a disturbing trend to medical practitioners who believe that autopsy "is the one place where truth can be sought, found, and told without conflicts of interest."[2] It is the unequivocal source of the cause of death.

Several reasons have been proposed for the current demand for private autopsy services: 1) Many hospitals don't have autopsy suites and can't provide the service; 2) city and county governments have cut budgets to coroners' offices; 3) many hospitals don't have trained technicians because there are no schools that teach them how to perform autopsies; 4) insurance companies don't cover them; 5) many doctors are concerned that autopsy results could be used against them or the hospital in malpractice suits; and 6) most hospitals will perform autopsies only for deaths under suspicious circumstances, not to determine such conditions as Alzheimer's disease, because the Joint Commission on Accreditation of Health Care organizations no longer requires hospitals to maintain a minimum autopsy rate.

A study published in the April 23, 1983, *New England Journal of Medicine* (*NEJM*) specifically refutes the notion that advanced imaging techniques obviate the need for autopsies: "We conclude that advances in diagnostic technology have not reduced the value of the autopsy." Numerous additional studies published in the *Journal of the American Medical Association* (*JAMA*) and *NEJM* in recent years revealed that autopsies turn up unexpected information about the cause of death approximately 20–40 percent of the time. In other words, autopsies often catch errors that skew vital statistics and priorities for funding disease research, which are typically drawn from death certificates.

Growing the Business

When Herrera was considering ways to meet the exploding demand for his services, the natural strategy was franchising. Autopsy/Post-Services can easily be duplicated, the demand is world-wide, and this franchise would probably face less competition because most franchisees "would rather open a restaurant or a yogurt shop than a dead body."[3] The typical franchisee candidates would be certified pathology assistants, autopsy technicians, embalmers, and doctors.

In 1995 alone, Herrera turned away 9,000 autopsy cases while doing around 900 cases a year without advertising. In 1998, he and his team were

---

[1] "Pathologists Request Autopsy Revival." *JAMA*, 273(24): 1889.
[2] Ibid.

[3] R. E. Howard, "Autopsy/Post-Services—A Sure Thing!" *The Stakeholder* (Sept. 1995).

performing five or more autopsies a day, generating more than $1 million for the business. The demand for his services led to the idea to franchise the business so that it could grow more quickly. He also knew that autopsy technicians, embalmers, pathologists, or pathology assistants were always looking for ways to grow their own businesses and increase their income. He built a model for the franchise and provided franchisees with thorough training, materials, techniques, and guidance. His manual provides checklists for every type of procedure possible.

To overcome the negative perception that many people have of the business and to find another way to grow it, Herrera began promoting the donation of tissues and organs for research. He firmly believes that all human tissue can be used for transplants or research to save lives and bring the cost of medical care down. Two particular areas of interest for Herrera are AIDS research and Alzheimer's disease. This is his way of showing that death is not necessarily bad, but merely a part of the cycle of life, and that when someone dies, someone else's life can be saved or otherwise helped by organ donation or tissue research.

But not everyone is so enthusiastic about Herrera's plans for his business. In October 2000, the city of Tujunga revoked his permit to operate a laboratory in a business district where neighboring businesses were restaurants and retail establishments. The planning department had decided that it had made a mistake six months after Herrera had spent thousands of dollars remodeling. While appealing the decision, Herrera refurbished the space into a fake morgue and began renting it to film studios for shooting TV shows and movies. When his appeal was denied on the grounds that his business would do harm to the surrounding businesses, he filed a lawsuit against the City of Los Angeles for $1 million for the right to open his laboratory.

Herrera is not one to let these challenges get him down and he continues to give back to the community through its various charities. Herrera's concerns now are several. What should he do if the city will not approve his laboratory site? How can he grow the business in a way that will maintain the level of quality and service he has become known for? What other sources of revenue can he develop for the business?

DISCUSSION QUESTIONS

1. Besides franchising, what is another way Herrera can effectively grow his business?

2. Who are Herrera's customers, and what is the most effective way to reach them?

3. With no established training centers for technicians, how can Herrera ensure a sufficient supply of qualified technicians?

4. What are the barriers to entry in this industry?

REFERENCES

AMA (1998). "Breathing New Life into Autopsies," *American Medical News,* 41 (10).

Manzano, R. (2000). "His Business Is Dead." *Los Angeles Times,* (Oct. 9).

Howard, R.E. (1995). "Autopsy/Post-Services—A Sure Thing!" *The Stakeholder* (Sept.).

Manzano, R.J. (2001). "Proposed Site for Autopsy Lab Rejected; Zoning: Planning Commission Sides with Retailers Who Say Tujunga Facility Would Be Too Close to Their Businesses." *Los Angeles Times,* (Jan. 5).

Medical News & Perspectives (1995).

"Pathologists Request Autopsy Revival." *JAMA,* 273 (24):1889.

Overnite Express

The overnight-delivery parcel industry is an integral part of today's fast-paced economy. As our "instant gratification" society moves forward, the importance of being able to ship and receive documents and packages in a dependable and timely manner can make or break a crucial business deal. The biggest players in this very important industry are United Parcel Service (UPS), Federal Express (FedEx), and the U.S. Postal Service. These companies offer next-day delivery to many parts of the country.

Background

Rob Ukropina graduated from the University of Southern California in 1976. Upon graduation, Ukropina began a two-year stint in the restaurant business working for the Velvet Turtle in a management capacity. In 1977, he turned his focus to the commercial printing industry while getting his feet wet as a salesman at Welsh Graphics in Pasadena. Ukropina spent the next two years at Welsh before going to work for Jeffries Banknotes Company in 1979. Jeffries specialized in financial printing such as prospectus' and stock certificates. It was during this period that he began laying the foundation of his network. Through his sales and managerial duties, Ukropina made numerous contacts with financial institutions and law firms that would serve him well in the future.

In 1983, Ukropina went to work for Pandick Printing, the largest financial printer in the United States. At age 30, he became a division president and ran the Orange County division from 1983 to 1989. Although he was successful at his job—his gross income in 1989 was $300,000—Ukropina found he was bored working for a large company and wanted to do something on his own. His first venture was to start a leasing company in which he served as the director of sales, marketing, and operations, while his partner put up the financial backing to support the endeavor. The company leased small equipment to

businesses and also financed small businesses. In addition to the leasing company, Ukropina ventured into the publishing business and started his own magazine, *Business for Sale*. The publication served as an "*Auto Trader*" of sorts for buying and selling small businesses.

In order to give his businesses the best possible chance to survive, Ukropina did not draw a salary for himself from 1989 to 1992. Everything he made he reinvested into the business. Unfortunately, due to many external factors (i.e., recession and a nonsupportive partner), Ukropina watched his net worth fall from $1.6 million in 1989 to zero in 1992. His family moved from their spacious 3,000 square-foot home in Newport Beach to a 1,000 square-foot apartment. In 1991, his wife went back to work to help the family afford food and clothing.

The Opportunity

There was little question that Ukropina would eventually run his own company again. He was brought up in an entrepreneurial family with his parents owning their own company. In addition to his own family, his in-laws were prominent entrepreneurs in the fields of engineering and real estate. Their influence would eventually entice his wife, Joyce, to start a successful company in advertising. Once he hit rock bottom in 1992, Ukropina decided to explore opportunities that he had encountered in his past.

Throughout Ukropina's career in the printing business, he had to deal with trying to make his bottom-line cost numbers dealing with distribution. While at Pandick, Ukropina was quoted in the February 1999 issue of *Traffic World:*

> It was a 24-hour, seven-day-a-week business where 25% of our bills came from distribution costs. To get documents printed and delivered for public offerings on time, the company would routinely spend $30,000 for pick-ups after 5 p.m. and some $5 million a year on Next Flight Out courier services. We're talking about spending $1,100 per five-pound package to deliver documents nationwide, because what's $1,100 when

This case is intended to be used as the basis for class discussion rather than an illustration of either effective or ineffective handling of the situation. This case was written by Matthew Benson, MBA, University of Southern California. Reprinted by permission.

you have a $110 million public offering that needs to be filed on time with the Securities and Exchange Commission?

He believed he could drastically cut those expenses if Pandick distributed on a regional, rather than strictly national, pattern. Ukropina's entire motivation was based on providing superior and less-costly service to his customers. He determined that UPS and FedEx did not deliver 3 percent of their packages due to sorting or having the wrong address. They also stopped pickups at 7:00 p.m., even though many businesses work much later into the evening trying to make deadlines. For many of these businesses, the only alternative was to use a ground messenger at a rate of $1 per mile.

Ukropina saw that there was an opportunity to fill a niche as a regional delivery service that was small enough to make corrections in mid-shipment if there were any logistics problems. If a package were addressed incorrectly, the driver would be able to call in and get proper directions for the destination. The larger companies would simply take it back to the hub and try to redeliver it the next day. There was definitely an opportunity to compete with the big boys in terms of flexible pickup times, quality, and service, something Ukropina took a lot of pride in.

From Opportunity to Business

The first thing that Ukropina did was to put together a five-year business plan in early 1992. Drawing from the experience of his failed leasing company and magazine, he knew that he needed a quality advisory board to help him start the company and invest in his idea. He did not look to load his board with a bunch of buddies but started calling on the business contacts he had made throughout his years in sales. Early members on the advisory board included a CEO of a healthcare network, an airline executive, and an executive from Peat Marwick.

In order to attract investors he offered 10 percent of Overnite Express for $150,000 and quickly brought the net worth of the company to $1.1 million. To get his first customers, Ukropina used a network of "friends." He called on all the law firms that he had done printing for in the past and explained what he was doing. He asked them if he could put an Overnite Express drop box in their offices and promised unparalleled service if they

would use it. Because they had known Ukropina for his service in the printing business, many of them agreed to take a chance on him.

Because he did not have an established delivery system in place, Overnite would pick up the packages in the drop boxes and subcontract a route courier service to deliver them to their destinations in an area that extended from Santa Barbara to the Mexico border. Ukropina claimed to have many a sleepless night in the beginning with crossed fingers praying that there would not be any problems. Luckily, everything went well and Overnite was able to start delivering on its own.

Nine months into the venture, Overnite Express had exhausted the original capital investment and Ukropina took on a partner, Doug Schneider. Together they managed to raise another $400,000 and in a year acquired another $100,000 through SBA financing. Also, through his trials and tribulations, Ukropina never allowed his credit to be adversely effected. In year three of business operations, Overnite Express secured a $300,000 receivable line of credit.

As Ukropina had learned from his other jobs, the only way to maintain a high level of quality is to ensure that the people who work for you are happy and enjoying what they do. He used his entrepreneurial philosophy in putting together an incentive plan that would allow him to keep good employees from becoming complacent, or worse, leaving the company. Everyone in the company, including Ukropina, is paid a permanently fixed salary. In addition to that, everyone is paid a percentage of the gross profits, along with an incentive-based bonus that is determined by the number of packages delivered and the time they are delivered. For example, a driver can make more money by delivering the majority of his packages before 11:00 a.m. than he can if he delivers them by 4:00 p.m., and he can make even more if he delivers them by 9:00 a.m. Thus, everyone in the company is an entrepreneur in his or her own right. Ukropina credits the entrepreneurial spirit that thrives throughout the company with the low employee turnover rate.

For nine years, Overnite Express has flourished in the regional Southern California market in which it operates. Ukropina is very proud to boast a 99.2 percent on-time rate for delivery and an astonishing 100 percent completion rate. In other words, every package gets to its destination, while only 0.8 percent arrive late.

In 1999, after constant pressure from clients to expand its delivery area to include Northern California, Ukropina performed a feasibility study to establish the profitability of such a venture. It turned out that many of Overnite's existing clients would choose a national courier if they had more than one package going out and did not know if Overnite delivered north of Bakersfield. Regardless of cost, it was less trouble to make one call instead of two. As Ukropina was quoted in the April 20, 2000 issue of *Orange County Metro:*

> Many of our customers ship most of their packages inside California. By expanding, we have made it easier for the customer. If it is easier for the customer it is a good business decision.... Now they don't have to think, since I have one package going to San Diego and another going to San Jose, I guess I will use FedEx for both. Now they can use us for both. Now it's simple—if you are shipping inside California, use Overnite Express.

Ukropina expected to get 28 percent more business by moving into Northern California and, at the same time, expand the Southern California business by 30 percent. In May 2000, he borrowed $200,000 to finance the expansion and estimated the break-even point to be approximately six months. To his pleasure and his surprise, the venture broke even in sixty days. Today, Overnite Express operates at a level of $10 million in annual sales, delivering 3,000 shipments per day. Overnite is merely a blip on the radar screen of UPS, which enjoys $40 billion in sales annually, and Ukropina likes that. He is able to provide service in a niche market in which the larger companies do not feel the need to compete.

The Future

When asked what he felt his future holds, Ukropina had to take a minute to answer. Then he had to qualify his answer by categorizing his future in terms of Overnite Express, his career, and his family. The growth strategy for Overnite Express is simple. He only wants it to grow in terms of being able to provide the greatest service to his clients. If the business warrants, the company will expand its operations as much as needed to maintain the current level of excellence. However, because of the niche that he enjoys and being the only delivery company that can boast 100 percent delivery rates while only servicing the state of California, he does not foresee the company expanding to a national level. As Ukropina likes to say, "We plan to stay humble and continue to operate below the radar screen of UPS and FedEx. The reality is that we have to offer better service here in California in order to compete with FedEx and UPS."

Overnite Express is faced with a challenge going forward. As business moves rapidly toward a dependence on electronic data, the company must find new sources for generating revenue, as document shipping will likely slow down. How can Overnite Express position itself for the changes that are sure to come?

As for his career, Ukropina considers himself a "builder" rather than a "maintainer." As long as the challenges are present to keep him motivated, he will stay with Overnite. The minute he feels that the company has grown to its potential, he will gladly step aside and move on to a new endeavor. So he must also position himself and the company for the time when he might take on a new challenge. There are many ways to exit a business either in part or completely. Ukropina wonders how he should prepare for that eventuality.

DISCUSSION QUESTIONS

1. How did Ukropina obtain his first customer and what did that tell him about his business?

2. What is Overnite's competitive advantage in an industry dominated by companies like Federal Express?

3. With the obvious move toward more electronic data transfer, what new sources of revenue should Ukropina consider developing?

4. Is it a wise decision to limit the company to California? Why, or why not?

5. What is Ukropina's growth strategy?

Beanos Ice Cream Shoppe

Terry Smith has spent the last six months preparing to purchase a Beano's Ice Cream franchise. Because his personal assets were limited, Smith needed a partner who could finance the purchase. After Smith found a prospective partner, Barney Harris, they negotiated a purchase price with Beanos. Then, Harris gave Smith a partnership proposal. As the case opens, Smith is evaluating the partnership proposal. His three choices are: to accept Barney Harris' partnership proposal, or to make a counter proposal, or to try to find a new partner.

Introduction

Two months ago, Terry Smith had been so confident that he would soon own his own Beanos Ice Cream franchise, that he had put an "I LOVE BEANOS ICE CREAM" bumper sticker on his Honda. As he looked at it now, he noticed how faded it had become in such a short time. He wondered if in fact it had been a short time—or a lifetime.

Until recently, Smith had rarely second-guessed himself. After carefully researching an issue, he would base his decision on the facts and then proceed—without looking back. Now, however, he knew he had to put all of the momentum from the past six months to one side. He had to forget about the months spent investigating franchises, selecting Beanos, writing his business plan, and looking for financing. He had to forget about the fact that he had found only one prospective partner who could finance the deal—Barney Harris—and that he and his partner had spent several more months negotiating to purchase the franchise. He had to push away his own emotional investment in the deal now and make one more critical decision: should he go into partnership with Harris?

If he signed the partnership proposal that Barney Harris had given him, Smith would get his franchise. If he did not sign the agreement, he may or may not ever see his dream come to life. It depended on whether he decided to make a counter offer, to look for a new partner, or to walk away from the deal altogether. It was that simple: sign it and get all the marbles, or risk everything for the chance to get something better.

Now, as Smith looked at his faded bumper sticker, he realized that he had to evaluate the proposal in the context of the whole franchise deal. The question was not just, "Is this a good partnership proposal?" The real question was, "Given the potential of this particular franchise, and given my financial and managerial needs, will this proposal help me reach my goals?"

Smith's Background

In the fall of 1995, Terry Smith, a 36-year-old marketing representative for a Fortune 500 telecommunications firm in Cleveland, was among the thousands of employees who were downsized.

At first, he investigated the possibility of working for other major corporations in Cleveland. His education (a B.S. in biology and an MBA) and experience made him very marketable. During the seven years he had spent with the telecommunications firm, he had developed a solid reputation in his field. In a relatively short time, he received several job offers for about $60,000 per year.

And yet . . . Smith felt reluctant to jump back into a large corporation. He realized that as a new employee, he would be among the first to be cut, if his employer experienced a downturn. Did he want to go through *that* again?

Smith had had a positive experience as an entrepreneur during the years he was in college getting his degrees. He had started a successful mobile music company. While it had not made him a millionaire, it had paid for his education and living expenses, even though he had worked only when he could take time away from his studies.

This case is intended to be used as the basis for class discussion rather than as an illustration of either effective or ineffective handling of the situation. This case was written by Todd A. Finkle, Department of Management, The William and Rita Fitzgerald Institute for Entrepreneurial Studies, University of Akron. Reprinted by permission.

One day, he found himself captivated by an article in *Entrepreneur* magazine. It pointed out that the number of downsized executives who were turning to entrepreneurship had doubled over the past two years. In 1993, between six and eight percent started their own businesses; in 1995, over 12 percent did so.

Smith decided that he needed to explore his options as an entrepreneur. He knew the down sides of owning a business: the long hours, the stress, problems with employees, paperwork, and a lack of benefits. However, he felt that these could be outweighed by the opportunity to make all of the important decisions himself.

After several months of research, he decided to seriously explore the purchase of an ice cream franchise in Gainesville, Florida called Beanos Ice Cream Shoppe, which cost $275,000 (see Exhibits 1–3 for the estimated costs and financial statements for a Beanos franchise). Smith had a net worth of $50,000 and a liquidity of $20,000, which meant that he had to obtain financing.

Background

Beanos was founded by Bill Hogan, Jeff Pricer, and Annie Aubey, three former executives who had grown weary of the corporate world. In 1968, they founded Beanos based on a secret ice cream recipe.

Since opening its first ice cream shop, Beanos has become one of the most respected ice cream companies in the U.S., selling superpremium ice cream, low-fat and non-fat frozen yogurt, and ice cream novelties. Sales and net income for Beanos have been increasing in recent years. Net sales have increased from $48 million in 1989 to $120 million 1993. Net income has increased from $1.5 million to $6.7 million over the same time period. In the last quarter of 1994, net sales totaled $27,193,000, up two percent from $26,532,000. Overall, 1994 net sales went up from $120,328,000 to $128,802,000, an increase of seven percent.

The company used the finest, high quality, all natural ingredients. They have differentiated themselves from the competition with: (1) superior ingredients, (2) new product development, (3) new market development, and (4) environmentally conscious behavior. These strategies have allowed Beanos several competitive advantages over the competition in the frozen dessert industry. Beanos has held the

number three market position in sales within the U.S.'s superpremium ice cream market for the past few years behind Haagen-Dazs and Ben and Jerry's. The company has two primary growth strategies: (1) international expansion and (2) increased domestic penetration.

Beanos had 300 franchises located all over the world, with the majority located in the United States. Five percent of the franchises were company-owned and 75 percent of the franchises were located in the Washington D.C.-Boston corridor and Southern California. More recently, the company has targeted warmer climates such as Florida, Texas, and Georgia.

The company has not had a franchise failure since 1991. Overall, only five percent of their franchises have failed. The average franchise had $350,000 in sales a year. However, in more successful markets, average sales were closer to $500,000. The company's domestic franchise agreements were generally for a ten-year term with an option for renewal. The agreements grant the franchisee an exclusive area to sell bulk ice cream and frozen yogurt, which the franchisee was required to purchase directly from the company.

Beanos provided the following to their franchisees: (1) a seven-day training seminar, (2) on-going operational support, which included access to a territory franchise consultant, (3) phone support, and (4) help with real estate and site selection. An input committee, comprised of five of the most successful franchisees, was developed to assist existing franchisees. There was also an annual franchisees' meeting, which included workshops. Finally, Beanos sent field consultants to visit each franchisee four times a year.

Industry Environment

In 1995, the U.S. Frozen Dairy Dessert Industry was in its mature stage of the industry life-cycle with the market segmented into the retail (dipping store-franchises) sector and the supermarket (take-home) sector. Estimated sales for 1998 were $12.8 billion, an increase of about 20 percent over 1993 sales. Two contrasting trends had developed in recent years: a movement towards full-fat products (which appeal to indulgent consumers) and a movement towards fat-free products (which appeal to health-conscious consumers). Brands, such as Healthy Choice, which were able to offer both rich taste and low-fat content, prospered.

Some of the consumer trends were: the fastest growing age group was the 45-54-year-olds, more two-income families, the U.S. annual population growth rate was expected to average 0.9 percent per year through the remainder of the decade, aging population, enhanced disclosure requirements for food labeling, more single-occupant and single-parent households, and health-conscious eating.

Ice cream has historically been one of the most popular dessert items. However, increased competitive pressures from entrants into supermarkets (Starbucks, Colombo, TCBY, and Swensen's) and new product development (novelty items like Haagen-Dazs' frozen yogurt bars) made the industry fiercely competitive.

Due to the fierce competitive environment, Baskin-Robbins, International Dairy Queen, Haagen-Dazs, and TCBY have increased their advertising. Finally, there has been a movement towards locating stores in non-traditional locations like airports, grocery stores, and in other franchises (such as Baskin-Robbins and Dunkin' Donuts).

Local Environment

Gainesville is located in north-central Florida. The city was ranked as *Money Magazine's* "Best Place to Live" in the U.S. for 1995. It had been ranked among Florida's most livable cities since 1991.

Employment growth in the 1990s had averaged 6.2 percent, which was nearly double the national average. Gainesville also had a low cost of living component compared to other cities of similar size in the U.S. In 1994, the unemployment rate was 2.8 percent, while the national average was 5.9 percent. In the past three years, Florida's economy has surpassed the national average. Florida was also one of nine states without a state income tax. Some of the statistics of Gainesville can be seen in Exhibit 4.

Prior marketing research efforts in Gainesville showed wide acceptance for Beano's products. Beano's had two promotional events in Gainesville, where ice cream was given to consumers. The feedback about the quality of the products was very positive, and the company had experienced success at selling products in local supermarkets.

Additionally, research showed that franchises located in college towns had sales averages that were surpassed only by resort areas. This made Gainesville very appealing, because the largest university in the South was located there. The University of Florida had an enrollment of 38,000 students and employed 15,500 people. Other institutions of higher education in Gainesville had a total enrollment of 20,000 students.

The population for Gainesville and Alachua County has increased 26 percent since 1980, an average increase of two percent a year (see Exhibit 5).

Exhibit 6 shows the Median Household Effective Buying Income Groups for Gainesville and Alachua County. The total effective buying income for Gainesville has risen from $627,766,000 in 1981 to $1,041,191,000 in 1992, an average increase of six percent a year. The average household income for Gainesville was $29,073.

Local Competition

Fifteen local dipping store competitors are listed in Exhibit 7, which includes information about each store's age, number of employees, and estimated sales. It should be noted that of these fifteen, three stores have sales of $500 thousand to one million.

In addition to these dipping stores, the local market also included supermarkets, convenience stores, restaurants, and an ice cream truck that parked near campus. Of these sources, three were seasonal. The ice cream truck, the campus food court, and a campus Freshen's Yogurt all operated only during the school year.

Four features were missing from the local competition. First, there were no national competitors of *superpremium* desserts in Gainesville. Second, no competitor had a place for customers to sit outside. Third, no competitor had a policy of "giving back to the community."

Fourth, there were no Haagen-Dazs stores. This was significant because Haagen-Dazs had been one of the first and strongest competitors, with sales peaking at $560 thousand at one location. A decline in sales prompted their withdrawal from the market.

A discussion of the four largest players in the local market follows.

Lauries Cafe

Lauries Cafe was a locally owned competitor that served superpremium ice cream, low-fat frozen yogurt, bagels, gourmet coffee, sandwiches, and salads. They had two stores and offered delivery services. The first store was located directly across from the University and had been there for three years. The second store was new and larger than the first.

TCBY

The city had three TCBY stores. Two of the franchises had sales between $500,000 and $1,000,000. These were located in the upper-income areas of Gainesville. The other store was younger (five years old) and located near campus. The stores sold soft-serve frozen yogurt and superpremium ice cream products along with novelty items. Currently, TCBY was marketing their "Treats" program heavily. Their Treats program featured candy mixed into their ice cream and frozen yogurt.

International Dairy Queen

Two successful Dairy Queen franchises were located in Gainesville. Dairy Queen sold hamburgers, hot dogs, barbecue, fish and chicken sandwiches, french fried potatoes, and onion rings. Their desserts consisted of cones, shakes, malts, sundaes and sodas, hardpacked products, and frozen ice cream cakes and logs.

Baskin-Robbins

Baskin-Robbins had two stores in Gainesville. One was located directly across from the main campus. It had standing room only. They recently remodeled this store and signed a ten-year lease. The other store was located one mile west of the University. Baskin-Robbins was known for their variety of flavors. They served both frozen yogurt and other ice cream products.

Smith's Goals and Financial Objectives

Smith saw an opportunity to obtain a franchise that had brand-name recognition and a history of success. Florida already had four Beanos franchises in Miami, Fort Lauderdale, Jacksonville, and Orlando. However, there were ample opportunities to open other stores in Florida.

Smith's goals were:

Phase I: Open one franchise in the Gainesville area in the fall of 1996. For the first two years of operation, the focus would be on the success of that store;

Phase II: Open a second store in Tallahassee in early 1998;

Phase III: open a third, fourth, and fifth store in consecutive years (1999, 2000, and 2001) in Orlando.

The financial objectives were:

Objective 1: Pay off any loans to each store by the sixth year.

Objective 2: Maintain an average return on investment of 20 percent for each store.

Objective 3: Maintain a positive cash flow starting in year one for each store.

Objective 4: Have sales of 2.5 million at the end of ten years.

The Search for Investors

Because Smith had already founded one company, he knew how difficult raising capital could be. He developed a list of people to talk with, and then proceeded as follows:

SBA Consultant

The Small Business Administration (SBA) consultant, Tom Hughes, was impressed with Smith's education, work experience, and detailed business plan. He stated that Smith would have no problem getting a loan of $175,000 as long as he had one-third of the loan amount in liquid assets. For example, if Smith wanted a loan of $175,000, he would need approximately $58,000 in liquid assets. However, Smith's liquidity had dropped to $7,000 over the past few months, due to living expenses. Consequently, he needed an investor(s).

Mr. Hughes also asserted that if Smith got an investor who owned 20 percent or more of the company, the SBA required that person to sign on the note. Smith realized that this could pose a problem because the investor(s) would be at risk for the entire investment of $275,000 if they put up $100,000. That could decrease their desire to invest in the venture. Mr. Hughes also explained that Smith could not receive an SBA loan in the state of Ohio. He would have to go through an SBA branch office located in Florida.

Banker

Smith's banker was Mike Tork, a casual friend. Tork was also impressed with Smith's credentials and affirmed that he should not have a problem getting an SBA loan for $175,000 if he got an investor(s) to put in $100,000. Tork stated the bank preferred to see the following before granting a loan: (1) quality management team, (2) likelihood of success, and (3) financial projections. Tork also stated that obtaining a loan would be easier due to Beanos' successful track record.

The bank required Smith to submit his business plan, tax returns for the past three years, and a current copy of his personal financial statement. Tork sent a copy of the business plan to the branch manager in Orlando, Florida, Don Pelham. Pelham told Smith that he might be willing to give him a conventional loan, which would exclude the SBA. Pelham stated, "We want you to be successful, and we will do whatever it takes. The more successful you become, the more successful we become." Pelham gave Smith two scenarios from which to choose.

The first scenario was an SBA loan guaranteed by the federal government. This would involve a lot of paperwork. Pelham estimated the interest rate to be around 9.25-9.5% or one to one-and-one-half percent above prime, plus a closing cost of $3,300. The terms of the loan would be worked out later, but Smith figured he would pay off the loan over a six or seven year period of time.

The second scenario would be a conventional loan from the bank. The time frame to obtain this loan was similar to the SBA's. However, the terms of this loan would be much more conducive to the needs of Smith's company. The loan would be broken down into operating and reducing lines of credit (both using variable interest rates). The exact interest rate percentages were not discussed. However, Smith learned through friends that these loans were usually structured at five points above prime.

The operating line of credit would be oriented towards short-term operations (working capital, inventory, and payroll). Pelham told Smith that they were very flexible on the terms. For instance, they would allow Smith to pay interest only during the first year. Pelham also said that he was willing to let Smith pay interest only for up to 36 months. However, the loan would have to be paid off over six-to-eight years.

The reducing line of credit would be used for equipment, renovation, and other fixed asset allocation. For this line, Pelham also stated that he would allow Smith to pay interest-only for up to two or three years, and Smith would have to pay off the note at the end of six-to-seven years.

SCORE Counselor

Smith's last meeting was with the local Service Corps of Retired Executives (SCORE) counselor, George Willis. Willis had worked for Dupont for 30 years in various marketing positions and had owned his own executive search franchise for 14 years. Willis had also consulted with several franchisees in the frozen dessert industry.

Willis told Smith to obtain two partners with an equity interest of 20 percent or less because having one partner with a 33 or 40 percent interest would put you at the mercy of that partner. What if that partner decided not to do the deal? What if something happened to that partner? Also, that partner would have too much control because he or she has the money. If you have two partners, you would have much more control. If one partner drops out, then you could get another. Smith stored this information and began his search for capital.

Family, Friends, and Savings

Remembering his days in graduate school, Smith sought out the number one source of financing for most startups: friends, family, and savings. He failed at finding resources there.

Business Professionals

Smith's next step was networking through his database of business professionals in the Cleveland area. The first person he contacted was an acquaintance, Barney Harris, whom he had met a year earlier through a friend. Harris was a very successful restaurateur. Smith called Harris to arrange a meeting. Harris agreed, but wanted a copy of the business plan a week in advance. Smith dropped off a copy of the plan and a confidentiality agreement contract the next day.

A week later, Smith and Harris met. Harris stated, "You know Terry, most of the people who come to see me with business deals just talk. They do not have a business plan, and they expect me to invest hundreds of thousands of dollars with them. Your business plan is excellent. I like how you examined the business from broad and narrow perspectives. This is exactly what I like to see." Harris was also impressed with Smith's intensity and ambition. Harris stated that he knew Smith had what it takes to become successful—"a fire in the belly." Harris told Smith that he was interested in becoming a potential partner, not an investor, and would be willing to put up $100,000.

After four months of hard work, Smith was excited at the opportunity of obtaining a partner. In his excitement, Smith stated that he was willing to give up 33 percent of the company in exchange for an investment infusion of $100,000. No further business professionals were contacted.

Beanos Selection Process

The selection process at Beanos required the potential franchisee(s) to send in an application form, psychological questionnaire, and personal financial statement. The next step was an independent phone interview that lasted one hour, followed by another half-hour for questions from the applicant. After this stage, there was a personal interview at Beanos' corporate headquarters in Phoenix, Arizona. The interview focused on the specifics of running a small business.

This process lasted approximately six weeks. After Smith and Harris passed, they received a letter that had a password in it that allowed them to contact any franchisee. Beanos also sent the potential franchisee a copy of their Uniform Franchise Offering Circular (UFOC), a legal document containing information on the company's history, management, finances, operations, and franchisees.

Smith quickly took advantage of this opportunity to gather more information by making a list of questions. He contacted ten franchisees and learned about sales, profitability, successful and unsuccessful marketing strategies, employees, and horror stories of partnership agreements. One of the franchisees from

Tucson, Arizona was kind enough to send Smith a copy of his financial statements from the previous year. After examining the differences between the franchisee's numbers and his projected proformas, Smith made some changes (see Exhibit 8 for revised expected scenario).

One of the most significant changes that Smith noticed was the cost of the franchise. Early on in the negotiation process, Smith estimated the cost of a franchise at $275,000. After talking with several franchisees in similar college towns, he estimated the cost of starting a franchise in Gainesville at $220,000, including working capital.

Smith also noticed that he initially overestimated the profitability of the business. In his original financial statements, Smith estimated the expected net income of the business at: $34,400, $91,800, $116,800, $135,700, and $138,300 for the years 1997-2001. He revised his figures to be: $29,000, $49,000, $67,600, $87,100, and $87,800. There was a significant difference, primarily due to his failure to include employee wages in the financial statements. This was a gross oversight.

Smith realized that he needed to get the partnership agreement out of the way as soon as possible. After all, they had been negotiating with Beanos for over five months now. Beanos had given Smith and Harris the green light. Now it was time for them to fulfill their side of the deal, to produce a partnership agreement and then to move forward with the construction of the franchise.

Harris's Partnership Proposal

Smith went to Harris and told him that it was time for them to draw up a partnership agreement. They had previously talked about a partnership proposal where Harris' percentage of the business would be 33 percent for an investment infusion of $100,000. Smith offered to write up the proposal. However, Harris insisted that he would write up the initial proposal. Two weeks later, Smith received it (see Exhibit 9) in the mail.

Smith found three surprises in this proposal. First, Harris changed the structure of the deal. Secondly, Harris charged him for accounting services, when Smith could do the bookwork himself. Third, the buy out clause proposed three times the cash flow of the business, averaged over the number of years they were in business, divided by the owner-ship percentage. Cash flow was not defined.

Smith was stunned. Quickly, he sketched out the proposal that he had expected to receive, so that he could compare them side by side (see Exhibit 10).

Conclusions

Terry Smith winced as he turned away from his "I LOVE BEANOS ICE CREAM" bumper sticker. He knew

he had three choices: take what Harris had offered in the proposal, even though it was not the proposal Smith had expected; give Harris a counter proposal that included the three changes Smith wanted, know-ing that there was a chance that Harris would back away from the deal altogether; or, start looking for a new partner. Smith started to walk across the parking lot, knowing it was time to make his next move.

DISCUSSION QUESTIONS

1. What were the internal strengths and external op-portunities that Smith's franchise would face? What were the internal weaknesses and external threats?

2. Should Smith and Harris go for an SBA loan or a conventional loan? Why? What problems will this cause for Smith?

3. Harris states that he wants 49 percent of the com-pany for a $90,000-95,000 loan at prime to be re-paid over a five-year period of time. Does this seem like a fair deal for Smith?

4. For the buy out arrangement, Harris wants three times the cash flow from the business averaged over the number of years the business has been open. This figure would then be divided by the ownership percentage of the person who is being bought out. Based on the financial material in the case, does this seem like a fair buy out clause? Why

or why not? If not, how would you devise a fair buy out clause based on the financial projections in this case?

5. After the franchiser approved Harris and Smith as partners, Smith began to work on the agreement. Is this the correct time to do this? Why or why not? Is there anything Smith should have done to pro-tect himself?

6. Smith states that one of the primary reasons he wants to go into business for himself was the fi-nancial rewards. Based on the figures in the case study, do you think that Smith has made the cor-rect decision to forgo his corporate job at $60,000 a year in exchange for a Beano's franchise?

7. Overall, do you think it would be wise for Smith to become a partner with Harris in this venture? Why or why not?

REFERENCES

Answers to Frequently Asked Questions about Fran-chising. *Franchising in the Economy.* Interna-tional Franchise Association (IFA), 1995.

Hill, T. and Jacobs, M. (1995). "Franchise Turnover Ratio Below Nine Percent." Frandata Corp. for the International Franchise Association's Education Foundation.

Top 50 Franchisers Ranked by System-Wide Sales. *Restaurant Business,* November 1, 1995.

Vaughn, B. (1976). The International Expansion of U.S. Franchise Systems: Status and Strategies. *Jour-nal of International Business,* Spring, pp. 65–72.

EXHIBIT 1

Investment Breakdown of Beanos Ice Cream Shoppe Franchise

Expenditure	Dollars
Franchise Fee	$ 30,000
Design & Architecture Fees	$ 15,000
Real Estate & Improvements	$ 80,000
Professional Fees	$ 2,000
Equipment	$ 40,000
Signage & Graphics	$ 15,000
Miscellaneous Opening Costs	$ 7,000
Initial Inventory	$ 11,000
Working Capital	$ 75,000
Total:	$275,000

EXHIBIT 2

Pro Forma Income Statement/Cash Flow Summary for the Years 1997–2001, Expected Scenario (in 000's)

	1997		1998		1999		2000		2001	
	$	% Sales	$	% Sales	$	% Sales	$	% Sales	$	% Sales
Sales	$300.0	100.0%	$400.0	100.0%	$450.0	100.0%	$490.0	100.0%	$500.0	100.0%
Cost of Sales	105.0	35.0	140.0	35.0	157.5	35.0	171.5	35.0	175.0	35.0
Gross Profit	195.0	65.0	260.0	65.0	292.5	65.0	318.5	65.0	325.0	65.0
Operational Expenses										
Employee Wages	21.0	7.0	28.0	7.0	31.5	7.0	34.3	7.0	35.0	7.0
Management Wages	30.0	10.0	31.5	7.9	33.1	7.4	34.8	7.1	36.5	7.3
Health Insurance	3.0	1.0	3.3	0.8	3.6	0.8	3.9	0.8	4.2	0.8
Rent	37.5	12.5	39.3	9.8	41.4	9.2	43.5	8.9	45.6	9.1
Utilities	5.3	1.8	5.4	1.3	5.6	1.2	6.2	1.3	6.5	1.3
Prop/Liability Insurance	4.5	1.5	5.2	1.3	5.1	1.1	5.5	1.1	5.9	1.2
Marketing	13.6	4.5	15.4	3.9	17.4	3.9	19.6	4.0	20.0	4.0
Accounting/Legal	2.0	0.7	2.4	0.6	2.6	0.6	2.8	0.6	2.9	0.6
Supplies	4.2	1.4	0.7	0.2	1.0	0.2	1.0	0.2	1.2	0.2
Repairs/Maintenance	1.4	0.5	1.8	0.5	2.1	0.5	2.4	0.5	2.8	0.6
Telephone	1.8	0.6	2.1	0.5	2.4	0.5	2.7	0.6	2.7	0.5
Bank Charges	0.3	0.1	0.3	0.1	0.6	0.1	0.7	0.1	0.8	0.2
Association/Chamber Dues	0.5	0.2	0.5	0.1	0.5	0.1	0.5	0.1	0.5	0.1
Auto	—	0.0	4.5	1.1	4.5	1.0	5.0	1.0	5.0	1.0
Depreciation	12.0	4.0	12.0	3.0	12.0	2.7	12.0	2.4	12.0	2.4
Miscellaneous Expenses	8.0	2.7	3.0	0.8	4.8	1.1	5.0	1.0	5.5	1.1
Total Operating Expenses	145.0	48.3	157.3	39.3	168.2	37.4	179.8	36.7	186.6	37.3
EBIT	50.0	16.7	102.7	25.7	124.7	27.7	138.7	28.3	138.4	27.7
Interest Income	0.6	0.2	1.2	0.3	1.2	0.3	2.0	0.4	2.0	0.4
Interest Expense	15.0	5.0	12.1	3.0	9.1	2.0	5.7	1.2	2.1	0.4
Earnings before Taxes	34.4	11.5	91.8	23.0	116.8	26.0	135.7	27.7	138.3	27.7
Add: Depreciation Expense	12.0	4.0	12.0	3.0	12.0	2.7	12.0	2.4	12.0	2.4
Cash From Operations	46.4	15.5	103.8	26.0	128.8	28.6	147.7	30.1	150.3	30.1
Debt Service	0	0.0	31.7	7.9	34.7	7.7	38.1	7.8	41.7	8.3
DISTRIBUTIONS	$46.4	15.5%	$72.1	18.0%	$94.1	20.9%	$109.6	22.4%	$108.6	21.7%

EXHIBIT 3

Pro Forma Financial Statement Assumptions 1997–2001

General: Projections are made on one store location in Gainesville, FL. The projections do not include additional store openings projected in the business plan. It appears that cash flow from first store operation is adequate for additional store(s) after Year 3. The timing of first store opening would affect the timing of the projections but would not adversely affect the revenues and expenses used in the forecast, only the timing.

Depreciation: Equipment purchased of $40,000 is depreciated over a five year life. Real Estate improvements and expenditures of $80,000 are depreciated over 31.5 years consistent with IRS tax depreciation laws.

Charitable/Advertising: Four Percent of sales after sales tax.

EBIT: Earnings Before Interest and Taxes

Interest Expense: Estimated at 9.25% applied to average outstanding debt balance.

Fixed Assets: Recorded at Historical Cost.

Debt Service: Initial borrowings of $275,000 at assumed rate of 9.25%. Payoff of debt service assumed to be made from internally generated funds and is forecasted to conclude in 2002. Extra funds will be used to pay off debt early.

EXHIBIT 4

Statistics for Gainesville, Florida

Gainesville (excluding students)	91,000
Area Population (Alachua County)	191,000
Total Labor Force	114,346
Cost of a Three Bedroom House	$82,000
Property Tax	$ 1,618
Retail Sales Tax (excluding food and medicine)	6%
State Personal Income Tax	0%
Franchise and Inventory Tax	0%
Unemployment	2.8%
Robberies/100,000	301
Annual Sunny Days	242
Mean Temperature (degrees F)	70.1
Average Sunshine/Day (hrs)	7.8
Annual Rainfall (inches)	49.9
Percent of population over 65	9.3%

Source: *Gainesville/Alachua County Community Overview 1994,* produced by The Council for Economic Outreach, Gainesville, Florida.

EXHIBIT 5

Area Population Trends

Year	Gainesville	Alachua County
1970	64,510	107,764
1980	81,370	151,369
1990	84,770	181,596
1995	91,000	191,000
2000	NA	208,900
2005	NA	221,600
2010	NA	233,900
2015	NA	245,200
2020	NA	256,200

Source: *Gainesville/Alachua County Demographics 1994,* produced by The Council for Economic Outreach, Gainesville, Florida.

EXHIBIT 6

Median Household Effective Buying Income Groups

Group	Gainesville (%)	Alachua County (%)	Florida (%)
Under $10,000	21.8	20.7	12.6
$10,000–19,999	20.6	19.7	18.0
$20,000–34,999	22.1	22.7	25.4
$35,000–49,999	14.2	15.1	18.8
$50,000–Over	21.3	21.8	25.2

Source: *Gainesville/Alachua County Demographics 1994,* produced by The Council for Economic Outreach, Gainesville, Florida.

EXHIBIT 7

Dipping Store Competitors in Gainesville

Store	Age	Employees	Sales
Dairy Queen	5 yrs	10–19	$500–1M
Dairy Queen	1	Unknown	Unknown
Baskin-Robbins	Pre 85	10–19	Less $500K
Baskin-Robbins	7	Unknown	Unknown
TCBY	10	5–9	$500–1M
TCBY	9	5–9	$500–1M
TCBY	5	5–9	Less $500K
Bresler's	5	5–9	Less $500K
Doug's Dairy Twirl	5	5–9	Less $500K
Fast Eddie's	7	1–4	Less $500K
Lauries Cafe	3	10–19	Less $500K
Lauries Cafe	2 months	Unknown	Unknown
Gator Ice Cream	1	5–9	Less $500K
Ice Cream Club	1	5–9	Less $500K
Real Italian Ice	Unknown	Unknown	Unknown

EXHIBIT 8

Revised Pro Forma Income Statement/Cash Flow Summary for the Years 1997–2001, Expected Scenario (in 000's)

	1997		1998		1999		2000		2001	
	$	% Sales	$	% Sales	$	% Sales	$	% Sales	$	% Sales
Sales	$340.0	100.0%	$385.0	100.0%	$435.0	100.0%	$490.0	100.0%	$500.0	100.0%
Cost of Sales	119.0	35.0	134.8	35.0	152.3	35.0	171.5	35.0	175.0	35.0
Gross Profit	221.0	65.0	250.3	65.0	282.8	65.0	318.5	65.0	325.0	65.0
Operational Expenses										
Employee Wages	46.9	13.8	52.0	13.5	57.6	13.3	64.9	13.3	66.8	13.4
Management Wages	30.0	8.8	31.5	8.2	33.1	7.6	34.8	7.1	36.5	7.3
Payroll Taxes	10.0	2.9	11.2	2.9	12.4	2.9	14.0	2.9	14.3	2.9
Worker Compensation	1.2	0.4	1.5	0.4	1.5	0.4	1.7	0.4	1.8	0.4
Health Insurance	3.0	0.9	3.3	0.9	3.6	0.8	3.9	0.8	4.2	0.8
Rent	37.5	11.0	39.3	10.2	41.4	9.5	43.5	8.9	45.6	9.1
Utilities	5.3	1.6	5.4	1.4	5.6	1.3	6.2	1.3	6.5	1.3
Prop/Liability Insurance	4.5	1.3	5.2	1.4	5.1	1.2	5.5	1.1	5.9	1.2
Marketing	13.6	4.0	15.4	4.0	17.4	4.0	19.6	4.0	20.0	4.0
Accounting/Legal	2.0	0.6	2.4	0.6	2.6	0.6	2.8	0.6	2.9	0.6
Supplies	4.2	1.2	0.7	0.2	1.0	0.2	1.0	0.2	1.2	0.2
Repairs/Maintenance	1.4	0.4	1.8	0.5	2.1	0.5	2.4	0.5	2.8	0.6
Telephone	1.8	0.5	2.1	0.5	2.4	0.6	2.7	0.6	2.7	0.5
Bank Charges	0.3	0.1	0.3	0.1	0.6	0.1	0.7	0.1	0.8	0.2
Association/Chamber Dues	0.5	0.1	0.5	0.1	0.5	0.1	0.5	0.1	0.5	0.1
Auto	—	0.0	4.5	1.2	4.5	1.0	5.0	1.0	5.0	1.0
Depreciation	12.0	3.5	12.0	3.1	12.0	2.8	12.0	2.4	12.0	2.4
Miscellaneous Expenses	8.0	2.4	3.0	0.8	4.8	1.1	5.0	1.0	5.5	1.1
Total Operating Expenses	181.5	53.4	192.9	50.1	217.7	50.0	226.6	46.2	234.3	46.9
EBIT	39.5	11.6	57.4	14.9	74.6	17.1	91.8	18.7	90.7	18.1
Interest Income	0.6	0.2	1.2	0.3	1.2	0.3	2.0	0.4	2.0	0.4
Interest Expense	10.9	3.2	9.6	2.5	8.2	1.9	6.7	1.4	5.0	1.0
Earnings before Taxes	29.0	8.5	49.0	12.7	67.6	15.5	87.1	17.8	87.8	17.6
Add: Depreciation Expenses	12.0	3.5	12.0	3.1	12.0	2.8	12.0	2.4	12.0	2.4
Cash From Operations	41.0	12.1	61.0	15.8	79.6	18.3	99.1	20.2	99.8	20.0
Debt Service	0	0.0	12.7	3.3	13.9	3.2	15.3	3.1	16.8	3.4
DISTRIBUTIONS	$41.0	12.1%	$48.3	12.5%	$65.7	15.1%	$83.8	17.1%	$83.0	16.6%

EXHIBIT 9

Barney Harris's Partnership Proposal

Short-term goal:	1 Store by Fall 1996
Long-term goal:	5 Stores
Incorporation:	Limited Liability Corporation
My Investment:	$100,000 with $5,000 going to equity in the company and $95,000 as a loan to the company. The loan would be repaid off in the next five years. I would receive quarterly interest at the prime rate for the loan. Also I would like to increase my equity position to 49% of the company.
Scoop Shop Operations:	Terry Smith agrees to spend 100% of his time operating the store.
Book Work:	I would like to have my accountant do all of the book work. Her fees are as follows: $2,000 to set up the books and $600/month thereafter, not including franchise reports, budgets, and forecasts.
Buy Out Arrangement:	I would like to propose three times the cash flow of the business, averaged over the number of years we are in business. This figure would then be divided by our ownership percentages. For example, if our partnership developed cash flows of $100,000/year and you wanted to purchase my interest, we would multiply the $100,000 times three for $300,000 times my ownership percentage of .49, meaning the purchase price would be $147,000.

EXHIBIT 10

Expected Proposal from Harris

Short-term goal:	1 Store by fall 1996
Long-term goal:	5 Stores
Incorporation:	Limited Liability Corporation
Your Investment:	Harris's investment would be $100,000 with $100,000 going towards a 33% equity position. The other $120,000 will be obtained through an SBA loan. All debt service must be current prior to distributions paid out to partners. The expansion of future stores will occur at a later date.
Scoop Shop Operations:	All day-to-day operations will be performed by Smith.
Book Work:	Smith will do the book work and have a payroll service do the taxes.
Buy Out Arrangement:	Two formulas will be used to estimate the value of the company:

Price-to-Sales
Discounted Cash Flow

Purchase price will be repaid over a five year period while the seller holds the note to the debt. The loan will be repaid on a quarterly basis at the current prime rate for that quarter (as quoted in the *Wall Street Journal*). I also propose that we each have a first right of refusal of our stock and neither party has the right to sell until after three years.

Earthlink.net: The Journey to Recognizing an Opportunity

In 1998, at 26 years old, Sky Dayton was listed on the Forbes "High Tech's 100 Wealthiest"—the third-youngest person ever to make the list. The company that he started in 1994, Earthlink®, had grown to nearly $175 million after an initial public offering in January 1997, which left Dayton with 14.3 percent of a company with a $1.8 billion market capitalization. In September 1999, Earthlink merged with Mind-Spring to become the number two Internet service provider after America Online (AOL).

Having no desire to remain in such a large organization, the young entrepreneur formed another company, eCompanies, in June 1999 with former Disney executive Jake Winebaum. E-Companies is an Internet start-up incubator that succeeded in raising $130 million in sixty days to create a venture fund. The dot com implosion led to a strategic change in the company and provided an important lesson to two entrepreneurs. How Sky Dayton began the journey that led to the creation of Earthlink is the subject of this case study.

The Early Years

Sky Dayton grew up with computers. With an interest that was sparked by his grandfather, an IBM fellow, he began hacking around writing programs and games at age 9. His first computer was a Timex Sinclair ZX-81, a "beast of a machine," as he recalls. It contained 1K of RAM and used a small black-and-white TV as its monitor. At Christmas that year, he received a 16MB upgrade kit, and he recalls that he actually had to program his games before he could play them. Then, when he turned off the computer, the program was lost, and he had to rewrite it before he could play the game again.

Dayton attended high school at the prestigious Delphi Academy in Oregon where at 15 he apprenticed at a computer animation shop. Upon graduation in 1988 at the age of 16, he was hired by an advertising firm in Hollywood where he worked his way into managing their computer graphics. Dayton did that for two years, but he had a burning desire to own his own business. He really liked the idea of getting strangers together to communicate and interact, so the logical business to start was a coffee house. In 1990, with an initial investment from his grandmother of $20,000, he founded Café Mocha in West Los Angeles on Melrose and ran it for a year.

Meanwhile, Dayton never lost his fascination and amazement with technology. In 1992, he decided that he was ready to open his own graphics design firm, Dayton Walker, to serve entertainment industry clients like Disney and Universal Studios.

In 1993, Dayton heard about the Internet and tried to find out more about it. Unfortunately, no one seemed to know anything. He could not find a business in Los Angeles with the word *Internet* in it. After much searching, Dayton managed to find a small service provider in San Diego who let him sign up after he claimed to be a UCLA student. Two days later, he received a list of instructions for how to connect to the Internet. Frustration overtook Dayton as he tried to get himself linked. It took about eighty hours to get online and figure everything out. Needless to say, it was a humbling experience. Yet, for reasons that he can't explain, a light went on in his head and he was sure that "this is probably the world's next communications medium, and somebody's got to make it easier."[1] He dropped everything he was doing and decided in that moment that he would be the one to make it possible for people to get connected to the Internet easily and quickly. Once, when asked if he was a technologist who built erector sets or an entrepreneur who sold lemonade, he replied, "I was out there selling erector sets."[2] He only sells what he builds.

Dayton first thought to create software to connect his customers and played with a program of his

---

This case is intended to be used as the basis for class discussion rather than as an illustration of either effective or ineffective handling of the situation.

[1] "Earth + Sky," http://www.zdnet.com/zdtv/thesite/0397w5/iview/iview442_032597.html, March 25, 1997.
[2] Biley Andrion, E. (1999). "The Accelerators." *The Zone News* (Oct.).

own design called "Internet Navigator." Then he called his ISP in San Diego to talk about his concept. The ISP told him simply that the Internet had already peaked and there was no opportunity there. This was in 1993.

A Brief History of Internet Time

In 1993, when Sky Dayton was contemplating starting a company that would make it possible for anyone to connect to the Internet easily and quickly, there were no World Wide Web sites on the Internet. The roots of the Web actually go back to the early 1960s in an obscure U.S. government research project, ARPA, the Advanced Research Projects Agency. The purpose of ARPA was to respond to the Russian launch of Sputnik in the late 1950s, which completely surprised the U.S. military, and put the United States on an equal footing with the Russians. It was essentially a command and control center or network for information about U.S. troop movements around the globe. Over time it became a network that allowed "host" computers in various locations (government and universities) to communicate with each other.

Between 1960 and 1990, the government invested $2 billion in a network of routers that created the Internet's backbone. Until the early 1980s, it was a classified system used only by academicians and scientists. There was no commercial content available. But many groups of scientists and computer types were beginning to see the potential of the Internet and looking for ways to increase its connectivity and user friendliness.

In the early 1990s, Cisco Systems bet on TCP/IP and Ethernet-based systems as the world standard for the new Internet, and, as a result, it experienced explosive growth. When Microsoft Corporation released Windows 3.0, Corporate America began rapidly expanding its networking capability. The development of the World Wide Web—a standard and graphical interface for accessing and sharing information—ignited the spark of popular interest in the Internet. While Corporate America was busy doing business on the Internet, the public was being introduced to it through proprietary online services with information, news, mail, software, games and other user-friendly applications. AOL and Compuserve became common brands. By 1997, however, AOL had

claimed the number one spot with fifteen million subscribers and eventually bought out Compuserve. But this was only the tip of the iceberg.

In 1992, a young hacker by the name of Marc Andreessen with his partner, Eric Bina, hacked out what was to be the first nonproprietary Internet browser, Mosaic. It was simple and logical and could display graphics automatically. For the first time, a web page looked like a magazine page instead of a computer page. They made it available free as a download in the spring of 1993, and within a month, they had distributed more than one million copies.

The potential of Mosaic was not lost on Silicon Graphics co-founder, Jim Clark. He contacted Andreessen, and the two decided to produce a commercial version of the Mosaic browser. Mosaic Communications was started in April 1994 and renamed Netscape later that year. Netscape benefited from the fact that by 1994 the Internet had reached critical mass; that is, enough people knew about it and appreciated its benefits that it was poised to explode. Netscape was there to create the explosion.

In June 1993, there were no web sites on the Internet. By June 1996, there were 200,000, and, by September 1997, there were 1,400,000 web sites and 25 million host computers.[3]

The Birth of Earthlink

Sky Dayton was determined to become part of the new Internet revolution. In 1994, he sold his stake in Dayton Walker and began writing a business plan to seek investors for his new Internet connection concept. With no experience or knowledge of how to go about writing a business plan, he decided to approach the task logically. Few people knew much about the Internet, so if he was going to get investors to understand his business concept, he had to bring them up to speed on the Internet. In about ten pages, he described the Internet and its huge potential as a communication medium. Then he talked about how he was going to make it easier for people to connect and use it. He figured he needed $100,000 to get the business up and running and 600 customers to break even.

---

[3]The Internet Society, http://www.isoc.org/.

Follow the Money

Dayton began talking to everyone he knew about his dream. Finally, the father of one of his boarding school friends, who was prominent in technology at that time, agreed to fund the venture in exchange for 40 percent of the company, and Earthlink was born in the spring of 1994. Feeling the burden of responsibility for his new investor, Dayton kept his overhead as low as possible. He focused his limited resources where they counted most—on the customer. His goal was to provide a trouble-free way to connect, superior technical support, and the highest levels of customer service. He charged $19.95 for unlimited access. On the first day in business, a potential customer called and signed up. Dayton didn't know what information to get from the customer, so he asked for the usual: name, address, and phone number. He then realized that he had no procedures in place. He dashed out and bought Quickbooks® to manage the money, and that's the way the business began.

The Growth Phase

Relatively quickly, Earthlink began to grow, and Dayton secured $75,000 for another 15 percent of the company. By 1996, the company was growing so fast that Dayton could barely keep up. With rapid growth came the usual problems. They frequently experienced what he calls "power meltdown." So much demand on the electrical system caused it to fail quickly and regularly, so he rented a backup diesel generator, parked it in the back of the building, and used it to run the power for the business when normal power went down. Dayton recalls one catastrophe that could have cost him the company. Today he jokingly refers to that time as the "Valentine's Day Massacre of 1996." The mother of all nightmares occurred when the entire database, including all their billing systems, failed. To add insult to injury, the backup device refused to load. The system was down for two long days. They had to fly in a database expert from San Diego who managed to recover 90 percent of the lost data and return operations to normal within forty-eight hours. After that, Dayton put systems in place so the problem would not happen again. His philosophy is that he never wants to solve the same problem twice.

It was easy to see that Earthlink had grown to the point where it needed professional management. It was no longer a one-man show. Dayton knew the value of hiring the best, so he brought on board Garry Betty, the youngest CEO on the NYSE as president and CEO of Digital Communications. Betty provided the balance that was needed because he was more conservative than Dayton in his business approach. Other executives were also recruited. Dayton's strategy was to hire from the top and let the company grow into its professional management. Soon, it was clear that Dayton was beginning to work himself out of a job. He assembled a professional board of directors and gave up more control.

With Dayton supplying the vision, and Betty at the controls, EarthLink grew from $3 million in revenues in 1995 to almost $175 million in 1998, a 5,700 percent increase. In 1997, Earthlink floated an initial public offering and soon thereafter achieved a market capitalization of about $1.8 billion. The company had gone from one person to about 2,300 in five years.

The Merger of Minds

MindSpring is a company that was born about the same time as Earthlink—actually, thirty days apart—with a similar pattern of growth and frustration. In September 1999, the two announced a synergistic merger that made the combo the number two ISP after AOL. The Earthlink brand would be the brand for the newly merged company. Dayton relinquished the chairman role to MindSpring founder Charles Brewer and retained a seat on the board. It was time for a new challenge.

The Birth of eCompanies

In 1997, about two years prior to the founding of eCompanies in 1999, Dayton met Jake Winebaum, chairman of Disney's Buena Vista Internet Group at an *LA Times* Roundtable. What sparked their mutual interest was not the Internet, but snowboarding. Both were avid snowboarders, and they quickly agreed to meet for some snowboarding. Over about a dozen snowboarding adventures, they got to know each other and began to discuss the possibility of some deals between Disney and Earthlink and also to look at the potential for the Internet. In May 1995,

Winebaum surprised Dayton with the news that he was leaving Disney. The two went to a local taco stand to discuss the news.

> So about three bites into an enchilada, Jake springs on me that he's thinking of leaving Disney and that he has an idea for a company he wanted to start. And here's a guy that I had known for a couple of years and that I had watched, [and] pretty much, at the time, was probably the most recruited CEO in the industry. He turned down every single job, from Geocities to, you know, you name it. Anyway . . . I was pretty impressed that he was willing to move on after building a multi-million dollar enterprise at Disney. About five bites into that enchilada, Jake said something that really impressed me. And this is Jake's line: that the Internet is only really 20% invented. And it really resonated with me. I had a lot of ideas that I wanted to do. About seven or eight bites into the enchilada—we don't exactly know where . . . it was somewhat of a blurry moment—but the idea of eCompanies was formed. And instead of starting one company or each of us starting another company, we decided to start a company that would start companies.[4]

And so eCompanies became a reality. Dayton and Winebaum decided to start the company in Los Angeles because they had both built companies there before; there was no shortage of talent or creativity. And most importantly, there was no shortage of capital. Southern California is considered by many to be the digital media industry leader because of its vigorous market at the center of global entertainment.

Located in Santa Monica near the ocean, eCompanies is a different kind of incubator for Internet ventures. It's known as an accelerator because of the speed at which it produces a new e-business—from concept to market in less than 180 days. Dayton and Winebaum, along with their senior vice president of strategy, came up with most of the ideas. Once they approve an idea, they take the business plan to their chief financial officer who builds budgets and generally takes care of all the financial issues related to

running the company and compensating those who work in it.

It is the job of the senior vice president of people to recruit and put together great teams, while the creative director oversees the creation of the web site. They build the user-interface first and then it goes to the chief technology officer who assembles all the back-end pieces. The senior vice president of marketing puts together a plan for creating customer awareness. The whole process takes 90 to 180 days.

Once the fledgling company is in the market, it has the potential to be funded by eCompanies Venture Group, which was formed by two venture partners they brought down from San Francisco who were experienced private equity venture investors. They put together eleven major limited partners and raised $130 million in less than sixty days. Dayton and Winebaum made sure that their investor partners could contribute expertise as well as money, so they included Sun America, Sprint, Disney, and Goldman Sachs, to name a few. eCompanies' first start-up, e-parties.com, launched on October 4, 1999 after only 100 days in incubation.

Epilogue

December 2000, eighteen months after the launch of eCompanies and the dot com bust of April 2000, none of eCompanies' incubatees had gone public. Many had simply died, or, like eParties, were sold for virtually nothing to other dot coms. So, the company that started with a flourish in 1999 was getting out of the Internet incubator business. Dayton and Winebaum shifted their focus to a newly formed wireless incubator, which was being developed in partnership with Sprint. Venture capitalists attributed the failure to unfortunate timing, hubris on the part of the founders, and the fact that the company focused on launching concepts rather than real businesses with a technological advantage of making things better, faster, or cheaper.

As of January 2002, Jake Winebaum was nursing Business.com (www.business.com), a business portal whose domain name cost the company $7.5 million, and Sky Dayton was doing the same with a wireless start-up called Boingo Wireless Internet Service (www.boingo,com). Both call the struggling eCompanies home along with two other companies, Jamdat (www.jamdat.com), a video gaming company,

---

[4]Biley Andrion E. (1999). "The Accelerators." *The Zone News* (Oct.).

and USBX (www.usbx.com), a financial services exchange. For anyone looking at incubators for accelerating start-up, the question remains, is there a viable future for business accelerators?

DISCUSSION QUESTIONS

1. How did Sky Dayton recognize the Earthlink opportunity and what steps did he take to exploit his opportunity?

2. What were some of the good decisions Dayton made when he began to grow Earthlink? Did he make any poor decisions? What were they and why?

3. Evaluate the benefits and effectiveness of incubators for accelerating the start-up of a new venture. In the light of the dot com debacle, is there still a role for incubators in the start-up process?

4. Given the experience and knowledge of Sky Dayton and Jake Winebaum, what would you advise that they do next?

RESOURCES

Bransten, L. (2001). "Danger Isn't Sharing Plans for Hand-Held Technology." *The Wall Street Journal* (May 14).

Brinsley, J. (2000). "Cyber Scrambling for Survival." *Los Angeles Business Journal* (Dec. 18).

Kumar, V. (2000). "eCompanies Lays Off 10, Refocuses on Wireless Deals." *The Industry Standard* (Dec. 7).

USC Entrepreneur of the Year (1999). Personal interview, video.

Highland Dragon

A true entrepreneur, Richard Fowler has relied on his strong network of people throughout the world, his experience and business knowledge, and his "sixth sense" of being able to recognize the time and the place for an opportunity. His goal of becoming independent, both professionally and financially, was realized early on in his career. But, his entrepreneurial sense of adventure and his yearning for new and exciting challenges continues on.

Growing up in Australia, Richard Fowler had aspirations of becoming a surgeon at an early age. However, he quickly dispelled the idea upon realizing the amount of study and schooling it would take. As a young man, he was restless and determined to get his life started. At the advice of his father, he decided to go into business. Fowler's father, Richard Fowler Senior, was a man who had worked his way up from being a fisherman to starting and running the largest and most successful fishing cooperative, South Australia Fishing Cooperative Limited (SAFCO). Fishing cooperatives were groups of fisherman in underdeveloped nations who joined together to be able to process and market their fish. Richard Fowler Senior was one of the most well-known men in the fishing industry and had developed ties with nearly every fishery in the world. He was an extremely hard-working man who believed in knowing every aspect of his business. He was the younger Fowler's biggest role model.

At age 18, Fowler started working at his father's company full-time. But, unlike most bosses' sons, he started at the very bottom. He began by offloading fish trucks, emptying trash, filleting fish, and cooking lobster. Working in various types of positions helped him earn the respect of other employees. He was, however, being groomed to take over the business and he worked his way up quickly through the different departments. In addition to working in a variety of positions, Fowler also spent a great deal of time overseas working with some of SAFCO's buyers and affiliates, including Van De Kamps and Chicken of the Sea. He worked in Africa, Europe, and North America getting to know both the people and the business inside and out.

By 1971, at age 29, Fowler was heading up the export department. He recalls that his salary was up for review. One week prior to the board meeting, he told the board members that he did not want another raise. Frustrated by the high tax rate, 66 percent at the time, he refused to give another penny of his salary to the government. In addition to the heavy taxes, he was becoming increasingly dissatisfied with the politics, the unions, and the attitude of the government. It was at this time he realized that he had put himself into a corner and he had to decide if he would stay and try to battle with the politics or leave the firm. He chose to leave.

The Industry

The seafood industry certainly isn't a glamorous one and not generally an area in which you'd expect to make millions. However, due to increased demand, the world fish and shellfish supply has doubled since 1965 (Exhibit 1). The United States only produces about 6 percent of the world supply and relies heavily on importing, particularly from Canada, Thailand, and China.

Imported seafood makes up more than half of the seafood consumed by Americans, with the majority of it being shrimp and tuna (Exhibit 2).[1] Approximately 1,000 companies currently import seafood into the United States. In 1998, these firms purchased more than 1.6 million tons of seafood valued at $8.2 billion making the United States the second largest seafood import market in the world.[2]

In 1998, after three years of decline, per capita consumption of seafood increased to 14.9 pounds

This case is intended to be used as the basis for class discussion rather than as an illustration of either effective or ineffective handling of the situation. This case was written by Barbara Plamondon, MBA University of Southern California. Reprinted by permission.

[1] H.M. Johnson & Associates (1998). "1998 Highlights." In *The 1999 Annual Report on the United States Seafood Industry,* http://www.hmj.com/highlights.html.
[2] National Fisheries Institute. "About Our Industry, Importing." http://www.nfi.org/industr5.html.

primarily due to a 0.3-pound increase in canned tuna. Americans consume more tuna than any other type of seafood (3.5 pounds per person per year) followed by shrimp (3.0 pounds per person per year).[3]

The Opportunity

In January 1972, Richard Fowler left Australia to travel to Asia. Having experienced many different cultures throughout the world, he found that he loved the attitude and the feeling of Asia. He felt there were plenty of opportunities for someone like himself trying to make his way in the world. He left his wife and two young daughters in Australia while he went to Indonesia, Singapore, Ceylon (now Sri Lanka), and China. He wasn't sure what he was going to do, but he was looking for a place that had little government involvement, good communication, and a strong financial system. He found all of these in Hong Kong. He believed that it was the most entrepreneurial location at that time. It had a strong banking system, an excellent location for transportation, easy communication, no government interference and *no taxes*!

Looking around for potential business, Fowler decided to stick to what he knew best, seafood. This is where he found his golden opportunity. What he found was that the United States had been trying to import fish from Asia with great difficulty. In the early 1970s, communication was very poor and very slow between the two continents. It was before the days of the fax machine, and telephone calls had to be booked twenty-four hours in advance. In order to purchase the seafood from Asia, Americans had to have their banks issue them a letter of credit that was sent to the Asian bank. Then, approximately one month later they would receive their shipment—if they were lucky. More often than not the quality of the seafood would be poor, not up to the size or weight of American standards. There were problems with the freezing and shipping. Often the product went bad. And, sometimes the Americans would open their newly shipped crate only to find dirt or rocks. So for Fowler, who was already very knowl-

edgeable in the fish export business and had excellent contacts throughout the United States, there was definitely an opportunity. If he could purchase the seafood from the Asian fisheries, inspect the product, and insure timely and quality delivery, he was sure that he could get the American companies to buy from him. He was right. Several of his America contacts enthusiastically agreed to buy the fish through him for a premium over what they had been paying. He then discovered a fishery in Thailand that he found was bringing in quality product and had people with whom he felt he could trust. Now, with Americans waiting to buy from him and the Thai fishery waiting to sell, his business was set. There was only one problem: he only had $2,200 to his name.

Without any money, Fowler realized that he would have to try to obtain a letter of credit from a Chinese bank based on his idea alone. With an American company willing to purchase a shipment of shrimp for $100,000 and the Thai company willing to sell the shipment for $90,000, there was definitely money to be made. However, the restrictions and regulations put into place by the Chinese banks were keeping him from realizing his dream. Then one night he was attending a party with a number of bankers. He met the only other English-speaking person in the room, a British man who worked at the Bank of Hong Kong. Fowler told him his idea and that night the British banker asked him what he could do to get his business. The next day Fowler pulled his pending letter of credit from the bank he was trying to deal with and met with the Bank of Hong Kong. Upon receipt of the American company's letter of credit, they issued a letter of credit to the Thai company's bank and the business was born.

The First Business

Judric was an instant success. The company name came from the first three letters of his wife's name, Judy, and the first three letters of his name. He soon had many willing buyers and suppliers. He moved his family to an apartment in Hong Kong and started to grow his business. He measured his success by the first million Hong Kong dollars he earned—about $200,000 U.S. dollars at the time, which was around August 1973, eighteen months after he had started his adventure. Much of his time was spent inspecting

---

[3]H.M. Johnson & Associates (1998). "1998 Highlights." In *The 1999 Annual Report on the United States Seafood Industry*, http://www. hmj.com/highlights.html.

potential suppliers throughout Asia. Fowler really felt the need to examine the product he was purchasing by doing physical inspections of the amount and quality of the fish being caught before going into business with the supplier. In addition to this, he relied heavily on face-to-face interviews with the company owners to get a feel for their honesty and ethics. He felt that knowing and respecting the Asian culture was essential in gaining their trust and compliance. One country he felt had a great deal of potential as a source of seafood was Vietnam. In fact, one of his buyers from the Liberty Fish Company in Philadelphia received a telex from Saigon telling him of the product there. Of course, at this time the Vietnam War was being fought so communication and organization were difficult. Fowler went to Saigon to see if there was any possibility of doing business there. He met up with two discharged American army men who were working for Sealand Shipping Company. They were "wheeler dealers" in the true sense of the word and eager to make some extra money. They agreed to send him the fish at an extremely low rate—particularly because they were using Sealand's containers to ship him the fish, unbeknownst to Sealand. Fowler found that in many of these countries business was carried out by the law of jungle. Businesses and governments alike could easily turn their heads on laws and regulations for the right price. This reinforced something that his father had taught him at an early age—not to be quick to trust anyone.

The Next Opportunity

When Vietnam fell in 1975, his two business associates left the country in search of new opportunities. It wasn't long before one of them, Tony Curatolo, was calling Fowler with a new possibility. He had heard that in the Philippines local fishermen were catching about ten tons of tuna per day. Fowler, knowing that Curatolo was the right man to really feel out the local people, sent him to the Philippines. There he got to know the Filipinos and built up good relationships. He confirmed that sometimes as much as ten tons of tuna a day was coming into the local market. However, the locals only purchased about five tons a day. After that, the price of the tuna plummeted because there simply wasn't enough demand. Fowler followed Curatolo to the Philippines and spoke with

the local fisherman. Knowing that they could catch not only the five tons that the locals demanded, but an additional ten tons, they agreed to sell to Fowler at an extremely low rate.

By late 1976 Fowler had built the first tuna cannery in the Philippines, Pacific Fisheries. Again he turned to the knowledge and advice of his father to get started. His father not only had the technical knowledge of how to start and run a cannery, but he also sent him a number of people from Thailand. With the assistance of his father's guidance and knowledge, Thailand had become the largest canner of tuna in the world. The Philippines soon took over the number two position, quickly surpassing the United States and Japan. Fowler had found a location that not only provided him an inexpensive price for tuna and cheap labor, but through Curatolo's relationships and with the assistance of a young local lawyer they had taken on, he managed to get the government to agree not to charge the company any taxes. Like Judric, Pacific Fisheries immediately became a huge success for Fowler.

A Fish Out of Water

In 1981, with his two growing daughters in mind, Fowler decided he needed to move out of Hong Kong because it offered very limited education in the upper grades for English-speaking students. Along with that decision, he also decided to sell the tuna cannery in the Philippines. He describes the combination of the move and the sale of Pacific Fisheries as the single worst business decision he has ever made. He sold the business to an Australian company and within two years the cannery was bankrupt. He attributes the failure of the cannery to the fact that the Australian firm started hiring union labor. Fowler had gone to great lengths to keep the union out of his business because in the Philippines the Communist party backed it. He felt that they intentionally tried to disrupt big businesses so that the government could come in and take over.

From Hong Kong the Fowlers moved to Honolulu and then Seattle looking for new opportunities. By 1988, communication between the continents had become much more advanced and trade was becoming so easy that literally anyone could sell seafood across continents. The benefits he had enjoyed—his strong network, his ability to communicate and negotiate with different cultures, and his industry knowledge—no longer gave him an attractive enough advantage over the competitors. His margins were shrinking fast and in 1989 he decided to close both the Los Angeles and Hong Kong offices of Judric.

For the ten years of relatively stagnant business, Fowler had lost a lot of incentive to use his entrepreneurial know-how, although he did invest in other companies during this time. In 1982 his father left SAFCO after it was sold to a new firm. Together they opened up Dover Fisheries in Australia, another cannery business. With Fowler funding the venture and his father running it, Dover became the biggest cannery in Australia at the time and was an excellent investment. He also got involved with a start-up company in Washington, Acorto, which makes fully automated expresso machines. The machines are used in airports, malls, and restaurants, such as McDonalds. Fowler was fully financing this project as well, and it was successful. However, the machines were extremely expensive and a lot of money needed to be put into marketing the product. He recently took on a partner in Washington with "very deep pockets" and turned over 80 percent of his stake in the company. At this point, Fowler, while obviously living an extremely comfortable life, still felt as if something was missing. He needed a challenge and an adventure in his life.

Highland Dragon: The New Adventure

In 1996 Fowler got a call from Gil Watts. Watts was one of the two ex-Army guys that he had worked with in Vietnam. Watts had returned to Vietnam in 1989 and had become one of the first American investors in that country when he started a fish farm. But, when Watts told him of the great opportunities in Vietnam since Clinton ended the trade embargo in 1994, Fowler decided to investigate. What he found was a country that had some of the hardest and best workers he had seen. He also admired their open-mindedness, a trait he felt was rare in Asian countries. So once again he looked to the fishing business. He checked the fishing ports several times a day and found they were bringing in a great deal of tuna. He checked through maps of the sea and the fish migration routes and found that there was definitely potential. In 1998 Fowler began building a tuna cannery in

Vietnam. Highland Dragon, as it was named, began as a partnership between Fowler and Watts. Fowler was completely funding the venture while Watts was to oversee it in Vietnam. They went in together as equal partners, which Fowler admits was generous since he was financing the company and doing all of the marketing, but he felt that due to their past relationship it was fair. However, the partnership didn't last and Fowler was forced to seek an attorney to find the best way of ending the partnership.

One positive outcome was an introduction to a Mr. Thanh, who, in a country bogged down with red tape and corruption, had a way of getting things done. For instance, Fowler discovered he needed to speak with the governor of Hanoi about some aspect of his business, a process that would typically take months—particularly for a foreigner. He called Mr. Thanh from the United States and asked him if he would set up a meeting as soon as possible. Mr. Thanh was a bit worried because it was Saturday in Vietnam and the governor wouldn't be in his office until Monday, but he said he would see what he could do. One hour later Fowler received a call back. They were to meet the governor at 9:00 Monday morning. Mr. Thanh had called him at home. Highland Dragon employees had great respect for Mr. Thanh and his hard work and honesty. As a result, Fowler made him the new general director, the position Watts once held.

Mr. Fowler is optimistic about the future of his new business. Once again his network of business associates has paid off. He called up old contacts that he hadn't spoken with in ten years and they were all eager to buy fish from Highland Dragon. U.S. canneries have recently been turning away tuna because they have all they can handle.[4] The Asian fish export business is looking better and better since labor is cheap and U.S. and worldwide consumption are up. In particular, Fowler loves the entrepreneurial feeling of Vietnam, which is somewhat reminiscent of Hong Kong in the early seventies.

However, there are also many obstacles ahead. The price of tuna is now the lowest it has been since 1966.[5] Asian firms are eager to sell to the booming

---

[4]"Asian Tuna Floods Canneries, Leaving U.S. Fleet in the Lurch." *The New York Times* (Sept. 6).
[5]Bair, J. (2000). "Too Much Tuna Cuts into Earnings." *The Associated Press* (Sept. 18).

U.S. economy, particularly with the decline in the Japanese economy. There has also been controversy about over-fishing and insuring that the tuna boats are dolphin-free. The high premiums Fowler enjoyed with his first ventures will now be unrealistic with the low prices and the large number of players in the market.

DISCUSSION QUESTIONS

1. How did Richard Fowler recognize the opportunity that led to the founding of Judric?

2. What expertise and experience did Fowler bring to the opportunity?

3. What caused Fowler to decide to close the offices of Judric in 1989, and what impact did that have on his entrepreneurial career?

4. What was the source of the opportunity for Highland Dragon?

5. What role did Mr. Thanh play in the success of Highland Dragon?

6. Given the declining price of tuna and the controversy surrounding over-fishing, where should Fowler take the business, and why?

EXHIBIT 1

World Fish and Shellfish Supply 1965–1996

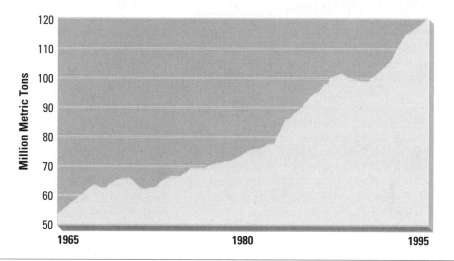

EXHIBIT 2

Leading U.S. Seafood Imports 1996–1997

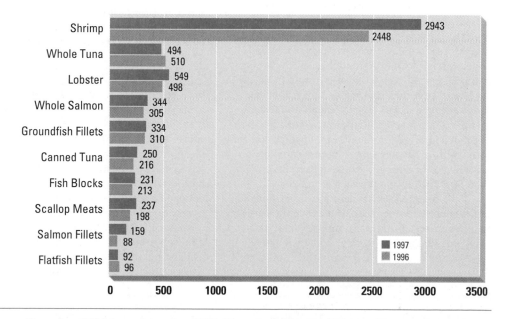

Figures from H.M. Johnson & Associates (1998). "About Our Industry." In *1998 Annual Report on the United States Seafood Industry,* National Fisheries Institute web page, http://www.nfi.org/industr5.html.

Roland International Freight Service

Roland International Freight Services (RIFS) was established in November 1991 as a privately owned, full-service transportation company geared toward providing reliable and dependable services to meet the domestic and international transportation needs of both importers and exporters. RIFS handles shipments by air, ocean, and multi-modal transportation in and out of the United States with a network of agents in sixty-two countries. The freight-forwarding business is a $30 billion industry. RIFS is a minor player in this industry, yet very successful because it focuses on areas that other freight forwarders either neglect or avoid.

Background

Roland Furtado started working in the shipping business on June 2, 1979. His aim in life was to become a pilot or an artist; however, after spending considerable time and effort in Kuwait and learning the freight business from the expatriates there, he soon found himself enamored with a business he did not want to abandon. Furtado's foray into entrepreneurship came about when a Taiwanese shipping company, for which he was working as a commissioned forwarder, released him because it was strapped for cash as a result of the crash in the Asian stock market. It then dawned on him that he had built a strong network base of clients and had the acumen to "go it alone." Rather than work as a commissioned forwarder for another individual company, Furtado made the decision to become an independent freight forwarder because he saw this challenge as an opportunity and pursued it.

While working for a freight forwarder, Furtado had studied the value chain of the freight forwarding business and realized that commission-based transactions provided greater margins and flexibility when negotiating contracts. The primary function of the freight forwarder is rather simple: forward freight from its source to its destination. Salespeople in this industry typically work on salary because the margins are small. They are expected to generate a gross profit three and a half times the amount of their salary. Furtado used this knowledge to become the first person to work solely on commission, making more money than his general manager at the time. Understanding the industry and constantly looking for "angles in the market" eventually let Furtado find a niche in the market in which to start a business.

Early on, Furtado understood that he possessed strong selling skills. "I never sell a rate to my customers. I sell a relationship!"[1] Furtado's early awareness of the need to build contacts, coupled with the skills he had refined in the freight forwarding industry over two decades, influenced him to start his business. Furthermore, he had built a client list and that also gave him the confidence to leave the security of a steady paycheck. Unlike other entrepreneurs who spend countless hours researching businesses and industries to find direction and opportunity for an innovation, Furtado was in the wrong place, at the wrong time, with the *right* mentality.

From Opportunity to Business

In November 1991, with little more than $100 to his name, Furtado borrowed $3,000 from a friend, rented an office in Westchester, Illinois, got his insurance bonding, and filed the required paperwork with the Maritime Commission. Furtado made a number of sacrifices to assure that success would come to his business. He "put his life on hold for this job."[2] As a bonded freight forwarder, Furtado began Roland International Freight Service (RIFS) by nurturing past relationships. He called upon the clients who knew him well from his tenure at other freight forwarders and assured them that they would receive quality service. One of the greatest assets of RIFS, which

---

This case is intended to be used as the basis for class discussion rather than as an illustration of either effective or ineffective handling of the situation. This case was written by Alexander N. Alvy, MBA, University of Southern California. Reprinted by permission.

[1]Interview with Roland Furtado (September 16, 2000). Roland International Freight Service, Westchester, IL.
[2]Ibid.

didn't appear on the balance sheet, was something that he had been building over the years: trust. Clients who had worked with Furtado trusted him more than the company for which he worked, because they interfaced primarily with him. In some cases, clients would soon forget with which business they were dealing, but would never forget Furtado.

As a small freight forwarder, Roland had the advantage of offering flexibility to his customers. Larger organizations that could reap the benefits of economies of scale were limited by the bureaucracy, structure, and protocol of their organizations. RIFS was small and more able to offer personal attention to clients who valued a service orientation. For example, RIFS offers consolidation services to customers purchasing a variety of goods from multiple suppliers.

The largest problem RIFS faced early on in 1992 was a lack of cash flow. Furtado had built his small office from the loan of a friend and had to manage the movement of every business dollar so that he would not become insolvent. In so doing, Furtado engaged in activities that could drive a business owner mad. For instance, since he could not afford to hire a staff, Furtado did all of the work himself with the exception of one apprentice, Joey. He felt that he could not delegate the administrative work to Joey because he did not want to run the risk of upsetting a single customer or of hurting any relationship he had spent years building.

Furtado was able to improve his cash flow situation by solving operational inefficiencies. For example, many freight forwarders ran up inventory costs by warehousing cargoes. By contrast, Furtado invested the time to negotiate contracts with clients to keep cargo with them as long as they could. As a result, Furtado did not have to own a single warehouse. Similarly, Furtado managed to broaden his service, offering to exploit opportunities other freight forwarders abandoned because those opportunities turned meager profits and required extra manpower. For example, Furtado bundled into his service offering the processing of letters of credit and the preparation of all documents for export shipment, which is required on all freight-forwarding services. Completing the paperwork is time consuming and requires that the freight forwarder be li-censed and bonded, but customers appreciated this extra service.

The Entrepreneur's Network

During the start-up of RIFS, Furtado found himself with many questions and few answers. Remarkably, key contributors to Furtado's early success were acquaintances within various unrelated industries. When he first moved to Los Angeles, Furtado had a small network of friends and associates. He would work hard but dine well. Early in the development of RIFS, he frequently visited a sushi restaurant with his many associates. There he engaged the head chef in conversation and slowly built a relationship that would later serve as a conduit between Furtado and what was to be a future client of RIFS.

Furtado's network did not end with his client list (e.g., Better Home Products, Kelley Toys, Cougar International, and Right Fashion). He had spent years working for various freight forwarders in the Middle East and in India. This experience had given him insight into the business, but more importantly it allowed him to build his personal network with other freight forwarders in the industry. He not only knew about the business practices in the industry, but he also knew the people in the industry with whom he could enter into strategic partnerships. For example, if a problem arose with a delivery to the Middle East, Roland could call upon associates of other freight forwarders to help resolve the conflict or to even take ownership of an account and see it through to its destination.

The Future

Furtado has never taken his company through a fiscal year without having turned a profit. In 2000, RIFS generated $670,000 in sales and is projecting a 25 percent increase in sales in 2001. With an insatiable drive to grow the business, Furtado seeks further expansion beyond its current one-man operation status to generate sales of $45 million annually within a five- to ten-year time horizon. Eventually, he would like to take the business public. These lofty goals are a function of the fact that credibility within the freight forwarding industry is relative to the number of branches within a firm. Moreover, the freight-forwarding business is witnessing mass consolidation and Furtado's defensive position can be targeted for an acquisition or for fierce competition (see Exhibit 1). "Ultimately, there will be fewer carriers. . . . Consolidation allows carriers to build economies of scale and eventually lower their costs of operation so they can provide the services customers are looking for."[3]

A second specialized business line Furtado is presently exploring is that of parcel shipping to India. Given his knowledge of rate schedules and parcel rates, Furtado can ship a $20'' \times 20'' \times 20''$ box of 100 pounds at a price of $100 to customers. Com-

parable carriers will charge the same for a 40-pound package of the same dimensions. Furtado's ability to "sniff out" small wins like this is what has kept his business both afloat and constantly improving. He has recently added a premium service of shipping human remains to his product offering. Although it is not the most glamorous work, people are willing to pay a premium for it, and Furtado has the infrastructure in place to take the business in-house. He also recently shipped a yacht for a sizable fee. Furtado is constantly looking for ways to grow the business, but his need to control the operations may stand in the way of that growth. How can he grow the business without risking the relationships he has so carefully nurtured?

---

[3] Orton, C. (2000). "Container Carrier Consolidation Continues." *World Trade* (Aug.):50–54.

QUESTIONS FOR DISCUSSION

1. What were the factors that impelled Furtado to finally start his own business?

2. How did Furtado recognize opportunity?

3. Describe the barriers to growth that Furtado faces. How can he overcome them?

4. What should Furtado's growth strategy be?

EXHIBIT 1

Top Participants (Miscellaneous Transportation)

	Company Name	Sales ($M)	Location	Ownership	Parent/Sub/ Division
1	Samskip Inc.	12,028	Norfolk, VA	Private	Subsidiary
2	New York City Transit Authority	4,096	Brooklyn, NY	Private	Subsidiary
3	Metropolitan Transportation Authority	3,733	New York, NY	Private	Parent
4	BAA plc	3,416	London, U.K.	Public	Parent
5	Johnson Controls World Services Inc.	2,960	Cape Canaveral, FL	Public	Subsidiary
6	Yellow Freight System, Inc.	2,591	Shawnee Mission, KS	Public	Subsidiary
7	Laidlaw, Inc.	2,263	United Kingdom	Public	Parent
8	C.H. Robinson Worldwide	2,261	Eden Prairie, MN	Public	Parent
9	GATX Corporation	1,859	Chicago, IL	Public	Parent
10	Stolt-Nielsen Transportation Group	1,800	Houston, TX	Private	Parent

Source: Figures are taken from OneSource.com's Industry profiler search engine (see link at http://businessbrowser.onesource.com/Browser/Compcia.asp?KeyID=L766643&Process=CP).

Note: OneSource lists "Arrangement of Transportation of Freight and Cargo" as a sub-category to the "Miscellaneous Transportation" industry. Consequently, the above named competitors may provide services that lie outside of the narrow industry of which RIFS is a part.

Alcoholes de Centroamerica, S.A. de C.V.

On a summer afternoon in 1995, Sr. Emin Barjum watched the faded-yellow Toyota pickup truck pull away from his loading dock in Tegucigalpa, Honduras. Sr. Barjum, founder and president of the Honduran liquor manufacturer Alcoholes de Centroamerica *(ALDECA), wondered if his plan would work. The truck was laboring under a load of* Yuscaran, *a competitor's brand of* aguardiente. *Sr. Barjum had purchased the* Yuscaran *for delivery to his most important customers, the large liquor distributors in San Pedro Sula, a major industrial city in northern Honduras.*

Sr. Barjum was doing this because Grupo Cobán, *a large conglomerate that had been able to establish a virtual monopoly in the Guatemalan* arguardiente *market, was planning to expand its business into Honduras. As an initial step in this process,* Grupo Cobán *had begun offering incentives to the largest San Pedro Sula liquor distributors in exchange for carrying its brands. Sr. Barjum was attempting to send a subtle message to these distributors. He wanted them to believe that ALDECA, which accounted for up to 80 percent of their business, could distribute its own brands, as well as those of the competition, directly to retailers. Sr. Barjum felt that this warning would provide leverage in his dealings with the distributors and might discourage them from doing business with* Grupo Cobán. *To make his message even stronger, Sr. Barjum was providing the* Yuscaran *to his distributors as a very low price. The distributors did*

not realize that ALDECA was actually losing money on each bottle of Yuscaran *it delivered to the San Pedro Sula.*

Sr. Barjum also faced other problems in August 1995. In addition to the Grupo Cobán *threat, the market for* aguardiente *was shrinking slowly, because Honduran preferences were shifting to lighter alcohols like wine and beer. Also,* Licorera de Boaco, *a Nicaraguan distillery with production facilities in Honduras, had proposed a merger. After a year of study a decision had to be made soon. The merger would give ALDECA additional capacity and could help fight the* Grupo Cobán *threat, but it would result in less direct control over marketing and operations. Was the additional capacity worth the loss of control? What other strategies might work? Sr. Barjum went back inside his office to speak with his son, Salomon "Tony" Barjum, about their company's future.*

History of Alcoholes de Centroamerica

Emin Barjum returned home in 1965 to Tegucigalpa, the capital city of Honduras, after receiving a B.B.A. from the University of Pennsylvania and an M.B.A. from the University of California at Berkeley. He began looking for business opportunities while working for the Honduran government's Economics Ministry. Sr. Barjum noticed that there was a lack of good-quality industrial alcohol in Honduras. To fill this gap, he founded ALDECA in 1967, with initial financing from the Barjum family and a group of friends. The plant was designed with the help of a Mexican consulting firm. Because the minimum efficient scale was greater than the local demand for industrial alcohol, Sr. Barjum had to go into the liquor business to make the project feasible. He obtained technical advice on fermentation, distillation, and other aspects of alcohol manufacturing from a retired Cuban distiller who lived in Miami, Florida. ALDECA then began producing small quantities of rum, vodka, gin, Scotch, and an inexpensive liquor called *aguardiente*.

This case was prepared by Richard L. Priem, Associate Professor, The University of Texas at Arlington College of Business Administration and K. Matthew Gilley of James Madison University. We thank Emin and Tony Barjum for their cooperation during the field research for this case, which was written solely for the purpose of student discussion. All data are based on field research and all incidents and individuals are real. The names of some ALDECA competitors have been disguised. All other rights reserved jointly to the authors and the North American Case Research Association (NACRA). Reprinted by permission from the *Case Research Journal*, volume 19, issue 1, pp. 1–22. Copyright © 1999 by Richard L. Priem and K. Matthew Gilley and the North American Case Research Association. All rights reserved.

With production established, Sr. Barjum began marketing his liquor by loading as many cases as possible into his car and driving northward from Tegucigalpa. Those early sales trips were very difficult because Honduras had only 1000 kilometers of roads (barely 100 kilometers were paved). At first, Sr. Barjum sold only a few cases per trip. However, his marketing efforts soon began showing results. He persuaded the owners of many northern cantinas to begin carrying ALDECA's rum and *aguardiente*. Sr. Barjum was successful in part because he was the only distillery owner who called directly on customers; other distilleries used salespeople. ALDECA's sales grew each year.

When Sr. Barjum began producing alcohol, there were about sixteen distilleries in Honduras, most of which were relatively small in terms of output and market share. Sr. Barjum believed that "it was easier for us to compete then, since we had many small competitors instead of a few very large ones." ALDECA's entry into the market changed liquor manufacturing in Honduras. Most of the competitors had been using raw sugar in the fermentation process, which was quite expensive. ALDECA, however, produced lower-priced products made with black-strap molasses. In 1995, only eight distilleries remained in Honduras; the rest had gone out of business. About half the survivors were forced to change to molasses to remain cost competitive.

ALDECA prospered until 1972, when a large Nicaraguan distillery, Licorera de Boaco, entered the Honduran rum market. Hondurans preferred internationally produced rums, and sales of ALDECA's rum declined rapidly. As a result, ALDECA changed its focus to *aguardiente* production. By the early 1990s, the company had developed a presence in the *aguardiente* market throughout the country and had captured approximately 50 percent of the market share (see Exhibit C for details). However, northern Honduras was ALDECA's most important market, comprising nearly 85 percent of its sales.

The Honduran Aguardiente Industry

The Product, Its Consumers, and Place of Consumption

Aguardiente is a clear, inexpensive, very strong liquor that is generally purchased by the glass in small cantinas by poor, uneducated males between the ages of 26 and 45. The small, family-owned cantinas usually have a maximum of six tables and a small bar. "The cantinas are traditionally the place where men meet after work to have a few drinks," states Sr. Barjum. "They are basically a haven for men." Women traditionally avoided consumption of *aguardiente* because those women who drank it were considered immoral. The serving size is typically 125 milliliters (approximately one-half cup), and the average consumer drinks three servings per cantina visit. About 60 percent of *aguardiente* consumers drink it straight, while roughly 40 percent follow it with lemon, salt, or a sip of a soft drink.

The product is traditionally sold to the cantinas in 750-milliliter and 1-liter bottles, from which the bartenders pour drinks for their customers. A trend is developing, however, toward smaller, 125-milliliter bottles. Some customers prefer the small bottles because, when they purchase one, they are guaranteed that the bartender did not "water down" the product. However, production of *aguardiente* in the smaller bottles is quite expensive, and price is an important factor in the purchase decision. The "best" combination of taste (smoothness) and strength (alcohol content) typically determine a consumer's brand preference.

The Competitors

There were three major players in the Honduran *aguardiente* market in the mid-1990s: ALDECA, which sold approximately 2.5 million liters of its brands per year; Destilleria Buen Gusto, which sold approximately 2.5 million liters of *Yuscaran* per year; and Licorera de Boaco, which sold 700,000 liters of its brands per year. There were several smaller competitors in Honduras, as well as many black-market operations.

Although ALDECA commanded nearly half the legal Honduran *aguardiente* market, the company did not fare well "brand-to-brand" with Destilleria Buen Gusto's Yuscaran brand. A recent ALDECA marketing survey revealed that, in the city of San Pedro Sula (within ALDECA's core northern market), 57 percent of the respondents preferred Yuscaran over ALDECA's Caña Brava. Sr. Barjum notes that, "If we combine all of our brands, then we win. But, brand against brand, they have a better share."

EXHIBIT A

Regional Map of Central America

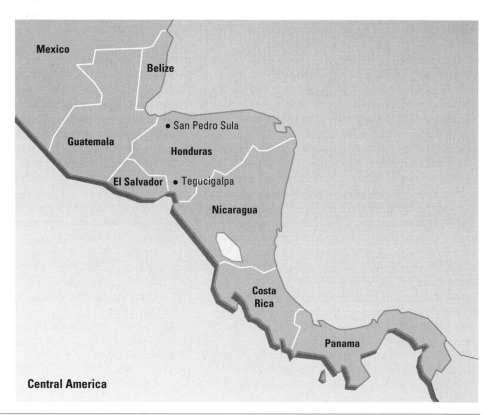

Central America

The General Environment in Honduras

Honduras is located in Central America between Guatemala, El Salvador, and Nicaragua. Although the Honduran political environment has been stable in recent years, more than 150 internal rebellions, civil wars, and governmental changes have occurred in Honduras since 1900. Its 6 million people live in a country that is approximately the size of Louisiana (see Exhibit A) and depend primarily on agriculture for employment. In the mid-1990s, Honduras was among the poorest countries in the western hemisphere, with per capita income of approximately $630 (U.S.). The country suffered from high popula-tion growth, high unemployment (15 percent) and underemployment (36 percent), high interest rates (approximately 36 percent), and high inflation (aver-aging 22 percent between 1990 and 1994). A weak infrastructure also was a problem. For example, there were only 1700 kilometers of paved roads in 1995, and water and electric service were very unreliable.

A lack of hard currency for foreign exchange also was a problem. In 1994, the Honduran Central Bank mandated that commercial banks, exchange houses, and businesses could not retain foreign currency. Rather, they were required to sell foreign currency to the Central Bank within 24 hours of its acquisition in exchange for *lempiras,* the Honduran currency. The

EXHIBIT B

ALDECA's Top Management Team

Name and Position	Age	Years at Company	Education	Experience
Emin Barjum Owner and general manager	53	28	M.B.A., University of California at Berkeley and B.B.A., University of Pennsylvania	Company president
Salomon "Tony" Barkum Assistant general manager	23	1	M.B.A. and B.B.A., The University of Texas at Arlington	Started here
Armando Leonel Aguilar Production manager	26	2	Chemical engineer and M.B.A., Honduras University	Assistant production manager at a sugar mill
Ileana Zelaya Head of Laboratory	24	1	Chemical engineer, Currently getting M.B.A., Honduras University	Head of lab at another company
Lesbia Argentina Nunez de Flores Head of accounting	41	21	CPA, Honduras University	Started here
Julio Valladares Sales manager	40	4	High school graduate	10 years in sales (liquor)

Central Bank then auctioned the foreign currency on the open market, but quotas limited the amount anyone could purchase per day. It took businesses quite some time, therefore, to obtain the currency necessary for foreign transactions.

Alcoholes de Centroamerica *in 1995*

Personnel

In 1995, Sr. Barjum was joined by his son, Tony, who was "learning the business" after completing a B.B.A. and an M.B.A. at The University of Texas at Arlington. Sr. Barjum's daughter, Patricia, provided some marketing advice to ALDECA as needed. Other top managers at ALDECA included Armando Leonel Aguilar, production manager; Ileana Zelaya, head of labora-

tory; Lesbia Agrentina Nunez de Flores, head of accounting; and Julio Valladares, sales manager. Exhibit B highlights the education and experience of ALDECA's top managers. The remainder of the 84 employees filled clerical and production positions. ALDECA had little trouble filling these lower-level positions because of the high Honduran unemployment and underemployment rates, as well as ALDECA's higher-than-average pay scale.

The importance of having a qualified, in-house chemical engineer was highlighted in the early 1990s when Sra. Zelaya discovered a virus living in the fermentation tanks. The elimination of this virus enhanced the efficiency of the fermentation process and increased ALDECA's production capacity by nearly one-third.

EXHIBIT C

Liters of *Aguardiente* Sold by ALDECA, 1987–1994

1987	1,944,000
1988	2,177,000
1989	2,342,000
1990	2,449,000
1991	2,801,000
1992	2,711,000
1993	2,554,000
1994	2,445,000

Product Lines

ALDECA produced seven brands of *aguardiente:* Caña Brava (its highest-quality and best-selling brand), Tic-Tac, Catrachito, Costeño, Torero, Favorito, and Bambu (see Exhibit D for details). The multibrand strategy was developed in part, Sr. Barjum noted, because "each cantina will carry only two or three brands. That's one of the reasons we're trying to get a lot of brands into the market, to confuse the markets. That way, our brands could stock a whole cantina."

ALDECA also manufactured small amounts of vodka and wine on a manual production line. A separate Barjum-controlled company produced a line of cosmetics (perfumes, deodorants, and lotions) made from excess alcohol. *Aguardiente* production, however, remained ALDECA's specialty.

Production Process

ALDECA produced all its alcohol from black-strap molasses, which was obtained from a few large sugarcane plantations in northern Honduras. Sr. Barjum signed contracts with these producers each year at the beginning of the harvest to ensure that ALDECA had enough molasses to last the entire year. However, since the molasses producers often promised more than they could manufacture, shortages were common toward the end of the year. ALDECA's attempts to resolve this problem were ineffective. Transportation costs prohibited the company from acquiring molasses from other countries, and large-capacity tanks, pipelines, and pumps would be very costly. Furthermore, it was impossible for ALDECA to build additional storage tanks in its current location because the land adjacent to the distillery had become developed in recent years.

Upon receiving the molasses from the manufacturers, ALDECA mixed the molasses with yeast and stored it in tanks, where it was allowed to ferment. After ALDECA's chemical engineer, Ileana Zelaya, determined that the mixture had achieved the proper level of fermentation, the molasses was pumped into distilling units, where it was converted into alcohol. The alcohol was then pumped into large vats, where it awaited the bottling process.

Following a standard practice in Honduras, ALDECA recycled all its bottles. The bottling process began at an enormous bottle-washing machine. Once the used bottles were washed, they were moved

EXHIBIT D

ALDECA *Aguardiente* Prices, 1990–1995 (In *lempiras* per 12-Bottle Case)

	1990	1991	1992	1993	1994	1995
Caña Brava	104	Not available	116	122	152	156
Tic-Tac	86	Not available	98	110	132	138
Castrachito	91	Not available	103	110	128	124
Costeña	95	Not available	107	114	129	115
Torero	99	Not available	111	117	135	124
Favorito	85	Not available	97	104	121	115
Bambu	85	Not available	97	104	116	93

one by one through the filling machine. They were then placed in boxes of twelve and were stored for shipment.

Although it may appear that ALDECA's production process was higly automated, it was still relatively labor-intensive. The bottles returned by the distributors were loaded manually into the bottle washer. After each bottle was filled, it was visually inspected for purity. Then, each bottle cap was started by hand before being tightened by the capping machine. Next, safety seals were secured by hand. Finally, the full bottles were boxed and stored manually.

In 1995, ALDECA was still using most of the same equipment with which it had begun production. Despite its age, the equipment remained simple, safe, efficient, flexible, and trouble-free. The bottling line was seldom interrupted by mechanical failures, and the interruptions that took place were usually solved within a few minutes.

Marketing

Marketing ALDECA's *aguardiente* was difficult. Nearly all *aguardiente* consumers were illiterate, so common vehicles for advertising such as newspapers and magazines, were ineffective. Advertising on television also was ineffective because the customers generally had no access to television. ALDECA used some radio advertising, since many cantinas (and some customers) had radios.

Most of ALDECA's marketing efforts, however, involved point-of-sale advertising. Each year, ALDECA developed a poster featuring a female model in a bathing suit. A 12-month calendar appeared at the bottom of the poster so that, according to Sr. Barjum, "the cantina owners will leave the poster on the wall all year." One year, ALDECA's advertising company failed to put the year itself on the calendar. As a result, that particular calendar remained on the walls of many cantinas for several years, even though the day/date designations were wrong! ALDECA also distributed to the cantinas, free of charge, disposable plastic cups with ALDECA's various product logos on the front and the serving sizes marked on the sides. Less successful marketing campaigns, such as neon signs for distributors and metal signs for cantinas, had been attempted at various times in the past.

ALDECA tried to improve the effectiveness of its advertising campaigns by hiring a well-respected local marketing firm to evaluate and revise its advertising. ALDECA gave this firm detailed information that included consumer demographics as well as frequency, amount, and location of consumption. The marketing firm then developed a multimedia campaign (television, radio, and print) that focused on a man consuming *aguardiente* at home. Sr. Barjum was disappointed with the result of the marketing firm's work because "we had given them all the marketing information we had, but they came out with a campaign which was completely out of the environment where people drink *aguardiente.*"

New product testing and introduction were handled through ALDECA's sales department. A sales representative typically visited the cantinas with the new *aguardiente* and offered the cantina owners several free bottles in exchange for permission to conduct a brief taste test. The free bottles were provided to the cantina owner as a show of goodwill and to offset revenues lost by the cantina during the test. The salesperson then offered cantina patrons free samples of the new product and asked for their opinions on how the new product compared to their favorite brands. A follow-up sales call was made later to secure the cantina's order.

Financial Performance

A cursory look at ALDECA's sales figures might lead one to believe that its bottom line had been suffering. Total factory sales dropped from 22 million *lempiras* in 1991 to 12 million *lempiras* in 1994. This drop, however, reflected an international response by ALDECA to changes in the taxation of *aguardiente* included a flat tax of 4.5 *lempiras* per liter. In April 1992, the Honduran government implemented a new tax system requiring that tax be paid on a *percentage* of the selling prince at the factory.

To remain competitively priced, ALDECA altered its transfer pricing. The company began selling its *aguardiente* to an in-house distributor at a lower price, thereby reducing the effect of taxes on the final price to wholesalers. The in-house distributor then provided ALDECA with the dividends shown at the bottom of ALDECA's income statement. Exhibits E and F provide more detailed information about ALDECA's financial performance.

EXHIBIT E

Alcoholes de Centroamerica Balance Sheet, 1990–1995 (In *lempiras*)

Activo Circulante	(Short-Term Assets)	1990	1991	1992	1993	1994
Caja Chica	(Petty cash)	500	500	500	500	500
Caja General	(Cash on hand)	8,266	133,771	128,265	3,586	17,111
Cuentas de Banea	(Bank accounts)	1,580,559	1,299,762	2,231,299	1,574,759	1,088,872
Total	(Total Cash)	1,589,325	1,434,033	2,360,064	1,578,845	1,106,483
Cuentas a Cobrar	(Accounts receivable)	505,077	453,648	1,370,009	1,723,785	2,500,668
Provision Cuentas in Cobrables	(Loss provision for A/R)	58,914	58,914	137,000	172,378	250,066
Total	(Total A/R)	446,163	394,734	1,233,009	1,551,407	2,250,602
Anticipos	(Employee advances)	159,795	59,588	80,127	48,003	220,489
Prestamos a Cobrar	(Loans receivable)	36,489	37,916	79,604	451,794	329,723
Reparos a Cobrar	(Dividends receivable)	1,308	1,308	1,308	1,308	1,308
Total	(Total)	197,592	98,812	161,039	501,105	551,520
Materias Primas	(Raw materials)	247,656	449,741	486,839	626,792	569,605
Envases	(Containers)	330,825	388,210	721,474	835,297	1,300,724
Timbres y Casquetes	(Caps, labels, etc.)	6,079	9,754	0	0	0
Combustibles	(Fuel)	16,661	30,416	16,606	28,003	47,960
Producto En Proceso	(Work in progress)	130,471	171,738	215,949	190,000	192,097
Porducto Terminado	(Finished goods inventory)	35,663	245,240	49,522	53,995	104,000
Total Inventarios	(Total Inventory)	767,355	1,295,099	1,490,390	1,734,087	2,214,386
Accesorarios	(Accessories)	35,996	29,487	114,846	118,433	127,386
Inv. En Transito	(Goods in transit)	0	0	0	1,837	0
Seguros Diferidos	(Prepaid insurance)	6,162	2,942	11,917	9,963	11,033
Publicidad Diferida	(Prepaid advertising)	4,924	0	9,057	18,911	5,234
Misc. Diferidos	(Prepaid misc.)	33,507	15,393	4,623	5,511	5,632
Impuestos Pagados	(Prepaid taxes)	8,233	9,094	26,662	5,300	25,562
Depositos Garanta	(Guaranteed deposits)	31,525	140,394	6,180	6,180	6,580
Envases En Circulacion	(Bottles in circulation)	179,989	266,131	353,205	370,306	350,222
Inversiones	(Short-term investments)	714,983	714,911	798,191	758,926	406,240
Total	(Total Other)	1,015,319	1,178,352	1,324,681	1,295,367	938,400
Total/Activo Circulante	(Total short-term assets)	4,015,754	4,401,030	6,569,183	6,660,881	7,061,391

EXHIBIT E *(continued)*

Alcoholes de Centroamerica Balance Sheet, 1990–1995 (In *lempiras*)

Activo Circulante	(Long-Term Assets)	1990	1991	1992	1993	1994
Terrenos	(Land)	297,004	297,004	297,004	317,246	317,246
Edificios	(Buildings)	485,880	485,880	485,880	595,949	595,949
Desp. Acum. Edificios	(Accumulated depr.—bldgs.)	151,411	163,486	175,561	197,195	224,160
Total	(Total)	631,473	619,398	607,323	716,000	689,035
Maquinaria	(Machinery)	1,582,256	1,824,121	2,180,582	2,386,341	2,884,602
Depr. acum.—maquinaira	(Accumulated depr.—mach.)	1,024,297	1,120,029	1,246,176	1,410,718	1,603,770
Total	(total)	557,959	704,092	934,406	975,623	1,280,832
Otras instalaciones	(Other installations)	193,708	248,695	285,469	398,005	455,890
Depr. Acum.—instalaciones	(Accumulated depr.—install.)	141,288	156,841	173,404	195,991	228,021
Total	(Total)	52,420	91,854	112,065	202,014	227,869
Mobiliario y equipo oficina	(Office equipment)	187,016	124,292	175,752	220,418	231,584
Depr. acum.—movil. Y equipo oficina	(Accumulated depr.—off.equip.)	114,983	92,025	102,134	118,466	138,593
Total	(Total)	72,033	32,267	73,618	101,952	92,991
Vehiculos	(Vehicles)	464,976	428,404	658,497	644,147	732,647
Depr. acum.—vehiculos	(Accumulated depr.—veh.)	353,718	353,298	416,043	446,155	516,949
Total	(Total)	111,258	75,106	242,454	197,986	215,698
Otros activos fijas	(Other L/T assets)	2,657	2,657	2,657	2,657	2,657
Depr. accu.—other activos fijas	(Accumulated depr.—L/T assets)	2,451	2,451	2,451	2,451	2,451
Total	(Total)	206	206	206	206	206
Total/activos fijas	(Total L/T assets)	1,425,349	1,522,923	1,970,072	2,174,188	2,506,631
Activos	(Total assets)	5,441,103	5,923,953	8,539,255	8,854,592	9,568,022

Pasivo Circulante	Liabilities	1990	1991	1992	1993	1994
Pasivo circulante	(Accounts payable)	210,435	137,030	73,186	113,791	214,013
Documentos por pagar	(Documents payable)	0	0	0	0	0
Prestamos por pagar	(Loans payable)	483,325	0	0	166,672	0

(continues)

EXHIBIT E *(continued)*

Alcoholes de Centroamerica Balance Sheet, 1990–1995 (In *lempiras*)

Pasivo Circulante	Liabilities	1990	1991	1992	1993	1994
Imp. S ventas recaudado	(Taxes payable)	202,211	247,576	1,779,839	1,695,078	1,845,644
Retencion empleados	(Employee benefits payable)	3,266	4,580	6,796	4,545	9,192
Imp. S renta a pagar	(Income taxes payable)	346,005	427,230	4,206	2,958	(12,861)
Dividendos por pagar	(Dividend payable)	3,476	3,476	454,781	3,476	3,476
Depositos de clientes	(Client deposits)	160,241	160,241	160,241	160,241	160,241
Total pasivo circulante	(Total liabilities)	1,408,959	980,133	2,479,049	2,146,761	2,219,705

Capital y Reservas	Equity	1990	1991	1992	1993	1994
Capital social 2,000,000	(Owner's equity)	2,000,000	2,000,000	2,000,000	2,000,000	2,000,000
Reserva legal	(Legal revenues)	441,543	17,127	611,690	688,818	774,696
Otras reservas	(Other reserves)	0	0	0	0	0
Utilidades no distribuidas	(Retained earnings)	522,553	915,001	1,556,925	2,476,507	4,573,621
Peridas y ganancias	(Net income)	1,068,048	1,511,692	1,891,591	1,542,506	0
Total capital y reservas	(Total equity)	4,032,144	4,934,820	6,060,206	6,707,831	7,348,317
Total pasivo, capital, y reservas	(Total liabilities and equity)	5,441,103	5,923,953	8,539,255	8,854,592	9,568,022

The Honduran Aguardiente *Market in 1995*

In the early 1990s, demand for *aguardiente* began to shrink after 15 years of relative stability. As a result, ALDECA only produced 2.4 million liters in 1994, compared with 2.8 million liters in 1991. Sr. Barjum explains the possible reason for this decline:

We feel that there is a market for softer, or less alcoholic, beverages, like wine or beer. We found out that the demand for beer in Honduras is 260 million 12-ounce bottles per ear. Wine imports have increased considerably. We don't have the exact figures because they aren't published, but we feel certain that these products have been taking some overall market share.

There were indications that demand for *aguardiente* was declining throughout Central America. As a result, competition within the industry was becoming more intense by the mid-1990s, as distilleries looked for ways to maintain profitability. Because of this, ALDECA was faced with a potential new competitor from Guatemala, as well as a merger offer from another Honduran distillery.

EXHIBIT F

Alcoholes de Centroamerica Income Statements, 1990–1995 (In *lempiras*)

Gastos de Ventas	Sales	1990	1991	1992	1993	1994	1995 Through 4/30
Aguardientes y rones	(Aguardiente and rum)	16,166,341	20,412,604	13,309,216	8,638,207	9,448,812	3,759,387
Otras bebidas	(Other drinks)	87,702	157,122	182,237	131,180	123,080	74,440
Vinos	(Wines)	49,720	38,880	97,268	118,564	95,642	56,230
Otros productos	(Other products)	860,260	155,764	1,062,047	1,262,978	1,959,433	844,051
Otros ingresos	(Other income)	438,591	512,147	364,106	454,011	484,937	225,735
Total ventas	(Total income)	17,602,614	22,276,507	15,014,874	10,604,940	12,111,904	4,959,844
Devoluciones y rebajas S/ventas	(Returned sales)	29,154	15,979	11,369	12,321	7,913	1,957
Total ventas e ing netos	(Net sales)	17,573,460	22,260,528	15,003,505	10,592,619	12,103,991	4,957,887
Costo de ventas	(Cost of goods sold)	13,826,979	16,957,738	8,591,248	4,898,314	6,397,587	2,798,326
Utilidad bruta	(Gross income)	3,746,481	5,302,790	6,412,257	5,694,305	5,706,404	2,159,561
Gastos de Fabrication	**(Manufacturing Costs)**						
Salarios	(Salaries)	212,244	330,425	403,930	407,991	437,602	134,938
Sueldos	(Wages)	93,656	132,244	126,339	110,098	166,959	85,331
Vacaciones	(Vacation)	12,390	15,751	20,265	21,782	27,876	10,820
Prestaciones sociales	(Severance pay)	39,000	16,057	57,873	55,215	50,972	38,184
Depr. maquinaria	(Depr. of equip.)	76,369	95,731	126,147	164,541	193,052	64,350
Depr. otras instalaciones	(Depr. of installations)	10,304	15,553	16,562	22,587	32,030	10,677
Mantenimiento	(Maintenance)	155,334	225,031	232,628	177,324	223,830	39,741
Combustibles	(Fuels)	4,110	70	8,128	2,776	64,275	13,328
Miscelanea	(Misc.)	6,027	13,768	14,286	13,413	17,488	5,360
Materiales	(Materials)	30,671	48,230	10,909	14,725	5,586	1,171
Herramientas	(Tools)	2,668	8,066	3,877	1,573	4,316	181
Energia electrica	(Electricity)	75,737	145,582	183,817	215,922	213,482	72,745
Agua	(Water)	71	3,382	10,206	11,279	4,145	2,114
Vigilancia	(Security)	64,408	155,468	199,906	218,460	220,762	96,396
Regalias	(Licensing fees)	38,282	28,569	48,144	36,882	6,019	0
Marcas de registros	(Brand registration fee)	2,499	1,419	2,501	22,187	3,338	1,171
Total	(Total)	823,770	1,235,346	1,465,518	1,496,755	1,671,732	576,507

EXHIBIT F *(continued)*

Alcoholes de Centroamerica Income Statements, 1990–1995 (In *lempiras*)

Gastos de Ventas	Sales	1990	1991	1992	1993	1994	1995 Through 4/30
Sueldos	(Wages)	8,423	20,256	43,616	46,400	49,050	12,700
Comisiones	(Commissions)	76,713	0	0	0	0	0
Vacaciones	(Vacations)	466	566	1,566	1,833	2,300	800
Prestacioines sociales	(Severance pay)	0	0	0	0	0	0
Depr. vehiculos	(Depreciation of vehicles)	34,069	32,296	62,475	77,954	70,791	23,597
Combustibles	(Fuels)	62,499	103,425	89,378	112,819	126,278	38,182
Mantenimiento	(Maintenance)	39,855	125,614	129,591	77,034	108,265	58,199
Seguros	(Insurance)	25,981	37,705	37,716	33,701	38,014	39,733
Otros gastos vehiculos	(Other vehicle expense)	23,966	24,634	32,441	31,864	38,950	11,484
Fletes	(Transportation fees)	187,674	265,800	103,092	155,563	225,189	93,456
Cuentas incobrales	(Bad debt exp.)	0	0	93,197	35,377	77,688	0
Gastos de viaje	(Travel expense)	11,438	16,479	23,473	28,001	20,175	2,405
Promocion	(Advertising)	254,662	351,225	520,997	506,214	622,613	43,151
Otros gastos de venta	(Other selling expenses)	48,258	77,305	61,251	54,486	43,542	7,878
Miscelaneos	(Misc. expenses)	475	599	2,682	586	484	136
Impuestos distr. S/ventas	(Taxes)	23,436	46,990	55,088	54,982	60,353	21,218
Total	(Total)	797,915	1,102,894	1,256,563	1,216,814	1,483,692	352,939

Gastos Admin. y Grales (Administrative Expenses)

Sueldos	(Wages)	189,707	219,926	238,788	246,322	284,979	115,513
Vacaciones	(Vacations)	6,663	5,341	5,305	5,169	8,172	1,689
Prestaciones sociales	(Severance pay)	27,066	0	0	0	566	0
Benef. empleados	(Empl. benefits)	96,926	133,039	133,962	168,490	195,830	52,610
Depr. edificios	(Building exp.)	12,075	12,075	12,075	21,634	26,965	8,988
Depr. mobiliario	(Depr.—furniture)	12,880	9,360	10,108	16,331	20,127	6,709
Mantenamiento	(Maintenance)	11,426	22,565	23,931	15,676	28,142	10,106
Seguro	(Insurance)	22,232	28,731	34,626	29,532	29,532	24,359

EXHIBIT F *(continued)*

Alcoholes de Centroamerica Income Statements, 1990–1995 (In *lempiras*)

Gastos de Ventas	Sales	1990	1991	1992	1993	1994	1995 Through 4/30
Arrendamiento equipos	(Lease-buyback expense)	0	20,060	60,979	53,123	39,193	0
Gastos de viaje	(Travel exp.)	0	34,905	34,928	25,892	38,254	10,072
Honorarios profesionales	(Legal fees)	15,061	52,524	33,625	20,870	19,210	56,308
Dietas y gastos de repres.	(Representation fees)	32,100	47,600	56,000	63,600	78,600	30,900
Papeleria y utiles	(Office supplies)	22,133	21,037	20,717	17,634	29,493	16,779
Correro, telgrafo, telefono	(Telephone and mail)	11,909	18,157	25,771	19,907	38,008	11,827
Donaciones	(Donations)	22,300	35,989	46,650	17,850	21,235	11,028
Miscelaneos	(Miscellaneous)	19,551	43,496	39,444	44,719	41,104	13,192
Otros impuestos distritales	(Taxes)	5,776	11,043	11,089	10,639	11,813	0
Otros gastos	(Other expenses)	0	0	0	0	0	0
Total	(Total)	507,805	715,848	787,998	777,388	911,223	370,082
Gastos financieros	(Financial exp.)						
Interese pagados	(Interest paid)	75,589	56,668	51,884	53,852	6,722	83,887
Gastos bancarias	(Bank comms.)	103,185	10,462	50,386	1,169	0	(9,728)
Total	(Total)	178,774	67,130	102,270	55,021	6,722	74,159
Gastos no deducibles	(Nondeductible expenses)						
Aportaciones INFOP	(Training institute tuition)	5,819	7,791	9,157	9,168	11,369	1,911
Multas, reparos, y otros	(Penalties)	378	989	423	352	128	0
Total	(Total)	6,197	8,780	9,580	9,520	11,497	1,911
Total gastos	(Total expenses)	2,314,461	3,129,998	3,621,929	3,555,498	4,084,866	1,375,598
Utilidad antes del I/S/renta	(Net income before taxes)	1,432,020	2,171,792	2,790,328	2,138,807	1,621,538	783,963
Impuestos S renta estimado	(Taxes)	523,876	823,073	1,071,835	809,715	597,306	0
Utilidad despues del I/S/renta	(Net income after taxes)	908,144	1,349,719	1,718,493	1,329,092	1,024,232	783,963
Dividendos recibidos	(Dividends received)	159,904	161,973	173,098	213,414	693,365	423,000
Utilidad neta	(Net income)	1,068,048	1,511,692	1,891,591	1,542,506	1,717,597	1,206,963

A New Threat

A Guatemalan conglomerate, Grupo Cobán, had recently made attempts to enter the Honduran *aguardiente* market. Sr. Barjum believed that Grupo Cobán was a major threat to ALDECA because it "has a monopoly on the Guatelmalan *aguardiente* market, producing 15 million liters per year. It has total control in Guatemala. It owns a bank and a sugar mill. It also has an interest in the Pepsi Cola manufacturing facilities in Guatemala, as well as beer. In addition, it has a cost advantage with respect to raw materials; both molasses and fuel oils are cheaper in Guatemala."

Grupo Cobán purchased a small distillery in Honduras, as well as the rights to use several brands of *aguardiente* that have been popular there. Sr. Barjum explains:

> The *[Grupo Cobán]* have purchased relatively new facilities. That is a disadvantage because they had to put up a lot of money for them. Right now, they are testing the market and testing what competitive reactions will be. If they give credit to distributors, for example, what are we going to do? If they give away bottles, how will we react? They are at that stage. They have not really come in full-strength. I think they are just at the initial testing stage.

Grupo Cobán's initial attempts to enter the Honduran market came in the form of enticements to ALDECA's distributors. Grupo Cobán executives offered one particularly attractive incentive; for initial orders, and for orders expanding a distributor's volume, Grupo Cobán would provide the reusable bottles free of charge. Normally, distributors wishing to carry a new manufacturer's *aguardiente* were required to either pay for the bottles up front or to provide acceptable used bottles for exchange. This represented a large initial cost for the distributors. Grupo Cobán's incentive shifted this cost from the distributor to the manufacturer. After the initial order was sold, the distributor would simply exchange the empty bottles to cover the bottle cost for the next order. However, while the bottles of most *aguardiente* manufacturers were interchangeable, thus minimizing the distributors' switching costs, Grupo Cobán's bottles were unique. Therefore, the distribu-

tors could only recover the value of these bottles by reordering Grupo Cobán brands.

Recently, Grupo Cobán invited ALDECA's four largest distributors in the San Pedro Sula area to visit Grupo Cobán's facilities in Guatemala. Two of the four declined that offer. The two distributors that accepted the offer reported some of the details of the meetings to Sr. Barjum. They were informed that Grupo Cobán was in the initial marketing stages in Honduras, confirming Sr. Barjum's suspicions. Later, Grupo Cobán was planning to introduce two new *aguardiente* brands into the Honduran market, each having a traditional Honduran name.

Unknown to ALDECA's distributors, Grupo Cobán had a history of entering markets in this way and then bypassing local distributors after its brands became established. Several of ALDECA's distributors indicated that they were considering Grupo Cobán's proposal, and Sr. Barjum was very concerned. He had been gathering and analyzing information of Grupo Cobán's entry into the Honduran market and identified several alternative courses of action for ALDECA. He explains:

> We can respond in-kind. To a certain extent, we can give credit to the wholesalers. We can also lower our prices. But, I'm trying to figure out some unique way to respond. One way might be to go to our distributors and tell them that they cannot take on different brands. If they choose to go with *Grupo Cobán,* then they can forget about us; we will begin selling directly to the cantinas. But, that would require a lot of change in our marketing department. We don't have too much experience with retailing.

An Opportunity

ALDECA also had the opportunity to merge with another Honduran distillery, Licorera de Boaco, which had recently approached Sr. Barjum with a merger proposal. Licorera de Boaco also was concerned about Grupo Cobán's entry into the Honduran *aguardiente* market and felt that a merger was the best way to handle the situation. According to Sr. Barjum:

> We have been off and on for about two years with the possibility of closing down our plant and manufacturing all of our products in their

facility, under our supervision, but using their technical procedures. We would give them all of our equipment, but we would keep the land and buildings. But, we are used to making decisions without talking too much with our board of directors. This merger would mean that nay decision would have to be mutually agreed upon. They have been in the market for about fifteen years and haven't really been successful. They have good marketing and distribution, but they have not done a good job with the product.

In 1995, ALDECA was running at 80 percent of capacity. ALDECA's plot of land was surrounded by other development and was too small for additional construction. Any large increase in output would require a shift in production to a different location. Licorera de Boaco, however, had the ability to produce three times more alcohol than ALDECA, and it had the potential to produce it at 15 to 20 percent lower cost. Sr. Barjum notes:

> If we united with *Licorera de Boaco,* that would mean that we would have larger storage facilities, or we could build larger storage facilities because they have more land than we have. That would give us an advantage of being able to get better prices for molasses because, at certain times of the year, the sugar mills are really pressed for storage. At that time, you will find two or three of them competing with each other. The thing is, though, I'll be frank with you. If I'm going to merge, I don't want more problems than I had to begin with. I'm going to have to look closely at their operation for the start and see what problems they are having. It is going to be more difficult for us, because I'm going to have their production problems. Tony cannot take care of that, because he is just starting to learn. I'll have to worry about that myself. I'll also have to be concerned with their marketing problems.

A major marketing problem was that Licorera de Boaco had not been able to establish a strong brand name for its *aguardiente*. If ALDECA chose not to merge, however, Licorera de Boaco might have continued to try to build strong brands itself Says Sr. Barjum:

They have their own sugar mill, they have 85 percent control of the Nicaraguan market, they have the technical know-how, and they have banks in the United States. So, they are a very powerful company. They also own the franchise for MasterCard in Central America. Financially, I think they may be more powerful than *Grupo Cobán,* and we are in the middle. We are like the cheese between the two slices of bread . . . everyone is trying to get us. So that's one of the reasons we thought about the possible merger with these people. But, that would mean we would have to close down shop here. Some of our personnel would be taken over there, and some of them would not. So, we would have to pay approximately 1.2 million *lempiras* in workers' compensation.

Some of the conditions of the merger proposal were as follows:

1. ALDECA would shift all of its production equipment to the Licorera de Boaco distillery.
2. The consolidated firm would have exclusive rights to the brand names of both ALDECA and Licorera de Boaco for 99 years.
3. The board of directors of the new firm would have seven members, three from ALDECA and four from Licorera de Boaco.

Details of the proposed equity arrangements for the merged company are provided in exhibit G. Additional portions of ALDECA's initial merger analysis are shown in Exhibit H.

Sr. Barjum's View of the Future

Sr. Barjum sat in his office with his son, Tony, late into the night trying to come to some conclusions about their situation. "I am reacting on a day-to-day basis," Sr. Barjum explained. "I have not determined where I want the company to go in, say, five years. How are we going to meet the new competition that is coming into the country? Maybe the way we've operated in the past is not correct for today."

They decided to call a meeting of their most important distributors to discuss the issue. Tony wanted to tell the distributors directly of Grupo Cobán's usual form of market entry and then give

EXHIBIT G

ALDECA's Merger Analysis

ALDECA sales (2,491,000 its/year)	L.	28,694,112.00
Licorera de Boaco direct costs (if produced 2,491,000 its.)		
Alcohol	L.	5,762,513.33
Bottle caps	L.	498,200.00
Labels	L.	163,990.83
Flavorings	L.	207,583.33
Security seal	L.	78,560.00
Direct labor	L.	398,560.00
Indirect expenses	L.	1,668,970.00
Total costs	**L.**	**8,778,377.49**
Profit margin distillery	L.	4,151,666.67
Sale price at the factory (2,491,000 its.)	L.	12,930,365.83
Add:		
44% Elaboration tax	L.	5,689,360.97
20% Consumption tax	L.	2,586,073.17
10% Sales tax	L.	2,120,580.00
Cost to distribution co.	L.	23,326,379.96
Dist. gross margin	L.	5,367,732.04
Less:		
Advertising (L. 4.00/box)	L.	830,333.33
Administration costs	L.	600,000.00
Sales exp.	L.	360,000.00
Transportation (L. 4.00/box)	L.	830,333.33
Other costs	L.	400,000.00
Total costs	L.	3,020,666.66
NI distribution co.	L.	2,347,065.37
NI liquor manufacturing	L.	4,151,666.68
ALDECA contribution	L.	6,498,732.04
Licorera de Boaco Contr. (their NI)	L.	1,100,000.00
Total	**L.**	**7,598,732.04**
45% Participation ALDECA	L.	3,419,429.42
1994 ALDECA	L.	3,592,181.26

EXHIBIT H

Consolidation Analysis

1. The equity structure of Licorera de Boaco S.A. and Distribuidora de Boaco S.A. is as follows:

Investor #1	10.2%
Investor #2	5.3%
Investor #3	5.3%
Familia Cortez	79.2%

   Note: Investor #3 is the general manager of Licorera and Distribuidora de Boaco.
2. Distribuidora de Boaco S.A. has 39% ownership of Distribuidora Puerto Barrias S.A., a large distribution company which had sales of 53 million lempiras last year.

Consolidation Proposal
1. ALDECA will transfer to Licorera de Boaco all its production machinery and equipment, including storage tanks and the electrical plant.
2. ALDECA will give Licorera de Boaco the exclusive authorization to produce and distribute its brand name products (a period of 99 years).
3. The owners of the brands that Licorera de Boaco currently manufactures and distributes would give the same authorization to the consolidation firm.
4. ALDECA would receive stock totaling 45% of the capital of Licorera de Boaco and Distribuidora de Boaco. The new capital structure would be the following:

Familia Cortez	45.0%
ALDECA	45.0%
Investor #1	5.0%
Investor #3	5.0%

5. The capital structure of Distribuidora Puerto Barrias will not be altered.
6. The board of directors will be chosen as follows:

Familia Cortez	3 directors
ALDECA	3 directors
Investor #1	1 director

7. The bylaws and articles of the corporation would be modified so that important decisions could be adopted with 90% of the stockholders approving a motion (for the General Assembly) and only with the vote of 6 of the 7 directors for the decisions pertaining to the Administrative Council.
8. The administration of Distribuidora de Boaco will correspond to Emin Barjum (CEO ALDECA).
9. The consolidated operations would yield the estimated income before taxes (taking into account current sales prices and costs):

For the fabrication and distribution of ALDECA products:	L. 6.5 million
For the fabrication and distribution of L. de Boaco products:	L. 1.1 million
Total	L. 7.6 million

   Note: Thje contribution by ALDECA seems substantially superior due to the fact that it has been calculated as a marginal contribution, the fixed costs are absorbed by the production of Licorera de Boaco products.
   The income before taxes of ALDECA in 1994 was of L. 3.6 million, with distributorship alcohol manufacturing and sales.

(continues)

EXHIBIT H *(continued)*

Consolidation Analysis

Advantages:
- Currently ALDECA has very little capability of increasing its production capacity without a substantial investment in equipment and buildings. The production capacity of ALDECA is 5000 liters of ethyl alcohol (12,500 liters of liquor) in 24 hours (currently operating at 80% of capacity).
- The production capability of Licorera de Boaco is 15,000 liters of ethyl alcohol (37,500 liters of liquor) in 24 hours.
- Due to superior technology, the direct fabrication costs of Licorera de Boaco are 10% lower than ALDECA's costs.
- The consolidation would strengthen ALDECA's competitive situation against Grupo Cobán, which currently bought a distillery in the north part of the country. (They not only want to produce rum, but also *aguardientes,* attacking ALDECA's core market.)
- The consolidated sales would represent 40% of the liquor market in Honduras.
- ALDECA would have a 17.5% (45% of 39%) direct participation in Distribuidora Puerto Barrias' operations.
- The very valuable location where ALDECA is currently located could be developed for housing or commercial purposes.

Disadvantages:
- Administrative autonomy would be lost.
- Would have to lay off many workers and pay approximately L. 900,000 as compensation. (This cost will be recovered by asking Licorera de Boaco to pay ALDECA L. 6.00 for every box of liquor produced for a period of 2–3 years.)
- The merger agreement would have to be drafted carefully, with a lot of emphasis on detail, to protect both parties, to avoid paralyzing the operations due to disagreement, etc.
- There is always risk of bad faith in the actions of the other party.

Financial:
ALDECA

Machinery and equipment	L. 1,281,000.00
Other installments	L. 228,000.00
Replacement parts and accessories	L. 129,000.00
Total	L. 1,638,000.00

Owners equity and retained earnings	
Licorera de Boaco	L. 4,720,000.00
Distribuidora de Boaco	L. 4,054,000.00
Total	L. 8,774,000.00

them an ultimatum: "Our brands or theirs, but not both." But what if the distributors did not believe that ALDECA could enforce the ultimatum? Sr. Barjum favored discussing the problem with the distributors and explaining to them some of the options that ALDECA was considering, like distributing *aguardiente* directly to the cantinas themselves. The implied threat should be enough to persuade the distributors to avoid Grupo Cobán's brands. Sr. Barjum hoped that the distributors did not know that ALDECA could only ship competitors' products, like the pickup-load of Yuscaran, at a loss.

DISCUSSION QUESTIONS

1. Describe the competitive environment for ALDECA in 1995. Use Porter's Five Forces Model as a framework for analysis.

2. What opportunities was ALDECA facing? Which of those opportunities seemed most feasible and beneficial to the company?

3. What challenges was ALDECA facing? How could the company overcome those challenges?

4. How should ALDECA respond to the entry of Grupo Cobán into the aguardiente market?

5. What the lessons that can be taken away from this case and applied in your business?

REFERENCES

Panet, J-P., Hart, L., and Glassman, O. 1994. *Honduras and Bay Islands Guide,* 2d ed. Washington: Open Road Publishing.

United Nations Economic Commission for Latin America and the Caribbean. 1996 *Report.*

U.S. Central Intelligence Agency. 1995. *World Fact Book.*

US. Department of Commerce. 1996. *National Trade Data Bank.*

U.S. International Trade Administration. 1995. *Country Commercial Guide: Honduras.*

Wizards of the Coast

The excitement was high among the top managers of Wizards of the Coast, the world's leading adventure gaming company, as they sat down to review progress over the first half of 1997. The company had just completed the acquisition of a major competitor, and with the opening of its first gaming entertainment center, it was pioneering a whole new retail concept. After three years of tremendous growth fueled by one hit product, followed by an unexpected downturn in revenues in 1996, Wizards looked to be on the rebound. But everyone knew that the company still had to prove that it had a sustainable growth strategy for the future.

Creating the Magic

In 1997, Wizards of the Coast was a privately held company best known for the world's leading adventure trading-card game, *Magic: The Gathering*®. Since its release in 1993, more than 5 million consumers worldwide had embraced the game, which was available in nine languages and played in over fifty-two countries. (See Appendix A for a description of *Magic*®.)

The Genesis

Wizards of the Coast was founded by Peter Adkison and a group of other young professionals in 1990 to develop role-playing games. Adkison had been intrigued by strategy and role-playing games ever since early childhood. He recalls playing games as a youngster all night long under the comforters of his bed using a flashlight, so that his mother would think he was asleep when she took a peek into the room during the early night hours. In high school, he devel-

This case is intended to be used as a basis for class discussion rather than as an illustration of either effective or ineffective handling of the situation. This case was prepared by Frank T. Rothaermel of Michigan State University and Suresh Kotha and Richard Moxon of the University of Washington. Charles Hill, "Wizards of the Coast— Update" from Charles Hill and Gareth Jones, *Strategic Management,* Fifth Edition. Copyright © 2001 by Houghton Mifflin Company. Used with permission.

oped a passion for the *Dungeons & Dragons*® (*D&D*) adventure role-playing game. (See Appendix B for a description of *D&D*.) It seemed natural to him to turn this hobby into a business. After graduating from college, Adkison worked for Boeing as a computer systems analyst but was eager to start his own venture. He recalls, "I was a small cog in a huge machine that itself was a small cog in a huge machine." Adkison and six of his friends kept their jobs but began developing role-playing games in their spare time.

In 1991, Adkison met Richard Garfield in a chat room on the Internet. At the time, Garfield was a doctoral student in combinational mathematics at the University of Pennsylvania and was known as an avid game player who had been designing his own games since he was a teenager. When the two got together at a game convention, the concept for *Magic*® was born. Adkison had the idea that there was a need for a fantasy role-playing game that was portable and could be played anywhere in no more than an hour. He thought that maybe it should be a card game. Garfield had also been interested in fantasy games since playing a game called *Cosmic Encounter* in the 1980s. One of the pieces in *Cosmic Encounter* had special powers. By invoking these powers, a player could change the rules of the game. This intrigued Garfield, and he wondered what would happen if all the pieces were magic, each one altering the game in some unique way. He believed that this idea could lead to a fantasy board game, but Adkison persuaded him to focus on cards instead and to think about a format in which players could trade cards.

Garfield came back a few weeks later with a prototype of *Magic: The Gathering*®. The idea was to combine a fantasy game concept, where players controlled the acts of mystical characters, with a trading-card format, where players could buy and sell collectible cards similar to those of their sports heroes. As Garfield remembers, "The concept of a trading-card game was one of the only 'Eureka!' experiences I've had." Adkison emphasizes the point that the first prototype of *Magic*® resembled very closely the later commercialized version of *Magic*®: "We still have the original, hand-drawn cards, and gosh, if you know how to play *Magic*®, you can play just fine with that very first game."

Operating out of the basement of Adkison's home as an eight-person company, Wizards of the Coast released *Magic: The Gathering*® in August 1993. The game became an overnight success. The first printing of 10 million cards, which was expected to last a year, sold out in just six weeks. According to one owner of a game store, "My initial order was for 24 units, my second order was for 572, and my third was to send everything you've got in the warehouse." With its sales success also came critical acclaim and the winning of several game and toy industry awards.

After *Magic*'s® instant splash, Garfield quit his new teaching position at Whitman College and began to pursue his true passion as a game inventor with Wizards of the Coast. Adkison made Garfield an equity partner in Wizards of the Coast and fully dedicated his then fledgling firm to creating fantasy card games. Adkison too quit his job at Boeing to become the president and CEO of Wizards of the Coast. (See Figure 1 for a timeline of Wizards of the Coast.)

Products and Customers

Magic® cards were sold in starter decks of sixty randomly selected cards for about $8.95, and booster packs of eight or fifteen cards for about $2.95 retail price. Even though these were the recommended retail prices, it was not uncommon for retailers to unbundle decks and to mark up the prices of highly demanded cards. The cards featured original artwork that appealed to fantasy-game players and collectors. As a consequence, *Magic*® cards were both collected and traded, with a card's price determined by its strategic role and its collector value. Each deck was unique, so no two players had identical sets of cards. Players traded cards in order to create a deck with desired characteristics.

According to the chief game developer for Wizards of the Coast, twenty-seven-year-old George Skaff Elias, the typical *Magic*® player is a person with a good education, disposable income, and an affinity for computers. While the game is most popular with males in their teens or twenties, the game also caught on with younger teens and with older men and women as well. College dormitories are a particular breeding ground for new "gamers." Compared with the typical player of a board game such as Monopoly, the player of *Magic*® sees the game more like a hobby, something on which to spend a significant amount of time and money.

Manufacturing and Distribution

Wizards contracted out the design, manufacturing, and packaging of its cards and other products. Most of its *Magic*® cards were designed by independent artists, who earned royalties from their sales by Wizards. The tremendous royalty payments due to the unexpected success of *Magic*® were initially a problem for Wizards, but it was solved in a friendly round of renegotiations with the artists. In the beginning, the company relied only on one supplier, Carta Mundi in Belgium, since no other firm could deliver the quality needed along with the ability to do the sophisticated card sorting that was required. During the first two years of booming popularity, manufacturing capacity was the single biggest constraint on the growth of Wizards. Carta Mundi was in 1997 still the largest supplier, but other suppliers were contracted as the game grew and as they were able to meet Wizards' standards.

Wizards built a widespread network to market its cards. Most adventure games were sold through small game, comic, or hobby shops, which were often mom-and-pop stores, supplied through relatively small distributors. These shops were critical for reaching the serious gamers and accounted for about 75 percent of the company's sales. Wizards allocated new card series to these stores, and there was often a feeding frenzy as consumers rushed to get an edge with new cards. As the popularity of *Magic*® rose, Wizards was able to enter national toy chains such as Toys 'R' Us, bookstores such as Barnes & Noble, and discounters such as Target. These stores did not have the same atmosphere and appeal as the small retailers but were more effective for reaching the mass market.

The Wizards Culture

While developing the systems needed to manage a much larger enterprise, Adkison was trying to pre-

FIGURE 1

Timeline of Wizards of the Coast

1990   Wizards of the Coast is formed as a sole proprietorship by Peter Adkison (May).
Wizards of the Coast is incorporated (December).

1991   Adkison meets Richard Garfield on the Internet.
First play-test version of *Magic: The Gathering®* is distributed.
Wizards acquires the Talislanta role-playing game line from Bard Games.

1992   Wizards releases its first new product, *The Primal Order®*.
Six other role-playing products are released.
Palladium sues Wizards for trademark infringement in its product *The Primal Order®*.
Garfield Games is formed to launch *Magic: The Gathering®*.

1993   Wizards lays off all its employees.
Everyone stays on to launch *Magic®*, being paid in stock.
The Palladium lawsuit is settled.
Magic: The Gathering® is launched to record sales.
The *Duelist Convocation (DCI)* is started to provide tournament play for *Magic®*.
All employees are hired back.
The company moves from "the basement" to real offices.
The *Duelist* magazine is launched.
Garfield Games and Wizards of the Coast merge.

1994   Five expansions for *Magic®* are released.
Jyhad®, the second trading-card game, based on the Vampire RPG, is released.
First world championships for *Magic®* are held in Seattle.
First European office is opened in Glasgow.

1995   *Netrunner®*, Wizards of the Coast's third trading-card game, is released.
The Everyway® role-playing game is released.
Wizards buys Andon, a convention management company.
The *Magic: The Gathering®* computer game is released by Microprose.
More than thirty employees are laid off in company's largest downsizing.
All game divisions are divested except for trading-card games.

1996   The *Magic: The Gathering®* $1,000,000 Pro Tour is launched in New York.
The Wizards of the Coast tournament center opens at corporate headquarters.
The BattleTech trading-card game is released.
Wizards gains the contract to run Origins, the second largest game convention in the United States.

1997   The Wizards of the Coast Game Center opens in Seattle.
Wizards acquires TSR Inc.
Wizards acquires Five Rings Publishing Group.
First Wizards retail store opens in Seattle.

serve the creative culture that was present when the company was formed. Leading by example, for many years he refused to have his own office or even a cubicle. On his business cards and memos, his position and title was stated as "CEO and janitor." He saw the company as similar to a small software firm, with a casual, creative atmosphere that tolerated individualism and creativity, expressed, for example, in eccentric clothing, body piercing, and frequent nerf wars among employees. But over the years, the atmosphere had become more reserved, and Adkison now even has a corner office.

Wizards' executives and employees tended to be very committed to the gaming concept. Garfield, the inventor of *Magic*®, sees adventure games as the "intellectual counterpart of sports—they keep you mentally fit." He believes that with playing *Magic*® comes "a lot of stealth education," whether it is art appreciation because of the beautiful cards or enhanced literacy because of the occasional quote from Shakespeare. Garfield also believes that *Magic*® is a strategic game that could be played successfully only when the player has a good understanding of strategy, probability, and chance.

Adkison, however, recognized that devoted gamers did not always make successful executives.

> There's nobody in the company who's ever managed a company this size, including me. We're trying to balance the desire for top-notch people to take us to the next level with the desire to stay true to people who founded the company. And that is very, very tough. We faced a lot of organizational problems when hiring people on top of an existing layer. None of the people who reported to me in 1993 report to me now. Many of them are still here, but experienced managers have come into the organization between them and myself. Our board of directors has evolved also, going from a board composed mainly of founders and management to a board with several outside directors, who have a lot of gray hair.

As Adkison pointed out, the firm hired experienced managers from established toy companies, used consultants on strategy and operational issues, and brought outsiders into its board of directors. In the meantime, Adkison himself completed an MBA degree in 1997 at the University of Washington Business School. He knew that he would need to continue strengthening the organization if it was to create a sustainable strategy for growth. Some of the newly hired professionals, who came with strong credentials, did not fit in well at Wizards and were asked to leave after a short time. Adkison made the transition from an entrepreneur to a traditional CEO as he deepened his theoretical understanding of business as well as his management skills and combined both with his intuitive feel for the gaming business.

The Adventure Gaming Industry

Wizards' executives defined the company as part of the adventure gaming industry, which is itself part of the much larger toy industry. They followed publications of the *Toy Manufacturers of America,* as well as the more specialized *Comics Retailer,* a monthly publication that had in-depth reports on gaming developments. Total U.S. toy industry sales in 1996 were estimated at more than $17 billion, of which the biggest single category was video games. Outside of video games, the games/puzzles category accounted for approximately $1.4 billion of sales. Role-playing, trading-card and war games, the segments in which Wizards competed most directly, accounted for about $350 million to $500 million in 1996 according to *Comics Retailer,* while the Game Manufacturers Association estimated gaming sales at $750 million.

The adventure gaming industry began in the 1960s with the development of a number of war games. The industry was revolutionized and began rapid growth in the early 1970s with the introduction of *Dungeons & Dragons*®, the first popular role-playing game. The game attracted players with its complexity and with the opportunity for players to exercise their creativity. The industry was revolutionized once again in the early 1990s with the introduction of *Magic*®. By 1997, *Dungeons & Dragons*® and *Magic*® were still the top-selling role-playing and trading-card games. The rest of the industry consisted of another major competitor, Games Workshop, a UK-based company with revenues of more than $100 million, and many smaller competitors. Industry observers estimated that the most serious potential future competition would come from companies invading adventure games from other industries.

Although there was no clear distinction between adventure and family games, what made adventure games unique was the fact that people pursued these games as a serious hobby, sometimes dedicating many hours a week to playing a certain game. In Adkison's words, "The Magic player is a hobby gamer, meaning it is a person that would rather game than do anything else. If this person could, he or she would play all the time. The constraint people are facing is the time they have to play." This commitment of hobby players led some critics to characterize players of *Dungeons & Dragons*® and *Magic*® as members of a cult.

Industry executives, however, feel that this is an unfair image and see most gamers as devoted to the intellectual and creative challenges offered by the games. According to a survey conducted by the *Game Manufacturers Association,* adventure game enthusiasts are young, literate and are doing well in scholastic endeavors. The survey results indicate that a majority of them are indeed very young—about 31 percent are between ten and fourteen years of age, about 37 percent are between fifteen and eighteen years old, and 32 percent are nineteen years or older. The survey also revealed that about 82 percent of the respondents indicated that they maintain a grade-point average of 3.0 or better in high school or college, and about 65 percent said that they read thirty-six or more books a year. About 80 percent described themselves as book readers.

Another issue facing the gaming industry is the rise of the Internet and of computer-based games. Most people in the industry regarded typical video games as representing completely different customer experiences: either lonely quests through fantasy worlds or "shoot-em-up" arcade-like games. But the Internet offered the possibility of role-playing and trading-cards in a virtual world.

Growing the Magic

The success of *Magic*® put Wizards on an explosive growth trajectory. Sales of about $200,000 in 1993 rocketed to $57 million in 1994 and $127 million in 1995. Adkison muses: "Our margins are fantastic, just like Microsoft's on software, because we basically sell

intellectual property. We have basically zero marginal cost." Wizards and Adkison had become instant entrepreneurial superstars. The company grew to about 500 employees and in 1996 moved to a brand-new, 178,000-square-foot office complex down the street from Boeing's job center in Renton, Washington. It had also opened several international sales offices.

Growth, however, brought problems. Staffing became close to chaotic. For instance, Adkison found that someone who had been on the payroll for several months had never really been hired by anybody. According to Adkison, "I've made so many mistakes, it's not even funny, and that is not counting the mistakes I made last week." Many of the gamers who started with the company were not ready to move into managerial roles. On the other hand, some managers who were brought in from outside could not work well with the gamers.

As it was already the dominant adventure trading-card game, there was not much growth potential for *Magic*® in taking an increasing share of this market. Wizards focused instead on extending the *Magic*® brand name into other products and in reaching the mass market to increase the overall size of the adventure trading-card industry. At the same time, Wizards had begun promoting *Magic*® tournaments in an effort to give the game added legitimacy and defend it from competing games.

Extending the Brand

Adkison was now attempting to leverage the *Magic*® brand name through licensing into books, computer games, and other products. With the popularity of *Magic*®, Wizards was able to pick and choose its opportunities. For example, *Magic*® appeared as a book series, published by Harper-Collins, with more than half a million copies sold. It was also out in two CD-ROM computer games. Wizards' executives felt that bookstores were a logical market for Wizards' products, since *Magic*® players tended to be heavy readers, and *Magic*® itself was often played in bookstores.

Magic® merchandise had been extended—through licensing into prepaid phone cards, clothing, card albums and protectors, a *Magic*® strategy guide and encyclopedia, and calendars. Wizards had also reached an agreement with an Internet development and design company to develop interactive CD-ROM products to serve as guides to the fantasy worlds created by Wizards. Wizards had also received movie and television offers, but no agreements had been reached so far. Licensing revenues were estimated to be about $1 million annually.

Going for the Mass Market

The dream of Wizards and other adventure game developers was the mass-market role-playing game. Selling a normal board game was a one-shot revenue of less than $10 to a game company, but customers could spend up to $500 per year on a role-playing game. A mass-market hit could easily create a billion-dollar company.

In the summer of 1997, Wizards introduced a more mainstream version of *Magic®* named *Portal®*. The game was targeted at a broader audience, such as younger teens and families, and was launched with a media campaign of close to $5 million. The aim was to move toward a consumer other than the core gamer, who had made *Magic®* a magical success. *Portal®* would be distributed through mass-market retailers such as Toys 'R' Us and Target. Wizards also introduced the so-called Arc System games. The Arc System game is a generic trading-card game system, which allows the development of card decks based on a variety of popular characters from television, such as Xena, the Warrior Princess. Those decks can also be intermingled.

But Wizards saw risks in the mass market as well. *Magic®* gamers were attracted to the atmosphere of game stores and to the experience of the game, not just the game itself. Mass-market retailers, on the other hand, saw games as "boxes." And given their tremendous buying power, Wizards would not enjoy the same margins that it did on its *Magic®* sales.

Developing Tournaments

To sustain and increase *Magic®* sales, Wizards was attempting to professionalize the activity of playing *Magic®*, transforming it into a legitimate sport. Noted Adkison, "It's been proven that sports are very sustainable. They hold people's attention for a long time." One part of the strategy was to create players with celebrity standing who could then push the game's popularity in the mass market.

Tournaments had been organized informally in the first years of *Magic®*, many of them held in and

sponsored by the game stores selling *Magic®*. And hundreds of tournaments were held each year. In 1996, the company organized a six-city professional tournament series that offered $1 million in prizes and scholarships. Wizards also created a computer-based global ranking for all professional players, accessible at the Wizards home page (www.wizards.com). In the United States, more than 50,000 tournament players competed in thirty leagues.

The *Magic®* World Championships generated such interest that they were carried on television by ESPN for the first time in 1997. Players from more than forty countries competed for individual and team titles and for $250,000 in prize money. Wizards was able to attract a corporate partner, MCI Telecommunications, to sponsor the world championships. According to one news analysis, the partnership gave legitimacy to Wizards and provided a mass audience, while MCI was able to tap an attractive audience by being associated with a "cool" event. According to the company that brokered the deal, *Magic®* players were especially attractive because of their passion for the game and their desire to collect everything associated with it. "You've never seen loyalty like this. It's unrivaled across any other product or service category," one analyst stated. MCI agreed to sponsor Wizard's *Magic®* tournaments in exchange for exclusive worldwide rights to produce and distribute *Magic®* prepaid telephone cards featuring the artwork of *Magic®* cards.

Wizards also published a variety of magazines connected with its games. *The Duelist* featured information on upcoming *Magic®* tournaments and articles and tips from celebrity players. The *Dragon* magazine, which came to Wizards with the acquisition of the *Dungeons & Dragons®* game, had been published since the 1970s.

Opening Game Centers

In May 1997, Wizards of the Coast opened its first retail and gaming store, a 34,000-square-foot Wizards of the Coast Game Center located in Seattle, close to the campus of the University of Washington. Designed as the first entertainment center solely aimed at adventure games, it offered an extensive array of arcade video games, sold games and associated merchandise, offered food and beverages, and provided a place to meet and compete with other trading-card gamers. It was also intended to be a site for tournaments. According to Adkison,

> The game center is sort of like Nike Town or Planet Hollywood. Playing is a serious hobby for the Magic player. Therefore, we decided to create the ultimate gaming and retail environment. This is a club, a hangout, a place for the devoted game players to go and know they can play any time. I was inspired by Starbucks' concept of the 'third place.' I wanted to create a third place for the gamer, a place between home and school or work. Starbucks inspired us but we want to make it even better.

Wizards hoped that game centers would create an even stronger game playing community. The company also hoped that game centers could expand the interest in games and encourage people to consider games as an entertainment choice, like going to the movies or out to dinner. Just as the Cineplex concept broadened to the moviegoing public, Wizards hoped that "gameplexes" could do the same thing for games. The first Wizards of the Coast Game Center carried many competitive games, but Wizards games were featured prominently.

Lisa Stevens, one of the original founders and vice president of Location-Based Entertainment, comments: "Our strategic intent was driven by the quest 'to make games as big as movies.' We were all inspired by that quest. And then we ask ourselves, what made the movies big? Basically, the invention of the Cineplex, where you could go as a group and see different movies. That is why we offer different games in our retail stores, even games from some of our competitors." Another objective behind game centers was to improve the retail distribution of the Wizards product line. The company was disappointed with the support given by traditional retailers to the games and felt that it knew better than retailers how to retail and support its games.

Wizards knew that the success of game centers was not a sure thing. Other companies, such as Gameworks, had introduced family entertainment centers with very limited success. Wizards was encouraged, however, by the success of the U.K.-based Games Workshop, with its gaming centers featuring the popular game *Warhammer*®. Adkison pointed out: "We have the brand but we need to improve

distribution. Target and other stores help sustain the sales but those stores don't create new players, that's what we do in our retail stores."

Product Development

Wizards had developed and marketed what was viewed as many great games, but none was able to replicate *Magic*'s® success. Although Adkison remained optimistic, he realized that repeating that tremendous success would be difficult. "We have several things we're working on in R&D that could turn out to be like *Magic*®. But in the gaming business, you can't bank on that success. We have to learn to make money with smaller releases."

The adventure game industry had developed largely as a result of two runaway hits, first *Dungeons & Dragons*®, and then *Magic*®. Adkison expected that another hit would one day revolutionize the industry once again. But it seemed unlikely that the same company would be responsible for the next revolution. Wizards needed to position itself to succeed even if it was not the one to develop this next hit.

Besides aggressively promoting *Magic*®, Wizards of the Coast had applied for a patent on *Magic*®, covering not the design of the cards but the method of play. It was set on collecting royalty payments from imitators, which had blossomed in recent years. Entry barriers to the game industry were relatively low, and Wizards estimated that there were more than 100 games trying to compete with *Magic*®.

Adkison recognized that Wizards of the Coast was still a one-product company, whose future was tightly linked to the success of *Magic*®: "*Magic*® provides over 90 percent of our cash flow. It is obviously our primary focus. The big strategic issue with *Magic*® is to develop its potential to become a 'classic game' that yields steady profits year after year. I wouldn't mind being a $500 million to $1 billion company. We want to make games as big as the movies."

Acquisitions

Wizards had recently completed two major acquisitions: Five Rings Publishing, the developer of the *Legends of the Five Rings*® trading-card game; and TSR, the creator of the pioneering *Dungeons & Dragons*® adventure game. The latter acquisition brought the number one (Wizards) and number three (TSR) of the adventure gaming industry under one roof in 1997. The number two of the industry is the publicly traded company Games Workshop from the United Kingdom. Adkison comments on Wizards' acquisition strategy:

> Looking at hobby gaming industry means that you need to look at a horizontally narrowed focused segment. And there are only three games in the hobby category out there: 1) *Magic*®, 2) *Dungeons & Dragons*®, and 3) *Warhammer*® [owned by Games Workshop]. And the sweet thing is that we own two of those three. One thing I have learned in my competitive analysis course in MBA-school is that it may be better to be a big player in a small market than to be a small player in a big market. And we want to be a big player.

However, integrating these acquisitions had been a major challenge for Wizards. It had to sort out TSR's very serious financial difficulties, and it moved the TSR operations and many of its staff from Wisconsin to its Seattle area headquarters.

Wizards had also confirmed reports that it had held discussions with Westend Games, which had the license for a Star Wars role-playing game, and another for a DC Comics role-playing game. There were other small game companies that might also make attractive acquisition candidates.

Global Expansion

Wizards estimated that *Magic*® was played in more than fifty countries by more than 5 million players. The company now had international offices in Antwerp, London, and Paris, and it planned to open other offices in Europe and Asia soon. Adkison noted that international sales had been very important in sustaining the company during the downturn in U.S. sales in 1996. The international market still had a lot of expansion potential.

Beyond Magic®: Challenges Facing Peter Adkison

In December 1995, Wizards had a round of downsizing as Adkison was attempting to focus the company on *Magic*®. Wizards divested itself of the product lines that were not primarily trading-card games. The company's growth came to a sudden halt in 1996,

when sales fell off to $117 million. According to Adkison, while the cause was partly the inevitable leveling-off in the growth of *Magic*'s® customer base, the downturn was also due to the fragmentation of the retail game stores. The success of *Magic*® had drawn many entrepreneurs into the game store business, but there was not enough room for all of them. The resulting shakeout caused some distributors to go under, and this hit Wizards too.

In addition, many imitators offered role-playing adventure games on-line, and Wizards' executives worried that such games might replace the face-to-face experience of Wizards' *Magic*® and *Dungeons & Dragons*®. Adkison recognized that the company would have to respond to the Internet challenge: "Currently, we are looking at e-commerce, and how to sell on-line. Should we ignore it or crush it?"

While sales in 1997 were expected to be close to the same level as in 1996, Adkison was aiming at future growth. "We certainly can operate at a slow growth mode and make nice profits," he said. "But we are focused on growing the company more rapidly in the future." Part of the pressure for growth was coming from its original investors. Many of them were friends of the original entrepreneurs, came from modest backgrounds, and had become rich from their investment in Wizards. But this wealth was all on paper, and many wanted to cash out some of their investments. But to take the company public at an attractive price, Wizards would need to have a good growth story for new investors. Hence it was critical to develop a sustainable growth strategy. This was the central issue facing Wizards' executives as they sat down in mid 1997 to discuss Wizards' future.

Appendix A: Magic: The Gathering®

The game *Magic: The Gathering*® combines elements of chess, bridge, and the 1970s role-playing game *Dungeons & Dragons*®. *Magic*® is a trading-card game in which the two players are rival wizards dueling for control of a magical "universe" called *Dominia*. Each player starts out with twenty life points, or lives. The goal is to reduce the opponent's life points from twenty to zero before the opponent has reduced your life points to zero.

Before starting the game, each player builds a deck of at least forty cards from his or her collection of cards and then plays that deck against the opponent's deck. Each player begins by shuffling his or her deck and drawing seven cards. The players take turns; each player's turn is made up of a series of actions, such as playing cards and attacking the opponent. There are several types of elaborately illustrated cards a player can choose from. For example, lands are the most basic, providing the magical energy a player needs to play all other cards. Creatures can fight for the player either by attacking the opponent or by fighting off the opponent's creatures. Other cards represent spells that a player can cast to hurt the opponent or help his or her creatures. The basic strategy of *Magic*® lies in choosing when to play what card and when to use what creatures to attack the opponent or protect yourself. More complex strategies involve combining cards to make them more powerful and choosing which cards to use in the player's deck to make it most effective. Games usually last between fifteen minutes and half an hour; however, some games can last up to several hours.

One of the key features of *Magic*® is that each game played is unique since each player starts out with a deck of 40 cards individually selected from among the more than 4,000 different cards sold. It is not uncommon for a player to own several hundred or even thousands of cards. Each player tries to assemble his or her favorite 40 cards out of the pool he or she owns according to the player's intended strategy. This ingenious twist encourages players to buy or trade for new cards to enhance their powers and strategic game options.

In addition, the game is in permanent evolution since new cards are constantly released and older cards are retired by Wizards of the Coast. These retired cards gain instant status as collectibles to be bought, sold, and traded in hobby stores, on college campuses, and on the Internet. New cards are issued in different sets and limited editions; many cards are even printed in limited numbers. These perpetual expansions have kept the game novel and contributed to its phenomenal growth as players engage in frantic buying and trading of cards in a fantasy arms race to create a competitive advantage in their individualist starter deck. Since most of the strategy in *Magic*® is assembling the unassailable deck, serious players have spent hundreds, if not thousands, of dollars to create their dream deck. This has led to the criticism that affluent players are more likely to win than their poorer counterparts.

With each expansion, *Dominia,* the fantasy multiverse where the wizards battle, also expands. "Think of *Dominia* as a beach," says Wizards spokeswoman Sue-Lane Wood. "Each expansion is a grain of sand on that beach, each its own universe." Currently, *Magic*® has undergone just a dozen or so extensions. However, the possible number of expansions is limited only by the imagination and the players' willingness to remain bewitched.

Appendix B: Dungeons & Dragons®

The *Dungeons & Dragons*® role-playing game, commonly known as *D&D,* evolved from historical war gaming, in which armchair generals lined up armies of painted miniature figurines on tabletops, decorated to look like battlefields, and staged skirmishes that were either historical or theoretical. Troop movements were negotiated with the help of rulers, and combat was resolved through the roll of dice and consultation of tables. Role-playing began with an idea to put aside the role of an entire army and take up the role of an individual character, who would infiltrate a castle through the sewers below to open the drawbridge and let in the invading army. This scenario proved so popular that the designer ran it repeatedly, for numerous friends and fellow wargamers, eventually substituting fantasy monsters for castle guards as obstacles to be overcome. Eventually, one of the players, Gary Gygax, volunteered to create standard rules for the new game, and he added rules for playing spell-casting wizards to offer an alternative to role-playing a warrior. These new rules were first published in Gygax's wargaming periodical *Chainmail,* but in 1974 he developed a full set of rules and called them *Dungeons & Dragons*®.

Over the next twenty-five years, *D&D* would be distributed in twenty-two countries and translated into more than a dozen languages. The *Advanced Dungeons & Dragons*® game expanded on the original in 1978, and the second-edition *AD&D*® game hit the market in 1989. Over a dozen *campaign settings*—distinct worlds in which to play *D&D*—were published over the years, and novels, computer games, board games, cartoons, comic books, and other media built upon the brand. Throughout its life, the *D&D* game frequently has been misunderstood, condemned, associated with nerds, and given up for dead, yet it retains near-universal brand recognition even among people who have never played it, and sales of the game are rising.

How D&D Is Played

Although computer games are simulating the traditional game with increasing efficiency, *D&D* is played with paper, pencil, dice, and rulebooks. A character is created by rolling dice to determine his or her basic physical and mental attributes, then the player chooses the character's profession (for example, fighter or wizard), equips the character for the road, joins with a group of friends who also have created characters, and goes on an adventure. One of the players takes on the special role of *Dungeon Master.* This person presents the situation at hand to the rest of the players, who react in character to cooperatively tell a story and enjoy the adventure together. For example, the Dungeon Master may say something like this, "You cross the drawbridge and enter the Castle of Nightmares, ready to seek and recover the famed *Staff of the Magi,* but a group of creatures steps from the shadows within to block your way. What will you do?" Each of the players in turn declares what his or her character intends to do—call out a greeting or threat, draw a weapon and prepare for battle, cast a spell, or anything else the player imagines the character might do under the circumstances—and then dice are rolled to determine the order in which actions take place and whether or not they are successful. (The Dungeon Master plays the role of every person and creature met by the adventuring party.) Rounds of action continue until the encounter is resolved. The player-characters then move on and continue to explore the castle until they achieve their goal (in this case, finding the Staff) or until their characters are either captured or killed by the inhabitants of the castle. Collectively, they tell the story of the adventure, and collectively they work to succeed (or fail). Assuming the party is successful, they gain *experience points,* grow more powerful, and move on to even more challenging scenarios. Ongoing campaigns may last for years, with groups playing every week for hours at a time.

Update[1]

Established in 1990 by Peter Adkison, Wizards of the Coast had experienced rapid growth largely on the strength of its best-selling trading card game, *Magic: The Gathering*®, reaching annual sales of around $150 million in 1998. Many skeptics familiar with the fashion-driven nature of the toy and game industry thought *Magic*® would be nothing more than a fad, and that in time Wizards would fade as sales of *Magic*® slumped. Adkison was determined to prove his critics wrong. In 1996 he formulated a three-pronged strategy to build Wizards into the premier brand in the hobby game industry.[2]

One aspect of Adkison's strategy was to broaden the appeal of *Magic*® and take the game into the mass market. This involved the development of a simpler version of *Magic, Portal*®, which was targeted at people who had never played *Magic*® before and was designed to be sold through mass market retailers such as Toys 'R' Us. Wizards also tried to keep its existing customers engaged in *Magic*® by organizing *Magic*® leagues and tournaments. According to Adkison, the objective of the organized game play was to turn the game into an "intellectual sport similar to chess."

A second leg of the strategy was to broaden the brand. Although Adkison would have liked to do this by developing new games internally, he also recognized that doing so was a difficult proposition. Lightning rarely strikes twice, and with *Magic*® Wizards had already had one lightning strike. Accordingly, in 1997 Wizards acquired TSR, creator of one of the more enduring games in the hobby arena, *Dungeons & Dragons*®. The third leg of the strategy involved forward integration into retail with the establishment of Wizards Game Centers. The game centers were designed to fulfill a dual role—they contained retail stores that sold games, including Wizards' offerings, and they promoted game play and helped to build the brand. To achieve this second role, space in the centers was set aside for people to meet and play games, and the centers were to become a site for hosting *Magic*® tournaments. The centers also had an area set aside for coin-operated video games.

---

[1]The source for much of the material in this case is interviews by Charles Hill with key players at Wizards, including CEO Peter Adkison.

[2]The author of this update, Charles Hill, assisted in the facilitation of strategic planning sessions at Wizards that helped to result in this strategy.

The Pokemon *Phenomenon*

With this strategy in place, Adkison believed that Wizards had a chance to achieve decent growth and become the dominant enterprise in the hobby game industry. Then lightning struck Wizards a second time: the *Pokemon*® phenomenon. *Pokemon*®, the endearing set of characters invented by Nintendo, had begun life in Japan as a game for Nintendo's N64 and *Game Boy*® video game platforms. In 1997, one of Nintendo's employees had developed the *Pokemon*® trading card game. The Nintendo employee was an avid player of *Magic: The Gathering*®, and he had simply taken the underlying structure of the *Magic*® game, referred to in the industry as the "game mechanic," and applied it to a new set of characters, those of the *Pokemon*® world. The resulting trading-card game was a sensation in Japan.

Seeing the potential, Nintendo decided to sell the trading-card game worldwide. Nintendo, however, faced two problems in selling *Pokemon*® trading cards outside Japan. First, it lacked the distribution required to sell the game. Second, Wizards of the Coast had applied for and received a patent on the game mechanic underlying *Magic*®. Since the *Pokemon*® trading-card game used the same game mechanic, it technically might have been in violation of this patent. The obvious solution to this dilemma was for Nintendo to license the ex-Japanese rights for the *Pokemon*® game to the company, with both the patent on the underlying game mechanic and with an established distribution system, brand name, and industry expertise—Wizards of the Coast.

The deal soon exceeded the expectations of both companies. *Pokemon*® quickly became a global phenomenon among the six- to twelve-year-old set. Sales of the trading cards rocketed along with sales of the video games and the growing popularity of an associated TV series. For Wizards, the result was an unexpected bonanza. The company's sales surged from $150 million in 1998 to an estimated $400 million in 1999. This was largely due to the popularity of *Pokemon*® trading cards, which accounted for some $225 million of this increase.[3] As with *Magic*®, the company quickly issued expansion sets for the basic *Pokemon*® game that emphasized new themes and generated incremental sales revenues from established customers. The collectible aspect of *Pokemon*® trading cards was, if anything, greater than that experienced with *Magic*®, with kids competing with one another to collect a full set of trading cards, including highly valued rare cards.

Another appealing aspect of the *Pokemon*® phenomenon was that it broadened the appeal of Wizards into a new demographic that it had not been able to reach with *Magic*®—six- to twelve-year-olds. The "dark themes" of *Magic*® had put off many parents while appealing to fourteen- to twenty-five-year-olds with a passion for strategy games. *Pokemon*® had the opposite effect, for the underlying mathematical aspect of the game intrigued some parents. At Wizards, a hope now emerged that kids would cut their teeth on *Pokemon*®, and then later, as they grew older, move onto *Magic*®. Moreover, *Pokemon*® allowed Wizards to widen its distribution system, selling in mainstream locations that had not sold *Magic*®.

The Hasbro Acquisition

With *Pokemon*® emerging as *the* theme of the 1999–2000 Christmas season, the success of Wizards attracted the attention of major players in the toy industry, including most notably, Hasbro. In September 1999, Hasbro made a $325 million bid to acquire Wizards, which the company quickly accepted.[4] Under the terms of the deal, Peter Adkison would continue as CEO of Wizards for at least another four years, the company would remain at its current location, and it would be granted a high degree of operating autonomy. Hasbro was looking to Wizards to broaden its offering of *Pokemon*® toys and games in advance of the upcoming holiday season. In addition, the growing presence of Wizards in the hobby niche of the game industry, along with its growing retail presence, were all appealing to Hasbro, which was suffering from stagnating sales among many of its traditional toy offerings.

From Wizards' perspective, the bid from Hasbro had a number of attractive features. Wizards had long planned to take the company public, but recognized that executing an initial public offering (IPO) might be very difficult given the skeptical view of the hobby game industry held on Wall Street. Many of

---

[3]J. Milliot, "Hasbro to Acquire Wizards of the Coast," *Publishers Weekly*, September 20, 1999, p. 12.
[4]J. Pereira and D. Golden, "Games: with Wizards and Dragons, Hasbro Expands Its Reach," *Wall Street Journal*, September 10, 1999, p. B1.

Wizards' key employees held significant stock in the company, but, absent of an IPO, this stock was not very liquid. The market was very thin given that there were only about 300 stockholders. The Hasbro bid allowed these employees to turn their illiquid Wizards stock into cold, hard cash, a very appealing option to many. Moreover, for Wizards, an acquisition by Hasbro gave the company the opportunity to use Hasbro's brand name to open certain doors, such as those of mass market retailers that had traditionally been reluctant to stock the products of the hobby game industry. Hasbro's financial muscle could also help Wizards to accelerate its retail store strategy, make further acquisitions in the industry, and fund the advertising required to grow its brand.

Strategy Going Forward

The acquisition by Hasbro did not signal any big change in strategy at Wizards. The company continued to take steps to build its *Magic*® and *Pokemon* trading-card games, hoping that, like *Monopoly*® and *Risk*®, these games would become "classic" and not just fads. These steps included an extension of the organized play concept to the *Pokemon*® game, issuing of more expansion packs and new editions for *Magic*®. In addition, the company continued to look for other opportunities to add to its franchise in the trading-card arena. In February 2000, the company announced that it had reached an agreement with Warner Publishing to create a *Harry Potter* trading-card game that would employ a game mechanic similar to that for *Magic*® and *Pokemon*®, and be targeted at ten- to fourteen-year-olds, the prime demographic for the best-selling *Harry Potter* books. The *Harry Potter* game was scheduled to be released in late 2000. Also in February 2000, the company announced that it had reached a deal with

the Major League Baseball Association and the Major League Baseball Players Association to create a trading-card game with a baseball theme that used MLB players as its central characters.[5]

Wizards also continued to aggressively pursue its retail strategy. Indeed, here Wizards had made a major strategic move prior to the Hasbro acquisition. In May 1999, Wizards acquired The Game Keeper Inc., which owned a chain of fifty-three retail stores selling chess, puzzles, backgammon, dominoes, and family board games. Most of the stores were located in malls on the West Coast. The plan was to add the full range of Wizards games to these stores and gradually convert them over to the Wizards brand name.[6] Wizards also continued to pursue its steady expansion of the bigger-destination Wizards Game Centers. In mid-1999 it had six game centers. By April 2000, the number had risen to eighteen and the company announced plans to open another thirty-four game centers in 2000. Of these thirty-four, six stores would be converted from Game Keeper stores, while the remaining centers would be net additions. Not all of the game centers would be as large as the original Seattle location, but the average size would still be around 2,700 square feet, again split among a retail store, an area for game play, and an area dedicated to coin-operated video games. The combination seemed to be a winning formula: the video game and game play area drawing in customers (and money in the case of the video games), who would then make purchases from the retail store.[7]

---

[5]S. P. Chan, "Wizards to make Harry Potter Cards," *Seattle Times,* February 12, 2000, p. B1.
[6]B. Ramsey, "Wizards Buys Chain of Stores," *Seattle Post Intelligencer,* May 6, 1999, p. D2.
[7]D. Scheraga, "Would You Like to Play a Game?" *Chain Store Age,* April 2000, pp. 50–51.

DISCUSSION QUESTIONS

1. What challenges did Wizard experience because of rapid growth? What would you have done differently?

2. Which sources of capital were available to Wizard when it was looking to grow? How did the management team decide on the most appropriate financing?

3. What was Wizard's growth strategy? Do you agree or disagree, given the times?

4. What was the impact of global expansion early in the game?

Notes

Chapter 1

[1]Reynolds, P.D. (2001). *National Panel Study of U.S. Business Start-Ups*. Kansas City, Mo: Kauffman Foundation/Entrepreneurship Research Consortium.

[2]The Internet Society, www.isoc.org.

[3]King, R. (2001). "Fallen Idol." *Business 2.0* (August 23): www.business2.com.

[4]Brockhaus, R.H. (1980). "Risk-taking Propensity of Entrepreneurs." *Academy of Management Journal,* 23: 509-520; Drucker, P.F. (1985). *Innovation and Entrepreneurship.* New York:Harper & Row.

[5]McClelland, D.C. (1965). "N-Achievement and Entrepreneurship: A Longitudinal Study," *Journal of Personality and Social Psychology,* 1: 389-392.

[6]Teal, E.J., and A.B. Carroll (1999). "Moral Reasoning Skills: Are Entrepreneurs Different?" *Journal of Business Ethics,* 19(3): 229-240.

[7]Greenberger, D.B., and D.L.Sexton (1988). "An Interactive Model of New Venture Initiation." *Journal of Small Business Management,* 1-7; Brockhaus, R., and P. Horowitz (1986). "The Psychology of the Entrepreneur." In *The Art and Science of Entrepreneurship,* edited by D. Sexton and R. Smilor. Cambridge, MA: Ballinger.

[8]Begley, T., and D. Boyd (1987). "Psychological Characteristics Associated with Performance in Entrepreneurial Firms and Smaller Businesses." *Journal of Business Venturing,* 2: 79-93.

[9]Shane, S., and S. Venkataraman (2000). "The Promise of Entrepreneurship as a Field of Research." *The Academy of Management Review,* 25(1): 217-226; Begley, T., and D. Boyd (1987). "Psychological Characteristics Associated with Performance in Entrepreneurial Firms and Smaller Businesses." *Journal of Business Venturing,* 2: 79-93.

[10]Gartner, W.B. (1988). "Who Is an Entrepreneur Is the Wrong Question." *American Journal of Small Business,* 11-31.

[11]Gartner, W.B., and C.B. Brush (1997). "Entrepreneurship: Emergence, Newness, and Transformation." Paper presented at the Academy of Management Entrepreneurship Division Doctoral Consortium, Boston, August.

[12]Caggiano, C. (2001). "E-tailing by the Numbers." *Inc. Technology* (1): 46. www.techreview.com.

[13]American Association of Home-Based Businesses, www.aahbb.org/.

[14]Reynolds, P.D. (1995). "Family Firms in the Start-up Process: Preliminary Explorations." Paper presented at the 1995 annual meetings of the International Family Business Program Association, Nashville, TN, July.

[15]Op.cit. Shane and Venkataraman (2000).

[16]Bhave, M.P. (1994). "A Process Model of Entrepreneurial Venture Creation." *Journal of Business Venturing* 9: 223-242; Reynolds, P.D., and B. Miller (1992). "New Firm Gestation: Conception, Birth, and Implications for Research." *Journal of Business Venturing,* 7: 405-417.

[17]Block, Z., and I.C. MacMillan (1985). "Milestones for Successful Venture Planning." *Harvard Business Review* 85(5): 184-188.

[18]Carter, N., W.B. Gartner, and P.D. Reynolds (1996). "Exploring Start-up Events Sequences. *Journal of Business Venturing* 11: 151-166.

[19]Birley, S., and P. Westhead (1993). "A Comparison of New Businesses Established by Novice and Habitual Founders in Great Britain." *International Small Business Journal,* 12(1): 38-60.

[20]Small Business Administration (1999). "Small Business Economic Indicators for 1999." Small Business Administration, Office of Advocacy, www.sba.gov.

[21]Ibid.

[22]Ibid. Provided by U.S. Department of Labor, Bureau of Statistics.

[23]Henderson, A.D. (1999). "Firm Strategy and Age Dependence: A Contingent View of the Liabilities of Newness, Adolescence, and Obsolescence." *Administrative Science Quarterly,* 44(2): 281-315.

[24]Aldrich H., and M. Fiol (1994). "Fools Rush In? The Institutional Context of Industry Creation." *Academy of Management Review,* 4(19): 645-670.

[25]Gross, N., P.C. Judge, O. Port, and S.H. Wildstrom (1998). "Let's Talk: Speech Technology Is the Next Big Thing in Computing." *Business Week* (Feb. 23): 61-80. www.businessweek.com.

[26]Op.cit. Shane and Venkataraman.

[27]Cohen, W., and R. Levin (1989). "Empirical Studies of Innovation and Market Structure." In *Handbook of Industrial Organization,* II, edited by R. Schmalensee and R. Willig. New York: Elsevier.

[28]Case, J. (1992). *From the Ground Up.* New York: Belknap Press, p. 44.

[29]Ibid., 46.

[30]Ibid., 64.

[31]Drucker, P.F. (1985). *Innovation and Entrepreneurship.* New York: Harper & Row.

[32]Finkle, T.A., and D. Deeds (2001). "Trends in the Market for Entrepreneurship Faculty During the Period 1989-1998." *Journal of Business Venturing,* 16(6) (June): 613.

[33]Ibid.

[34]Venkataraman, S. (1997). "The Distinctive Domain of Entrepreneurship Research: An Editor's Perspective." In *Advances in Entrepreneurship, Firm Emergence, and Growth,* edited by J. Katz and R. Brockhaus. Greenwich, Conn.: JAI Press.

[35]Op. cit. Shane and Venkataraman (2000).

[36]Carroll, G., and E. Mosakowski (1987). "The Career Dynamics of Self-employment." *Administrative Science Quarterly,* 32(4): 570-589.

[37]Amit, R., L. Glosten, and E. Muller (1993). "Challenges to Theory Development in Entrepreneurship Research." *Journal of Management Studies,* 30 (5): 815-834.

[38]Kirzner, I. (1997). "Entrepreneurial Discovery and the Competitive Market Process: An Austrian Approach." *Journal of Economic Literature,* 35(1): 60-85.

[39]Schumpeter, J. (1934). *Capitalism, Socialism, and Democracy.* New York: Harper & Row.

[40]Kaish, S., and B. Gilad (1991). "Characteristics of Opportunities Search of Entrepreneurs Versus Executives: Sources, Interests, and General Alertness." *Journal of Business Venturing,* 6: 45-61.

[41]Baumol, W. (1993). "Formal Entrepreneurship Theory in Economics: Existence and Bounds. *Journal of Business Venturing,* 8: 197-210.

[42]Kirzner, I. (1973). *Competition and Entrepreneurship.* Chicago: University of Chicago Press.

[43]Evans, D., and L. Leighton (1989). "Some Empirical Aspects of Entrepreneurship." *American Economic Review,* 79(3): 519-535; Aldrich, H., and C. Zimmer (1986). "Entrepreneurship Through Social Networks." In *The Art and Science of Entrepreneurship,* edited by D. Sexton and R. Smilor. Cambridge, MA: Ballinger.

[44]Cooper, A., C. Woo, and W. Dunkelberg (1989). "Entrepreneurship and the Initial Size of Firms." *Journal of Business Venturing,* 4: 317-332; Carrol, G., and E. Mosakowski (1987). "The Career Dynamics of Self-employment." *Administrative Science Quarterly,* 32(4): 570-589.

[45]Khaneman, D., and D. Lovallo (1994). "Timid Choices and Bold Forecasts: A Cognitive Perspective on Risk Taking." In *Fundamental Issues in Strategy: A Research Agenda,* edited by R.P. Rumelt, D.E. Schendel, and D. Teece, 71-96. Boston: Harvard Business School Press.

[46]Busenitz, L.W., and J.B. Barney (1997). "Differences Between Entrepreneurs and Managers in Large Organizations: Biases and Heuristics in Strategic Decision-Making." *Journal of Business Venturing,* 12(1): 9-30.

[47]Aldrich, H., and C. Zimmer (1986). Entrepreneurship Through Social Networks." In *The Art and Science of Entrepreneurship,* edited by D. L. Sexton and R.W. Smilor. Cambridge, MA: Ballinger.

[48]Granovetter, M. (1982). "The Strength of Weak Ties: A Network Theory Revisited." In *Social Structure and Network Analysis*, edited by P.V. Marsden and N. Lin. Beverly Hills, CA: Sage.

[49]Fisher, D., and S. Vilas (2000). *Power Networking: 59 Secrets for Personal and Professional Success.* Marietta, GA: Bard Press.

Chapter 2

[1]Collins, J., and J. Porras (1997). *Built to Last: Successful Habits of Visionary Companies.* New York: HarperBusiness.

[2]Ibid., 76.

[3] Nash, L. (1988). "Mission Statements—Mirrors and Windows." *Harvard Business Review,* (March-April): 155-156; Schermerhorn Jr., J.R., and D.S. Chappell (2000). *Introducing Management.* New York: John Wiley.

[4] Barrier, M. (1988). "Doing the Right Thing." *Nation's Business* (March). www.findarticles.com.

[5]Anderson, D., and K. Perine (2000). "Marketing the DoubleClick Way." *The Industry Standard Magazine* (Mar. 6). www.thestandard.com.

[6] Freeman, R.E. (1984). *Strategic Management: A Stakeholder Approach.* Englewood Cliffs. NJ: Prentice-Hall.

[7]Evan, W., and R.E. Freeman (1983). "A Stakeholder Theory of the Modern Corporation: Kantian Capitalism." In *Ethical Theory and Business*, edited by T. Beauchamp and N. Bowie. Englewood Cliffs, NJ: Prentice-Hall; Wicks, A.C., D.R. Gilbert Jr., and R.E. Freeman (1994). "A Feminist Reinterpretation of the Stakeholder Concept." *Business Ethics Quarterly,* 4(4): 475-498.

[8]Longenecker, J.G., J.A. McKinney, and C.W. Moore (1989). "Ethics in Small Business." *Journal of Small Business*, 27: 27-31.

[9]McDonald, G.M., and R.A. Zepp (1989). "Business Ethics: Practical Proposals." *Journal of Business Ethics*, 81: 55-56.

[10]McNamara, C. *Complete Guide to Ethics Management: An Ethics Toolkit for Managers.* Free Management Library, www.mapnp.org/library/topics.htm.

[11]Cavanaugh, G.F., D.J. Moberg, and M. Valasquez (1981). "The Ethics of Organizational Politics." *Academy of Management Review*, 6(3): 363-374.

[12]"Introduction to Corporate Social Responsibility," *Business for Social Responsibility Report.* www.bsr.org.

[13]Greco, S. (1997). "Volunteering: The New Employee Perk." *Inc.* (Sept. 1). www.inc.com.

[14]Ibid.

[15]Muoio, A. "Ways to Give Back," *Fast Company,* 12 (December 1997–June 1998), p. 113

[16]Boyd, D.P., and D.E. Gumpert (1983). "Coping with Entrepreneurial Stress." *Harvard Business Review* (March-April): 44-64.

[17]Bird, B.J. (1989). *Entrepreneurial Behavior.* Glenview, IL: Scott Foresman.

Chapter 3

[1]Drazin, R.D. (1999). "Multilevel Theorizing about Creativity in Organizations: A Sensemaking Perspective." *Academy of Management Review,* 24(2) (April): 286; Drazin, R. (1990). "Professionals and Innovation: Structural-Functional versus Radical-Structural Perspectives." *Journal of Management Studies*, 27(3): 245-263; Amabile, T.M. (1988). "A Model of Creativity and Innovation in Organizations." In *Research in Organizational Behavior*, vol. 10, edited by B.M. Staw and L.L. Cummings. Greenwich, CT: JAI Press, 123-167.

[2]Ibid. Drazin (1999); Woodman, R.W., J.E. Sawyer, and R.W. Griffin (1993). "Toward a Theory of Organizational Creativity." *Academy of Management Review* 18(2): 293-321.

[3]Singh, B. (1986). "Role of Personality versus Biographical Factors in Creativity." *Psychological Studies*, 31: 90-92; Barron, F., and D.M. Harrington (1981). "Creativity, Intelligence, and Personality." *Annual Review of Psychology*, 32: 439-476; Gardner, H. (1993). *Frames of Mind.* New York: Basic Books.

[4]Amabile, T.M. (1988). "A Model of Creativity and Innovation in Organizations." In *Research in Organizational Behavior*, vol. 10, edited by B.M. Staw and L.L. Cummings. Greenwich, CT: JAI Press, 123–167; Oldham, G.R., and A. Cummings (1996). "Employee Creativity: Personal and Contextual Factors at Work." *Academy of Management Journal*, 39: 607–634; Mumford, M.D., and S.B. Gustafson (1988). "Creativity Syndrome: Integration, Application, and Innovation." *Psychological Bulletin*, 103: 27–43; Payne, R. (1990). "The Effectiveness of Research Teams: A Review." In *Innovation and Creativity at Work*, edited by M.A. West and J.L. Farr. Chichester, England: Wiley, 101–122.

[5] Woodman, R W., J.E. Sawyer, and R.W. Griffin (1993). "Toward a Theory of Organizational Creativity." *Academy of Management Review*, 18(2): 293–321.

[6] Klein, K.J., F. Dansereau, and R.J. Hall (1994). "Levels Issues in Theory Development, Data Collection, and Analysis." *Academy of Management Review*, 19(2): 195–229.

[7]Giddens, A. (1994). *Central Problems in Social Theory: Action, Structure and Contradiction in Social Analysis*. Berkeley, CA: University of California Press; Kazanjian, R.K. (1988). "Relation of Dominant Problems to Stages of Growth in Technology-based New Ventures." *Academy of Management Journal*, 31: 257–279; Peterson, M.F. (1998). "Embedded Organizational Event: The Units of Process in Organizational Science." *Organization Science*, 9: 16–33.

[8]Siler, T. (1996). *Think Like a Genius*. New York: Bantam Books.

[9]Ibid.

[10]Op. cit. Amabile (1988).

[11]Hills, G.E. (1985). "Market Analysis in the Business Plan: Venture Capitalists' Perceptions." *Journal of Small Business Management* (Jan.): 38–46.

[12]McLain, D.L. (2001). "Job Forecast. Internet's Still Hot." *New York Times* (Jan. 30): 9. www.nytimes.com.

Chapter 4
[1]Churchill, N.C., J.A. Hornaday, B.A. Kirchhoff, O.J. Krasner, and K.H. Vesper (1987). "Venture Survivability." In *Frontiers of Entrepreneurship Research*. Wellesley, MA: Babson Center for Entrepreneurial Studies.

[2]Starbuck, W.H. (1976). "Organizations and Their Environments." In *Handbook of Industrial and Organization Psychology*, edited by M.D. Dunnette. Chicago: Rand McNally; Pfeffer, J., and G.R. Salancik (1978). *The External Control of Organizations*. New York: Random House.

[3]Downes, L., and C. Mui (1997). *Unleasing the Killer App: Digital Strategies for Market Dominance*. Cambridge: Harvard University Press.

[4]Porter, M.E. (1980). *Competitive Strategy: Techniques for Analyzing Industries and Competitors*. New York: Free Press, p. 3.

Chapter 5
[1] Buchanan, L. (2001). "The Rules." *Inc.* (Jan.): 70–72. www.inc.com.

Chapter 6
[1]Hall, J.A. (1991). *Bringing New Products to Market*. New York: AMACOM.

[2]Pruden, D.R. (2000). "Customer Research, Not Marketing Research." *Marketing Research*, 2 (Summer).

[3]Pritibhushan, S. (2000). "Determination of Reliability of Estimations Obtained with Survey Research: A Method of Simulation." *International Journal of Market Research*. 42(3): 311–317.

[4]Gray, R. (2000). "The Releventless Rise of Online Research." *Marketing* (May 18).

[5]Couper, M.P. (2000). "Web Surveys: A Review of Issues and Approaches." *Public Opinion Quarterly*, 64(4): 464–494.

Chapter 7
[1]Clark, K., and T. Fujimoto (1991). *Product Development Performance*. Boston: Harvard Business School Press.

[2]Pine II, B.J. (1993). *Mass Customization*. Boston: Harvard Business School Press.

[3]von Braun, C. (1990). "The Acceleration Trap." *Sloan Management Review*, 32(1): 49.

[4]Ibid., 21.

[5]Quinn, J.B. (2000). "Outsourcing Innovation: The New Engine of Growth." *Sloan Management Review*, 41(4) (Summer): 13–29.

[6]Huxley, M. (2001). "Rapid Prototyping Cuts Time to Market." *CADalyst* (May). www.findarticles.com.

[7]Schmitz, B. (2000). "Tools of Innovation." *Industry Week* (May 15).

[8]*Diamond v. Chakrabarty,* 447 U.S. 303 (1980).

[9]"Qualifying for a Patent." *NOLO Law for All.* www.nolo.com/encyclopedia/articles/pts/pct3.html#FAQ-294.

[10]U.S. Patent and Trademark Office: Design Patents. www.uspto.gov/web/offices/pac/doc/general/design.html.

[11]Bonisteel, S. (2001). "Bounty Hunters Get Bonus for Effort on Amazon Patent." *Newsbytes* (March 14).

[12]*State Street Bank & Trust v. Signature Financial Group Inc.,* 149 F.3d 1368, 47 USPQ2d 1596 (Fed. Cir. 1998).

[13]Love, J.J., and W.W. Coggins (2001). "Successfully Preparing and Prosecuting a Business Method Patent Application." Presented at AIPLA, Spring 2001. www.uspto.gov/web/menu/pbmethod/aiplapaper.rtf.

[14]U.S. Patent and Trademark Office: Disclosure Document Program. www.uspto.gov/web/offices/com/sol/notices/disdo.html.

[15]U.S. Patent and Trademark Office, www.uspto.gov/web/offices/pac/disdo.html.

[16]Ibid.

[17]Paris Convention for the Protection of Industrial Property, 21 U.S.T 1583, 828 U.N.T.S. 305 (1967).

[18]Patent Cooperation Treaty, 28 U.S.T. 7645 No. 8733 (1970).

[19]Oddi, A.S. (1996). Un-unified Economic Theories of Patents: The Not-Quite-Holy Grail. *Notre Dame Law Review,* 71: 267–327.

[20]Trademark Act of 1946, 15 U.S.C. § 1127.

[21]Brown, J.D., and J.E. Prescott (2000). "Product of the Mind: Assessment and Protection of Intellectual Property." *Competitive Intelligence Review,* 11(3): 60.

[22]Ibid.

[23]*Whelan v. Jaslow,* 797 F.2d 1222; 21 Fed. R. Evid. Serv. (Callaghan) 571: U.S. Court of Appeals for the Third Circuit (1986).

Chapter 8
[1]Van de Ven, A.H., R. Hudson, and D.M. Schroeder (1984). "Designing New Business Start-ups." *Journal of Management,* 10(1): 87–108.

[2]Aldrich, H., and C. Zimmer (1986). "Entrepreneurship through Social Networks." In *The Art and Science of Entrepreneurship,* edited by D.L. Sexton and R.W. Smilor. Cambridge, MA: Ballinger, pp. 3–23.

[3]Moss Kanter, R. (2001). "A More Perfect Union," *Inc.* (Feb.): 93–98, www.inc.com.

[4]Dubini, P., and H. Aldrich (1991). "Personal and Extended Networks Are Central to the Entrepreneurial Process." *Journal of Business Venturing,* 6(5): 305–313.

[5]Ibid.

[6]Kidwell, R.E., and N. Bennett (1993). "Employee Propensity to Withhold Effort: A Conceptual Model to Intersect Three Avenues of Research. *Academy of Management Review,* 18(3): 429–456.

[7]Goodstein, J., K. Gautam, and W. Boeker (1994). "The Effects of Board Size and Diversity on Strategic Change." *Strategic Management Journal,* 15(3): 241–250.

[8]Jonovic, D.J. "Professionalizing: The Key to Long-Term Shareholder Value, Part 1." Baylor University. http://hsb.baylor.edu/html/cel/ifb/legacies/jonovic.htm.

[9]Ibid.

[10]Michael F. Corbett & Associates (1999). *The 1999 Outsourcing Trends Report.* New York: Michael F. Corbett & Associates Ltd. The company surveyed the opinions of U.S. private-and public-sector executives and industry experts.

[11]Barthelemy, J. (2001). "The Hidden Costs of Outsourcing." *MIT Sloan Management Review,* 42(3) (Spring): 60–69.

[12]Sovereigh, K.L. (1999). *Personnel Law.* 4th ed. Upper Saddle River, NJ: Prentice-Hall.

Chapter 10
[1]Cort S.G. (1999). "Industry Corner: Industrial Distribution: How Goods Will Go to Market in the Electronic Marketplace." *Business Economics* (Jan.). www.findarticles.com.

[2]Gates, B. (1999). *Business @ the Speed of Thought.* New York: Warner Books.

[3]Shapiro, C., and H.R. Varian (1999). *Information Rules.* Boston: Harvard Business School Press.

[4]Downes L., and C. Mui (1998). *Unleashing the Killer App.* Boston: Harvard Business School Press.

[5]Rayport, J.F., and J.J. Sviokla (1994). "Managing in the Market-space." *Harvard Business Review* (Nov.-Dec.): 141–150.

[6]Slywotzky, A.J. (1996). *Value Migration.* Boston: Harvard Business School Press.

[7]Fein, A.J. (1999). "Manage Consolidation in the Distribution Channel." *Sloan Management Review,* 1 (Fall): 61–73.

[8]Anderson, E.A., G.S. Day, and V.K. Rangan (1997). "Strategic Channel Design." *Sloan Management Review,* 38 (Summer): 59–69.

[9]Westland, J.C., and T.H.K. Clark (1999). *Global Electronic Commerce.* Cambridge, MA: MIT Press.

[10]Munson, C.L., Rosenblatt, M.J., and Rosenblatt, Z. (1999). "The Use and Abuse of Power in Supply Chains." *Business Horizons* (Jan.-Feb.). www.findarticles.com.

[11]Ibid.

[12]Stern, L.W., and A.I. El-Ansary (1988). *Marketing Channels.* 3rd ed. Englewood Cliffs, NJ: Prentice-Hall.

Chapter 11

[1]Lawton, J. (1999). "The Just-Right Business Plan." *Entrepreneur's Byline* (March 1). www.entreworld.org/Content/Entrebyline.cfm?ColumnID=75.

[2]Walton, K. (1999). "A Business Plan with Heart." *EntreWorld.org.* (March 1). www.entreworld.org/Content/Entrebyline.cfm?ColumnID=76.

[3]Brown, B.D. and E. Robinson. (2000). "Building a Dot-Com from the Ground Up." *Oracle Magazine* (Apr. 10). www.oracle.com/oramag/webcolumns/2000/index.htm?brownrobl.html.

[4]Smilor, R. "The Entrepreneur's Rosetta Stone: How to Read a Business Plan." *Entrepreneur's Byline,* EntreWorld.org, www.entreworld.org/Content/EntreByline.cfm?ColumnID=197.

[5]Hankin, R.N. "Creating and Realizing the Value of a Business." *Entrepreneur's Byline,* EntreWorld.org, www.entreworld.org/Content/EntreByline.cfm?ColumnID=198.

[6]Brush, C.G., P.G. Greene, M.M. Hart, and H.S. Haller (2001). "From Initial Idea to Unique Advantage: The Entrepreneurial Challenge of Constructing a Resource Base." *The Academy of Management Executive,* 15(1): 64–78.

[7]Block, Z., and I.C. Macmillan (1992). "Milestones for Successful Venture Planning." In *The Entrepreneurial Venture,* edited by W.A. Sahlman and H.H. Stevenson. Boston: Harvard Business School Publishing, pp. 138–148.

[8]McWilliams, B. (1996). "Garbage In, Garbage Out." *Inc. Magazine* (Aug. 1). www.inc.com.

[9]Rich, S.R., and D.E. Gumpert (1992). "How to Write a Winning Business Plan." In *The Entrepreneurial Venture,* edited by W.A. Sahlman and H.H. Stevenson. Boston: Harvard Business School Publishing.

[10]Kelly, P., and M. Hay (2000). "The Private Investor-Entrepreneur Contractual Relationship: Understanding the Influence of Context." In *Frontiers of Entrepreneurship Research,* edited by E. Autio et al., Wellesley, MA: Babson College.

[11]Mason, C.M., and R.T. Harrison (2000). "Investing in Technology Ventures: What Do Business Angels Look for at the Initial Screening Stage?" *Frontiers of Entrepreneurship Research,* edited by E. Autio et al., Wellesley, MA: Babson College, p. 293.

Chapter 12

[1]Greco, S. (2001). "Balancing Act." *Inc.* (Jan.): 56–60. www.inc.com.

[2]"Partnership Basics." *NOLO Law for All.* www.nolo.com/encyclopedia/articles/sb/partnerships.html.

[3]"Partnership Basics." *NOLO Law for All.* www.nolo.com/encyclopedia/articles/sb/buy_sell.html.

Chapter 13

[1]Reed, M.I., and M. Hughes, eds. (1992). *Rethinking Organizations: New Directions in Organization Theory and Analysis.* London: Sage; Hassard, J., and M. Parker (1993). *Postmodernism and*

Organizations. London: Sage; Boje, D.M. (1996). *Postmodern Management and Organization Theory.* Thousand Oaks, CA: Sage.

[2]Hatch, M.J. (1999). "Exploring the Empty Spaces of Organizing: How Improvisational Jazz Helps Redescribe Organizational Structure." *Organization Studies* (Winter); Brown, S.L., and K.M. Eisenhardt (1998). *Competing on the Edge: Strategy as Structured Chaos.* Boston: Harvard Business School Press.

[3]Eisenberg, E.M. "Jamming: Transcendence Through Organizing." *Communication Research,* 17(2): 139–164.

[4]Pape, W.R. (1998). "Virtual Manager: Mastering Business in a Networked World." *Inc. Magazine* (Sept. 15).

[5]Barker, E. (2000). "Best Cities: The Location Advantage." *Inc. Magazine* (Dec. 1). www.inc.com.

[6]Myers, R. (1995). "Temporary Tenant." *Nation's Business* (Aug.): 39.

[7]Krackhardt, D., and J.R. Hanson (1993). "Informal Networks: The Company Behind the Chart." *Harvard Business Review*, 71(4): 105.

[8](1993). *Inc. Magazine* (Oct.): 86.

[9]Katzenbach, J.R., and D.K. Smith (1993). *The Wisdom of Teams.* Boston: Harvard Business School Press.

[10]Osborne, R.L. (1992). "Minority Ownership for Key Employees: Dividend or Disaster?" *Business Horizons,* 35(1): 76.

Chapter 14
[1]Chang, M. (Nov. 1995). "Turning Raw Materials into Finished Products." *Laser Focus World.* http://lfw.pennnet.com.

[2]Trebilcock, B. (2001). "E-Manufacturing Gets Started." *Modern Materials Handling* (May 15). www.manufacuring.net.

[3]Ibid.

[4]Anderson, E., and B. Weitz (1992). "The Use of Pledges to Build and Sustain Commitment in Distribution Channels." *Journal of Marketing Research,* 29 (Feb.): 18–34; Doney, P.M., and J.P. Cannon (1997). "An Examination of the Nature of Trust in Buyer-Seller

Relationships." *Journal of Marketing,* 61 (Apr.): 35–51.

[5]Anderson, E., and A.T. Coughlan (1987). "International Market Entry and Expansion Via Independent or Integrated Channels of Distribution." *Journal of Marketing,* 51 (Jan.): 71–82.

Mohr, J., R.J. Fisher, and J.R. Nevin (1996). "Collaborative Communication in Interfirm Relationships: Moderating Effects of Integration and Control." *Journal of Marketing,* 60 (July): 103–115.

[6]Lusch, R.F., and J.R. Brown (1996). "Interdependency, Contracting, and Relational Behavior in Marketing Channels." *Journal of Marketing,* 60 (Oct.): 19–38.

Noordewier, T.G., G. John, and J.R. Nevin (1990). "Performance Outcomes of Purchasing Arrangements in Industrial Buyer-Vendor Relationships." *Journal of Marketing,* 54 (Oct.): 80–93.

[7]Emshwiller, J.R. (1991). "Suppliers Struggle to Improve Quality as Big Firms Slash Their Vendor Rolls." *The Wall Street Journal* (Aug. 16): B1, B2.

[8]Magnet, M. (1994). "The New Golden Rule of Business." *Fortune* (Feb. 21): 60–64.

[9]Cannon, J.P. (1999). "Buyer-Seller Relationships in Business Markets," *Journal of Marketing Research,* 36(4) (Nov.): 439–461.

[10]"Feigenbaum's 40 Steps to Quality Improvement," In *Federal Quality Management Handbook,* Appendix IA: "How to Get Started." June 1990. http://deming.eng.clemson.edu/pub/tqmbbs/prin-pract/feig40.txt.

[11]Ibid.

[12]Hopper, K. (1982). "Creating Japan's New Industrial Management: The Americans as Teachers." *Human Resource Management,* 21(2–3): 13–34.

[13]Bartholomew, D. (2001). "Cost v. Quality." *Industry Week* (Sept.). www.industryweek.com.

[14]Terry, R. (2002). "Training Toys." *Washington Techway* (July 23). www.washtech.com.

[15]Op. cit. Feigenbaum (1990), 1.

[16]Challener, C. (2001). "Six Sigma: Can the GE Model Work in the Chemical Industry?" *Chemical Market Reporter* (July 16). www.findarticles.com.

[17]Boswell, C. (2001). "Technically, Inc. Boosts Process Development with Six Sigma." *Chemical Market Reporter* (July 16). www.findarticles.com.

[18]Dolan, K.A., and R. Meredith (2001). "Ghost Cars, Ghost Brands." *Forbes* (Apr. 30): 106–112. www.forbes.com.

Chapter 15

[1]Wind, J. (1999). "Marketing Strategy in the Global Information Age." Knowledge@Wharton (Oct. 13). http://knowledge.wharton.upenn.edu.

[2]Peppers D., and M. Rogers (1993). *The One to One Future: Building Relationships One Customer at a Time.* New York: Currency/Doubleday.

[3]Ibid., 36.

[4]"Ask the Marketing Doctors." (1995). *Inc. Magazine* (Oct.): 68. www.inc.com.

[5]Op.cit. Peppers and Rogers (1993), 83.

[6]"Big-Time Marketing on a Small Budget." (2000). *Inc. Magazine* (Oct. 11). www.inc.com.

[7]Levinson, J.C. (1993). *Guerrilla Marketing.* Boston: Houghton Mifflin.

[8]Stansell, K. "Inspire People to Talk about You." *Bootstrapper's Success Secrets.* www.kimberlystansell.com/archives.htm.

[9]Bianchi, A. (1997). "Something for Nothing." *Inc. Magazine* (Mar. 1). www.inc.com.

[10]Levinson, J.C. (1993). *Guerrilla Marketing.* Boston: Houghton Mifflin.

[11]"Firms Now Spend More on Old, Not New, Customer." (1994). *Los Angeles Times* (Nov. 1), p. 3.

[12]Mardesich, J. (2001). "Too Much of a Good Thing." *The Standard* (Mar. 19). www.thestandard.com.

[13]Gunther, M. (1998). "The Internet Is Mr. Case's Neighborhood." *Fortune* (Mar. 30): 69–80.

[14]Demarco, D. (2001). "What's in a Name?" *Insight* (July 30).

[15]Nybert, A. (2001). "Privacy Matters." *CFO* (July).

Chapter 16

[1]Kolb R.W., and R.J. Rodriguez (1996). *Financial Management.* 2nd ed. Cambridge, MA: Blackwell Business.

[2]Ibid.

[3]Mills, J.R. (1998). "The Power of Cash Flow Ratios." *Journal of Accountancy* (Oct.), p. 53.

Chapter 17

[1]Mangelsdorf, M.E. (2000). "Analysis of the 2000 *Inc. 500.*" *Inc. Magazine* (Oct. 15).

[2]Ibid.

[3]"The 2000 *Inc. 500* Almanac." (2000). *Inc. Magazine* (Oct. 15).

[4]Bishop, S. (1999). "The Strategic Power of Saying No." *Harvard Business Review* (Nov./Dec.).

[5]Roberts, M.J. (1999). "Managing Growth." *New Business Venture and the Entrepreneurs.* New York: Irwin/McGraw-Hill.

[6]Hannan, M., and J. Freeman (1984). "Structural Inertia and Organizational Change." *American Sociological Review,* 49: 149–164; McKelvey, B., and H. Aldrich (1983). "Populations, Natural Selection, and Applied Organizational Science." *Administrative Science Quarterly,* 28(1): 101–128.

[7]Kuratko, D.F., and R.M. Hodgetts (1989). *Entrepreneurship: A Contemporary Approach.* Chicago: Dryden Press.

[8]Terpstra, D.E., and P.D. Olson (1993). "Entrepreneurial Start-up and Growth: A Classification of Problems." *Entrepreneurship Theory & Practice* (spring): 5–20.

[9]Osborne, R.L. (1994). "Second Phase Entrepreneurship: Breaking Through the Growth Wall." *Business Horizons* (Jan./Feb.): 80–86.

[10]Ibid.

[11]Lafontaine, F. (1998). "Franchising Growth and Franchisor Entry and Exit in the U.S. Market: Myth and Reality." *Journal of Business Venturing,* 13:95–112.

[12]Shealy, J. (2000). "Update—The Top 10 Hottest New Franchises." *Success Magazine* (Dec.).

[13]Bates, T. (1999). Franchising Testimony of Dr. Timothy Bates to the U.S. House of Representatives Judiciary Committee's Subcommittee in Commercial and Administrative Law, U.S. Government Printing Office; Shane, S. (1996). "Hybrid Organizational Arrangements and Their Implication for Firm Growth and Survival: A Study of New Franchisors." *Academy of*

Management Journal (Feb.): 216–231; Op. cit. Lafontaine (1998).

[14]Huff, F.S. (2001). "Let's Kick It Up a Notch." www. BlackEnterprise.com (April).

[15]Buss, D.D. (1995). "Growing More By Doing Less." *Nation's Business* (Dec.): 18.

[16]Ibid.

[17]Austin, N.K. (1999). "Sailor's Delight." *Inc. Magazine* (Nov. 1).

[18]U.S. Department of Commerce (2000). U.S. Export Statistics. www.census.gov/foreign-trade/www/.

[19]Oviatt, B.M., and P. McDougall (1995). "Global Start-ups: Entrepreneurs on a Worldwide Stage." *The Academy of Management Executive,* 9(2) (May): 30–44.

[20]Ibid.

[21](1995). "It's a Small (Business) World." *Business Week* (Apr. 17): 96–101. www.businessweek.com.

[22]Schwartz, N.D. (1999). "Secrets of Fortune's Fastest-Growing Companies." *Fortune* (Sept.) 72–86. www.fortune.com.

Chapter 18
[1]Venkataraman, S. (1997). "The Distinctive Domain of Entrepreneurship Research." *Advances in Entrepreneurship Research: Firm Emergence and Growth,* 3: 119–138; Gompers, P. (1997). "An Examination of Convertible Securities in Venture Capital Investments." Working Paper, Harvard University.

[2]Shane, S. (1998). "Social Relationships and the Financing of New Ventures." Working Paper, Sloan School of Management, MIT, Cambridge, MA.

[3]Bhide, A. (1992). "Bootstrapping Finance: The Art of Start-Ups." *Harvard Business Review,* 70(6): 109–117.

[4]Mamis, R.A. (1997). "Power of Poverty." *Inc. Magazine* (Aug.): 40. www.inc.com.

[5]Ibid.

[6]Reynolds, P., and S. White (1997). *The Entrepreneurial Process.* Greenwich, CT: Greenwood Press.

[7]Freear, J., and W. Wetzel Jr. (1990). "Who Bankrolls High-Tech Entrepreneurs?" *Journal of Business Venturing* (March): 77–89.

[8]Fraser, J.A. (1999). "20 Tips for Finding Money Now." *Inc.* (March): 37. www.inc.com.

[9]Brinsley, J. (2000). "Incubator Becoming Dirty Word in Net Business." *Los Angeles Business Journal* (May).

[10]Kaufman, L. (2000). "Incubators Still Cooking Up Hot Ideas for Businesses." *Los Angeles Business Journal* (Oct. 16). www.cbjonline.com.

[11]Hoffman, H., and J. Blakely (1987). "You Can Negotiate with Venture Capitalists." *Harvard Business Review* (Mar.-Apr.): 6–24.

[12]Ibid.

[13]Birchard, B. (1999). "Intangible Assets Plus Hard Numbers Equals Soft Finance." *Fast Company,* (28): 316. www.fastcompany.com.

[14]Ibid., 68.

[15]White, M.C. "The Valuation of Newly-Formed Technology Companies." White & Lee, www. whiteandlee.com/valuatn.htm.

[16]Tuller, L.W. (1994). *Small Business Valuation Book.* Holbrook, MA: Bob Adams, Inc., p. 43.

Chapter 19
[1]Kahn, A.D. (1999). "Facing the Reality of Succession Planning." *The CPA Journal* 69(9): 66–67.

[2]Matthews, C. (2001). "Planning for Succession." *Inc. Magazine* (Oct. 17), www.inc.com.

[3]ABI World (2001). U.S. Bankruptcy Filing Statistics, October 29. www.abiworld.org/stats/newstatsfront.html.

Index

Note: f indicates figure and *p* indicates profile.